Dearest Reader,

How lovely of you to come to my one hundredth book! After all, you were there when it all began, and I certainly couldn't have done any of this without you. It's hard to believe that seventeen years have passed since I stepped out of the shower, seven months pregnant with my second child, to take a phone call from my agent that would change my entire life. She'd called to tell me I'd sold my first novel, *Tried and True,* to Silhouette Desire. The struggling writer had finally made it to the gates of the Promised Land. The rest, as they say, is history. A very long and fruitful history for which I never stop being grateful. Although I've had my favorites, I can truly say that I loved writing each and every story that found its way to the Silhouette imprint. I've tried to write the kind of stories that I've always enjoyed reading, stories with warmth and humor, and that leave me with a smile at the end. I sincerely hope they do the same for you and that they have found a place in your hearts the way they have in mine.

Now, if you'll excuse me, I have to start on the second hundred. Thanking you from the bottom of my heart for always being there, I wish you happiness and love.

Sincerely yours,

Marie Ferrarella

Dear Reader,

You asked for more ROYALLY WED titles and you've
got them! For the next four months we've brought back
the Stanbury family—first introduced in a short story by
Carla Cassidy on our eHarlequin.com Web site. Be sure to
check the archives to find Nicholas's story! But don't forget to
pick up Stella Bagwell's *The Expectant Princess* and discover
the involving story of the disappearance of King Michael.

Other treats this month include Marie Ferrarella's one
hundredth title for Silhouette Books! This wonderful, charming
and emotional writer shows her trademark warmth and humor
in *Rough Around the Edges*. Luckily for all her devoted readers,
Marie has at least another hundred plots bubbling in her
imagination, and we'll be seeing more from her in many of
our Silhouette lines.

Then we've got Karen Rose Smith's *Tall, Dark & True*
about a strong, silent sheriff who can't bear to keep quiet
about his feelings any longer. And Donna Clayton's heroine
asks *Who Will Father My Baby?*—and gets a surprising answer.
No Place Like Home by Robin Nicholas is a delightful read
that reminds us of an all-time favorite movie—I'll let you guess
which one! And don't forget first-time author Roxann Delaney's
debut title, *Rachel's Rescuer*.

Next month be sure to return for *The Blacksheep Prince's
Bride* by Martha Shields, the next of the ROYALLY WED
series. Also returning are popular authors Judy Christenberry
and Elizabeth August.

Happy reading!

Mary-Theresa Hussey

Mary-Theresa Hussey
Senior Editor

Please address questions and book requests to:
Silhouette Reader Service
U.S.: 3010 Walden Ave., P.O. Box 1325, Buffalo, NY 14269
Canadian: P.O. Box 609, Fort Erie, Ont. L2A 5X3

Marie Ferrarella

ROUGH AROUND THE EDGES

SILHOUETTE *Romance*®

Published by Silhouette Books

America's Publisher of Contemporary Romance

To Leslie Wainger and Pat Teal,
with me at one and still with me at one hundred.
Thank you, with love and gratitude,
Marie

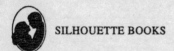 SILHOUETTE BOOKS

ISBN 0-373-19505-2

ROUGH AROUND THE EDGES

Visit Silhouette at www.eHarlequin.com

Printed in U.S.A.

Chapter One

The wide, gregarious smile that had become his trademark faded the moment Shawn Michael O'Rourke stepped outside the Irish-style pub he'd discovered his second weekend in Bedford, California.

There was nothing to smile about and no reason to pretend any longer. There was no one to see him. His friends were all inside.

Ordinarily, meeting and sharing a pint or two at the Shamrock with his friends would smooth over whatever was troubling O'Rourke at the time. He wasn't a happy-go-lucky man, but he met life head-on, facing what it brought and moving on. But this was no ordinary situation and he was worried.

Worried clear down to the bone, as his grandmother used to say.

The light showers that were falling when he'd entered the pub had turned into a full-fledged storm while he'd been inside. He turned the collar of his jacket up, but it did little to keep the March rain off his neck. He hunched his shoulders in. But it was more than the rain that was making him feel beaten down.

There had to be something he could do.

He knew that if he didn't come up with a solution—and soon—everything he'd worked for these past few years, everything he'd dreamed of over these past ten years, would mean nothing. He'd be done for. It didn't seem fair that a random act of birth could have such an effect on a man's life, a man's future and that of his family's.

O'Rourke hurried to the rear of the building, to the postage-stamp-size parking lot that was filled to capacity tonight. He dug into his pocket for his car keys.

Had he been born on the other side of the Atlantic, today would have been just another day in his life, a day in which he was working toward the culmination of his dream.

Instead, it was one day less he had. One day closer to when he had to leave. Leave the country, leave his hopes and his dreams. Sure, he could attempt to start over again back home in Ireland. After all, the dream had begun there, in his head. But it was right here, in a converted loft in Bedford's Industrial Plaza, that all the visible components were housed.

To Shawn Michael O'Rourke, America really was the land of opportunity. He'd found everything he'd needed on this side of the ocean: the education he required and the financial backers, both men of experience and dreamers like himself. Dreamers who weren't content only to dream, but to do.

All that wouldn't mean anything anymore come thirteen days from today. That was his deadline. In thirteen days, he was to be gone from these shores. To return home just another failed dreamer.

Muttering words under his breath he knew his late, sainted mother would have taken a very dim view of, O'Rourke got into his van. The rain followed him in, covering the steering wheel and everything else in its path with a fine layer of mist before he shut the door. He hardly noticed. He jammed his key into the ignition and turned it. The motor hummed to life, along with the CD he'd left in his CD player, a compilation of songs from the seventies and eighties. He loved everything American.

Gloria Gayner began extolling the need to find some "hot stuff" as he drove out of the parking lot. He didn't need any hot stuff, he thought. He needed a miracle, pure and simple.

O'Rourke frowned as he looked out the windshield. It wasn't the state of his brain but the rain that was beating down that made it hard for him to see. Had he imbibed enough at the Shamrock to cloud his mind, he would have happily continued until he would have gotten good and drunk.

No, he wouldn't have, he thought, turning down another street. Drinking to the point where his problem no longer seemed important was only a temporary fix, one with a huge price tag on in. Namely the morning after. Tying one on with his friends would only bring him a huge headache and interfere with his being able to think.

He needed to be clearheaded. There were responsibilities weighing on his shoulders, people depending on him, both here and in Ireland. People he was going to let down in thirteen days. Not that anyone would say anything. But *he'd* feel as if he was letting them down.

Damn, there had to be a way.

Without realizing it, he fingered the St. Jude medal he wore, a last gift from his mother, as he waited for the light to change. St. Jude, patron saint of lost causes. That had been him, once, a lost cause, until something had brought him around, taking him away from a life of carousing to something far more steady. His mother swore it was her prayers to the saint whose medal he wore around his neck. He figured it was his finally coming to grips with his father's death that had done it.

Maybe if he thought long enough and hard enough, he'd come up with a solution. One that would keep him from being sent back to his native Ireland with his tail between his legs now that his visa, and every single extension he could put on it, was finally up.

The streets he was driving through were close to being deserted, even though it was only a little after nine in the evening. On a night like tonight, people stayed in their homes.

And that's where he should be, O'Rourke decided. Home. For as long as it still was home to him.

He noticed that the rain seemed to be coming down harder. Angel's tears, his mother used to say. She also said the angels were shedding the tears because of him.

He could see her, even now, fixing him a look with those deep blue eyes of hers, her arms crossed before her as she watched him come staggering in in the wee hours of the morning. Following the same path his late father had before him.

"When are you ever going to amount to something,

Shawn Michael? You're my firstborn, boyo. What am I going to say to my Maker when the time comes to face him and let him know what I did with the life he sent me to guide?''

O'Rourke smiled now, his mother's words echoing in his head as clearly as if she'd actually spoken them. "You died before I could show you, eh, Mum?'' he murmured to the memory that existed in his mind. "Except, I guess I won't be showing you at that, not if this fine government has its way,'' he added with a sigh as he turned down the next block.

Kitt Dawson didn't think the day could get much worse. But each time she had thought that today, fate, with its twisted sense of humor, had gone out of its way to prove her wrong.

Kitt gritted her teeth together, grabbing on to the steering wheel even though she wasn't moving. Here it came, another one. Another killer contraction. She held her breath, praying for it to end.

The top of her head felt as if it was going to come off. And then the contraction ebbed away, leaving her shaken, sweaty and scared.

She loosened her fingers from around the steering wheel. The baby wasn't due for another two weeks. The fact that it was coming didn't really surprise her, not beyond the initial salvo of disbelief when her water broke fifteen minutes ago. Nothing was going the way it should have gone today, why should this be any different?

It was a day for the record books. She'd lost her job because the aerospace company she was working for had lost its contract. She'd come home, hoping for a word of comfort, only to discover that she'd lost the foundation of her life as well. Jeffrey, the man to whom she'd given her heart, not to mention half her apartment, had left. Cleaned out the apartment the way he never had while they were living together. He'd taken everything of worth, including the new car he was supposed to have taken in for an oil change today. Taken it and every single dime she had in the world. He'd cleaned out the joint bank account as neatly as he had the apartment.

It had been her bank account, really. She'd been the one to put the money in. The only time he touched it was to take money out. She'd made herself a million excuses, saying things would get better once Jeffrey was back on his feet again.

He'd found his feet all right, she thought now. Found them and used them to run off with her things and the leggy brunette down the hall.

She should have seen it coming, Kitt upbraided herself. Maybe she had at that, but had refused to acknowledge it because love was blind. And she had loved Jeffrey. Dearly.

And now she was paying for it. Also dearly.

Okay, so love was blind, but she was supposed to have brains.

She was also supposed to have an umbrella, she thought as she looked through the windshield of her dead car with mounting exasperation.

It was raining. Not drizzling the way the weatherman had laughingly promised, but raining. Building-an-ark-and-collecting-two-of-everything kind of raining. And her car, the second-hand lemon that had actually belonged to Jeffrey, had just died a few feet passed the intersection, refusing to come back to life.

Just like Jeffrey after he'd discovered that she was pregnant, she thought, struggling hard not to give in to bitterness.

Well, the car was not about to suddenly rise from the dead and the rain was not about to abate. She had no choice but to get out and walk.

"It just keeps getting better and better," she muttered, snapping off her seat belt.

Opening the door, Kitt wiggled out from behind the steering wheel she was wedged against. Another contraction began to build. Kitt froze. The pain that ran through her felt almost lethal, stealing her breath away with a vengeance. She had to get to the hospital. *Now.* She was in no mood to give birth on the corner of MacArthur and Fairview.

The way her luck was running, the next thing that would happen would be a flash flood.

With growing despair, she looked up and down the street. Nothing.

Why didn't they have cabs prowling the streets here? She'd heard they did that in the big cities, why was that a restricted practice? For that matter, where was a police car when you needed one? If she'd gone through that light, she bet one would have popped out of the ground with a pre-printed ticket on the dashboard.

Maybe that wasn't fair, but she didn't feel very fair right now. She felt angry and cheated and in pain.

The rain lashed at her from all directions, pushed around by the wind that went first one way, then another. Kitt struggled to keep her orientation. She started to feel dizzy.

Thoughts began to slip in and out of her head like pulses of lights on a faulty circuit.

Maybe she could find a phone and call 911. The police were bound to get here faster than any cab she'd call.

Now all she had to do was find a phone.

Now all she had to do was see in this godforsaken awful weather, she amended. It seemed as if actual sheets of rain were coming down, wiping out any visibility beyond two, maybe three feet. Squinting, Kitt could barely make out the traffic signal across the street.

A haloed green ball of light shone like a feeble beacon. Kitt stepped off the curb, praying she could get across the street before another contraction hit, incapacitating her. Biting her lower lip, her head down against the wind, she tried to cross the intersection as quickly as possible.

Her own bulk combined with the lashing rain slowed her down. The light turned yellow just as she'd made it hardly more than halfway across the street. Pushing herself, she strove to move faster. Her eyes were half closed, trying to keep the rain at bay.

The squeal of brakes from the oncoming vehicle had her screaming in response. The next second, there was water hitting her not just from above, but from the street as well, drenching her legs as her foot made contact with the sidewalk.

Everything started to swirl around in her head. Kitt reached out to steady herself, but there was nothing to grab onto. She vaguely thought she heard a man's voice shouting at her.

Or maybe that was to her, she wasn't sure. It didn't seem important.

Her outstretched hands made contact with cement. Hard. Tearing at the fleshy part of her palms and making them sting.

She'd fallen.

The thought telegraphed itself through her brain at the same instant the pain registered. The next second, she felt someone cradling her.

"Are you all right?" There was a hint of a lilting accent in the deep voice. There was more than a hint of concern.

With effort, Kitt managed to bring the world back into focus. Some man she'd never seen was holding her against him.

"No, I'm not all right. I'm pregnant," she snapped. Angry at the world at large and frightened, Kitt tried to sit up. She couldn't. The man asking the stupid question was holding her.

My God, he'd almost hit a pregnant woman with his van, O'Rourke thought, trying to shake off the numbing fear the realization created. Rapidly pulling his wits about him, O'Rourke looked at her, searching for signs of bleeding.

"You came out of nowhere."

"I came out of my car," she contradicted him curtly. "And I was trying to cross the street. Didn't anyone ever teach you how to drive?" She yanked her arm away from him and tried vainly to gain her feet. She felt like a turtle flipped onto its back. A huge, pregnant turtle.

"I didn't hit you, did I?" Swiftly, O'Rourke ran

his hands up and down her limbs, checking for any damage. "I mean—"

Where the hell did he come off, trying to touch her? What was wrong with him? Again she tried to get to her feet, but between the rain, her labor pains and the exhaustion that was sinking in, it was beginning to feel like an impossible feat.

"Look, I'm in labor." At least she could manage to push his hands away, which she did. "I would really, really prefer if you didn't try to cop a feel or mug me right now."

O'Rourke sat back on his heels, ignoring the rain falling into his eyes. "I'm just checking for broken bones—" His mouth fell open. "Labor?"

She bit her lower lip, trying very hard to focus on something other than the pain. Trying very hard not to get hysterical.

"Yes, labor," she ground out.

What the hell was she doing wandering around in her condition? "You shouldn't be out on a night like this." O'Rourke looked around, trying to spot someone who might have been with her. But there was no one on the street and only one car had passed since he'd darted out of his van. "Especially not alone."

"Not my choice," she bit off. Turning, she tried to get to her knees. The pain had her gasping. And then suddenly, just like that, in the middle of her contraction, she was airborne. The pain left. The surprise didn't. The stranger had picked her up.

Rising to his feet, O'Rourke couldn't help marveling at the woman in his arms. She didn't feel as if she weighed enough to be having a baby, not even sopping wet. But there certainly was no arguing with the huge mound that met his eye. The woman was definitely swollen with life. Stepping back with her, he took momentary shelter under the awning of a shop that sold bridal gowns.

O'Rourke glanced down the length of the block. He saw a car, its hazard lights on, in the opposite intersection. "Is that your car?"

Kitt nodded her head. "It's dead. I need 911. An ambulance," she added when he said nothing.

The pain came again, harder and faster than before. Bent on breaking her in half from the inside out. Without realizing it, Kitt dug her fingers into his arm, squeezing hard.

Even through his jacket, he could feel the intensity of her grasp. For a little woman, her strength was surprising.

"How far apart are they?" She looked at him with wide, dazed eyes. "The contractions," he prompted. "How far apart are you having them?"

Her breath and voice returned as the pain receded. She all but went limp in the stranger's arms. "I haven't timed them."

"Guess."

She said nothing, but grasped his arm again, harder this time.

"Okay, I'll guess for you," O'Rourke said, a sinking feeling taking hold of the pit of his stomach. "Not far apart at all."

Released from the contraction's viselike grip, Kitt began to pant. That had been an exceedingly hard one. How much worse was this going to get? She was afraid to find out. Really afraid.

"Good guess," she rasped, trying valiantly to maintain a brave front. "Do you have a cell phone?"

"Not yet." It was something he'd been promising himself to get. Now there didn't seem to be any reason. Not if they deported him.

She closed her eyes, searching for strength. It only made the spinning in her head intensify. Kitt opened her eyes again, looking directly at the man who was still holding her.

"Great, the only other person in Southern California without a cell phone and I had to run into him." She looked toward what she'd thought was a public phone from across the street. But there was an Out of Order sign taped across it. "We need to get to a phone. I need an ambulance."

He heard the hitch of rising hysteria in her voice. And then she was clutching at him again, her nails digging into his chest this time. Less than one minute had elapsed between contractions. She was going to give birth any second.

"You need more than that, ma'am." O'Rourke looked around, but everything looked closed for the night. "You're having the baby."

"That's what I'm trying to tell you."

"Now," he emphasized. He saw panic beginning to etch its way into her features even though he'd only put into words what he knew she had to already be thinking. "Don't worry, I'll help you," he promised.

There was no place else to go. He had to put her in the back of his van. At least she could lie down there. As long as he pushed back some of the computer equipment he'd packed on the van's floor.

"Are you a doctor?" she asked warily.

Something else his mother had wished unsuccessfully. O'Rourke smiled as he shook his head.

"No, a brother."

Her head was swimming again. Kitt desperately tried to make sense of what she was hearing. Rain was falling in her face again. They had moved out from under the shelter of the awning. Was that a good thing?

"You mean like some religious order?"

Leaning her against him, he did a quick balancing act and opened the rear doors of his van. "No, like a sibling who saw a fair number of his brothers and sisters come into the world."

"This isn't exactly a spectator sport," she said.

As gently as possible, he lay her on the floor of his van, then hopped up in beside her. There was no blanket available. Stripping off his jacket, O'Rourke turned it inside out and bunched it up, creating a makeshift pillow for her head.

Lifting her head slightly, he slipped his jacket beneath her. "Don't worry, I know what to do." At least, he hoped he remembered. He gave the woman what he hoped was his most confident smile. "My mother used to give birth so fast, there was no time to get her to the doctor or have the midwife come to her."

Kitt could feel another contraction taking root. She licked incredibly dry lips and wished she was six again. Six and sitting in her family room, watching cartoons. Or eighteen and taking her college boards. Any place but here, any time but now.

"So you helped?" she heard herself ask as she

mentally tried to scramble away from the pain there was no escaping.

O'Rourke saw the look in her eyes and took her hand, holding it tight. She held it tighter. "I was the oldest of six."

She felt as if she was in a doomed race. Kitt began to breathe hard. "You're sure you're...not some... weirdo who gets...off...on this kind of thing?"

She was pretty, he thought. Even in pain, with her blond hair pasted against her face, she was pretty. Leaning forward, he brushed the wet hair from her forehead, wishing there was some way to make her comfortable. "Not very trusting, are you?"

That was a laugh. "I have absolutely no reason to *be-e-e-e*." Arching, she rose off the floor and screamed the last part against his ear.

O'Rourke took a deep breath, shaking his head as if that could help him get rid of the ringing. "So much for tuning pianos," he quipped, drawing back. She was shaking. The only thing he had to offer her was his sweater. "I know it's not comfortable, but it's the best I can do right now."

Her eyes widened as she saw him stripping off the sweater. He *was* some kind of weirdo. A weirdo with what looked like a washboard stomach.

Her purse, where was her purse? She had pepper spray in there if she could just get to it. "What are you doing?"

He tucked his sweater around her upper torso as best he could. It wasn't much, but it was better than nothing. "Trying to keep you warm."

He sat back on his heels, taking her hand again. "What's your name?"

"Kitt—with two t's. Kitt Dawson."

"Please to meet you, Kitt with two t's." Shifting his hand so that hers slipped into his, he shook it. "I'm Shawn Michael O'Rourke."

It was coming. Another contraction. She tried to brace herself. "That's some mouthful."

He grasped her hand again, sensing another contraction was about to seize her. "My friends call me O'Rourke."

Her eyes met his. It was blurry inside his van. "And are we going to be friends?"

He grinned. "Well, Kitt-with-two-t's, we're certainly going to be something after tonight."

In response, Kitt screamed again.

Chapter Two

Kitt's scream echoed in his head, making his ears ring.

"I guess this means it's showtime, so to speak," O'Rourke said, bracing himself.

He only hoped he was up to this.

True, he'd helped his mother when it came to be her time, but Sarah O'Rourke gave birth so easily it was almost as if she were a mother hen laying eggs. There was nary a whimper out of her, not even once. Just biting down on what she'd come to call her "birthing stick" and within a half an hour, O'Rourke found himself with a new little brother or sister. He always felt that his mother had simply had him in attendance, off to the side, on the off chance that something went wrong. He'd held her hand, mostly, and mopped her brow.

His father was never around for the momentous occasions. James O'Rourke was too busy trying to earn enough money to support all the hungry little mouths he and Sarah kept bringing into the world.

Standing there, holding his mother's hand, O'Rourke had thought little of it then. It was just the circle of life continuing, nothing more. The impact of it was never as great as it was at this moment. This was some strange woman he was helping.

What if...?

O'Rourke refused to let his mind go there. He had no time for "what-ifs." The woman was screaming again like a bloody banshee, arching so that she looked as if she was trying to execute some incredibly convoluted yoga position from the inside out.

O'Rourke tried to think, to remember. His mother had always seemed so calm about it.

"Gravity'll help you, Kitt." Suddenly inspired, he grasped Kitt by the shoulders and positioned her so that her shoulders were propped up against the wall of boxes in the van.

Wearing a thin cotton blouse that was soaked clear down to the skin, Kitt felt the rough cardboard digging into her back. For the first time, as the twisting corkscrew of pain abated for a moment, she noticed her surroundings. There were boxes everywhere. Big boxes. Was he some kind of bootlegger?

"What...what is all this?" She tried to crane her neck, her hands resting protectively around her swollen belly. "Are...you...a...smuggler?"

O'Rourke bit back a laugh. "Why? Do I look like a smuggler?"

She looked at him with eyes that were beginning to well up with pain again. "You...look..." She searched for a word. "Dangerous."

He'd certainly never thought of himself in that light. "Dangerous?"

She hadn't meant to insult him. He was trying to help her. "The…good…kind of…dangerous."

Amusement curved his mouth even as she clutched at his hand again, squeezing his fingers hard. "There's a good kind?"

"Yes…like you." With his black hair and bright blue eyes, half naked, he made her think of some kind of tortured, poetic hero. "Dangerous…the kind who…lives…on the edge." She blew out a long, cleansing breath, knowing another contraction was about to smash into her. She talked quickly, wanting to get it all out before she couldn't. "Makes a woman's heart flutter. That's my problem. I'm attracted to the window dressing—only to find out that the sale's been over…for months."

The pain was making her delirious, O'Rourke decided. Maybe this wasn't such a piece of cake as he'd hoped. Stories he'd heard from his mother about two-day-long labors came back to him.

He looked past the woman's head toward the front of the van. Maybe there was time to drive her to some hospital after all.

Kitt grabbed his attention and his arm, digging in her nails and crying out.

And then again, maybe not, he amended.

"I'm breaking," she screamed to him. "I'm… breaking…in half…. Someone's…taking one leg…and pulling it…one way…and…the other's… snapping…off."

He'd heard his mother describe it that way. It was when his brother Donovan had made his appearance in the world. Donovan had come in at just under twelve pounds. His father's chest had stayed puffed up for a week despite his mother's choice words about the experience.

"Nobody's pulling either leg, Kitt," he told her as gently as he could while still keeping his voice raised so that she could hear him. "It's your body telling you it's almost time."

"Almost time?" she echoed incredulously, able to focus on his face for a second. "My body's... in...overtime! I've been...in...agony since before...I...left...the house."

He didn't doubt it. She looked like a strong woman, despite her small frame. Good breeding stock, his grandmother would have probably called her. He figured maybe he should put what she was going through in perspective for Kitt. "Women have been known to be in labor for thirty-six hours."

That's not what she wanted to hear at a time like this, when she felt like a ceremonial wishbone. "If I'm going to die," she ground out between tightly clenched teeth, "you're...going with me."

He laughed as he wiped an unexpected bead of perspiration on his forehead with the back of his wrist. "Not at your best under pressure, are you, Kitt-with-two-t's?"

"Yes," she gasped as the pain began again. "I am...but there's only...so much...pressure a person should...have to...take." Her eyes flew open. This was the worst ever. She didn't know if she could get past this latest wave. "Oh-God-oh-God-oh-God."

He could tell by the way she was arching her back that this one had to be a doozy. He had to get her to focus her attention on something else.

"Now, you listen to me. Look at me." When she

didn't, he took her chin in his hand and physically made her look in his direction. "Right here, focus your eyes and look at me." O'Rourke pointed to his own eyes as he released her face. "We're going to have this baby and we're going to be done with it right quick, do you hear me? When I say 'push' I want you to bear down and push to the count of ten and then stop. Ready?" He said it with firm authority, belying his own queasy feelings.

She panted several times before she had enough energy to answer. "Ready."

"Okay." He braced himself. "Now push. Two-three-four…" He continued counting until he reached ten. "Okay, stop."

As if all the air had been let out of her, Kitt collapsed, her head rolling to the side. She lay so still O'Rourke thought she'd fainted until he saw her tense again. Another contraction had taken hold, he thought. "Bear down, Kitt, bear down."

"I *am* bearing down," she spat out, her entire face scrunching up.

Agony was imprinted on her every feature. Her hands fisted, leaning down hard on her knuckles, Kitt hunched forward and pushed for all she was worth. Gasping, trying desperately to get in enough air to keep from passing out, she fell back before O'Rourke reached ten.

She'd stopped when he'd reached eight. This wasn't going to get them anywhere. "Ten, Kitt, you stop at ten, not before."

The man was a tyrant, a tall, good-looking, pig-headed tyrant. She didn't even have enough strength to level a dirty look at him. "You stop at ten, I ran out of steam. As a matter of fact," she said, her energy returning to some degree, "you have the baby. You're better at this than I am."

O'Rourke's eyes narrowed as he looked at her. The uncanny instinct that had brought him to these shores and steered his career in the right direction told him what to do. "You didn't tell me you were a slacker, Kitt-with-two-t's."

If she had the energy, she would have hit him. "You...didn't...ask."

"Kitt—"

The words of encouragement he was about to resort to never had the chance to be spoken. Kitt groaned and then whimpered. The desperate sound wrenched his heart. Another contraction was coming and it was obvious she had no strength for it.

She was going to pass out on him, he realized suddenly, his mind scrambling frantically for a course of action. She had to be up to this, there was no other way. O'Rourke took her hand, wrapping it in both of his.

"Come on, Kitt-with-two-t's," he coached earnestly, "you can do this. Mothers have been doing it since the beginning of time."

"Fine...get one of...them...to do...it."

He focused his eyes on hers, willing her to remain looking at him. "You know better than that, Kitt. It's your baby, you have to do it."

There were tears in her eyes as she dug her fists in on either side of her. "Okay, okay, okay...here comes...another one. *E-e-e-e!*" She shrieked for all she was worth, her body jolting from the force that slammed into her.

"Push," he ordered. "Push like a life depended on it. Harder, harder—" He saw it then, the crown of the head. His heart began to beat as rapidly as he thought hers undoubtedly was. "He's coming! He's coming, Kitt. Your baby's coming!"

"He?" she questioned breathlessly. "That…part's coming out…first?"

Slightly giddy himself, perspiration falling into his eyes, O'Rourke laughed at the image that created. "No. The head, Kitt-with-two-t's, the head's coming out first. Now push! One…two…three…"

She could hardly hear him counting. Kitt bore down, her head swirling again as she fought for consciousness and against the pain that was shredding her into tiny pieces. "Then…how…do you…know it's a…boy?"

"Just a pronoun, nothing more, Kitt."

Wasn't the baby out yet? It felt as if she'd been pushing since the beginning of time. "How *big*…is this…head?"

He should have been keeping her up to speed on progress. But he was so awed by the miracle of life, he'd forgotten.

"Shoulders, we have shoulders." He looked up and saw that she was close to completely collapsing. "Come on, Kitt, we're almost done, just a little more, push a little more—"

Her eyes squeezed shut, Kitt bore down and pushed as hard as was humanly possible for her.

And then she heard it. The lusty howl of a life entering the world.

Her baby. He was here.

Finally.

Exhausted beyond belief, she fell back against the stack of cardboard boxes like a used, limp cleaning rag. "Is he…is he all right?"

O'Rourke's heart was pounding with exhilaration as he looked down at the tiny life-form howling in his hands. He'd held larger computer manuals.

They'd done it. They'd really done it. O'Rourke felt himself grinning like a fool and not caring.

"Your son's a girl, Kitt-with-two-t's. A beautiful, fairylike little girl with soft downy hair and eyes the color of sapphires kissed by the sun."

"A girl?" The wonder of it sliced through the pain that still bracketed her body, allowing her a touch of freedom. "I have a daughter?"

"That you do." Grinning, he looked up at Kitt. "She's a mite messy, but anyone with eyes can see she's a beauty like her mother." Very carefully, O'Rourke handed the tiny being to her mother. "Say hello to your mama, love," he coaxed.

Drenched in perspiration, relief and joy, Kitt accepted the precious bundle into her arms. The instant she held her daughter, she felt her heart swelling.

"So this is what all the fuss was about," she murmured quietly, looking down into the face of her newborn child.

Was it possible to fall in love so fast? In the blink of an eye? She supposed it had to be, because she'd just fallen in love with her daughter.

You're a fool, Jeffrey, to be walking away from this. You have no idea what you're missing.

Now that the excitement was over, O'Rourke became aware of the temperature within the van. It was downright chilly outside and that was seeping its way into the vehicle.

Leaning over both of them, he moved the sweater he'd tried to cover Kitt with. It had fallen in a heap on the side during the birthing.

"Maybe you'd better wrap my sweater around your little girl," he suggested. "It's big enough to cover her completely and it's a wee bit cool for her."

With the sweater wrapped around the small body, Kitt curved her arm around the baby. She looked up at O'Rourke. "What about you?" For the second time, her eyes slid over his body. And for the first time she realized how really close he was. "We've only left you your pants."

He glanced down at himself, as if he'd forgotten that he wasn't wearing anything from the waist up. The grin grew broader. "Good thing you weren't having twins."

The next moment, someone was opening the rear of the van and shining a flashlight inside, nearly blinding O'Rourke.

"Everything all right in here?"

The question and the beam of blinding light were both coming from the heavyset policeman in his late forties who was peering into the van.

The man's curious expression transformed to one of surprise as the sight of O'Rourke's semiunclad body and Kitt's compromising position registered. "Hey, just what the heck's going on here?"

Thinking quickly, O'Rourke pulled Kitt's skirt back down, covering her, then placed his body in between the man and Kitt, summoning his most genial expression. Years of practice from living on the shadier side of the straight and narrow made all this second nature to him.

O'Rourke rocked back on his heels. "You're just in time, Officer. Do you have any matches on you?" He pulled out an Exacto knife from his pants pocket as he asked. The policeman raised one thick eyebrow in silent question, his other hand moving over to his gun and holster. "I've yet to cut the cord between mother and daughter and I need something to sterilize the blade." He held the Exacto knife up for the man's inspection.

The policeman's face paled a little, the full impact of what he was looking at registering. "You mean she's just...?"

O'Rourke nodded as solemnly as an altar boy. "Just this minute, yes. Had you been here a couple of minutes sooner, you could have lent a hand in bringing about life's biggest miracle, Officer." He put out his hand to the man, holding the Exacto knife in the other. "Do you have those matches, sir?"

The policeman shook his head. "The wife made me give up smoking. Called it an anniversary present. It was cheaper than buying her that gold bracelet she fancied—but twice as hard."

O'Rourke nodded knowingly. "That it would be," he said sympathetically. "Never mind, then," he consoled the policeman. "I've got a cigarette lighter I can use. Provided it works," he added almost under his breath. "Never had any use for it myself."

Looking embarrassed now for his intrusion, the policeman withdrew from the van, the flashlight dangling by his side. "Um, I'll go call for an ambulance," he said, jabbing a thumb in the air behind him toward his squad car.

"You do that, Officer," O'Rourke encouraged him from the front of the van.

"O'Rourke?" Kitt called to him weakly.

"In a minute, love." Waiting a moment after pushing the lighter in, he pulled it out again and passed the glowing red circle over the shaft of the Exacto knife blade. He blew on it to cool it. "There, that should do it."

He popped the cigarette lighter back into place, then snaked his way back to Kitt and the baby. Sitting on his heels again, he blew out a breath. He didn't exactly relish this part, but it had to be done.

"This won't hurt a bit," he promised Kitt. Or so his mother had said. His eyes went from her to the baby she held against her breast. Nothing prettier than that, he thought. "Either of you."

Kitt pressed her lips together apprehensively. It wasn't herself she was thinking of, but the baby. The way O'Rourke phrased his assurance told her he'd read her thoughts. "How did you know?"

"You've got that new-mother, protective look about you. I've seen it often enough to be familiar with it." Taking the umbilical cord, he made a quick cut, severing the connection. Then, with a bit of thread, he tied it around the tiny part left above the baby's navel.

"Where did you get the thread?"

The grin flashed again. "I'm a handy man to have around. Never know what's up my sleeve—so to speak," he added with a wink.

Probably a lot of tricks, she thought. She knew his type. As handsome as the day was long and as honest as a leprechaun's promises.

The policeman returned, popping his head in. "Ambulance is on its way," he told them. This time he made his way into the interior to keep the rain from coming in. "Here, I think you could use this." Stripping off his raincoat, he handed it to O'Rourke. "You don't want a bed right next to your wife's in the hospital, do you?'' He followed the question up with a hearty chuckle that turned into a belly laugh.

O'Rourke put on the rain slicker. ''She's not my wife,'' he corrected the policeman.

Although he'd been in love with someone once, he thought as he glanced at Kitt, who looked a great deal like her. Susan O'Hara. Susan got tired of waiting for him to propose and married the banker's son as soon as she was out of high school, he recalled with a touch of nostalgia. Last he'd heard, they had four children and were expecting a fifth. He hoped she was happy.

''We're not married,'' Kitt chimed in.

The policeman, his attention almost completely captivated by the smallest person in the van, shook his head at the information. Looking from one to the other, he seemed genuinely disappointed.

''I know it's not supposed to be necessary in this day and age, having a marriage license and all, but believe me, inside—'' he thumped his barrel chest ''—you'll both feel a whole lot better if you give this little guy a stable home and a full-time mother and father he can have around him every night.''

''She,'' O'Rourke corrected him before Kitt had a chance to do the same.

''She,'' the policeman repeated with a nod of his head. ''Even more important, then. Girls need good examples to help keep them on the straight and narrow.'' He eyed O'Rourke. ''You wouldn't want her having babies of her own without a wedding ring and a loving husband somewhere in the picture, now, would you?''

No, he supposed he wouldn't, O'Rourke thought. If the little doll in Kitt's arms was his. ''But you don't understand,'' he began.

The policeman laughed dismissively. "Hey, just because I've got a few years on you doesn't mean I don't know what it's like to be young. I do. I remember it real well." Shifting toward O'Rourke, he slung one arm around his shoulders in camaraderie. "But marriage is better, trust me. There's something great about having one person to come home to. One person to turn to no matter what." He smiled at Kitt. "Now, you might say that you can do all that without a silly piece of paper, but if it's so silly, I say, what's the harm in having it? Right? And believe me, in the end, it'll come to mean a lot to you. It's the thing that makes you try one more time when you think you've had it and it's time to go your own way." He sighed deeply, as if remembering. "I know what I'm talking about. Why, if it wasn't for my marriage license—"

This had the earmarks of going on even longer than the storm outside, O'Rourke thought. "Officer—" he began, trying to explain.

"Gary," the policeman interjected. "Officer Gary Brinkley."

"Gary," O'Rourke allowed. "You don't understand. We're two strangers."

The smile on the round face turned knowing. "Everyone feels like that sometime or other. Hell…" He stopped abruptly, slanting a look at Kitt. "Excuse me, heck, my wife and I feel that way, too, sometimes. But it's the long haul that counts." He fixed O'Rourke with a look, then swept it toward Kitt. "Promise me you two'll think about it."

O'Rourke and Kitt exchanged glances and both smiled as if on cue.

"Okay," O'Rourke allowed, knowing there was no

other way to call a halt to the kindly lecture. "We promise we'll think about it. Won't we, love?"

She was aching and exhausted. Why being addressed by a generic term should have caused a small thrill to dance through her made absolutely no sense to Kitt. So she didn't even try to figure it out.

Chapter Three

O'Rourke stood outside his van in the rain as the two ambulance attendants, a maternal-looking woman named Martha and a thin-faced man of about thirty, quickly placed Kitt and her baby onto a stretcher.

Because no one seemed to be doing anything to try to keep the rain away from them, O'Rourke took off the rain slicker and held it above Kitt and the baby. He succeeded in keeping their faces dry.

The smile she flashed him made up for the fact that he was now soaked clear down to the bone.

"Can't seem to keep you dressed, can we?" the policeman commented. But as O'Rourke glanced back at him, he could see that Gary approved of the gallant gesture.

O'Rourke slipped the rain slicker onto his now-drenched arms. He might still be a wee bit rough around the edges, he thought, remembering something his mother had once said about him, but at least chivalry wasn't entirely dead within his heart.

"You coming?" the female attendant asked as her partner stabilized the stretcher inside the rear of the ambulance.

O'Rourke shook his head. Chivalry notwithstanding, his part in all this was technically over now that there were more competent people on the scene. Time for the Good Samaritan to be finding his own way home. He began to back away.

"No, I—"

"Sure, he's coming," Gary told the woman, putting out one hand to stop her from closing the ambulance doors. "He's the daddy."

Time to set this man straight. "Actually—" But O'Rourke got no further.

Like a conspirator, unmindful of the rain, Gary lowered his head in close to O'Rourke. His voice was nothing if not sympathetic. He spoke like a man with years of domesticity behind him.

"Now, you don't want to go planting seeds of doubt and discord with the little mother at a time like this, do you? She's been through a great deal." Gary arched a knowing, shaggy brow. "Whatever went down between you from your first time together to now's all in the past. She needs you, boy." The policeman all but pushed him toward the ambulance. "Go hold her hand and tell her she's beautiful."

With rain plastering his hair to his head and pouring down his face, O'Rourke stared at the other man incredulously. In his experience, policemen didn't stand around, doling out advice like some kind of psychologist. "What?"

"Beautiful. Tell her she's beautiful," Gary repeated, raising his voice as the wind began to pick up. "A woman needs to hear stuff like that, especially when she looks as if she could scare the paint right off the walls." He looked toward the interior of the ambulance. The female attendant was scowling at him, waiting to close the door he wasn't releasing. "She's just had your kid, and it looks like she's done a great job, if you ask me. Give her the support she needs. Believe me, you'll come out a winner in the end."

Before O'Rourke had a chance to say anything to protest the blatant assumptions the policeman had made, Gary propelled him into the ambulance.

"Got one more for you, Martha," Gary announced triumphantly.

Suddenly, O'Rourke found himself inside the ambulance. The doors behind him were being closed and Kitt was looking up at him in dazed confusion. He had no choice but to take a seat beside the strapped-in gurney.

"I'll follow you in." The policeman's voice wedged itself into the ambulance just before the rear doors were shut. "It's a slow night."

Not for everybody, O'Rourke thought.

The next second he heard the siren wailing as the ambulance driver picked up speed. They were on their way to the hospital. This evening was definitely one he was going to tell the others about when he phoned home.

Or arrived home, he amended, thinking of the deportation notice on his desk at the apartment.

Was she imagining it, or was the stranger with the washboard stomach at her side again? Kitt blinked twice, trying to clear her vision. The man remained sitting where he was.

"What are you doing in here?"

O'Rourke laughed shortly, trying to stay out of the attendant's way as Martha monitored Kitt's vital signs. "I'm asking myself the same question." He glanced toward the closed doors, wondering if the policeman was making good his claim and was following the ambulance. "The good constable seems to think you need moral support."

His attention drawn back to the woman who was the reason for all the mayhem he'd found himself in in the last half hour, O'Rourke looked at her. There was no doubt that she was exhausted, but there was also no need for him to serve up empty platitudes about her appearance the way Gary had suggested. Despite what she had just been through, wet hair notwithstanding, Kitt Dawson looked radiant. Above and beyond the call of new motherhood. There was something in her face that transcended her ordeal.

O'Rourke had a sneaking suspicion that, fixed up, Kitt Dawson immediately became the center of attention in every room she entered.

Moral support, Kitt thought dully. She could certainly do with some of that right about now. Too exhausted to concentrate, she knew she was going to have to puzzle out what her next move was going to be—and sooner than later.

When she was discharged from the hospital, she could probably stay with Sylvia, her best friend, in her Newport Beach studio apartment. But two people—two and a half people, Kitt silently amended, looking at the sleeping bundle in her arms—living in such close quarters got awfully old fairly quickly.

But at least it would give her a little time to think. And hopefully come up with a viable plan. Right now, she had nothing.

Her Good Samaritan was talking to her, she realized. Concentrating as best she could, Kitt tried to absorb what he was saying to her and not think about how much she hurt. Physically and emotionally.

"Besides," O'Rourke was saying, "you've still got my sweater and my jacket and I sort of thought I'd be taking them back by and by, once they have you settled in at the hospital." He figured it was as good an excuse as any. Besides, the sweater had been Beth's going-away gift to him. His youngest sister would be hurt if she thought he'd just given it away.

Kitt realized that the sweater was still wrapped around her baby. The jacket had somehow managed to come along with her when the attendants had transferred her from the van to the gurney. She felt beneath her head now.

"Your things," she acknowledged with a note of embarrassment. "They'll probably need a lot of work before you can wear them again."

"Don't be worrying about that." As the attendant withdrew, O'Rourke unconsciously drew in closer to Kitt, placing his hand over hers in a silent bond that was as natural to him as breathing. "My mother taught me how to take care of my things well and make them last," he told her with a smile. She'd had to, he added silently, doffing his cap to his mother. When there were six children, money only stretched so far. Fabric stretched farther. "So, what're you going to call her?" He nodded toward her sleeping bundle.

Kitt tightened her arm around the bundle instinctively. She hadn't thought of names, at least not girls names. Something inside of her had been convinced she was going to give birth to a boy. Just like something inside of her had been convinced that Jeffrey was going to make a miraculous turnaround and suddenly become responsible.

Good thing she didn't make her living as a fortune teller, she thought sarcastically. She would have starved to death a long time ago.

Looking down at the bit of heaven in her arms, Kitt sighed now. "I don't know yet."

He'd had a sibling or two who'd had to wait for a moniker, O'Rourke thought. As if sensing she was the topic of conversation, the baby opened her eyes and looked directly at him.

O'Rourke felt his heart being claimed in an instant. "So you're nameless, are you, little one?" he whispered to her softly.

As if in response, the baby made a noise and then closed her eyes again.

Very gently, taking care to only touch his hand lightly along the downy hairs, O'Rourke passed his hand over the small head. "I supposed this qualifies as our first conversation."

Kitt found she couldn't say anything in response. There was suddenly a large lump in her throat, blocking any words.

The next moment, the ambulance had stopped, its rear doors parallel with the doors leading into Harris Memorial's emergency room. The doors flew open. Kitt and her baby were engulfed in a sea of activity as the attendants quickly took her out of the ambulance. An awning sheltered them from the rain.

As a nurse hurried out from the hospital to flank one side of the gurney, an emergency room physician took the other while Martha rattled off Kitt and the baby's vital signs to them.

O'Rourke found himself swept up in the wave, hurrying along to keep up, although logically he knew he should just drop back and let the natural progression of things take over and sweep Kitt and the baby away from him. After all, he wasn't needed any longer.

Feeling foolish, reminding himself that he was facing a huge dilemma of his own and that Kitt and her baby were in good hands now, he slowed down. But as he did so, a hand came down on his shoulder, generating an intense sensation of déjà vu.

O'Rourke didn't have to turn around to know that when he did, he'd be looking down into Officer Gary Brinkley's face.

"What are you doing here?" O'Rourke asked, only mildly surprised.

Gary jerked a thumb back toward the rear of the hospital parking lot where presumably his squad car was standing. "Thought maybe the new dad would need a ride back to his car. Besides—" the policeman nodded at his torso "—you've got my rain slicker."

O'Rourke looked down at his chest. He'd almost forgotten he was walking around in the oversize black slicker. "Oh, right." He began shrugging the slicker off his shoulders.

The hand was back on his shoulder, stopping him. "No, hang on to it until you get something else to wear," Gary urged.

O'Rourke looked after the disappearing gurney. He'd accomplished nothing by coming along. Except maybe to push aside his own problem for a short while longer. But that hadn't erased it. It was time to get going.

He turned to look at the policeman next to him.

"I'll take that ride now, Constable. If you're sure that it won't be taking you away from anything more pressing you have to do—''

The idea of there being something more urgent on tap made the policeman laugh again. He clamped a fatherly arm around O'Rourke's shoulders.

"Hey, this is Bedford.'' He nodded at the disappearing gurney. "That's probably the most exciting thing that's going to happen around here all night.'' He paused, hesitating before venturing back outside. "Don't you want to see your little woman before you go?''

To try to explain one last time to the policeman that Kitt Dawson wasn't *his* little woman and that he had only happened by at an opportune time for her seemed completely futile to him. For simplicity's sake, and because he wanted to get home sometime before midnight, O'Rourke resigned himself to going along with the charade.

"No, I thought I'd give her a chance to get cleaned up a little—and I'd like to do the same before coming back to see her and the baby,'' he added for good measure, having absolutely no intention of doing the latter even if Kitt did have some of his clothing in her possession. It wasn't as if that was his last jacket or sweater, and despite his words to the contrary, she was right. There probably was no way he could get them cleaned at this point. Beth would just have to understand.

The answer had the desired effect on the policeman. He seemed obviously pleased. Nodding his head, Gary steered O'Rourke around toward the rear doors. "Okay, then let's get going.''

* * *

The trip back to his van was not one undertaken in silence.

O'Rourke hadn't really thought that it would be. Officer Gary Brinkley strongly reminded him of Shamus O'Brien, a distant cousin of his mother's in the old country. It wasn't that the two men looked alike, but Shamus could talk the hands off a grandfather clock and not take any note of it as he just kept on going. Not because the man liked to hear the sound of his own voice, but because Shamus truly felt that everything he said was important, gleaned on the battlefields of life. He felt it his duty to share those lessons with those who hadn't had a chance to experience them yet.

And after what sounded like an endless twenty years on the police force, first in Los Angeles County, then here in Bedford, it sounded as if the good constable had a great many lessons of life to impart as well. And O'Rourke found himself the lucky recipient tonight.

It occurred to O'Rourke that he might have been better off walking back to the van in the rain. It would have been a great deal wetter and longer, but on the up side, it would have been a great deal more peaceful.

The topic the police force veteran had settled on was marriage and family. Gary was definitely pushing for the pros. At length.

O'Rourke had a headful of cons to oppose him with, albeit—not wanting to prolong the diatribe any longer than absolutely necessary—he listed them silently. In no uncertain terms, marriage and the family that followed had been both his parents' undoing. And while O'Rourke loved his siblings with a fierceness that would have made the hearts of the creators of greeting cards swell with joy, there was no doubt in his mind that it was the burden of these same siblings, and himself as well, that had first killed off his father, then his mother. Sarah O'Rourke had died of nothing short of a broken heart a little over two years after her husband's demise. Leaving the business of family-raising squarely on O'Rourke's shoulders.

"Nothing like it in the world," Gary was saying for what seemed like the fourth or fifth time. "But hell," the man said, turning in his seat, "I don't have to convince you of that, do I?"

"And why's that?" O'Rourke heard himself asking the question as curiosity got the better of him.

"Because I saw the look in your eyes when you looked down at that baby. You feel it already, don't you?"

Mystified, O'Rourke asked, "Feel what?"

"That tug on your heart." He thumped his chest with his fisted hand. "The one that anchors you in their harbor and makes you vow to do everything in your power to see to it that they get every chance in the world to have the things you didn't. To be happy and healthy and all that other stuff."

Turning another corner, Gary pulled up his squad car in front of the van. The rain had subsided, falling steadily and sedately now rather than in sheets and gusts.

"Here's your van," Gary pointed out needlessly. He twisted around in his seat. "So, you going to do it? Are you going to make an honest woman of her?"

Now, there was a term he hadn't heard in a long time, O'Rourke thought. Not since before he left Ireland. Then it had come from Susan, telling him that

Patrick was going to be making one of her. An honest woman. It was Patrick's baby she was carrying, all the while he'd been thinking that she belonged to him. He'd felt his heart crack a little then, but told himself it hadn't. He'd known that the kind of life he'd planned for himself didn't include having someone like Susan in it. She needed attention he couldn't spare.

He'd wished her luck and shut his heart. Just another sacrifice he'd made to get to where he wanted to be. A man who could take care of his own, meaning the family that already was, not the one that might be, if things were different.

Problem was, he hadn't gotten there yet.

A whimsical smile played on his lips as he looked at the policeman next to him. "Are you a Catholic, Constable?"

The shaggy black-and-gray brows drew together in one formidable hairy line. "What? No. Why?"

"Pity." O'Rourke unhooked his seat belt. "You'd have made an excellent priest. Father Donnelley back home couldn't have held a candle to you." Another man dedicated to long-winded sermons, he thought.

Gary hadn't gotten to where he was in life by not knowing when he was being given the slip. "So, is that a yes or a no?"

O'Rourke grinned. "Not a candle," he repeated, getting out. "Thank you for the ride and the advice. And the rain slicker." Shedding the aforementioned garment, he left it on the passenger seat, then closed the door. He could almost hear the man inside the squad car sigh as he pulled away.

O'Rourke's grin widened.

It faded when he realized he'd left his van keys in

his jacket. The jacket that was now with a dewy-eyed, sharp-tongued woman in Harris Memorial, some fifteen or so miles away.

One of O'Rourke's many dubious talents, garnered during his wild-oats-sowing period before he'd settled down to the business of creating a stable life for his siblings, was gaining access to cars that weren't his own. He'd done it mainly as a challenge, not to steal anything more substantial than a joyride or two. A brush with the law had rid him of that inclination, but he was glad he'd retained the talent, rusty though it was. It got him into his van, which he then hot-wired to get him home.

Home had presented yet another challenge, but he'd picked the lock and finally gotten inside. Happily, he kept a spare set of keys in the apartment so hot-wiring and breaking and entry were not to become a permanent part of his life. But that also meant that he had to go back to the hospital, he realized.

It was the last thought on his mind before he dropped into a restless sleep.

Though the threat of deportation weighed heavily on his soul, his dreams that night were governed by visions of a tiny baby. A tiny, downy-haired baby who laughed up at him, her big eyes fixed on his face. No matter how many times he woke up during the night, each time he fell back asleep, he dreamed of the child.

Deirdre would have been able to make sense of it, he reasoned, thinking of his sister when he finally gave up and stumbled out of bed the next morning. Deirdre always claimed to be able to interpret dreams.

It took no great scholar to broach the surface of it, he thought, pouring coffee into his mug and gulping it down. Last night had remained foremost on his mind, despite his dilemma.

But now it was morning and it was time to try to come to terms with his dilemma: he faced utter disaster if he didn't find a way to remain in the glorious United States with its promise of success and riches.

Clutching his mug, O'Rourke went back to his bathroom and walked into the shower. He remembered to leave the mug outside a second before he turned on the water. He was down to thirteen days. Thirteen days in which to come up with a sudden-death plan or put everything on hold. The latter wasn't an option.

He knew what the market was like these days. If you stopped dancing, you lost your place on the floor. He wasn't about to lose his place. He just needed someone to help him fill up his dance card.

Showered and shaved, O'Rourke went to the converted loft where he had set up the offices of Emerald Computers, a dream still in the making, and tried to put in a full day's work into five hours.

Maybe while he worked, he hoped, something would come to him. The best ideas snuck up on you when you least expected it.

None did.

He figured he might as well make that trip to the hospital and collect his keys, if not his jacket. No sense in having an extra set floating around. Although just possibly, in thirteen days, the keys would belong to an empty apartment.

He wasn't going to let himself think that way, O'Rourke insisted sternly. He wasn't going to be his father, giving up and giving in. There had to be a way.

"I'm taking lunch, Simon," he said to the dark-haired man who was his best friend, as well as his assistant.

Preoccupied, Simon glanced up from the schematic he was studying. The look on his face was pure surprise once O'Rourke's words had sunk in. "You?"

O'Rourke grinned. He didn't ordinarily take a break until it was way past time for calling it a day. Food came to him as an afterthought, thanks to one person or another in the office who shared their own lunch or thought to bring him something back from wherever it was they'd gone. It wasn't something he normally gave much attention to himself. He thrived on energy, not food. Work was far more important to him.

"I've got a friend in the hospital" was all he said as he left. A friend, he added, who had his house and car keys.

She didn't know what to do.

She'd had the foresight to preregister at the hospital just two days ago, so the paperwork and the rest of it were all taken care of. Her insurance, the employee relations woman at the aerospace firm had assured her upon her "outplacement" yesterday, was good to the end of the month. That meant that at least the hospital bill and the doctor's fee were taken care of.

But what about after that?

Kitt chewed on her lower lip. She had no job, no money. There was Sylvia, who'd just left after visiting all morning. The woman had a giant heart and had opened her door to her instantly, after calling Jeffrey a variety of names, some of which Kitt was completely unfamiliar with. But Sylvia was a struggling freelance writer who was just making her own ends meet. There was no way she was going to impose on her best friend for more than a couple of days. She loathed doing even that, but her back was against the wall.

If only there was some way to make the wall come down, Kitt thought in desperation.

There was a light rap on her door. Probably the nurse to bring the baby in for her feeding, she thought. She began slipping the shoulder of her hospital gown down. "Come in."

The next moment, she found herself looking at the man who had come to her aid last night.

O'Rourke.

He'd come in carrying a large bouquet of carnations in one hand. And a tiny bouquet of daisies in the other.

Chapter Four

Kitt suddenly realized that she was perilously close to becoming half nude in another second. Despite the experience they'd shared last night, a rosy hue began to climb up her cheeks. Quickly, she tugged her gown up over her shoulder again.

"Hi." Her throat felt dry. Kitt stared at the man who filled the doorway, a half bemused, half embarrassed look on his face. "What...what are you doing here?"

She'd never expected to see him again, though now that she thought of it, she remembered she'd had a fuzzy dream about him last night. It returned to her in a haze, its edges unclear. She supposed that was the result of the dire circumstances under which they'd been thrown together. There seemed to be no other reason for her to dream about a complete stranger. She couldn't even pinpoint what the dream was about, only that he'd been part of it.

Feeling oddly uncomfortable, O'Rourke launched

into his explanation. "Well, the truth of it is, you have my keys. Both for the house and the van. They were in the pocket of the jacket."

Her eyes widened and she looked toward the closet where the nurse had placed both the jacket and the ruined sweater. The latter was in a sealed plastic bag. "Oh, I'm sorry—how did you get home? Did your wife...?"

"No wife. I've a few talents my sainted mother wished I didn't have. But I'll be taking the keys now if you don't mind, as well as the jacket itself and the sweater." He paused as a thought hit him. "You do still have them, don't you?"

"In the closet." She pointed.

He realized she was looking at the flowers he'd brought. The ones he'd thought to pick up at the gift shop downstairs. The ones he'd forgotten he was holding the instant he'd seen that bare shoulder of hers and the hospital gown dipping down temptingly over the swell of her breast.

Fumbling mentally, O'Rourke paused before opening the closet. "Oh, these. To celebrate you being my first nonfamily delivery, I brought you flowers." Crossing to her bed, he handed her the large bouquet.

How long had it been since she'd had flowers from anyone? The last time she recalled, it had been for her high school graduation and it was her father who'd given them to her.

"And those?" she nodded at the tiny one he still held. "Did your flowers give birth, too?"

Now that he thought of it, the notion that had prompted him to pick up the smaller bouquet seemed foolish. He shrugged, trying to seem casual.

"I got them for the little one. Flowers from her

first admirer, so to speak." He turned away in case Kitt wanted to laugh, pretending to look around. "Is there a vase someplace?"

Kitt felt her eyes begin to smart. She couldn't remember when she'd been so touched.

"You can use the water pitcher," she suggested quietly. Her throat felt as if it was closing up. "And the little bouquet can go into the glass."

She had absolutely no idea why a tiny handful of flowers would affect her so. There were tears threatening to spring into her eyes. Maybe it was because the baby's father hadn't even wanted to stick around to see her born, much less bring her flowers.

Or maybe it was just postpartum depression, Kitt told herself. Why else would she suddenly feel so weepy over tiny white and purple daisies?

Deciding the jacket and sweater could wait, O'Rourke laid the large bouquet on its side on the counter, took the pitcher and filled it halfway with water. He did the same with the glass, then tucked the appropriate bouquets into each.

"I hope your husband won't mind my bringing you flowers." Lucky thing the man wasn't here, O'Rourke realized. The situation could have become rather sticky. He knew he wouldn't exactly appreciate someone bringing flowers to his wife if he had one.

The lump in Kitt's throat grew a little larger and she called herself an idiot to waste any emotion on a man who wouldn't waste the time of day on her. Sheer will made the lump dissolve.

She laughed shortly under her breath. "I don't think there's anything to worry about on that score."

There was something in her voice that caught his attention. O'Rourke turned around, the water pitcher in one hand, the glass in the other. Flowers bowing their heads from each.

"You're not married."

It wasn't a question. As soon as he said it, he had got the distinct feeling that she wasn't.

Kitt raised her chin in an unconscious, defiant gesture. It wasn't by choice she found herself in this situation, she thought, squelching the pang she felt. She came from old-fashioned people with old-fashioned values. You married the person you loved and made babies with. Jeffrey hadn't quite seen it her way. But she'd hung on, hoping. Which probably made her a fool in most people's books, she imagined.

"No, I'm not."

There was a gruffness in her voice, a defensiveness. He'd gone somewhere he wasn't supposed to, he thought.

O'Rourke figured it wasn't a good idea for a new mother to get upset so soon after delivery. Setting both bouquets of flowers down on the counter that ran against the wall where she could see them, he attempted to sound disinterested.

"No one's judging you, love. It was just a question. Just didn't want to be getting my head bashed in by some jealous husband, that's all."

There was a brief flash of kindness in his eyes as he looked at her.

What was the matter with her? Kitt upbraided herself. He was only being nice. She looked for a way to change the subject. "Irish, right? Your accent, I mean," she added when he didn't say anything.

"Yes, Irish. County Cork, specifically. Born and

raised. But I thought my accent was sublimated after all this time. I've been here four years.''

"No, it's not." She thought his accent rather charming, and though it wasn't exactly thick enough to cut with a knife, it was still very much there. "Why would you want to lose it?"

He lifted one shoulder in a careless shrug. "Not lose it, just put it on hold for a while. Natives tend to have more faith in dealing with natives than foreigners. It only stands to reason.''

"Not if the foreigners have more to offer than the natives. What is it that you do?"

What did he call himself? Entrepreneur? Computer visionary? Dreamer? Not exactly sure where to begin, he settled for mystery. "It's complicated."

Kitt frowned. Even in this so-called enlightened day and age, she still ran into prejudice in her field. Was he like that, given to believing inherently in male superiority? "I didn't push out my brains along with Shawna. Try me."

Any thought of explanations were suddenly aborted. "Shawna?"

That's right, he didn't know, she realized. She'd made the decision during the morning feeding.

"My baby. Since I didn't have a name picked out for her, I thought it only fitting that she be named after the man who helped bring her into the world. You don't mind, do you?"

"Mind?" O'Rourke echoed. "No." It hit him funny, creating a small, odd feeling in the pit of his stomach. A little like what he'd experienced when he'd first held the tiny being in his arms last night, except more so. Shawna. He liked it. "Huh. Never had anyone named after me before."

"Then consider it a first." They were getting away from the topic and she was suddenly consumed with curiosity. "You were about to tell me what you do."

He sighed, looking out the window. He could see the harbor from where he stood. The ocean seemed calm. He'd be crossing an ocean soon himself if things didn't turn around for him.

"Not much of anything if the government has its way." He saw her looking at him oddly. "I'm about to be deported."

Kitt's mind jumped to the documentary she'd watched the other night on gangland criminals from the 1930s. Lucky Luciano had been deported. "You're an undesirable?"

O'Rourke's lips curved in a slightly lopsided smile. "That all depends on your definition of undesirable, I suppose." Since he'd mentioned it, there was no point in keeping her in the dark about the actual reason. "My visa's up in thirteen days."

He didn't seem very happy about that, she noted. Maybe he had nothing to go back to. She knew how that was. She wouldn't have wanted to go back to her old home, either. Her parents were both gone and her only brother had moved away to Oregon a couple of years ago. Nothing left but memories. "Can you get an extension?"

He laughed softly. "Those are up, too."

She had no idea why, but it made her sad to think of his leaving. "Then you have to go back?"

Pushing his hands into his pockets, he looked out the window again and stared at cottony clouds that seemed to be pasted in the sky. There *had* to be a solution, he was just missing it. "Looks that way."

"And you don't want to."

No, he didn't want to, he thought. O'Rourke looked at her, trying to keep his tone light. "I'm not nearly ready. The work I'm doing—" No point in getting into that. "Well, it's complicated."

They'd come full circle. "So you said." She thought of her own circumstances. "Well, at least you have somewhere to go to. Count yourself lucky."

Years of playing both mother and father to his siblings while trying to juggle his own life had made him keenly attuned to nuances, though he never admitted as much outright. "Why, don't you?"

"Yes, of course I do." Hearing herself snap had Kitt relenting as she offered him a contrite smile. "At least, temporarily." Because he'd told her some of his problem, she suddenly felt the need to open up herself. The strain of keeping it bottled up was suddenly too much. "You want to compare hard-luck stories? I'll give you a hard-luck story. Try coming back home after being laid off, or 'outplaced' as they whimsically call it at the company where I work, excuse me, worked, to find out that the man you've given your heart, not to mention your paychecks, to has decided that the aerobic instructor down the hall was more suited to him than the slightly overweight, now-out-of-work aerospace engineer he'd been living with, so he's run off with her." She'd been an idiot to call Jeffrey with the news, expecting sympathy. But how was she to know he'd suddenly bolt? "Run off with her, most of my things and all of my joint bank account. The rent's not even paid. It hasn't been for the last three months and the landlady said I have to move out immediately." She struggled to keep the bitterness, as well as the panic, out of her voice. "As of right now, I have no permanent address."

Forgetting that she was a stranger, O'Rourke took the tone he used with his siblings whenever one of them messed up. "Are you daft, woman? How could you have a joint bank account with a man who wasn't your husband?"

She took umbrage at his tone. "Where I come from, they call it being in love."

O'Rourke snorted. "Where I come from, they call it being stupid."

She didn't need this abuse. She'd upbraided herself enough on her own. Served her right for opening up to a total stranger. What was she thinking?

That was the problem, she wasn't thinking, only feeling. Big mistake. Not one she meant to repeat.

"Well, thank you for your flowers," she said coldly, "but I think you'd better leave now."

He'd insulted her. O'Rourke tried to look properly contrite. It was an expression he couldn't ever quite manage.

"Sorry, I didn't mean for that to come out. I have a habit of speaking my mind a little too bluntly." He could almost hear his mother's voice in his head. "My mother used to say it's what made me so rough around the edges. I tend to plow right into the thick of things instead of looking for the door and opening it first. Sorry," he repeated.

Kitt blinked back tears, annoyed with herself for suddenly unloading and then for getting upset about it. Talk about hormones running amok and being out of whack.

She waved away his apology. "Not your fault. I'm just a poor judge of character."

O'Rourke looked around for a box of tissues,

knowing there had to be one somewhere in the room. He spotted it on the counter beside the sink.

"You're not the first one to have that problem, or the last." He picked up the box and brought it over to Kitt. "Fell for the wrong person myself, I did. Problem was, I thought she'd wait for me while I got our future together. Turns out she went on to another man because she got tired of waiting for me." O'Rourke stopped, surprised to hear himself tell her that. It wasn't something he talked about, not even with his friends.

Reaching, Kitt took a tissue out of the box in his hand and wiped the dampness from around her eyes. He was matching her woe for woe. She looked up and studied him for a moment.

"Have you always had this competitive problem?" she asked. "This need to out-misery someone?"

O'Rourke frowned, thinking himself a dolt. Why had he just said all that? It had to be the deportation weighing heavily on his mind that was making him lose his grip this way. Otherwise, why would he just talk about things best left unsaid?

He tossed the box back on the counter. "I was just trying to make you feel better."

"Sorry." She wiped a last stray tear that had trickled out. "It worked." Kitt balled the tissue up in her palm, then sighed. "Temporarily at least." A knock on her door interrupted whatever she was going to add. "Come in."

The door slowly opened and a cheery-looking nurse entered, pushing a small bassinet with a small occupant before her.

"Someone here to see you." The nurse's brown

eyes lit up when she looked at the man standing beside her patient. "And her daddy, too."

"Oh, I'm not—"

The nurse brought the bassinet to a halt at the foot of the bed. "Sterile, no, but that can be taken care of quickly enough," she assured him, crossing to the far wall with its cupboards and closets. "Not sterile in the traditional sense, of course," she chuckled. "That little darling there proved that handily enough."

Chattering away happily, the nurse opened up the cupboard beneath the sink and took out what looked like a flat blue paper towel. Deftly, she shook it out and the "towel" transformed into a paper gown intended to cover the length of its wearer. She held it out to him.

"Here, you put this on and then you can hold your daughter." After a beat, O'Rourke took it from her. She interpreted his look her own way. "Probably seems silly to you, seeing as how you held her without that to begin with. We all heard about the delivery," she confided with a wink. "Very impressive. Lots of fathers fold at the first sign of blood. They go down like a stone. You're a lucky lady," she told Kitt, patting her arm a moment before she went to pick up the baby.

Holding the infant to her, the nurse looked at O'Rourke expectantly. He was still holding the blue paper gown in his hand.

"Well, what are you waiting for? An invitation? Put it on." She waved him to it. "I can't let you hold her until you have the gown on," she reiterated. "And wash your hands. Rules."

It was either put on the gown, or launch into an explanation that, the story making the rounds notwithstanding, he wasn't the father. O'Rourke didn't feel like getting into that. It hadn't worked with the well-meaning policeman last night and he had a feeling it wasn't going to convince the nurse now.

Besides, he wasn't adverse to holding the baby again. The truth was, he rather liked it. There was something special about babies. They represented innocence untouched, potential untapped. That spoke to him, making him hopeful about the future.

No, there was nothing better than holding a newborn in his arms.

Unless it was helming his own company. His own solvent company.

O'Rourke put his arms through the blue gown and pulled the ends together behind him as best he could.

"All right," he pronounced, holding out his arms. "I'm ready for her."

The nurse transferred the baby into his arms. Watching him, a knowing look came into her eyes. "This isn't your first, is it?"

He thought of the others. "No, not my first."

He'd been barely eight the first time he'd held a newborn in his arms. Bridgette. The experience had felt almost mystical to him. Somehow, he placed himself beyond the blood and the obvious detractions, coming to a feeling like no other. The best way he could describe it was to say it was a bonding. A bonding that transcended the everyday and made him feel, for the first time in his young, poverty-stricken life, that there was something beyond the confines of his small town.

Beyond the island he'd been born to, even. It also made him feel that no matter where he went in the world, a part of him would always remain grounded within the babe he'd held in his arms.

That tiny babe was twenty-three now. Twenty-four next June.

Funny how all that came back to him suddenly as he held the child of a woman he didn't know. Held a child he was no part of.

Stirring, Shawna looked up at him with her huge blue eyes, just like the first time. And just like the first time, he felt himself being taken captive by the diminutive being. A captive just as surely as if she'd snatched him into the palm of her hand and held him fast there.

Holding her to his chest, O'Rourke saw Shawna begin to root at his paper gown, locking her rosebud mouth around it. A dampness began to spread out from where contact had been made.

Very gently, he separated her mouth from the paper before she could tear it off. He had a feeling disposable hospital gowns were not on the list of required nutrients for newborns.

"Ah now, love, you won't be finding anything there to satisfy your hunger, I'm afraid. That's your mama's department." He glanced up toward Kitt.

As if on cue, the nurse took the infant from him and briskly presented Shawna to her mother.

"Always makes me misty, seeing a brand-new father with his baby." She cleared her throat. "Didn't know my own," she confided. "This makes me feel that there's hope for the world. You make a lovely couple and now you make an even lovelier family. Core of our culture, the family. Used to be nothing more solid. Time for that to happen again."

So much for protesting that O'Rourke wasn't the

father, Kitt thought. She would have felt like the person who announced to a five-year-old that there was no Santa Claus. Still, she wasn't about to nurse Shawna in front of O'Rourke.

She shook her head. "No, I—"

The nurse looked at her knowingly. "I understand." She lowered her voice. "It's perfectly normal to feel a little awkward about this. Here, let me show you a little trick." Deftly, she positioned her body between the woman in the bed and the man she had assumed was her husband before going to work.

Not that she had to block out his view. Tempting as the woman might be, O'Rourke had averted his eyes to give Kitt the privacy she deserved. A man had to have certain standards.

"This way," he heard the nurse telling Kitt triumphantly, "you can even feed your daughter in public and no one'll be the wiser for it."

"Unless they start to wonder why there's a pair of tiny legs sticking out from under the blanket I have thrown over my shoulder," Kitt quipped. It was an awkward bit of camouflage at best, she thought, looking down at the way the blanket was arranged over her.

The nurse said something in reply, but it was lost on O'Rourke. He'd stopped listening to the exchange as he replayed something the nurse had said earlier in his mind. He'd called them a family. A solid core.

Maybe this was it. The opportunity he was praying for. Why not?

Excitement began to pulse through his veins as the idea took on shape. Granted, it wasn't a new idea. It was actually something that one of his friends at the pub had thrown his way last night before he'd left, half in jest, half because the other man was in his cups and going down for the third time.

At the time, the idea had been laughably ludicrous. He'd put it out of his mind two seconds after it was out of O'Brien's mouth.

But now it was back again and taking on a life of its own.

Desperate men discovered they were capable of desperate things and he was no different. Bridgette had called him just before he'd left this morning to tell him that Brennan had been accepted by the university. Another dream in jeopardy. Going to the university meant books and tuition. The money had to come from somewhere.

Right, from big brother who was on the cusp of being a success in California.

All he needed was a little more time.

Turning the instant the nurse left the room, O'Rourke looked at Kitt and spoke before his courage flagged or his common sense took over.

"Kitt, would you like to marry me?"

Shawna squealed as her mother's arm tightened around her.

Chapter Five

"Excuse me?" It took effort for Kitt to keep her jaw from dropping. She *had* to have misheard him. And yet, he was looking at her as if he expected an answer. "Did you just say...?"

O'Rourke nodded, moving closer to her bed. "Will you marry me? Yes, I did."

She moved her arm more protectively around the baby nursing at her breast, taking care to keep the cotton blanket covering her in place. Kitt never took her eyes off his face. He was playing some kind of cruel joke.

Her mouth hardened. "Aren't you a little early for April Fool's Day?"

He'd never been much of a salesman. He'd always let the facts and ideas speak for themselves. But in this case, Kitt didn't know the facts, so it was up to him to tell her. And convince her that this wasn't all an insane scheme.

O'Rourke had no idea where someone with polish

would begin. He did what he normally did, he just plunged in. "The only thing I'm trying to be early for is my deportation—by derailing it." That just served to confuse her, he thought, seeing the look in her eyes. "Look, I realize that this probably must sound just a little crazy to you—"

"Just a little," she allowed, trying to make sense out of what he was saying. She didn't know whether to be insulted or just vaguely amused. Because he'd come to her aid when she'd really needed someone, Kitt decided to choose the latter.

"And maybe it is," he agreed, hooking his thumbs in his back pockets as he looked at her, "but the way I see it, we've both got a problem—"

Very carefully, she shifted Shawna over to her other breast, then raised her eyes to look at O'Rourke. He had to see how ridiculous this all sounded.

"The way *I* see it, you're the one with the bigger problem if you go around proposing to women you don't know."

He hadn't phrased it right, he thought, annoyed with himself. O'Rourke tried again. "This isn't a marriage proposal—"

Maybe there was something wrong with him after all and she was being a little too blasé, Kitt thought. "Funny, I thought the words 'will you marry me' were a dead giveaway that it was a marriage proposal."

The woman was never going to get married to anyone if she kept interrupting people who were spilling out their guts to her like this. "No," he contradicted her firmly, "it's a business proposal. As in a business arrangement," O'Rourke clarified. "You need a place to stay and some financial help to get you back on your feet. I need a wife to remain in this country—''

Okay, he wasn't dangerous, just a little deranged. Kitt said the first thing that occurred to her. "Isn't getting married to stay here rather a drastic step to take?''

He laughed shortly. Yes, it was drastic, but what choice did he have? "Believe me, if there were any other way to do this, I would be doing it.''

Well, she'd certainly set herself up for that one. He made her sound as if she was a last resort. Kitt looked down at the top of her daughter's head, all that was visible as she nursed Shawna. "There's that head-turning, Irish charm again.''

O'Rourke dug his hands deep into his pockets again and swore silently. He wasn't any good at this.

"Sorry, that didn't come out quite right, but I am a man in a desperate situation.'' As if he was working with a blueprint, he laid it all out for her. "I've sunk every dime I have into making a go of this business I've started, and if I have to leave the country now, then I'll lose everything.''

This man meant nothing to her, she argued with herself. There was no reason to feel guilt creeping in. And yet, she did. Guilt because he was asking her to help and she wasn't jumping in to do it. O'Rourke's fate was temporarily in her hands and she didn't like that feeling.

"I'm sure that if you appeal to someone—''

His eyes held hers and he saw her for what she was. His last hope. "I'm appealing to you.''

Yes, you are.

The thought came to her out of the blue, snatching her breath away. Where had that come from and what was the matter with her? She'd just given birth and lost everything. Being attracted to a man, even in a minor way, should be the last thing on her mind.

Shutting out the thought, she concentrated on making sense out of what he was saying to her. "I mean appeal to someone in the government. Talk to someone at immigration. Someone has to listen."

She didn't look that naive, he thought. "No, they won't," he contradicted. "And even if they did listen, it'd be too late. These things, if they evolve at all, take time. Time's the one thing I don't have. I've got thirteen days to find a way to stay in this grand and glorious country of yours." And he felt every one of those precious minutes as they ticked away, forever slipping out of his grasp. "Thirteen days in which to find a solution so that Brennan can attend the university and Bridgette can go on with her nursing school and Donovan can—"

Finished nursing, Kitt eased Shawna away from her breast, sliding the gown back into place before moving the cotton blanket. Very gently, she placed the infant against her shoulder and patted the tiny back, waiting for a telltale burp.

"Who are all these people?" He was rattling off names that meant nothing to her. "Friends of yours?"

"Relatives of mine," he corrected her. "My brothers and sisters."

O'Rourke'd sounded as if he was about to pick up steam when she'd interrupted him. "Just how many brothers and sisters are there?"

"Five, not counting me." He watched Kitt pat concentric circles along the baby's back. "I told you that last night."

The baby emitted a small sound that was close

enough to a burp to satisfy Kitt. She released the breath she'd been holding.

"I was a little busy at the time. I didn't take in everything you said. Five, huh?" Because of what she'd just been through, Kitt's sympathy immediately went out to O'Rourke's mother.

"Yes, and I'm the oldest." He raised his eyes to hers in silent query, indicating Shawna. When she nodded, he took the infant from her. But instead of returning her immediately to the bassinet, he held the now dozing baby in his arms for a moment, gazing down at the small, round face. His siblings had all been this size once, and he'd held almost all of them the way he was now holding Shawna. "The one they're counting on."

And in truth, he knew he wouldn't have it any other way. He was the patriarch of the family and it was a position he had both made peace with and wanted.

O'Rourke looked up at Kitt, waiting for her response.

He had beautiful eyes, she realized. She felt a little like a deer, caught in the headlights of an oncoming car, except that there was no fear involved. There was, instead, a fascination that made it almost impossible for her to look away.

"So, if you don't stay in this country..." She let her voice trail off.

"All their dreams get put on hold because mine are," he concluded. He placed Shawna back into her bassinet. The infant went on sleeping. "If not destroyed forever." He was being dramatic and he knew it, but he needed to get her on his side.

Kitt folded her hands in her lap before her, sighing. "Boy, you sure know how to work a guilt trip with the best of them, don't you?'' she quipped. "My grandmother had nothing on you.'' And Nana had been a veteran, she recalled.

She paused, knowing that what she was considering was crazy. But marriages had been undertaken for less. Some people married at the end of a short, whirlwind romance punctuated by wild, passionate joinings. She knew one couple who had married after knowing each other for only a month. They'd lived to repent the rash move for the rest of their lives.

How much worse than that was this? Not much, in her book. Maybe it was even better. At least it seemed nobler.

Kitt slanted her glance toward O'Rourke. "If I say yes—*if*,'' she emphasized, putting her hand up to forestall any words from him until she was ready to relinquish the floor. "How long will this 'marriage' be for and what do I get out of it in exchange?'' She knew she was being cold, but that was the only way she could get herself to deal with any of this. Cold and detached. "And before we go any further, exactly what sort of 'expectations' are you going to have of me?''

He knew what she was asking. If she had to worry about him getting any amorous inclinations toward her. "You'll be my wife in name only.'' He wanted to be completely up front with her. "The only time you'll have to pretend any sort of affection toward me is when the INS agent questions us.''

She'd completely forgotten about that part. "We're going to be interrogated?'' In general she did well under pressure, but not when it came to doing something that could place her on the wrong side of the law.

"In a manner of speaking," O'Rourke answered offhandedly. "The INS frowns on bogus marriages entered into for the sole purpose of keeping an alien in the country."

Which described their proposed union to a tee. "Frowns I can handle. What else do they do?"

He didn't want to spend the afternoon being the INS's press secretary. Or sabotaging his only chance. "That's not important. If we convince them that this is an actual love match, there shouldn't be a problem." He glanced at the sleeping baby. Funny how some things just came together when you needed them. He'd wished for a miracle last night and now it seemed that he might have just gotten one. As long as the miracle agreed. "And your just having given birth helps to make things believable."

How convenient for her to give birth at such an opportune time, she thought sarcastically. "You intend to say you're the father?"

O'Rourke shrugged. It wasn't that far-fetched. "Everyone else is already saying it—"

Who was he trying to convince, her or himself? "One wanna-be advise-columnist policeman and a nurse who made a natural mistake do not technically qualify as 'everybody.'"

He realized he was rationalizing. Worse, he was clutching at straws. That wasn't like him.

O'Rourke made himself back away and give her breathing space, at least emotionally.

"You're right," he told her, taking her hands in his. "They don't matter. The only one who matters in this is you." He made his best pitch. "If you do me this favor, there'll be a substantial amount of money at the end of the allotted time for you. Until then, I'll give you a roof over your head and provide for you and the baby.''

Her independent streak bristled, but she left her hands where they were. "I'm perfectly capable of earning a living for myself and Shawna."

As he spoke, he slowly ran his thumbs along the inside of her hands, underscoring his point. And managing to unsettle himself in the bargain. ''No one's disputing that, but you said you were out of a job and until you find one, by your own admission, you're out of funds."

She hated this, hated being in this position. Raising her head, she could feel everything within her rebelling. "So what you're saying is that I'm basically selling myself to you—"

"Leasing," O'Rourke corrected her, struggling not to just throw his hands up and say the hell with it.

He wasn't accustomed to begging, not even when the recipient of his pleas was a woman who would have easily gladdened the heart of any normal man with normal inclinations. Something he couldn't allow himself to experience until he brought his dream to successful fruition.

"I prefer the term 'leasing,'" he reiterated. "And it would be getting me out of one huge jam, not to mention saving—"

"—Bridgette, Brennan, Donovan and who knows who else, yes, I know," she said.

Kitt sighed, drawing her hands away, damning Jeffrey for putting her in a position to even consider this. She shut her eyes. She had to be crazy. She *was* actually considering it.

But what choice did she have? With no money, no job and nowhere to go, she wasn't exactly chock-full of options here herself. Their friendship aside, staying with Sylvia would feel too much like charity to her.

Here at least she would be "paying" for what she was getting. Kitt opened her eyes to find him watching her. Something fluttered in her stomach.

That was probably a sign to turn him down. She ignored it. "And you won't be expecting any connubial rights?"

"I have no connubial rights," he told her flatly. "What I have are obligations." He read what looked like doubt in her eyes. "Besides, someone once said I didn't have the time to kiss a woman, much less do anything else with her."

"I hope it wasn't a girlfriend who said it."

One corner of his mouth lifted slightly in amusement. And remembrance. "It was."

She was on the verge of saying yes. "Maybe I will be safe at that."

He took her hand to silently seal the agreement. "You'll be safe, Kitt-with-two-t's, I promise you that." He *wanted* her to feel safe. "I can give you a list of references to check out so that you can assure yourself you're not throwing your lot in with some madman newly escaped from the insane asylum."

His choice of disclaimers amused her. She felt herself beginning to relax. Maybe this was a good thing she was doing. "Comforting."

By nature he wasn't all that talkative. But he felt immensely relieved right now, as if a huge boulder had been removed from his chest. That sort of thing tended to make a mute man verbose.

"I mean it to be." He looked into her eyes earnestly. "I need help, Kitt-with-two-t's, and I'll be everlastingly grateful if I receive it. I mean to make my fortune here, as well as the fortunes of those depending on me. I can't let a little thing like deportation get in the way." He took a deep breath. "So, what do you say? Will you marry me?"

The irony of it struck her full force. "You know, I've waited all my life to hear those words." She laughed softly. That would teach her to be a dreamer. "I never expected it to sound like a business merger."

He felt his sympathies aroused. A woman like Kitt deserved better, she deserved to be proposed to by a man who meant to give her a real home and a family, not just shelter.

"I can make it sound more romantic if you like, Kitt, but you'll know it'll be a lie."

She had to stop being such a dreamer. The real world was a demanding place. Hadn't she learned that yet?

"Yes, I know." She told herself to look at the bright side and make the best of things. "And I appreciate your being so honest with me, especially after what I've just gone through with Jeffrey." Kitt made up her mind. She was going to go along with this, she thought. But she needed more information. "If I say yes, how long does this 'arrangement' have to go on?"

"A little more than a year." The rules demanded a year. He figured a little longer than that would be playing it safe. "After that, you're free to divorce me any time you want."

"A little more than a year," she repeated.

It sounded like a long time to some, but she had no plans for the next year or so on the romantic front. No plans for the rest of her life, really, other than raising Shawna and being the best mother possible. She'd learned her lesson when it came to men. It could be summed up in two words: *stay clear.*

A little more than a year. That provided a great deal of leeway. Marrying O'Rourke would free her up not to jump at the first job she found. It would allow her the luxury of looking for something that had a good future with it. And the luxury to enjoy her baby for a few weeks without feeling guilty about it—or feeling guilty because she'd had to rush back to work in order to put food on the table and diapers on Shawna's little bottom.

In reality, this was a godsend, she reasoned. They would each get what they wanted. She'd get her breathing space and he would get the time he said he needed to finish whatever it was he needed to finish. She was going to have to ask him to go into greater detail about that. But not right now.

"All right, Shawn Michael O'Rourke, I accept." She put out her hand to seal the bargain. "I'll be your wife. In name only."

His fingers closed around hers. "Absolutely," he said, raising his other hand in a solemn promise. "I'll only touch you if someone's looking."

Her eyes narrowed as she drew her hand away. "Define *touch.*"

Rather than waste a lot of words, he showed her instead.

"Like this." Briefly, he took her hand again. "Or this." O'Rourke cupped her elbow as if escorting her from a car. "Or maybe, if the INS man is boring suspicious holes into us, like this." He slid his fingers along her cheek in a gesture he remembered seeing shared between his parents on those rare occasions when they had a moment to themselves and the responsibilities weren't crushing them beneath their weight.

Something small and intense moved through her, unfurling fledgling wings that still managed to flap strongly. She dismissed the feeling as something associated with the after-effects of giving birth. What else could it be?

"All right," she agreed quietly, praying she wasn't going to live to regret this. "Do what you have to do. I'll marry you."

As a surge of pure, unadulterated joy and triumph spiked through him, O'Rourke fought the very real urge to kiss her.

But he didn't, knowing it would be misinterpreted and ruin everything.

Simon Gallagher abandoned the programming equation that had his eyes almost crossing and rose from his desk like a man who had suddenly found he'd been transported to a foreign land when he wasn't looking. He stared at O'Rourke, a man he'd known almost from the first moment the latter had arrived in the country.

"You want me to be what?"

"My best man," O'Rourke repeated. He would have preferred having this exchange after hours, over two bottles of dark beer at the Shamrock, but time was of the essence and he couldn't afford to waste any. Throwing a wedding together took time. "You're the best I can find on such short notice," he told the smaller man dryly, "so you'll have to do."

Simon shook his head, mystified. "O'Rourke, O'Rourke, O'Rourke, you're going too fast for me.

You left here two hours ago to have lunch and then you come back—just after I've made up my mind to drag Newport Bay looking for your body because you've never been more than fifteen minutes away from your desk since we found this loft—to tell me that you're planning to get married." Getting up from his desk, he came around to his best friend's side, more than a little concerned. "What happened to you while you were gone? Did some alien creatures abduct you like in that show Mavis is always watching?"

O'Rourke was well aware of Simon's sister's viewing preferences. The choice of words seemed almost ironic to him.

"No, but I'm trying to avoid being 'abducted' as an alien and sent on my way." He had, and always would have, strong ties to Ireland. He wanted to go home, but to visit and of his own free will, not because he was being forced to go.

Simon crossed his arms before his chest, studying his friend and business associate. "So I take it this isn't a love match?"

"The only thing I love is my work and my family, not necessarily in that order. And I tolerate you on occasion," he added.

Simon ignored the barb. "And this woman you're marrying, she understands that?"

They were alone in this section of the loft. Nonetheless, O'Rourke lowered his voice even more. "It's a business arrangement," he allowed. "But that's just something between you, me and her, understood? As far as everyone else is concerned, I'm marrying the mother of my child and living up to my responsibilities."

O'Rourke glanced back toward the other end of the loft, where the rest of his crew was working. He intended to have them all attend the wedding, every last mother's son and daughter of them. To bear witness to the marriage.

Though he'd been trying to find a solution to O'Rourke's problem himself, Simon played devil's advocate. "Thirteen days before you're scheduled deportation. Seems a mite convenient, don't you think?"

"Nine," O'Rourke corrected him. He couldn't arrange to get the church before then, and if he was going to pull this off, he had to include as many trappings in this wedding as possible. "And life's a lot stranger than fiction."

Maybe this might work at that. Who knew? "That it is, boyo, that it is," Simon agreed, affecting a strong brogue. "Okay, you can count on me to stand up for you." He clapped O'Rourke on the back. "I just hope you know what you're doing."

"Do you have any idea what you're doing?" Horror echoed in Sylvia Mason's voice.

"Yes. I'm getting married," Kitt told her simply.

Sylvia had come by just before visiting hours were over for the night to see how she was doing and if she could cheer Kitt up. The last thing in the world she expected was to be invited to Kitt's wedding.

"I've never known giving birth could make a person go insane." Sylvia shook her head incredulously. "Who is he, Kitt? Do you know anything about him? How do you know he won't slit your throat while you're sleeping?"

That was *not* what she needed to hear. She had

enough doubts plaguing her. "You have got to get yourself assigned to another news desk, Sylvia."

Sylvia frowned. "You're not answering my question, Kitt."

No, and she wasn't going to. She wasn't about to start entertaining absurd thoughts. Her mind was made up. It had to be. For Shawna's sake. "I wanted you for my maid of honor, not my interrogator."

"You're in luck, I'm having a two-for-one sale." She grabbed both of Kitt's hands, forcing her best friend to look at her. "Look, my friend, I'm not going to be your maid of honor, I'm not even letting you out of this hospital room tomorrow until you tell me who this guy is and why you're marrying him."

She knew Sylvia meant well. She was just concerned about her. "I already told you. He's the man who delivered my baby. The man I named Shawna after."

"So?" Sylvia didn't see that as an explanation for the drastic step Kitt was proposing to take. "Send him a gift basket with a thank-you card attached. Don't marry him, for God's sakes."

Kitt hesitated, debating with herself. She could trust Sylvia. "Sylvia, you have to promise me that what I'm about to tell you doesn't leave this room."

"You're beginning to sound like a cheap thriller. Okay, okay." Sylvia raised her hand in solemn promise. "Not leaving the room, not a word. Now, tell me. What's the big mystery?"

Kitt took a deep breath. "He's about to be deported—"

"Oh, great. And he's marrying you to stay in this country."

In the face of Sylvia's annoyance, Kitt suddenly

felt protective of O'Rourke, although for the life of her she wouldn't have been able to explain why. The man didn't really mean anything to her.

"And I'm marrying him so that I can take a little time getting back on my feet."

Sylvia cut her short. "You can do that in my apartment."

Kitt smiled at the other woman. "You don't have enough room in your apartment for two fleas to go square dancing, Sylvia. Believe me, this is for the best." Her resolve wavering, she needed support, not arguments. "Don't give me a hard time, Sylvia. Just say you'll be my maid of honor." She raised her eyes in silent supplication. "I really need you in my corner about this."

"Okay." Sylvia sighed loudly, relenting. "But I plan to make periodic checks on you to make sure he hasn't stuffed you into a planter or something."

Relieved, Kitt laid back against her pillows. "I can trust him, Sylvia."

Sylvia frowned. "As I remember, you said the same thing about Jeffrey."

"I was in love with Jeffrey, Sylvia. I'm not in love with O'Rourke."

Sylvia sighed, shaking her head. "Perfect way to start a marriage, no love, no expectations."

"No disappointment," Kitt interjected.

"I hope you know what you're doing, Kitt."

So did she, Kitt thought. So did she.

Chapter Six

"It's not much." Opening the door to his apartment, O'Rourke pocketed his key and stepped back to allow Kitt and the baby room to come in.

He glanced at his watch as he closed the door behind her. He'd taken precious time off to pick her up at the hospital and bring her and the baby directly here. There was a conference call he had to be back for within the hour.

Instinctively, Kitt held the infant in her arms closer to her. She felt as if she'd stepped right into the heart of pure chaos. There were books and papers everywhere, intermixed with empty pizza boxes, journals and clothes that had fallen miles short of making it into the laundry hamper.

Kitt's eyes widened as she took it all in. How could anyone live like this? There were things on every surface as far as the eye could see.

"Oh, I don't know," she replied. "Looks like a lot to me."

"You're talking about the mess," he guessed, chagrined. He'd meant to clean it all up last night, but he'd stayed too late at the loft. The trouble was, he had good intentions, but good intentions took time and he never had any of that. Work ate it all up.

She turned to stare at him. He didn't look like a slovenly man. "You didn't tell me you lived in a frat house."

He wasn't sure exactly what she was alluding to, but he figured it had something to do with the state of his living quarters. He supposed that any cryptic comment was probably well deserved. He'd never gotten the knack of keeping house.

O'Rourke paused to set down the suitcase he was carrying, the one that he'd discovered Kitt had hastily thrown together just before attempting to drive herself to the hospital. He'd gone back to retrieve it for her yesterday, taking a mechanic friend of his along to see what could be done about her car. A new alternator had resurrected it and brought it back to the land of the living. He'd had it driven over to his apartment complex, where it now resided in guest parking.

Shrugging, he looked around, trying to see it through her eyes. It did look pretty awful. "This is the first time I've had this much room to myself and I guess I got a little carried away."

In Kitt's estimation, he looked slightly embarrassed. There was hope for him, she decided. Her brother had attracted chaos like this and had thought nothing of it. She'd always felt sorry for whoever wound up marrying Perry.

O'Rourke picked up a pair of underwear and tucked it out of sight beneath a shirt that straddled the arm of the sofa. "I was going to clean up, but there was this bug at the office."

Probably some here, too, she thought, looking around cautiously. "Bug? As in something needing to be exterminated?"

It took him a second to catch the misunderstanding. "No, as in glitch." He tried again. "As in an impediment." He never had gotten around to telling her what he was working on. Maybe it was time. He picked up her suitcase again. "You might as well know something about the man you're marrying...."

His voice seem to fade slightly as the phrase jumped out at her.

The man you're marrying.

It almost sounded surreal to her. She was marrying someone because she had to. It was like something out of the nineteenth century. With effort, Kitt pulled herself back, trying to focus on what O'Rourke was saying to her. Something about computer systems and innovations. Speed. RAM. All the buzz words that were so important to the Silicon Valley generation. Somehow they had all become of secondary importance to her in the last few days.

She looked down at the sleeping baby in her arms. Now there was nothing more important in her life than Shawna.

Raising her eyes to O'Rourke again, Kitt tried to look as if she was interested in what he was saying.

She didn't fool him for a second. "Your eyes are glazing over." He laughed. "Sorry, I tend to get carried away when I'm talking about Emmie."

"Emmie?"

His mind was always jumping ahead to things. At times it was hard keeping track of what he had and what he hadn't already said. And what he'd only thought he'd said out loud.

"That's what we've nicknamed the prototype computer. Short for Emerald. The company's name is Emerald Computers."

Well, that made sense, seeing where he was from, she thought. "Good thing to know." She looked around uncertainly at the wall-to-wall mess. "Um, where are we going to be staying?"

"We?"

Lowering her eyes, Kitt indicated the baby in her arms. "Shawna and I." She was almost afraid to venture out of the living room into the hall. "There is something beyond this, isn't there?"

Caught up in his explanation about his work, he'd almost forgotten why she was here. There were times when his mind felt as disorganized as his apartment was. "Oh, right, sure. This way."

Careful to circumvent the three-foot-high stack of technical books that were doing a shaky imitation of the Leaning Tower of Pisa in the center of the room, O'Rourke led the way to the rear of the apartment. He brought them to a room that looked as if it was little bigger than an expanded broom closet. A very crowded expanded broom closet, now that he looked at it through her eyes.

"There's no bed in it now," he apologized. "But I can get one. Right now I've made it into my den."

She wouldn't have known what to call it herself, other than a disaster. Trying not to jostle Shawna, she peered cautiously into the room. "How can you tell?"

He laughed under his breath. He had that coming, too. "Housekeeping was never my long suit."

She looked at him. "I don't think I would have had trouble guessing that one."

O'Rourke made a hasty reassessment, then mentally retraced his steps and pointed to the room opposite the den. "Maybe for the time being, you'd better stay in the bedroom."

She looked at him suspiciously, still not a hundred percent convinced that she had made the right move, agreeing to come here, much less to marry him. Sylvia's studio apartment was looking better and better to her all the time. Sylvia knew where to find the trash can. "Where will you be sleeping?"

"On the sofa." He nodded in the general direction. "In the living room."

She tried to remember actually seeing one. "There was a sofa out there?"

"It's not as bad as all that," he protested, then paused. "All right, I suppose it is as bad as all that, but I haven't had the time to fix things up, what with working and planning the wedding and all."

Kitt turned around to look at him. "You're 'planning' the wedding? I thought we'd just go to some justice of the peace...." She'd envisioned something that involved the three of them and two witnesses, Sylvia and whoever he decided to bring with him. This sounded as if it had the potential for a great deal more.

As O'Rourke moved into the room, he began to clear things away. It was a task steeped in futility. As one heap became smaller, another grew larger. "It'll look better if it's done in a church, with friends looking on." He tossed several shirts into a corner, out of the way for the time being. "Speaking of which, have you got any friends you'll be wanting to invite?"

She and Jeffrey had moved here a little more than a year ago from San Francisco. She hadn't had time to make many friends other than Sylvia. Jeffrey and her career had taken up a great deal of her time.

Fat lot of good that had done her, she thought.

Kitt fought back the wave of self-pity that threatened to overcome her. If she could just keep ahead of it every time it reared its head, eventually she would outlast it, she promised herself. The trick was to keep tap dancing as fast as she could.

And to remember never to trust another man as long as she lived.

"Just a few," she told him. Shawna stirred, but to Kitt's relief, the infant went on sleeping. Kitt began to rock slightly as she looked around the room again. "We're going to need a crib."

He set her suitcase down in front of the pile of shirts. "You haven't got one in your apartment?"

She shook her head. "Never got around to buying one." The reason for it was silly, she supposed. "My mother handed down this superstition—buy things for the baby and maybe the baby—"

"Won't come," he finished, nodding his head as he substituted a euphemism for the final word. There was no need to explain superstitions to him. He'd grown up with them. "My mother had the same superstition. Of course, she didn't have a chance to get rid of the baby things for years after I was born. Didn't stop the little ones from coming."

Moving around her, O'Rourke opened the bottom drawer of his bureau and shook out the contents onto the floor. Socks, all singular, spread out on the carpet as he went out into the hall and began to rummage through the linen closet.

Now what? She followed him out into the hall. "Um, don't you think there're enough things on the floor already?"

"I'll find a place for them," he promised, walking back into the bedroom. He ignored the pile of socks and crouched down over the drawer he'd just removed. Carefully, he spread out first two towels and then a folded sheet in it. "Right now, we need a place for the baby to sleep."

She stared at the wooden rectangle. "The drawer?" she asked incredulously.

He glanced at Kitt over his shoulder. Obviously the woman had never had to make do. He was an expert at it.

O'Rourke rose to his feet. "According to my da, that was where I spent the first month and a half of my life until he and Ma got enough money together to buy a secondhand crib."

It sounded like something out of a fairy tale. "You slept in the drawer?"

"Like a baby," he quipped, taking hers from her. "All right, love," he whispered softly to the infant, "this is your new bed, at least for tonight." Gently, he laid Shawna down in her newly arranged bed. She looked like an angel, he thought. Rising, he stood back to admire his handiwork. Shawna continued sleeping. "She likes it."

"I suppose it's all right for now," Kitt allowed guardedly. She looked toward the king-size bed that dominated the room. Like the rest of the apartment, it was littered with books, papers and discarded clothing. "You're absolutely sure there's a bed under there somewhere."

He winked at her, sending a sudden, unannounced

shiver shimmying down her spine. "I have it on the best authority." And now, he thought, looking at his watch again, it was time to get going if he was going to make that conference. He began backing out. "I've had your car brought around. It's parked in guest parking. There's a box of diapers there," he pointed vaguely to an opposite corner of the room. "And here's an extra set of keys to the apartment." He'd almost forgotten to give them to her. "Take-out numbers are posted above the phone in the kitchen. Order anything you want. You'll find money in the drawer next to the knives. I have to go."

He was leaving her? And who kept money in a kitchen drawer with the utensils? "Go? Go where?" she asked as she followed him out of the room.

"Back to work."

Hurrying to the front door, he stopped just as he opened it. He realized that it probably seemed as if he was abandoning her, but he had little choice. The call was going to be coming in soon and he had to be there to take it. Doubling back, he squeezed her arm awkwardly.

"Get some rest," he instructed gruffly. "And make yourself at home."

And then he was gone.

"Sure," she said, addressing her words to the closed door. "If home was a pigsty."

Turning slowly around to face the turmoil that surrounded her, she sighed deeply. Alice in Disasterland. At least he'd had the presence of mind to bring her car here.

Still, despite the car and the diapers, she was far from comforted. "Oh, God, Kitt, what have you gone and gotten yourself into?"

* * *

The first thing that occurred to O'Rourke after he'd let himself in late that night was that somehow, his key had fit into the wrong lock.

He was in the wrong apartment. He had to be.

What other explanation was there? There was no pile of shirts stacked by the door, waiting for an opportune moment to be carried off to the laundry room at the other end of the complex. No overturned laundry basket he meant to pick up in the corner. The coffee table was out and in plain sight rather than lost beneath an ocean of newspapers and technical journals.

Like a man in a trance, O'Rourke took a few steps forward, pocketing his key again.

The sofa was visible as well, without a single textbook sinking into any of its cushions. And as for the carpet, it was completely unmarred by anything except furniture.

It was as if a tornado had gone through the room and rather than leave debris in its path, had neatly sucked out everything that didn't ordinarily belong in a living room.

Had to be the wrong apartment.

He looked around again. No, this was his apartment all right. He recognized the furniture.

Awed, O'Rourke made his way into the darkened room slowly, then stopped to slant a glance toward the kitchen. He'd left it looking like a near-survivor in a three-day, all-male chili cook-off competition. Every dish, pot and utensil he owned had been out, either in the sink or on the counter and table, remnants of meals past evident somewhere on their surface.

They were all gone, every last one of them.

Washed, dried and put away from the looks of it when he explored the interior of kitchen cabinets he'd long since left empty. They were full now. Full and organized.

No pungent order of decaying plant and/or animal life met his nose when he opened the refrigerator. It was also gleaming in its emptiness. If she'd ordered out, there was no telltale evidence of it, no drooping, half-sealed container wilting on one of the shelves the way there had been when he'd left this morning.

O'Rourke shook his head in complete amazement.

As he made his way to the bathroom, nothing got in his way on the floor, blocking progress. Whatever he'd left on the floor had been picked up and disposed of in some manner or other. Even the shower looked clean.

Peeking into the room he had offered her to begin with, O'Rourke saw that it once again looked like a den. Books were back on the shelves, even the ones from the living room. Papers were neatly stacked on the desk and the small daybed against the wall was not only visible, it was accessible.

He'd forgotten all about that, losing it in the clutter of books, papers and magazines. He had somewhere to sleep now, other than the sofa.

He felt like a visitor to a foreign land. Because he was bone-tired, he lay down on the daybed, promising himself that he was only going to close his eyes for a minute.

The crying woke him.

It crept into his dreams, pushing them apart until they disappeared without a trace. High-pitched crying, the kind that belonged to a newborn just testing its lungs and power.

"Deirdre?" he murmured. No, Deirdre wasn't a baby anymore, he thought thickly. Deirdre was eighteen now. "Beth?" he mumbled, sitting up.

The moment he did, the cobwebs evaporated from his brain and he remembered. His sisters and brothers were a continent and an ocean away. The crying was coming from his bedroom.

Shawna.

He was on his feet, stumbling for the doorway before he was completely awake. That he wasn't stubbing his toes on various objects in his path registered vaguely as he found his way to his bedroom.

He almost entered before he remembered he wasn't supposed to. It wasn't his room now, it belonged to Kitt and they had an agreement.

Feeling slightly frustrated at being kept out of his own bedroom, O'Rourke leaned against the door so his voice would carry without making it seem as if he was shouting at her.

"Kitt, it's O'Rourke. Is everything all right in there?"

The next thing he knew, the door was opening and he found himself face-to-face with Kitt, her hair mussed and wild about her shoulders, her eyes ever so slightly puffy from lack of sleep. The robe she had on was partially undone at the waist and a light blue nightgown was peeking out, teasing his attention.

He caught himself thinking he'd never seen anything lovelier in his life before he hastily banished the thought. If he started letting himself go that route, this arrangement between the two of them was never going to work. In return for her help, he'd offered Kitt shelter, not lechery, and he might have his faults, but lying wasn't one of them. He was an honorable man and he stuck to his word. A bargain was a bargain. Even if it might not be an easy one.

She'd heard him come in earlier and wondered if he'd knock on her door before going to bed. She never slept well in a new place, and even if she had been so inclined, a certain six-pound, three-ouce princess wasn't about to let her get more than a few minutes of sleep at a time. It felt as if she'd been up all night and she probably looked it, Kitt thought, though she was sure it didn't matter to the man standing in the doorway.

"She's just wet," Kitt told him. She turned around and led the way back to the bed, the baby in her arms. "I never realized babies leaked so much."

He grinned, dragging one hand through his hair to get it out of his eyes.

"That they do, love," he assured her. "You no sooner fill up one end than the other end starts making room for more."

Kitt put Shawna down on the bed and began changing her. O'Rourke looked around the room. It was the same in here as it had been throughout the rest of the house. He hardly recognized it. Everything was so neat, it looked as if it was waiting for a photographer to come and immortalize it on film.

He looked in Kitt's direction, about to comment on the transformation, but his words dried up in his mouth. She was bending over the baby, completely oblivious to the fact that he had a very clear, very tantalizing view of her breasts. It took him a moment before he finally found his tongue.

"What did you *do* to the place?"

She spared him a glance before putting the finishing touches on Shawna's tiny diaper. She thought it odd that he was staring at the opposite wall.

"I made it livable. I had some time on my hands," she told him, quickly disposing of the soggy diaper by throwing it into a wastebasket he realized had once been in the bathroom.

O'Rourke cleared his throat, feeling suddenly awkward. "I thought you were supposed to rest while the baby was sleeping."

It hadn't quite worked out that way. Unable to stand the mess, she'd started to pick up just a few things. One thing had led to another until she'd finally cleaned up the entire apartment. Even with all that work behind her, she still hadn't been able to sleep.

She shrugged. "I got restless. I'm not much good at sitting around."

"Neither am I, but I never felt the urge to clean anything." Redirecting his attention to the work she'd accomplished rather than to the woman herself, he found himself relaxing again. "You're a miracle worker, woman. It didn't look this good the day I moved in."

"I can well believe that." She looked up to find him staring at her, waiting for an explanation to go along with her comment. "I found things growing in the refrigerator that looked as if it had been brought by the dinosaurs before the Ice Age. Don't you *ever* clean out the refrigerator?"

"I thought you did that when you ate everything that was in it," he said wryly.

His voice drifted away as he turned toward the bureau. When he'd left, it was cluttered with clothes and a copy of the program for the hardware he was trying to complete. Those had disappeared, replaced with a collection of small framed photographs positioned equidistant from one another.

Kitt saw what had taken away his attention and caught her lower lip between her teeth. Had she overstepped her bounds in her zeal to make the place less likely to attract the attention of the health department?

"I found those under the bed when I was vacuuming. I thought you might like them better if they were on the bureau."

He'd wondered where the photographs had gotten to. Picking up the one of his youngest sister, Beth, O'Rourke paused for a second before replacing it and looking back at Kitt.

"Thanks, I've been meaning to do that," he mumbled. Expressing gratitude always put him on shaky grounds.

She nodded. "I figured as much. Interesting storage place," she couldn't resist adding. "Oh, by the way, if you're looking for your clothes in the morning, you'll find them either in the bureau or in the closet. I found your filing system of leaving them all over the apartment too complicated to remember once I washed them."

His mouth fell open. That wasn't in the bargain, either. "You washed them?"

She nodded, picking up the baby and resting her against her shoulder. "It was either that, or bury them by the roadside."

He laughed, shaking his head. "You've got a sharp tongue on you, Kitt-with-two-t's. My mother would have liked you."

The words hung in the air long after he had retreated back to the den to claim the last few hours of sleep before he had to go back to the office.

Kit wasn't quite sure what to make of them. Or of him.

Or the very odd feeling that was moving around inside her, trying to find a resting place for itself.

Chapter Seven

Kitt pushed the tiny bouquet of baby carnations strapped to Shawna's wrist back, away from her face. In protest, Shawna squirmed against her chest, mewling a protest.

Probably because her heart was hammering so loud, it was frightening the baby, Kitt thought. One arm around her daughter, she was holding her own bouquet of carnations with the other. Both had been a gift from O'Rourke. He'd taken care of everything, right down to purchasing the wedding outfit for her and, incredibly enough, a similar one for Shawna. He'd claimed not to know what he was doing, but for a man supposedly without a clue, he was doing brilliantly well.

Kitt's heart pounded harder as, listening to the priest, she heard him coming to the home stretch. The all-important words that, business arrangement or not, would bind her to this tall, dark, handsome stranger at her side.

She hadn't thought she'd be nervous. After all, this was just supposed to be a business arrangement, nothing more. Something circumstances had forced her into for the sake of her own self-respect.

Yes, she was an aerospace reliability engineer, and yes, she would be working again and soon, but the fact of it was that she was still a female aerospace reliability engineer and a new mother to boot. Because of government rules and regulations, employers pretended that all things were equal, but in reality, on an unspoken level, they weren't. People were still people, and in the eyes of those who counted, because of her age, sex and circumstances, she could very well be a liability at the present time. That made getting a job in her field not impossible, but not as easy as falling off a log, either.

And she needed to fall off that log, quickly, because she only had the money that had been in her purse—Jeffrey hadn't left her any. Not a single, worn-out thin dime.

So here she was, standing at the altar of a perfectly lovely church in Bedford, with a cherubic-looking man in clerical robes reading words aloud she had dearly hoped to hear in earnest, rather than because it was all part of a complex charade.

As they came to the part where they exchanged their vows and their rings, Kitt glanced at the man standing beside her. Despite her butterflies, or maybe because of them, she couldn't help thinking that O'Rourke cleaned up nicely. He was wearing a black tuxedo and looked, for all the world, just like a beautiful bridegroom.

Her bridegroom.

Kitt almost laughed then, just as O'Rourke was

saying that he took her for his lawful wedded wife. Too bad this was all make-believe. Too bad the words weren't real.

"And do you, Katherine Ann Dawson, take this man..."

Don't go there, don't even think it, she warned herself. She couldn't think of this as anything but what it was, an unorthodox sort of employment. She was going to have absolutely no feelings for this man, other than for a sense of loyalty. And gratitude, she added, because he had given her a way to save face.

"...Shawn Michael O'Rourke as your..."

Not altruistically, she conceded, because she was, after all, helping him, but still the arrangement was mutually beneficial to them both. If he was very easy on the eye, that had absolutely no bearing on the situation whatsoever.

"...lawfully wedded husband?"

She realized the priest, as well as everyone else, was waiting for her to give an answer.

"I do." The words almost stuck in her throat.

A wife. Who would have ever thought it? O'Rourke almost shook his head in the wrong place, as the priest continued to say the words that would eventually tie them to each other in the sight of God and the INS.

A wife, he marveled again. He never thought he'd be at this place in his life at this time. Granted, he'd been in love with Susan and maybe they would have gone to the altar eventually, but he'd never really been a man who was out for a wife and family. He was far too busy for a wife, as Susan had pointed out, and God knew he had already had family enough to spare.

"Repeat after me," the priest instructed O'Rourke. "With this ring, I thee wed."

He took a deep breath, taking the ring that Simon held out to him. "With this ring…"

Funny how life pulls strings to make things happen. He raised his eyes from the ring he was slipping onto Kitt's finger to her face. For a moment, everything seemed to freeze. Were those tears in the woman's eyes? Women cried at the strangest times. You'd think she was actually getting married.

"…I thee wed…"

This wasn't real, he reminded himself. Legal, but not real. The woman beside him was his business partner, his associate, nothing more. He was going to have to think of her in the same light he thought of Simon.

Simon would never look this good in the outfit she was wearing. He'd picked it out because it seemed practical. That wasn't exactly the way he would have described it once he saw it on her. The pearl-white, street-length, two-piece suit adhered nicely to her body, tempting his eye with just a hint of cleavage. She'd woven some of the baby's breath from her bouquet into her hair. It made her look a little like a wood nymph.

A wood nymph with a baby in her arms. His little namesake was getting a front-row seat to her mother's marriage to the man who was going to give her a legal last name. It had already been entered on the birth certificate, after a long debate on Kitt's part.

Shawna O'Rourke. It had a nice ring to it, he thought.

So did Kitt O'Rourke.

Don't go there, he warned himself. It was nothing

more than a merger for the sheer purpose of keeping him in this country for the next year. One more year would be more than enough time to get Emerald Computers on its feet and turning a healthy profit. After that, all their fortunes would be made, he was certain of it. The concept was too good to fail. And so was he.

He slanted a glance at Kitt. He hadn't imagined it. There were still tears in her eyes.

All their fortunes, he underscored, because he aimed to take care of her, too, for giving him this opportunity. He had always made it a point never to forget a good turn.

His heart suddenly racing, O'Rourke slid the ring all the way down her finger. It seemed to gleam at him in its new place.

"Psst, look this way," Jeremy Lathom hissed at them, waving his hand to get their attention and have them look in his direction.

Jeremy, his video specialist, was manning a camcorder. For good measure, O'Rourke thought to have the wedding videotaped in case there were any questions later on. He wanted everything on the up-and-up, so that there was no room for future snags or loopholes. He had no intentions of being tripped up. A risk-taker in his early years, he'd learned that "better safe than sorry" had a firm place in his life.

Folding his hands beatifically before him, the priest looked out at the people sitting in the pews. "If there is any among you who would object to this union between Shawn Michael and Katherine, speak now or forever hold your piece."

Kitt slanted a glance to her left, praying Sylvia wouldn't suddenly be struck with an overwhelming qualm of conscience and feel compelled to raise an objection. The seconds ticked by. Sylvia remained silent. Kitt released the breath she was holding.

"Then by the power vested in me by the state of California and in the sight of Almighty God, I now pronounce you husband and wife." The jovial-looking priest waited a bit for nature to take its course. When neither nature nor the couple before him did, he stepped forward again and urged, "You may kiss the bride," in something louder than a stage whisper.

Kiss. Kitt felt herself stiffening. She'd forgotten about that part. For the sake of the video, she knew she couldn't protest or demur.

Okay, here goes.

Dutifully, she handed Shawna to Sylvia and then turned to the man who was now for all intents and purposes her husband. She raised her mouth to his, not really knowing what to expect, hoping she wouldn't suddenly burst into tears because she was suddenly feeling strangely emotional and somehow very cheated.

O'Rourke placed a hand on either of her shoulders and lowered his mouth to hers, determined to make this look like an authentic love match for anyone watching the videotape.

What happened was that he forgot about the fine line between real and make-believe, and as he endeavored to make the kiss seem real, it became real. So real that he discovered it captured him squarely in its grip and held him fast.

A sweetness was released within his veins, a sweetness coupled with a rush that sent his head spinning and had him questioning his own hold on reality, which admittedly at this moment was none too firm.

He lingered over her lips, trying to get his bearings. As if they belonged to someone else, he felt his hands tightening ever so slightly on her shoulders, even as his own body tightened like the string of an archery bow.

Oh boy, oh boy, oh boy. The refrain echoed in her head like an endlessly looped tape, destined to go on forever.

What had she gotten herself into? What was happening to her? Where had her knees gotten to? The second O'Rourke had started kissing her, her knees had suddenly numbered themselves among the missing and everything inside of her had gone utterly haywire. Was this part of the postpartum experience, too? Was that the reason why the floor was suddenly the ceiling and the ceiling the floor?

Though she fought to pull everything back into focus, it seemed to have inverted on her, throwing her into complete disorientation. Had his hands not been on her shoulders, holding her up, Kitt was certain that she probably would have discovered herself sitting unceremoniously on the church floor.

Still and all, it was delicious for all its disorienting powers. She felt herself leaning into the kiss, holding on to it just a beat longer.

Somewhere in the distance, she heard someone clearing their throat.

"You may now stop kissing the bride," the priest chuckled, then pretended to fan himself with the white, gilt-edged Bible he was holding. "I'm not sure if as a man of the cloth I'm supposed to be allowed to witness such displays of affection firsthand."

Tucking the Bible under one arm, he moved forward and took each of them by the hand. He beamed at them as he held their hands for a second. "I have a very good feeling about this." And then he released their hands. "Go, be happy."

Kitt wasn't sure when she had felt so confused and so guilty all at one time, in her life.

The scent of cologne subtly seeped into her senses. There was something about the way he was holding her as they danced that telegraphed itself through her entire consciousness, making every fiber of her body aware of O'Rourke.

Aware of them together.

It wasn't as if he was holding her too close. He was being a complete gentleman about it.

And yet...

And yet there was this nervousness dancing along with her, claiming her as its partner. It was their first dance together as husband and wife. That was the way the leader of the small band had announced it. Another tradition she'd hoped to meet under different circumstances.

Desperate for conversation, for distraction, she grabbed on to the first thing she could think of. "This is a very nice restaurant."

Lame, Kitt, lame.

O'Rourke nodded, trying very hard not to notice the way the woman in his arms felt, leaning into his body. As if she belonged there. Which was an absolutely absurd thought, one he'd attribute to too much beer or wine—except that, beyond the few sips he'd had in acknowledgment of Simon's toast to them, he hadn't had any.

"It belongs to Simon's third cousin on his mother's side. Simon reserved the room. It's his wedding present to us." He hadn't been able to talk Simon out of it, despite the fact that they both knew it wasn't a real marriage. Simon's argument had been that if he was deported, then they would all be out of work, including him. Simon had maintained it was a small-enough investment to make against the future.

Relative or not, Kitt figured it couldn't have been cheap to have this room reserved for the reception. "Very generous of him. Did Simon find the band, too?" She nodded toward the trio playing on the far side of the room.

O'Rourke nodded, glancing at the musicians. "Another cousin, I think."

Kitt laughed. She felt a little giddy despite the fact that the only thing she'd had to drink, because she was nursing, was ginger ale when Simon had made his toast. "Lucky thing Simon has such a big family."

She'd always wanted a big family. Now she was down to just a brother with wanderlust. The last she'd heard, he was in Oregon, but that was five months ago.

And she had the baby, of course. "If it'd been up to my connections, the reception would have been kept at McDonald's with some old man playing songs on the kazoo."

The mention of the children's instrument made O'Rourke smile. "Better than on a comb."

"On a comb?"

"Sure." He looked at her and realized she didn't know what he was talking about. He sincerely doubted that the makeshift musical "instrument" was something restricted to his part of the world. "Haven't you ever done that, hummed something on a comb with a bit of tissue paper draped over it? It sounds a bit like a kazoo, actually."

Kitt shook her head, amused. Since O'Rourke had mentioned it with such feeling, she assumed he'd played the thing himself. Try as she might, she couldn't visualize that.

"I'm afraid my musical experience is limited to playing the radio."

For a second, in his mind's eye he was back home again, surrounded by siblings he'd always claimed were annoying, siblings he loved dearly.

"I used to play songs for my sisters and brothers on the comb to keep them entertained."

He thought of the years they all did without, and how that had finally broken his father. In his own way, he'd tried his best to help. His best hadn't been nearly good enough.

But it had to be now, he resolved.

He found himself looking down into Kitt's eyes and struggling to keep track of what he was saying. "There wasn't much money for things like entertainment when we were very young."

A comb and tissue paper. The man knew how to make do. A hint of admiration nudged itself forward. "You sound like a very resourceful person."

He'd never done well with compliments. They made him self-conscious. Looking away, he shrugged. "You do what you have to."

Which included marrying her. The next moment she wondered where the thought, draped as it was in sadness, had come from. Why should there be sadness? Had to be hormones, she decided. When were they finally going to level off and leave her a sane person?

Sylvia came up behind them, laying a hand on Kitt's shoulder. "Hate to break this up," she interjected, nodding at O'Rourke, "but it looks as if someone's hungry."

His lips curved slightly. "Help yourself to anything on the buffet, Sylvia."

"I mean the baby."

O'Rourke flashed a grin so quickly, it was gone almost before it registered. "I know that." Releasing Kitt, he stepped back.

"You know," Sylvia mused, looking after O'Rourke as he walked across the floor to a cluster of people. "With a little bit of work, he might not be half bad."

Kitt took her daughter from her friend. "No one's going to be working on him, Sylvia, so stop thinking what you're thinking right now."

Sylvia was the soul of innocence. "How do you know what I'm thinking?"

Though she had never come right out and said so to her, Sylvia had never cared for Jeffrey. Kitt could see that O'Rourke was beginning to fare far better in her friend's eyes.

"Because I know you." Kitt turned her attention to more important things. She chucked Shawna under the chin and the infant ceased fussing for a moment. Kitt hoped there was a chair in the ladies' room. "C'mon, sweetie, time to fill you up again."

"It was a lovely reception." Kitt's voice sounded a little hollow to her ears as they walked into O'Rourke's apartment.

Their apartment now, she corrected.

The door closed behind her with a finality that echoed in her head.

It was different somehow, different coming here tonight than it had been all the other times these last few days, despite the fact that O'Rourke brought over all the things Jeffrey hadn't taken from her apartment so she could feel more at home here. Different from even the first time when she had walked into the living pigsty and shock had greeted her, intensifying with every second that passed and every new place she looked.

She couldn't put her finger on why, but it definitely felt different to her.

Just nerves, she told herself. After all, she was the man's wife in the legal sense.

What if he...?

Without meaning to, she drew her breath in and held it.

O'Rourke saw the look Kitt slanted toward him. Felt the tension that vibrated around her like some large, vaporous cloud. It mystified him and then he realized what was going through her head.

She was afraid.

Of him?

The thought made him angry and he felt insulted that Kitt would actually believe he would try something with her.

What kind of a man did she think he was?

Granted, that kiss in the church had all but scorched the socks right off his feet, but that was no reason for her to think that he—

Had she felt something then, too? Was it something that not only he had experienced, but she had as well?

Was that it? Was she afraid now that he would press his advantage?

The shock of the idea that she might have felt something made him let the anger go.

He took a breath himself before answering. "I've been to better," he acknowledged. "Jimmy Allen had a wedding reception the Sunday before I left Ireland that went on for three days."

"Three days?" she echoed. She thought of the bride and groom. "Weren't they tired? Didn't they want to…?"

Kitt stopped abruptly, realizing that she had let her tongue get ahead of her brain again. She didn't want to be giving him any ideas.

If he hadn't known where she was going with this to begin with, the vivid blush on her cheeks would have told him. "They slipped off to their honeymoon around midnight of the first day. The rest of us just carried on in their honor." The reception had been in Jimmy's father's house. A widower, the man had more than welcomed the company. "Wasn't a sober man left standing in County Cork by the time it was over."

Both of her parents had been teetotalers, and if her brother drank, she didn't know about it. The concept of getting pleasantly loaded was completely foreign to her. "Is that what you consider a good time?"

He could tell by the innocent query in her voice that she was completely unacquainted with spirits. He didn't really drink anymore, but he didn't want any lectures, either. Would she be the kind to lecture? he wondered, looking at her.

He found himself getting trapped in her eyes. "It has its place. But it doesn't compare to being with the right woman." With effort, he drew his attention away. "Or so they tell me."

He'd aroused her curiosity and she forgot about being tired. "There's never been a right woman for you?"

He didn't feel like talking about Susan. That was something that happened long ago and far away. "I never went looking."

Neither had she. She thought of Jeffrey. They'd literally bumped into each other running for shelter from a sudden shower and winding up in the same spot. "Sometimes you don't have to look. Sometimes you just get found."

He wondered about the man who had walked out on her. It wasn't his place to ask.

"Never been found, either. Listen, I know it's late and you're tired." Shawna was beginning to stir in her arms. She'd slept through a great deal of the reception—storing up energy, no doubt. "If you'd like, I can take the little one for the night, let you get some sleep."

He'd made the suggestion gruffly, but she appreciated the gesture nonetheless. "Aren't you going in to work tomorrow?"

He shrugged carelessly, slipping off the tuxedo jacket and undoing the tie. "Yes, but that doesn't matter. Getting up for the baby doesn't bother me." He saw her hesitating. Was it that she didn't trust him, or didn't want to impose? "It's not like I haven't done it before."

She slid out of her shoes and instantly became four inches shorter. "I'm not sure what to make of you, Shawn Michael."

Only his mother had called him that. His siblings

had used just the first name. "The name's O'Rourke, if you don't mind," he corrected her. "And there's no reason to try to make anything of me at all." He spread his arms out for her. "What you see is what you get. I'm a simple sort of man."

Simple, huh? She wasn't all that convinced. She began walking toward her bedroom. "Thanks for the offer, but I think I'll just keep her for the night."

He shrugged, turning away. "Suit yourself."

No, she thought, she didn't know what to make of him at all. Maybe he was right, maybe she shouldn't even try. In any event, she was too tired to analyze anything tonight.

With a shrug, Kitt took her daughter to their room and closed the door.

Chapter Eight

On his way out to the office, O'Rourke paused to hand Kitt a sheet of paper he'd agonized over in the wee hours of the night when sleep had decided to remain elusive, finding no place for itself in a head filled with other thoughts. Thoughts that were increasingly making space for a diminutive blond-haired woman.

It had been five days since their wedding, five days that had found them settling into a routine of sorts. He hadn't really known what to expect, maybe that nothing would actually change since they weren't really married in each other's eyes.

But there had been changes. Subtle changes. There was a different feeling when he came home at night, no matter how late. A feeling of sharing. It wasn't his home any longer, there were two other people in it now, albeit that one of them was a tiny people, but that still didn't change the fact that he was no longer alone.

But it wasn't really an awkward sharing of space, even though he was by and large a private man when it came to his personal life. And, after all, for most of his life, he'd shared space with more than a couple of other bodies. There'd been his brothers and sisters. The six of them had shared one house, bursting to the seams. Granted, as the oldest, he'd had his own bedroom once his mother had passed on.

That hadn't changed, either, he thought with a smile creeping over his lips. He still had his own room.

But this time he felt restless about it.

Perfectly natural itch, he supposed, for a man being in the same apartment with an attractive woman. It was just that he'd always been too busy to notice attractiveness, or varying degrees thereof.

He wasn't too busy lately.

Especially since the attractive woman knew how to cook. That had been something else he hadn't expected. Kitt had had meals waiting for him. He wasn't accustomed to that any longer, not since he'd left Ireland.

Shifting Shawna to her other side, Kitt took the sheet of paper O'Rourke held out to her, curiosity nudging itself forward.

He'd hardly touched his breakfast, she noted, looking over his shoulder toward the kitchen table and the single plate that sat there. She had meant to join him, but Shawna had decided to recycle her breakfast earlier than usual and she'd had to go and change a very pungent diaper before it ruined breakfast for O'Rourke.

It appeared she didn't have to bother.

Kitt glanced at the lengthy, handwritten sheet. "What's this?"

He rather thought that was self-evident, seeing as how he'd carefully written down the general subject and its specific match right beside it.

"Can't you tell?" Turning the sheet around in her hand so that it faced him, O'Rourke indicated the first line, which read, "Favorite color: blue." "It's a list of my likes and dislikes."

Her brows drew together. "And I'm getting this because...?"

She was going to make him late. Bad enough he'd gotten little sleep last night, letting his mind wander to places it shouldn't and then suffering the consequences of that wandering by finding himself miserably fully awake. "Because it's what you should know about me if the INS agent should happen to ask," he told her, his voice short.

Someone had obviously gotten up on the wrong side of the daybed, she thought. She looked up from the sheet. "Why don't you just tell me?"

He didn't see the point. Words could be forgotten. Hadn't Susan forgotten the words he'd once said to her, in the shadow of the Forever Tree, where people had come since forever to pledge their hearts? *Wait for me, Susan. I'm going to make us a wonderful life.* "This way's more efficient."

She glanced at the list. It appeared rather comprehensive. And cold.

"More impersonal, if you ask me." If that was the way he wanted it... With a sigh, she folded it with one hand, then slipped it into the front pocket of her jeans. "Does this mean you want me to write a list, too?"

About to leave, he stopped in his tracks. "Why?"

The man had tunnel vision, Kitt thought, amused. And yet, there was almost something appealing about the way he thought of himself as the problem....

Don't go there, she warned herself. Tender feelings weren't called for here. Hadn't tender feelings caused her to overlook so many warning signs about Jeffrey? *This is just a business arrangement, think like a businesswoman.*

"Well, won't this agent be asking you things about me as well? Marriage is a two-way street, you know," she added for good measure.

Damn, but she was right. He hated overlooking things. "I forgot about that."

"What?" Kitt cocked her head, looking at him. "That marriage is a two-way street, or that you're supposed to know something about me?"

Amusement was curving her lips. It took him a second before he could draw his eyes away and get his mind back on the subject.

"The latter." He thought of his parents' life together. The untroubled moments were precious few and far between. "Marriage isn't a two-way street, it's a superhighway, with things coming at you from all sides when you least expect them."

There was bitterness in his voice. Just how much did she know about this man she had agreed to lie for? "Are you sure you weren't married before?"

"No, just a witness." He crossed to the door. By now he should have been in his car, halfway to work. "Okay, make up a list."

A witness. She thought that an odd thing to say, but she could tell that questioning him wasn't going to shed any further light on the subject, at least not now.

Holding Shawna, she followed him to the door. "I'd rather tell you."

It was two days before they had to meet with the INS agent. "I'm not sure when I can find the time to talk," he told Kitt honestly, pausing to lightly run his hand over the baby's head. She cooed in response. "If you give me a list, I can memorize it in my spare moments."

Kitt's eyes held his for a split second. "You sound like you're cramming for an exam."

"I am."

The next moment, O'Rourke was gone, leaving her to sigh, shake her head and have the rest of her breakfast alone.

She waited up for him. Instead of seven, the hour he usually seemed to come home, O'Rourke didn't come in until half past ten. She'd begun to worry about him, then laughed herself out of it. If she didn't know better, she would have said she was beginning to behave like a real wife. She was only concerned the way one friend was concerned about another, she insisted, using Shawna as a sounding board.

"No reason to think anything else, right, love?"

It had hit her a second later that she'd used the same term of endearment for her daughter that O'Rourke did. She didn't know if that was a bad sign or a good one.

The moment he walked in through the door that night, she was at his side. She presented her own list of likes and dislikes to him. His had been committed to memory easily enough. She'd done it during the space of one of Shawna's many mininaps.

"They're going to want to know something more, you know. The INS people," she added when he looked at her blankly.

He'd thought that she'd be in bed by now. Hoped it really. Something had been riding him all day and he wasn't sure what it was. He'd thought that it was the upcoming INS meeting, but in the center of his being, where he'd always been honest with himself, he knew that it wasn't. He just didn't want to speculate as to what it was.

But an ounce of prevention...

The ounce hadn't been taken. She'd remained up, lying in wait for him. He tossed his jacket toward the coatrack. It missed. "Such as?"

Seeing that he was about to go into the living room, she caught his sleeve and tugged in the direction of the kitchen. His dinner was being kept warm in the oven. Holding him by one sleeve, she stooped to pick up the jacket. She saw a flash of guilt cross his face and took it as a hopeful sign.

"Such as how we met, how long we were together before we got married." Picking up two pot holders, Kitt opened the oven and took out the plate, putting it on the table at the place she'd left set for him. "Anything unusual in our relationship," she continued, looking at him. "You know, things that make people people."

A whimsical look had entered her eyes and he found himself being captivated by it. "I guess this is called getting our stories straight."

Pouring herself a cup of coffee, she took a seat opposite him at the table. "Something like that."

Pot roast, he realized. She'd made pot roast. With tiny potatoes and carrots around it. His favorite. She'd read the list, all right.

He had trouble keeping the smile from finding his lips. "All right, how did we meet?"

She laced both hands around her mug. "We were both running for the same awning during a sudden cloudburst and we bumped into each other." Her eyes met his. "You caught me and we've been together ever since."

The pot roast was excellent. He waited until the meat all but melted on his tongue before commenting. "Very nice. Did you just think of that?"

"No." She looked down into the mug, telling herself it was foolish to dwell on the past except for what it could teach her about the future: Not to trust her heart. "It's how Jeffrey and I met." Her mouth curved in a self-deprecating smile. "All except the last part."

She was hurting. It didn't take an expert to see that. O'Rourke's hand tightened around his fork. He had no idea where the protective feeling came from. Probably something left over from the way he felt about his sisters, he reasoned. The excuse didn't quite ring true, but he ignored that.

"Ask me, the lout doesn't deserve you."

The reaction, coming from nowhere, had her smiling. "And why's that?"

His scowl was almost frightening. It was something she knew men probably didn't want to find themselves on the receiving end of. "Anyone who can run out on a pregnant woman like that, taking her things and all, should be filleted in the middle of town square."

From some distant place, a warmth began to creep forward, curling itself around her heart. "We don't have a town square in Bedford, but I like the rest of it." She finished her coffee, then set her mug down. "You always been a white knight?"

He laughed shortly. "My mother used to call me a blackguard."

But it had been said with affection, Kitt decided. If she'd learned nothing else about the man in the last few days, it was that he was very family-oriented. One of the few conversations they'd had had been about his brothers and sisters. Anyone would have heard the love in his voice when he spoke of them.

"I don't think she meant it," Kitt said softly.

"Neither do I." He cleared his throat, then waved her on gruffly. "All right, let's get on with this, shall we? What else do you want to add?"

He didn't seem to mind her taking over. Given his gruff nature, that surprised her. Pleased, she launched into the rest of it, giving him the scenario she'd created in her head.

"All right, we've been together two years and you've been somewhat marriage-shy, but you took one look at Shawna after she was born and decided the time had come to make an honest woman of her mother."

She'd said it exactly the way the policeman had that night Shawna was born. He laughed and there was admiration in his voice when he said, "You're very good."

"Thank you." The compliment pleased her more than she'd expected it to. "It's the creative side of me that doesn't get used very much."

"And why's that?"

This was going to require more coffee. She rose to refill her cup, then realized that she didn't want to inadvertently keep Shawna awake after the next feeding. Reluctantly, she crossed to the refrigerator and poured a glass of orange juice instead, consoling herself that at least it was healthy for the baby if not entirely pleasurable for her.

"Reliability aerospace engineers don't get to be creative in the general sense of the word," she told him, sitting down again. She noted that he was making short work of the dinner she'd prepared. That pleased her, too. "We're supposed to come through with worst-case scenarios and calculate the probability that they'll happen."

He studied her for a moment. "Doesn't sound like something you'd be doing."

She'd had her sights set on another branch of engineering, but she'd taken the work as it came up. A woman without funds, with student debts to pay off, couldn't afford to be overly choosy.

"I didn't start out that way, just something that seemed to develop."

"Why don't you do something different if you don't like what you're doing now?" He thought of the huge risk he'd taken. His had been leaving a mining town and the place that had been waiting for him once he'd finished high school. But he had other plans, plans that had required tightening his belt even more and asking for sacrifices of the others. Plans that had included college and a dream. "Especially since you're out of work." It seemed the perfect time to him for her to be choosy.

She shrugged. Easier said than done. The words on her résumé locked her into a specific area. And marriage charade or not, she didn't want to be dependent on O'Rourke for her livelihood. She wanted to find something as soon as she could leave Shawna with a sitter. "Once you're in a niche—"

"You break out," he told her firmly. She looked at him in surprise. "You try something different until you find something that works for you."

Picking up his plate, she took it to the sink and rinsed it off. "You know, I wouldn't have said that optimism was something I'd expect from you, either."

"It's not optimism. It's practical."

Wiping her hands as she turned from the sink, she looked at him. "If you say so."

"I do."

Very carefully, Kitt took the paper with his likes and dislikes on it from her pocket and wrote across the top: "Must have final word."

Leaning over her shoulder, he read what she'd written. "Do not," he said.

She merely smiled, her point taken.

He blew out a breath, then laughed. "This might work after all, love."

Calls me "love" instead of using my name, she added to the list mentally.

The warmth that curled around her heart rose up another half a degree.

The Immigration and Naturalization Service office was located in a very modern-looking federal building in the heart of Orange County.

Nothing about the eight-story edifice looked intimidating, but Kitt still felt a nervous flutter in the pit of her stomach as she got out of the van two days later. O'Rourke was already out on his side, unstrapping Shawna's car seat restraints.

He frowned as he did so. He didn't really condone using the infant as a prop, even though he knew her very presence would instantly strengthen his case for him. There just seemed something wrong about involving someone so small in the middle of a lie. She wasn't his daughter, as he would claim before the man doing the interview, and he wasn't in love with her mother, although if he had the time, things could...

No, they couldn't, he told himself firmly, taking Shawna into his arms. He closed the rear passenger door. There was no use thinking that. He hadn't the time, or the expertise when it came down to it. He was best suited for building computers, not relationships. Hadn't he already had enough proof of that?

"Wait." Hurrying up the steps of the federal building beside him, Kitt was suddenly struck with a thought.

He looked at her. Had she suddenly lost her courage? Was she going to back out on him now? He'd gotten a few days' extension, the last ever, Henry Rutherford, the agent, had told him, because O'Rourke had said his new baby was colicky, which prevented Kitt from coming in. This was the last possible day he had to plead his case. One more day and he'd be in violation of the law.

Trying not to sound irritated, O'Rourke asked, "What's the matter?"

She was beside him in a step. "What am I supposed to call you?" He raised an eyebrow as if he didn't follow her. "I've been calling you O'Rourke, but that's not exactly what a wife would call her husband."

The memory brought a smile to his lips. "Well, actually, that was what my mother called my father, but if you think it makes things more authentic-sounding to call me Shawn Michael, I suppose it's all right for the interview."

Which meant that he didn't want her calling him that once they got home, she thought. Why that bothered her so much, she couldn't really put her finger on. But it did. It was as if he was reinforcing a wedge that had to exist between them.

Well, why shouldn't there be a wedge? They were strangers, weren't they? Strictly speaking.

"Shawn Michael it is," she agreed. "Now, if I can just keep all the other details about you straight in my mind…"

O'Rourke slipped his arm around her, guiding her up the stairs. He wasn't sure if she was pulling his leg or not. He forced himself to remain calm. As if his entire future, not to mention the future of his brothers and sisters and all the people who'd come to depend on him and his dream, wasn't riding on this.

"There's not that much to remember," he assured her calmly. "We'll be done before you know it."

He'd lied to her.

This wasn't a quick session, over in a blink of an eye. It was a lengthy, prolonged one that felt as if it was to go on indefinitely. In addition, she hadn't expected to be separated from O'Rourke the moment the interview officially began. But the agent, a tall, thin man who looked as if he would snap at the first sign of a good wind, had explained it was policy to interview them separately and then together.

It had been O'Rourke's turn first. She'd had time to grow progressively more nervous.

When it came to be her turn, Kitt tried to read the man's face as he asked her question after question, attempting to gauge whether or not he was satisfied with her answers. He had a face that was neither friendly nor off-putting. It was just there, entirely emotionless. Even when he looked at Shawna and asked her questions about the baby.

Everything she said was being noted and written down. To use against her? she wondered.

And then the man laid down his pen. It looked as if the session was about to come to an end.

"You seem uncomfortable, Mrs. O'Rourke," the agent observed, closing his folder. "Is there any particular reason for that?"

Kitt began to protest, then thought better of it. She was always best when she fell back on the truth, so she decided to bluff it out rather than to deny the observation.

Slipping a pacifier into Shawna's questing mouth, she looked at the agent. "Well actually, there is—" she read his name from the plate before him "—Mr. Rutherford. This feels a little like that police drama on television where they separate supposed suspects and interrogate them in different rooms to see if their stories match."

There was no hint of either recognition or humor in the dark brown eyes that bore into her. "Is that what you feel like, a suspect?"

Kitt raised her chin. "No, I don't. I do feel like a maligned person, though. Just because I chose to fall in love with a good man whose only failing was that he wasn't fortunate enough to be born in this country, I have to be subjected to a battery of questions I wouldn't have had to answer if I'd married, say, a recent parolee who'd been sent to prison for armed robbery of a gas station.'' She realized that only part of her indignation was an act. It occurred to her that she really did feel irritated on O'Rourke's behalf. ''I just don't think it's fair, that's all.''

''Life isn't fair, Mrs. O'Rourke. The only shot we have at making it remotely fair is by adhering to rules. This meeting is about one of those rules.'' The eyes behind the rimless glasses narrowed. ''You do know we frown on people who enter into marriage for the sole purpose of allowing one or the other so-called spouse to remain in this country.''

''Yes,'' she said tersely and with the proper amount of indignation, ''I do know that.''

The INS agent didn't appear to accept her answer at face value. ''And that there are substantial penalties attached to staging such a marriage—''

The butterflies in her stomach tightened, but her expression remained unchanged. ''My daughter needed her father.''

''So you say.'' With a slight nod of his head, Rutherford rose from behind the desk. Then, without saying anything further to her, he stepped out of the room.

Nerves knitted themselves together into a huge, tangled ball. Holding Shawna closer to her, Kitt prayed the agent wasn't going to get one of the U.S. marshals she saw in the building when she and O'Rourke had taken the escalator up to the second-floor INS office.

But when Rutherford returned, he was accompanied by O'Rourke rather than an officer of the law. She breathed a silent sigh of relief. O'Rourke slanted a quick look at her. There was compassion in his eyes as he placed his hand over hers and took the chair beside her.

Rutherford sat down behind his desk and looked at them, his small brown eyes regarding them in prolonged silence.

"Your answers to all the questions were identical," he finally said. "Some might say too identical." He paused, allowing his words to sink in. And then he permitted himself the smallest hint of a smile to grace his lips. "Off the top of my head, I can only say that I wish my wife knew as much about me as you know about your husband, Mrs. O'Rourke. I see no reason to continue 'interrogating' the two of you."

Kitt cheered silently, relieved to have the ordeal finally over with. O'Rourke raised a brow, then looked at her. Kitt realized that Rutherford had picked up on the word she'd used. Was this going to jeopardize the interview?

"I didn't mean—" she began,

But the agent raised his hand. "No, you're quite right," he told her primly. "This is an interrogation of sorts. No thumbscrews, but if we can make you squirm, then maybe you'll give up the lie if there's one to give up." He paused again, his eyes scanning them slowly. Kitt decided that she was never going to feel at ease in the man's presence. "But even though you have convinced me that this marriage was undertaken to give this little girl a proper home, there will be a few spot checks in the next year to make certain that everything is aboveboard."

O'Rourke nodded. He'd expected nothing less.

"And if we discover somewhere down the line in the next year that this is a bogus marriage—"

O'Rourke picked up Kitt's hand, noting that it felt icy, and laced his fingers through it. He brought it to his lips, kissing her knuckles while keeping his eyes on the agent. He never noticed the slight change in Kitt's expression. "It's not."

"For your sakes, I hope that's true, because quite frankly, you do look rather good together. I've been in this department a long time and I have rarely met a couple who looks as if they belong together as much as you two do. I suppose the baby helped create that image." He smiled benevolently at Shawna. And then he leaned back in his chair and eyed the two of them one last time. "All right, I've decided to grant your petition to remain in this country, Mr. O'Rourke. Normally, if you'd come to this country with the sole intent of marrying Mrs. O'Rourke, there'd be a three-year waiting period before you could become a citizen. However, since you've already been in this country close to four years, that will be waived. There's naturally some paperwork to put through, but for all intents and purposes, you may consider yourself a citizen of the United States.

"However," he added ominously, "should you decide sometime within the next year that you are not suited for each other and petition for a divorce, you will be deported, Mr. O'Rourke. And quickly. Do I make myself clear?"

"Absolutely." O'Rourke had no doubt that the man meant exactly what he said.

Rutherford waved them on their way, reaching for

the next folder in his stack. "All right, then go and take this pretty little girl home."

On his feet already, O'Rourke slipped his arm around Kitt's waist. "I intend to."

Rutherford raised his eyes to the couple. "I was referring to the baby." But there was a hint of a smile again on the agent's lips as he said it.

They left the room quickly.

Chapter Nine

Barely able to contain his exuberance, O'Rourke still managed to wait until he and Kitt had left not only the INS office but the federal building as well and were at his van in the parking lot before he threw his arms around Kitt. Embracing her, baby and all, he picked them both up and spun them around in a jubilant circle.

"You did it," he cried. "You did it." God, but he was relieved. A couple of times back there, as Rutherford had sat frowning at him, he'd been certain that the jig was up.

Setting her down again, incredibly high on triumph, O'Rourke took Kitt's face in his hands and, with the baby still between them, kissed her soundly on the mouth.

Kissed her soundly while blotting out all the other surrounding sounds of the world around her, including her own baby's gurgling.

Including the hammering of her own heart and the

racing of her pulse. Blotting it out not as a result of any small, airborne experience, but because he was kissing her.

Her head was spinning around something fierce and her bearings were down to nonexistent.

Careful, you've been down this trail before, she tried to upbraid herself.

But she hadn't. Not like this. Not with this degree of disorientation and confusion. And certainly not with a man who had no real need of her in any manner except on paper.

Jeffrey had wooed her and wanted things from her. Her understanding when his acting jobs dried up, one after another. Her loyalty when he wasn't up to taking any job but what he deemed was his true calling, something that seemed to have few to no openings as time went on. And her money when things became progressively tighter for him. Full of promise at the outset, Jeffrey had only taken things from her.

All this man wanted from her was a lie. There was no reason to give him anything else. Certainly not any of her feelings.

But Kitt wasn't all that sure if she had a say in the matter, even though she wanted to. Something within her melted every time he kissed her. "Melted" was a very difficult position from which to take any sort of concrete stand.

O'Rourke realized belatedly that he'd let himself get carried away, but what was the harm of it? He was supposed to be her husband, and husbands and wives kissed in parking lots sometimes. He didn't think she could hold it against him.

As long as he didn't hold on to it himself.

Releasing her, smiling down at the baby who

looked up at him, a bubble forming on her lips, O'Rourke asked, "What do you say we celebrate, love? I can come home early tonight."

She wished he'd stop calling her that. Love. She could get used to hearing the word. And familiarity bred belief, something that was dangerous to a woman in as vulnerable a position as she was right now. Vulnerable because she had been hurt by a man she had believed loved her. Vulnerable because she was beginning to have feelings for a man she knew she shouldn't.

"A night on the town?" she suggested half teasingly.

A look of concern entered his eyes as he looked at Shawna. "What about the baby?"

Now, there was something Jeffrey would have never allowed to give him a second's pause. Children weren't obstacles to reckon with for him, they were obstacles to be ignored. "Sylvia can watch her. Sylvia's been dying to watch her."

Why not? What was the harm in it? The woman had certainly earned a reprieve from cooking him dinner, though he'd never once asked her to.

Still, the bottom line was that she did it and it was time she had a break.

"A night out it is, then." He unlocked the passenger side for her, holding the rear door open while she placed Shawna in her infant seat. "Provided we're home by midnight."

Straightening, Kitt looked at him. He didn't seem like a man who'd be in by midnight. More like midmorning of the following day. "Conference call, Cinderella?"

He rounded the hood, then got in on his own side. "I was thinking more like a baby feeding."

Kitt buckled her seat belt. "They have things called breast pumps now, they—"

Wincing, O'Rourke left the car key dangling in the ignition as he pretended to cover his ears with his hands. "Spare me."

Kitt closed her mouth, turning to face front in her seat as he started the car. The idea that he could actually be squeamish tickled her.

"A date with your husband, what a novel idea." Sylvia thrust a dress toward her.

Sylvia had arrived half an hour earlier than Kitt had asked her to, haunting her every step and taking it upon herself to first veto the dress she'd selected, then pick out one she felt was more appropriate for the evening ahead.

She held the dress up against Kitt, then turned her toward the wardrobe mirror. "If more couples did that, think of the marriages that could be saved."

Kitt sighed. She didn't need this. It was hard enough trying not to let her thoughts get the better of her and lead her astray. "None of your sarcasm, Syl."

Sylvia dramatically placed a hand to her indignant breast.

"Who's being sarcastic?" And then she smiled, taking the dress from Kitt and placing it on the bed so that it wouldn't get wrinkled. "I think it's great. A woman should get out with her husband once in a while."

Maybe she shouldn't be going. Maybe it would give off the wrong vibrations or start a precedent. She didn't want him thinking that she thought…what Sylvia seemed to be thinking.

"Syl, he's not my husband. I mean, he is but he's—" Exasperated, she threw up her hands. "Why are you making this difficult?"

"I'm not making anything difficult," Sylvia said innocently. "I'm just trying to make the best of it." Pausing, she ceased her search along the closet floor for Kitt's shoes and rose to her feet. "You know, the man has a head on his shoulders—and as for those shoulders, not to mention that butt—"

Kitt's mouth dropped open. "You've been checking out his butt?"

Sylvia's grin was positively wicked by any standards. Her eyes glinted as she looked at Kitt. "Butt, nothing, I've been checking out all of him and I don't know what's wrong with the women where he comes from, but where I come from, you throw a net over a guy like that and stake your claim before he gets away."

She knew where Sylvia was heading with this. They'd already had this discussion, or a theme and variation of it, before. "This is an arrangement, Syl—"

Sylvia went back to her search for the black high heels. "The nice thing about the English language is that so many of its words can have such a broad meaning. 'Arrange' something tonight." Triumphant, she rose again, shoes in hand. She held them up for Kitt's perusal before setting them on the floor before the bed. "Make yourself irresistible to the guy. He's got a future, why can't it be your future, too?" She stopped fussing and looked at Kitt squarely. "A hundred years ago, a lot of marriages were arranged.

What the people doing the arranging hoped was that love would bloom afterward. You told me that you've always liked historicals," she reminded Kitt.

Sylvia would bring that up. Served her right for sharing too much. "To read, not to live." She caught Sylvia's arm as the other woman made a beeline for her makeup case. Enough was enough. "Look, Syl, I appreciate what you're trying to do, but I have a horrible track record when it comes to men and I'd rather just sit this dance out."

Sylvia appeared unconvinced and undeterred. "One mistake doesn't make a record."

But Kitt knew better. She'd lived it. *Was* living it. "One really bad mistake makes you gun-shy."

Sylvia caught her by the shoulders, forcing Kitt to look at her. "I don't want you to shoot him, I want you to get to know him. You deserve to be happy. So does Shawna."

Very gently, Kitt drew Sylvia's hands away from her. "Just watch her for me and I'll be happy."

Sylvia shook her head. "You are a very stubborn woman."

Kitt merely smiled at her, relieved at the reprieve. "So they tell me."

He didn't remember until an hour after the fact that he was supposed to have gone home by five if not before. He'd been jammed up on a conference call that had gone over, and then Alfred, the part-time computer wizard he'd hired straight out of the eleventh grade had come to inform him of a major glitch that had just cropped up. Thoughts of dinner and Kitt had temporarily been moved to the rear of his brain.

But they were back now, back with a vengeance. And with guilt.

Picking up the receiver and jabbing out the numbers of his home phone on the keyboard, O'Rourke listened to the telephone on the other end ring three times before Kitt finally answered it.

"Hello?"

She sounded sad, he thought, and wondered if there was anything wrong with the baby. Not bothering with a greeting, he launched into his excuse immediately. "Look, love, this is O'Rourke. I'm sorry, we've come up with another bug and I just didn't notice the time."

He wasn't sure, but he thought he heard her stifling a sigh.

"That's all right, I already sent Sylvia home." She didn't add that it was over Sylvia's very vocal protest. There seemed no point in saying that. "The baby's fussing, anyway. Colic, most likely." She was trying very hard to remain on top of things in this brand-new world of motherhood she found herself in. "I would have been poor company, anyway. I wouldn't have been able to keep my mind on dinner. I'll see you later."

They were disconnected. O'Rourke looked at the receiver before hanging up, thinking. She was disappointed, he decided, replacing the receiver. And, in an odd way, so was he. He had to admit, when he'd thought of it, the idea of dinner with her was not without its appeal.

Maybe it was just as well that he had gotten caught up in things and forgotten about dinner. There was no sense, he told himself, in opening up doors to rooms he wasn't allowed to enter.

* * *

An hour later, with a bouquet of carnations like the ones in her wedding bouquet in one hand, a bottle of champagne to toast their success in the other, O'Rourke arrived home.

Feeling a little sheepish without the slightest idea why, he closed the door behind him and called Kitt's name, taking care not to be too loud just in case the baby was asleep.

Kitt came out of the kitchen, wiping her hands on an apron that had seen better times. He made a mental note to replace it for her.

And not to envision her wearing only that.

Kitt looked at the flowers. Remembering them, he thrust the bouquet toward her.

"What's that for?"

O'Rourke cleared his throat, deliberately focusing his attention on the bottle of champagne he still held. "To celebrate…" His eyes met hers. He'd been raised to face up to things he'd done. "And to say I'm sorry."

Funny how an apology could soften her. Jeffrey used to apologize all the time, she reminded herself, desperately trying to harden a heart she feared had already been breached.

She took the flowers from him. "You've nothing to apologize for. We can reschedule."

As if it was a business meeting, he thought. Good, that was how they were supposed to view it. If they kept it unmuddled, then there would be no problems, no hurt feelings. No misunderstandings at the end.

Leading the way to the kitchen and the glasses, he slanted a glance at Kitt over his shoulder. There was something about the way she looked at him… No, this wasn't absolutely cut and dried, or was it?

"You're just saying that to make me feel guilty."

A soft, teasing grin appeared on her lips that he found utterly irresistible. He'd guessed right. "How am I doing?"

Taking out a corkscrew, O'Rourke paused and laughed. "Damn. How does someone with the face of an angel get to be so devious?"

She tried not to allow the compliment to get to her. That way lay danger. She couldn't start believing him, believing in things. It would lead to her downfall again.

"Self-preservation. And practice." Turning toward the oven as he occupied himself with the corkscrew, she took two pot holders in her hand. "I've got to get your dinner out of the oven before it decides to turn stone cold on you."

"You made dinner?" The cork popped, punctuating his query. He set the cork and corkscrew on the counter. "I thought we were supposed to go out."

"We were, but when you didn't show up, I decided to get creative with what we had in the refrigerator." She placed the casserole on the counter, next to the glasses he was filling. "My mother taught me how to make do with almost anything."

"Stone soup," he commented, remembering a story his mother had once read to him.

She was acquainted with the story, vaguely recalling a children's show-hostess reading it to her pint-size audience.

"No, that's being clever and conning people out of things in order to make a good soup. I just work with what's there." She didn't know exactly what prompted her to look at him that instant, but she did.

Was he being put on notice? Was he what she was

planning on working with next? Or was he just reading things into her words?

Probably the latter.

He finished pouring the champagne into the glasses. "I could use some dinner," he agreed.

"Good, because I waited to eat with you."

Kitt carried over the casserole dish and placed it in the middle of the dining room table. For the first time, he noticed that there were candles in the candlestick holders. And they were lit. Atmosphere? Or was she just being frugal?

"You waited?" Picking up the two glasses, he followed her into the room on her second pass. "With dinner canceled, I might not have been home for hours."

She shrugged away the observation. Nothing she hadn't thought of herself. "I took a chance. I figured I'd give you until ten before I started without you." Sitting down, she shook out the napkin before putting it on her lap. "It's nice to have company for a meal."

Yes, he thought, taking the chair opposite her, *it was.*

It was going smoothly.

Maybe, if he were the superstitious type like his mother before him, he might have said things were going too smoothly. For perhaps the first time in his life, both his work and his home life were on an even keel. The alarm due to the discovered glitch was over, things at the office were progressing at an ever-increasing pace, and it looked as if Emerald Computers might actually become a success sooner than he'd expected. The bugs in his program for the new line of computer were dropping…well, like flies, and things were looking good. Awfully good.

And at home, well, he knew that was an artificial situation in reality, but it certainly did feel real. At times he literally forgot it wasn't supposed to be. No matter what time of the night he came home, the smell of food was waiting to greet him when he walked in.

He didn't have to scrounge around, looking for something to throw together in order to create something that passed for a meal. He didn't have to scrounge at all, not for food, or clothes or even the notes to his program that he brought home to work on on occasion. Somehow, things were always being straightened for him. Available when he needed them. Always within reach.

He wasn't accustomed to that.

A man could get accustomed to that.

But if he did, what then? he questioned himself silently as he drove along the thoroughfare, heading home. When the agreement was over, when Kitt could finally safely leave him and get on with her life and he with his, what then? Getting accustomed to life the way it was now would make the future that much harder for him to bear, that much harder to function in.

He wasn't a marrying man, certainly, but there was no disputing that he was a family man, and as much as he claimed to enjoy unobstructed freedom, the truth of it was that he did miss having a family around him. Having Kitt and her daughter around for the last month had filled a void he hadn't been aware of having.

Being made aware made it harder.

So? When the day came that Kitt finally left, he told himself, he'd get one of his brothers or sisters to come to Bedford to live.

Hell, he amended, taking a turn to get into his apartment complex, he'd bring them all to America. Wasn't that the ultimate plan once he got his company up and running? To have his entire family come out here to live? Working alongside of him, maybe, but most assuredly living in this country, enjoying all the fine benefits that went hand in hand with being a citizen of the United States.

He liked the sound of that.

Taking another corner, O'Rourke laughed at himself. He was beginning to sound just like an infomercial.

That was because for the last two days, when they weren't working on the actual computer design, he and Simon were meeting with and listening to the ideas of a pitchman who was going to help them get an infomercial on the air in order to make the public aware of their product. When the time came. He was putting the horse before the cart.

But damn, the horse was eager to run.

It was all coming together, he thought, a grin forming on his lips. The ideas, the backers, the dream, all of it was coming together.

Part of him was afraid that it would all turn to dust on him at the last minute. There was only so much luck to go around and he had a fear that perhaps, just perhaps, it would be used up before it became his turn to dip into the magic well.

Or surely before anything came of it.

As God was his witness, he swore silently, he didn't intend to be a failure. Failure was for other men, not him. He wouldn't stand for it. He'd paid his dues and worked as hard as any man—harder—just so his dream could become a reality. For him and for everyone.

It occurred to O'Rourke as he let himself into the house quietly that night, that Kitt had become part of that inner circle. She'd become part of "everyone."

He couldn't help wondering if she'd want to be, once she knew.

The sound he'd heard just as he walked up to the first-floor garden apartment, the sound he'd taken to be a cat somewhere in the distance, protesting some grave injustice against it, turned out to be coming from within his apartment.

They didn't have a cat.

It was the baby.

The thought hit him just as he turned the key and opened the door. The baby was crying like that, like something was very wrong with her.

O'Rourke felt his heart speed up just a little. "Kitt? Kitt, it's me, O'Rourke. I'm home." He pocketed his key, looking around the room. "Where are you?"

She came into the living room then, her eyes huge, haunted and frightened. She was carrying the baby, rocking the infant as she walked.

"It's Shawna," she told him needlessly, every word etched with concern. "She's been crying all afternoon, all night," she amended. She felt so helpless, so powerless to do anything. Kitt hated the feeling. "I don't know what to do to make her stop." Trying very hard to keep the edginess from her voice, she told him, "I've been walking the floor with her for hours."

She looked it, he realized. Appearing far more

worn and tired than even when he'd first seen her. He held out his arms to her.

"Here, give the baby to me. You sit down and get some rest," he ordered, taking Shawna from her. There was not even a glimmer of recognition in the baby's eyes, the way there had begun to be in the last week. He felt his heart sink a little.

"She won't eat," Kitt told him. "And she hasn't slept all day except for a couple of minutes at a time. Every time I start to put her down, she wakes up and starts to cry all over again, even harder."

There was nothing to be alarmed about, he told himself. Babies did this all the time. Still, all he could remember was Mrs. Flannery and Tara. Tara had died at two months from causes no one could ascertain. Mrs. Flannery was never the same again.

"Why don't you call the doctor?" he suggested, beginning to pace.

"I did." That had come out too loudly. Getting hold of herself, Kitt continued. "I put in a call to her pediatrician an hour ago. I got his answering service. They said they'd relay the message, but he hasn't called me back."

O'Rourke looked down at the little girl in his arms. She felt warm to him, warmer than he was willing to accept. "All right, if Mohammed won't call the mountain, the mountain is going to call Mohammed." He began to head for the door. "You drive to the hospital, I'll be in the back seat with the baby."

It took a second for his words to sink in. She'd half expected him to laugh off her concern. She was incredibly relieved that he hadn't, that he seemed as concerned as she was. But that also made her frightened. It meant that he thought there was something wrong, too.

"You?"

He nodded. There was no room for discussion here. He didn't like the baby's color. "I know infant CPR."

It didn't seem like something he should be familiar with. "How...?"

"It wasn't an entirely backward town I lived in," he said. "The local nurse specialized in CPR. It was something she thought I should know." He hoped and prayed that it didn't come down to that, that he wouldn't need to use CPR on the infant. He didn't know if he could stand it if he had to.

Chapter Ten

"**D**amn."

The bitten-off curse rang in her ears. Her heart already hammering harder than she thought possible, Kitt darted her eyes darted toward the rearview mirror, praying everything was all right.

It wasn't.

O'Rourke was unstrapping Shawna's restraints and taking the small body out of the infant seat. Her daughter was limp.

"What are you doing?" Kitt demanded.

"Just drive," O'Rourke ordered, not sparing the necessary second to glance in her direction. There wasn't time.

Schooling himself to go slow and to remember the steps, he began giving the baby CPR the instant he had her lying on her back. It took him a beat to recall the differences in technique for infants. Fingers pressed against tiny chests instead of hands and puffs of air gently administered instead of mouth-to-mouth contact. He counted mentally before starting the cycle again, more quickly this time.

Watching Shawna intently since the moment he had gotten into the car with her, he'd seen the infant's color drain away and then her tiny chest cease its movement altogether. The baby had stopped breathing.

There was no time to speculate why. All he knew was that he had to get her breathing again.

"Oh, my God," Kitt said, craning her neck and turning around. "She's stopped breathing, hasn't she?"

Frightened, agitated and feeling more helpless than she had ever felt in her life, Kitt barely missed plowing into the green-and-white moving van making a turn in front of her. Working the brakes, she managed to turned the wheel just in time to narrowly avoid the collision.

She could feel her heart slamming into her rib cage, not because of the near miss, but because of the drama being played out in the back seat.

"Is she...is she...?"

Trying to push out the word, Kitt couldn't make herself say it. It was too horrible to even contemplate. Saying it would make it real.

The silence from the back seat was only because O'Rourke couldn't spare the breath to answer her, not because her worst fears were being realized, Kitt insisted fiercely.

Blinking back tears, numbing her mind, she drove exactly the way she felt—like someone trying to outrace death.

The hospital seemed as if it was located an eternity away instead of the few miles it actually was. By the time Kitt had made it to the emergency room parking lot, she was shaking so badly, she wasn't sure if her legs could support her.

There wasn't time to think about herself.

Slamming on the brakes, she fled the car before the engine had ceased its final revolution.

"I need help here!" she shouted as she burst into the room, bumping against electronic doors that were still yawning open. "My baby's stopped breathing! She's in the parking lot!"

The next moment, she was moving out of the way of the ER team that hurried past her: a physician dressed in periwinkle-blue scrubs, followed by a nurse.

The latter was a blur to her. As she followed them, Kitt saw that O'Rourke was already at the doors, Shawna in his arms.

"I got her to breathe again." Infinite relief throbbed in the declaration.

The physician took Shawna from him. Words were buzzing around Kitt's head, words aimed at her as well as O'Rourke. She saw him looking at her oddly. She was having trouble assimilating the questions. Nothing seemed to penetrate or make sense.

"Ma'am?"

"Kitt?"

The world was swiftly receding from her, blanketing itself in darkness until all that remained was a tiny spotlight, no larger than the head of a pin. And then that almost disappeared, too.

But then it held on. Just as the strong arms that closed around her held on. Catching her. Sheltering her.

The spotlight disappeared.

* * *

A voice seemed to reach out to her, coming from a great distance that seemed almost insurmountable at first. Bit then it began growing closer and closer.

The voice took on texture.

She began to understand.

"Kitt, the baby's going to be all right. Kitt, can you hear me? She's dehydrated, but she's going to be all right. Kitt, damn it, wake up, do you hear me? Wake up this minute."

She heard concern beneath the rough words. Or did she only think she did? Things were still swimming together, but there was light now, light and feeling and sound.

Someone was rubbing her hands.

O'Rourke.

The realization came to her a moment before she actually opened her eyes and focused. She was lying on a stretcher. No, a gurney, it was a gurney, and O'Rourke was standing over her. He was scowling, but she saw a glimmer of concern and then relief in his eyes as she looked up at him.

He was holding her hand in his.

Suddenly everything came flooding back to her. "Shawna," she cried, trying to sit up. A large, strong hand pushed her back, making her lie down. "Is she...?"

"Just fine," the ER physician informed her, pushing back the white curtain that surrounded the hospital bed as he came in. "Your daughter's going to be fine. I just stopped in to see how you are feeling."

"Very foolish," she admitted, this time successfully managing to sit up.

She was still a little woozy, but she struggled against giving in to the feeling. It was only after a beat that she realized that O'Rourke, instead of trying to keep her down, had placed his hand at her back and was propping her up.

Kitt flushed, embarrassed at the scene she must have caused. "I've never fainted before."

The doctor nodded, taking a second pulse reading. "So your husband said. If he hadn't caught you, you'd be checking in for the night right now along with your daughter."

Husband. It felt so odd to hear that word in connection with herself. Odd and yet very comforting at the same time. She supposed it was just because she'd been raised to buy into the whole "happily ever after" scenario. That had been a disservice her parents had done her, making her believe that there was a marriage in store in everyone's future.

And then the rest of what the doctor had said penetrated.

"You're admitting Shawna?"

"Only overnight," the older man was quick to reassure her. "To make sure her fluid levels are back to normal and remain that way. She was a little dehydrated. There was a mild strain of flu going around a few weeks ago. Looks like your little girl caught the tail end of it."

Kitt dug her fisted hands into the mattress on either side of her. She wanted everything crystal clear and spelled out. "But she's all right?"

"Almost perfect," the doctor guaranteed. "If you'd like, I can have a nurse take you up to the pediatric ward once you're ready and you can see for yourself just how almost perfect she is."

"Thank you." Kitt swung her legs over the side of the immobilized gurney, sitting up.

The physician made a notation on the chart and signed it. "There, you're free to go. You know, you two came in with Shawna just in time." Kitt looked at him quizzically. "Lucky thing your husband knows CPR." The older man looked at O'Rourke. "You saved her life."

A chill went over Kitt's heart.

Telling the doctor they knew the way to the pediatrics ward and that there was no need to have a nurse leave the floor to accompany them, Kitt and O'Rourke left the emergency room area. Walking beside him to the elevators in the rear of the building, Kitt was silent as the physician's words sank in.

She could have lost her daughter. Just like that. From something as common as the flu.

Gratitude filled her until there was no room for anything else. She took O'Rourke's hand in hers as the elevator doors opened.

"That's twice now," she told him softly.

He pressed the button for the appropriate floor. The doors began to close. They were alone in the elevator. "Twice?"

She pressed her lips together. "That you saved Shawna."

It took him a second to understand what she was referring to. "The first really doesn't count. I was just there to help her be born."

He was being unduly modest. She'd noticed that about him. He didn't like taking credit, even when it was due him.

"Either way, that makes her yours officially."

Gratitude made him uncomfortable. He never knew what to say, so he shrugged it off. "She's already mine," he reminded her. "We put my name on the birth certificate, remember?"

That had been done to strengthen his claim that he was Shawna's father. Since the baby's real father had wanted nothing to do with Shawna, Kitt hadn't raised any objections when the subject had come up. They'd returned to the hospital the day after the wedding to place his name in the space she'd left empty on the form. In her heart, Kitt had a feeling that, rough around the edges or not, O'Rourke seemed far better suited to the role of father than Jeffrey ever would have been.

"Yes, I know, but this makes it real. You breathed life back into her." Tears sprang up to her eyes as they reached their floor. "If you hadn't been there..."

They stepped out of the elevator and he paused to look at her. Tears always undid him, even tears that were only threatening to be shed.

"But I was," he told her firmly, taking hold of her arms. He wanted to hold her but was afraid. Afraid that if he did, he wouldn't let go. "Don't go there, Kitt-with two-t's," he told her softly. "Don't plague your mind with 'what-ifs.' It's a waste of time and it settles and solves nothing." He looked at her, his expression solemn. "Always keep your face forward. It's the only way any of us can ever make it in this world."

She knew what he was doing. She'd learned a little about this stranger the rain had swept into her life. He was trying to keep her at bay because her gratitude made him uncomfortable. Too bad.

"That still doesn't stop me from being grateful." Rising up on her toes, she brushed her lips against his cheek.

The same warm wave of sweetness washed over him, just as it had when he'd first kissed her at the altar. O'Rourke felt his gut tightening while other parts of him demanded attention and tribute.

He ignored the demands. It wasn't going to go that way, he told himself. A deal was a deal. He'd given his word and his word was his bond. He wasn't about to start behaving like a real husband, no matter how much a part of him wanted to.

"No harm in being grateful," he told her crisply. He fooled neither of them.

Three hours later, O'Rourke closed the door behind Kitt as they walked into the apartment. Kitt's arms were empty. Per the physician's suggestion, backed up by Shawna's own pediatrician, Dr. Rafe Saldana, Shawna remained overnight at Harris Memorial for observation. With O'Rourke holding her hand, Kitt had agreed that it was the safest way to go. Knowing that didn't make the ache she felt now any the easier to bear.

O'Rourke pocketed his keys as he turned on the light. It seemed dreary in here now. And quiet. He hadn't realized how quiet the house would feel without the baby in it.

Planted in the middle of the living room, he slipped his hands into his pockets and looked around, as if seeing the place for the first time.

"Listen," he said to her after a beat.

"To what?" There was nothing to hear, she thought, cocking her head to see if she'd missed something. It had gotten to the point where she could sense a second before Shawna got ready to let out with a wail.

But there was nothing to listen for now. Her baby wasn't here.

"To the silence." He turned around to look at Kitt. "Who would have thought something so tiny could leave behind such a huge void?" And she had, he thought. He felt Shawna's missing presence acutely.

Would it be the same with her mother? Down the line, when they were both out of his life, would it feel this way to come home and know that that was all there was? Just him and the walls?

It gave him sincere pause, O'Rourke thought. He was not happy about the direction his thoughts were taking.

The comment, especially coming from him, surprised Kitt. Surprised her because it was so sensitive. Surprised her because it had been exactly what she was thinking.

She smiled at him. "Don't look now, O'Rourke, but someone's going to start accusing you of being sensitive."

One corner of his mouth rose in bemusement. Sensitive was the last thing he'd ever be accused of. "There's an entire town back in Ireland that might take exception to that."

She stepped out of her shoes, wondering if the dinner she'd forgotten about, warming in the oven, was ruined yet. Would it be worth the effort to try to save it?

"Then they're all wrong." She rethought his protest. "And I don't think they would, anyway. I think that your family knows exactly the kind of man you are."

Her naiveté made his mouth curve in earnest. "Ah, but that's where you're wrong, love. Nobody really knows the kind of man I am, deep down. The real me." He saw her begin to protest and he knew what she was going to say. That he could read her thoughts was a fact he just accepted without exploration. "Those things I put down on paper for you to memorize, that's just the surface me."

She knew that. It was their living together these last weeks that had given her an inkling of what was inside. "And the inner you?"

He had a sudden thirst that took him away from her and to the kitchen. "Will stay that way."

She followed him. "You're afraid of being soft, aren't you?"

Opening the refrigerator, he helped himself to a bottle of beer. It occurred to him that since this bogus marriage had taken place, he hadn't taken himself down to the Shamrock but once. He was going to have to do something about that, he decided.

"Aren't you?" he echoed.

Kitt flipped the dials on the oven to the off position, then took the bottle from him and took a healthy swig before handing it back. Ordinarily, she didn't care for beer, but tonight she had a craving. She didn't think a single sip would hurt anything. It'd be out of her system by the time she had Shawna back.

She'd have her daughter back thanks to him, she thought.

Her eyes pinned his as she slipped the bottle into his hand. "I asked you first."

He shrugged, taking another long pull. Trying not to think about the fact that her lips had been on the bottle a moment earlier. "Soft people get walked on in this world and nobody's ever going to walk on me."

She stared at him. "Funny, you just said what I promised myself just before we 'ran into' each other."

He wished she wouldn't look at him like that. With eyes so blue that they almost hurt him. Inside, where it counted. He tried to sound disinterested. "That proves we're two smart people."

Because he'd turned away, she moved until she was in his line of sight again. "Does it?"

Her voice undulated through him. O'Rourke cupped her cheek, telling himself that contact was a fatal tactical error.

He still didn't pull back.

"Sometimes too smart for our own good," he murmured. Drawing back his hand, O'Rourke slid his fingers along her cheek.

Soft, so soft.

The next thing he knew, he was kissing her. Kissing Kitt with all the pent-up passion that he'd been storing up all these years without even being aware of it. It became too much to bear. Only half conscious of what he was doing, he took her into his arms, molding her to his body. Hungering for her. For the taste of her mouth, for the sweet temptation of her breath along his face. For the heat of her body as it touched his.

He could feel things sizzling within him, urgently begging for release.

Damn but he wished…

Wished for things he knew couldn't happen.

The wisest thing he could do right at this moment was to break away. To step back and introduce space between them. Space and reason.

But he wasn't one who could be accused of always

doing the wisest thing, he recalled. There were teachers in his past who could easily testify to that.

His arms tightened around Kitt as his kiss deepened. For a moment longer, he gave himself permission to be nothing more than a simple man, enjoying the kiss of a woman he found everything but resistible.

Her moan excited him further.

The moan had surprised her, escaping the way it had. But she couldn't stop it, couldn't help herself. There was this rush of sensations taking over her body like pillaging Vikings, leaving nothing untouched. Nothing unscathed.

Standing up on her toes, Kitt pressed herself further into the madness that all this represented. Into the madness and against him. She could have sworn that she was never going to want what she was wanting at this moment. That she was never going to find herself falling for another man, not after what she'd gone through with Jeffrey.

But this wasn't Jeffrey.

This was some man she couldn't figure out. A man who came through for her like a white knight when she needed one, and then regressed into less-than-knightly behavior when the need was gone. A man who had formed a business deal with her and then made her want to form a relationship instead.

Best way to make him back away, she thought, her brain slipping further into a haze. *Ask for a relationship. No man wants a relationship, no matter what he says. Besides, your batting average is way below acceptable, Kitt,* she reminded herself. There was no getting away from the fact that when it came to men, she was a rotten judge of character.

None of it mattered.

The man had a mouth like sin and she couldn't resist wanting it. She felt his hands begin to slid down her sides, felt her body begin to hum like a tuning fork that had suddenly been struck.

She wanted him. Wanted to make love with him. Wanted to be wanted by him. Her heart racing, she began to tighten her arms around his neck.

And then there was air.

Air and space and a sudden feeling of loss she couldn't begin to put into words. Stunned, she realized that he'd withdrawn his mouth from hers and had dropped his hands from her body as if she'd suddenly blistered his skin.

Damn, why was this so hard? he berated himself. He wasn't some animal that needed appeasing. He was a man with willpower. And a memory. This was wrong, what he'd almost allowed to happen. Wrong.

It didn't stop him from wanting it.

Shoving his hands into his pockets before he was tempted to touch her again, O'Rourke took another step back. "It's late, Kitt-with-two-t's. Maybe we should go to bed."

She stood looking at him, her eyes uncertain as to his meaning.

"Separately," he added.

She pulled air into her lungs. Slowly. Then nodded. "All right." Her voice was devoid of any emotion. "That's a good idea."

But she really didn't think so as she turned to go into her room.

Neither did he.

Chapter Eleven

Passing the small cubbyhole that had generally been accepted as O'Rourke's space, Simon retraced his steps and looked in. It was a little before seven in the morning. Simon had thought he'd get a jump-start on the day, but obviously O'Rourke had beaten him to it. From the looks of the wilting breakfast muffin on the desk, he'd been here for some time.

As he had been for the last few weeks, Simon noted. For a while there, he'd hoped that O'Rourke had finally met a force of nature greater than his own stubbornness. That it appeared now that he hadn't was disappointing to Simon.

Sensing someone was there, O'Rourke looked up, a scowl firmly imprinted on his handsome face. Unable to walk away from a computer problem, he'd been wrestling with the newest bug in the hardware program for the last two hours and it was giving him one hell of a headache.

"What?"

O'Rourke had fairly spat out the word. Simon nonetheless took it as an invitation and walked into the alcove. "Is it my imagination, O'Rourke, or have you been haunting the office even more than usual in the last few weeks?"

O'Rourke lifted one shoulder in a half shrug, dismissing the question. Right now, his disposition was somewhere south of surly. It took effort to be civil, even though none of this was Simon's fault.

It wasn't anyone's fault but his own, he supposed. There hadn't been another way open to him, except for the marriage, but he hadn't expected the consequences to be so serious. He hadn't expected to feel anything for the woman who was helping him with this charade, at least, nothing beyond gratitude and perhaps a small amount of friendship.

He hadn't expected to feel his whole body heating at the sight of her in the morning—her hair in her eyes, the faded Packers football jersey she slept in teasing the tops of her thighs. Teasing him as well. And he hadn't expected to have his thoughts turning to her at the strangest times during the day, for no other apparent reason than she had just popped into his head.

It was no way to conduct a business arrangement.

He hadn't anything more to offer Kitt than he had to Susan, and Susan hadn't seen fit to want it. Of course, there was the promise of money now, but Kitt wasn't the type to be swayed by money. A woman like that needed attention and he couldn't give it to her.

Not that she'd probably want it from a man who'd used her to stay in this country so that he could make his dreams come true.

It was a moot point.

His scowl deepened as he tried to concentrate on his work and failed. Again. What the hell had crawled into his brain lately? Why couldn't he seem to think straight anymore?

He had the answer to that, too. And he didn't like it. "No, it's not your imagination. I've been here more than usual."

Leaning a hip against O'Rourke's desk so that the man was forced to look at him, Simon said, "Mind if I ask why?"

O'Rourke hardly spared him a look. "I've got work to do," he said tersely.

That part was obvious and he wasn't asking about that. They now had, thanks to the financial backing they'd just secured at the beginning of the month, enough manpower to work that out without O'Rourke dedicating his every waking moment to being here. O'Rourke had been the father to the idea, now it was time to do some serious delegation.

"Why?" Simon repeated. The look O'Rourke gave him was dark. "I know you well enough to know that something's bothering you. What is it?"

"Nothing," O'Rourke snapped, then instantly regretted it. Simon deserved better. Hell, so did he.

Pushing back from his desk, O'Rourke rose, towering over Simon as he ran his hand along the back of his neck. God, but he felt at a loss, hemmed in by his own damn integrity.

For the most part, he believed in keeping his own counsel. But it wasn't working this time.

He faced Simon squarely. "I think I'm in love."

O'Rourke expected to hear Simon hooting with

laughter. That he didn't surprised him. So did the look of concern on his friend's face.

"In love?" Simon blew out a long breath. "That's bad. Does Kitt know?"

O'Rourke laughed shortly. Therein lay the whole irony. "It *is* Kitt."

Puzzled, confused, Simon ventured cautiously. "Well, that's good, then." He peered at O'Rourke's face. "Isn't it?"

O'Rourke's frown only became more so. "No, not really."

Lost, Simon shook his head. "In love with the woman you're married to—is that a bad thing where you come from?"

O'Rourke sighed deeply. He shouldn't have said anything. "It is if you're supposed to have a strictly business relationship."

"So it got a little friendlier. Sometimes that happens with 'business relationships.' What's so wrong with that?"

O'Rourke pinned him with a black look, warning him not to venture any further into his thoughts than he already had. "It didn't get *that* friendly, so get your mind out of the gutter—"

"Bedroom," Simon interjected.

"Especially there. And I'll have you know there's *everything* wrong with it." One look at Simon told him his friend clearly wasn't following this. "Don't you see, if I do anything, she'll think I tricked her. I can't even make a move without being guilty—"

"O'Rourke—"

But O'Rourke wasn't listening. His head was too full of thoughts, of objections as well as desires that refused to allow themselves to go quietly.

"Besides, what kind of a husband would I make, anyway?" He was pacing around the small area like an oversize, trapped panther. "Always working. She'll leave me."

"Whoa, don't you think you're getting a little ahead of yourself here? You haven't even given her a chance to 'stay' in the right sense of the word and you've already got her leaving you." Reaching a little, Simon laid a hand on O'Rourke's shoulder. "Maybe she'd like seeing her husband only on a limited basis." O'Rourke looked at him quizzically. "We call that quality time here."

O'Rourke remained unconvinced. "Where I come from, they call it being self-absorbed and that's what it'll seem to her that I am."

"You could change, then," Simon commented.

There was no use making promises that he would not keep. O'Rourke knew the kind of man he was. It was all or nothing. And this was more than just his dream. He wasn't the only one involved anymore.

"I'm not going to change—"

Simon had a feeling it wasn't all written in stone the way his friend seemed to believe. "For the right woman—"

Stifling an angry huff, O'Rourke stood over him. "Why are you doing this?"

Smaller by five inches and twenty pounds, Simon held his ground. Their friendship, formed in the last year in college, went deep, and he didn't want to see O'Rourke throw something meaningful away. "Because from the little I've seen of her, I think Kitt's a great girl and she's taken some of that surly edge off you."

Steely eyes narrowed until his brows touched. "What surly edge?"

Simon held his hands up. "Sorry, I meant your Irish charm." The grin faded as his expression became sober. "So, what are you going to do?"

That remained the big question. The one O'Rourke didn't have an answer to. Wanting Kitt wasn't enough. "I don't know. Work it out, I guess."

Simon clapped him on the back. "Just as long as the work you're doing isn't all here."

Simon had bullied him into coming home at a decent hour by calling him a coward, the one word guaranteed to turn him into a stubborn sixteen-year-old, bent on disproving his accuser.

Putting his key into his pocket now, O'Rourke smiled to himself. Kitt was in the living room, concentrating so hard on something she had on the coffee table, she didn't seem to hear him come in.

He wondered what had absorbed her attention so fully. "What's that?"

Startled, she looked up and then smiled her greeting. "Hi. I didn't hear you come in." Because he was looking at the paper she'd been filling out, she turned it around so that he could see it. "It's a job application. I went down for an interview today."

A job interview. It was starting. Pretty soon, with the hours he kept, even if he got home sooner, they wouldn't be in the same place at the same time.

Well, what the hell had he expected, for her to turn into some barefoot and pregnant woman waiting on him hand and foot? He wouldn't have wanted that, anyway.

Except maybe the pregnant part.

He stopped himself in time.

He tried to look disinterested as he shrugged out of his windbreaker. "Oh?"

She nodded, but the excitement she'd felt earlier this afternoon, during the actual interview, was growing fainter. She hadn't a clue as to why. Work used to mean so much to her. It defined what she was, where she was coming from. She liked being her own person.

Now it didn't mean quite as much. Was she still in the final throes of postpartum depression?

"Hellenic Industries." Rising, she took the jacket he'd just draped over the back of the sofa and walked with it to the coatrack by the door. "They've just landed a new contract for work on the space station." She hung the jacket up. "I think they liked me."

"What's not to like?" The damn wolves probably took one look at her and began tossing coins as to who would devour her first.

The thought surprised him. What the hell was wrong with him? He didn't think like that and he didn't know anyone else who thought like that. He forced a reassuring smile to his lips, though he was feeling nothing of the kind.

His comment made her pause and she looked at him. Was that a compliment, or a crack? God, but he was so hard to read. Not that she was any good at that sort of thing, she reminded herself, thinking of how wrong she'd been about Jeffrey.

But O'Rourke only added to her confusion. He'd all but disappeared these last few weeks. Right after he'd kissed her the night they'd taken Shawna to the hospital. Kissed her senseless and made her think that they were going to…going to make…

It didn't matter what she had thought. *He* had thought something different. Any idiot could see that he was backing away from her. Pronto.

She'd thought that he was different. The day after, when they'd brought Shawna home from the hospital, he'd been so attentive to the baby that she'd thought, hoped really, that she'd actually found a decent man she could slowly build a life with.

But then he backed away so quickly it made her head spin. And her heart.

Served her right for letting herself dream a little. This would teach her. The only one she could depend on was herself. It was time she pulled herself back up on her feet. Two months was long enough to drift. She needed to get back to work. To be her own person.

And not to rely on any man, no matter what.

"Well, they might not have liked my credentials," she pointed out matter-of-factly.

He wasn't thinking of her credentials. He was thinking of what it would be like to come home and not find her here. And that would be where this would lead. He had no doubts that she would stick to the bargain, stay the year. But the second it was up, she'd be gone.

And he, he realized, didn't want her to be. "Have you ever thought about being something other than an aerospace engineer?"

"Such as?"

"Oh, I don't know. Maybe a business of your own," he said.

"Making my own space station?" she asked, tongue in cheek.

"No, I mean—" He didn't know what he meant.

He was rambling, O'Rourke thought in disgust. "Never mind, it was just a passing thought."

She didn't like not being in the loop. He had something to say and, good or bad, she wanted to hear it. "Well, let it pass this way and maybe I can answer you better."

He shrugged, not wanting to pursue the matter. It had been a stupid one at that, he thought. "What about Shawna?"

She stiffened her shoulders unconsciously. "What about her?"

He'd have thought that would have been the first question she'd think of. "Who'll watch her if you go back to work?"

"Sylvia works at home most of the time." She'd already broached the matter to Sylvia when she'd returned from the interview. Sylvia had stayed with Shawna for the afternoon and was more than willing to turn that into an on-going event. "She can watch her."

He knew all about the hours that Sylvia kept. They were highly irregular. "Most of the time," he echoed. "What about when she's out? Are you going to have someone else raise your baby?"

"Why are you interrogating me this way?" she demanded. "What's it to you if Sylvia watches the baby or I have a sitter for her?"

"Because...because..." The right words weren't coming. The doorbell rang at that moment, preventing the wrong ones from emerging. Frustrated, he shot her a look as he crossed to the door. "This isn't over yet."

"What isn't over yet?" she asked, confused and annoyed at the tone he had taken with her.

He didn't trust himself to answer her civilly. If someone had asked him, he wouldn't have been able to explain what was going on inside him now—or why there was this overwhelming urge, as he yanked open the door, to just keep walking until he'd put her and these feelings all behind him.

The man standing in the doorway quickly sent thoughts of prolonged walks or a drive to the Shamrock out of his head.

"Mr. Rutherford."

Framed by the doorway, the INS agent appeared even smaller than he had in his office. He gave the impression of peering over O'Rourke's shoulder without moving a muscle. "Is this a bad time?"

O'Rourke struggled for composure. Was there something wrong with his application for citizenship? Had the paperwork been turned down after all? "No, why?"

Rutherford kept his expression bland and unreadable, save for a small, obligatory smile. "I thought I heard raised voices coming from here just as I rang the bell."

"I was shouting to make myself heard over the doorbell and the radio," O'Rourke told him. Realizing that he was blocking the way, O'Rourke stepped back to admit the agent into the apartment. His eyes found Kitt's. "Look who's here, love."

Instantly alert, Kitt smiled brightly at the INS agent, completely burying any residual annoyance she'd just felt. It was showtime and O'Rourke needed her—the big, dumb jerk.

Coming forward, she put out her hand. "Hello, Mr. Rutherford."

"Hello. Mrs. O'Rourke." He shook her hand, looking around. "What radio?" he asked O'Rourke. "I don't hear a radio."

Kitt jumped in quickly. "That's because I shut it off when I realized the doorbell was ringing. We like to play the radio. It helps soothe Shawna in the evening."

She saw the look of gratitude in O'Rourke's eyes and it pleased her.

"How is your daughter?" Rutherford asked. Like the investigator he sometimes was, the man drifted around the room, observing, making mental notes.

The best way to handle this was straightforwardly, Kitt decided. "Come see for yourself." Beckoning him to follow her, Kitt led Rutherford to the bedroom so he could see the baby.

"You keep her in your room?" Rutherford asked Kitt.

The baby stirred but continued sleeping. Kitt nodded toward the doorway, taking O'Rourke's hand as she moved out of the room again.

Rutherford made note of that, too.

"For now," she told the agent quietly, answering his question. "She's been sick and O'—Shawn Michael," she corrected herself quickly, "wanted to be able to hear her if she started to cry." She smiled, remembering how kind O'Rourke had been that evening they'd rushed to the hospital. Whatever else the man was, she had to give him his due. He was good to her daughter. And just because he was distancing himself from her didn't mean he wasn't a good man.

She was quick on her feet, O'Rourke thought, tipping his hat to her. Aware that she was still holding his hand, he threaded his fingers through it and smiled at her when she looked at him.

They were in the living room now. Rutherford felt it was all right to cease talking in whispers. "Sounds like you're turning out to be a good father."

"He's a natural," Kitt told the man as O'Rourke self-consciously shrugged away the observation.

Surprised at the feeling behind her words, O'Rourke raised his eyes to Kitt's. Her smile widened.

The silent communication was not lost on the INS agent. Looking around the room, he saw the application form Kitt had been filling out when O'Rourke had walked in. He raised a quizzical brow and nodded at the form. "What's this?"

"A job application." Picking it up, she handed it to the man, making sure that he noticed what she had filled in as to her marital status. "I was thinking of going back to work."

His attention was drawn to O'Rourke rather than to her. "Oh?"

Trying to cull the man's good graces, she still felt herself resenting the implication that the decision of whether or not she return to work rested with her so-called husband. They'd come a long way since the Dark Ages.

"I'm the independent kind, Mr. Rutherford," she told him. "I like pulling my own weight. Just because I'm married doesn't mean I expect my husband to provide for me. I like the idea of being able to bring something to the table, so to speak, as well."

Rutherford studied her for a long moment. His expression gave nothing away. The silence was driving Kitt crazy. Her hand tightened in O'Rourke's.

"So, everything's going well?" Rutherford finally asked. "In general," he added.

"Very well," Kitt told him with feeling, deciding that maybe she'd better play up the role of the supportive wife. After all, this was about O'Rourke, not her. "Shawn Michael's got that backing he needed after all."

"Really?" For the first time, there was genuine interest and a smattering of pleasure on the other man's lean face.

O'Rourke was relieved to be able to discuss something he knew about. "Someone my father once knew back in Ireland has connections here and—" He realized he was about to become long-winded. "To make a long story short, we have the funding to finish the work on the computers. The Emerald computers should be on the market before Thanksgiving."

"And these are different from hundreds of other brands how?" Rutherford asked, curious.

O'Rourke felt himself getting revved up. "Mine use a different kind of processor. One that's extremely affordable for smaller businesses. They're four times as fast as the standard computer on the market today and—" O'Rourke stopped. "You really want to hear this? I can get pretty carried away."

"That he does," Kitt put in, gently caressing O'Rourke's cheek. "Work consumes a lot of his time. But he's always there for the baby and me when we need him," she added quickly.

There was such feeling in her voice that again, Rutherford stopped to study her for a long moment. "I see. And is this marriage everything you'd hoped it would be, Mrs. O'Rourke?"

If she laid it on too thickly, she knew he would be suspicious. So she brushed a kiss against O'Rourke's cheek and wove her arms through his.

"We're still in the period of adjustment, Mr. Ruth-erford, but yes, I think we're on our way to making a strong marriage."

"That's not what I asked," Rutherford said.

"It's what I answered." Kitt tossed her hair over her shoulder. "And I think my answer is actually bet-ter than your question."

Rutherford raised a brow, then looked at O'Rourke. "I see you have your hands full, Mr. O'Rourke."

O'Rourke laughed and there was pleasure in his voice. "You don't know the half of it."

"Maybe I do." They both looked at him quizzi-cally. "I'll be honest with you. When I gave my seal of approval to the matter of your wedding, I had some reservations. I've seen too many bogus marriages not to. But I also saw something in the two of you that made me think that maybe, just maybe, this one was on the level." He allowed himself a half smile. "I don't mind telling you that I'm relieved I wasn't wrong."

Kitt exchanged looks with O'Rourke, relieved that for now, they'd cleared another hurdle. "Would you like to stay for dinner, Mr. Rutherford?"

The question took the agent by surprise and he didn't answer at first. "You know, in all my years of doing this, not a single couple has ever asked me to break bread with them. They're always in a hurry to hand me my hat and see me on my way."

"That's because they're afraid of you," she told him honestly. "You're the man who could put an end to their hopes."

"And you don't feel that way?" he asked her, his eyes shifting to take in O'Rourke as well.

"No, I don't feel that way. And neither does Shawn

Michael." She looked at him, waiting for O'Rourke to agree. "We're all responsible for ourselves in this world, Mr. Rutherford. We're the ones who can make our own dreams come true—or not."

He liked her spirit and her philosophy. Slanting a look at O'Rourke, Rutherford had a feeling he wasn't alone. "You have yourself a wonderful woman, here, Mr. O'Rourke."

O'Rourke slipped his arm around Kitt's waist. "Yes, I'm just beginning to fully appreciate that."

There was something in O'Rourke's voice that gave Kitt pause and she looked at him.

You're just reading things into his voice, she told herself.

Looking toward the kitchen, Rutherford hesitated for a moment, then made his decision. "Much as I'd like to stay and as convinced as I am that the wonderful aroma I detect coming from your kitchen far surpasses anything that Mrs. Rutherford might have waiting for me on my arrival home, the way I've made my marriage work is always to be home when I said I would be."

O'Rourke opened the door for him. Rutherford raised his eyes to O'Rourke's as he crossed the threshold. "You might want to keep that in mind."

"Absolutely," O'Rourke agreed. "Nice to see you again."

And nice to see you leave, he added silently as he closed the door behind the man.

O'Rourke didn't know whose sigh of relief was louder, his or Kitt's.

Chapter Twelve

O'Rourke turned to Kitt after a moment, a myriad of feelings moving through him, jockeying for space and recognition.

He owed her, he thought, he owed her a great deal. But it wasn't gratitude that was rising to the top right now. It was something else. And he wasn't any surer of what he wanted to do about it now than he had been all the other times he'd felt it making its presence known.

"You think well on your feet."

Relieved that the INS agent had decided not to take her up on her impromptu dinner invitation and had left, Kitt looked at the man she'd put herself on the line for and wondered if she was making a big mistake again.

Somehow, she didn't think so. Her mouth curved in amusement at his comment. "I think well in any position. What are you referring to, specifically?"

He followed her back to the living room. "Coming up with a reason for the crib in the room."

She lifted her shoulder, shrugging off the accomplishment as next to nothing. The peasant blouse she had on slid down, exposing her shoulder.

"Piece of cake."

Her words dried in her mouth as he pushed the material back into place before she had a chance to. She could feel his fingers moving up her shoulder slowly. Fanning fires that were supposed to remain dormant.

His eyes held hers. Did she feel it? Did she feel that spark between them?

Spark, hell, it was a forest fire waiting to go out of control. "And that bit about me being a good father was a nice touch."

His eyes were holding hers. She was finding it difficult to breathe. A sensible woman would have stepped back by now. But a sensible woman probably wouldn't have gotten herself into this situation—any of it—in the first place.

"I meant it."

O'Rourke fought the very real urge to bring the peasant blouse back down until it was around her waist. He wanted to hold her. To touch her. "I never thought of myself as the father type."

"You should," she told him softly, wishing he would kiss her. "You've all the qualifications for it."

He didn't want to crowd her. Just because he was having trouble wrestling with urges he hadn't dealt with since he was a teenager, didn't mean she had to put up with them.

O'Rourke stepped back. "Why? Because I know CPR for infants? I already told you—"

Space, why was there always space between them? Didn't he find her attractive? She tried to concentrate on what they were talking about and not on what was ricocheting all through her.

"You're a caretaker," she contradicted. "Why does that bother you so much?"

Before he knew what he was doing, he was telling her. Telling her things he didn't talk about with anyone because it was his business, his and his family's. But he was telling her, anyway. "Because my father was a caretaker and it killed him. Working double shifts in the mine to provide for kids he shouldn't have had. At least, not all of them."

"Oh? And which ones should he have cut out?"

O'Rourke looked at her, taken aback by the passion in her voice, confused by her question. "What?"

"Your brothers and sisters, which one would you have left out of the mix? If you could pick which ones should never have been born, who would you choose?"

"I can't choose—" O'Rourke snapped, annoyed.

"Then you like them all."

"Of course I like them all, but—"

Did she have to hit him over the head with it, or was he being deliberately obtuse just to bait her? "Maybe so did your father."

He sighed. She had a point, he supposed, but he wasn't about to say so. Whether or not James O'Rourke loved all his children—and he did—didn't matter. The end result was still the same. "He died too young."

Kitt's eyes locked with his. "Everyone dies too young."

She'd made another valid point, he thought, not knowing whether to be impressed or irritated. He settled for a little of both. "You know, woman, you do have an antagonistic way about you."

She grinned, the mood lightening. "So I've been told. I wasn't trying to make friends, I was trying to show you that you're wrong."

He bristled at that and felt the need to retreat from the thought he'd been entertaining himself. "Well, if anyone's wrong, it's Rutherford."

She started to sit down again, to finish filling out the rest of the application, but he'd sparked her curiosity. "About?"

"Saying that he had a feeling when he saw us that we might be the couple who would 'make it.'"

So he thought that was wrong, did he? Kitt felt something tightening inside her. And something hurting. Damn it, what was wrong with her? Why did she insist on doing this to herself? Why did she insist on letting the strings around her heart loosen to the point that she was in jeopardy of being hurt? Wasn't once enough? Hadn't she learned anything?

"So you thought he was wrong?" she asked stiffly.

"Of course I did." O'Rourke tried to read her reaction and failed miserably. "Didn't you?"

"Sure." She glanced up. "The baby's crying." And for once, Kitt blessed her for it. She needed an excuse to get away from O'Rourke before she did something stupid like cry. God, but she'd thought she was made of sterner stuff than this. "I'd better go to her."

He frowned, cocking his head slightly as he listened. "I don't hear anything."

"Deaf as well as blind," she muttered before she could stop herself. "Not much of a prize, are you?"

"What the hell are you talking about?" He found himself talking to her retreating back.

"Nothing," she shot back over her shoulder, annoyed with her lack of control, "absolutely nothing."

Left standing alone in the living room, O'Rourke shook his head. What the hell had just happened here? Had they been in the same conversation? And where had all this tension come from?

But she'd certainly put him in his place, he thought, agreeing as to how wrong Rutherford had been in his whimsical estimation that they looked like a couple who actually belonged together.

The thought was really absurd.

And yet wasn't that what he'd just been thinking himself? Still, one of them thinking that wasn't enough. It took two...

Kitt found herself blinking back tears as she changed the baby.

This was stupid, she upbraided herself. Reaching for the baby powder, she dusted the newly dried bottom. She didn't know what was wrong with her. She hadn't been this emotional while she was pregnant. Why was she having such a hard time harnessing her emotions now, after the baby was born?

Powder container met bureau with more force than it should have, sending up a white cloud. It had been two months now, shouldn't things have gotten back to normal by now?

Normal, right, she laughed at herself. Here she was, living in some strange man's apartment, pretending to be his wife....

No, she wasn't pretending, Kitt corrected herself silently. She was his wife. The words were legal, the document was legal. What she was pretending about were the feelings...

No, she admitted to herself quietly, she wasn't pretending about those, either. They were there, all right.

But she was going to have to ignore them. She folded one diaper tab into place, then the other. Shawna kicked bowed legs that were becoming chubby in glee. Kitt smiled in response, her heart heavy. Certainly O'Rourke didn't feel anything for her. Except maybe gratitude, and even that was hard to tell, once he got a burr under his saddle and growled his way through the day.

With a sigh, she picked Shawna up from the bed. "There, nice and dry. Try staying that way for more than five minutes." She nuzzled the soft little neck.

Since the baby was wide awake, she decided to take her out into the living room. She could use the company. And the interference. O'Rourke always seemed to be nicer when he was around Shawna.

Strapping Shawna into the infant seat, Kitt walked out of the bedroom and into the living room. A noise from the kitchen caught her attention.

The first thing she noticed was that the table was set. She didn't remember doing that.

Because she hadn't, she realized. He had. She looked at O'Rourke with a silent question in her eyes. Why was he doing this?

"You set the table."

"You were busy."

The timer had gone off on the stove while she was in the bedroom. It gave him something to do. With two pot holders buffering the pan, he took the roast beef she'd been making out of the oven and placed it on the counter. With less than deft movements, O'Rourke transferred the roast onto a large platter, then brought that to the table.

"And I thought turnaround was fair play."

He looked out of place doing that, she thought, amusement curving her mouth. "Do men set the table in your part of the world?"

"They do if they're hungry and everyone else is busy," he told her gruffly, feeling suddenly like a bull in a china shop. "I'm not completely Neanderthal."

She set down the infant seat on the floor near the table so that the baby could see them both. "I never said you were."

Taking two glasses down from the cupboard, he spared her a look. "Not in so many words."

Kitt took the glasses from him and placed them on the table. "Not in any words."

Forgetting to use the pot holders, he took out the two baked potatoes she'd put in alongside the pan and instantly regretted it. It took effort to put them down on the counter rather than drop them.

"Here, let me see that," she ordered. She looked at his hands, then took out a small tube of aloe ointment she'd stored in the drawer. "It's not bad," she commented, rubbing in the ointment. "But you could have done a lot of damage to your hands. Pay attention to what you're doing."

The slow movement of her fingers along his skin,

rubbing in the ointment, dissolved his embarrassment. "Then what is it you do think of me?" he asked, going back to their previous conversation. She looked at him quizzically, and he added, "Just so I know."

She chose her words deliberately. Carefully. "I think you're a good man who's decent and kind and so damn afraid to take a chance on life he's wrapped himself up completely in his work and he'll bite the head off anyone who'll approach him with the truth." It wasn't what he'd expected to hear, she thought smugly. "Just so you know," she finished, paraphrasing him.

He drew his hands away from her, annoyed at his own stupidity. "I'm wrapped up in my work, as you put it, in order to make a go of this company so that there'll be money to send my brothers and sisters through school and give them the life they deserve."

She took out a can of soda for herself and a bottle of beer for him. "Maybe they want to make their own lives. Maybe they don't want things handed to them any more than you do."

He could argue that no one had handed him anything, that he'd had to work for everything he had, but it didn't have to be that way for the others.

"I don't want to see them struggle the way I did," he insisted, taking the bottle she'd opened from her. "Waiting tables and sweeping out pubs after hours just to have enough for books…"

There was no denying that it had been a hard way to go, Kitt thought, but it had contributed to making him the man he was now. "Didn't seem to hurt you any. Other than to close you off."

"It wasn't the waiting and the sweeping that did that," he snorted.

She watched as he sliced the roast beef into even servings. The man had an eye and a hand for precision. "Then what did?"

"Watching my father die by inches." It was painful to talk about, even now, after all these years. "Watching my mother waste away because he was gone. Getting Susan's Dear John letter."

She might not have witnessed her parents struggling to put food on the table, but she knew about being hurt by someone she cared about. "Looks like we both have people in our past who liked to leave notes in their wake."

He'd been so wrapped up in his own world, he hadn't realized that she had a universe of her own as well. That she'd been hurt in her world. Oh, he knew all right, the way he knew that the sun rose and set and that there were plants that you didn't touch unless you wanted to spend the next week scratching. But the knowledge hadn't penetrated where he lived. Deep in the soul of him.

It did now.

O'Rourke studied her face, thinking of the woman who sat opposite him in a completely different light: as a person with feelings, with hopes and dreams of her own. A person who had fought her way to be where she was. A person, like him, who wouldn't knuckle under.

"Yeah, well, it served to teach us something, didn't it?" he said. "It served to teach us not to put our faith in something that could blow up in our faces without any warning."

His voice had gone up and he was scowling so hard, he looked like a thundercloud. "Why are you so angry?" She hadn't said anything to set him off.

"I'm not angry," he snapped.

The hell he wasn't, she thought. "Then why are you shouting?"

"I'm not shouting, I'm just talking." Realizing that his voice was raised, he lowered it. "Loudly."

"Oh." Kitt raised a napkin to her lips, afraid that she was going to laugh at him. There was almost something endearing about the way he was struggling to control his temper—even though she hadn't a clue as to why it had erupted in the first place.

The scowl on his face deepened. "And you needn't be trying to hide that smirk."

Kitt put the napkin back down on the table. "You *want* me to smirk?"

He felt his temper fraying and he still couldn't fathom what had set him off like this. All those emotions butting up against one another inside of him were to blame. How the hell did a man cap that off?

O'Rourke drew himself up. He knew one way. "I want you to do whatever you want to do. I think there's been a great deal of pussyfooting around and maybe we should stop pretending and start being honest with each other."

Putting down her fork, she stared at him. "Well, now you've really lost me—"

"Maybe that's just the trouble."

"Come again?"

"That job application," he said, nodding toward the living room. The form was still on the coffee table where she'd left it earlier, half filled out. "Is that the first step?"

Kitt placed her glass down again. "The first step to what?"

It cost him to be this exposed. It would have cost him more if he wasn't. "To your leaving."

Now his anger was starting to make sense to her. It instigated her own. "Is that it? Are you afraid I'll go and then you'll be deported? We had an agreement. I don't renege on agreements," she said heatedly. "And besides, from the sound of it, you're well on your way to becoming an enterprising capitalist who—"

This was all new to him, explaining his feelings. He was a lot better at troubleshooting motherboards and confounding processors.

"Damn it, I'm not talking about being deported, or putting up a front for some INS agent who pops up like toast whenever he feels like it. I know you won't back down on your agreement."

"Then what are you talking about?"

He threw up his hands. How much plainer could he make it? "Tomorrow."

She cocked her head, but his meaning remained obscure. "Tomorrow?"

He blew out an annoyed breath. "And the day after that, and the day after that."

She was beginning to lose her own patience. "If you don't start being any clearer—"

He was navigating through turbulent waters without a compass, but he gave it his best. "You want clear? All right, I'll be clear. Katherine Dawson, will you marry me?"

"Did you sleep through the first ceremony? I already did."

He shook his head. She didn't understand. "I mean really marry me."

She was trying to follow him, she really was. "That was a fake priest?"

Unable to sit any longer, he got up from the table and crossed to her. "He was a real priest and stop confusing the issue. I mean marry me with your heart—"

She was on her feet instantly, refusing to be intimidated or browbeaten this way. "You leave my heart out of this."

He'd come too far to back down now. Taking her hands in his, he refused to let her move away.

"I can't. Any more than I can leave mine out." He looked into her eyes. "You confuse me and you infuriate me and you make me pine—I figure we've got the makings of a fine match right there. Now all I need is for you to say yes."

"All?"

He heard the dangerous edge in her voice and knew he probably hadn't said it right. "Maybe I shouldn't have put it that way."

"Maybe." Her eyes narrowed. "If this is about having an itch, I suggest you go somewhere else to scratch it."

He shook his head, but he still didn't follow her. "An itch?"

He was playing dumb and she didn't like it. "Sex, O'Rourke, sex."

He turned her so that her back was to the baby.

"Don't go using that kind language in front of the little one."

She'd had enough. Kitt pulled her hands away from his. "I wasn't the one who brought it up."

"Yes," he told her firmly, "you were. Because it's not about that word, or an itch, or whatever it is you want to call it. I can get someone to satisfy those kind of things any day of the week. It's the rest of it that I'm talking about."

"The rest of it," she repeated, afraid to put her own meaning to his words. Afraid of being wrong again.

"Damn it, woman, I want an independent soul. I want someone I can respect who can respect me and what I need." He took her hands again, pleading his case with his eyes. "I need a woman I can depend on to be her own person. And if that woman should be packaged up in a body the angels fought over to make their own, with a face that makes a man's heart skip a beat, well, so much the better."

She wanted to be perfectly clear on all this. "And this is me you're talking about," she said slowly.

He smiled. Maybe there was hope yet. "This is you I'm talking about."

He left her mystified. "When, exactly, did this awareness suddenly take place?"

That was easy enough to answer. "The first time I looked at you."

Now she knew he was putting her on. "The first time you looked at me, I looked like a half-drowned, overstuffed sausage about to burst apart."

He grinned, drawing her into his arms. "Aye, you did at that. But it got better."

She felt her heart begin to beat hard. "So you're saying what, that you want to be my husband in every sense of the word?"

"If you'll let me." Feeling on slightly safer ground, he opened his heart to her. "I didn't set out wanting a wife, Kitt-with-two-t's. I set out wanting an excuse to stay in this country. But I found myself wanting you. All the time. I don't expect you to love me—"

"Why?" she interrupted.

It took him a second to collect himself. "Because that would be too much to ask—" His business was finally going well, his siblings would be in this country soon. He didn't expect to be lucky in every aspect of his life.

"Ask," she told him.

Was she serious? "Do you?"

Kitt batted her lashes at him, feigning innocent ignorance. "Do I what?"

"Do you love me, damn it, woman?"

She almost laughed out loud. "Yes, I love you, damn it, man."

It was his turn to ask. "Why?"

The grin settled into a smile on her lips. She cupped his cheek with her hand. "Because you need me and I need that. Because you're there when I need you. And because you won my heart the minute I saw you walking into my hospital room with two bouquets in your hand. I knew then that you had a heart of a poet."

A poet. Now, there was something no one had accused him of being. "Then you knew more than me."

"Women generally do know more than a man,

Shawn Michael," she told him, a smile playing on her lips.

"We'll have that discussion later," he promised. "Right now, all I want you to know is that I love you, Kitt-with-two-t's. And I plan on loving you until my dying day."

"Only that long?" she asked.

His eyes smiled at her. "Something else to discuss. Later."

Kitt's smile burned away in the heat of his kiss. It took them a long time to get back to the discussion.

* * * * *

Look for Marie Ferrarella's next book,
THE M.D. MEETS HIS MATCH, on sale in
Silhouette Special Edition in June 2001.

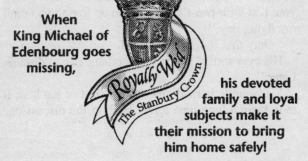

SILHOUETTE *Romance*™

*Experience
the power of love....*

Feel the breathless connection....

*Fall in love as though it were
the very first time....*

Come to where favorite authors—such as
Diana Palmer, Stella Bagwell,
Marie Ferrarella, Carolyn Zane
*and many more—deliver pulse-pounding
romance, genuine emotion and stories straight
from the heart!*

*Silhouette Romance—
From first love to forever!*

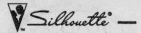

REGENCY
ROMANCE

Visit the elegant English countryside,
explore the whirlwind of London Society
and meet feisty heroines who tame roguish
heroes with their wit, zest and feminine
charm, in...The Regency Collection.

Available in March 2001 at your favorite retail outlet:

TRUE COLOURS
by Nicola Cornick

THE WOLFE'S MATE
by Paula Marshall

MR. TRELAWNEY'S PROPOSAL
by Mary Brendan

TALLIE'S KNIGHT
by Anne Gracie

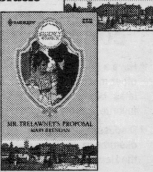

QUINTUS CURTIUS

II

QUINTUS CURTIUS

WITH AN ENGLISH TRANSLATION BY
JOHN C. ROLFE, Litt.D.
UNIVERSITY OF PENNSYLVANIA

IN TWO VOLUMES
II
BOOKS VI–X

CAMBRIDGE, MASSACHUSETTS
HARVARD UNIVERSITY PRESS
LONDON
WILLIAM HEINEMANN LTD
MCMLXXXV

American
ISBN 0-674-99407-8

British
ISBN 0 434 99369 7

First printed 1946
Reprinted 1956, 1962, 1976, 1985

Printed in Great Britain

CONTENTS OF VOLUME II

QUINTUS CURTIUS RUFUS

BOOK VI

CONTENTS OF BOOK VI

2

The soldiers are aroused by his eloquence and bid him lead them wherever he will. He takes advantage of their enthusiasm and marches through Parthienê to Hyrcania. A description of the Stiboetes river. Nabarzanes in a letter asks for pardon, which is granted. A description of the Caspian Sea (iv).

Alexander receives Artabazus with great courtesy, spares the Greeks who had aided Darius, defeats the Mardi, and entertains a queen of the Amazons (v).

The Macedonians are offended by Alexander's habits. To prevent a mutiny he plans to make war upon Bessus. He must first put down a revolt of Satibarzanes, whom he had made satrap of the Arii. He drives the barbarians from the mountains, takes Artacana, and marches against the Drangae (vi).

Dymnus reveals a conspiracy against Alexander to Nicomachus, who through his brother Cebalinus reports it to Alexander. Dymnus kills himself (vii).

Philotas, son of Parmenion, is charged by Alexander's friends with forming the conspiracy. He is arrested and taken to the king's quarters (viii).

Alexander addresses the soldiers about the conspiracy. Some of the leaders make charges against Philotas. When the accused is asked whether he wishes to make his defence in the Macedonian language or in Greek, he prefers to reply in Greek (ix).

Philotas denies the charges (x).

Bolon rouses the soldiers against Philotas. A confession is forced from him by torture, and he is stoned to death with the other conspirators (xi).

QUINTUS CURTIUS RUFUS

HISTORIARUM ALEXANDRI MAGNI MACEDONIS

LIBER VI

Dum haec in Asia geruntur, ne in Graecia quidem Macedoniaque tranquillae res fuere. Regnabat apud Lacedaemonios Agis, filius Archidami, qui Tarentinis opem ferens occiderat eodem die quo Philippus Athenienses ad Chaeroneam vicit ; is Alexandri virtutis aemulus cives suos stimulabat, ne Graeciam servitute Macedonum diutius premi paterentur ; nisi in tempore providerent, idem iugum ad ipsos transiturum. Adnitendum igitur, dum aliquae Persis ad resistendum vires essent ; illis oppressis, adversus immanem potentiam frustra avitae libertatis memores futuros. Sic instinctis animis, occasionem belli movendi captabant. Prospero igitur eventu Memnonis invitati consilia cum eo miscere aggressi sunt et, postquam ille rerum laetarum initia intempestiva morte destituit, nihilo remissius agebant.

Sed ad Pharnabazum et Autophradaten profectus, Agis triginta argenti talenta decemque triremes impetravit, quas Agesilao fratri misit, ut in Cretam navigaret, cuius

---

[a] 338 B.C.   [b] See iii. 1. 21.

4

QUINTUS CURTIUS RUFUS

HISTORY OF ALEXANDER THE GREAT OF MACEDON

BOOK VI

*While this was happening in Asia, not in Greece either
nor in Macedonia was there complete quiet.   There was
ruling among the Lacedaemonians Agis, son of Archi-
damus, who, while bearing aid to the Tarentines, was
slain on the same day that Philip defeated the Athenians
at Chaeronea.*ᵃ   *Agis, a rival of Alexander in valour,
was spurring on his citizens not to allow Greece to be
longer oppressed by slavery to the Macedonians ; unless
they took precaution betimes, the same yoke would pass to
them.   They ought therefore to bestir themselves while the
Persians still had some strength for resistance ; when
they were crushed, the Lacedaemonians, faced by an
immense power, would in vain be mindful of their ancestral
freedom.   When their minds had been thus aroused, the
Lacedaemonians sought for an opportunity of beginning
war.   Accordingly, encouraged by Memnon's ᵇ successful
result, they began to join in his plans, and after he was
taken off in the beginning of a prosperous career by an
untimely death, they did not act with any less vigour.*

*But Agis went to Pharnabazus and Autophradates, and
obtained thirty talents of silver and ten triremes, which he
sent to his brother Agesilaüs, in order that he might sail*

5

nsulae cultores inter Lacedaemonios et Macedonas diversis studiis distrahebantur. Legati quoque ad Dareum missi sunt, qui ad bellum ampliorem vim pecuniae pluresque naves peterent. Atque haec eorum consilia clades ad Issum—nam ea intervenerat—adeo non interpellavit, ut etiam adiuvaret. Quippe fugientem insecutus Alexander in loca in dies longinquiora rapiebatur, et ex ipso proelio mercennariorum ingens multitudo in Graeciam fuga se receperat; quorum octo milia Persica pecunia conduxit Agis eorumque opera plerasque Cretensium urbes recepit.

Cum deinceps Menon in Thraciam ab Alexandro missus barbaros ad defectionem impulisset atque Antipater ad eam conprimendam exercitum ex Macedonia in Thraciam duxisset, opportunitate temporis strenue usi, Lacedaemonii totam Peloponnesum, paucis urbibus exceptis, ad suas partes traxerunt, confectoque exercitu viginti milium peditum cum duobus milibus equitum, Agidi summam imperii detulerunt. Antipater, ea re comperta, bellum in Thracia, quibus potest condicionibus, componit raptimque in Graeciam regressus ab amicis sociisque civitatibus auxilia cogit. Quibus convenientibus, ad quadraginta milia militum recensuit. Advenerat etiam ex Peloponneso valida manus; sed quia dubiam eorum fidem cognoverat, dissimulata suspicione, gratias egit, quod ad defendendam a Lacedaemoniis Alexandri dignitatem adfuissent; scripturum se id regi, gratiam in tempore relaturo. In praesens nihil opus esse maioribus copiis; itaque domos redirent, foederis necessitate expleta. Nuntios deinde ad Alexandrum mittit, de motu

6

to Crete, the inhabitants of which island were divided by conflicting interests between the Lacedaemonians and the Macedonians. Envoys were sent also to Darius, to ask for a greater sum of money for carrying on the war and more ships. And these plans of theirs the defeat at Issus —for that had meanwhile happened—was so far from interrupting, that it even helped them. For Alexander, in his close pursuit of the fleeing king, was being hurried to more distant places, and from the battle itself a great number of mercenaries had fled to Greece ; and of these Agis with his Persian money hired 8000, and by their help recovered numerous cities of the Cretans.

Next, after that, when Menon, sent by Alexander into Thrace, had stirred up the barbarians to revolt, and Antipater, to suppress it, had led an army from Macedonia into Thrace, promptly taking advantage of the opportune time, the Lacedaemonians brought over to their side the entire Peloponnesus with the exception of a few cities, and mustering an army of 20,000 infantry and 2000 cavalry, conferred the chief command upon Agis. Antipater, on learning of this action, settled the war in Thrace on the best terms he could make, and hastily returning to Greece, got together what troops he could from the friendly and allied cities. When these had assembled he counted a force of 40,000 soldiers. A strong band also had come from the Peloponnesus ; but since he knew that their loyalty was doubtful, concealing his suspicion, he thanked them for having come to defend the prestige of Alexander against the Lacedaemonians ; he said that he would write this to the king, who in due time would requite them. That at present there was no need of greater forces ; therefore they might return to their homes, having fulfilled the obligation of their treaty. Then he sent messengers to Alexander, to inform him of the uprising in Greece.

7

Graeciae certiorem facturus. Atque illi regem apud Bactra demum consecuti sunt, cum interim Antipatri victoria et nece Agidis in Arcadia res transacta esset.

Rex iam pridem tumultu Lacedaemoniorum cognito, quantum tot terrarum spatiis discretus potuit, providerat; Amphoterum cum Cypriis et Phoeniciis navibus in Peloponnesum navigare, Meneta tria milia talentum ad mare deferre iusserat, ut ex propinquo pecuniam Antipatro subministraret, quanta illi opus esse cognovisset. Probe enim perspexerat, quanti ad omnia momenti motus istius inclinatio futura esset; quamquam postea, accepto victoriae nuntio, cum suis rebus illam dimicationem comparans, murium eam pugnam fuisse cavillatus est. Ceterum principia eius belli haud improspera Lacedaemoniis fuere. Iuxta Corrhagum, Macedoniae castellum, cum Antipatri militibus congressi victores exstiterant; et rei bene gestae fama etiam, qui dubiis mentibus fortunam spectaverant, societati eorum se adiunxerunt. Una ex Eleis Achaeisque urbibus Pellene foedus aspernabatur et in Arcadia Megalopolis, fida Macedonibus propter Philippi memoriam, a quo beneficiis affecta fuerat. Sed haec circumsessa non multum a deditione aberat, nisi tandem Antipater subvenisset. Is postquam castra castris contulit seque numero militum alioque apparatu superiorem conspexit, quam primum de summa rerum proelio contendere statuit; neque Lacedaemonii detrectavere certamen.

Ita commissa est pugna, quae rem Spartanam maiorem in modum afflixit. Cum enim angustiis locorum in qui-

---

[a] The battle of Megalopolis, 331 **B.C.**

These at last overtook Alexander at Bactra, when in the meantime the revolt had been ended by Antipater's victory in Arcadia and the death of Agis.

The king, having learned long beforehand of the rebellion of the Lacedaemonians, had provided for it so far as he could when separated by the extent of so many lands; he had ordered Amphoterus with Cyprian and Phoenician ships to sail to the Peloponnesus, Menes to take 3000 talents to the sea-coast, in order that from near at hand he might supply Antipater with as much money as he should learn that he needed. For he had rightly perceived how greatly that move would tip the scales of Fortune's balance for all his plans; although later, after having received news of Antipater's victory, he jestingly remarked, comparing that battle with his own exploits, that it had been a fight with mice. However, the first stages of that war had not been without success for the Lacedaemonians. Near Corrhagum, a fortress of Macedonia, having encountered Antipater's soldiers, they had come off victors; and because of the fame of that success those also who had looked upon the fortune of the rebels with doubting minds had allied themselves with them. Pellenê alone of the cities of Elis and Achaia rejected the league, and in Arcadia Megalopolis, being faithful to the Macedonians because of the memory of Philip, from whom they had received favours. But that city was besieged and was on the point of surrender, had not Antipater at last come to their aid. He, after comparing camp with camp and seeing that he was superior in number of men and in other equipment, decided to fight a decisive battle as soon as possible; and the Lacedaemonians did not decline the contest.

Accordingly, a battle[a] took place, which greatly damaged the Spartan cause. For when, trusting to the narrowness

9

bus pugnabatur confisi, ubi hosti nullum multitudinis
usum futurum credebant, fortissime congressi essent, ac
Macedones impigerrime resisterent, multum sanguinis
fusum est. Sed postquam Antipater integram subinde
manum laborantibus suis subsidio misit, impulsa Lacedae-
moniorum acies gradum paulisper retulit. Quod con-
spicatus, Agis cum cohorte regia, quae ex fortissimis
constabat, se in medium I. pugnae discrimen immisit,
obtruncatisque qui promptius resistebant, magnam
2 partem hostium propulit. Coeperant fugere victores
et,[1] donec avidius sequentes in planum deduxere,
inulti cadebant ; sed ut primum locus in quo stare
3 possent fuit, aequis viribus dimicatum est. Inter
omnes tamen Lacedaemonios rex eminebat, non
armorum modo et corporis specie, sed etiam magni-
4 tudine animi, quo uno vinci non potuit. Undique
nunc comminus, nunc eminus petebatur, diuque arma
circumferens, alia tela clipeo[2] excipiebat, corpore
alia vitabat, donec hasta femina perfossa plurimo
5 sanguine effuso destituere pugnantem. Ergo clipeo
suo exceptum armigeri raptim in castra referebant,
iactationem vulnerum haud facile tolerantem.
6   Non tamen omisere Lacedaemonii pugnam et, ut
primum sibi quam hosti aequiorem locum capere
potuerunt, densatis ordinibus effuse[3] fluentem in se
7 aciem excepere. Non aliud discrimen vehementius

---

[1] et *Modius; A omits.*
[2] clipeo *I;* clypeo *BFP V;* clippeo *L; so below.*
[3] effuse *Acidalius;* effusi *A.*

---

* *Cf.* vii. 4. 33 ; Tac. *Ann.* i. 53 *manibus aequis.*

*of the plain in which they fought, where they believed that
the enemy would have no advantage from their superior
numbers, they attacked most valiantly and the Macedonians resisted most vigorously, there was great bloodshed. But after Antipater from time to time sent a fresh
force to aid his hard-pressed men, the army of the
Lacedaemonians was forced to give way, and drew back
for a while. Agis, on seeing this, with the royal cohort,
which was made up of his bravest men,* I. plunged right
into the danger-point of the fight, and cutting down
those who resisted most bravely, drove a great part
2 of the enemy before him. The victors had begun to
flee, and until they brought the enemy, who pursued
them too eagerly, down into the level ground, they
were falling unavenged; but no sooner was there
standing-room, than they fought on equal terms.[a]
3 Among all the Lacedaemonians, however, their king
was conspicuous, not only for the excellence of his
arms and his person, but also for the greatness of his
4 courage, in which alone he was unsurpassed. On all
sides, now hand to hand, now at long range, he was
attacked, and for a long time, turning his arms now
here, now there, he caught some of the weapons with
his shield and avoided others by his agility; but at
last his thighs were run through by a lance and from
5 great loss of blood failed him as he fought. Therefore his guards laid him upon his shield and quickly
carried him back to his camp, hardly able to endure
the effect of the jolting on his wounds.
6 Yet the Lacedaemonians did not give up the fight,
but as soon as they could gain ground more favourable to themselves than to the enemy, they took
close order and met their line of battle as it poured
7 like a flood upon them. That no contest was ever

fuisse memoriae proditum est. Duarum nobilissimarum bello gentium exercitus pari Marte pugnabant ;
8 Lacedaemonii vetera, Macedones praesentia decora intuebantur, illi pro libertate, hi pro dominatione pugnabant, Lacedaemoniis dux, Macedonibus locus
9 deerat. Diei quoque unius tam multiplex casus modo spem, modo metum utriusque partis augebat, velut de industria inter fortissimos viros certamen
10 aequante Fortuna. Ceterum angustiae loci in quo haeserat pugna non patiebantur totis ingredi viribus ; spectabant ergo plures, quam inierant proelium, et qui extra teli iactum erant clamore invicem suos
11 accendebant. Tandem Laconum acies languescere, lubrica arma sudore vix sustinens, pedem deinde
12 referre coepit. Ut urgente hoste apertius fugere,[1] insequebatur dissipatos[2] victor et emensus cursu omne spatium, quod acies Laconum obtinuerat, ipsum Agin persequebatur.
13 Ille ut fugam suorum et proximos hostium conspexit, deponi se iussit ; expertusque membra an impe-
14 tum animi sequi possent, postquam deficere sensit, poplitibus semet excepit, galeaque strenue sumpta, clipeo protegens corpus, hastam dextera vibrabat, ultro provocans[3] hostem, si quis iacenti spolia demere
15 auderet. Nec quisquam fuit qui sustineret comminus congredi ; procul missilibus appetebatur, ea ipsa in hostem retorquens, donec lancea nudo pec-

---

[1] fugēre *Bentley;* fugeret *A.*
[2] dissipatos *Lauer;* dissipatus *A.*
[3] provocans *Hedicke;* uocans *A.*

---

[a] Cf. iv. 6. 25.   [b] A vivid description in Diod. xvii. 63. 4.

more desperate is a matter of record. The armies of the two nations most famed in war were fighting
8 on even terms; the Lacedaemonians had an eye to their ancient, the Macedonians to their present glory, the one side was fighting for freedom, the other, for dominion, the Lacedaemonians lacked a
9 leader, the Macedonians room for fighting. Also, so many shifting changes in a single day increased now the hope, now the fear of both sides, as if Fortune were purposely balancing a struggle between the
10 bravest of men. But the narrowness of the place in which the battle remained fixed did not allow them to engage with their full strength; therefore more looked on at the contest than took part in it, and those who were out of range of a weapon urged on
11 their men in turn by their acclamations. At last the army of the Laconians, who were barely able to hold their weapons slippery with sweat,[a] began to weaken,
12 then to retreat. Next, when they fled more openly, as the enemy pushed on, the victor followed them closely, scattered as they were, and passing at the double over all the space which the Laconians' army had held, was in pursuit of Agis himself.
13 He, when he saw the flight of his men and the foremost of the enemy, gave orders to be put down, and having tried whether his limbs could follow the
14 desire of his spirit, and feeling that they failed him, he sank upon his knees, and quickly putting on his helmet, and protecting his body with his shield, he brandished a spear in his right hand, actually challenging anyone who would dare to despoil him as he lay
15 there.[b] But there was no one who could endure to engage with him hand to hand. He was assailed from a distance with weapons, hurling the same ones back

tori infixa est. Qua ex vulnere evolsa, inclinatum
ac deficiens caput clipeo paulisper excepit, dein,
linquente spiritu pariter ac sanguine, moribundus in
16 arma procubuit. Cecidere[1] Lacedaemoniorum v
milia et ccc, ex Macedonibus haud amplius M; ceterum vix quisquam nisi saucius revertit in castra.

Haec victoria non Spartam modo sociosque eius,
sed etiam omnis qui fortunam belli expectaverant[2]
17 fregit. Nec fallebat Antipatrum dissentire ab animis
gratulantium vultus ; sed bellum finire cupienti opus
erat decipi, et, quamquam fortuna rerum placebat,
invidiam tamen, quia maiores res[3] erant quam quas
18 praefecti modus caperet, metuebat. Quippe Alexander hostes vinci voluerat. Antipatrum vicisse ne
tacitus quidem indignabatur, suae demptum gloriae
19 existimans quidquid cessisset alienae. Itaque Antipater, qui probe nosset spiritus eius, non est ausus
ipse agere arbitria victoriae, sed concilium Grae-
20 corum quid fieri placeret consuluit. A quo Lacedaemonii nihil aliud quam ut oratores mittere ad regem
liceret, Tegeatae[4] veniam defectionis praeter auctores
impetraverunt, Megalopolitanis, quorum urbs obsessa
erat a defectionis sociis,[5] Achaei et Elei[6] centum xx
21 talenta dare iussi sunt. Hic fuit exitus belli, quod

[1] Cecidere *Lauer;* excidere *A.*
[2] belli expectaverant *Hedicke;* bellam spectauerant *A.*
[3] maiores res *C;* maiores *P m. pr.*
[4] Tegeatae *Bentley;* geatae *A (in C corr. added* precati *in marg.; V has in text* peccati geatae *; L ***** geatae).*
[5] sociis *Zumpt;* eius *A.*
[6] Achaei et Elei *Gronov;* achas eteli *A.*

[a] 3500 in Diod. xvii. 63. 3.
[b] Especially that of Alexander ; *cf.* x. 10. 14.
[c] *arbitria victoriae,* formed on the analogy of *arbiter pacis et belli,* Justin xxii. 2. In a different sense in viii. 1. 34.

at the enemy, until at last a lance was implanted in his naked breast. When this had been pulled from the wound, he rested his bent and failing head upon his shield for a moment, then, as his breath and his blood left him together, he fell dying upon his
16 armour. There fell of the Lacedaemonians 5300 ; of the Macedonians, not more than a thousand[a] ; but hardly anyone returned to the camp without a wound.

This victory broke the spirit, not alone of Sparta and her allies, but of all those who had awaited the
17 fortune of the war. Antipater did not fail to notice that the expression of those who congratulated him did not correspond with their feelings, but since he desired to end the war, he was constrained to let himself be deceived, and although the success of the affair pleased him, yet he feared envy,[b] for what he had done was more important than suited the limita-
18 tions of a prefect. For Alexander had wished the enemy to be defeated, but that Antipater had conquered them was so displeasing to him, that he could not even be silent, thinking that whatever had fallen to the glory of another had been taken from his own.
19 Hence Antipater, who perfectly understood the king's disposition, did not himself venture to act as arbiter[c] of his victory, but summoned a council of the Greeks and consulted it as to what was best to
20 be done. From the council the Lacedaemonians obtained nothing except permission to send envoys to the king, the people of Tegea, except the ringleaders, were granted pardon for their revolt, to those of Megalopolis, whose city had been besieged by the participants in the revolt, the Achaeans and the
21 Eleans were ordered to pay 120 talents. Such was

QUINTUS CURTIUS

repente ortum, prius tamen finitum est quam Dareum
Alexander apud Arbela superaret.

II. Sed ut primum instantibus curis laxatus est animus militarium rerum quam quietis otiique patientior,
excepere eum voluptates, et quem arma Persarum
2 non fregerant vitia vicerunt : tempestiva[1] convivia
et perpotandi pervigilandique insana dulcedo, ludique
et greges pelicum.   Omnia in externum lapsa morem.
Quem ille[2] aemulatus, quasi potiorem suo, ita popularium animos oculosque pariter offendit, ut a pleris-
3 que amicorum pro hoste haberetur.   Tenaces quippe
disciplinae suae, solitosque parco ac parabili victu
ad implenda naturae desideria defungi, in peregrina
4 et devictarum gentium mala impulerat.   Hinc saepius
comparatae in caput eius insidiae, secessio militum,
et liberior inter mutuas querellas dolor, ipsius deinde
nunc ira, nunc suspiciones, quas excitabat inconsultus
pavor, ceteraque his similia, quae deinde dicentur.
5 Igitur cum tempestivis conviviis dies pariter noctesque consumeret, satietatem epularum ludis inter-
pellabat, non contentus artificum quos e Graecia
exciverat turba[3]; quippe captivae iubebantur suo
ritu canere inconditum et abhorrens peregrinis auribus carmen.

---

[1] tempestiva *Heusinger;* tempestatiua *P m. pr.;* intempestiva *C.*
[2] Quem ille *Hedicke;* quemque *A.*
[3] turba *J. Froben;* turbae *A.*

---

[a] See note on *de die,* v. 7. 2.
[b] For *perpotandi cf.* Cic. *Verr.* v. 33. 87 ; for *pervigilandi*
Ovid, *Fasti* vi. 326.   The two compounds with *per-* add to
the effect ; *cf.* v. 5. 1 *praealtae praecipitesque.*
[c] *Cf.* vi. 6. 9.   [d] *Cf. parabili cultu corporis,* iii. 5. 2.

the outcome of the war, which broke out suddenly, yet was ended before Alexander overcame Darius at Arbela.

II. But Alexander, as soon as a mind which was better qualified for coping with military toil than with quiet and ease was relieved of pressing cares, gave himself up to pleasures, and one whom the arms of the Persians had not overcome fell victim to their vices :
2 banquets begun early,[a] the mad enjoyment of heavy drinking and being up all night,[b] sport, and troops of harlots. There was a general slipping into foreign habits. By emulating these, as if they were preferable to those of his country, he so offended alike the eyes and the minds of his countrymen, that by many of
3 his former friends he was regarded as an enemy. For men who held fast to[c] their native discipline, and were accustomed with frugal and easily obtained[d] food to satisfy the demands of nature, he had driven to the
4 evil habits of foreign and conquered nations. Hence the more frequent making of plots against his life, mutiny of the soldiers, and freer expression of resentment amid mutual complaints, then on his own part now anger, now suspicions aroused by groundless fear, and other similar evils, of which an account will
5 be given later. Alexander, therefore, when he was wasting days and nights alike in early and prolonged banquets, used to relieve the satiety of his feasts with entertainments, not content with a throng of artists[e] whom he had summoned from Greece ; for captive women were bidden to sing after their manner a song discordant and hateful to foreign ears.[f]

---

[e] Including τεχνῖται Διονυσιακοί; cf. Plut. Alex. xxix. 2-3.
[f] Cf. Cic. De Orat. iii. 18. 66 abhorrens ab auribus vulgi ; De Off. i. 18. 83.

6 Inter quas unam rex ipse[1] conspexit maestiorem quam ceteras et producentibus eam verecunde reluctantem. Excellens erat forma, et formam pudor honestabat ; deiectis in terram oculis et, quantum licebat, ore velato, suspicionem praebuit regi nobiliorem esse, quam ut inter convivales[2] ludos deberet 7 ostendi. Ergo interrogata quaenam esset, neptim se Ochi, qui nuper regnasset in Persis, filio eius genitam esse respondit, uxorem Hystaspis fuisse. Propinquus hic Darei fuerat, magni et ipse exercitus 8 praetor. Adhuc in animo regis tenues reliquiae pristini moris haerebant ; itaque fortunam regia stirpe genitae et tam celebre nomen Ochi reveritus, non dimitti modo captivam, sed etiam restitui ei suas opes iussit, virum quoque requiri, ut reperto coniugem 9 redderet. Postero autem die praecepit Hephaestioni ut omnes captivos in regiam iuberet adduci. Ibi singulorum nobilitate spectata, secrevit a vulgo quorum eminebat genus. M hi fuerunt ; inter quos repertus est Oxathres, Darei frater, non illius fortuna quam indole animi sui clarior.

10 XXVI milia talentum proxima praeda redacta[3] erant, quis e[4] duodecim milia in congiarium militum absumpta[5] sunt, par huic pecuniae summa custodum

[1] ipse *A;* saepe *Hedicke.*
[2] convivales *P m. pr.;* conuiuiales *C.*
[3] redacta *J. Froben;* reducta *A.*
[4] quis e *A;* omnino *Hedicke.*
[5] absumpta *J. Froben;* adsumpta *A.*

---

[a] *Regiam* probably here, as elsewhere, for *praetorium*, the king's headquarters.

[b] *Congiarium*, originally a gift of wine or oil (*cf. congius*, a liquid measure), used also in a general sense.

6   Among these women the king himself noticed one more sad than the others, who modestly resisted those who would lead her forward. She was of surpassing beauty, and her modesty enhanced her beauty; with downcast eyes and with her face covered so far as she was allowed, she aroused in the king a suspicion that she was of too high birth to be exhibited amid

7 entertainments at a banquet. On being accordingly asked who she was, she replied that she was the granddaughter of Ochus, who had lately been king of the Persians, being the daughter of his son, and that she had been the wife of Hystaspes. He had been a kinsman of Darius and himself the commander

8 of a great army. There still lingered in the king's mind slight remains of his former disposition; and so, respecting the ill-fortune of a lady born of royal stock, and so famous a name as that of Ochus, he not only gave orders that the captive should be set free, but also that her property should be returned to her; likewise that her husband should be looked for, in order that when he had been found, he might restore

9 his wife to him. Moreover, on the following day he ordered Hephaestion to cause all the prisoners to be brought to the palace.[a] There, having inquired into the rank of each one, he separated from the common herd those who were of high birth. There were a thousand of these; among them was Oxathres, brother of Darius, no more distinguished because of the rank of that king than for his own mental endowments.

10   Twenty-six thousand talents were amassed from the recent booty, and of these 12,000 were spent in largess[b] to the soldiers, and a sum equal to this was embezzled by the great dishonesty of those who

11 fraude subtracta est. Oxydates[1] erat nobilis Perses,
qui a Dareo capitali supplicio destinatus, cohibebatur
in vinculis ; huic liberato satrapeam Mediae áttribuit
fratremque Darei recepit in cohortem amicorum,
omni vetustae claritatis[2] honore servato.

12 Hinc in Parthienen perventum est, tunc ignobilem
gentem, nunc caput omnium qui post Euphraten et
13 Tigrim amnes siti Rubro mari terminantur. Scythae
regionem campestrem ac fertilem occupaverant,[3]
graves adhuc accolae. Sedes habent et in Europa et
in Asia ; qui super Bosphorum colunt asscribuntur
Asiae, at qui in Europa sunt a laevo Thraciae latere
ad Borysthenem atque inde ad Tanaim recta plaga
14 attinent. Tanais Europam et Asiam medius interfluit. Nec dubitatur, quin Scythae qui Parthos
condidere non a Bosphoro, sed ex Europae regione
penetraverint.

15 Urbs erat ea tempestate clara Hecatompylos,[4] condita a Graecis ; ibi stativa rex habuit commeatibus
undique advectis. Itaque rumor, otiosi militis vitium,
sine auctore percrebruit,[5] regem contentum rebus
quas gessisset in Macedoniam protinus redire sta-

---

[1] Oxydates *Aldus;* oxidates *A.*
[2] claritatis *I;* caritatis *A.*
[3] occupaverant *Hedicke;* occupauerunt *A.*
[4] Hecatompylos *J. Froben;* haecathouphilos *A.*
[5] percrebruit *Zarotus;* percrebuit *A.*

---

[a] Referring not only to the treasurer, but also to others
through whose hands the booty had passed.
[b] Apparently meaning " the Companion Cavalry," the
agema, cf. vii. 5. 40. [c] *i.e.* as Parthia.
[d] *i.e.* the Scythians, not the Parthians.
[e] *i.e.* east of ; cf. Pliny, *N.H.* v. 110.
[f] The Cimmerian Bosphorus (Strait of Kertsch) ; the

11 had charge of it.[a] Oxydates was a Persian noble, who was being kept in bonds, because he had been destined by Darius for capital punishment. Alexander freed him and conferred upon him the satrapy of Media, and the brother of Darius he received into the band of his friends,[b] with the maintenance of all the honour due to his ancient lineage.

12 From there they came to Parthienê, then an obscure nation, but now[c] the head of all those who dwell beyond the Euphrates and Tigris Rivers and extend
13 as far as the Red Sea. The Scythians had taken possession of the level and fertile part of the region, and are still dangerous neighbours. They[d] have homes both in Europe and in Asia; those who dwell above[e] the Bosphorus[f] are assigned to Asia, but those who are in Europe extend from the left side of Thrace to the Borysthenes[g] and from there in a direct
14 course to the Tanais.[h] The Tanais flows between Europe and Asia. There is no doubt that the Scythians, from whom the Parthians are descended, made their way, not from the Bosphorus, but from the region of Europe.

15 There was at that time a famous city called Hecatompylos,[i] founded by the Greeks; there the king remained for several days, after having supplies brought there from every side. As a result, gossip, the vice of idle soldiery, spread without authority that the king, content with what he had accomplished,
16 had decided to return forthwith to Macedonia. They

adjective is often omitted where it is evident from the context which Bosphorus is meant.

[g] the Dnieper.   [h] the Don.
[i] See Diod. xvii. 75. 1. According to Pliny (*N.H.* vi. 113) it was the residence of Arsaces and his successors.

16 tuisse. Discurrunt lymphatis similes in[1] tabernacula
et itineri sarcinas aptant ; signum datum crederes,
ut vasa colligerent totis castris. Tumultus hinc
contubernales suos requirentium, hinc onerantium
17 plaustra perfertur ad regem. Fecerant fidem rumori
temere vulgato Graeci milites redire iussi domos ;
quorum equitibus singulis denarium sena milia cum
data essent, peditibus singula milia,[2] ipsis quoque
18 finem militiae adesse credebant. Haud secus quam
par erat territus, qui Indos atque ultima Orientis
peragrare statuisset, praefectos copiarum in praetorium contrahit, obortisque lacrimis, ex medio
gloriae spatio revocari se, victi magis quam victoris
19 fortunam in patriam relaturum, conquestus est ; nec
sibi ignaviam militum obstare, sed deum invidiam,
qui fortissimis viris subitum patriae desiderium ad-
movissent, paulo post in eandem cum maiore laude
famaque redituris.

20 Tum vero pro se quisque operam suam offerre,
difficillima quaeque poscere, polliceri militum quoque
obsequium, si animos eorum leni et apta oratione
21 permulcere voluisset ; numquam infractos et abiectos
recessisse, quotiens ipsius alacritatem et tanti animi
spiritus haurire potuissent. Ita se facturum esse

---

[1] in *added in I; A omits.*
[2] cum data . . . milia *added by Hedicke.*

---

[a] A regular expression for collecting the baggage as a
preliminary to marching ; *cf.* Caes. *B.G.* i. 66 ; iii. 37 *vasa
conclamare* ; figuratively, Sen. *Epist.* xix. 1 *vasa in senectute
colligere.*
[b] The *denarius* is reckoned as equal to the *drachma* ;
hence the whole sum amounted to a talent.
[c] Said not with reference to the external form, but to the
contents ; *cf.* Cic. *Partit.* vi. 19 *sententiae aptae opinionibus
hominum et moribus.*

ran as though crazed to their tents and made ready their packs for the journey; you would believe that the signal to march[a] had been given throughout the whole camp. Here the noise of those looking for their tent-mates, there of those loading the wagons, was
17 borne to the king's ears. The Greek soldiers who had been bidden to return to their homes had gained credence for the report which had been circulated without reason; since 6000 denarii[b] had been given to each of their horsemen, and 1000 to every man of their infantry, the rest of the army believed that the end of military service was at hand for themselves
18 also. Alarmed, as was natural, the king, who had determined to traverse the lands of the Indi and the remotest parts of the Orient, summoned the leaders of his forces to his tent, and, with tears in his eyes, complained that he was being recalled from the mid-course of his glory, to take back to his native land the fortune of one who was vanquished rather than
19 that of a victor; that it was not cowardice on the part of his soldiers that stood in his way, but the envy of the gods, who had inspired in the bravest of men a sudden longing for their native land, to which they would return a little later with greater glory and fame.
20 Then indeed each general individually offered his service, demanded the most difficult tasks, promised also the obedience of the soldiers, if the king would consent to soothe their feelings by a mild and appro-
21 priate[c] address; that they had never held back spiritless and downcast, whenever they had been able to draw upon his enthusiasm and the inspiration of so great a mind. Alexander replied that he would do it; only let them in advance prepare the ears of

23

respondit ; illi modo vulgi aures praepararent sibi.
Satisque omnibus quae in rem videbantur esse compositis, vocari ad contionem exercitum iussit, apud
quem talem orationem habuit :

III. " Magnitudinem rerum quas gessimus, milites,
intuentibus vobis minime mirum est et desiderium
2 quietis et satietatem gloriae occurrere. Ut omittam
Illyrios, Triballos, Boeotiam,[1] Thraciam, Spartam,
Achaeos, Peloponnesum, quorum alia ductu meo,
3 alia imperio auspicioque perdomui, ecce orsi[2] bellum
ab Hellesponto Ionas, Aeolidem servitio barbariae
impotentis eximimus, Cariam, Lydiam, Cappadociam,
Phrygiam, Paphlagoniam, Pamphyliam, Pisidas,
Ciliciam, Syriam, Phoenicen, Armeniam, Persidem,
4 Medos, Parthienen habemus in potestate. Plures
provincias complexus sum, quam alii urbes ceperunt,
et nescio an enumeranti mihi quaedam ipsarum
5 rerum multitudo subduxerit. Itaque si crederem
satis certam esse possessionem terrarum, quas tanta
velocitate domuimus, ego vero, milites, ad penates
meos, ad parentem sororesque et ceteros cives, vel
retinentibus vobis, erumperem, ut ibi potissimum
parta vobiscum laude et gloria fruerer, ubi nos uber-
rima victoriae praemia expectant, liberum, coniugum
parentumque laetitia, pacis quies, rerum per virtutem
partarum secura possessio.
6   " Sed in novo et, si verum fateri volumus, precario

---

[1] Boeotiam *Aldus;* boetiam *A.*   [2] orsi *I;* orsum *A.*

---

[a] *Cf.* Diod. xvii. 74. 3.
[b] He has already mentioned Sparta and Achaia in the
Peloponnesus.
[c] The singular is as common in such expressions as the
plural ; see Livy iii. 42. 2 ; iv. 20. 6, etc.

the common soldiers for what he was to say. When everything that seemed to be to the purpose had been sufficiently arranged, he ordered the army to be called to an assembly, and delivered to it a speech in the following terms [a] :

III. " When you look back, soldiers, upon the greatness of the deeds which we have done, it is not surprising that you feel a desire for repose and a 2 satiety of glory. To say nothing of the Illyrians, the Triballi, Boeotia, Thrace, the Achaeans, the Peloponnesus in general,[b] some of whom I have subdued under my own leadership, others under my 3 command and auspices,[c] lo ! beginning war at the Hellespont, we have freed the Ionians and Aeolis from slavery to a savage barbarian, we have made ourselves masters of Caria, Lydia, Cappadocia, Phrygia, Paphlagonia, Pamphylia, the Pisidians, Cilicia, Syria, Phoenicia, Armenia, Persia, the Medes, 4 and Parthienê. The provinces of which I have taken possession outnumber the cities which others have captured, and I verily believe that in enumerating our exploits their very number has caused me to 5 forget some of them. Therefore, if I believed that the possession of the lands which we have so quickly subdued were wholly secure, I myself, my soldiers, even if you wished to hold me back, would rush to my home, to my mother and sisters, and to the rest of our fellow countrymen, in order that there rather than elsewhere I might enjoy with you the praise and glory which we have won, where the richest rewards of victory await us, the happiness of our children, wives and parents, the repose of peace, the carefree possession of the fruits of our valour.

6   " But in a new and, if we wish to confess the truth,

imperio, adhuc iugum eius rigida cervice subeuntibus
barbaris, tempore, milites, opus est, dum mitioribus
ingeniis imbuuntur et efferatos melior consuetudo
7 permulcet. Fruges quoque maturitatem statuto
tempore expectant; adeo etiam illa sensus omnis
8 expertia tamen sua lege mitescunt. Quid? creditis
tot gentes alterius imperio ac nomine assuetas, non
sacris, non[1] moribus, non commercio linguae nobiscum
cohaerentes eodem proelio domitas esse quo victae
sunt? Vestris armis continentur, non suis moribus
et,[2] qui praesentes metuunt, in absentia hostes erunt.
Cum feris bestiis res est, quas captas et inclusas, quia
9 ipsarum natura non potest, longior dies mitigat. Et
adhuc sic ago, tamquam omnia subacta sint armis,
quae fuerunt in dicione Darei. Hyrcaniam Nabarzanes occupavit, Bactra non possidet solum parricida
Bessus, sed etiam minatur, Sogdiani, Dahae, Massagetae, Sacae, Indi sui iuris sunt. Omnes hi, simul
10 terga nostra viderint,[3] illos sequentur[4]; illi enim
eiusdem nationis sunt, nos alienigenae et externi.
Suis quisque[5] autem placidius paret, etiam cum is
praeest, qui magis timeri potest. Proinde aut quae
cepimus[6] omittenda sunt, aut quae non habemus
occupanda.
11   "Sicut in corporibus aegris, milites, nihil quod

---

[1] non *added by Lauer;* A *omits.*
[2] et *Modius;* sed A.   [3] viderint *I;* uiderunt A.
[4] illos sequentur *Jeep;* sinequentur P *m. pr.;* sisequentur C.
[5] suis quisque *Modius;* suisque A.
[6] cepimus *J. Froben;* coepimus A.

---

[a] *Cf.* v. 8. 12.
[b] *Cf.* Florus iv. 12. 2 *inflataeque cervices*; Amm. xiv. 6. 5
post superbas efferatarum gentium cervices oppressas.

insecure [a] empire, to whose yoke the barbarians still submit with obdurate [b] necks, there is need of time, my soldiers, until they are trained to milder dispositions, and until better habits appease their 7 savage temper. The fruits of the earth also look forward to ripeness at its appointed season, so true is it that even those things, devoid of sense as they are, nevertheless grow soft in accordance with a law 8 of their own. Well, then ! Do you believe that so many nations accustomed to the rule and name of another, united with us neither by religion, nor customs, nor community of language, have been subdued in the same battle in which they were overcome ? [c] It is by your arms that they are restrained, not by their dispositions, and those who fear us when we are present, in our absence will be enemies. We are dealing with savage beasts, which lapse of time only can tame when they are caught and caged, 9 because their own nature cannot tame them. And I am so far speaking as if our arms had subdued everything that was under the sway of Darius. Nabarzanes has taken possession of Hyrcania, the murderer Bessus not only holds Bactra, but he also threatens us ; the Sogdiani, Dahae, Massagetae, Sacae, and Indi are independent. All these, as soon as they see our backs, 10 will follow them ; for they are of the same nation, we are of an alien race and foreigners. Moreover, everyone obeys his own rulers with better grace, even when he who dominates them can be more feared. Accordingly, we must either give up what we have taken, or we must seize what we do not yet hold.

11   " Just as in ailing bodies, my soldiers, physicians

  [c] Cf. Florus iv. 12. 30 *Germani victi magis quam domiti erant.*

27

nociturum est medici relinquunt, sic nos quidquid
obstat imperio recidamus. Parva saepe scintilla contempta magnum excitavit incendium. Nil tuto in
hoste despicitur ; quem spreveris, valentiorem negle-
12 gentia facias. Ne Dareus quidem hereditarium Persarum accepit imperium, sed est[1] in sedem Cyri
beneficio Bagoae, castrati hominis, admissus ; ne vos
magno labore credatis Bessum vacuum regnum occu-
13 paturum. Nos vero peccavimus, milites, si Dareum
ob hoc vicimus, ut servo eius traderemus imperium,
qui ultimum ausus scelus, regem suum, etiam ex-
ternae opis egentem, certe cui nos victores pepercis-
semus, quasi captivum in vinculis habuit, ad ultimum,
14 ne a nobis conservari posset, occidit. Hunc vos
regnare patiemini ? Quem equidem cruci affixum
videre festino, omnibus regibus gentibusque et fidei
15 quam violavit meritas poenas solventem. At, hercules,[2] si mox eundem Graecorum urbes aut Hellespontum vastare nuntiatum erit vobis, quo dolore
afficiemini Bessum praemia vestrae occupavisse victoriae ! Tunc ad repetendas res festinabitis, tunc
arma capietis. Quanto autem praestat territum
adhuc et vix mentis suae compotem opprimere !
16 " Quadridui nobis iter superest, qui tot proculca-
vimus nives, tot amnes superavimus, tot montium
iuga transcucurrimus. Non mare illud, quod exaes-

---

[1] est *added by Hedicke.*
[2] hercules *P m. pr.;* hercule *C.*

---

[a] A frequent comparison in the schools of rhetoric ; *cf.*
v. 9. 3 ; Sulp. in Cic. *Ad Fam.* iv. 5 ; Cic. *Pro Cluent.* xxi. 57.
[b] See Diod. xvii. 5. 3 ff. [c] *Cf.* vii. 5. 40.
[d] Curtius usually omits *suae* in this expression ; Cicero
sometimes has the possessive adjective, sometimes not ; *cf.*
In Pisonem xx. 48 and xx. 47.

leave nothing which will do harm,[a] so let us cut away whatever stands in the way of our rule. Often to have ignored a tiny spark has roused a great conflagration. Nothing is safely despised in an enemy; one whom you have scorned you make stronger by 12 neglect. Not even Darius received the rule of the Persians by right of succession, but he was admitted to the throne of Cyrus by the favour of Bagoas, a eunuch [b]; so do not suppose that it will be hard 13 labour for Bessus to seize a vacant kingdom. We certainly committed a sin, soldiers, if we conquered Darius for the purpose of turning over the sovereignty to his slave, who, having dared the worst of crimes, held his king in fetters, like a captive, even when he was in need of aid from without, and whom we, the victors, would surely have spared, and finally slew 14 him in order that he might not be saved by us. Will you suffer such a man to rule? A man whom I, for my part, am in haste to see nailed to a cross,[c] thus paying a well-deserved penalty to all kings and 15 nations, and to loyalty, which he desecrated. But, by Heaven! if presently it shall have been announced that the same wretch is laying waste the cities of the Greeks and the Hellespont, what grief will you feel that a Bessus has robbed you of the fruits of your victory! Then you will hurry to recover what is yours, then you will take up arms. But how much better it is to crush him while he is still in fear and almost beside himself.[d]

16 " A march of four days [e] is left for us, who have trodden so many snows, have passed over so many rivers, crossed the heights of so many mountains. Not that sea, which with its rising tide covers the

[e] The actual distance was 3700 stadia; Pliny, *N.H.* vi. 45.

tuans iter fluctibus occupat, euntes nos moratur, non
Ciliciae fauces et angustiae includunt ; plana omnia
et prona sunt. In ipso limine victoriae stamus.
17 Pauci nobis fugitivi et domini sui interfectores super-
sunt. Egregium, mehercule, opus et inter prima
gloriae vestrae numerandum posteritati famaeque
tradetis, Dareum quoque hostem, finito post mortem
illius odio, parricidae caede[1] esse vos ultos, neminem
18 impium effugisse vestras manus. Hoc perpetrato,
quanto creditis Persas obsequentiores fore, cum in-
tellexerint vos pia bella suscipere et Bessi sceleri,
non nomini suo irasci ? "

IV. Summa militum alacritate iubentium[2] quo-
2 cumque vellet ducere, oratio excepta est. Nec rex
moratur[3] impetum, tertioque per Parthienen die ad
fines Hyrcaniae penetrat, Cratero relicto cum eis
copiis quibus praeerat et ea[4] manu quam Amyntas
ducebat, additis DC equitibus et totidem sagittariis,
ut ab incursione barbarorum Parthienen tueretur.
3 Erigyium[5] impedimenta, modico praesidio dato,
campestri itinere ducere iubet. Ipse cum phalange
et equitatu CL stadia emensus, castra in valle qua
Hyrcaniam adeunt communit. Nemus praealtis den-
sisque arboribus umbrosum est, pingue vallis solum
rigantibus aquis quae ex petris imminentibus manant.

---

[1] parricidae caede *Bentley;* parricidas *A.*
[2] iubentium *J. Froben;* subeuntium *A* (subcuncium *V*).
[3] moratur *Hedicke;* moratus *A.*
[4] ea *Freinshem;* ex *A.*
[5] Erigyium *J. Froben;* phrygum *P;* phrigum *BV;*
prhigum *L;* frigum *F.*

---

[a] *Cf.* v. 3. 22. [b] This is not true.
[c] *Cf. impia bella,* iv. 1. 12.
[d] The account of this march against Hyrcania is more
clearly given by Arr. iii. 23. 2 ff.

road with its waves,[a] delays our march, not the passes and narrows of Cilicia shut us in, the whole country is level and easy.[b] We stand on the very
17 threshold of victory. A few runaways and slayers of their master remain for us. A noble work, by Heaven! and one to be numbered among the chief of your glorious deeds you will hand down to posterity and to fame, namely, that you have avenged even Darius, your enemy, having ended your hatred of him after his death, by slaying his murderer, and
18 that no impious man has escaped your hands. When this has been accomplished, how much more submissive do you think that the Persians will be, when they know that you undertake pious wars,[c] and that it is the crime of Bessus, not the Persian name, that inflames your wrath?"

IV. The address was received with the greatest enthusiasm of the soldiers, who bade him lead them
2 whithersoever he wished. Nor did the king delay their ardour, but two days later he made his way through Parthienê to the borders of Hyrcania,[d] having left Craterus with the forces under his command and the band which Amyntas was leading, besides 600 horsemen and the same number of archers, to protect Parthienê from any inroad of the
3 barbarians. He ordered Erigyius to conduct the baggage by the route through the plains, having given him a moderate escort. He himself with the phalanx and the cavalry, after traversing 150 stadia, fortified a camp in the valley through which one enters Hyrcania. There is a grove shaded by a dense growth of very tall trees, where the rich soil of the valley is watered by streams which flow from
4 the overhanging rocks. From the very roots of the

31

4 Ex ipsis radicibus montium Stiboetes[1] amnis effunditur, qui tria fere stadia in longitudinem universus
fluit, deinde saxo, quod alveolum interpellat, reper-
cussus, duo itinera velut dispensatis aquis aperit.
5 Inde torrens et saxorum per quae incurrit asperitate
violentior, terram praeceps subit. Per ccc stadia
conditus labitur rursusque, velut ex alio fonte con-
ceptus, editur et novum alveum intendit priore sui
6 parte spatiosior—quippe in latitudinem x et trium
stadiorum diffunditur—rursusque angustioribus coercitus ripis iter cogit. Tandem in alterum amnem ca-
7 dit; Rhidagno nomen est. Incolae affirmabant, quaecumque[2] demissa[3] essent in cavernam quae propior
est fonti rursus ubi aliud os amnis aperitur existere;
itaque Alexander boves,[4] qua subeunt aquae terram, praecipitari iubet, quorum corpora, ubi rursus
erumpit, expulsa videre qui missi erant ut exciperent.
8 Quartum iam diem eodem loco quietem militi
dederat, cum litteras Nabarzanis, qui Dareum cum
Besso interceperat, accepit, quarum sententia haec
erat : se Dareo non fuisse inimicum, immo etiam
quae credidisset utilia esse suasisse et, quia fidele
9 consilium regi dedisset, prope occisum ab eo. Agi-
tasse Dareum custodiam corporis sui contra ius fasque
peregrino militi tradere, damnata popularium fide,
quam per ducentos et triginta[5] annos inviolatam

---

[1] Stiboetes *Hedicke;* ziobetis *A* (ziobecis *L*).
[2] quaecumque *I;* quicumque *A.*
[3] demissa *Kinch;* dimissa *P.*
[4] boves *Bentley;* duos *A.*
[5] ducentos et triginta *J. Froben;* ii et ccc *A.*

---

[a] See Arr. iii. 23. 3 ff.
[b] This expression is used also of direct quotations ; *cf.*
Sall. *Jug.* ix. 1 ; so also *summa,* Curt. vi. 9. 14.

mountains the Stiboetes River gushes forth, which flows as a single stream for a distance of nearly three stadia, then, dashed against a rock which obstructs its little channel, it forms two branches, as if by 5 a distribution of its waters. From there a torrent, made more violent by the rough stones over which it runs, it plunges headlong under the earth. For 300 stadia it glides on in a hidden course, and again, as if reborn from another source, it comes to the surface and cuts a new channel, wider than its former 6 one—for it expands to a width of thirteen stadia— and once more contracts its course within narrower banks. At last it empties into another river ; it is 7 called the Rhidagnus. The natives asserted that whatever articles had been thrown into the cavern which is nearer the river's source come out where the other mouth of the river opens ; therefore Alexander gave orders that oxen be thrown in where the waters go under the earth, and those who were sent to intercept them saw their bodies thrown out where the river bursts forth again.

8   Alexander had already given the soldiers a rest for the fourth day in the same place,[a] when from Nabarzanes, who with Bessus had taken Darius prisoner, he received a letter, of which this was the purport [b] : That he had not been an enemy of Darius, quite on the contrary, he had given him what he believed to be salutary advice, and because he had given the king faithful counsel, he had barely escaped 9 with his life. That Darius had meditated handing over the guardianship of his person to foreign soldiers, contrary to what was just and right, distrusting the loyalty of his own subjects, which for two hundred and thirty years they had preserved inviolate to their

10 regibus suis praestitissent.   Se, in praecipiti et lubrico stantem, consilium a praesenti necessitate re-
petisse.   Dareum quoque, cum occidisset Bagoan,
hac excusatione satisfecisse popularibus, quod in-
11 sidiantem interemisset.   Nihil esse miseris mortalibus
spiritu carius ; amore eius ad ultima esse propulsum.
Sed ea magis esse secutum quam optasse.[1]   In communi calamitate suam quemque habere fortunam.
12   Si venire se iuberet, sine metu esse venturum.
Non timere ne fidem datam tantus rex violaret ;
13 deos a deo falli non solere.   Ceterum si cui fidem
daret videretur indignus, multa exsilia patere fu-
gienti ; patriam esse ubicumque vir fortis sedem
14 sibi elegerit.   Nec dubitavit Alexander fidem, quo
Persae modo accipiebant, dare, inviolatum, si venis-
set, fore.
Quadrato tamen agmine et composito ibat, specu-
latores subinde praemittens, qui explorarent loca.
15 Levis armatura ducebat agmen, phalanx eam sequebatur, post pedites erant impedimenta.   Et gens
bellicosa et naturae situs difficilis aditu curam regis
16 intenderat.   Namque perpetua vallis iacet usque ad
mare Caspium patens, quo[2] terrae eius velut brachia
excurrunt ; media flexu modico sinum faciunt lunae

---

[1] quam optasse *Bentley;* quae optasset A.
[2] quo *Stangl;* duo *A.*

---

[a] See vi. 3. 12.
[b] *Cf.* vi. 5. 4 ; Diod. xvi. 43. 4.
[c] *i.e.* in order of battle, since he did not trust Nabarzanes.
[d] This does not conflict with vi. 4. 3.   The reference is to
the part of the baggage which was needed on the march.
[e] This refers to the southern part of the Caspian Sea.

10 kings. For his own part, standing as he was on
dangerous and slippery ground, he had taken counsel
from his immediate necessity. Darius also, when he
had killed Bagoas,[a] had satisfied his countrymen with
this excuse, that he had killed the eunuch because
11 he was plotting against him. That nothing was more
precious to wretched mortals than life ; that it was
from love of this that he had been driven to extremi-
ties. But those acts he had yielded to, rather than
desired. In a general calamity each man's fortune
was his own.
12 If Alexander should order Nabarzanes to come
to him, he would come without fear. He had no
apprehension that so great a king would violate a
pledge which he had given; the gods were not wont
13 to be deceived by a god. But if Nabarzanes should
be thought unworthy of receiving a pledge, many
places of exile were open to his flight ; wherever a
brave man has chosen his home, there is his native
14 land. Alexander did not hesitate to give a pledge,
in the manner in which the Persians were wont to
receive them,[b] that if he should come, he would be
unharmed.

Nevertheless Alexander went on with his army in
square formation [c] and in good order, sending scouts
ahead from time to time, to reconnoitre the country.
15 The light-armed troops led the march, the phalanx
followed them, after the infantry was the baggage.[d]
Both the warlike race and the nature of their position, which was difficult of access, had put the king
16 on his guard. For there is a continuous valley extending as far as the Caspian Sea, to which arms, so
to speak, of that land jut forth [e] ; these, bending
slightly in the middle, form a curve very like the

maxime similem, cum eminent cornua, nondum
17 totum orbem sidere implente. Cercetae et Mossyni
et Chalybes[1] a laeva sunt et ab altera parte Leucosyri
et Amazonum campi ; et illos qua vergit ad septen-
18 trionem, hos ad occasum conversa prospectat. Mare
Caspium dulcius ceteris ingentis magnitudinis serpentes alit ; piscium in eo longe diversi ab aliis
colores.[2] Quidam Caspium, quidam Hyrcanium appellant ; alii sunt, qui Maeotiam paludem in id
cadere putent et argumentum afferant[3] aquam, quod
dulcior sit quam cetera maria, infuso paludis humore
19 mitescere. A septentrione ingens in litus mare in-
cumbit longeque agit fluctus et magna parte exaestuans stagnat ; idem alio caeli statu recipit in se
fretum eodemque impetu, quo effusum est, relabens
terram naturae suae reddit. Et quidam credidere
non Caspium mare esse, sed ex India in Hyrcaniam
Oceanum[4] cadere, cuius fastigium, ut supra dictum
est, perpetua valle submittitur.
20 Hinc rex xx stadia processit semita propemodum
invia, cui silva imminebat, torrentesque et eluvies
iter morabantur ; nullo tamen hoste obvio, pene-

---

[1] Chalybes *J. Froben;* calibes *A.*
[2] colores *Koehler;* colorem *A.*
[3] adferant *Hedicke;* adferent *A.*
[4] Oceanum *added by Hedicke.*

---

[a] *i.e.* the crescent moon. [b] *i.e.* westwards.

[c] vi. 5. 24 shows that Curtius had in mind the Amazons
of Themiscyra on the Pontus; but it was a different group
which dwelt on the Caspian.

[d] Curtius is more cautious and more accurate than Pliny,
who says (*N.H.* vi. 45 f.) *haustum ipsius maris dulcem esse et
Alexander Magnus prodidit.*

[e] The fact is, that different names are applied to different

moon with its horns standing out when that heavenly
17 body does not yet fill out its complete orb.[a] The
Cercetae and the Mossyni, and the Chalybes are on
the left,[b] and on the other side the fields of the
Leucosyri and the Amazons [c]; and it looks towards
the latter where it slopes towards the north, to the
18 former when it is turned towards the west. The
Caspian Sea, which is fresher than others,[d] breeds
serpents of huge size; the colours of the fish in it
are very different from others. Some call it Caspian,
others Hyrcanian [e]; there are still others who think
that the Maeotic pool empties into it, and they advance as evidence the water, because it is fresher
than the other seas, since the water from the pool
which has flowed into it tempers its saltness.
19 Towards the north a great sea rushes upon the
shore, drives its waves far, and like a rising tide
forms a pool of great extent; but in another condition of the weather [f] the sea retires into itself,
and with the same force with which it poured in,
it flows back and restores the land to its natural
condition. And some have thought that this is not
the Caspian Sea, but that the Ocean makes its way
from India into Hyrcania,[g] whose high land, as was
said before, sinks into an uninterrupted valley.
20 From here the king proceeded for twenty stadia
by an almost impassable path, which a forest over-
hung, while torrents and floods delayed the march;

parts of the sea; Mela (v. 3. 19) mentions also *Scythicum.*
Cf. Arr. vii. 16. 2 ff.
[f] That is, a different direction of the wind.
[g] A popular belief was that the northern Ocean lay not
far north of India, the Caspian, and Hyrcania, and had an
inlet into the Caspian.

tratum¹ tandemque ad cultiora² perventum est.
21 Praeter alios commeatus, quorum tum copia regio
abundabat, pomorum quoque ingens modus nascitur,
22 et uberrimum gignendis uvis solum est. Frequens
arbor faciem quercus habet, cuius folia multo melle
tinguntur, sed, nisi solis ortum incolae occupaverint,
vel modico tepore sucus extinguitur.
23   xxx hinc stadia processerat, cum Phrataphernes ei
occurrit, seque et eos qui post Darei mortem profugerant dedens ; quibus benigne exceptis, ad oppidum Arvas pervenit. Hic ei Craterus et Erigyius³
24 occurrunt. Praefectum Tapurorum gentis, Phrada-
tem, adduxerant ; hic quoque in fidem receptus,
multis exemplo fuit experiendi clementiam regis.
25 Satrapen deinde Hyrcaniae dedit Amminaspin⁴; exul
hic regnante Ocho ad Philippum pervenerat. Tapu-
rorum⁵ quoque gentem Phradati reddidit.

V. Iamque ultima Hyrcaniae intraverat, cum
Artabazus, quem Dareo fidissimum fuisse supra diximus, cum propinquis Darei ac suis liberis modicaque
2 Graecorum militum manu occurrit. Dextram venienti obtulit rex ; quippe et hospes Philippi fuerat,
cum Ocho regnante exsularet, et hospitii pignora in
regem suum ad ultimum fides conservata vincebat.
3 Comiter igitur exceptus : " Tu quidem," inquit,
" rex, deos quaeso, perpetua felicitate floreas ; ego

¹ penetratum *Bentley;* penetrat *C;* penetrant *P m. pr.*
² cultiora *I;* *ultiora *P;* ulteriora *BFL;* ultierora *V.*
³ Erigyius *J. Froben;* eriguus *A.*
⁴ Amminaspin *Fuhr;* manapin *P m. pr.;* manapi *C.*
⁵ Tapurorum *Aldus;* Taurorum *A.*

ᵃ *Cf.* Pliny, *N.H.* xii. 8. 18 ; identified by some with
manna.
ᵇ *Cf.* Arr. iii. 22. 1.   ᶜ See v. 9. 1.

yet since no enemy met them, they passed through,
21 and finally came to more cultivated places. Besides
other supplies, of which the region then had an
abundance, a huge amount of fruits is grown, and
22 the soil is very rich in producing grapes. A kind of
tree which is common there resembles an oak, the
leaves of which are bedewed with a great deal of
honey [a]; but unless the natives gather it before sunrise, the sap is destroyed by even a moderate warmth.
23 From there Alexander had advanced for thirty
stadia, when Phrataphernes met him, surrendering
himself and those who had fled after the death of
Darius; having received them courteously, the king
came to the town of Arvae. There Craterus and
24 Erigyius met him. They had brought Phradates,
governor of the tribe of the Tapuri; he also was
received under protection, and was an example to
many in entrusting themselves to the king's clemency.
25 Then Alexander made Amminaspes [b] satrap of Hyrcania; he had come to Philip as an exile during the
reign of Ochus. Alexander also restored the tribe
of the Tapuri to Phradates.

V. And already the king had entered the farthest
part of Hyrcania, when Artabazus, who, as we have
said before,[c] had been most faithful to Darius, met
him with his own children and the relatives of Darius,
2 as well as with a small band of Greek soldiers. On his
arrival the king offered him his right hand; for he
had been a guest of Philip when he was in exile in the
reign of Ochus, but the loyalty to his king, which he
had maintained to the end, prevailed over the pledges
3 of guest-friendship. Being therefore affably greeted,
he said : " May you for your part, king, I pray the
gods, enjoy perpetual happiness; I, though in all

39

ceteris laetus hoc uno torqueor, quod praecipiti
4 senectute diu frui tua bonitate non possum." Nona-
gesimum et quintum annum agebat. Novem iuvenes,
omnes eadem matre geniti, patrem comitabantur;
hos Artabazus dexterae regis admovit, precatus ut
5 tam diu viverent donec utiles Alexandro essent. Rex
pedibus iter plerumque faciebat; tunc admoveri sibi
et Artabazo equos iussit, ne ipso ingrediente pedibus
senex equo vehi erubesceret.
6   Ut deinde castra sunt posita, Graecos quos Artabazus adduxerat convocari iubet; at illi, nisi fides
Lacedaemoniis quoque et Sinopensibus[1] daretur, respondent se quid[2] agendum ipsis foret deliberaturos.
7 Legati erant Lacedaemoniorum missi ad Dareum;
quo victo, applicuerant se Graecis mercede apud
8 Persas militantibus. Rex, omissis sponsionum fideique pignoribus, venire eos iussit, fortunam quam
ipse dedisset habituros. Diu cunctantes plerisque
consilia variantibus tandem venturos se pollicentur.
9 At Democrates Atheniensis, qui maxime Macedonum
opibus semper obstiterat, desperata venia, gladio se
transfigit. Ceteri, sicut constituerant, dicioni Alex-
10 andri ipsos se permittunt. M et D milites erant,
praeter hos legati ad Dareum missi XC. In supplementum distributus miles, ceteri remissi domum

----

[1] Sinopensibus *Modius;* est inopensibus *A.*
[2] se quid *Giunta;* si quid *A.*

----

[a] *Cf.* Livy iv. 9. 13 *praecipiti die.*
[b] For *admovit cf.* iii. 12. 26; viii. 3. 3; etc.
[c] *Cf.* Arr. iii. 24. 4.
[d] *i.e.* indecision rather than difference of opinion.
[e] Otherwise unknown; Kirchner, *Pros. Att.* 3513.
[f] So both Arrian (iii. 23. 9) and Diodorus (xvii 76. 2).

40

other respects happy, am grieved by this alone, that
because of hastening [a] old age I cannot long enjoy
4 your kindness." He was in his ninety-fifth year.
Nine young men, all born of the same mother, accompanied their father ; these Artabazus caused to take [b]
the king's right hand, praying that they might live
5 so long as they might be helpful to Alexander. The
king generally made a journey on foot ; on that occasion he ordered horses to be brought for himself and
Artabazus, in order that the aged man might not
feel ashamed to ride a horse while the king himself
went on foot.

6 Then, after a camp had been pitched, the king
ordered the Greeks whom Artabazus had brought
to be called together ; but they replied that unless
a pledge of safety was given also to the Lacedaemonians and to the men of Sinopê,[c] they would con-
7 sider what step they ought to take. These had been
sent as envoys of the Lacedaemonians to Darius, and
after the defeat of that king had attached themselves
to the Greeks who were serving as mercenaries with
8 the Persians. The king, having given them no
pledges of protection nor promises, ordered them to
come to him and to accept such fortune as he himself
would give them. After long hesitation and many
changes of mind,[d] they finally promised that they
9 would come. But Democrates,[e] an Athenian, who
had always been prominent in opposing the Macedonian power, despairing of pardon, fell upon his
sword. All the rest, as they had decided, surrendered
10 at discretion to Alexander. They numbered 1500
soldiers,[f] and besides these, ninety who had been
sent as envoys to Darius. The soldiers were distributed as additions to the king's troops, the rest were

41

praeter Lacedaemonios, quos tradi in custodiam
iussit.

11 Mardorum erat gens confinis Hyrcaniae, cultu
vitae aspera et latrociniis assueta ; haec sola nec
legatos miserat nec videbatur imperata factura. Itaque rex indignatus, si una gens posset efficere ne
invictus esset, impedimentis cum praesidio relictis,

12 valida[1] manu comitante procedit. Noctu iter fecerat,
et prima luce hostis in conspectu erat ; tumultus
magis quam proelium fuit. Deturbati ex collibus
quos occupaverant, barbari profugerunt, proximique

13 vici ab incolis deserti capiuntur. Interiora regionis
eius haud sane adiri sine magna vexatione exercitus
poterant ; iuga montium, praealtae silvae rupesque
inviae saepiunt, ea quae plana sunt novo munimenti

14 genere impedierant barbari. Arbores densae sunt
de industria consitae ; quarum teneros adhuc ramos
manu flectunt, quos intortos rursus inserunt terrae ;

15 inde velut ex alia radice laetiores virent trunci. Hos,
qua Natura fert, adolescere non sinunt ; quippe alium
alii quasi nexu conserunt. Qui ubi multa fronde
vestiti sunt, operiunt terram. Itaque occulti ramo-
rum velut laquei perpetua saepe iter cludunt.[2]

16 Una ratio erat caedendo aperire saltum, sed hoc
quoque magni operis. Crebri namque nodi dura-
verant stipites, et in se implicati arborum rami,

---

[1] valida *Mützell;* inuicta *A.*
[2] cludunt *Modius;* cludi**t *P;* cludit *C.*

---

[a] Mardi or Amardi; *cf.* Strabo xi. 508, Pliny, *N.H.* **vi.** 36
(Amarbi mss.).
[b] *Cf. tumultuariae manus,* iv. 16. 24.

sent home except the Lacedaemonians whom he ordered to be held under guard.

11 The Mardi were a race bordering on Hyrcania,[a] a people of rude habits of life and accustomed to brigandage ; they alone had neither sent envoys, nor seemed likely to be obedient to orders. Hence the king, piqued by the thought that one race might prevent him from having been "invincible," having left the baggage with a guard, went on, accompanied

12 by a strong force. He had made the march by night, and at daybreak the enemy was in sight ; it was rather a tumult[b] than a battle. Dislodged from the hills of which they had taken possession, the barbarians fled, and the nearest villages, deserted by their inhabitants,

13 were taken. The interior parts of that region, however, could not be approached without greatly fatiguing the army ; ranges of mountains, lofty forests, and impassable rocks shut them in, and such parts as are level the barbarians had obstructed by a novel

14 kind of fortification. Trees are purposely planted close together ; while their branches are still tender, they bend them down with their hands, twist them together, and again insert them in the earth ; then, as if from another root, more vigorous trunks spring.

15 They do not allow these to grow in the direction which Nature carries them, but they join them together, as if interlacing them. When they are clad in abundant foliage, they hide the ground ; and so the secret snares, so to speak, of the branches

16 shut in the road by a continuous hedge. The only expedient was to cut an opening into the woods, but this too was a task of great difficulty. For the many knots had hardened the trunks, and the interlaced branches of the trees, like so many

43

suspensis circulis similes, lento vimine frustrabantur
ictus.

17 Incolae autem ritu ferarum virgulta subire soliti,
tum quoque intraverant saltum occultisque telis hostem lacessebant. Ille venantium modo latibula
scrutatus plerosque confodit, ad ultimum circumire
saltum milites iubet, ut, si qua pateret, irrumperent.

18 Sed ignotis locis plerique oberrabant, exceptique
sunt quidam, inter quos equus regis—Bucephalam
vocabant—, quem Alexander non eodem quo ceteras
pecudes animo aestimabat. Namque ille nec in
dorso insidere suo patiebatur alium, et regem, cum
vellet escendere, sponte genua submittens excipiebat

19 credebaturque sentire quem veheret. Maiore ergo
quam decebat ira simul ac dolore stimulatus, equum
vestigari iubet et per interpretem pronuntiari, ni
reddidissent, neminem esse victurum. Hac denun-
tiatione territi, cum ceteris donis equum adducunt.

20 Sed ne sic quidem mitigatus, caedi silvas iubet,
aggestaque humo e montibus, planitiem ramis im-

21 peditam exaggerari. Iam in[1] aliquantum altitudinis
opus creverat, cum barbari desperato regionem quam
occupaverant posse retineri, gentem suam dedidere.
Rex obsidibus acceptis Phradati parere[2] eos iussit.

22 Inde quinto die in stativa revertitur. Artabazum

---

[1] in *added by Acidalius.*
[2] parere *Freinshem;* tradere *A.*

---

* *Cf.* Arr. v. 19. 5 ; Diod. xvii. 76. 5 ff.

suspended festoons, by their tough interwoven shoots would bring to naught the strokes of the axe.

17 The natives, however, being accustomed to crawl under the thickets like wild beasts, then also had entered the woods and from concealment were assailing their enemy with weapons. Alexander, tracing them to their lairs as hunters do, slew many of them, and finally ordered the soldiers to encircle the forest, and to rush in if they could find an opening anywhere;

18 but in the unknown country many of them strayed and lost their way, and some were captured, among them the king's horse—they called him Bucephalas [a] —which Alexander valued more highly than all other animals. For he would not allow anyone else to sit upon his back, and when the king wished to mount him, he knelt down of its own accord to receive him,

19 and seemed to know whom he was carrying. Therefore aroused with greater anger than was seemly and at the same time with grief, the king gave orders that the horse should be traced, and that proclamation should be made through an interpreter, that unless it should be returned, not a man would be left alive. Terrified by this threat, along with other

20 gifts they brought the horse. But not even by this made milder, the king ordered the woods to be cut down and earth to be brought from the mountains and heaped upon the plain which was made impass-

21 able by the branches. And this work had already risen to a considerable height, when the barbarians, despairing of being able to hold the region which they had occupied, surrendered their nation. The king, after having received hostages, ordered them to submit to Phradates.

22 Then, four days later, the king returned to his

deinde, geminato honore quem Dareus habuerat ei,
remittit domum. Iam ad urbem Hyrcaniae in qua
regia Darei fuit ventum erat; ibi Nabarzanes accepta
23 fide occurrit, dona ingentia ferens. Inter quae
Bagoas erat, specie singulari spado atque in ipso flore
pueritiae, cui et Dareus assuerat[1] et mox Alexander
assuevit; eiusque maxime precibus motus Nabarzani
ignovit.

24 Erat, ut supra dictum est, Hyrcaniae finitima gens
Amazonum, circa Thermodonta amnem Themiscyrae
25 incolentium campos. Reginam habebant Thalestrin,
omnibus inter Caucasum montem et Phasin amnem
imperitantem. Haec, cupidine visendi regis accensa,
finibus regni sui excessit et, cum haud procul abesset,
praemisit indicantes venisse reginam adeundi eius
26 cognoscendique avidam. Protinus facta potestas est[2]
veniendi. Ceteris iussis subsistere, trecentis feminarum comitata processit atque, ut primum rex in
conspectu fuit, equo ipsa desiluit duas lanceas dex-
27 tera praeferens. Vestis non tota[3] Amazonum corpori
obducitur; nam laeva pars ad pectus est nuda, cetera
deinde velantur. Nec tamen sinus vestis, quem nodo
28 colligunt, infra genua descendit. Altera papilla
intacta servatur qua muliebris sexus liberos alant;

---

[1] adsuerat *Hedicke* fuerat *P;* adsuetus fuerat *C.*
[2] potestas est *Hedicke;* potestate *A.*
[3] tota *Hedicke;* toto *A.*

---

[a] Probably Arvae (Zadracarta, Arr. iii. 23. 6); *cf.* vi. 4. 23.
[b] See x. 1. 25.   [c] See vi. 4. 17, note.
[d] On the probability of this story see Plut. *Alex.* xlvi.

permanent camp. From there he sent Artabazus home, after conferring on him double the honour which Darius had paid him. Now they had come to the city of Hyrcania in which the palace of Darius had been [a]; there Nabarzanes, having received a safe
23 conduct, met him, bringing great gifts. Among these was Bagoas,[b] a eunuch of remarkable beauty and in the very flower of boyhood, who had been loved by Darius and was afterwards to be loved by Alexander; and it was especially because of the boy's entreaties that he was led to pardon Nabarzanes.
24 There was, as was said before,[c] neighbouring on Hyrcania, a race of Amazons, inhabiting the plains of
25 Themiscyra, about the river Thermodon. They had a queen, Thalestris, who ruled all who dwelt between the Caucasus mountains and the river Phasis. She, fired with a desire to visit the king,[d] came forth from the boundaries of her kingdom, and when she was not far away sent messengers to give notice that a queen had come who was eager to meet him and to become acquainted with him. She was at once given permis-
26 sion to come. Having ordered the rest of her escort to halt, she came forward attended by three hundred women, and as soon as the king was in sight, she herself leaped down from her horse, carrying two
27 lances in her right hand. The clothing of the Amazons does not wholly cover the body; for the left side is nude as far as the breast, then the other parts of the body are veiled. However, the fold of the robe, which they gather in a knot,[e] does not
28 reach below the knee. One nipple is left untouched, and with it they nourish their female children [f] ; the

* Cf. Virg. Aen. i. 320.
f The males were given to the fathers to rear.

aduritur dextera, ut arcus facilius intendant et tela
vibrent.

29   Interrito vultu regem Thalestris intuebatur, habitum eius haudquaquam rerum famae parem oculis
perlustrans ; quippe omnibus barbaris in corporum
maiestate veneratio est, magnorumque operum non
alios capaces putant, quam quos eximia specie donare

30 natura dignata est.   Ceterum interrogata num aliquid petere vellet, haud dubitavit fateri ad com-
municandos cum rege liberos se venisse, dignam ex
qua ipse regni generaret heredes ; feminini sexus se

31 retenturam, marem reddituram patri.   Alexander an
cum ipse militare vellet interrogat ; at illa causata
sine custode regnum reliquisse, petere perseverabat

32 ne se irritam spei abire pateretur.   Acrior ad vene-
rem feminae cupido quam regis, ut paucos dies subsisteret perpulit. xiii dies in obsequium desiderii
eius absumpti sunt. Tum illa regnum suum, rex
Parthienen petiverunt.

    VI. Hic vero palam cupiditates suas solvit con-
tinentiamque et moderationem, in altissima quaque
fortuna eminentia bona, in superbiam ac lasciviam

2 vertit.   Patrios mores disciplinamque Macedonum
regum salubriter temperatam et civilem habitum
velut leviora magnitudine sua ducens, Persicae regiae

3 par deorum potentiae fastigium aemulabatur; iacere

---

    a A delicate expression. In Diod. xvii. 77. 2 she frankly
says παιδοποιίας ἕνεκεν ἥκω.
    b So also Plut. *Alex.* xxxviii; Diod. xvii. 72. 2 ; Justin
xii. 3.   Hence apparently from one source and less credible.
    c *Civilem, cf.* Tac. *Ann.* i. 72 (of Tiberius) ; i. 33 (of
Germanicus).

right is seared, in order that they may more easily stretch their bows and hurl their spears.

29 With fearless expression Thalestris gazed at the king, carefully surveying his person, which did not by any means correspond to the fame of his exploits ; for all the barbarians feel veneration for a majestic presence, and believe that only those are capable of great deeds whom nature has deigned to adorn with

30 extraordinary physical attractiveness. However, on being asked whether she wished to make any request, she did not hesitate to confess that she had come to share children with the king,[a] being worthy that he should beget from her heirs to his kingdom; that she would retain any female offspring but would return

31 a male to his father. Alexander asked her whether she wished to serve in war with him ; but she, giving as an excuse that she had left her realm without a guard, persisted in asking that he should not suffer

32 her to go away disappointed in her hope. The passion of the woman, being, as she was, more keen for love than the king, compelled him to remain there for a few days. Thirteen days were spent in satisfying her desire. Then she went to her kingdom, and the king to Parthienê.

VI. It was in fact at this time [b] that Alexander gave loose rein to his passions, and changed continence and self-control, eminent virtues in every exalted fortune, to haughtiness and wantonness.

2 Regarding his native customs and the discipline of the Macedonian kings, wholesomely restrained and democratic,[c] as too low for his grandeur, he strove to rival the loftiness of the Persian court, equal to

3 the power of the gods; he demanded that the victors over so many nations in paying their respects

humi venerabundos[1] ipsum paulatimque servilibus
ministeriis tot victores gentium imbuere et captivis
4 pares facere expetebat.[2] Itaque purpureum diadema distinctum albo, quale Dareus habuerat, capiti
circumdedit vestemque Persicam sumpsit, ne omen
quidem veritus, quod a victoris insignibus in devicti
5 transiret habitum. Et ille se quidem spolia Persarum
gestare dicebat, sed cum illis quoque mores induerat,
superbiamque habitus animi insolentia sequebatur.
6 Litteras quoque, quas in Europam mitteret, veteris
anuli gemma obsignabat, eis, quas in Asiam scriberet,
Darei anulus imprimebatur, ut appareret unum ani-
7 mum duorum non capere fortunam. Amicos vero
et equites unaque[3] principes militum, aspernantes
quidem, sed recusare non ausos, Persicis ornaverat[4]
8 vestibus. Pelices ccc et lxv,[5] totidem quot Darei
fuerant, regiam implebant, quas spadonum greges,
et ipsi muliebria pati assueti, sequebantur.
9 Haec luxu et peregrinis infecta moribus veteres
Philippi milites, rudis natio ad voluptates, palam
aversabantur, totisque castris unus omnium sensus
ac sermo erat, plus amissum victoria quam bello esse
10 quaesitum ; cum maxime vinci ipsos deditos[6] alienis
moribus et externis. Quo tandem ore[7] domos quasi
in captivo habitu reversuros ? Pudere iam sui regem ;

[1] venerabundos *Vindelinus;* uenerabundus *A.*
[2] expetebat *I;* expectabat *A.*
[3] unaque *Bentley;* hii namque *C;* hi*namque *P.*
[4] ornaverat *Vindelinus;* onerauerat *A.*
[5] ccc et lxv *Vogel;* cccc et lx *A.*
[6] deditos *Bentley;* dedique *A.*
[7] quo tandem ore *Jeep;* quo tante more *A.*

a The *cidaris,* see iii. 3. 19.
b *i.e.* the Companion Cavalry, οἱ ἑταῖροι ἱππεῖς ; *cf.*
vi. 2. 11, note, and Diod. xvii. 77. 5.

to him should prostrate themselves upon the ground, and gradually sought to accustom them to servile
4 duties and to treat them like captives. Accordingly, he encircled his brow with a purple diadem, variegated with white ^a such as Darius had worn, and assumed the Persian garb, not even fearing the omen of changing from the insignia of a victor to the
5 dress of the conquered. In fact, he used to say that he was wearing the spoils of the Persians ; but with them he had assumed also their customs, and insolence of spirit accompanied the magnificence of his
6 attire. The letters also which were to be sent to Europe he sealed with the device of his former ring ; on those which he wrote to Asia, the ring of Darius was impressed, so that it appeared that one mind was not equal to the fortune of the two realms.
7 Moreover, he compelled his friends, the cavalry,^b and with them the leaders of the soldiers, to wear the Persian dress, which was indeed repugnant to them,
8 but which they did not dare to refuse. Three hundred and sixty-five concubines, the same number that Darius had had, filled his palace, attended by herds of eunuchs, also accustomed to prostitute themselves.
9 These practices, corrupted by luxury and foreign customs, were openly detested by the veteran soldiers of Philip, a people novices in voluptuousness, and in the whole camp the feeling and the talk of all was the same, namely, that more had been lost by victory
10 than had been gained by war ; that it was then above all that they themselves were conquered men, when they had surrendered themselves to alien and foreign habits. With what face, pray, would they return to their homes, as if in the attire of prisoners ? The king was already ashamed of them since resemb-

victis quam victoribus similiorem, ex Macedoniae
11 imperatore Darei satrapen factum. Ille, non ignarus
et principes amicorum et exercitum graviter offendi,
gratiam liberalitate donisque reparare temptabat.
Sed, opinor, liberis pretium servitutis ingratum
12 est. Igitur, ne in seditionem res verteretur, otium
interpellandum erat bello, cuius materia opportune
13 alebatur. Namque Bessus, veste regia sumpta,
Artaxerxen appellari se iusserat Scythasque et ceteros Tanais accolas contrahebat.

Haec Satibarzanes nuntiabat ; quem receptum in
14 fidem regioni quam antea obtinuerat praefecit. Et
cum grave spoliis apparatuque luxuriae agmen vix
moveretur, suas primum, deinde totius exercitus
sarcinas, exceptis admodum necessariis, conferri[1]
15 iussit in medium. Planities spatiosa erat, in quam[2]
vehicula onusta perduxerant. Expectantibus cunctis
quid deinde esset imperaturus, iumenta iussit abduci,
suisque primum sarcinis face subdita, ceteras incendi.[3]
16 Flagrabant exurentibus dominis, quae ut intacta ex
urbibus hostium raperent, saepe flammas restinxer-
ant, nullo sanguinis pretium audente deflere, cum
17 regias opes idem ignis exureret. Brevi deinde ratio
mitigavit dolorem, habilesque militiae et ad omnia

---

[1] conferri *Lauer;* referre *A.*
[2] quam *Lauer;* qua *A.*
[3] incendi praecepit *A;* praecepit *deleted by Kinch.*

---

[a] For *alebatur cf.* vii. 7. 17 *bellum alemus.*
[b] *Cf.* Arr. iii. 25. 3.

ling the vanquished rather than the victors, he had changed from a ruler of Macedonia to a satrap of
11 Darius. The king, not unaware that the chief of his friends, and the army as well, were grievously offended, tried to win back their favour by liberality and by bounty. But, in my opinion, the price of
12 slavery is hateful to free men. Therefore, that the situation might not result in mutiny, it was necessary to put an end to their leisure by war, the material for which was opportunely increasing.[a]
13 For Bessus, having assumed regal attire, had given orders that he should be called Artaxerxes,[b] and was assembling the Scythians and the rest of the peoples dwelling by the Tanais.

This was announced by Satibarzanes, whom Alexander had received under his protection and had made satrap of the region which he had formerly governed.
14 And since the army, laden with spoils and the equipment of luxury, could with difficulty be moved, he ordered first his own baggage, then that of the whole army, to be gathered together in their midst, except
15 what was absolutely necessary. There was a spacious plain, into which they had driven the loaded wagons. When all were wondering what the king was going to order next, he commanded that the animals be led away, and, when he had first applied a torch to his
16 own pack, that the rest be burned. There were consumed, set on fire by their owners, the riches to save which unharmed from the cities of the enemy they had often extinguished flames, and no one dared to weep for the price of his blood, when the
17 same fire was consuming the king's wealth. Then in a short time reason soothed their grief, and, prepared for military service and ready for everything, they

parati laetabantur sarcinarum potius quam disciplinae
fecisse iacturam.

18 Igitur Bactrianam regionem petebant. Sed Nicanor, Parmenionis filius, subita morte correptus,
19 magno desiderio sui affecerat cunctos. Rex, ante
omnis maestus, cupiebat quidem subsistere funeri
adfuturus, sed penuria commeatuum festinare cogebat ; itaque Philotas cum duobus milibus et DC
relictus, ut iusta fratri persolveret, ipse contendit
ad Bessum.
20 Iter facienti ei litterae afferuntur a finitimis[1]
satraparum, e quibus cognoscit Bessum quidem hostili
animo occurrere cum exercitu, ceterum Satibarzanen,
quem satrapeae[2] Ariorum ipse praefecisset, defecisse
21 ab eo. Itaque quamquam Besso imminebat, tamen
ad[3] Satibarzanen opprimendum praeverti optimum
ratus, levem armaturam et equestres copias educit,
totaque nocte itinere strenue facto improvisus hosti
22 supervenit. Cuius cognito adventu, Satibarzanes
cum duobus milibus equitum—nec plures subito
contrahi poterant—Bactra perfugit, ceteri proximos
23 montes occupaverunt. Praerupta rupes est, qua
spectat occidentem, eadem, qua vergit ad orientem,
leniore summissa fastigio ; multis arboribus obsita
perennem habet fontem, ex quo large aquae manant.
24 Circuitus eius xxx et duo stadia comprehendit. In
vertice herbidus campus ; in hoc multitudinem im-

---

[1] finitimis *I;* finibus *A.*
satrapeae *Hedicke;* satrapem *P;* satrapham *C.*
[3] ad *added by Vindelinus; A omits.*

---

a ab eo: this use of *is* instead of the reflexive is fairly
common in Curtius.

rejoiced that jettison had been made of their packs,
and not of their discipline.

18 Therefore they were making for the region of
Bactra. But the carrying off of Nicanor, son of Parmenion, by a sudden death had been a cause of great
19 grief to all. The king, saddened more than the
others, desired to halt in order to be present at his
funeral, but scarcity of supplies caused him to
hasten ; therefore, leaving Philotas with 2600 men
to perform the due rites for his brother, he hurried
on to meet Bessus.

20 As he was on his way, letters were brought to him
from the neighbouring satraps, from which he learned
that Bessus was in fact coming to meet him with
hostile intent with his army, but also that Satibarzanes, whom he himself had given charge of the
21 satrapy of the Arii, had revolted from him.[a] Therefore, although eager to meet Bessus, yet thinking it
best to make it his first business [b] to crush Satibarzanes, he led out his light-armed troops and his
cavalry forces, and marching swiftly all ni_ t, came
22 unexpectedly upon the enemy. On learni.._ of his
arrival [c] Satibarzanes with 2000 horsemen— 'or he
had not been able in his haste to muster more—fled
for refuge to Bactra, the rest took possession of the
23 neighbouring mountains. There is a rock, very steep
on its western side, but towards the east sinking
with a gentler slope ; covered with many trees, it
has a perennial fount, from which there is an
abundant flow of water. Its circuit covers thirty-
24 two stadia. On its summit is a grass-covered plain ;

[b] On *praeverti cf.* Tac. *Ann.* ii. 56 *praeverti ad Armenios
instantior cura fuit* ; iv. 32.
[c] *Cf.* Arr. iii. 25. 7.

bellem considere iubent. Ipsi qua rupes sedit[1]
arborum truncos et saxa obmoliuntur. XIII milia
25 armata erant. In quorum obsidione Cratero relicto,
ipse Satibarzanen sequi festinat. At,[2] quia longius
abesse eum cognoverat, ad expugnandos eos qui edita
26 montium occupaverant[3] redit. Ac primo repurgari
iter[4] iubet quidquid ingredi possent, deinde, ut occurrebant inviae cotes praeruptaeque rupes, irritus labor
27 videbatur obstante Natura. Ille, ut erat animi semper obluctantis difficultatibus, cum et progredi arduum
et reverti periculosum esset, versabat se ad omnes
cogitationes, aliud atque aliud—ita ut fieri solet ubi
prima quaeque damnamus—subiciente animo.

Haesitanti, quod ratio non potuit fortuna consilium
28 subministravit. Vehemens favonius erat, et multam
materiam ceciderat miles, aditum per saxa molitus.
29 Haec vapore torrida flamma arserat[5]; ergo aggeri
alias arbores iubet et igni dari[6] alimenta, celeriterque,
stipitibus cumulatis, fastigium montis aequatum est.
30 Tunc undique ignis iniectus cuncta comprehendit.
Flammam in ora hostium ventus ferebat, fumus
ingens velut quadam nube absconderat caelum.
31 Sonabant incendio silvae, atque ea quoque quae non
incenderat miles, concepto igne, proxima quaeque
adurebant. Barbari suppliciorum ultimum, si qua

sedit *Hedicke;* erat *A.*   [2] At *Hedicke;* et *A.*
    [3] occupaverant *Vindelinus;* occupauerunt *A.*
            [4] iter *added by Capps.*
        [5] flamma arserat *Hedicke;* iam inauerat *A.*
            [6] dari *Aldus;* dare *A.*

<hr>

[a] For *iter repurgare cf.* Livy xliv. 4.

on this they ordered those who were not fit for war to
take their places. They themselves piled tree-trunks
and stones against the slope of the rock. They
25 numbered 13,000 armed men. Leaving Craterus to
blockade these, he hastened in pursuit of Satibarzanes. But because he had learned that the barbarian was a long distance away, he returned to storm
those who had taken possession of the mountain
26 heights. And first he ordered to be cleared whatever road they would be able to traverse[a]; then, when
impassable crags and precipices presented themselves, the labour seemed hopeless against the op-
27 position of Nature. But Alexander, being always of
a mind to wrestle with difficulties, since to advance
was a hard task and to return dangerous, considered
all kinds of expedients as his mind suggested one
after another—as is usual when we reject every first
thought.

As he was at a loss, chance offered a plan which cal-
28 culation could not suggest. There was a strong west
wind, and the soldiers had cut a great amount of
wood when trying to make an approach over the
stones. This, dried by the heat, had caught fire ;
29 therefore he ordered other trees to be piled on, and
fuel to be given to the flames, and soon, as the
trunks were heaped up, they equalled the height of
30 the mountain. Then fire was thrown upon it from
every side and kindled the whole mass. The wind
drove the flames into the faces of the enemy, a great
31 smoke had hidden the sky as if by a cloud. The
woods roared from the conflagration, and those parts
also to which the soldiers had not set fire, took fire
themselves, and burned everything that was near
them. The barbarians tried to escape the worst of

57

intermoreretur ignis, effugere temptabant, sed qua
32 flamma dederat locum hostis obstabat. Varia igitur
caede consumpti sunt ; alii in medios[1] ignis,[2] alii
petris praecipitavere se, quidam hostium manibus
obtulerunt, pauci semustulati venere in potestatem.
33 Hinc ad Craterum, qui Artacana obsidebat, redit.
Ille, omnibus praeparatis, regis exspectabat adven-
34 tum captae urbis titulo, sicut par erat, cedens. Igitur
Alexander turres admoveri iubet ; ipsoque aspectu
barbari territi e muris supinas manus tenderes,
orare coeperunt ; iram in Satibarzanen, defectionis
auctorem, reservaret, supplicibus semet dedentibus
parceret. Rex data venia non obsidionem modo
solvit, sed omnia sua incolis reddidit.
35 Ab hac urbe digresso supplementum novorum
militum occurrit ; Zoilus[3] D equites ex Graecia adduxerat, III milia ex Illyrico Antipater miserat,
Thessali equites c et xxx cum Philippo erant, ex
Lydia II milia et sescenti, peregrinus miles, advene-
36 rant, ccc equites gentis eiusdem sequebantur. Hac
manu adiecta adit[4] Drangas ; bellicosa natio est.
Satrapes erat Barzaentes,[5] sceleris in regem suum
particeps Besso ; is suppliciorum quae meruerat
metu profugit in Indiam.
VII. Iam nonum diem stativa erant, cum externa
vi non tutus modo rex, sed invictus, intestino facinore

---

[1] medios *I;* medio *A.*   [2] ignis *C;* ignes *P.*
                [3] Zoilus *J. Froben;* Zolus *A.*
        [4] adit *added by Hedicke;* *A omits.*
[5] Barzaentes *Modius;* barzaenses *P m. pr.;* barzanenses *C.*

---

[a] Cannot be exactly located ; apparently the principal
city of the Arii; *cf.* Arr. iii. 25. 6, where Artacoana.
[b] *Cf.* iv. 4. 1 *soluta obsidione.*
[c] Arr. iii. 25. 3.

torments, if the fire died down anywhere, but where
the flames gave a passage the enemy awaited them.
32 Hence they were destroyed by varied forms of
death ; some threw themselves into the midst of
the flames, others down from the rocks, some offered
themselves to the hands of the enemy, a few, half
roasted, came into their power.

33 From there he returned to Craterus, who was
besieging Artacana.[a] He, having prepared everything beforehand, was awaiting the coming of the
king, leaving to him the honour of capturing the city,
34 as was right. Therefore Alexander ordered towers
to be brought up; and at the mere sight the terrified
barbarians on the walls, stretching out their hands,
palms up, began to entreat him to reserve his
anger for Satibarzanes, the ringleader of the revolt,
and to spare the suppliants who surrendered themselves. The king pardoned them, and not only put
an end to the siege,[b] but returned all their property
to the inhabitants.

35 When he had left this city, a reserve[c] of new
soldiers met him ; Zoïlus had brought 500 soldiers
from Greece, Antipater had sent 3000 from Illyricum,
with Philip there were 130 Thessalian cavalry, from
Lydia 2600 foreign troops had come, and 300 horse-
36 men of the same race followed. With the addition
of these forces he entered the land of the Drangae,
a warlike tribe. Their satrap was Barzaentes, an
accomplice with Bessus in the crime against his king ;
he, fearing the punishment which he had deserved,
fled to India.

VII. Already Alexander had been encamped for
nine days in the same place, when, being not only
safe from force from without, but unconquered, he

59

2 petebatur. Dymnus, modicae apud regem auctori-
tatis et gratiae, exoleti cui Nicomacho[1] erat nomen,
amore flagrabat, obsequio uni sibi dediti corporis
3 vinctus. Is, quod ex vultu quoque perspici poterat,
similis attonito remotis arbitris cum iuvene secessit
in templum, arcana se et silenda afferre praefatus,
4 suspensumque expectatione per mutuam caritatem
et pignora utriusque animi rogat, ut affirmet iure-
5 iurando quae commisisset silentio esse tecturum. Et
ille ratus nihil quod etiam cum periurio detegendum
6 foret indicaturum, per praesentes deos iurat. Tum
Dymnus aperit in tertium diem regi insidias comparatas seque eius consilii fortibus viris et illustribus
7 esse participem. Quibus iuvenis auditis se vero
fidem in parricidio dedisse constanter abnuit, nec ulla
8 religione ut scelus tegat posse constringi. Dymnus,
et amore et metu amens, dexteram exoleti complexus et lacrimans, orare primum ut particeps con-
9 silii operisque fieret ; si id sustinere non posset,
attamen ne proderet se, cuius erga ipsum benivolentiae praeter alia hoc quoque haberet fortissimum
pignus, quod caput suum permisisset fidei adhuc
inexpertae.
10   Ad ultimum aversari scelus perseverantem mortis
metu terret ; ab illo capite coniuratos pulcherrimum

---

[1] Nicomacho *Aldus;* nichomacho *P;* nichomaco *C.*

---

was attacked by a crime within his own household.
2 Dymnus, a man of slight weight and favour with the
king, burned with love for a catamite named Nicomachus, bound by the compliance of a body devoted
3 to him alone. He, as if in great alarm, as could
clearly be seen also from his expression, without witnesses withdrew with the youth into a temple, first
saying that he had something secret and confidential
to communicate, and when the youth was on tiptoe
4 of expectation, he besought him by their affection for
each other, and by the pledges which they had both
exchanged, to declare under oath that he would
keep silent about what Dymnus should reveal to him.
5 Nicomachus, not supposing that he would tell him
anything which it would be incumbent on him to disclose even at the cost of breaking his word, took oath
6 by the gods in whose temple they were. Then Dymnus
revealed that a plot against the king had been arranged for the third day thereafter, and that he shared
in that design with some brave and distinguished men.
7 The youth, on hearing this, steadfastly denied that he
had pledged his faith to take part in treason,[a] and
said that he could not be bound by any religious obli-
8 gation to keep the crime secret. Dymnus, mad both
with love and with fear, seizing the youth's hand and
weeping, begged first that he would take part in the
9 design and its execution ; if he could not bring himself to do that, at least he would not betray him,
whose goodwill towards Nicomachus, besides all the
rest, had this very evident proof, that he had trusted
his life to his loyalty without previously testing it.
10 Finally, when the youth persisted in expressing
abhorrence of the crime, Dymnus tried to terrify him
by fear of death, saying that the conspirators would

61

11 facinus incohaturos. Alias deinde effeminatum et
muliebriter timidum, alias proditorem amatoris appellans, nunc ingentia promittens, interdumque regnum quoque, versabat animum tanto facinore procul
12 abhorrentem. Strictum deinde gladium modo illius,
modo suo admovens iugulo, supplex idem et infestus,
expressit tandem[1] ut non solum silentium, sed etiam
13 operam polliceretur. Namque abunde constantis
animi et dignus qui pudicus esset, nihil ex pristina
voluntate mutaverat, sed captum Dymni amore
14 simulabat nihil recusare. Sciscitari inde pergit, cum
quibus tantae rei societatem inisset; plurimum
referre, quales viri tam memorabili operi admoturi
15 manus essent. Ille et amore et scelere male sanus,
simul gratias agit, simul gratulatur quod fortissimis[2]
iuvenum non dubitasset se adiungere, Demetrio,
corporis custodi, Peucolao,[3] Nicanori; adicit his
Aphobetum, Iolaum,[4] Theoxenum,[5] Archepolim,
Amyntam.
16 Ab hoc sermone dimissus Nicomachus ad fratrem—
Cebalino erat nomen—quae acceperat defert. Placet
ipsum subsistere in tabernaculo, ne, si regiam intrasset non assuetus adire regem, coniurati proditos se
17 esse rescincerent. Ipse Cebalinus ante vestibulum
regiae—neque enim propius aditus ei patebat—

---

[1] expressit tandem ut C (V omits tandem); expressit ut
tandem P.
[2] fortissimis P; fortissimus C.
[3] Peucolao Modius; peuculao A.
[4] Iolaum Vogel; ioceum A.
[5] Theoxenum Hedicke; idoxenum P m. pr.; idioxenum C
(adioxenum V).

11 begin their glorious deed by taking his life. Then
calling him now effeminate and womanishly timid,
and now the betrayer of his lover, now making vast
promises, sometimes even royal power, he worked
upon a mind to which such a deed was utterly abhor-
12 rent. Then applying a drawn sword, now to Nicomachus' throat and now to his own, at the same time
a suppliant and an enemy, Dymnus at last forced
him to promise, not only silence, but even support.
13 Yet the lad, being of a most steadfast spirit—indeed he
should have been chaste—had made no change in his
former resolution, but pretended that, overcome with
14 love for Dymnus, he could refuse him nothing. Then
he went on to inquire with whom he had entered
upon an association of so great importance ; it made
a great deal of difference, he said, what sort of men
were going to put their hands to so memorable an
15 enterprise. Dymnus, almost crazed by love and
guilt, at the same time thanked him, and also congratulated him that he had not hesitated to join
with the bravest of men, Demetrius, one of the
body-guard,[a] Peucolaüs, Nicanor ; to these he added
Aphobetus, Iolaüs, Theoxenus, Archepolis, Amyntas.
16 On being dismissed from this conference, Nicomachus reported to his brother—his name was
Cebalinus—what he had heard. They agreed that
Nicomachus should stay in his brother's tent, for fear
that, if he, who was not accustomed to approach the
king, should enter the royal apartment, the conspirators might learn that they had been betrayed.
17 Cebalinus himself stood before the vestibule of the
tent—for nearer access was not allowed him—waiting

[a] *Cf.* Arr. iii. 27. 5, which indicates that Demetrius was one
of the seven of the highest rank among the body-guard.

consistit, opperiens aliquem ex prima cohorte amico-
18 rum, a quo[1] introduceretur ad regem. Forte, ceteris
dimissis, unus Philotas, Parmenionis filius—incertum
quam ob causam—substiterat[2] in regia ; huic Cebalinus ore confuso magnae perturbationis notas prae
se ferens aperit quae ex fratre compererat, et sine
19 dilatione nuntiari regi iubet. Philotas, collaudato
eo, protinus intrat ad Alexandrum, multoque invicem
de aliis rebus sermone consumpto, nihil eorum quae
20 ex Cebalino cognoverat nuntiat. Sub vesperam eum
prodeuntem in vestibulo regiae excipit iuvenis, an
mandatum exsecutus foret requirens. Ille, non
21 vacasse sermoni suo regem causatus, discessit. Postero die Cebalinus venienti in regiam praesto est,
intrantemque admonet pridie communicatae cum
ipso rei. Ille curae sibi esse respondet ; ac ne tum
22 quidem regi quae audierat aperit. Coeperat Cebalino esse suspectus ; itaque non ultra interpellandum
ratus, nobili iuveni—Metron erat ei nomen—super
armamentarium posito, quod scelus pararetur indicat.
23 Ille, Cebalino in armamentario abscondito, protinus
regi, corpus forte curanti, quid index detulisset osten-
24 dit. Rex ad comprehendendum Dymnum missis
satellitibus, armamentarium intrat. Ibi Cebalinus
gaudio elatus : "Habeo te," inquit, "incolumem ex
25 impiorum manibus ereptum." Percontatus deinde

---

[1] a quo *J. Froben;* quo *C* (*P m. pr. omits*).
[2] substiterat *Lauer;* subsisterat *P;* subsisteret *C.*

---

[a] See vi. 2. 11, note *b.*

for someone of the first rank *a* of the king's friends,
18 to admit him to Alexander's presence. It happened
that when the rest had been dismissed, Philotas, son
of Parmenion, alone—it is not known for what reason
—had remained in the royal apartment ; to him
Cebalinus, in confused words and showing signs of
great perturbation, disclosed what he had learned
from his brother, and asked that it be reported to the
19 king without delay. Philotas, after strongly com-
mending him, at once went in to Alexander, and
having talked with him for some time about other
matters, reported nothing of what he had learned
20 from Cebalinus. Towards evening the young man
met Philotas in the vestibule of the royal apartment, as he was coming out, and asked him whether
he had done what he requested. Philotas alleged
that the king had had no time to talk with him,
21 and went away. On the following day Cebalinus
was on hand when Philotas came to the royal apartment, and reminded him, as he entered, of the
matter which he had communicated to him the day
before. Philotas replied that he was attending to
it, but did not even then disclose to the king what he
22 had heard. Cebalinus began to suspect him, and so,
thinking that there ought to be no further obstruc-
tion, he told a young nobleman—his name was
Metron—who had charge of the armoury, of the
23 crime which was being planned. He, after having
concealed Cebalinus in the armoury, at once revealed
to the king, who chanced to be taking a bath, what
24 the informer had reported. The king sent his attendants to arrest Dymnus, and entered the armoury.
There Cebalinus, transported with joy, said : " I
have you safe, snatched from the hands of impious

Alexander quae noscenda erant, ordine cuncta cog
noscit. Rursusque institit quaerere, quotus dies esset
ex quo Nicomachus ad eum detulisset indicium.
26 Atque illo fatente iam tertium esse, existimans haud
incorrupta fide tanto post deferre quae audierat vin-
27 ciri eum iussit. At[1] ille clamitare coepit eodem
temporis momento quo audisset, ad Philotan decucurrisse[2]; ab eo operiri comperta.[3]

28   Rex identidem[4] quaerens an Philotan adisset, an
institisset ei ut pervenirent ad se, perseverante eo
affirmare quae dixerat, manus ad caelum tendens,
manantibus lacrimis hanc sibi a carissimo quondam
29 amicorum relatam gratiam querebatur. Inter haec
Dymnus haud ignarus quam ob causam accerseretur
a rege, gladio quo forte erat cinctus graviter se
vulnerat occursuque satellitum inhibitus, perfertur in
30 regiam. Quem intuens rex : " Quod," inquit, " in
te, Dymne, tantum cogitavi nefas, ut tibi Macedonum regno dignior Philotas me quoque ipso videretur ? " Illum iam defecerat vox ; itaque edito
gemitu vultuque a conspectu regis averso subinde
collapsus exstinguitur.

31   Rex, Philota venire in regiam iusso : " Cebalinus,"
inquit, " ultimum supplicium meritus, si in caput
meum praeparatas insidias biduo texit[5] ; sed huius

---

[1] iussit. At *Hedicke;* iussit *P;* iusserat *C.*
[2] decucurrisse *Kinch;* de∗∗currisse *P;* decurrisse *C.*
[3] operiri comperta *Jeep;* perconperta *P;* percomperta *C.*
[4] identidem *Freinshem;* item *C (V omits);* idem *P m. pr.*
[5] texit ; sed *Hedicke;* texisset, teẍit, texi, tex, *etc. MSS.*

25 men." Then Alexander, after inquiring about all
the particulars, learned the whole matter in detail.
And again the king went on to inquire how long it
was since Nicomachus had given him the informa-
26 tion. And when Cebalinus admitted that it was two
days before, Alexander, thinking him of doubtful
loyalty in reporting so long afterwards what he had
27 heard, ordered that he be put in fetters. But Cebalinus began to cry out that at the very moment that
he had heard of it he had run to Philotas; that it
was by him that what he had learned was concealed.
28 When the king asked again and again whether he
had gone to Philotas, and whether he had urged him
that they should go to Alexander, and Cebalinus
persisted in affirming what he had said, the king,
raising his hands to heaven, with flowing tears began
to lament that such requital had been made him by
one who had formerly been the dearest of his friends.
29 In the meantime Dymnus, well aware why he was
summoned by the king, gave himself a severe wound
with a sword which he chanced to be wearing,
and being stopped by the guards who ran up, was
30 brought into the royal apartment. The king, looking him in the eye, said : " What great wrong have
I planned against you, Dymnus, that you should
think Philotas more worthy to rule the Macedonians,
than I am myself ? " But speech had already failed
Dymnus ; and so, uttering a groan and averting his
face from the king's gaze, he forthwith swooned and
died.
31 The king, having ordered Philotas to come to the
royal tent, said : " Cebalinus deserved the extreme
penalty, if he concealed for two days a plot aimed
at my life ; but he has substituted Philotas as

67

criminis Philotan reum substituit, ad quem protinus
32 indicium detulisse se affirmat. Quo propiore gradu
amicitiae me contingis, hoc maius est dissimulationis
tuae facinus, et ego Cebalino magis quam Philotae
id convenire fateor. Faventem habes iudicem, si
quod admitti non oportuit[1] saltem purgari[2] potest."

33 Ad haec Philotas haud sane trepidus, si animus
vultu aestimaretur, Cebalinum quidem scorti sermonem ad se detulisse, sed ipsum tam levi auctore
nihil credidisse respondit, veritum ne iurgium inter
amatorem et exoletum non sine risu aliorum detulis-
34 set ; cum Dymnus semet interemerit, qualiacumque
erant, non fuisse reticenda. Complexusque regem
orare coepit ut praeteritam vitam potius quam culpam, silentii tamen, non facti ullius, intueretur.
35 Haud facile dixerim credideritne ei rex an altius iram
suppresserit ; dexteram reconciliatae gratiae pignus
obtulit et contemptum magis quam celatum indicium
esse videri sibi dixit.

VIII. Advocato tum[3] consilio amicorum, cui tamen
Philotas adhibitus non est, Nicomachum introduci
2 iubet. Is eadem quae detulerat frater[4] ad regem
ordine exposuit. Erat Craterus regi carus in paucis,
et eo Philotae ob aemulationem dignitatis adversus,
3 neque ignorabat saepe Alexandri auribus nimia iacta-

[1] oportuit *J. Froben;* potuit *A.*
[2] purgari *Jeep;* negari *A.*
[3] tum *Zumpt;* tamen *A.*   [4] frater *added by Vogel.*

the one guilty of that offence, since he declares that
he immediately reported the information to him.
32 The closer the degree of friendship which you have
with me, the greater is the crime of your secrecy,
and I at any rate admit that such action becomes
Cebalinus rather than Philotas. You have a favourable judge, if what ought not to have been done can
at least be excused."

33 To these words Philotas, in no wise disturbed, if
his feelings were judged from his expression, replied
that Cebalinus had, it was true, reported to him the
talk of a wanton, but that he himself put no trust in
an authority of so little weight, fearing besides lest
he should be laughed at by the rest if he reported
34 a quarrel between a lover and his favourite ; but
since Dymnus had made away with himself, it ought
not to have been passed over in silence, whatever its
nature was. Then, throwing his arms about the king,
he began to entreat him to have regard to his past
life rather than to a fault which, after all, was only
35 one of silence, and not of any action. I could not
readily say whether the king believed him, or suppressed his anger deep in his heart ; he offered him
his right hand as a pledge of renewed favour, saying
that it appeared to him that the information was
scorned rather than concealed.

VIII. Then, having called a council of his friends,
to which however Philotas was not invited, he ordered
2 Nicomachus to be brought before it. The youth set
forth in order the same information that his brother
had given to the king. Craterus was dearer to
Alexander than most of his friends, and for that
reason less friendly to Philotas, as his rival in import-
3 ance, he was well aware too that Philotas had often

69

tione[1] virtutis atque operae gravem fuisse et ob ea
non quidem sceleris, sed contumaciae tamen esse
4 suspectum.   Non aliam premendi inimici occasionem
aptiorem futuram ratus, odio suo pietatis praeferens
speciem : " Utinam," inquit, " in principio quoque
5 huius rei nobiscum deliberasses ! Suasissemus, si
Philotae velles ignoscere, patereris potius ignorare
eum quantum deberet tibi, quam usque ad mortis
metum adductum saepius de periculo suo quam de
tuo cogitare beneficio.   Ille enim semper insidiari
tibi poterit, tu non semper Philotae poteris ignoscere.
6 Nec est quod existimes eum, qui tantum ausus est,
venia posse mutari.   Scit eos qui misericordiam con-
7 sumpserunt amplius sperare non posse.   At ego,
etiam si ipse vel paenitentia vel beneficio tuo victus
quiescere volet, patrem eius Parmenionem, tanti
ducem exercitus et inveterata apud milites suos
auctoritate haud multum infra magnitudinis tuae
fastigium positum, scio non aequo animo salutem
8 filii sui debiturum tibi.   Quaedam beneficia odimus.
Meruisse mortem confiteri pudet ; superest, ut malit
videri iniuriam accepisse quam vitam.   Proinde scito[2]
9 tibi cum illis de salute esse pugnandum.   Satis hostium superest, ad quos persequendos ituri sumus ;
latus a domesticis hostibus muni.   Hos si summoves,
nihil metuo ab externo."
10   Haec Craterus.   Nec ceteri dubitabant quin

---

[1] iactatione *J. Froben;* actione *A.*
[2] scito *Modius;* scio *A.*

wearied the ears of Alexander by excessive vaunting
of his valour and his services, and hence was sus-
4 pected, not indeed of crime, but of arrogance. Thinking that there would be no more advantageous
opportunity of ruining his enemy, disguising his
hatred under a pretence of loyalty, he said : " I only
wish that at the very beginning of this matter you
5 had deliberated with us ! We should have persuaded
you, if you wished to pardon Philotas, to suffer him to
be ignorant how much he was indebted to you, rather
than, after he had been brought even to the very fear
of death, to think more often of his own danger than
of your kindness. For he will always be able to plot
against you, you will not always be able to pardon
6 Philotas. There is no reason for you to think that
one who has dared so much can be changed by a
pardon. He knows that those who have exhausted
7 mercy can no longer hope for it. But even if he himself, either through change of heart or overcome by
your kindness, shall wish to remain quiet, I at any rate
know that his father Parmenion, the leader of so great
an army, and because of his long-continued influence
with his soldiers holding a position not much below
the height of your greatness, will not with equanimity
8 owe his son's life to you. There are some favours
which we hate. One is ashamed to admit that one
has deserved death ; therefore, Philotas would prefer
to seem to have suffered an injury rather than to have
been granted his life. Therefore be sure that you
9 will have to fight with those men for your life. There
are enemies enough left, in pursuit of whom we are
about to go ; guard yourself against domestic foes.
If you get rid of these, I fear nothing from without."
10 Thus spoke Craterus. And the rest did not doubt

71

coniurationis indicium suppressurus non fuisset nisi
auctor aut particeps. Quem enim pium et bonae
mentis, non amicum modo, sed ex ultima plebe, auditis
quae ad eum delata erant, non protinus ad regem
11 fuisse cursurum ? ne Cebalini quidem exemplo, qui
ex fratre comperta ipsi nuntiasset, commotum esse[1]
Parmenionis filium, praefectum equitatus, omnium
arcanorum regis arbitrum ! Simulasse etiam, non
vacasse sermoni suo regem, ne index alium internun-
12 tium quaereret. Nicomachum, religione quoque
deum astrictum, conscientiam suam exonerare pro-
perasse ; Philotam consumpto per ludum iocumque
paene toto die, gravatum esse pauca verba pertinentia
ad caput regis tam longo et forsitan supervacuo
13 inserere sermoni. At eum non credidisse[2] talia
deferentibus pueris ! Cur igitur extraxisset biduum,
tamquam indicio haberet fidem ? Dimittendum
14 fuisse Cebalinum, si delationem eius damnabat. In
suo quemque periculo magnum animum habere ;
cum de salute regis timeretur, credulos esse debere,
vana quoque deferentis admittere.
15 Omnes igitur quaestionem de eo, ut participes
sceleris indicare cogeretur, habendam esse decernunt.
Rex admonitos uti consilium silentio premerent di-
mittit. Pronuntiari deinde iter in posterum iubet,

[1] commotum esse *added by Hedicke; A omits.*
[2] eum non credidisse *Hedicke;* enim si non credidisset *C;*
enim non credidisse *P m. pr.*

---

[a] *Cf.* vi. 9. 21 ; Arr. iii. 11. 8 ; vi. 6. 1.
[b] With *conscientiam exonerare cf.* v. 13. 22, vi. 9. 9.

that Philotas would not have suppressed the evidence of the conspiracy, unless he had been its ringleader or a participant in it. For who, if a loyal man, and of good intention, not to say a friend, but even one of the lowest condition, on hearing what had been revealed to Philotas, would not at once have hastened
11 to the king ? To think that the son of Parmenion, as commander of the cavalry [a] a confidant of all the king's secrets, was not moved even by the example of Cebalinus, who had announced to him what he had learned from his brother ! That he also pretended that the king had no time to talk with him, for fear that the informer might seek another intermediary !
12 Nicomachus, even though bound by an oath to the gods, had hastened to unburden his conscience [b] ; Philotas, after spending the whole day in amusement and merriment, had found it difficult to find room, in so long and perhaps superfluous a talk, for a few words
13 relating to the life of his king ! But, he says, he did not believe mere boys who brought such information. Why then did he prolong the time for two days, as if he had faith in their testimony ? Cebalinus ought to have been dismissed, if Philotas rejected his in-
14 formation. In the time of his own danger every-one ought to have great courage ; when fears were felt for the safety of their king, they ought to be credulous and to listen even to those who bring false information.
15 All therefore decided that Philotas should be put to the torture, in order that he might be forced to name the participants in the crime. The king dis-missed them, after admonishing them to keep silent about his plans. Then he ordered a march to be announced for the following day, lest any indication

16 ne qua noxiis[1] initi consilii daretur nota. Invitatus
est etiam Philotas ad ultimas ipsi epulas, et rex non
cenare modo, sed etiam familiariter colloqui cum eo
17 quem damnaverat sustinuit. Secunda deinde vigilia,
luminibus extinctis, cum paucis in regiam coeunt
Hephaestio et Craterus et Coenus et Erigyius, hi
ex amicis, ex armigeris autem Perdiccas et Leonnatus.
Per hos imperatum ut qui ad[2] praetorium excubabant
18 armati vigilarent. Iam ad omnes aditus dispositi
erant equites, itinera quoque obsidere iussi, ne quis
ad Parmenionem, qui tum Mediae magnisque copiis
19 praeerat, occultus evaderet. Atarrhias[3] autem cum
ccc armatis intraverat regiam ; huic decem satellites
adduntur,[4] quorum singulos deni armigeri sequeban-
20 tur. Hi ad alios coniuratos comprehendendos dis-
tributi sunt, Atarrhias cum trecentis ad Philotam
missus, clausum aditum domus moliebatur, l iuvenum
promptissimis stipatus ; nam ceteros cingere undique
domum iusserat, ne occulto aditu Philotas posset elabi.
21 Illum sive securitate animi sive fatigatione resolutum
somnus oppresserat ; quem Atarrhias torpentem
22 adhuc occupat. Tandem ei sopore discusso cum
inicerentur catenae : " Vicit," inquit, " bonitatem
tuam, rex, inimicorum meorum acerbitas." Nec
plura elocutum capite velato in regiam adducunt.

---

[1] noxiis *Jeep;* noni *A.* [2] ad *added by I.*
[3] Atarrhias *Hedicke;* atarras *A.*
[4] adduntur *Hedicke;* traduntur *A.*

---

[a] There is confusion between *armigeri* and *satellites* ; the
latter is used of the body-guard in iii. 12. 10, both together
in iv. 7. 21.

[b] *Moliebatur* both in verb and tense implies effort ; *cf.*
iv. 7. 7 ; viii. 10. 30.

of the decisions entered on should be given to
16 the guilty parties. Philotas was even invited to a
banquet, which was his last, and the king had the
heart, not only to dine with him, but even to talk
familiarly with the man whom he had condemned.
17 Then in the second watch, when the lights had been
put out, there came to the king's tent, with a few
others, Hephaestion, Craterus, Coenus, and Erigyius,
these from the number of his friends, and from the
body-guard Perdiccas and Leonnatus. By these it was
ordered that those who were on guard at the king's
18 tent should remain on watch and under arms. Already
cavalry had been stationed at all the entrances, and
they had been ordered also to beset the roads, in
order that no one might secretly go out to Parmenion,
who was then governing Media and was in command
19 of great forces. Atarrhias, moreover, with 300 armed
men had entered the royal tent ; to him were given
besides ten attendants,[a] each followed by ten men-
20 at-arms. These were sent in different directions to
arrest the other conspirators. Atarrhias was sent
with 300 men to Philotas and set about breaking
open [b] the closed entrance to his house, attended by
fifty of the bravest of his soldiers; for he had ordered
the rest to surround the house on all sides, for fear
that Philotas might be able to slip out by a secret
21 door. But he, either through absence of anxiety or
worn out by fatigue, had been overcome by sleep :
Atarrhias seized him while he was still drowsy.
22 When at last he was fully awake and chains were put
upon him, he said : " O Sire, the bitterness of my
enemies has prevailed over your kindness." And
without further words on his part they led him with
veiled head into the king's quarters.

23 Postero die rex edixit omnes armati coirent. vi
milia fere militum venerant, praeterea turba lixarum
24 calonumque impleverant regiam. Philotan armigeri
agmine suo tegebant, ne ante conspici posset a vulgo
25 quam rex allocutus milites esset. De capitalibus
rebus vetusto Macedonum modo inquirebat rex,
iudicabat[1] exercitus—in pace erat vulgi—, et nihil
potestas regum valebat, nisi prius valuisset auctoritas.
26 Igitur Dymni primum cadaver infertur, plerisque
quid parasset quove casu extinctus esset ignaris.
IX. Rex deinde in contionem procedit vultu praeferens dolorem animi. Amicorum quoque maestitia
2 expectationem haud parvam rei[2] fecerat. Diu rex
demisso in terram vultu, attonito stupentique similis
stetit. Tandem recepto animo :

" Paene," inquit, " milites, hominum scelere vobis
ereptus sum ; deum providentia et misericordia vivo.
Conspectusque vestri venerabilis coegit,[3] ut vehementius parricidis irascerer, quoniam is primus,[4]
immo unus vitae meae fructus est, tot fortissimis viris
et de me optime meritis referre adhuc gratiam posse."
3 Interrupit orationem militum gemitus, obortaeque
sunt omnibus lacrimae. Tum rex :

" Quanto," inquit, " maiorem in animis vestris
motum excitabo, cum tanti sceleris auctores osten-

---

[1] rex, iudicabat *added by Hedicke; A omits.*
[2] rei *I;* ei *A.*
[3] coegit *J. Froben;* cogit *FBL;* coget *V (P omits).*
[4] is primus *G. Hermann;* spiritus *A.*

23 On the following day the king made proclamation that all should assemble under arms. About 6000 soldiers had come, besides these a crowd of camp-servants and batmen had filled the royal quarters.
24 The men-at-arms covered Philotas with their troop, in order that he might not be seen by the general
25 throng until the king had addressed the soldiers. In accordance with the ancient custom of the Macedonians, the king conducted the inquiry into criminal cases, and the army passed judgement—in time of peace it was a duty of the common people—and the power of the king availed nothing, unless his influence
26 had earlier had weight with them. Accordingly, the corpse of Dymnus was first brought in, the greater number being ignorant what he had attempted or by what chance he had been killed. IX. After this the king entered the assembly, manifesting his sorrow by his expression. The sadness of his friends also caused
2 no slight expectation of what was to take place. For a long time the king stood with his eyes fixed upon the ground, like one amazed and at a loss. At last, having recovered his spirits, he said :

"Almost, my soldiers, have I been wrested from you by the wickedness of certain men ; for it is by the providence and mercy of the gods that I still live. And the sight of your revered assembly has forced me to be more violently angry with the traitors, since the first, nay, the sole enjoyment of my life is to be able still to requite so many valiant men who have the
3 highest claim upon my gratitude." His speech was interrupted by the soldiers' lamentations, and tears sprang to the eyes of all. Then the king continued :

"How much greater emotion shall I rouse in your minds, when I reveal the authors of so great a crime !

77

dero! Quorum mentionem adhuc reformido et,
4 tamquam salvi esse possint, nominibus abstineo. Sed
vincenda est memoria pristinae caritatis et coniuratio
impiorum civium detegenda. Quomodo autem tantum nefas sileam? Parmenio, illa aetate, tot meis,
tot parentis mei meritis devinctus, omnium nobis
amicorum vetustissimus, ducem se sceleri tanto prae-
5 buit. Minister eius Philotas Peucolaum[1] et Demetrium et hunc Dymnum, cuius corpus aspicitis,
ceterosque eiusdem amentiae in caput meum subor-
6 navit." Fremitus undique indignantium querentium-
que tota contione obstrepebat, qualis solet esse
multitudinis et maxime militaris, ubi aut studio
7 agitur aut ira. Nicomachus deinde et Metron et
Cebalinus producti, quae quisque detulerat exponunt. Nullius eorum indicio Philotas ut[2] particeps sceleris destinabatur. Itaque, indignatione expressa,
vox invicem[3] silentio excepta est.
8 Tum rex: " Qualis," inquit, " ergo animi vobis
videtur, qui huius rei delatum indicium ad ipsum[4]
suppressit? Quod non fuisse vanum Dymni exitus
9 declarat. Incertam rem deferens tormenta non
timuit Cebalinus, nec Metron[5] ne momentum quidem
temporis distulit exonerare se, ut eo ubi lavabar
10 inrumperet; Philotas solus nihil timuit, nihil credidit.
O magni animi virum! Iste regis periculo commo-

---

[1] Peucolaum *J. Froben;* leucolaum *A.*
[2] ut *Bentley;* in *A.*   [3] invicem *Jeep;* indicium *A.*
[4] ad ipsum *Freinshem;* id ipsum *A.*
[5] nec Metron *added by Hedicke.*

---

[6] *Cf.* the same expression above, vi. 8. 12.

From the mention of these I still shrink, and I refrain from calling their names, as if they could be saved. 4 But I must overcome the memory of my former affection, and the conspiracy of impious citizens must be brought to light. For how can I be silent about such an abomination? Parmenion, old as he is, bound by so many favours of mine, so many of my father's, the eldest of all our friends, offered himself as the leader 5 in so great a crime. His tool, Philotas, has suborned against my life Peucolaüs, and Demetrius, and this Dymnus, whose body you see before you, and the 6 others infected by the same madness." On all sides cries of indignation and lament broke out in the whole assembly, such as are wont to be uttered by a multitude, and especially one of soldiers, when they 7 are moved by devotion or by anger. Then Nicomachus and Metron and Cebalinus were brought forward, and set forth what each of them had reported. By the testimony of none of these was Philotas designated as a participant in the crime. Therefore after forceful expression of indignation the rest of the speech was heard in silence.

8 The king continued : " What, then, seems to you to be the spirit of a man who suppressed the information which was brought to him about this matter— information which the death of Dymnus shows not 9 to have been unfounded ? Cebalinus, when reporting an uncertain matter did not fear torture, and Metron was so far from putting off even for a single moment the freeing *a* of his mind, that he even forced his way 10 into the place where I was bathing. Philotas alone had no fear, believed nothing. O the great courage of the man ! Would such a man be moved by the danger to his king, would he change countenance,

veretur, vultum mutaret, indicem tantae rei sollicitus
11 audiret! Subest nimirum silentio facinus, et avida
spes regni praecipitem animum ad ultimum nefas
impulit. Pater Mediae praeest ; ipse apud multos
copiarum duces meis praepotens viribus, maiora quam
12 capit spirat. Orbitas quoque mea, quod sine liberis
sum, spernitur. Sed errat Philotas. In vobis liberos,
parentes, consanguineos habeo ; vobis salvis orbus
13 esse non possum." Epistulam deinde Parmenionis
interceptam, quam ad filios Nicanorem et Philotan
scripserat, recitat, haud sane indicium gravioris con-
14 silii praeferentem. Namque summa eius haec erat :
" Primum vestri curam agite, deinde vestrorum ; sic
15 enim quae destinavimus efficiemus." Adiecitque rex
sic esse scriptam, ut, sive ad filios pervenisset, a
consciis posset intellegi, sive intercepta esset, falleret
ignaros.
16 " At enim Dymnus, cum ceteros participes sceleris
indicaret, Philotan non nominavit! Hoc quidem
illius non innocentiae, sed potentiae indicium est,
quod sic ab eis timetur etiam a quibus prodi potest,
ut, cum de se fateantur, illum tamen celent. Cete-
17 rum Philotan ipsius indicat vita. Hic Amyntae, qui
mihi consobrinus fuit et in Macedonia capiti meo
impias comparavit insidias, socium se et conscium
18 adiunxit. Hic Attalo, quo graviorem inimicum non

---

a On *summa cf.* vi. 4. 8, note.
b *Cf.* vi. 10. 24; he was the son of Perdiccas, brother
of Philip.

would he listen anxiously to the informer of so great
11 a matter ?   No doubt this silence conceals a purpose,
and the eager hope for royal power drove his mind
headlong to the worst of abominations.   His father
governs Media ; he himself, because of the great
power which through my influence he has with many
leaders of our forces, aspires to greater things than
12 are within his capabilities.   He scorns even my
bereavement, in that I have no children.   But Philotas is mistaken.   In you I have children, relatives,
kinsmen ; while you live, I cannot be without off-
13 spring."   Then he read an intercepted letter which
Parmenion had written to his sons Nicanor and
Philotas, which did not, it is true, furnish evidence of
14 any serious design.   For this was its substance[a] :
" First, look out for yourselves, then for yours ; for
thus we shall accomplish what we have planned."
15 And the king added that the letter was written in
such terms, in order that, if it should reach his sons,
it could be understood by their accomplices, or if it
should have been intercepted, it would deceive those
who knew nothing of the plot.   Then the king
continued :
16   " But, it may be said, Dymnus, when he revealed
the other participants in the crime, did not name
Philotas.   This, in fact, is a sign, not of his innocence,
but of his authority, because he was so feared even by
those by whom he could be betrayed, that when they
confessed their own guilt, they nevertheless did not
name him.   Furthermore, his own life shows the
17 character of Philotas.   He it was who, when Amyntas,
my own cousin,[b] in Macedonia made an impious plot
against my life, joined with him as an ally and an
18 accomplice.   He gave his sister in marriage to

81

habui, sororem suam in matrimonium dedit. Hic,
cum scripsissem ei pro iure tâm familiaris usus atque
amicitiae qualis sors edita esset Iovis Hammonis
oraculo, sustinuit rescribere mihi se quidem gratulari,
quod in numerum deorum receptus essem, ceterum
misereri eorum quibus vivendum esset sub eo qui
19 modum hominis excederet. Haec sunt et iam[1] pridem
animi alienati a me et invidentis gloriae meae indicia.
Quae equidem, milites, quamdiu licuit, in animo meo
pressi. Videbar enim mihi partem viscerum meorum
abrumpere, si in quos tam magna contuleram viliores
20 mihi facerem. Sed iam non verba punienda sunt ;
linguae temeritas pervenit ad gladios. Hos, si mihi
creditis, Philotas in me acuit, si ipsi, admisit.

    " Quo me conferam, milites ? cui caput meum
21 credam ? Equitatui, optimae exercitus parti, principibus nobilissimae iuventutis, eum[2] praefeci, salutem,
spem, victoriam meam fidei eius tutelaeque commisi.
22 Patrem in idem fastigium in quo me ipsi posuistis
admovi ; Mediam, qua nulla opulentior regio est, et tot
civium sociorumque milia imperio eius dicionique
subieci. Unde praesidium petieram, periculum ex-
23 stitit. Quam feliciter in acie occidissem, potius hostis
praeda quam civis victima ! Nunc servatus ex periculis quae sola timui, in haec incidi quae timere non

---

[1] et iam *Bentley:* etiam *A.*   [2] eum *Hedicke;* unum *A.*

[a] See Plut. *Alex.* ix. **4** ; Diod. xvii. 2. **3.**
[b] *Cf.* vi. 1. 17 for *modus* in this sense.
[e] See on vi. 6. 7 and *cf.* Arr. iii. 27. **4.**

Attalus,[a] than whom I had no more dangerous enemy. He, when I had written to him, by right of so close a familiarity and friendship, the nature of the reply which had been given by the oracle of Jupiter Ammon, had the impudence to reply that he for his part congratulated me that I had been received into the number of the gods, but that he pitied those who would have to live under one who rose above the

19 limitations [b] of a man. These are tokens of a mind which is both long since alienated from me and is also envious of my glory. These things, soldiers, so long as it was possible, I buried in my own thoughts. For it seemed to me that I was tearing away a part of my own flesh, if I should make those upon whom I had conferred such great favours more worthless in my

20 sight. But it is no longer mere words that must be punished; rashness of language has passed on to swords. These, if you believe me, Philotas has whetted against me, if you believe him, he has allowed it.

"Whither shall I turn, soldiers? to whom shall I

21 trust my life? I have put him in command of the cavalry,[c] the best part of my army, the elite of our noblest young men, I have entrusted to his loyalty

22 and protection my life, my hope, my victory. His father I have raised to the same high rank as that in which you have placed me. I have put under his command and sway Media, than which no region is richer, and so many thousands of citizens and allies. Where I had looked for protection danger has

23 arisen. How happily would I have fallen in battle, the prey of an enemy rather than the victim of a fellow-citizen! Now, saved from the only dangers which I feared, I have met with those which I ought not

83

24 debui. Soletis identidem a me, milites, petere ut
saluti meae parcam. Ipsi mihi praestare potestis,
quod suadetis ut faciam. Ad vestras manus, ad
vestra arma confugio ; invitis vobis salvus esse nolo,
volentibus non possum, nisi vindicor."

25   Tum Philotan, religatis post tergum manibus, ob-
soleto amiculo velatum iussit induci. Facile appare-
bat, motos esse tam miserabili habitu non sine invidia

26 paulo ante conspecti. Ducem equitatus pridie viderant, sciebant regis interfuisse convivio ; repente
reum quidem, sed iam[1] damnatum, immo vinctum

27 intuebantur. Subibat animos Parmenionis quoque,
tanti ducis, tam clari civis, fortuna, qui modo duobus
filiis, Hectore ac Nicanore, orbatus, cum eo quem
reliquum calamitas fecerat absens diceret causam.

28 Itaque Amyntas, regius praetor, inclinatam ad
misericordiam contionem rursus aspera in Philotan
oratione commovit : proditos eos esse barbaris ;
neminem ad coniugem suam in patriam et ad parentes
suos esse[2] rediturum, velut truncum corpus dempto
capite sine spiritu, sine nomine aliena terra ludi-

29 brium hostis futuros. Haudquaquam pro spe ipsius
Amyntae oratio grata regi fuit, quod coniugum,
quod patriae admonitos pigriores ad cetera munia
exsequenda fecisset.

30   Tum Coenus, quamquam Philotae sororem matri-

---

[1] iam *Jeep;* etiam *A.*   [2] suos esse *Hedicke;* fuisse *A.*

---

[a] Hence not *sine praeiudicio* ; *cf.* vii. 1. 20.
[b] See vii. 2. 33 ; vi. 8. 7.   [c] See iv. 8. 7, vi. 6. 18.

24 to have feared. You are wont, soldiers, ever and anon
to ask me to be careful of my life. You yourselves
can furnish me with the means of doing what you
advise. To your hands, to your weapons I flee for refuge ; I do not wish to be safe, if you do not wish it,
if you do wish it, I cannot be unless I am avenged."

25 Then he ordered Philotas to be brought in with his
hands bound behind his back and his head veiled in
a worn-out cloak. It was readily apparent that
men were touched by the wretched plight of one
who shortly before had been looked upon with envy.

26 The day before they had seen him the commander
of the cavalry, they knew that he had been present
at a banquet with the king ; suddenly they beheld
him on trial, it is true, but already condemned, nay,

27 even in bonds.[a] There entered their minds also the
ill-fortune of Parmenion, so great a general,[b] so
distinguished a citizen, who, recently bereft of two
sons, Hector and Nicanor,[c] would, though absent,
make his plea along with the only son whom

28 calamity had left him. Accordingly Amyntas, one
of the king's generals, again aroused the assembly,
which was inclined towards pity, by a harsh speech
against Philotas, saying that they had been betrayed
to the barbarians, that no one would return to his
wife, to his native land, to his parents, but that like
a body bereft of its head, without life, without name,
in a foreign land they would be the sport of their

29 enemies. The speech of Amyntas was by no means
so pleasing to the king as the author of it had hoped,
since by having reminded them of their wives and of
their native land he had made them less alert for
performing the tasks which remained.

30 Then Coenus, although he had joined Philotas'

monio secum coniunxerat, tamen acrius quam quisquam in Philotan invectus est, parricidam esse regis,
31 patriae, exercitus clamitans, saxumque, quod forte
ante pedes iacebat, corripuit[1] emissurus in eum, ut
plerique crediderunt, tormentis subtrahere cupiens.
Sed rex manum eius inhibuit dicendae prius causae
debere fieri potestatem reo nec aliter iudicari pas-
32 surum se affirmans. Tum dicere iussus[2] Philotas,
sive conscientia sceleris sive periculi magnitudine
amens et attonitus, non attollere oculos, non hiscere
33 audebat. Lacrimis deinde manantibus, linquente
animo in eum a quo tenebatur incubuit; abstersisque
amiculo eius oculis, paulatim recipiens spiritum ac
34 vocem, dicturus videbatur. Iamque rex intuens
eum : " Macedones," inquit, " de te iudicaturi sunt ;
quaero, an patrio sermone sis apud eos usurus."
35 Tum Philotas : " Praeter Macedonas," inquit,
" plerique adsunt, quos facilius quae dicam percep-
turos arbitror, si eadem lingua fuero usus qua tu
egisti, non ob aliud, credo, quam ut oratio tua intel-
36 legi posset a pluribus." Tum rex : " Ecquid videtis
adeo etiam sermonis patrii Philotan taedere ? Solus
quippe fastidit eum discere. Sed dicat sane utcumque ei cordi est, dum memineritis aeque illum a

---

[1] corripuit *I;* eripuit *A.*
[2] iussus *Modius;* rursus *P;* orsus *C.*

---

[a] For *attollere oculos* and *hiscere* together *cf.* Livy vi. 16.
3 ; for *hiscere* Livy xxxix. 12. 5, Amm. xxiii. 6. 80.
[b] Even in the time of Alexander Macedonian was not
understood by the Greeks, if Curtius is to be trusted.

sister to himself in marriage, inveighed against him
more savagely than anyone else, shouting that he
31 was a traitor to king, to country, to the army, and
catching up a stone which chanced to be lying at his
feet, he was on the point of hurling it at him, as many
thought because he desired to save him from torture.
But the king stayed his hand, declaring that the
accused ought to be given the opportunity of first
pleading his cause, and that otherwise he would not
32 allow him to be judged. Then Philotas, when
ordered to speak, either through consciousness of
guilt or beside himself and thunderstruck by the
greatness of his peril, did not venture to lift his eyes
33 or to open his mouth.[a] Then, with a flood of tears, he
swooned and fell into the arms of the man who was
holding him ; and when his eyes had been dried with
the cloak which he was wearing, he gradually recovered his breath and his voice and seemed about to
34 speak. And now the king, looking intently at him,
said : " The Macedonians are about to pass judgement upon you ; I wish to know whether you will use
their native tongue [b] in addressing them." There-
35 upon Philotas replied : " Besides the Macedonians
there are many present who, I think, will more easily
understand what I shall say if I use the same language
which you have employed,[c] for no other reason, I
suppose, than in order that your speech might be
36 understood by the greater number." Then said the
king : " Do you not see how Philotas loathes even
the language of his fatherland ? For he alone disdains to learn it. But let him by all means speak in
whatever way he desires, provided that you remember
that he holds our customs in as much abhorrence as

[c] The Greek κοινή.

87

nostro more quam sermone abhorrere." Atque ita
contione excessit.

X. Tum Philotas : " Verba," inquit, " innocenti
reperire facile est, modum verborum misero tenere
2 difficile. Itaque, inter optimam conscientiam et
iniquissimam fortunam destitutus, ignoro quomodo
3 et animo meo et tempori pareo. Abest quidem
optimus causae meae iudex ; qui cur me ipse audire
noluerit non, mehercule, excogito, cum illi, utrimque
cognita causa, tam damnare me liceat quam absol-
vere, non cognita vero, liberari absenti[1] non possum
4 qui a praesente damnatus sum. Sed quamquam
vincti hominis non supervacua solum sed etiam
invisa defensio est, qui iudicem non docere videtur,
sed arguere, tamen, utcumque licet me dicere, memet
ipse non deseram nec committam, ut damnatus etiam
5 mea sententia videar. Equidem, cuius criminis reus
sim non video ; inter coniuratos nemo me nominat,
de me Nicomachus nihil dixit, Cebalinus plus quam
6 audierat scire non potuit. Atqui coniurationis caput
me fuisse[2] credit rex ! Potuit ergo Dymnus eum
praeterire quem sequebatur, praesertim cum quaerenti socios vel falso fuerim nominandus, quo facilius
7 qui temptabatur posset impelli ? Non enim detecto
facinore nomen meum praeteriit, ut possit videri
socio pepercisse ; Nicomacho,[3] quem taciturum ar-

---

[1] absenti *Hedicke;* absente *A.*   [2] fuisse *I;* fecisse *A.*
[3] Nicomacho *Acidalius;* nicomachus *P;* nichomachus *C.*

---

[a] This, like other things in Curtius, is unfair to Philotas.
[b] *Ex-* is intensive ; *cf. exputo* in Cic. *Ad Fam.* x. 24. 6.
[c] See vi. 7. 14-15.

our language." [a] And with these words he left the assembly.

X. Then Philotas said : " It is easy for an innocent man to find words, it is difficult for a wretched man to
2 keep his words within bounds. Therefore, abandoned between the best of consciences and the most unfavourable of fortunes, I do not know how to suit what I shall say both to my feelings and to the situa-
3 tion. In fact, the best judge of my cause is not present; why he should not wish to hear me himself, I cannot, by Heaven ! imagine,[b] since after having heard both sides of the case, he can as readily condemn me as acquit me, but if he has not heard both sides, I cannot be acquitted in his absence since I
4 was condemned by him when he was present. But although the defence of a man in fetters is not only superfluous but also odious, since he seems not to inform the judge but to accuse him, nevertheless, in whatever manner I am allowed to speak, I shall not myself fail, nor let myself seem to have been con-
5 demned by my own voice as well. For my part, I do not see with what crime I am charged; no one among the conspirators names me, Nicomachus said nothing about me, Cebalinus could not know more than he
6 had heard. And yet the king believes me to have been the head of the conspiracy ! Could Dymnus then fail to mention the one whose follower he was, especially when I ought to have been named, even falsely, to Nicomachus, who asked [c] who were his associates, in order that the man who was being
7 tempted might be more easily persuaded ? For when the crime was disclosed, he did not leave out my name in order that he might seem to have spared an associate; for when he confessed to Nicomachus, who he

cana de semetipso credebat, confessus, aliis nominatis
8 me unum subtrahebat.   Quaeso, commilitones, si
Cebalinus me non adisset, nihil me de coniuratis scire
voluisset, num hodie dicerem causam, nullo me nomi-
9 nante ?   Dymnus sane ut[1] vivat[2] adhuc et velit[3]
mihi parcere, quid ceteri ?   Qui de se confitebuntur,
me videlicet subtrahent !   Maligna est calamitas, et
fere noxius, cum suo supplicio crucietur, acquiescit
10 alieno.   Tot conscii ne in eculeum quidem impositi
verum fatebuntur ?   Atqui nemo parcit morituro nec
cuiquam moriturus, ut opinor.

11   "Ad verum crimen et ad unum revertendum mihi
est ; ' cur rem delatam ad te tacuisti ? cur tam securus
audisti ? '   Hoc, qualecumque est, confesso mihi, ubicumque es, Alexander, remisisti ; dexteram tuam
amplexus, reconciliati pignus animi, convivio quoque
12 interfui.   Si credidisti mihi, absolutus sum, si peper-
cisti, dimissus : vel iudicium tuum serva.   Quid hac
proxima nocte, qua digressus sum a mensa tua, feci ?
quod novum facinus delatum ad te mutavit animum
13 tuum ?   Gravi sopore acquiescebam, cum me malis
indormientem mei[4] inimici vinciendo excitaverunt.
Unde et parricidae et prodito[5] tam alti quies somni ?
14 Scelerati conscientia obstrepente condormire[6] non
possunt ; agitant eos Furiae cogitato[7] modo, nedum[8]

---

[1] ut *Jeep;* et *A.*
[2] vivat *Aldus;* uiuet *P m. pr.;* uiueret *C.*
[3] velit *Aldus;* uelut *A.*   [4] mei *Hedicke;* meis *A.*
[5] prodito *Acidalius;* proditori *A.*
[6] condormire *Modius;* comdormire *P m. pr.;* cum dor-
mire *C.*   [7] non cogitato *A;* non *deleted by Hedicke.*
[8] nedum *Hedicke;* sed etiam *A.*

believed would keep in silence the secrets about him-
8 self, having named others, me alone he left out. Pray,
fellow-soldiers, if Cebalinus had not come to me, if
he had wished me to know nothing about the conspirators, would I to-day be pleading my cause, when
9 no one named me? Suppose that Dymnus were still
alive and wished to spare me, what of the rest?
Those who will confess their own guilt will of course
be silent about me! Calamity is malign, and as a
rule a guilty person, when suffering his own torture,
10 assents to that of another. Will so many accomplices not confess the truth even when placed upon
the rack? And yet no one spares one who is about
to die, and in my opinion one who is about to die
spares no one.

11   "I must return to the real and only accusation
against me: 'Why did you keep silence about the
matter which was reported to you? why did you
hear it with so little concern?' This, such as it is,
you, Alexander, wherever you are, pardoned when I
confessed it; grasping your right hand, as a pledge
of restored friendship, I even was present at your
12 banquet. If you believed me, I was acquitted, if you
spared me, I was dismissed; pray abide by your decision. What have I done during this last night, when
I left your table? what new crime has been reported
13 to you and changed your mind? I was resting in
heavy sleep, when, as I had fallen asleep over my misfortunes, my enemies awakened me by binding me.
Whence did such deep sleep come to a traitor and
14 one who had been betrayed? The wicked cannot
sleep soundly because of the clamours of conscience;
the Furies torment them when their treason is merely
planned, much more when it has been accom-

consummato parricidio. At mihi securitatem primum innocentia mea, deinde tua dextera obtulerat ;
non timui, ne plus alienae crudelitati apud te liceret
15 quam clementiae tuae. Sed ne te mihi credidisse
paeniteat, res ad me deferebatur a puero, qui non
testem, non pignus indicii exhibere poterat, imple-
16 turus omnes metu, si coepisset audiri. Amatoris et
scorti iurgio interponi aures meas credidi infelix,
et fidem eius suspectam habui, quod non ipse deferret
17 sed fratrem potius subornaret. Timui ne negaret
mandasse se Cebalino et ego viderer multis amicorum
18 regis fuisse periculi causa. Sic quoque, cum laeserim
neminem, inveni qui mallet perire me quam incolumem esse ; quid inimicitiarum creditis excepturum
19 fuisse, si insontes lacessissem ? At enim Dymnus se
occidit ! Num igitur facturum eum divinare potui ?
Minime. Ita, quod solum indicio fidem fecit, id me,
cum a Cebalino interpellatus sum, movere non poterat.
20 At hercules, si conscius Dymno tanti sceleris fuissem,
biduo illo proditos esse nos dissimulare non debui ;
Cebalinus ipse tolli de medio nulloque negotio potuit.
21 Denique post delatum indicium quod operturus[1]
eram, cubiculum regis solus intravi, ferro quidem
cinctus. Cur distuli facinus ? An sine Dymno non
22 sum ausus ? Ille igitur princeps coniurationis fuit,

[1] quod operturus *Jeep;* operiturus *FP m. pr.;* opperitu-
rus *BLV.*

92

plished. But to me, first my blamelessness, then your right hand, had brought freedom from care ; I had no fear that more would be allowed on your part 15 to the cruelty of others than to your clemency. But to prevent you from regretting your belief in me, let me say that the matter was reported to me by a mere boy, who could show me no witness nor proof of his information, and who would fill all with fear if he should begin to be heard. Unhappily I believed that my ears had 16 been exposed to a quarrel of a wanton and his boy, and besides I suspected his truthfulness because he did not himself bring the report, but employed his 17 brother instead. I feared lest he should deny having given instructions to Cebalinus, and I should seem to have been the cause of danger to many of the king's 18 friends. Even as it is, although I have injured no one, I have found one who preferred that I should perish rather than be unharmed ; what enmities do you think I should have incurred, if I had attacked blameless 19 persons ? But, you will say, Dymnus killed himself ! Could I have divined that he would do so ? Certainly not. Hence the only thing which has given assurance to this information could not influence me when I was 20 accosted by Cebalinus. But, by Heaven, if I had been an accomplice with Dymnus in so great a crime, I ought not to have concealed for those two days my knowledge that we had been betrayed ; Cebalinus himself could have been put out of the 21 way, and with no trouble. Finally, after the information which I was going to conceal had been made known, I entered the king's bedroom alone, and wearing a sword. Why did I put off the deed ? Was 22 it that I did not dare to do it without Dymnus ? He then was the leader of the conspiracy and I, Philotas,

sub illius umbra Philotas latebam, qui regnum Macedonum affecto ! Ecquis e vobis corruptus est donis ? Quem ducem, quem praefectum impensius colui ?

23 " Mihi quidem obicitur quod societatem patrii sermonis asperner, quod Macedonum mores fastidiam. Sic ego imperio quod dedignor, immineo ! Iam pridem nativus ille sermo commercio aliarum gentium exolevit ; tam victoribus, quam victis peregrina

24 lingua discenda est. Non, mehercule, ista me magis laedunt, quam quod Amyntas, Perdiccae filius, insidiatus est regi. Cum quo quod amicitia fuerit mihi, non recuso defendere, si fratrem regis non oportuit

25 diligi a nobis. Sin autem in illo fortunae gradu positum etiam venerari necesse erat, utrum, quaeso, quod non divinavi, reus sum, an impiorum amicis insontibus quoque moriendum est ? Quod si aequum est, cur tam diu vivo ? si iniustum, cur nunc tamen[1]

26 occidor ? At enim scripsi misereri me eorum quibus vivendum esset sub eo qui se Iovis filium crederet. Fides amicitiae, veri consilii periculosa libertas, vos me[2] decepistis ! vos quae sentiebam ne reticerem,

27 impulistis ! Scripsisse me haec fateor regi, non de rege scripsisse.[3] Non enim faciebam invidiam, sed pro eo timebam. Dignior mihi Alexander videbatur, qui Iovis stirpem tacitus agnosceret quam qui

28 praedicatione iactaret. Sed quoniam oraculi fides certa est, sit deus causae meae testis ; retinete me

---

[1] tamen *Eberhard;* demum *A.*
[2] vos me *I;* me *A.*   [3] scripsisse *deleted by Aldus.*

---

[a] Used freely of a cousin, see vi. 9. 17.
[b] That is, it was not criticism, but advice, as explained in the next sentence.

who aspire to the throne of Macedonia was lurking
under his shadow ! Has anyone of you been bribed
by gifts ? To what general, to what prefect did I
show too marked attention ?

23   " It is even charged against me that I scorn association with my native language, that I disdain the
customs of the Macedonians. So then I aspire to the
rule of something which I hold in contempt. It is
long ago that that native tongue has gone out of use
through intercourse with other nations ; a foreign
language has to be learned as well by the victors as by

24 the vanquished. Those charges, by Heaven ! are no
more injurious to me than it is that Amyntas, son of
Perdiccas, plotted against the king. The charge that
I was on friendly terms with him I do not refuse
to meet, provided it was our duty not to love the king's

25 brother.[a] But if it was necessary even to venerate
one in that lofty position, am I, pray, guilty because
I did not have the power of divination, or must the
innocent friends of guilty men also die ? But if that
is just, why have I lived so long ? if unjust, why am

26 I nevertheless to die now ? But, it may be said, I
also wrote that I pitied those who had to live under
a man who believed himself the son of Jupiter.
O loyalty to friendship, O dangerous freedom in
giving true counsel, it is you that played me false ! It
was you that impelled me not to keep silent about

27 what I thought. I confess that I wrote this to
the king, but not about the king.[b] For I did not
seek to rouse ill-will against him, but I feared for
him. It seemed to me more worthy of Alexander
to recognize in silence the parentage of Jupiter, than

28 to boast of it publicly. But since the truth of the
oracle is sure, let the god bear witness in my case ;

in vinculis, dum consulitur Hammo, num[1] arcanum et
occultum scelus inierim.[2] Qui regem nostrum dignatus est filium, neminem eorum qui stirpi suae insidi-
29 ati sunt latere patietur. Si certiora oraculis creditis
esse tormenta, ne hanc quidem exhibendae veritatis
fidem deprecor.

30 "Solent rei capitis adhibere vobis parentes. Duos
fratres ego nuper amisi, patrem nec ostendere possum
nec invocare audeo, cum et ipse tanti criminis reus
31 sit. Parum est enim tot modo liberum parentem, in
unico filio acquiescentem, eo quoque orbari, nisi ipse
32 in rogum meum imponitur. Ergo, carissime pater, et
propter me morieris et mecum; ego tibi vitam adimo,
ego senectutem tuam exstinguo. Quid enim me
procreabas infelicem adversantibus diis ? an, ut hos
33 ex me fructus perciperes, qui te manent ? Nescio,
adulescentia mea miserior sit an senectus tua ; ego
in ipso robore aetatis eripior, tibi carnifex spiritum
adimet, quem, si fortuna expectare voluisset, natura
34 poscebat.   Admonuit me patris mei mentio quam
timide et cunctanter quae Cebalinus detulerat ad me
indicare debuerim. Parmenio enim cum audisset
venenum a Philippo medico regi parari, deterrere
eum voluit epistula scripta, quo minus medicamentum
35 biberet quod medicus dare constitueret. Num creditum est patri meo ? num ullam auctoritatem eius
litterae habuerunt ? Ego ipse quotiens quae audie-

[1] Hammo, num *Hedicke;* ammodum *A.*
[2] inierim *Jeep;* interim *A.*

[a] *Cf.* vi. 11. 23 *qui Philippum dedignatur patrem,* vi. 11. 5
Alexandrum filium agnoscentis; Virg. *Aen.* iv. 536.
[b] See iii. 6. 4.

keep me in fetters while Hammon is asked whether
I planned a secret and hidden crime. He who has
recognized[a] our king as son will not suffer those
who have plotted against his stock to be concealed.
29 If you believe tortures to be more trustworthy than
oracles, I do not refuse even that testimony for bringing the truth to light.

30   " Those who are charged with a capital offence are
accustomed to bring their relatives before you. I
have recently lost two brothers, my father I cannot
bring before you, nor do I dare to appeal to him, since
31 he himself is accused of this great crime. For it is
not enough that he who was lately the father of so
many sons, and now takes comfort in but one, should
be bereft of him too, unless he himself is placed upon
32 my funeral pyre. Therefore, dearest father, you will
die both because of me and with me ; it is I who am
taking your life from you, I who am extinguishing you
in your old age. Why, pray, did you beget unhappy
me under adverse gods ? Was it that you might reap
33 from me these fruits which await you ? I know not
whether my youth or your old age is the more
wretched. I am taken off in the very flower of my
strength, from you the executioner will take the life
which, if Fortune had been willing to wait, Nature
34 was demanding. The mention of my father has
reminded me how timidly and hesitatingly I ought to
have revealed what Cebalinus had reported to me.
For Parmenion, when he had heard that poison was
being prepared for the king by his physician Philip,[b]
wrote him a letter and tried to prevent him from
drinking the potion which the physician had decided
35 to give him. Was my father believed ? His letter
had no weight, had it ? As for myself, how often

ram detuli et cum ludibrio credulitatis repulsus sum !
Si et, cum indicamus, invisi et, cum tacemus, suspecti
36 sumus, quid facere nos oportet ? "   Cumque unus e
circumstantium turba exclamasset : " Bene meritis
non insidiari ! "   Philotas : " Recte," inquit, " quis-
37 quis es, dicis.   Itaque si insidiatus sum, poenam non
deprecor et finem facio dicendi, quoniam ultima verba
gravia sunt visa auribus."   Abducitur deinde ab eis
qui custodiebant eum.

XI.   Erat inter duces manu strenuus Bolon quidam,
pacis artium et civilis habitus rudis, vetus miles, ab
humili ordine ad eum gradum in quo tunc erat
2 promotus ;   qui tacentibus ceteris stolida audacia
ferox admonere eos coepit, quotiens suis quisque
deversoriis quae occupassent proturbatus esset ut
purgamenta servorum Philotae reciperentur eo, unde
3 commilitones expulissent.   Auro argentoque vehicula
eius onusta totis vicis stetisse, ac[1] ne in viciniam
quidem deversorii[2] quemquam commilitonum receptum esse, sed per dispositos quos supra somnum
habebat, omnis procul relegatos, ne femina illa murmurantium inter se silentio verius quam sono ex-
4 citaretur.   Ludibrio ei fuisse rusticos homines,
Phrygasque et Paphlagonas appellatos, qui non
erubesceret, Macedo natus, homines linguae suae

---

[1] ac *Freinshem;* at *A.*
[2] deversorii *Hedicke;* diuersorii *A.*

---

[a] An example of the speaker's *stolida audacia,*=" that
coward."
[b] Races who provided many slaves;   *cf.* Aristophanes'
appellation of Cleon as ὁ Παφλαγών in the *Knights.*

have I reported what I had heard and been repulsed
with mockery of my credulity ! If we are both disliked when we report anything, and suspected when
36 we keep silence, what are we to do ? " And when
one of the throng of bystanders had exclaimed " not
plot against your benefactors ! ", Philotas replied :
37 " You speak rightly, whoever you are. Hence, if I
have so plotted, I do not beg for immunity from
punishment, and I make an end of speaking, since
my last words have seemed to displease your ears."
Philotas was then led away by the men who were
guarding him.

XI. There was among the generals one Bolon,
valiant in deeds of arms, but unacquainted with the
arts of peace and with civil manners, an old soldier,
who had risen from a humble rank to the position
2 which he then held ; he, when the rest were silent,
rudely and with coarse audacity began to remind
them how often they had been put out of the quarters
which they had occupied in order that the off-
scourings of Philotas' slaves might be received in the
places from which they had driven out his fellow-
3 soldiers. That his wagons laden with gold and silver
had stood in whole sections of the city, and that not
one of his fellow-soldiers was admitted even to the
neighbourhood of his lodging, but they were all
removed to a distance by those whom he had placed
in their positions to watch over his sleep, lest that
she-man *a* might be disturbed by what is more truly
described as the silence than the sound of those who
4 whispered together. That the rustic men had always
been objects of his mockery, and were called Phry-
gians and Paphlagonians *b* by one who, though born
a Macedonian, did not blush that men of his own

99

5 per interpretem audire. Nunc eum[1] Hammonem
consuli velle ; at[2] eundem Iovis arguisse mendacium
Alexandrum filium agnoscentis, scilicet veritum ne
6 invidiosum esset quod dii offerrent. Cum insidiaretur
capiti regis et amici, non consuluisse eum Iovem ;
nunc ad oraculum mittere, dum pater eius sollicitet
quibus[3] praesit in Media, et pecunia cuius custodia
commissa sit perditos homines ad societatem sceleris
7 impellat. Ipsos missuros ad oraculum, non qui
Iovem interrogent[4] quod ex rege cognoverint, sed qui
gratias agant, qui vota pro incolumitate regis optimi
persolvant.

8   Tum vero universa contio accensa est, et a corporis
custodibus initium factum, clamantibus discerpendum
esse parricidam manibus eorum.   Id quidem Philotas,
qui graviora supplicia metueret, haud sane iniquo
9 animo audiebat ; at[5] rex in contionem reversus, sive
ut in custodia quoque torqueret, sive ut diligentius
cuncta cognosceret, concilium in posterum diem distulit et, quamquam in vesperam inclinabat dies,
10 tamen amicos convocari iubet. Et ceteris quidem
placebat, Macedonum more obrui saxis, Hephaestio[6]
autem et Craterus et Coenus tormentis veritatem

[1] Nunc eum *Bentley;* mecum *L m. pr. P;* necum *BFL
m. sec. V.*
[2] velle ; at *Hedicke;* uellet *A.*
[3] sollicitet quibus *Hedicke;* sollicitet qui *P;* sollicitetur
qui *C.*
[4] non qui Iovem interrogent *Giunta;* qui Iovem interrogent non *C;* qui Iovem interrogent *P.*
[5] at *added by Freinshem.*
[6] Hephaestio *Hedicke;* ephestio *A* (euphestio *B m. pr.*).
100

language heard his words through an interpreter.
5 Now he wished Hammon to be consulted ; but that
same man accused Jupiter of lying when he acknowledged Alexander as his son, fearing, forsooth, lest
what the gods offered should be an object of envy !
6 When he was plotting against the life of his king and
his friend, he did not consult Jupiter ; now he would
send to the oracle, in order that in the meantime his
father may arouse those whom he governs in Media,
and with the money entrusted to his charge may
7 induce abandoned men to share in his crime. They
themselves would send to the oracle, not to ask
Jupiter what they had learned from the king, but to
thank him, and pay the vows which they had made
for the safety of the best of kings.
8   Then truly the whole assembly was inflamed, and
a beginning was made by the body-guards, who
shouted that the traitor ought to be torn to pieces by
their own hands. This indeed Philotas, who feared
severer tortures, heard by no means reluctantly ;
9 but the king, having returned to the assembly,
either that he might also [a] torture him in prison, or
that he might investigate the whole matter more
carefully, adjourned the council to the following day,
and although the time was approaching evening, he
nevertheless ordered his friends to be called together.
10 And the rest for their part recommended that Philotas
be stoned to death, according to the ancient custom
of the Macedonians, but Hephaestion and Craterus
and Coenus said [b] that the truth ought to be forced

---

[a] *Quoque* refers to the following word, which is unusual
in Curtius ; but *cf.* however vi. 6. 5 ; iv. 10. 15.
[b] The plural verb shows unanimity and throws doubt on
Coenus' purpose suggested in vi. 9. 31.

exprimendam esse dixerunt ; et illi quoque qui aliud
11 suaserant in horum sententiam transeunt. Consilio
ergo dimisso, Hephaestio cum Cratero et Coeno ad
12 quaestionem de Philota habendam consurgunt. Rex
Cratero accersito et sermone habito, cuius summa
non edita est, in intimam deversorii partem secessit
et remotis arbitris in multam noctem quaestionis
expectavit eventum.

13   Tortores in conspectum Philotae omnia crudelitatis
14 instrumenta proponunt. Et ille ultro : " Quid
cessatis," inquit, " regis inimicum, interfectorem
confitentem occidere ? Quid quaestione opus est ?
cogitavi, volui." Craterus exigere, ut, quae con-
15 fiteretur, in tormentis quoque diceret. Tum[1] cor-
ripitur et, dum obligantur oculi, dum vestis exuitur,
deos patrios, gentium iura nequiquam apud surdas
aures invocabat. Per ultimos deinde cruciatus,
utpote et damnatus et inimicis in gratiam regis tor-
16 quentibus, laceratur. Ac primo, quamquam hinc
ignis, illinc verbera iam non ad quaestionem, sed ad
poenam ingerebantur, non vocem modo, sed etiam
17 gemitus habuit in potestate ; sed postquam intumescens corpus ulceribus flagellorum ictus nudis ossibus
incussos ferre non poterat, si tormentis adhibituri
modum essent, dicturum se quae scire expeterent
18 pollicetur. Sed finem quaestioni fore iurare eos per
Alexandri salutem volebat removerique tortores. Et

[1] tum P; dum C.

_____

[a] Apparently used without reference to any particular law.

102

from him by torments; and those also who had recommended the other course went over to their
11 opinion. Therefore the council was dismissed, and Hephaestion with Craterus and Coenus arose to put
12 Philotas to the question. The king, having summoned Craterus and had a talk with him, the subject of which has not been made public, withdrew into the inner part of his quarters, and dismissing all witnesses awaited until late at night the result of the inquisition.
13   The torturers laid out all their instruments of
14 cruelty before the eyes of Philotas. And he, of his own accord, said: "Why do you delay to kill the king's enemy, the murderer who confesses that he wished to kill him? What is the need of an inquisition? I planned it, I wished it." Craterus demanded that what he confessed he should also say under torture.
15 Then he was seized, and while his eyes were being bound, while his clothing was being taken off, he called upon his country's gods and on the law of nations,[a] but vainly to deaf ears. Then he was torn by the utmost torments, inasmuch as he had been condemned and his personal enemies were torturing
16 him to gratify the king. And at first, although now fire, and now the lash was used upon him, no longer for the purpose of seeking the truth, but as a punishment, he kept not only words but even groans under
17 control; but when his body, swollen with wounds, could no longer endure the blows of the scourges upon his bare bones, he promised that if they would moderate his tortures, he would tell them what they
18 wished to know. But he wished them to swear by Alexander's life that there would be an end to the torments, and the torturers removed. And when

103

utroque impetrato : " Cratere,"[1] inquit, " dic quid
19 me velis dicere." Illo indignante ludificari eum
rursusque revocante tortores tempus petere coepit
dum reciperet spiritum, cuncta quae sciret indica-
20 turus. Interim equites, nobilissimus quisque et ii
maxime qui Parmenionem propinqua cognatione
contingebant, postquam Philotan torqueri fama vulgaverat, legem Macedonum veriti, qua cautum erat
ut propinqui eorum qui regi insidiati essent cum ipsis
necarentur, alii se interficiunt, alii in devios montes
vastasque solitudines fugiunt, ingenti per tota castra
terrore diffuso, donec rex, tumultu cognito, legem se
de[2] supplicio coniunctorum sontibus remittere edixit.
21 Philotas verone an mendacio liberare se a cruciatu
voluerit anceps coniectura est, quoniam et vera con-
fessis et falsa dicentibus idem doloris finis ostenditur.
22 Ceterum : " Pater," inquit, " meus Hegelocho quam
familiariter usus sit non ignoratis ; illum dico Hege-
lochum qui in acie cecidit ; omnium malorum nobis
23 is[3] fuit causa. Nam cum primum Iovis filium se
salutari iussit rex, id indigne ferens ille : ' Hunc
igitur regem agnoscimus,' inquit, ' qui Philippum
dedignatur patrem ? Actum est de nobis si ista
24 perpeti possumus. Non homines solum sed etiam
deos despicit qui postulat deus credi. Amisimus
Alexandrum, amisimus regem ; incidimus in super-

---

[1] Cratere *Zumpt;* cratero *A.*
[2] de *added by Scheffer.*
[3] is *added by Vogel; A omits.*

---

[a] Followed by the infinitive because only the substance of
the law is given.
[b] It is uncertain which of three men of this name is meant ;
probably the one named in iv. 5. 14.

both things were granted, he said : " Tell me, Cra-
19 terus, what you wish me to say."   And when Craterus
was indignant that Philotas was mocking him, and
was calling the torturers back again, Philotas began
to ask for time until he could recover his breath,
after which he would tell everything which he knew.
20 Meanwhile the cavalry, all those of the noblest
birth and especially such as were nearly related to
Parmenion, after the report had spread abroad that
Philotas was being tortured, fearing the law of the
Macedonians by which it was provided that the
relatives of those who had plotted against the king
should be put to death with the guilty parties, some
killed themselves, others fled to out-of-the-way
mountains and to lonely desert places, while great
terror spread through the entire camp, until the
king, learning of the tumult, made proclamation *a*
that he remitted the law providing for the punishment of those related to the guilty parties.
21   Whether Philotas wished to free himself from
further torture by telling the truth or by a falsehood,
it is difficult to divine, since the same end to suffering
is offered to those who have confessed the truth and
22 to those who say what is false.   At any rate, Philotas
said : " How intimate my father was with Hegelochus
you know well ; I mean the Hegelochus who fell in
battle *b* ; he was the cause of all our misfortunes.
23 For as soon as the king gave orders that he should be
saluted as the son of Jupiter, Hegelochus, indignant
at that, said : ' Are we then to recognize this king,
who disdains Philip as his father ?   It is all over with
24 us if we can endure that.   He scorns, not only men,
but even the gods, who demands to be believed a god.
We have lost Alexander, we have lost our king ; we

biam nec dis, quibus se exaequat, nec hominibus,
25 quibus se eximit, tolerabilem. Nostrone sanguine
deum fecimus qui nos fastidiat ? qui gravetur mortalium adire concilium ? Credite mihi, et nos, si viri
26 sumus, a dis adoptabimur. Quis proavum huius
Alexandrum, quis deinde Archelaum, quis Perdiccan
occisos ultus est ? Hic quidem interfectoribus patris
ignovit.'
27 " Haec Hegelochus dixit super cenam ; et postero
die prima luce a patre accersor. Tristis erat
et me maestum videbat ; audieramus enim, quae
28 sollicitudinem incuterent. Itaque, ut experiremur
utrumne vino gravatus effudisset illa an altiore con-
cepta consilio, accersi eum placuit. Advenit ille,[1]
eodemque sermone ultro repetito,[2] adiecit se, sive
auderemus duces esse, proximas a nobis partes vin-
dicaturum, sive deesset animus, consilium silentio
29 esse tecturum. Parmenioni vivo adhuc Dareo intempestiva res videbatur ; non enim sibi, sed hosti esse
occisuros Alexandrum, Dareo vero sublato praemium
regis occisi Asiam et totum Orientem interfectoribus
esse cessura. Approbatoque consilio in haec fides
30 et data est et accepta. Quod ad Dymnum[3] pertinet
nihil scio, et haec confessus intellego non prodesse
mihi quod praesentis[4] sceleris expers sum."

[1] Advenit ille *Hedicke;* acuenire *A.*
[2] repetito *I;* petito *A.*   [3] Dymnum *I;* damnum *A.*
[4] praesentis *Hedicke;* persus *A.*

---

[a] Alexander Philhellen, of the time of Darius and Xerxes ;
no one speaks of his death.
[b] A contemporary of Socrates and Euripides, who wrote
his *Bacchae* at his court ; Arist. *Polit.* v. 8. 11.
[c] *Cf.* Justin vii. 5.

have fallen under a tyranny endurable neither to the
gods, to whom he makes himself equal, nor to men,
25 from whom he separates himself. Have we at the
price of our blood created a god who disdains us,
who is reluctant to enter into council with mortals ?
Believe me, we too, if we are men, shall be adopted by
26 the gods. Who avenged the death of Alexander,[a]
the ancestor of this one, who afterwards that of
Archelaüs,[b] who of Perdiccas ?[c] He himself pardoned the murderers of his father.'[d]

27 " These were the words of Hegelochus at dinner[e] ;
and on the dawn of the following day I was summoned by my father. He was troubled and saw that
I was sad ; for we had heard what struck anxiety
28 into our hearts. Therefore, in order to learn whether
Hegelochus had blurted out those words when heavy
with wine, or whether they were inspired by some
deeper design, we decided to have him summoned. He
came, and after repeating the same sentiments of his
own accord, he added that if we dared to take the
lead, he would claim from us the honour of seconding
our plan, or if we lacked the courage, he would bury
29 the plan in silence. To Parmenion the plan seemed
premature while Darius still lived : for they would
be killing Alexander, not for themselves, but for the
enemy ; but if Darius were out of the way, as a reward for killing the king Asia and the entire Orient
would fall to his slayers. This advice was approved,
and a pledge to that end was given and received.
30 So far as Dymnus is concerned, I know nothing,
but I know that after this confession it does not
avail me that I have no part in the present crime."

[d] Cf. iv. 7. 27.
[e] *Super cenam* is usual in such a connexion.

31 Illi rursus tormentis admotis, cum ipsis quoque
hastis os oculosque eius everberarent, expressere ut
32 hoc quoque crimen confiteretur. Exigentibus deinde
ut ordinem cogitati sceleris exponeret, cum diu
Bactra retentura regem viderentur, timuisse respondit, ne pater LXX natus annos, tanti exercitus dux,[1]
tantae pecuniae custos, interim exstingueretur, ipsi-
que spoliato tantis viribus occidendi regis causa non
33 esset. Festinasse ergo se, dum praemium in manibus haberet, repraesentare consilium ; cui patrem
afuisse[2] nisi crederent, tormenta, quamquam iam
34 tolerare non posset, tamen non recusare.[3] Illi col-
locuti satis quaesitum videri, ad regem revertuntur,
qui postero die et, quae confessus erat Philotas,
recitari et ipsum, quia ingredi non poterat, iussit
35 afferri. Omnia agnoscente eo, Demetrius,[4] qui
proximi sceleris particeps esse arguebatur, producitur.
Multa affirmatione animique pariter et constantia et
vultus[5] abnuens, quicquam sibi in regem cogitatum
36 esse, tormenta etiam deposcebat in semetipsum ; cum
Philotas circumlatis oculis, ut incidere in Calan[6]
quendam haud procul stantem, propius eum iussit
accedere. Illo perturbato et recusante transire ad
eum : " Patieris," inquit, " Demetrium mentiri rur-
37 susque me excruciari ? " Calan vox sanguisque
defecerant, et Macedones Philotan inquinare inno-
xios velle suspicabantur, quia nec a Nicomacho nec

---

[1] dux tantus *A;* tantus *deleted by Vindelinus.*
[2] cui patrem afuisse *Hedicke;* cuius patrem fuisse *A.*
[3] recusare *Vindelinus;* recusaret *A.*
[4] eo Demetrius] eodem et prius *FP;* ei demetrius *V m. sec.*
[5] vultus *Heinse;* uultu *A.*   [6] Calan *Hedicke;* calin *A.*

---

[a] That is, Parmenion.

31 They again applied tortures, and striking at his face and eyes with their own spears as well, they forced him to plead guilty to that crime also.

32 Then, when they required him to set forth the order of the proposed deed, he replied that since it seemed that Bactra would detain the king for a long time, they feared that his father,[a] being seventy years old, the leader of so great an army and custodian of so great a treasure, might meanwhile die, and that he himself, robbed of so great strength, would have

33 no reason for killing the king. That therefore he had hastened to carry out promptly the design while he had the prize in his hands; unless they believed that his father had no part in the present design, although he could no longer endure tortures, yet he did not

34 refuse them. They, after talking together, thinking that sufficient question had been made, returned to the king, who gave orders that on the following day what Philotas had confessed should be read, and that he himself should be carried in, since he could not walk.

35 When he had acknowledged everything, Demetrius, who was accused of sharing in the latest conspiracy, was led in. He stoutly denied, with equal assurance of mind and of countenance, that he had formed any design against the king, and even demanded that he

36 himself should be put to the question; when Philotas, turning his eyes on all sides, as they fell upon a certain Calas, standing near by, bade him approach nearer. When he was troubled and refused to cross over to him, Philotas said : " Will you allow Demetrius

37 to lie, and me to be tortured again ? " Calas turned pale and lost the power of speech, and the Macedonians suspected that Philotas wished to besmirch the innocent with guilt, since the youth had not been

ab ipso Philota, cum torqueretur, nominatus esset
adulescens ; qui ut praefectos regis circumstantes se
vidit, Demetrium et semetipsum id facinus cogitasse
38 confessus est. Omnes ergo a Nicomacho nominati,
more patrio, dato signo saxis obruti sunt.

39   Magno non salutis, sed etiam invidiae[1] periculo
liberatus erat Alexander ; quippe Parmenio et Philotas, principes amicorum, nisi palam sontes, sine
indignatione totius exercitus non potuissent damnari.

40 Itaque anceps[2] quaestio fuit dum infitiatus est
facinus ; crudeliter torqueri videbatur post con-
fessionem ; et iam[3] Philotas[4] amicorum misericordiam
meruit.[5]

[1] invidiae *Ruben;* uitae *A.*
[2] anceps q. f. dum *A;* dum anceps q. f. dum *Vogel.*
[3] et iam *Post,* etiam neque *C,* etiam eq *V in ras.;* iam
neque *Vogel.*
[4] Philotas *FP;* Phylotas *BLV;* amicorum Philotas *Vogel.*
[5] *Punctuation and interpretation of* Itaque . . . meruit
Post and Lockwood.

---

[a] Arrian (iii. 26) seems to believe in the guilt of Philotas,
citing the opinion of Ptolemy son of Lagus and of Aristobulus, who accompanied Alexander and wrote a life of him

named by Nicomachus nor by Philotas when he was being tortured; but when he saw himself surrounded by the king's prefects, he confessed that Demetrius

38 and he himself had planned that crime. Therefore all who had been named by Nicomachus were stoned to death on a given signal, after the usage of their country.

39 Alexander had been freed from great danger, not indeed of death, but of hatred; for Parmenion and Philotas, the chief men among his friends, unless clearly shown to be guilty, could not have been condemned without exciting the indignation of the

40 whole army. Thus the issue of the case was doubt ful as long as he denied the crime; that his torture was continued after the confession was considered an act of cruelty; and now Philotas merited the compassion of his friends.[a]

which is one of the chief sources of later biographers. So also Diodorus (xvii. 80) and Plutarch (*Alex.* xlviii.-xlix.). But Justin (xii. 5) condemns the king. Curtius' opinion is left uncertain by the text here given (*et iam*), but is definitely adverse to Philotas in that favoured by Vogel (*iam neque*), " not even of his friends."

BOOK VII

CONTENTS OF BOOK VII

114

about war with the Scythians. Aristander interprets the omens in accordance with the wishes of Alexander. Menedemus is defeated and slain with a loss of 2500 horsemen. Alexander conceals the disaster (vii).

While Alexander is preparing for war, envoys arrive from the Scythians and deliver an address proposing peace (viii).

Alexander, having dismissed the envoys, croses the Iaxartes and attacks the Scythians. Having defeated them, he treats them generously. He receives the Sacae in surrender and then pursues Spitamenes, who had defeated Menedemus (ix).

Sogdiana is recovered; the high spirit of its nobles. Alexander returns to Bactra. Bessus is sent to Ecbatana to suffer punishment. Six cities are founded near Margiana (x).

The crag of Arimaza, almost impregnable from its situation and from the nature of the country, is captured by Alexander. Because of his obstinate defence its commander, Ariamazes, along with his relatives and other nobles, is scourged and crucified (xi).

LIBER VII

I. Philotan sicut recentibus sceleris eius vestigiis
iure affectum supplicio censuerant milites, ita, postquam desierat esse quem odissent, invidia in miseri-
2 cordiam vertit.   Moverat et claritas iuvenis et patris
3 eius senectus atque orbitas.   Primus Asiam aperuerat
regi, omnium periculorum eius particeps semper
alterum in acie cornu defenderat, Philippo quoque
ante omnes amicus et ipsi Alexandro tam fidus, ut
occidendi Attalum non alio ministro uti mallet.
4 Horum cogitatio subibat exercitum, seditiosaeque
voces referebantur ad regem.   Quis ille haud sane
motus satisque prudens otii vitia negotio discuti,
edicit ut omnes in vestibulo regiae praesto sint.
5 Quos ubi frequentes adesse cognovit, in contionem
processit.

Haud dubie ex composito Atarrhias postulare
coepit ut Lyncestes Alexander, qui multo ante quam
6 Philotas regem voluisset occidere, exhiberetur.   A
duobus indicibus, sicut supra diximus, delatus, ter-

---

   a This is an exaggeration, in spite of Parmenion's services
in general.
   b On *defenderat* for *tuebatur* in this sense *cf.* iv. 13. 35.
   c *Cf.* Plut. *Alex.* xlix. 7 ;   *De Fort. Alex.* ii. p. 339 E.
Otherwise this fact is not mentioned.
   d Apparently a proverb; *cf.* Senec. *Ep.* lvi. 9.

BOOK VII

I. Although while the traces of his crime were fresh, the soldiers believed that Philotas had been justly punished, yet after the man whom they hated had 2 ceased to live, hatred changed to pity. The distinction of the young Philotas affected them, and the 3 old age and bereavement of his father. Parmenion had been the first to open Asia to the king,[a] and as his partner in all dangers had had charge [b] of one wing of the army in battle ; he had also been first of Philip's friends,[c] and was so faithful to Alexander himself that Alexander preferred to use no other 4 emissary in killing Attalus. The thought of these things occurred to the army, and mutinous words were reported to the king. He, being not greatly disturbed by these, and well aware that the faults of idleness are dispelled [d] by activity, made proclamation for all to appear at the entrance of his head-5 quarters.[e] When he learned that they were present there in great numbers, he entered the assembly.

Atarrhias, undoubtedly by previous arrangement, began by asking that Lyncestes Alexander, who long before Philotas had wished to kill the king, should be 6 brought before them. He had been charged with this by two informers, as we have said above,[f] and

---

[e] This seems to be here, as often, the meaning of *regia.*
[f] In Book II (lost); *cf.* Arr. i. 25. 3 ff.

tium iam annum custodiebatur in vinculis. Eundem
in Philippi quoque caedem coniurasse cum Pausania
pro comperto fuit, sed quia primus Alexandrum
regem salutaverat, supplicio magis quam crimini
7 fuerat exemptus ; tum quoque Antipatri soceri eius
preces iustam regis iram morabantur. Ceterum
recruduit suppuratus dolor ; quippe veteris periculi
8 memoriam praesentis cura renovabat. Igitur Alexander ex custodia educitur iussusque dicere, quamquam toto triennio meditatus erat defensionem,
tamen haesitans et trepidus pauca ex his quae composuerat protulit, ad ultimum non memoria solum,
9 sed etiam mens eum destituit. Nulli erat dubium
quin trepidatio conscientiae indicium esset, non
memoriae vitium. Itaque ex eis,[1] qui proximi ad-
stiterant, obluctantem adhuc oblivioni lanceis
confoderunt.
10   Cuius corpore ablato, rex introduci iussit Amyntam
et Simian ; nam[2] Polemon, minimus ex fratribus,
11 cum Philotan torqueri comperisset, profugerat. Omnium Philotae amicorum hi carissimi fuerant, ad
magna et honorata ministeria illius maxime suffraga-
tione producti, memineratque rex summo studio ab
eo conciliatos sibi, nec dubitabat huius quoque ultimi
12 consilii fuisse participes. Igitur queritur[3] olim sibi
esse suspectos matris suae litteris, quibus esset ad-

---

[1] iis *Vindelinus;* his *A.*
[2] Simian ; nam *Hedicke;* simannam *A.*
[3] Igitur queritur *Hedicke;* igitur *A.*

---

* Both sons of Andromenes, also Attalus and Polemon,
v. 1. 40, Arr. iii. 27. 1; *cf.* also Curt. vi. 11. 20.

was now spending the third year of his imprisonment
in fetters. It was regarded as certain that he had
also, with Pausanias, conspired to kill Philip, but
because he had been the first to hail Alexander as
king, he was exempted from punishment rather than
7 from guilt; then too the prayers of his father-in-law
Antipater were delaying the king's just anger. However, the resentment which had been coming to a
head broke out anew, since anxiety from the present
danger revived the memory of the one of long stand-
8 ing. Therefore Alexander (Lyncestes) was brought
out of prison, and when ordered to speak, although
for three whole years he had practised a defence, yet
hesitating and trembling he presented only a few
words of what he had composed, and finally, not
9 only his memory, but his thoughts failed him. No
one doubted that his alarm was an indication of a
guilty conscience and not of a failure of memory.
Accordingly, some of those who stood nearest to
him ran him through with their lances as he was still
struggling with forgetfulness.
10 When his body had been taken away, the king
ordered Amyntas and Simias [a] to be brought in, for
Polemon, the youngest of the brothers, had fled
when he heard that Philotas was being tortured.
11 These had been the dearest of all Philotas' friends,
and had been advanced to important and honourable
positions mainly through his influence, and the king
remembered that Philotas had recommended them
to him with the greatest urgency, and did not doubt
that they had been participants also in this last design
12 of his. Therefore he complained that they had long
since been objects of his suspicion because of letters
of his mother, in which he had been warned to protect

monitus ut ab his salutem suam tueretur ; ceterum
se invitum deteriora credentem nunc manifestis
13 indiciis victum iussisse vinciri. Nam pridie quam
detegeretur Philotae scelus, quin in secreto cum eo
fuissent non posse dubitari.[1] Fratrem vero, qui
profugerit cum de Philota quaereretur, aperuisse
14 fugae causam. Nuper praeter consuetudinem, officii
specie amotis longius ceteris, admovisse semetipsos
lateri suo nulla probabili causa, seque mirantem quod
non vice sua tali fungerentur officio, et ipsa trepida-
tione eorum perterritum, strenue ad armigeros, qui
proxime sequebantur, recessisse.

15 Ad haec accedere, quod, cum Antiphanes, scriba
equitum, Amyntae denuntiasset, pridie quam Philotae scelus deprehensum esset, ut ex suis equis more
solito daret[2] eis[3] qui amisissent equos, superbe respondisset,[4] nisi incepto desisteret, brevi sciturum
16 quis ipse esset. Iam linguae violentiam temerita-
temque verborum, quae in semetipsum iacularentur,
nihil aliud esse quam scelesti animi indicem ac testem.
Quae si vera essent, idem meruisse eos quod Philotan,
17 si falsa, exigere ipsum ut refellant. Productus deinde
Antiphanes de equis non traditis et adiectis etiam
18 superbe minis indicat. Tum[5] Amyntas facta dicendi
potestate: "Si nihil," inquit, "interest regis, peto ut,

---

[1] dubitari *I;* dubitare *A.*
[2] daret *Aldus;* darent *A.*   [3] iis *I;* his *A.*
[4] respondisset *Letellier;* respondisse *A.*
[5] indicat. Tum *Freinshem;* inde captum *A.*

---

[a] *Vice sua* is ablative for the more common accusative ;
see vii. 2. 5, below.
[b] A scribe, γραμματεύς, who kept a list of the soldiers and
an account of their receipts and expenditures.

his life against them ; but that although he had been
unwilling to believe unfavourable reports, now forced
by clear proofs, he had ordered them to be im-
13 prisoned. For it could not be doubted that the day
before the crime of Philotas was revealed they had
been with him in secret. Moreover, their brother
who had run away during the inquisition of Philotas
14 had made clear the reason for his flight. Lately,
under the pretence of rendering service, they had
removed all other persons to a distance, and contrary
to custom had attached themselves to his side without any plausible reason, and because he was surprised
that they performed such service out of their turn,[a]
and alarmed by their very confusion, he had quickly
taken refuge with his guards who were following
close after him.

15 It was added to this, that when Antiphanes, com-
missary of the cavalry,[b] had given orders to Amyntas,
the day before the crime of Philotas had been discovered, that, as was usual, he should turn over some
of his horses to those who had lost theirs, Amyntas
had replied insolently, that unless Antiphanes gave
up his attempt, he would soon know who Amyntas
16 was. That now his violent tongue and the rash
words that were hurled at the king himself were
nothing other than an indication of, and testimony
to, an evil design. If these charges were true, those
men deserved the same treatment as Philotas, if false,
he himself demanded that they should refute them.
17 Then Antiphanes, being brought forward, gave testimony about the failure to deliver the horses and also
18 that Amyntas had arrogantly added threats. Then
Amyntas, on being given permission to speak, said :
" If it makes no difference to the king, I ask that,

dum dico, vinculis liberer." Rex solvi utrumque
iubet desiderantique Amyntae, ut habitus quoque
redderetur armigeri, lanceam dari iussit.

19 Quam ut laeva comprehendit, evitato eo loco, in
quo Alexandri corpus paulo ante iacuerat : " Qualiscumque," inquit, " exitus nos manet, rex, confitemur
prosperum tibi debituros, tristiorem fortunae im-

20 putaturos. Sine praeiudicio dicimus causam liberis
corporibus animisque ; habitum etiam in quo te
comitari solemus reddidisti. Causam non possumus,
fortunam timere desinemus.[1]

21 " Et, quaeso, permittas mihi id primum defendere,
quod a te ultimum obiectum est. Nos, rex, sermonis
adversus maiestatem tuam habiti nullius conscii
sumus nobis. Dicerem iam pridem vicisse te invidiam, nisi periculum esset ne alia malignius dicta

22 crederes blanda oratione purgari. Ceterum etiam si
militis tui vel in agmine deficientis et fatigati vel
in acie periclitantis vel in tabernaculo aegri et vulnera
curantis aliqua vox asperior esset accepta, meruera-
mus fortibus factis, ut malles ea tempori nostro

23 imputare quam animo. Cum quid accidit tristius,
omnes rei sumus[2] ; corporibus nostris, quae utique
non odimus, infestas admovemus[3] manus ; parentes,
liberis[4] si occurrant, et ingrati et invisi sunt. Contra
cum donis honoramur, cum praemiis onusti reverti-
mur, quis ferre nos potest ? quis illam animorum

---

[1] desinemus *Vindelinus;* desiemus *A.*
[2] sumus *Bentley;* sunt *A.*
[3] infestas admovemus *Aldus;* infectas admouemus *BFL;*
infectus admouemus *V; P omits.*
[4] liberis *A, defended by Post;* liberi *Eberhard.*

---

[a] See Quint. v. 2. 1. Here there is a contrast with the
condition in which Philotas made his defence.

while I am speaking I may be freed from fetters."
The king ordered both to be released, and when
Amyntas desired that the apparel of a guard also
be restored to him, he ordered that a lance be given
him.

19 When he took this in his left hand, shunning the
place in which the body of Alexander Lyncestes had
lain a short time before, Amyntas said : " Whatever
outcome awaits us, Sire, we confess that if it is favourable, we shall owe it to you ; that if it is less so, we
20 shall attribute it to ill-fortune. We plead our cause
without prejudice,ᵃ bodies and minds both free ; you
have also even restored the apparel in which we are
accustomed to attend you. We cannot distrust our
cause, we shall cease to fear ill-fortune.

21 " And, I pray you, allow me to meet first the
charge which you last made against me. We, Sire,
are conscious of no language directed against your
majesty. I would say that you have long since risen
superior to ill-will, if there were not danger lest you
might believe that other more malicious words were
22 being purged away by flattering language. But even
if some harsher speech had been heard from a soldier
of yours, either when wearied and worn out on the
march or encountering danger in battle, or in his
tent when ailing and attending to his wounds, we
have deserved by brave deeds that you should prefer
to impute it to our exigency rather than to ill-will.
23 Whenever anything especially sad happens, we are
all criminals ; we turn hostile hands against our own
bodies, which we in no way hate ; parents, if they
oppose their children, become disliked and hated.
On the other hand, when we are honoured by gifts,
when we return loaded with prizes, who can endure

24 alacritatem continere ? Militantium nec indignatio
nec laetitia moderata est ; ad omnes affectus impetu
rapimur. Vituperamus laudamus, miseremur iras
cimur, utcumque praesens movit affectio ; modo
Indiam adire et Oceanum libet, modo coniugum et
liberorum patriaeque memoria occurrit.

25 " Sed has cogitationes, has inter se colloquentium
voces signum tuba datum finit ; in suos quisque
ordines currimus, et quidquid irarum in tabernaculo
conceptum est in hostium effunditur capita. Utinam

26 Philotas quoque intra verba peccasset ! Proinde ad
id revertar propter quod rei sumus. Amicitiam
quae nobis cum Philota fuit adeo non eo infitias, ut
expetisse quoque nos magnosque ex ea fructus per-

27 cepisse confitear. An vero Parmenionis, quem tibi
proximum esse voluisti, filium omnes paene amicos
tuos dignatione vincentem cultum a nobis esse mira-

28 ris ? Tu, hercules, si verum audire vis, rex, huius
nobis periculi es[1] causa. Quis enim alius effecit ut
ad Philotan decurrerent qui placere vellent tibi ?
Ab illo traditi, ad hunc gradum amicitiae tuae ascendi-
mus ; is apud te fuit, cuius et gratiam[2] expetere et

29 iram timere possemus. Si non propemodum in tua
verba, at tui[3] omnes te praeeunte[4] iuravimus, eosdem
nos inimicos amicosque habituros esse, quos tu haberes.
Hoc sacramento pietatis obstricti, aversaremur[5]

---

[1] periculi es *I;* periculis *P;* pericules *C m. pr.*
[2] et gratiam *Bentley;* *ē* gratiam *P;* gratiam *C.*
[3] in tua verba, at tui *Bentley;* tuo uerberatu ei *A.*
[4] praeeunte *Lauer;* praetereunte *A.*
[5] aversaremur *Modius;* obuersaremur *A.*

---

[a] *periculum,* in the legal meaning of κίνδυνος.
[b] The regular soldiers' oath, as well as that of a surrendering people ; see Livy xxxvii. 1. 5.

24 us ? who can master that enthusiasm of spirit ? With
soldiers neither their indignation nor their joy is
restrained; we are carried away with violence to all
emotions. We blame, we praise ; we pity, we show
anger, just as the present emotion affects us ; now
it pleases us to go to India and the Ocean, now
the memory of wives and children and of fatherland
causes opposition.

25 " But to these thoughts, these words of those who
talk together, the signal given by the trumpet puts
an end; we hasten each to his own place in the ranks,
and whatever anger had been conceived in the tent
is discharged upon the heads of the enemy. Would
that Philotas also had confined his wrongdoing to

26 words ! Therefore let me return to the matter about
which we are being accused. The friendship that we
had with Philotas I am so far from denying, that I
admit that we both sought from it and gained from it

27 great fruitage. Or indeed do you wonder that the
son of Parmenion, whom you have been pleased to
have next in rank to yourself, surpassing almost all

28 your friends in distinction, was courted by us ? You,
by Heaven !, if you are willing to listen to the truth,
Sire, are the cause of our present jeopardy.[a] For
who else brought it about that those who wished to
please you should run to Philotas ? It is because we
were recommended by him that we have mounted to
our present rank in your friendship ; he held such a
place in your estimation, that we might seek his

29 favour and fear his anger. Have we not, all of us
soldiers, sworn, if not almost in your own words,
at least in the form dictated by you, that we would
regard the same men as enemies and friends as
yourself ?[b] Bound as we were by this oath of

30 scilicet quem tu omnibus praeferebas ! Igitur, si hoc
crimen est, paucos innocentes habes, immo, hercules,
neminem. Omnes enim Philotae amici esse voluerunt, sed totidem quot volebant esse non poterant
Ita, si a consciis amicos non dividis, ne ab amicis
quidem separabis illos, qui idem esse voluerunt.

31 "Quod igitur conscientiae affertur indicium ? Ut
opinor, quia pridie familiariter et sine arbitris locutus
est nobiscum. At ego purgare non possem, si pridie
quicquam ex vetere vita ac more mutassem. Nunc
vero, si, ut[1] omnibus diebus, illo quoque qui suspectus
est fecimus, consuetudo diluet crimen.

32 "Sed equos Antiphani non dedimus, et pridie
quam Philotas detectus est. Hic[2] mihi cum Anti-
phane res erit. Qui si nos suspectos facere vult, quod
illo die equos non dederimus, semetipsum, quod eos
33 desideraverit, purgare non poterit. Anceps enim
crimen est inter retinentem et exigentem, nisi quod
melior est causa suum non tradentis quam poscentis
34 alienum. Ceterum, rex, equos decem habui[3] e quibus Antiphanes octo iam distribuerat eis[4] qui amise-
rant suos, omnino duos ipse habebam ; quos cum
vellet abducere homo[5] superbissimus, certe iniquissi-
mus, nisi pedes militare vellem, retinere cogebar.
35 Nec infitias eo liberi hominis animo locutum esse me

---

[1] si, ut *I;* sicut *A.*   [2] hic *P;* haec *C.*
[3] habui *V corr.;* habui habeo *F;* obui abeo *L;* habeo *BP.*
[4] iis *P;* his *C.*
[5] *The frag. Einsidlense (E) begins with* -cere homo.

loyalty, we were, forsooth, to be unfriendly to one
30 whom you preferred to all others! Therefore, if this
is a crime, you have few who are blameless, nay, by
Heaven, not one. For all wished to be friends of
Philotas, but not all those who wished to be could
be. So, if you do not distinguish his friends from
the guilty, you will not separate, either, from his
friends those who have wished to be such.

31 " What evidence of guilty knowledge, then, is
brought against us? I suppose it is because the
day before he talked with us familiarly and without
witnesses. But I could not excuse myself, if on that
day I had made any change in my former life and
custom. So, now that on that day also which is the
object of suspicion we did what we did every day,
adherence to custom will free us from guilt.

32 " But we did not hand over the horses to Antiphanes, and that too on the day before Philotas was
unmasked. This will be a matter between me and
Antiphanes. If he wished to expose us to suspicion
because on that day we did not give him the horses,
he will not be able to justify himself because he asked
33 for them then. For the guilt is in doubt as between
him who retained them and him who demanded
them, except that the cause of one who did not give
up what was his own is better than that of one who
34 demanded what belonged to another. As a matter
of fact, Sire, I had ten horses, of which Antiphanes
had already distributed eight to those who had lost
their own and I myself had left but two in all; when
that most insolent man, at any rate the most unfair,
wished to lead away these, I was forced to retain
35 them unless I wished to fight on foot. And I do not
deny that I spoke to him in the spirit of a free man,

cum ignavissimo et hoc unum militiae ius[1] usurpante,
ut alienos equos pugnaturis distribuat. Huc enim
malorum ventum est, ut verba mea eodem tempore
et Alexandro excusem et Antiphani!

36   " At, hercule, mater de nobis inimicis tuis scripsit.
Utinam prudentius esset sollicita pro filio et non
inanes quoque species anxio animo figuraret![2] Quare[3]
enim non ascribit metus sui causam? denique non
ostendit auctorem? Quo facto dictove nostro mota,
37 tam trepidas tibi litteras scripsit? O miseram condicionem meam, quia forsitan non periculosius est
tacere quam dicere! Sed utcumque cessura res est,
malo tibi defensionem meam displicere quam causam.
Agnosces autem quae dicturus sum; quippe memi-
nisti, cum me ad perducendos ex Macedonia milites
mitteres, dixisse te, multos integros iuvenes in domo
38 tuae matris abscondi. Praecepisti igitur mihi ne
quem praeter te intuerer, sed detrectantes militiam
perducerem ad te. Quod equidem feci et liberius
quam expediebat[4] mihi executus sum tuum imperium.
Gorgiam et Hecataeum et Gorgidan,[5] quorum bona
39 opera uteris, inde perduxi. Quid igitur iniquius est
quam me, qui, si tibi non paruissem, iure daturus fui
poenas, nunc perire, quia parui? Neque enim ulla
alia matri tuae persequendi nos causa est, quam quod
40 utilitatem tuam muliebri praeposuimus gratiae. VI

[1] ius *Bentley;* suae *A.*
[2] figuraret] fugararet *apparently P m. pr.;* figuraretur *E.*
[3] quare] quae *E.*   [4] expediebat *E;* expedibat *A.*
[5] Gorgidan *Hedicke;* gorgatan *AE.*

---

[6] These scribes in general were looked down upon by the
soldiers, as non-combatants; they were usually of low condition and often slaves.

128

addressing one of the basest [a] and one who enjoyed only this privilege of military service, of distributing the horses of others to those who were going to fight. For it has come to this condition of evils, that I must excuse my words at the same time both to Alexander and to Antiphanes !

36   " But, by Heaven ! your mother has written that we are your enemies. Would that her solicitude for her son had been accompanied by more prudence, and that she had not through anxiety of mind pictured vain phantoms ! For why does she not add the reason for her fear ? finally, why does she not reveal the authority for it ? By what deed or word of ours was 37 she moved to write you so agitated a letter ? O wretched fortune of mine, since perhaps it is not more dangerous to be silent than to speak ! But whatever the result may be, I prefer that it should be my manner of defence rather than my cause that displeases you. But you will admit what I am about to say ; for you remember that when you sent me to bring soldiers from Macedonia, you said that there were many young men fit for service who were hidden 38 away in your mother's palace. Therefore you instructed me that I should regard no one except you, but should bring to you those who declined military service. This I did, and I executed your order with more zeal than was expedient for me. I brought from there Gorgias, Hecataeus, and Gorgidas, who 39 are rendering you good service. What, then, is more unjust than that I, who, if I had not obeyed you, would justly have suffered punishment, should now die because I did obey ? For your mother has no other reason for persecuting us than that we preferred 40 your advantage to a woman's favour. I brought 6000

milia Macedonum peditum et DC equites adduxi ;
quorum pars secutura me non erat, si militiam de-
trectantibus indulgere voluissem. Sequitur ergo, ut,
quia illa propter hanc causam irascitur nobis, tu
mitiges matrem, qui irae eius nos obtulisti."

II. Dum haec Amyntas agit, forte supervenerunt
qui fratrem eius Polemonem, de quo ante est dictum,
fugientem consecuti, vinctum reducebant. Infesta
contio vix inhiberi potuit quin protinus suo more
saxa in eum[1] iaceret. Atque ille sane interritus[2] :
2 " Nihil," inquit, " pro me deprecor, modo ne fratrum
innocentiae fuga inputetur mea. Haec si defendi
non potest, meum crimen sit. Horum ob id ipsum
melior est causa, quod ego, quia[3] profugi, suspectus
3 sum." At haec elocuto universa contio assensa est ;
lacrimae deinde omnibus manare coeperunt, adeo in
contrarium repente mutatis, ut solum pro eo esset
4 quod maxime laeserat. Iuvenis erat primo aetatis
flore pubescens, quem inter equites tormentis Philotae conturbatos[4] alienus terror abstulerat ; desertum eum a comitibus et haesitantem inter revertendi
fugiendique consilium, qui secuti erant occupaverunt.

---

[1] meum in eum *E*.   [2] interritus *C;* territus *EP*.
[3] quia *Bentley;* qui *AE*.
[4] conturbatos] conturbatis *EP;* conturbato *E*.

---

[a] See v. 1. 40, where the number of cavalry is given as
500 ; Diodorus has 600, as here.
[b] vii. 1. 10. Arrian iii. 27. 2 differs in details. Curtius
130

Macedonian infantry and 600 horsemen [a] ; a part of these would not have followed me, if I had been willing to show indulgence to those who shrank from military service. Therefore it follows that, because it is for that reason that she is angry with us, you should soothe your mother, since it is you who have exposed us to her anger."

II. While Amyntas was making this plea, those chanced to arrive who had pursued his brother Polemon, of whom mention has been made before,[b] and whom, being in flight, they were bringing back in bonds. The incensed assembly could hardly be restrained from at once stoning him to death, according to their custom. But he, quite unterrified, said :
2 " I ask no mercy for myself, provided my flight be not prejudicial to the innocence of my brothers.[c] If this cannot be defended, let the guilt be mine. Their cause is the better for the very reason that I was
3 suspected because I took flight." But when he had said this, the whole assembly sympathized ; now they all began to shed tears, and were suddenly so changed to the opposite opinion that what had especially damaged his cause was the only thing that was
4 in his favour. He was a young man just come to maturity and in the first bloom of his youth, one of the horsemen who had been terrified by the torture of Philotas and whom the alarm of others had led to flee ; deserted by his companions, and wavering between the purpose of returning and of fleeing, he was overtaken by those who had followed him.

uses the tradition which he follows to make a very vivid picture, in much fuller detail than Arrian.

[c] That is, if his flight will not be interpreted as evidence of the guilt of his brothers, who also fled.

5 Is tum flere coepit et os suum converberare, maestus
non suam vicem, sed propter ipsum periclitantium
fratrum.[1]

6 Moveratque iam regem quoque, non contionem
modo, sed unus erat implacabilis frater, qui terribili
vultu intuens eum : " Tum," exclamat,[2] " demens,
lacrimare debueras, cum equo calcaria subderes,
fratrum desertor et desertorum comes. Miser, quo
et unde fugiebas ? Effecisti, ut reus capitis accusa-
7 toris uterer verbis." Ille peccasse sese[3] gravius in
fratres quam in semetipsum fatebatur. Tum vero
neque lacrimis neque adclamationibus quibus studia
sua multitudo profitetur temperaverunt. Una vox
erat pari emissa consensu, ut insontibus et fortibus
viris parceret. Amici quoque, data misericordiae
occasione, consurgunt flentesque regem deprecantur.
8 Ille silentio facto : " Et ipse," inquit, " Amyntan
mea sententia[4] fratresque eius absolvo. Vos autem,
iuvenes, malo beneficii mei oblivisci quam periculi
vestri meminisse. Eadem fide redite in gratiam
9 mecum qua ipse vobiscum revertor. Nisi quae delata
essent excussissem, aliquid de dissimulatione mea
suspicari potuissetis[5] ; satius est purgatos esse quam
suspectos. Cogitate neminem absolvi posse, nisi qui

---

[1] ipsum periclitantium fratrum] ipsos periclitantes fratres E.
[2] exclamat Hedicke; ait AE.
[3] sese Hedicke; se sed C; sese sed P; sese set E.
[4] mea sententia] frag. E ends with these words.
[5] aliquid . . . potuissetis Hedicke; ualde dissimulatio mea
superare potuisset sed A.

5 He then began to weep and to beat his face, not grieving on his own account,[a] but on that of his brothers, who were endangered through him.

6 And now he had affected the king also, and not only the assembly, but his brother alone was inexorable, and gazing at him with a terrifying expression, exclaimed : " Then, madman, is when you ought to have wept, when you were applying spurs to your horse, a deserter of your brothers and a companion of deserters. Wretch, whither were you fleeing and from whom ? You have forced me, on trial for my life, to use the words of an accuser." Polemon con-

7 fessed that he had sinned more grievously against his brothers than against himself. Then truly the soldiers did not moderate their tears and the acclamations [b] by which a crowd expresses its favour. One cry was uttered by common consent, that the king should pardon these brave and blameless men. His friends also, when opportunity for mercy had been

8 given, arose and with tears appealed to the king. He, having silenced them, said : " I myself by my vote acquit Amyntas and his brothers. But as for you, young men, I prefer that you should forget my kindness rather than remember your danger. Return to favour with me with the same confidence with which

9 I myself return to favour with you. If I had not examined what had been reported to me, you might have been able to feel some suspicion of my silence ; it is better to be justified than to be suspected. Remember that no one can be acquitted unless he has

---

[a] The accusative is more common than the ablative, which occurs in vii. 1. 14 ; cf. Livy viii. 25. 1, etc.

[b] Acclamations sometimes expressed disapproval; see x. 7. 6.

QUINTUS CURTIUS

10 dixerit causam. Tu, Amynta, ignosce fratri tuo.
Erit hoc simpliciter etiam mihi reconciliati animi
tui pignus."

11 Contione deinde dimissa, Polydamanta vocari
iubet. Longe acceptissimus Parmenioni erat, proxi-
12 mus lateri in acie stare solitus. Et quamquam conscientia fretus in regiam venerat, tamen, ut iussus
est fratres suos exhibere admodum iuvenes et regi
ignotos ob aetatem, fiducia in sollicitudinem versa,
trepidare coepit, saepius quae nocere possent quam
13 quibus eluderet reputans. Iam armigeri, quibus
imperatum erat, produxerant eos, cum exsanguem
metu Polydamanta propius accedere iubet, sum-
motisque omnibus : " Scelere," inquit, " Parmenionis
omnes pariter appetiti sumus, maxime ego ac tu,
14 quos amicitiae specie fefellit. Ad quem persequendum puniendumque—vide quantum fidei tuae credam
—te ministro uti statui. Obsides, dum hoc peragis,
15 erunt fratres tui. Proficiscere in Mediam et ad
praefectos meos litteras scriptas manu mea perfer.
Velocitate opus est, qua celeritatem famae[1] antecedas.
Noctu pervenire illuc te volo, postero die quae scripta
16 erunt exsequi. Ad Parmeniona quoque epistulas
feres, unam a me, alteram Philotae nomine scriptam.
Signum anuli eius in mea potestate est. Si pater
credet a filio impressum, cum te viderit, nihil metuet."

17 Polydamas, tanto liberatus metu, impensius etiam

[1] famae *added by Vindelinus.*

---

[a] *Cf.* iv. 11. 22; Cael. in Cic. *Ad Fam.* viii. 6. 1.
[b] See iv. 15. 6 ; Arr. iii. 26. 3.
[c] *exhibere,* a juristic term; *cf.* vii. 1. 5.
[d] For *eluderet cf.* Cic. *De Opt. Gen. Orat.* vi. 17.

134

10 pleaded his cause. Do you, Amyntas, pardon your brother. This will be a pledge that your feelings are sincerely [a] reconciled with me also."

11 Then he dismissed the assembly and ordered Polydamas [b] to be called. He was by far the dearest of Parmenion's friends, accustomed to stand by his side

12 in battle. And although, relying on a clear conscience, he had come to headquarters, yet when he was ordered to produce [c] his brothers, who were very young and unknown to the king because of their youth, his confidence changed to anxiety and he began to be afraid, considering more frequently what could harm them than by what means he could parry

13 such attacks. [d] And now the guards who had been ordered to do so had brought them in, when the king ordered Polydamas, deathly pale with fear, to draw nearer, and, removing all witnesses, said : " We have all alike been attacked by the crime of Parmenion, especially you and I, whom he has deceived by the

14 guise of friendship. To pursue and punish him—see how much I trust to your loyalty—I have decided to use you as my instrument. While you are doing

15 this, your brothers will be hostages. Set out for Media and take letters, written in my own handwriting, to my prefects. There is need of great speed, in order to outstrip the swiftness of rumour. I wish you to arrive there by night, and on the following

16 day to carry out what has been written. You will also take letters to Parmenion, one from me, the other written in the name of Philotas. The seal of his ring is in my possession. If his father believes that this was impressed by his son, he will fear nothing when he sees you."

17 Polydamas, relieved from so great fear, promised

quam exigebatur promittit operam conlaudatusque
et promissis oneratus, deposita veste quam habebat
18 Arabica induitur. Duo[1] Arabes, quorum interim
coniuges ac liberi, vinculum fidei, obsides apud regem
erant, dati comites. Per deserta etiam ob siccitatem
loca camelis undecimo die quo destinaverat per-
19 veniunt. Et priusquam ipsius[2] nuntiaretur adventus,
rursus Polydamas vestem Macedonicam sumit et in
tabernaculum Cleandri—praetor hic regius erat—
20 quarta vigilia pervenit. Redditis deinde litteris,
constituerunt prima luce ad Parmenionem coire.
Iamque[3] ceteris quoque litteras regis attulerat, iam
ad eum venturi erant, cum Parmenioni Polydamanta
21 venisse nuntiaverunt. Qui dum laetatur adventu
amici, simulque noscendi quae rex ageret avidus—
quippe longo intervallo nullam ab eo epistulam
acceperat—Polydamanta requiri iubet.
22 Deversoria[4] regionis illius magnos recessus habent
amoenosque nemoribus manu consitis ; ea praecipua
23 regum satraparumque voluptas erat. Spatiabatur in
nemore Parmenion, medius inter duces quibus erat
imperatum litteris regis ut occiderent. Agendae
autem rei constituerant tempus, cum Parmenio a
24 Polydamante litteras traditas legere coepisset. Polydamas procul veniens, ut a Parmenione conspectus

---

[1] Duo *Lauer;* duc *P;* dux *C.*
[2] ipsius *Vindelinus;* ipsi *A.*
[3] Iamque *Hedicke;* namque *A.*
[4] Deversoria *Hedicke;* diversoria *A.*

his help even more earnestly than was demanded of
him, and after being highly commended and loaded
with promises, he put off the dress which he was
18 wearing and put on an Arab costume. Two Arabs,
whose wives and children were meanwhile as a
pledge of loyalty held as hostages with the king,
were given him as companions. They arrived at the
designated place on the eleventh day,[a] traversing
on camels places which were even made desert by
19 dryness. And before his arrival could be reported,
Polydamas again assumed Macedonian dress and
went to the tent of Cleander—he was one of the
20 king's generals—in the fourth watch. Then, having
delivered the letter, they decided to go together
to Parmenion at daybreak. And now Polydamas
had delivered the king's letters to the others as well,
and already they were on the point of going to
Parmenion, when it was announced to him that Poly-
21 damas had come. He, rejoicing in the arrival of his
friend, and at the same time being eager to have news
of what the king was doing—for he had received
no letter from him for a long time—ordered that
Polydamas be looked for.
22 The residences in that region [b] have extensive,
charming, and secluded parks with groves artificially
planted; these were the special delight of both kings
23 and satraps. Parmenion was walking about in a
grove, surrounded by his officers, who had been ordered by the king's letters to kill him. And they had
arranged to do the deed at the time when Parmenion
had begun to read the letters delivered by Polydamas.
24 As Polydamas came near and was seen by Parmenion

[a] Remarkably quick time ; in fact, incredibly so.
[b] Cf. Xen. Oecon. iv. 13.

137

est, vultu laetitiae speciem praeferente, ad com-
plectendum eum cucurrit, mutuaque[1] salutatione
facta,[2] Polydamas epistulam a rege scriptam ei tradi-
25 dit. Parmenio vinculum epistulae solvens, quidnam
rex ageret requirebat. Ille ex ipsis litteris cognitu-
26 rum esse respondit. Quibus Parmenio lectis:
"Rex," inquit, "expeditionem parat in Arachosios.
Strenuum hominem et numquam cessantem! Sed
tempus saluti suae, tanta iam parta gloria, parcere."
27 Alteram deinde epistulam Philotae nomine scriptam
laetus, quod ex vultu notari poterat, legebat; tum
eius latus gladio haurit Cleander, deinde iugulum
ferit, ceteri exanimum quoque confodiunt.
28 Et armigeri, qui ad primum aditum[4] nemoris ad-
stiterant, cognita caede, cuius causa ignorabatur, in
castra perveniunt et tumultuoso nuntio milites con-
29 citant. Illi armati ad nemus in quo perpetrata
caedes erat coeunt et, ni Polydamas ceterique eiusdem noxae participes dedantur, murum circumdatum
nemori eversuros denuntiant omniumque sanguine
30 duci parentaturos. Cleander primores eorum intro-
mitti iubet litterasque regis scriptas ad milites recitat,
quibus insidiae Parmenionis in regem precesque, ut
31 ipsum vindicarent, continebantur. Igitur, cognita
regis voluntate, non quidem indignatio, sed tamen
seditio compressa est. Dilapsis pluribus, pauci re-

---

[1] mutuaque *Lauer;* mutuata *C;* mutuatu *P.*
[2] salutatione *Hedicke;* gratulatione *A.*
[3] facta *Bentley;* functi *A.*
[4] qui . . . aditum *Hedicke;* quid aditum *P;* qui aditum *C.*

---

[a] *Cf.* Nepos, *Paus.* iv. 1 ; Ovid, *Trist.* iv. 7. 7.
[b] See vii. 3. 4.   [c] *Cf.* x. 4. 3.

to have an expression presenting the appearance of joy, he ran to embrace him, and after they had exchanged greetings, Polydamas handed him the letter
25 written to him by the king. Parmenion, as he loosed the fastening ^a of the letter, asked what the king was doing. Polydamas replied that he would learn from
26 the letter itself. Parmenion, after reading the letter, said: "The king is preparing an expedition against the Arachosii.^b An active man, who never rests! But it is time for him to show consideration for his own welfare, after having already gained so much glory."
27 Afterwards he was reading the second letter, written in the name of Philotas, with pleasure, as could be seen from his expression; then Cleander plunged his sword into his side and struck him again in the throat, and the others stabbed him even after he was lifeless.
28 And the guards, who were posted at the entrance of the grove, on learning of the murder, the cause of which was unknown to them, came into the camp and aroused the soldiers with the alarming message.
29 They armed themselves and went in a body to the grove in which the murder had been committed, threatening that unless Polydamas and the rest who had shared in the same outrage ^c were delivered to them, they would throw down the wall surrounding the grove and offer expiation for the death of their
30 leader with the blood of all. Cleander ordered their leaders to be admitted, and read to the soldiers the letters which the king had written, in which were contained an account of the plots of Parmenion against the king and Alexander's prayers that they
31 should avenge him. Accordingly, when the wish of the king was known, the mutiny of the troops was checked, but nevertheless not their indignation.

manserunt, qui saltem ut corpus ipsis[1] sepelire per-
32 mitterent precabantur. Diu id negatum est Cleandri
metu ne offenderet regem. Pertinacius deinde pre-
cantibus, materiem consternationis subtrahendam
ratus, capite deciso truncum humare permisit ; ad
regem caput missum est.

33   Hic exitus Parmenionis fuit, militiae domique clari
viri. Multa sine rege prospere, rex sine illo nihil
magnae rei gesserat. Felicissimo regi et omnia[2] ad
fortunae suae exigenti modum satisfecit. LXX natus
annos iuvenis ducis et saepe etiam gregarii militis
munia explevit[3] ; acer consilio, manu strenuus, carus
34 principibus, vulgo militum acceptior. Haec impule-
rint illum ad regni cupiditatem an tantum suspectum
fecerint, ambigi potest, quia Philotas, ultimis cruci-
atibus victus, verane dixerit quae facta probari non
poterant, an falsis tormentorum petierit finem, re
quoque recenti, cum magis[4] posset liquere, dubita-
tum est.

35   Alexander, quos libere mortem Parmenionis con-
questos esse compererat separandos a cetero exercitu
ratus, in unam cohortem secrevit ducemque his
Leonidam dedit, et ipsum Parmenioni quondam

---

[1] ipsis *Vogel;* ipsius *A.*
[2] et omnia *Lauer;* et ad omnia *A.*
[3] explevit *Freinshem;* explicuit *A.*
[4] magis *Lauer;* magnis *A.*

---

[a] The sketch of Parmenion's life is only general ; the
interest of later historians in Alexander, and the effort to
exalt his exploits, made it difficult to give a fuller characterization ; *cf.* Arr. iii. 26. 4.

[b] An unjustified statement ; Curtius is more rhetorical
than historically accurate.

[c] *Cf.* Arr. iii. 26. 4.

When many of them had slipped away, a few remained, who prayed that at least they might be per-
32 mitted by them to bury the body. This was for a long time refused through Cleander's fear that he might thus offend the king. Then, when they besought more persistently, thinking that occasion for disturbance ought to be removed, Cleander cut off the head and allowed them to bury the body ; the head was sent to the king.

33 Such was the end of Parmenion,[a] a man illustrious in war and in peace. He had achieved many successes without the king, the king had done no great deed without him.[b] He satisfied a king who was most fortunate and who required that all things should match the greatness of his good fortune. At the age of seventy he fulfilled the duties of a leader in the prime of life and often even those of a common soldier ; keen in counsel, vigorous in action, he was dear to the leading men and still more so to the common soldiers.
34 Whether these qualities [c] drove him to a desire for royal power, or merely made him suspected of such a design, may be doubted ; for it was uncertain, even when the affair was recent and could more easily be made clear, whether Philotas, overcome by the violence of his tortures, told the truth about matters which could not be proved, or by a false confession sought an end to his torments.

35 Alexander, thinking [d] that those who, as he had learned, had freely deplored the death of Parmenion ought to be separated from the rest of the army, put them apart in one cohort and gave them as their leader Leonidas,[e] who had himself formerly

[d] Cf. Diod. xvii. 80. 4 ; Justin xii. 5.
[e] Otherwise unknown.

36 intima familiaritate coniunctum. Fere idem erant
quos alioqui rex habuerat invisos. Nam cum experiri
vellet militum animos, admonuit qui litteras in Macedoniam ad suos scripsisset eis[1] quos ipse mittebat
perlaturis[2] cum fide traderet. Simpliciter ad neces-
sarios suos quisque scripserat quae sentiebat ; aliis
gravis erat, plerisque non ingrata militia. Ita et
agentium gratias et querentium litterae exceptae
37 sunt. Et, qui forte taedium laboris per litteras erant
questi, hanc seorsus cohortem a ceteris tendere
ignominiae causa iubet, fortitudine usurus in bello,
libertatem linguae ab auribus credulis remoturus.
Id consilium, temerarium forsitan—quippe fortissimi
iuvenes contumelia[3] irritati erant—sicut omnia alia
38 felicitas regis excepit. Nihil illis ad bella promptius
fuit ; incitabat virtutem et ignominiae demendae
cupido et quia fortia facta in paucis latere non
poterant.

III. His ita compositis, Alexander, Arsame Drangarum satrape constituto, iter pronuntiari iubet in
Arimaspos,[4] quos iam tunc mutato nomine Euergetas
appellabant, ex quo frigore victusque penuria Cyri
exercitum affectum tectis et commeatibus iuverant.
2 Quintus dies erat, ut in eam regionem pervenerat.
Cognoscit Satibarzanem,[5] qui ad Bessum defecerat,

---

[1] eis · *Vindelinus;* si *A.*
[2] perlaturis *Vindelinus;* perlaturus *A.*
[3] contumelia *Modius;* contumelias *L m. pr. PV;* con-
tumeliis *BFL m. sec.*
[4] Arimaspos *Wesseling;* armatos *A.*
[5] Satibarzanem *Aldus;* satibazanem *A.*

---

[a] " Benefactors "; *cf.* Diod. xvii. 81 and Arr. iii. 27. 4.

36 been an intimate friend of Parmenion. These were about the same as those whom he had for other reasons disliked. For once, when he wished to sound the feelings of the soldiers, he told any who had written letters to their people in Macedonia to hand them to the messengers whom he himself was sending, who would faithfully deliver them. Each man had written frankly to his relatives what he had thought ; to some military service was burdensome, to most it was not disagreeable. In this way Alexander got hold of the letters of those who had written favourably and of those who complained.

37 And he ordered a cohort of those who chanced in their letters to have complained of the irksome military service to encamp apart from the rest by way of disgrace, saying that he would use their bravery in war, but would remove loose talking from credulous ears. This plan, perhaps rash—for the bravest of men had been irritated by the insult—like everything else, the

38 good fortune of the king made successful. Nothing was more enthusiastic for war than those men ; their valour was enhanced both from the desire of wiping out disgrace, and because brave deeds could not be concealed among a few.

III. When these matters had been thus arranged, Alexander, having made Arsames satrap of the Drangae, ordered a march to be proclaimed against the Arimaspi, whom even at that time they called the Euergetae,ᵃ having changed their name from the time when they had aided with shelter and supplies the army of Cyrus, when it was almost worn out by

2 cold and lack of food. It was the fifth day since he had come into that region. He learned that Satibarzanes, who had revolted and gone over to Bessus,

eum equitum manu irrupisse rursus in Arios.[1] Itaque
contra eum misit[2] Caranum et[3] Erigyium cum Artabazo et Andronico ; eos[4] vi milia Graecorum peditum,
3 dc equites sequebantur. Ipse lx diebus gentem
Euergetarum ordinavit, magna pecunia ob egregiam
in Cyrum fidem donata.

4 Relicto deinde qui eis praeesset Amedine—scriba
is Darei fuerat—Arachosios, quorum regio ad Ponticum mare pertinet, subegit. Ibi exercitus qui sub
Parmenione fuerat occurrit. Sex milia Macedonum
erant et cc nobiles et v milia Graecorum cum equitibus
5 dc, haud dubie robur omnium virium regis. Arachosiis datus Menon praetor, iiii milibus peditum et dc
equitibus in praesidium relictis.

Ipse rex nationem ne finitimis quidem satis notam,
quippe nullo commercio colentem[5] mutuos usus, cum
6 exercitu intravit. Parapanisadae[6] appellantur, agreste hominum genus et inter barbaros maxime
inconditum. Locorum asperitas hominum quoque
7 ingenia duraverat. Gelidissimum septentrionis axem
ex magna parte spectant, Bactrianis ab occidente

---

[1] Arios *Acidalius;* alios *A.*
[2] contra eum misit *added by Hedicke.*
[3] et *added by Aldus.*   [4] eos *Hedicke;* et *A.*
[5] colentem *Acidalius;* nolentem *C;* uolantem *P.*
[6] Parapanisadae *Hedicke;* paramedesidem *A.*

---

[a] Cf. vii. 4. 32 ; Arr. iii. 28. 2.
[b] Arr. iii. 23. 9.
[c] That is, established a government among them.
[d] The last datable point was the death of Darius in July,
330 b.c. (Arr. iii. 22. 2).

with a force of cavalry had again invaded Aria.
Therefore he sent against him Caranus [a] and Erigyius
with Artabazus and Andronicus [b]; they were followed
3 by 6000 Greek infantry and 600 cavalry. He himself
set in order [c] the race of the Euergetae within sixty
days,[d] and gave them a great sum of money because
of their splendid loyalty to Cyrus.

4 Then, after having left Amedines to govern them
—he had been Darius' secretary—he subdued the
Arachosii, whose territory extends to the Pontic Sea.[e]
There he met the army which had been commanded
by Parmenion. It consisted of 6000 Macedonians,
200 nobles, 5000 Greeks, with 600 cavalry, beyond
5 doubt the flower of all the king's forces.[f] Menon was
made governor of the Arachosii, and 4000 infantry
and 600 cavalry were left as a garrison.

The king himself with his army entered a nation
not very well known even to their neighbours, since,
having no commerce with them, they practised no
6 borrowed customs. They are called the Parapanisadae,[g] a rude race of men and especially uncultivated
even among barbarians. The harshness of their
climate had hardened the nature also of the inhabit-
7 ants. They look in great part toward the very cold
northern pole,[h] on the west they are adjacent to the

---

[e] This, the Black Sea, is of course absurd. Warmington
suggests that, by an error, *Ponticum* may have arisen from
πόντος,=*mare* or perhaps ὠκεανός; hence "to the Red Sea,"
or "to the Indian Ocean." The Arachosii were in eastern
Iran or Baluchistan.   [f] An exaggeration.

[g] Named from the mountain Parapanisus,=Hindū Kush.

[h] For this poetic term *cf.* Virg. *Aen.* viii. 26 ff. ; Diod.
xvii. 82. 2. The Pole Star is meant: it is the last star in
the tail of Ursa Minor, which seems to stand still, while the
rest of the heavens turn about it.

coniuncti sunt, meridiana regio ad mare Indicum
8 vergit.   Tuguria latere crudo[1] struunt et, quia sterilis
est terra materia, nudo etiam montis dorso, usque
ad summum aedificiorum fastigium eodem laterculo
9 utuntur.   Ceterum structura latior ab imo paulatim
incremento operis in artius cogitur, ad ultimum in
carinae maxime modum coit.   Ibi foramine relicto
10 superne lumen admittunt.[2]   Vites et arbores, si quae
in tanto terrae rigore durare potuerunt, obruunt
penitus; hieme defossae[3] latent, cum discussa aperire
11 humum coepit, caelo solique redduntur.   Ceterum
adeo altae nives premunt terram, gelu et perpetuo
paene rigore constrictae, ut ne avium quidem feraeve
ullius vestigium exstet.   Obscura caeli verius umbra
quam lux, nocti similis, premit terram, vix ut quae
12 prope sunt conspici possint.   In hac tum[4] omnis
humani cultus solitudine destitutus exercitus, quidquid malorum tolerari potest pertulit, inopiam, frigus,
13 lassitudinem,   desperationem.   Multos   exanimavit
rigor insolitus nivis, multorum adussit pedes, pluri-
morum oculos.   Praecipue perniciabilis fuit fatigatis;
quippe in ipso gelu deficientia corpora sternebant,
quae cum moveri desissent, vis frigoris ita astringe-
bat, ut rursus ad surgendum coniti,[5] non possent.
14 A commilitonibus torpentes excitabantur, neque
aliud remedium erat, quam ut ingredi cogerentur;

---

[1] crudo *Hedicke;* primo *A.*
admittunt *Zumpt;* admedium *A.*
[3] defossae *Vindelinus;* defossa *A.*
[4] tum *Freinshem;* tamen *A.*
[5] coniti *Lauer;* contineri *A.*

Bactriani, on the south their territory slopes toward
8 the Indian sea. They build huts of unbaked brick, and
because the land is destitute of timber, since even the
ridge of the mountain is bare, they use the same
9 brick up to the very top of their buildings. But
their structure is broader at the base and gradually
becomes narrower as the work grows, and finally it
comes together very much like the keel of a ship.[a]
There they leave an opening and let in light from
10 above. Vines and trees, if any have been able to
live in such a frozen soil, they bury deep in the
ground; in winter these remain dug in, and when
the end of winter begins to open the earth, they are
11 restored to the sky and to the sun. But such deep
snows cover the ground and are bound so fast by ice
and almost perpetual cold, that no trace is to be found
even of birds or of any wild beast. What may be
called a dim shadow of the sky rather than light, and
resembling night, broods over the earth, so that
objects which are near at hand can hardly be made
12 out. The army, then, abandoned in this absence of
all human civilization, endured all the evils that could
13 be suffered, want, cold, fatigue, despair. The unusual
cold of the snow caused the death of many, to many it
brought frost-bite of the feet, to very many blindness
of the eyes. It was especially harmful to those who
were fatigued; for when their strength gave out, they
stretched themselves on the very ice, and when they
ceased to move, the force of the cold so bound them
fast, that when they struggled to rise again, they could
14 not do so. But they were roused from their torpor
by their fellow-soldiers, for there was no other cure
than to be forced to go on; then only, when their

[a] See Sall. Jug. xviii. 4-5.

tum demum, vitali calore moto, membris aliquis
redibat vigor.

15 Si qui tuguria barbarorum adire potuerunt, celeriter refecti sunt. Sed tanta caligo erat, ut aedificia
16 nulla alia res quam fumus ostenderet. Illi, numquam
ante in terris suis advena viso, cum armatos repente
conspicerent, exanimati metu, quidquid in tuguriis
erat afferebant, ut corporibus ipsorum parceretur
17 orantes. Rex agmen circumibat pedes, iacentes quosdam erigens et alios, cum aegre sequerentur, adminiculo corporis sui excipiens. Nunc ad prima signa,
nunc in medio,[1] nunc in ultimo agmine itineris multi-
18 plicato labore aderat. Tandem ad loca cultiora
perventum est commeatuque largo recreatus exercitus ; simul et qui consequi non potuerant in illa castra
venerunt.

19 Inde agmen processit ad Caucasum montem, cuius
dorsum Asiam perpetuo iugo dividit ; hinc simul
mare, quod Ciliciam subit, illinc Caspium fretum et
amnem[2] Araxen nobiliaque[3] regionis Scythicae[4]
20 deserta spectat. Taurus, secundae magnitudinis
mons, committitur Caucaso ; a Cappadocia se attol-
lens Ciliciam praeterit Armeniaeque montibus
21 iungitur. Sic inter se iuga velut serie cohaerentia
perpetuum habent dorsum, ex quo Asiae omnia fere

---

[1] medio *I*; medium *A*.   [2] et amnem] etiam nem *P*.
[3] nobiliaque *Hedicke*; et alia quae *P*; aliaque *C*.
[4] Scythicae *Hedicke*; schythiae *P*; scithiae *C*.

---

[a] Not what is to-day known as the Caucasus, but the
Parapanisus, or Hindu Kush, which at first the Macedonians
thought was the Caucasus. The Hindu Kush was also
taken to be a part of a long transverse east-west ridge

natural warmth was aroused, did any strength return
to their limbs.

15 If any could reach the huts of the barbarians, they
were quickly restored. But such was the darkness
that the only thing which revealed the buildings was
16 their smoke. When the natives, who had never
before seen a stranger in their country, suddenly
caught sight of armed men, they were paralysed with
fear and brought them whatever they had in their
17 huts, begging them to spare their lives. The king
went about on foot among his troops, lifting up some
who were lying prostrate, and, by the aid of his body,
supporting those who were following with difficulty.
Now in the van, now in the centre, now at the rear
of the army he was everywhere present with manifold
18 toil. At length they came to more cultivated places
and the army was revived by an abundance of supplies ; at the same time also those who had not been
able to keep up came into the camp which they had
pitched.

19 From there the army proceeded to the Caucasus
mountains,[a] whose range divides Asia by a continuous
ridge. It looks on one side to the sea which washes
Cilicia, on the other to the Caspian Sea, the river
Araxes, and the well-known deserts of the Scythian
20 region. Taurus, a mountain of second rank in height,
joins the Caucasus ; rising from Cappadocia, it passes
by Cilicia, and unites itself with the Armenian moun-
21 tains. Thus the ranges, as if connected in a series,
form a continuous chain, from which almost all the
rivers of Asia flow, some into the Red Sea,[b] others

stretching from the Mediterranean to the " eastern Ocean,"
and the whole ridge was often called Taurus.
  [b] *i.e.* Persian Gulf, Arabian Sea and Indian Ocean.

flumina, alia in Rubrum, alia in Caspium mare, alia
in Hyrcanium et Ponticum decidunt. XVII dierum
22 spatio Caucasum superavit exercitus. Rupes in eo x
in circuitu stadia complectitur, IIII in altitudinem
excedit, in qua[1] vinctum Promethea fuisse antiquitas
23 tradidit. Condendae in radicibus montis urbi sedes
electa est. VII milibus subactarum nationum[2] et
praeterea militibus quorum opera uti desisset per-
missum in nova urbe considere. Hanc quoque
Alexandream incolae appellaverunt.

IV. At Bessus Alexandri celeritate perterritus, dis
patriis sacrificio rite facto, sicut illis gentibus mos est,
cum amicis ducibusque copiarum inter epulas de bello
2 consultabat. Graves mero suas vires extollere, hostium nunc temeritatem, nunc paucitatem spernere
3 incipiunt. Praecipue Bessus ferox verbis, et parto
per scelus regno superbus ac vix potens mentis, dicere
orditur : socordia Darei crevisse hostium famam.
4 Occurrisse enim in Ciliciae angustissimis faucibus,
cum retrocedendo posset perducere incautos in loca
naturae situ tuta,[3] tot fluminibus obiectis, tot montium latebris, inter quas deprehensus hostis ne fugae
quidem, nedum resistendi occasionem fuerit habi-
5 turus. Sibi placere in Sogdianos recedere ; Oxum[4]

---

[1] qua *Vindelinus;* quo *A.*
[2] subactarum nationum *Hedicke;* seniorum macedonum *A.*
[3] situ tuta *Bentley;* sit aut *A.*
[4] Oxum *Lauer;* exum *A.*

---

[a] *i.e.* the Caspian and Black Seas.

into the Caspian, and still others into the Hyrcanian and Pontic.[a] The army passed over Caucasus
22 in a space of seventeen days. There is a crag in the mountain, embracing ten stadia in circumference and rising to four stadia in height, on which ancient
23 fable reports that Prometheus was chained. A site for founding a city was chosen at the foot of the mountain and seven thousand from the subdued nations were permitted to settle in the new city, as well as those soldiers whose services the king had ceased to make use of. This city also its inhabitants called Alexandria.

IV. But Bessus, greatly terrified by Alexander's speed, after having duly performed a sacrifice to the gods of the country, as is the custom with those nations, was feasting and holding council with his friends and with the leaders of his forces about the
2 war. Heavy with wine, they began to boast of their strength, and to express scorn, now of the rashness
3 of the enemy, now of their small numbers. In particular Bessus, in insolent language and so proud of a sovereignty gained by murder as hardly to be in his right mind, began by saying that the reputation of the enemy had increased through the incapacity
4 of Darius. For he had encountered them in the narrowest part of the passes of Cilicia, when by drawing back he might have taken them off their guard and led them into places which the nature of the country made safe, since so many rivers lay in the way and there were so many hiding-places in the mountains that if surprised among these the enemy would have had not even an opportunity for flight,
5 much less for resisting. That it was his intention to withdraw into the land of the Sogdiani ; he would

amnem velut murum obiecturum hosti, dum ex
6 finitimis gentibus valida auxilia concurrerent. Venturos autem Chorasmios et Dahas[1] Sacasque[2] et Indos
et ultra Tanain amnem colentes Scythas ; quorum
neminem adeo humilem esse, ut humeri eius non
possent Macedonis militis verticem aequare.
7   Conclamant temulenti unam hanc sententiam salu-
brem esse ; et Bessus circumferri merum largius
8 iubet, debellaturus super mensam Alexandrum. Erat
in eo convivio Gobares,[3] natione Medus, sed magicae
artis—si modo ars est, non vanissimi cuiusque ludibrium—magis professione quam scientia celeber,
9 alioqui moderatus et probus. Is cum praefatus esset,
scire servo utilius esse parere dicto quam afferre
consilium, cum illos qui pareant idem quod ceteros
maneat, qui vero suadeant proprium subeant[4] periculum ; Bessus eum dicere iussit intrepidum,[5] pocu-
10 lum etiam, quod habebat in manu, tradidit. Quo
accepto, Gobares : " Natura," inquit, " mortalium
hoc quoque nomine prava et sinistra dici potest, quod
in suo quisque negotio hebetior est quam in alieno.
11 Turbida sunt consilia eorum, qui sibi suadent. Obstat
metus, alias[6] cupiditas, nonnumquam naturalis eorum
quae excogitaveris amor ; nam in te superbia non

[1] Dahas *Aldus;* deas *A.*
[2] Sacasque *J. Froben;* sagasque *A.*
[3] Gobares *Stangl;* cobares *A.*
[4] subeant *Hedicke;* sibi *A.*
[5] Bessus . . . intrepidum *added by Halm.*
[6] alias *Bentley;* aliis *A.*

---

[a] *i.e.* the Amu Darya.
[b] This is not the river (Don) which was generally known
by that name, but the Iaxartes (Syr Darya).

oppose the Oxus [a] River like a wall to the enemy, until powerful auxiliaries should assemble from the
6 neighbouring nations; the Chorasmii would come to him and the Dahae and Sacae, and the Indians and the Scythians dwelling beyond the river Tanais,[b] not one of whom was so short of stature that he was not a head taller than a Macedonian soldier.

7 His drunken companions shouted in chorus that this plan alone was sound; and Bessus ordered wine to be served more abundantly, as if intending to
8 vanquish Alexander at the table. There was present at that banquet Gobares,[c] a Mede by nationality, but a dabbler in the art of magic—if only that is an art, and not the illusion of all the greatest liars —more celebrated in his pretension than in his actual knowledge, but in other respects modest and upright.
9 He, by way of preface, said that he knew that it was more expedient for a slave to obey orders than to offer counsel, since the same fate awaits those who obey which awaits the rest, but those who advise undergo a particular peril of their own.[d] Bessus bade him speak fearlessly and even handed him the cup which he had
10 been holding in his hand.[e] Having taken the cup, Gobares said : "The nature of mortal men may be called perverse and vicious under this head also, that each one is less keen-sighted in his own business than
11 in that of another. The counsels of those who advise themselves are confused. Fear opposes them, at another time their desire, sometimes the natural love of their own plans; for presumption does not apply to you. You have, in truth, learned by ex-

<hr />

[c] The name is not certain.
[d] That is, the result is charged against them.
[e] As being the speaker.

cadit. Expertus es utique[1] quod ipse reppereris **aut**
12 solum aut optimum ducere. Magnum onus sustines
capite, regium insigne ; hoc aut moderate perferen-
dum est, aut, quod abominor, in te ruet. Consilio,
13 non impetu, opus est." Adicit deinde, quod apud
Bactrianos vulgo usurpabant, canem timidum vehementius latrare quam mordere altissimaque[2] flumina
minimo sono labi. Quae inserui, ut qualiscumque
inter barbaros potuit esse prudentia traderetur.
14 Ille[3] his audientium expectationem suspenderat[4] ;
tum consilium aperit utilius Besso quam gratius.
" In vestibulo," inquit, " regiae tuae velocissimus
consistit rex ; ante ille agmen quam tu mensam
15 istam movebis. Nunc ab Tanai exercitum accerses
et armis flumina oppones. Scilicet, qua tu fugiturus
es hostis sequi non potest ! Iter utrique commune
est, victori tutius. Licet strenuum metum putes
16 esse, velocior tamen spes est. Quin validioris occupas
gratiam dedisque te, utcumque cesserit, meliorem
17 fortunam deditus quam hostis habiturus ?[5] Alienum
habes regnum, quo facilius eo careas. Incipias[6]
forsitan iustus esse rex, cum ipse fecerit, qui tibi et
18 dare potest regnum et eripere. Consilium habes
fidele, quod diutius exsequi supervacuum est. Nobilis
equus umbra quoque virgae regitur, ignavus ne

---

[1] utique *Hedicke;* utramque *A.*
[2] altissimaque *Hedicke;* altissima quaeque *A.*
[3] Ille *Hedicke, ed. min.;* in *A.*
[4] suspenderat *J. M. Palmer;* sui spem dederat *A.*
[5] habiturus *Lauer;* habituros *A.*
[6] Incipias *Hedicke;* incipiens *A.*

---

[a] *Cf.* vii. 8. 14-16.
[b] *Cf.* Pliny, *Epist.* ii. 20. 3 ; Amm. xxi. 1. 2.
[c] *Cf.* Livy xxxvi. 22. 11 ; Quint. i. 5. 4.

perience to consider as the only or the best plan
12 whatever you yourself have devised. You sustain a
great burden on your head, a kingly crown; this
must either be borne with moderation or, which I
pray the gods to avert, it will fall in ruins upon you.
There is need of prudence, not of impetuosity."
13 Then he added a proverb in common use among the
Bactriani, that a timid dog barks more violently than
it bites, and that the deepest rivers flow with the
least sound. This I have quoted, in order that whatever wisdom could exist among barbarians[a] might be
recorded.

14 By these words Gobares had left in suspense the
expectation of his hearers[b]; then he disclosed his
advice, which was more expedient for Bessus than
pleasing to him. "At the entrance[c] of your kingdom,"
said he, "stands the swiftest of kings; he will advance
his army before you put away that table of yours.
15 Now you will summon an army from the Tanais, and
you will oppose rivers to his arms. Of course the
enemy cannot follow to whatever place you shall flee!
The route is common to both, safer for the victor.
Although you may think that fear is swift, yet hope
16 is more rapid. Why do you not hasten to gain the
favour of the stronger and give yourself up, since
however it may turn out, you will have better fortune
in having surrendered than you will have as his
17 enemy? You are holding the kingdom of another,
hence it will be easier to do without it. You would
perhaps begin to be a legitimate king when he himself
has made you one who can give you royal power, or
18 wrest it from you. You have faithful advice, which
it would be superfluous to set forth at greater length.
A noble horse is guided by the mere shadow of the

19 calcari quidem concitari potest." Bessus et ingenio
et multo mero ferox, adeo exarsit ut vix[1] ab amicis
quo minus occideret eum—nam strinxerat quoque
acinacem—contineretur. Certe convivio prosiluit
haudquaquam potens mentis. Gobares inter tumultum elapsus ad Alexandrum transfugit.

20 VIII milia Bactrianorum habebat armata Bessus.
Quae quamdiu propter caeli intemperiem Indiam
potius Macedonas petituros crediderant, oboedienter
imperata fecerunt; postquam adventare Alexandrum compertum est, in suos quisque vicos dilapsi,

21 Bessum reliquerunt. Ille cum clientium manu, qui non
mutaverant fidem, Oxo[2] amne superato, exustisque
navigiis quibus transierat, ne isdem hostis uteretur,
novas copias in Sogdianis contrahebat.

22 Alexander Causcasum quidem, ut supra dictum est,
transierat, sed inopia frumenti quoque prope ad

23 famem ventum erat. Suco ex sesima[3] expresso haud
secus quam oleo artus perunguebant, sed huius suci
ducenis quadragenis denariis amphorae singulae,
mellis denariis trecenis nonagenis, trecenis vini aesti-
mabantur; tritici nihil aut admodum exiguum

24 reperiebatur. Siros vocabant barbari, quos ita sollerter abscondunt, ut nisi qui defoderunt invenire
non possint; in his conditae fruges erant. In quarum
penuria milites fluviatili pisce et herbis sustinebantur.

25 Iamque haec ipsa alimenta defecerant, cum iumenta

---

[1] vix *I;* vis *A.*   [2] Oxo *Lauer;* mox *A.*
[3] sesima *Hedicke* (*perhaps* sesama, *Plin.* N.H. *xviii.*
10. 22); sesema *A.*

---

[a] *Cf.* Arr. iii. 28. 8.   [b] See vii. 3. 19, note.
[c] See Varro, *R.R.* i. 57. 2.

whip, a worthless one cannot be aroused even by
19 the spur." Bessus, headstrong by nature, and made
still more so by much wine, so burned with anger
that he was with difficulty restrained by his friends
from killing the speaker—for he had even drawn
his scimitar. At any rate, he leaped up from the
banquet-table, quite beside himself. Gobares escaped
amid the confusion and deserted to Alexander.
20   Bessus had 8000 [a] Bactriani under arms. These, so
long as they believed that the Macedonians because
of the rigour of the climate would be more likely to
go to India, carried out his orders obediently ; after
they learned that Alexander was coming against
them, they slipped away each to his own village and
21 deserted Bessus. He with a band of his clients who
had not changed their allegiance passed over the
river Oxus, and after burning the boats in which he
had crossed, in order that the enemy might not use
them, was levying fresh forces among the Sogdiani.
22   Alexander had crossed the Caucasus,[b] as was said
above, but had almost been reduced to starvation
23 through lack of grain. With the juice pressed from
sesame they anointed their bodies in lieu of oil, but
each amphora of this juice was valued at 240 denarii,
an amphora of honey at 390, and of wine at 300 ; of
24 wheat very little or nothing was found. For the barbarians had pits which they call *siri*,[c] which they
conceal so skilfully, that only those who dug them
can find them ; in these their crops were stored away.
In lack of these supplies the soldiers lived on fish from
25 the river and on herbs.[d] And now even these foods
had failed them, whereupon they were ordered to

[d] Especially *silphium* (species of *Ferula*) ; this shows that
the march was made in the spring.

quibus onera portabant caedere iussi sunt ; horum
carne, dum in Bactrianos perventum est,[1] traxere
vitam.

26 Bactrianae terrae multiplex et varia natura est.
Alibi multa arbor et vitis largos mitesque fructus alit,
solum pingue crebri fontes rigant, quae mitiora sunt
frumento conseruntur, cetera armentorum pabulo
27 cedunt. Magnam deinde partem eiusdem terrae
steriles harenae tenent ; squalida siccitate regio non
hominem, non frugem alit. Cum vero venti a Pontico
mari spirant, quidquid sabuli[2] in campis iacet con-
verrunt; quod ubi cumulatum est, magnorum collium
procul species est, omniaque pristini itineris vestigia
28 intereunt. Itaque, qui transeunt campos, navigan-
tium modo, noctu sidera observant, ad quorum cursum iter dirigunt ; et propemodum clarior est noctis
29 umbra quam lux. Ergo interdiu invia[3] est regio,
quia nec vestigium quod sequantur inveniunt et nitor
siderum caligine absconditur. Ceterum si quos ille
ventus qui a mari exoritur deprehendit, harena
30 obruit. Sed, qua mitior terra est, ingens hominum
equorumque multitudo gignitur. Itaque Bactriani
31 equites xxx milia expleverant. Ipsa Bactra, regionis
eius caput, sita sunt sub monte Parapaniso. Bactrus
amnis praeterit moenia. Is urbi et regioni dedit
nomen.

32 Hic regi stativa habenti nuntiatur ex Graecia

---

[1] est *added by Hedicke.*
[2] sabuli *Lauer;* pabuli *C;* paulo *P.*
[3] interdiu invia *Lauer;* interdium uia *P;* inde inuia *C.*

---

[a] In the fruitful plains and on the lower slopes of the
mountains.
[b] For this meaning *cf.* Amm. xxvi. 1. 10.

kill the pack-animals which carried their baggage ; on the flesh of these they managed to exist until they reached the Bactriani.

26 The land of the Bactriani is of a manifold and varied nature. In one part many trees and vines produce plentiful and mellow fruits, frequent brooks irrigate the rich soil, the milder parts *a* of this they sow with grain, the rest they leave for pasture for the flocks.

27 Farther on a great part of the same land is occupied by sterile sands ; because of its frightful *b* dryness the region is uninhabited and produces no fruit. Indeed, when the winds blow from the Pontic sea,*c* they sweep together whatever sand lies on the plains ; when this is piled up, it looks from a distance like great hills, and all traces of the former road disappear.

28 Accordingly, those who cross the plains watch the stars and direct their course by them, as do those who sail the sea ; and the shade of night is almost brighter

29 than daylight. Therefore the region is impassable in the daytime, because they find no traces to follow, and the light of the stars is hidden in darkness. Moreover, if the wind which arises from the sea overtakes

30 any, it buries them in the sand. But where the land is milder it breeds a great multitude of men and horses. Therefore the cavalry of the Bactriani had

31 amounted to 30,000. Bactra *d* itself, the capital of the region, is situated at the foot of Mount Parapanisus. The Bactrus River *e* flows at the foot of its walls. The river gave its name to the city and to the region.

32 While the king was holding a stationary camp

c He should have said the Caspian or the Indian Ocean. See page 145, note *e*.   *d* Modern Balkh.

e The Dehâs or Balkhâb ; it diminishes in size until it nearly disappears.

Peloponnesiorum Laconumque defectio—nondum
enim victi erant, cum proficiscerentur tumultus eius
principia nuntiaturi—et alius praesens terror affertur,
Scythas, qui ultra Tanaim amnem colunt, adventare
Besso ferentis opem.   Eodem tempore, quae in gente
Ariorum[1] Caranus[2] et Erigyius gesserant perferuntur.
33 Commissum erat proelium inter Macedonas Ariosque.
Transfuga Satibarzanes[3] barbaris praeerat ; qui cum
pugnam segnem utrimque aequis viribus stare vidis-
set, in primos ordines adequitavit, demptaque galea
inhibitis qui tela iaciebant, si quis viritim dimicare
vellet, provocavit ad pugnam ; nudum se caput in
34 certamine habiturum.   Non tulit ferociam barbari
ducis Erigyius,[4] gravis quidem aetate, sed et animi
et corporis robore nulli iuvenum postferendus.   Is
galea dempta canitiem ostentans : " Venit," inquit,
" dies, quo aut victoria aut morte honestissima quales
35 amicos et milites Alexander habeat ostendam." Nec
plura elocutus equum in hostem egit.
Crederes imperatum ut acies utraeque tela cohi-
berent ; protinus certe recesserunt dato libero spatio,
intenti in eventum non ducum[5] modo, sed etiam suae
36 sortis, quippe alienum discrimen secuturi.   Prior
barbarus emisit hastam ; quam Erigyius modica

---

[1] Ariorumque *Lauer;* arionum *A* (alionum *V*).
[2] Caranus *J. Froben;* cauranus *P;* caurarus *C.*
[3] Satibarzanes *Vindelinus;* sartibazes *A.*
[4] ducis Erigyius *Zumpt;* dux illius exercitus *A.*
[5] ducum *Freinshem;* duorum *A.*

---

[a] Arr. iii. 29. 1 fills in the gap in the narrative.

[b] See Diod. xvii. 83. 5 f. ; but *cf.* Arr. iii. 28. 3, who says
nothing about a challenge.

[c] The plural *utraeque* is unusual, but *cf.* Livy xxxiii.
18. 12 ; xxxvi. 16. 10 ; etc.

there,[a] news came from Greece of the revolt of the
Peloponnesians and the Laconians—for they had not
yet been vanquished when those who were to report
the beginnings of that uprising set forth—and another
cause of alarm near at hand was reported, namely,
that the Scythians who dwell beyond the river Tanais
were coming and bringing aid to Bessus. At the same
time news was brought of what Caranus and Erigyius
33 had accomplished in the land of the Arii. A battle
had been fought between the Macedonians and the
Arii. The traitor Satibarzaneṣ commanded the barbarians ; when he saw that the battle was almost at
a standstill with the forces equal on both sides, he
rode into the foremost ranks, and taking off his helmet
and checking those who were hurling weapons, he
challenged to battle anyone who wished to fight in
single combat [b] ; he said that he would fight bare-
34 headed. Erigyius, advanced in years, it is true, but
in vigour of both mind and body not to be deemed
inferior to any of the young men, could not endure
the bravado of the barbarian. He, having taken off
his helmet and displaying his white hair, said : " The
time has come for me to show either by victory or
by a glorious death what sort of friends and soldiers
35 Alexander has." Without more words he drove his
horse against the foe.

You would believe that the order had been given
for both [c] armies to cease fighting ; certain it is that
they at once drew back and left a free space, intent
upon the fate, not only of the leaders, but their own
also, since they were bound to share the outcome of
36 another's fight.[d] The barbarian was the first to hurl
his spear. Erigyius avoided it by a slight movement

[d] That is, their own fight would not decide their fate.

capitis declinatione evitavit[1] atque ipse infestam
sarisam,[2] equo calcaribus concitato, in medio barbari
37 gutture ita fixit, ut per cervicem emineret. Prae-
cipitatus ex equo barbarus adhuc tamen repugnabat.
Sed ille extractam e vulnere hastam rursus in os
dirigit. Satibarzanes manu complexus, quo maturius
38 interiret, ictum hostis adiuvit. Et barbari, duce
amisso, quem magis necessitate quam sponte secuti
erant, tunc haud immemores meritorum Alexandri
39 arma Erigyio tradunt. Rex his quidem laetus, de
Spartanis haudquaquam[3] securus, magno tamen
animo defectum eorum tulit, dicens non ante ausos
consilia nudare quam ipsum ad fines Indiae pervenisse
40 cognossent. Ipse Bessum persequens copias movit ;
cui Erigyius barbari caput, opimum[4] belli decus,
praeferens occurrit.

V. Igitur Bactrianorum regione Artabazo tradita,
sarcinas et impedimenta ibi cum praesidio relinquit,
ipse cum expedito agmine loca deserta Sogdianorum[5]
2 intrat, nocturno itinere exercitum ducens. Aquarum,
ut ante dictum est, penuria prius desperatione quam
desiderio bibendi sitim accendit. Per cccc stadia ne
3 modicus quidem humor exsistit. Harenas vapor
aestivi solis accendit ; quae ubi flagrare coeperunt,
haud secus quam continenti incendio cuncta torren-

---

[1] evitavit *I;* uitauit *A.*

[2] sarisam *Hedicke;* sarissam *C;* sarassam *P.*

[3] haudquaquam *Lauer;* haud quamquam *BFP;* haut q.
L; aut q. *V.*

[4] barbari caput, opimum *Bentley;* barbaricae optimum *P;*
barbarici optimum *C.*

[5] Sogdianorum *Glareanus;* susitanorum *A.*

---

[a] *Defectus* in this sense is very rare ; *cf.* Capitol. *Opilius
Macrinus* viii. 2.

[b] This was not true at the time when he said it.

of his head, and putting spurs to his horse, drove his lance straight into the middle of the barbarian's throat, so that it came out at the back of his neck.

37 The barbarian, though thrown from his horse, yet still continued to fight. But Erigyius, drawing the spear from the wound, directed it again at his face. Satibarzanes seized it with his hand, in order to die more

38 quickly, and aided the enemy's stroke. The barbarians, having lost their leader, whom they had followed rather on compulsion than voluntarily, and then not unmindful of the merits of Alexander,

39 surrendered to Erigyius. The king, rejoicing in this success, although by no means free from anxiety about the Spartans, yet bore their revolt *a* with great courage, saying that they had not dared to reveal their design until they knew that he had come to

40 the confines of India.*b* He himself moved his forces in pursuit of Bessus ; Erigyius met him, displaying the head of the barbarian, as a glorious spoil of war.*c*

V. Therefore having entrusted the region of the Bactriani to Artabazus, he left there the packs and baggage with a garrison, and himself with a light-armed force entered the desert places of the Sogdiani

2 leading his army by night.*d* The scarcity of water, mentioned above,*e* sets up a burning thirst through despair of finding it, before it does so by desire for drinking. For 400 stadia not even a drop of water

3 is to be found. The heat of the summer sun makes the sands hot, and when they began to glow, everything is burned as if by a continuous conflagration.

---

c The language suggests the Roman *spolia opima* ; see iii. 11. 7, note.

d To travel by night in summer is usual in Turkestan.

e vii. 4. 27.

4 tur.   Caligo deinde, immodico terrae fervore excitata, lucem tegit, camporumque non alia quam vasti
5 et profundi aequoris species est.   Nocturnum iter
tolerabile videbatur, quia rore et matutino frigore
corpora levabantur.   Ceterum cum ipsa luce aestus
oritur, omnemque naturalem absorbet humorem[1]
6 siccitas ;   ora visceraque penitus uruntur.   Itaque
primum animi, deinde corpora deficere coeperunt ;
7 pigebat et consistere et progredi.   Pauci, a peritis
regionis admoniti, praeparaverant aquam ;   haec
paulisper repressit sitim, deinde crescente aestu
rursus desiderium humoris accensum est.   Ergo,
quidquid vini oleique erat omnibus[2] ingerebatur,
tantaque dulcedo bibendi fuit, ut in posterum sitis
6 non timeretur.   Graves deinde avide hausto humore,
non sustinere arma, non ingredi poterant, et feliciores
videbantur, quos aqua defecerat, cum ipsi sine modo
infusam vomitu cogerentur egerere.

9   Anxium regem tantis malis circumfusi amici, ut
meminisset orabant, animi sui magnitudinem unicum
10 remedium deficientis exercitus esse ;   cum ex eis qui
praecesserant ad capiendum locum castris, duo occurrunt utribus aquam gestantes, ut filiis suis, quos in
eodem agmine esse et aegre pati sitim non ignora-
11 bant, succurrerent.[3]   Qui cum in regem incidissent,

[1] absorbet humorem] arbor betum orem *P m. pr.;* a. b.
morem *P corr.*   [2] omnibus *Hedicke;* hominibus *A.*
[3] succurrerent *Heinse;* occurrerent *A.*

[a] To judge from his description, Curtius must have seen
such mirages or learned of them from authentic sources.

4 Then too a mist, aroused by the excessive warmth of the ground, obscures the light, and the aspect of the plain is not unlike that of a vast and deep sea.[a]

5 By night the march seemed endurable, since their bodies were relieved by the dew and by the early morning coolness.[b] But with the very daylight the heat returns, and dryness consumes all their natural moisture; mouths and innermost vitals are

6 parched. As a result, first their courage and then their strength began to give out, they were reluc-

7 tant either to stand still or to go on. A few, advised by those who knew the region, had provided themselves with water beforehand; this for a time appeased their thirst, then, as the heat increased, the desire for water was kindled again. Therefore what wine and oil there was was lavished upon all, and so great was the pleasure of drinking, that they

8 did not fear thirst for the future. Later, heavy from drinking greedily, they could not carry their arms nor march, and those seemed more fortunate who had had nothing to drink, since those who had were forced to get rid of by vomiting up what they had poured down without moderation.

9 The king, worried by such troubles, was surrounded by his friends, who begged him to remember that the greatness of his own courage was the sole remedy for

10 the weakness of the army; when two of those who had gone ahead to choose a place for a camp met them, bringing water in skins, in order to aid their sons who were in that same army and whom they

11 knew to be suffering severely from thirst. When they met Alexander, one of them opened one of the

[b] In the sandy desert there is a great fall of temperature at night, from 100° to 70° or 60°.

alter ex his, utre resoluto, vas, quod simul ferebat,
implet, porrigens regi. Ille accipit ; percontatus
12 quibus aquam portaret, filiis ferre cognoscit. Tunc
poculo pleno, sicut oblatum est, reddito : " Nec
solus," inquit, " bibere sustineo nec tam exiguum
dividere omnibus possum ; vos currite et liberis
vestris quod propter illos attulistis date."
13 Tandem ad flumen Oxum ipse pervenit prima fere
vespera. Sed exercitus magna pars non potuerat
consequi ; in edito monte ignes iubet fieri, ut ei qui
aegre sequebantur haud procul castris ipsos abesse
14 cognoscerent, eos autem qui primi agminis erant,
mature cibo ac potione firmatos, implere alios utres,
alios vasa, quibuscumque aqua portari posset, ac suis
15 opem ferre. Sed qui intemperantius hauserant,
intercluso spiritu exstincti sunt, multoque maior
16 horum numerus fuit quam ullo amiserat proelio. At
ille thoracem adhuc indutus, nec aut cibo refectus aut
potu, qua veniebat exercitus constitit nec ante ad
curandum corpus recessit quam praeterierat omne[1]
agmen, totamque eam noctem cum magno animi
17 motu perpetuis vigiliis egit. Nec postero die laetior
erat, quia nec navigia habebat nec pons erigi poterat,
terra circum[2] amnem nuda[3] et materia maxime sterili.
Consilium igitur quod unum necessitas subiecerat init.
18 Utres quam plurimos stramentis refertos dividit ; his

---

[1] praeterierat omne *Hedicke;* praeterierant qui *A.*
[2] terra circum *Hedicke;* circum *A.*
[3] nuda *Hedicke;* nudo *A.*

---

* This story is told by others for other occasions, the
pursuit of Darius, the march through Cedrosia, etc. ; Frontinus, *Strat.* i. 7. 7, lays its scene in Africa.

skins, filled a cup which he was carrying with him, and offered it to the king. He took it; then, having asked for whom he was bringing the water, he learned 12 that he was bringing it for his sons. Thereupon, returning the full cup, just as it had been offered to him, the king said : " I cannot endure to drink alone, and I cannot distribute so little among all ; do you hasten and give to your children what you have brought for them." [a]

13 At length Alexander came to the river Oxus at about sunset. But the great part of the army had been unable to keep up with him ; hence he ordered fires to be lighted on a high hill, in order that those who were following with difficulty might know that 14 they were not far from the camp, but that of those who were in the front of the army, after speedily refreshing themselves with food and drink, some should fill skins, others whatever other vessels could 15 hold water, and bring aid to his men. But those who had drunk too intemperately, had a choking fit [b] and died, and the number of these was much greater 16 than the king had lost in any battle. But he, still wearing his cuirass and refreshed neither with food nor drink, stood on the road by which the army was coming, nor did he retire to refresh himself until the whole army had passed by, and he spent that whole 17 night without sleep in great trouble of mind. Nor was he more cheerful on the following day, because he had no boats, nor could a bridge be set up, since all the land around the river was bare and especially lacking in timber. Therefore he adopted the only 18 expedient that necessity had suggested ; he distributed as many skins stuffed with straw as possible ;

[b] *Cf.* iii. 6. 13.

incubantes transnavere amnem, quique primi transierant in statione erant, dum traicerent ceteri. Hoc
modo sexto demum die in ulteriore ripa totum exercitum exposuit.

19 Iamque ad persequendum Bessum statuerat progredi, cum ea quae in Sogdianis[1] evenerant[2] cognoscit.
Spitamenes erat inter omnes amicos praecipuo[3]
20 honore cultus a Besso; sed nullis meritis perfidia
mitigari potest, quae tamen iam minus in eo invisa
esse poterat, quia nihil ulli nefastum in Bessum,
interfectorem regis sui, videbatur. Titulus facinori[4]
speciosus praeferebatur, vindicta Darei, sed for-
21 tunam, non scelus oderat[5] Bessi. Namque ut
Alexandrum flumen Oxum superasse cognovit,
Dataphernem et Catanen,[6] quibus a Besso maxima
fides habebatur, in societatem cogitatae rei asciscit.
Illi promptius annuunt[7] quam rogabantur, assumptis-
que VIII fortissimis iuvenibus, talem dolum intendunt.
22 Spitamenes pergit ad Bessum et remotis arbitris
comperisse ait se, insidiari ei Dataphernen et Catanen, ut vivum Alexandro traderent; agitantes a
semet occupatos esse et vinctos teneri.

23 Bessus, tanto merito, ut credebat, obligatus, partim
gratias agit, partim avidus expetendi[8] supplicii ad-
24 duci eos iubet. Illi, manibus sua sponte religatis, a
participibus consilii trahebantur; quos Bessus truci

---

[1] Sogdianis *Freinshem;* susianis *A.*
[2] evenerant *Hedicke;* erant *A.*
[3] praecipuo *B corr. L corr. V corr.;* praecipue *A.*
[4] facinori *Acidalius;* facinoris *A.*
[5] oderat *Acidalius;* oderant *C;* oderan *P.*
[6] Catanen *Kinch;* catenen *P;* catenem *C.*
[7] adnuunt *Jeep;* addunt *A.*
[8] expetendi *Vogel;* explendi *A.*

lying upon these, they swam [a] across the river, and those who had crossed first remained on guard until the rest had passed over. In this way he brought his whole army on the farther bank after five days.

19 And now he had decided to go on in pursuit of Bessus, when he learned what had happened in the country of the Sogdiani. Spitamenes was most
20 highly honoured by Bessus among all his friends, but treachery cannot be tamed by any services, a thing which nevertheless might have been less odious in his case, since it seemed that no wrong could be done by anyone to Bessus, the murderer of his king. A specious pretext for his crime was offered, namely, the avenging of Darius, but it was the fortune, not the evil
21 deed, of Bessus that he hated. For when he learned that Alexander had crossed the river Oxus, he enrolled Dataphernes and Catanes, in whom Bessus had the greatest confidence, as accomplices in the conspiracy which he had planned. They consented more promptly than they were asked, and taking with them eight very strong young men, they laid the
22 following snare. Spitamenes went to Bessus and in a private conference said that he had learned that Dataphernes and Catanes were plotting against him, in order to deliver him alive to Alexander; that he had anticipated their conspiracy and was holding them in fetters.

23 Bessus, under obligation for this great service, as he thought it, both thanked them and, eager to inflict punishment, ordered the two men to be brought
24 to him. They, with their arms voluntarily bound, were dragged in by the accomplices in the plot; Bessus, gazing fiercely at them, arose, evidently unable to

[a] See Arrian iii. 29. 3-4.

vultu intuens, consurgit, manibus non temperaturus.
Atque illi simulatione omissa circumsistunt eum et
frustra repugnantem vinciunt, derepto[1] ex capite
regni insigni[2] lacerataque veste, quam e spoliis occisi
25 regis induerat. Ille deos sui sceleris ultores adesse
confessus, adiecit non Dareo iniquos fuisse quem sic
ulciscerentur, sed Alexandro propitios, cuius[3] vic-
26 toriam semper etiam hostes adiuvissent. Multitudo
an vindicatura Bessum fuerit incertum est, nisi illi
qui vinxerant iussu Alexandri fecisse ipsos ementiti,
dubios adhuc animi terruissent. In equum imposi-
tum Alexandro tradituri ducunt.
27 Inter haec rex, quibus matura erat missio electis
nongentis fere, bina talenta equiti dedit, pediti terna[4]
denarium milia, monitosque ut liberos generarent,
remisit domum. Ceteris gratiae actae, quod ad
reliqua belli navaturos operam pollicebantur.
28 Dum Bessum persequitur,[5] perventum erat in par-
vulum oppidum. Branchidae[6] eius incolae erant;
Mileto quondam iussu Xerxis, cum e Graecia rediret,
transierant et in ea sede constiterant, quia templum[7]

[1] derepto *Wakefield;* direpto *A.*
[2] insigni *Lauer;* insigne *A.*
[3] cuius *Giunta;* insecutos *A.*
[4] terna *J. Froben;* ter *A.*
[5] dum Bessum persequitur *Hedicke;* dum bessus perducitur *P;* tum Bessum perducitur *C.*
[6] Branchidae *J. Froben;* brancidae *A.*
[7] templum *Lauer;* templa *A.*

[a] According to Ptolemy in Arr. iii. 30. 1-2, Spitamenes and
Dataphernes lost their courage, and Bessus fell into the
hands of those whom Alexander had sent.
[b] According to Aristobulus (Arr. *l.c.*), the conspirators
delivered him to Ptolemy.

refrain from laying hands upon them. Then they, laying aside pretence, surrounded him, and in spite of his vain attempts at resistance bound him, tearing from his head the royal tiara and rending the clothes which he had put on from the spoils of the murdered
25 king. Bessus, confessing that the gods had come as avengers of his crime, added that they had not been unfavourable to Darius, whom they thus avenged, but propitious to Alexander, since even his enemies
26 always aided his victory. Whether the populace would have rescued Bessus is uncertain, had not those who had bound him, by falsely saying that they had done so by order of Alexander,[a] terrified them while their minds were still wavering. The conspirators placed him on a horse and took him to be delivered to Alexander.[b]
27 Meanwhile [c] the king, having selected about 900 of those whose discharge was due, gave two talents to each of the cavalry and to each of the infantry 3000 denarii, and sent them home after exhorting them to beget children. To the rest he gave thanks, because they promised to render good service for the remainder of the war.
28 While the king was pursuing Bessus, they arrived at a little town. It was inhabited by the Branchidae [d]; they had in former days migrated from Miletus by order of Xerxes, when he was returning from Greece, and had settled in that place, because to gratify

[c] According to Arr. iii. 29. 5, it was before crossing the Oxus.

[d] See Amm. xxix. 1. 31, note; Strabo xi. 11. 4. Their oracle was on the foothill Posidion, twenty stadia from the shore, and 180 from Miletus: see also Hdt. vi. 19. The story of Alexander's savage act is discredited by many modern scholars.

quod Didymeon[1] appellatur in gratiam Xerxis viola-
29 verant. Mores patrii nondum exoleverant, sed iam
bilingues erant, paulatim a domestico externo sermone degeneres. Magno igitur gaudio regem excipiunt, urbem seque dedentes. Ille Milesios qui
30 apud ipsum militarent convocari iubet. Vetus odium
Milesii gerebant[2] in Branchidarum gentem. Proditis
ergo sive iniuriae sive originis meminisse mallent,
31 liberum de Branchidis permittit arbitrium. Variantibus deinde sententiis, se ipsum consideraturum quid
optimum factu esset ostendit.

Postero die occurrentibus Branchidis[3] secum procedere iubet, cumque ad urbem ventum esset, ipse
32 cum expedita manu portam intrat ; phalanx moenia
oppidi circumire iussa et dato signo diripere urbem,
proditorum receptaculum, ipsosque ad unum caedere.
33 Illi inermes passim trucidantur, nec aut commercio
linguae aut supplicum[4] velamentis precibusque inhiberi crudelitas potest. Tandem, ut deicerent,
fundamenta murorum ab imo moliuntur, ne quod
34 urbis vestigium extaret. Nemora[5] quoque et lucos
sacros non caedunt modo, sed etiam extirpant, ut
vasta solitudo et sterilis humus, exustis[6] etiam radici-
35 bus, linqueretur. Quae si in ipsos proditionis auctores

[1] Didymeon *Freinshem;* didimaon *A.*
[2] Milesii gerebant *Freinshem;* miles gerebant *P;* miles
gerebat *C.*
[3] Branchidis *Madvig;* brachiadas *A* (barchiadas *L*).
[4] supplicum *J. Froben;* supplicio cum *A.*
[5] Nemora *Acidalius;* nec mora *A.*
[6] exustis *Hedicke;* excussis *A.*

---

[a] Of Apollo, near Miletus.
[b] *Cf.* Livy xxiv. 30. 14 ; xxv. 25. 6.

Xerxes they had violated the temple ^a which is
29 called the Didymeon. They had not ceased to follow
the customs of their native land, but they were
already bilingual, having gradually degenerated from
their original language through the influence of a
foreign tongue. Therefore they received Alexander
with great joy and surrendered their city and themselves. He ordered the Milesians who were serving
30 with him to be called together. They cherished a
hatred of long standing against the race of the
Branchidae. Therefore the king allowed to those
who had been betrayed free discretion as to the
Branchidae, whether they preferred to remember
31 the injury or their common origin. Then, since their
opinions varied, he made known to them that he
himself would consider what was best to be done.

On the following day when the Branchidae met
him, he ordered them to come along with him, and
when they had reached the city, he himself entered
32 the gate with a light-armed company ; the phalanx
he ordered to surround the walls of the town and at
a given signal to pillage the city, which was a haunt
of traitors, and to kill the inhabitants to a man.
33 The unarmed wretches were butchered everywhere,
and the cruelty could not be checked either by community of language or by the draped olive branches ^b
and prayers of the suppliants. At last, in order that
the walls might be thrown down, their foundations
were undermined, so that no vestige of the city might
34 survive. As for their woods also and their sacred
groves, they not only cut them down, but even pulled
out the stumps, to the end that, since even the
roots were burned out, nothing but a desert waste
35 and sterile ground might be left. If this had been

QUINTUS CURTIUS

excogitata essent, iusta ultio esse, non crudelitas
videretur ; nunc culpam maiorum posteri luere, qui
ne viderant quidem Miletum, adeo[1] et Xerxi non
potuerant prodere.

36 Inde processit ad Tanain amnem. Quo perductus
est Bessus non vinctus modo, sed etiam omni vela-
mento corporis spoliatus. Spitamenes eum tenebat
collo inserta catena, tam barbaris quam Macedonibus
37 gratum spectaculum. Tum Spitamenes : " Et te,"
inquit, " et Dareum, reges meos, ultus, interfectorem
domini sui adduxi, eo modo captum, cuius ipse fecit
exemplum. Aperiat ad hoc spectaculum oculos
Dareus ! exsistat ab inferis, qui illo supplicio indignus
38 fuit et hoc solacio dignus est ! " Alexander, multum collaudato Spitamene, conversus ad Bessum :
" Cuius," inquit, " ferae rabies occupavit animum
tuum, cum regem de te optime meritum prius vin-
cire, deinde occidere sustinuisti ? Sed huius parri-
cidii mercedem falso regis nomine persolvisti tibi."[2]
39 Ille facinus purgare non ausus regis titulum se usurpare dixit, ut gentem suam tradere ipsi posset ;
quippe,[3] si cessasset, alium fuisse regnum occu-
paturum.
40 Et Alexander Oxathren,[4] fratrem Darei, quem
inter corporis custodes habebat, propius iussit accedere tradique Bessum ei, ut cruci affixum, mutilatis
auribus naribusque, sagittis configerent barbari

    [1] adeo *J. Froben;* ideo *A.*   [2] tibi *Acidalius;* ibi *A.*
              [3] quippe *Hedicke;* qui *A.*
        [4] Oxathren *Snakenburg;* oxathen *P;* oxaten *C.*

    [a] *Cf.* Plut. *De sera num. vind.* 557 B.
    [b] Here, as often before and later, the Iaxartes (Syr Darya)
is meant. The order of events differs from that of Arr. iii.
30. 6, who seems to be right.
174

designed against the actual authors of the treason, it would seem to have been a just vengeance and not cruelty ; as it was, their descendants [a] expiated the guilt of their forefathers, although they themselves had never seen Miletus, and so could not have betrayed it to Xerxes.

36 Then Alexander advanced to the river Tanais.[b] Thither Bessus was brought, not only bound, but stripped of all his clothing. Spitamenes held him with a chain [c] placed about his neck, a sight as pleas-

37 ing to the barbarians as to the Macedonians. Then Spitamenes said : " Avenging both you and Darius, my kings, I have brought you the slayer of his lord, captured in the manner of which he himself set the example. Would that Darius might open his eyes to behold the spectacle. Would that he might rise from the lower world, since he did not deserve such a

38 fate and merits this consolation." Alexander, after having highly praised Spitamenes, turned to Bessus and said : " Of what wild beast did the frenzy enter your mind when you had the heart, first to bind, and then to kill the king who was your greatest benefactor ? But the reward for this parricide you have

39 paid yourself by the false name of king." Bessus, not daring to deny his crime, said that he had used the title of king in order that he might be able to hand over his nation to him ; for if he had delayed, another would have seized the rule.

40 But Alexander ordered Oxathres, the brother of Darius, whom he had among his body-guard, to come nearer, and that Bessus be delivered to him, in order that, bound to a cross after his ears and his nose had been cut off, the barbarians might pierce him with

[c] Arr. iii. 30. 3-5.

asservarentque corpus, ut ne aves quidem contin-
41 gerent. Oxathres cetera sibi curae fore pollicetur;
aves non ab alio quam a Catane[1] posse prohiberi
adicit, eximiam eius artem cupiens ostendere; namque adeo certo ictu destinata feriebat, ut aves quoque
42 exciperet. Nunc[2] forsitan, sagittarum[3] celebri usu,
minus admirabilis videri ars haec possit; tum ingens
visentibus miraculum magnoque honori Catani fuit.
43 Dona deinde omnibus qui Bessum adduxerant data
sunt. Ceterum supplicium eius distulit, ut eo loco
ipso, quo Dareum ipse occiderat, necaretur.

VI. Interea Macedones, ad petendum pabulum
incomposito agmine egressi, a barbaris, qui de proximis montibus decurrerunt, opprimuntur pluresque
2 capti sunt quam occisi; barbari autem captivos prae
se agentes rursus in montem recesserunt. xx milia
latronum erant; fundis sagittisque pugnam invadunt.
3 Quos dum obsidet rex, inter promptissimos dimicans
sagitta ictus est, quae in medio crure fixa reliquerat
4 spiculum. Illum quidem maesti et attoniti Macedones in castra referebant, sed nec barbaros fefellit
subductus ex acie—quippe ex edito monte cuncta
5 prospexerant—; itaque postero die misere legatos ad
regem. Quos ille protinus iussit admitti, solutisque
fasciis, magnitudinem vulneris dissimulans, crus bar-
6 baris ostendit. Illi iussi considere affirmant non

---

[1] Catane *Kinch;* catene *A.*
[2] Nunc *Bentley;* nam *P;* namsi *C.*
[3] sagittarum *Hedicke;* sagittis tam *A.*

---

[a] Apparently he shot them on the wing.
[b] See Arr. iii. 30. 11; Plut. *De Fort. Alex.* i. p. 327 B;
Alex. xlv. 3.
[c] This is not mentioned by Arrian, and does not suit the
character of the Sogdiani. It is apparently one of the
romantic additions of later writers.

arrows and so guard his body that not even the birds
41 could touch it. Oxathres answered that he would
take care of the rest; he added that the birds could
not be kept off by anyone else than Catanes, desiring
to show the man's remarkable skill; for he struck his
mark with so sure an aim that he even brought down [a]
42 birds. Nowadays perhaps, when the use of arrows
is frequent, such skill may seem less wonderful, but at
that time it was a great wonder to those who saw it
43 and gained Catanes great repute. Gifts were given
to all who had brought in Bessus. But Alexander
postponed his execution, in order that he might
be slain in that very place where he had killed
Darius.

VI. Meanwhile some of the Macedonians, who had
gone forth in a disorderly band to forage, were fallen
upon by the barbarians, who rushed down from the
mountains near by, and more were captured than
2 were killed; but the barbarians, driving their
prisoners before them, withdrew again to the mountains. The brigands numbered 20,000, and they
3 entered battle with slings and arrows. While the
king was besieging them, as he fought among the
foremost he was struck by an arrow, which had left its
4 point fixed in the middle of his leg.[b] The sorrowing
and amazed Macedonians carried him back into
the camp, but it did not escape the barbarians
that the king had been carried from the field—for
from their lofty mountain they had seen everything
5 —and so on the following day they sent envoys to
the king.[c] He at once ordered them to be admitted,
and taking off the bandages, but concealing the severity of the wound, showed his leg to the barbarians.
6 The envoys, when bidden to be seated, declared that

Macedonas quam ipsos tristiores fuisse cognito vulnere ipsius ; cuius si auctorem repperissent, dedituros fuisse ; cum dis enim pugnare sacrilegos tantum.
7 Ceterum se gentem in fidem dedere, superatos vulnere illius. Rex, fide data et captivis receptis,
8 gentem in deditionem accepit. Castris inde motis, lectica militari ferebatur. Quam pro se quisque eques pedesque subire certabant ; equites, cum quibus rex proelia inire solitus erat, sui muneris id esse censebant, pedites contra, cum saucios commilitones ipsi[1] gestare assuevissent,[2] eripi sibi proprium officium tum potissimum, cum rex gestandus esset, querebantur.
9 tur. Rex in tanto utriusque partis certamine et sibi difficilem et praeteritis gravem electionem futuram ratus, invicem subire eos iussit.
10 Hinc quarto die ad urbem Maracanda[3] perventum est ; LXX stadia murus urbis amplectitur, arx alio[4] cingitur muro. Mille praesidio urbis relictis, proximos vicos depopulatur atque urit
11 Legati deinde Abiorum[5] Scytharum superveniunt, liberi ex quo decesserat Cyrus, tum imperata facturi. Iustissimos barbarorum constabat ; armis abstinebant nisi lacessiti, libertatis modico et aequali usu

[1] ipsi *J. Froben;* ipse *A.*
[2] adsuevissent *J. Froben;* adsueuisset *A.*
[3] Maracanda *J. Froben;* marupenta *A.*
[4] alio *Heinse;* illinc *A.*
[5] Abiorum *Freinshem;* aulorum *A.*

[a] Samarcand.
[b] See Arr. iv. 5. 1 ; Amm. xxiii. 6. 53 ; *Iliad* xiii. 6.

the Macedonians had not been more sorrowful than they themselves on hearing of the wound ; that if they could have discovered who had inflicted it, they would have given him up ; for that only the impious

7 warred with the gods. Furthermore, they said, that overcome by his wound, they surrendered their race into his protection. The king, having pledged his faith and recovered his men who had been taken

8 prisoner, received the race in surrender. Then camp was broken and he was carried in a soldier's litter. All the cavalry and the infantry vied with one another as to who should carry it ; the cavalry, with whom the king had been wont to enter battle, thought that it was a part of their privilege, the infantry on the other hand, since they themselves had been accustomed to carry their injured comrades, complained that their proper duty was being taken from them just at the

9 very time when the king had to be carried. Alexander, in so great a contention between the two parts of the army thinking that a choice would be difficult for him and displeasing to those who were passed over, ordered them to carry him by turns.

10 From there on the fourth day they came to the city of Maracanda [a] ; this city is begirt by a wall of seventy stadia, and the citadel is enclosed by another wall. Having left 1000 men as a guard of the city, he ravaged and burned the neighbouring villages.

11 Then envoys of the Abii, who are Scythians,[b] arrived, who had been free since the death of Cyrus and were then ready to submit to Alexander. They were commonly regarded as the most just of the barbarians ; they abstained from warfare except in self-defence, and because of their moderate and impartial practice of freedom they had made the

179

12 principibus humiliores pares fecerant. Hos benigne
allocutus, ad eos Scythas qui Europam incolunt
Derdam[1] quendam misit ex amicis, qui denuntiaret
his, ne Tanain amnem iniussu regis transirent. Eidem
mandatum, ut contemplaretur locorum situm et illos
quoque Scythas qui super Bosphorum colunt[2] viseret.
13 Condendae urbi sedem super ripam Tanais elegerat,
claustrum et iam perdomitorum et quot[3] deinde adire
decreverat ; sed consilium distulit Sogdianorum nuntiata defectio, quae Bactrianos quoque traxit. VII
14 milia equitum erant, quorum auctoritatem ceteri
sequebantur.

Alexander Spitamenen[4] et Catanen, a quibus ei
traditus[5] erat Bessus, haud dubius quin eorum opera
redigi possent in potestatem, coercendo[6] qui novave-
15 rant res, iussit accersi. At illi, defectionis ad quam
coercendam evocabantur auctores, vulgaverant fama
Bactrianos equites a rege omnes, ut occiderentur,
accersi, idque imperatum ipsis non sustinuisse tamen
exsequi, ne inexpiabile in populares facinus admitterent. Non magis Alexandri saevitiam quam Bessi
parricidium ferre potuisse. Itaque sua sponte iam
motos metu poenae haud difficulter ad arma con-
citaverunt.

---

[1] Derdam *Hedicke;* pendam *A.*
[2] Bosphorum colunt *Acidalius;* bosphoro incolunt *P*
bosforo incolunt *C.*
[3] quot *Hedicke;* quod *A.*
[4] Spitamenen *Snakenburg;* spitamen *A.*
[5] ei traditus *Lauer;* et traditus *C* (traditus *F m. pr.*)
et raditus *P.*
[6] coercendo *added by Freinshem;* cohercendo *C.*

---

[a] Really the Iaxartes (Syr Darya), which is confused with
the real Tanais (the Don).

12 humblest equal to the chief men.   Having addressed
them courteously, Alexander sent one of his friends,
Derdas, to those Scythians who dwell in Europe ; he
was to command them not to cross the Tanais *a* river
without the king's order.   He charged the same
messengers to reconnoitre the country and to visit
those Scythians also who dwell above *b* the Bosphorus.

13 He had chosen a site for founding a city on the bank
of the Tanais,*c* as a barrier both to those who had
already been subdued and to those whom he had
decided to attack later; but his design was put off
by the reported revolt of the Sogdiani, which also

14 involved the Bactriani.   These consisted of 7000
cavalry, whose authority the rest followed.

Alexander ordered Spitamenes and Catanes to be
summoned, by whom Bessus had been delivered to
him, not doubting that by their aid they *d* could be
reduced into his power by the suppression of those

15 who had stirred up a revolt.   But they, being the
ringleaders of the revolt to the suppression of
which they were summoned, had spread abroad the
report that all the Bactrian cavalry were being sent
for by the king, in order that they might be slain,
but that they however could not bring themselves to
execute this order which had been given them, for
fear of committing an inexpiable crime against their
countrymen.   That they had been no more able to
endure the savage cruelty of Alexander than the
parricide of Bessus.   Therefore they aroused to
arms without difficulty those who were already of
their own accord alarmed by fear of punishment.

b That is, east and north of the Cimmerian Bosphorus.
c *Cf.* Arr. iv. 1. 3 ; apparently Khojend on the Iaxartes.
d *i.e.* the Sogdiani and the Bactriani.

16 Alexander, transfugarum defectione comperta,
Craterum obsidere Cyropolim iubet ; ipse aliam
urbem regionis eiusdém corona capit, signoque ut
puberes interficerentur dato, reliqui in praedam
cessere victoris. Urbs diruta est, ut ceteri cladis
17 eius exemplo continerentur. Memaceni, valida gens,
obsidionem non ut honestiorem modo, sed etiam ut
tutiorem ferre decreverant ; ad quorum pertinaciam
mitigandam rex L equites praemisit, qui clementiam
ipsius in deditos simulque inexorabilem animum in
18 devictos ostenderent. Illi nec de fide nec de clementia[1] regis ipsos dubitare respondent equitesque
tendere extra munimenta urbis iubent ; hospitaliter
deinde exceptos gravesque epulis et somno, intem-
19 pesta nocte adorti interfecerunt. Alexander haud
secus quam par erat motus, urbem corona circumdedit, munitiorem quam ut primo impetu capi posset.
Itaque Meleagrum et Perdiccan in obsidionem iun-
git ; ipse ad Craterum[2] pergit, Cyropolim, ut ante
dictum est, obsidentem.[3]
20 Statuerat autem parcere urbi conditae a Cyro ;
quippe non alium gentium illarum magis admiratus
est quam hunc regem et Samiramin, quos et magnitudine animi et claritate rerum longe emicuisse
21 credebat. Ceterum pertinacia oppidanorum iram
eius accendit ; itaque captam urbem diripi iussit.

[1] clementia *Modius;* clementiā *P m. pr.;* potentia *C* (po-
tentiā *F*).
[2] ipse . . . Craterum *added by Hedicke.*
[3] obsidentem *Mützell;* obsidentes *A.*

---

[a] Nothing is known of these or of the variant Nenaceni.
[b] *Cf.* Pliny, *N.H.* vi. 18 (49).

16 Alexander, on learning of the rebellion of the deserters, ordered Craterus to besiege Cyropolis; he himself took another city of the same region by circumvallation, and when the order had been given that all the men fit for service should be killed, the rest became booty for the victor. The city was razed, in order that the rest might be held to their allegiance

17 by the example of its destruction. The Memaceni,[a] a powerful race, had decided to stand a siege, as not only more honourable, but also as safer; to tame their obstinacy, the king sent ahead fifty horsemen, to make known to them his clemency towards those who surrendered and his inexorable spirit towards

18 the vanquished. They replied that they did not doubt the good faith and clemency of the king and ordered the horsemen to encamp outside the fortifications of the city; then, having entertained them hospitably, they attacked them in the dead of night, when they were heavy with feasting and sleep,

19 and slew them. Alexander, incensed as was quite natural, surrounded the city with a line of troops, since it was too well fortified to be taken at the first assault. Therefore he united Meleager and Perdiccas in its siege, and he himself rejoined Craterus, who was besieging Cyropolis, as was said before.

20 However, he had decided to spare this city, since it was founded by Cyrus; for there were no other of those nations whom he admired more than that king and Semiramis,[b] who he believed had far excelled all others in the greatness of their courage and the glory

21 of their deeds. But the obstinacy of the inhabitants so inflamed his anger, that, after taking the city, he ordered it to be ravaged. Having destroyed it,

Deleta ea,[1] Memacenis[2] haud iniuria infestus,[3] ad
22 Meleagrum et Perdiccam redit. Sed non alia urbs
fortius obsidionem tulit; quippe et militum promptissimi cecidere et ipse rex ad ultimum periculum
venit. Namque cervix eius saxo ita icta est, ut oculis
caligine offusa collaberetur, ne mentis quidem compos ; exercitus certe velut erepto iam eo ingemuit.
23 Sed invictus adversus ea quae ceteros terrent, nondum percurato vulnere acrius obsidioni institit,
naturalem celeritatem ira concitante. Cuniculo ergo
suffossa moenia ingens nudavere spatium, per quod
irrupit, victorque urbem dirui iussit.
24 Hinc Menedemum cum tribus milibus peditum et
dccc equitibus ad urbem Maracanda[4] misit. Spitamenes transfuga, praesidio Macedonum inde deiecto,
muris urbis eius incluserat se, non adeo[5] oppidanis
consilium defectionis approbantibus ; sequi tamen
25 videbantur, quia prohibere non poterant. Interim
Alexander ad Tanain amnem redit et, quantum soli
occupaverat[6] castris, muro circumdedit ; LX stadiorum urbis murus fuit. Hanc quoque urbem Alex-
26 andriam appellari iussit. Opus tanta celeritate
perfectum est, ut XVII die quam munimenta excitata
erant tecta quoque urbis absolverentur. Ingens
militum certamen inter ipsos fuerat, ut suum quisque
27 munus—nam divisum erat—primus ostenderet. In-

[1] Deleta ea *Hedicke;* delete *A.*
[2] Memacenis *Acidalius;* macedones *A.*
[3] infestus *Acidalius;* infestos *A.*
[4] Maracanda *J. Froben;* maracandam *A.*
[5] non adeo *Hedicke;* haud *A* (aut *V*).
[6] occupaverat *Vogel;* occupauerant *A.*

[a] Arrian (iv. 2. 3) does not mention undermining.
[b] Called Alexandria on the Iaxartes.

not unreasonably filled with indignation against the
Memaceni, he returned to Meleager and Perdiccas.
22 But no other city withstood siege more stoutly; for
the bravest of his soldiers fell and the king himself
was exposed to extreme danger. For his neck was
struck with a stone with such force that darkness
veiled his eyes and he fell and even lost consciousness ; the army in fact lamented as if he had already
23 been taken from them. But unconquered in the
face of what terrifies other men, he pressed on the
siege before the wound had yet been wholly healed,
anger spurring on his natural speed. Therefore,
his men having undermined [a] the walls and opened
a great breach, he burst through it into the city, and
when victor ordered it to be razed.

24   Next he sent Menedemus with 3000 infantry and
800 cavalry to the city of Maracanda. Within the
walls of this city the deserter Spitamenes, after driving
out the Macedonian garrison, had shut himself,
although the inhabitants did not fully approve of his
design of revolt; yet they were thought to consent to
25 it, since they could not prevent it. Meanwhile Alexander returned to the Tanais and surrounded with a
wall all the space which he had occupied with his
camp ; the wall of the city measured sixty stadia.
This city also he ordered to be called Alexandria.[b]
26 The work was completed with such speed, that seventeen days [c] after the fortifications were raised the
buildings of the city also were finished. There had
been great rivalry of the soldiers with one another,
that each band—for the work was divided—might be
27 the first to show the completion of his task. As

* Arrian (iv. 4. 1) says twenty ; Justin (xii. 5) agrees with
Curtius.

colae novae urbi dati captivi, quos, reddito pretio dominis, liberavit ; quorum posteri nunc quoque non apud eos tam longa aetate propter memoriam Alexandri exoleverunt.

VII. At rex Scytharum, cuius tum ultra Tanaim imperium erat, ratus eam urbem, quam in ripa amnis Macedones condiderant, suis impositam esse cervicibus, fratrem, Carthasim nomine, cum magna equitum manu misit ad diruendam eam proculque amne sub-
2 movendas Macedonum copias. Bactrianos Tanais ab Scythis quos Europaeos[1] vocant dividit, idem Asiam et Europam finis interfluit. Ceterum Scy-
3 tharum gens haud procul Thracia sita ab oriente ad septentrionem se vertit Sarmatarumque, ut quidam
4 credidere, non finitima, sed pars est. Recta deinde regione saltum[2] ultra Istrum iacentem colit, ultima Asiae, qua Bactra sunt, stringit. Habitant quae septentrioni propiora sunt ; profundae inde silvae vastaeque solitudines excipiunt. Rursus quae Tanain et Bactra spectant, humano cultu haud disparia sunt primis.[3]
5 Cum hac gente non provisum bellum Alexander gesturus, cum in conspectu eius obequitaret hostis, adhuc aeger ex vulnere, praecipue voce deficiens, quam et modicus cibus et cervicis extenuabat dolor,
6 amicos in consilium advocari iubet. Terrebat eum

---

[1] Europaeos *Aldus;* europeas *A.*
[2] saltum *Jeep;* alium *A.*   [3] primis *Bentley;* primus *A.*

---

[a] Justin (xii. 5) says that they were the inhabitants of the three cities which Cyrus had founded. But *cf.* Arr. iv. 4. 1.
[b] *Cf.* Amm. xxix. 2. 21 ; xxxi. 7. 12.

inhabitants for the new city prisoners *a* were chosen, whom he freed by paying the masters their price ; even now their posterity after so long a time have not ceased to enjoy consideration among those peoples because of the memory of Alexander.

VII. But the king of the Scythians, whose rule at that time extended beyond the Tanais, thinking that this city which the Macedonians had founded on the bank of the river was a yoke upon their necks,*b* sent his brother, Carthasis by name, with a large force of cavalry to demolish it and drive off the Macedonian 2 forces away from the river. The Tanais separates the Bactriani from the so-called European Scythians, and 3 is also the boundary between Asia and Europe.*c* But the Scythian race which is situated not far from Thrace extends from the east towards the north, and is not a neighbour of the Sarmatians, as some have 4 believed, but a part of them.*d* Then keeping straight on, it inhabits the forest lying beyond the Danube, and borders the extremity of Asia at Bactra. They inhabit the parts which are nearer to the north, then dense forests and desert wastes meet them. Again, the parts which look towards the Tanais and Bactra in human cultivation are not unlike the first.

5 Alexander, about to wage an unforeseen war with this race, when the enemy rode up in sight of him, although still ailing from his wound, and especially feeble of voice, which both moderation in food and the pain in his neck had weakened, ordered his friends to 6 be called to a conference. It was not the enemy that

c The Iaxartes, confused with the real Tanais, which flows into the Maeotic Gulf (Sea of Azov).
d Strabo xi. 2. 1 reckons the Sarmatians as a part of the Scythians.

non hostis, sed iniquitas temporis; **Bactriani** defecerant, Scythae etiam lacessebant, ipse non insis-
tere in terra, non equo vehi, non docere, non hortari
7 suos poterat. Ancipiti periculo implicitus, deos quoque incusans querebatur, se iacere segnem, cuius
velocitatem nemo antea valuisset effugere; vix suos
8 credere non simulari valitudinem. Itaque, qui[1] post
Dareum victum hariolos et vates consulere desierat,
rursus ad superstitionem, humanarum mentium[2] ludibrium,[3] revolutus, Aristandrum, cui credulitatem
suam addixerat,[4] explorare eventum rerum sacrificiis
iubet. Mos erat haruspicibus exta sine rege spectare
et quae portenderentur referre.
9 Inter haec rex, dum fibris pecudum explorantur
eventus latentium rerum, propius[5] ipsum considere
de industria[6] amicos iubet, ne contentione vocis cica-
tricem infirmam adhuc rumperet. Hephaestio et[7]
Craterus et Erigyius erant cum custodibus in taber-
10 naculum admissi. "Discrimen," inquit, "me occupavit meliore hostium quam meo tempore; sed
necessitas ante rationem est, maxime in bello, quo
11 raro permittitur tempora eligere.[8] Defecere Bactriani in quorum cervicibus stamus, et quantum in
nobis animi sit alieno Marte experiuntur. Haud
dubia fortuna; si omiserimus Scythas ultro arma

[1] qui *added by Hedicke.*
[2] mentium *Iunius;* gentium *A.*
[3] ludibrium *Hedicke;* ludibrio *A.*
[4] addixerat *Lauer;* adduxerat *A.*
[5] propius *J. Froben;* prius *A.*
[6] de industria *Hedicke;* deinde *A.*
[7] et *added by Hedicke;* A *omits.*
[8] tempora eligere *Hedicke;* temporelegere *A.*

<hr>

[a] For *humanarum mentium* cf. Amm. xiv. ii. 25.

alarmed him, but the unfavourable condition of the times ; the Bactriani had revolted, the Scythians also were provoking him to battle, he himself could not stand on his feet, could not ride a horse, could not 7 instruct nor encourage his men. Involved as he was in a double danger, accusing even the gods, he complained that he, whose swiftness no one had before been able to escape, was lying idle ; even his own men hardly believed that he was not feigning illness. 8 Therefore he, who after vanquishing Darius had ceased to consult soothsayers and seers, lapsing again into superstition, that mocker of men's minds,[a] ordered Aristander, to whom he had consigned his faith,[b] to examine by sacrifices into the outcome of his affairs. It was the custom of the diviners to examine the entrails without the presence of the king, and to report what these portended. 9 Meanwhile the king, while they were trying by inspection of the entrails of the victims to learn the result of hidden events, purposely bade his friends to sit very near him, in order that he might not, by exerting his voice, break the scab of his wound, which was still tender. Hephaestion, Craterus, and Erigyius, with his body-guard, had been admitted to his 10 tent. To them he said: "Danger has surprised me at a time better for the enemy than for myself; but necessity outstrips calculation, especially in war, where a man is seldom allowed to choose his own times. 11 The Bactriani have revolted, on whose necks we are standing, and are trying through a war waged by others to learn how much spirit we have. Our fortune is not doubtful; if we disregard the Scythians, who

[b] For *addixerat* see Cic. *Verr.* ii. 1. 52. 137, on the general idea v. 4. 2. Aristander, *peritissimus vatum*, iv. 2. 14.

inferentes, contempti ad illos, qui defecerunt, re-
12 vertemur ; si vero Tanaim transierimus et ubique
invictos esse nos Scytharum pernicie ac sanguine
ostenderimus, quis dubitabit parere etiam Europae[1]
13 victoribus ? Fallitur qui terminos gloriae nostrae
metitur spatio quod transituri sumus. Unus amnis
interfluit ; quem si traicimus, in Europam arma
14 proferimus. Et quanti aestimandum est, dum Asiam
subigimus, in alio quodam modo orbe tropaea statuere
et quae tam longo intervallo Natura videtur diremisse
15 una victoria subito committere ? At, hercule, si
paulum cessaverimus, in tergis nostris Scythae haere-
bunt. An soli sumus qui flumina transnare possumus ? Multa in nosmetipsos recident quibus adhuc
16 vicimus. Fortuna belli artem victos quoque docet.
Utribus amnem traiciendi exemplum fecimus nuper ;
hoc ut Scythae imitari nesciant, Bactriani docebunt.
17 Praeterea unus gentis huius exercitus adhuc venit,
ceteri expectantur. Ita bellum vitando alemus et
quod inferre possumus accipere cogemur.
18 " Manifesta est consilii mei ratio ; sed an permis-
suri sint mihi Macedones animo uti meo dubito,
quia, ex quo hoc vulnus accepi non equo vectus sum,
19 non pedibus ingressus. Sed si me sequi vultis, valeo,
amici. Satis virium est ad toleranda ista ; aut, si
iam adest vitae meae finis, in quo tandem opere

---

[1] Europae *Letellier;* europen *A.*

---

[a] This method of crossing rivers seems to have been
general with Asiatic peoples.

are attacking us without provocation, we shall return
12 an object of contempt to those who have revolted ; if
however we cross the Tanais and show by the defeat
and slaughter of the Scythians that we are everywhere invincible, who will hesitate to obey those who
13 are victors even over Europe also ? He is deceived
who measures our glory by the space which we are
about to cross. A single river flows between us ; if
14 we cross that, we carry our arms into Europe. And
how highly must it be regarded, while we are subjugat-
ing Asia, to set up trophies in what might be called
another world, and suddenly to join in one victory
places which Nature seems to have separated by so
15 great a space ? But, by Heaven ! if we delay even a
short time, the Scythians will be close at our backs. Are
we the only ones that can swim across rivers ? Many
inventions will recoil upon us by which we have so far
16 been victorious. The fortune of war teaches its art
even to the vanquished. We have lately set them
the example of crossing a river on skins *a* ; even if the
Scythians do not know how to imitate this, the Bac-
17 triani will teach them. Besides, only one army of
this nation has yet arrived, the rest are expected.
Hence by avoiding war, we shall give it strength,
and in a war in which we can take the offensive
we shall be reduced to defence.
18   " The reasonableness of my plan is clear ; but I
doubt whether the Macedonians will allow me to use
my judgement, because, as the result of this wound
which I have suffered, I have neither ridden nor gone
19 on foot. But if you are willing to follow me, I am
strong, my friends. I have sufficient strength to
endure the dangers which I have suggested ; or, if the
end of my life is already at hand, in what exploit,

20 melius exstinguar ? " Haec quassa adhuc voce sub-
deficiens vix proximis exaudientibus dixerat, cum
omnes a tam praecipiti consilio regem deterrere
21 coeperunt, Erigyius maxime, qui haud sane auctoritate proficiens apud obstinatum animum, superstitionem cuius potens non erat rex incutere temptavit
dicendo deos quoque obstare consilio magnumque
22 periculum, si flumen transisset, ostendi. Intranti
Erigyio tabernaculum regis Aristander occurrerat
tristia exta fuisse significans ; haec ex vate comperta
Erigyius nuntiabat.

23 Quo inhibito, Alexander non ira solum, sed etiam
pudore confusus, quod superstitio quam celaverat
24 detegebatur, Aristandrum vocari iubet. Qui ut
venit, intuens eum : " Non rex," inquit, " sed priva-
tus clam[1] sacrificium ut faceres mandavi ; quid eo
portenderetur cur apud alium quam apud me professus es ? Erigyius arcana mea et secreta te
prodente cognovit, quem certum, mehercule, habeo
25 extorum interprete uti metu suo. Tibi autem, qui
sapis,[2] quam potest denuntio ipsi mihi indices quid
ex eis[3] cognoveris, ne possis infitiari dixisse, quae
26 dixeris." Ille exsanguis attonitoque similis stabat,
per metum etiam voce suppressa, tandemque eodem
metu stimulante ne regis exspectationem moraretur :
" Magni," inquit, " laboris, non irriti discrimen instare praedixi ; nec me tam[4] ars mea quam beni-

---

[1] clam *Hedicke;* sum *A.*
[2] qui sapis *Jeep;* qui saepius *FP;* saepius *BLV.*
[3] ex eis *Kinch;* extis *A.*
[4] me tam *Bentley;* mea *A.*

20 pray, shall I die more nobly?" So much had he spoken in a voice faltering, broken all the time and with difficulty to be heard by those who were beside him, when all began to deter the king from so rash a
21 plan, Erigyius especially, who, unable by his influence to check his obstinate purpose, tried to arouse his superstition, which was the king's weak point, by saying that even the gods opposed his plan, and that great danger menaced him, if he should cross the
22 river. Erigyius, as he entered the king's tent, had been met by Aristander, who told him that the signs of the victims had turned out unfavourable; this, which he had learned from the seer, Erigyius reported.
23 Having silenced him, Alexander, confused, not by anger alone, but also by shame because the superstition which he had concealed was revealed, ordered
24 Aristander to be summoned. When he came, the king, gazing sternly at him, said: "Not as king, but secretly as a private person, I ordered you to offer a sacrifice. Why did you announce what was portended by it to another rather than to me? Through your indiscretion Erigyius knew my private and secret affairs, and, by Heaven! I feel sure that he uses his
25 own fear as an interpreter of the victim's vitals. But I give you, who know, a solemn warning to indicate to me personally what you have learned from those sacrifices, so that you may not be able to deny having
26 said what you shall tell me." Aristander stood pale and as if thunderstruck, and although through fear he lost his voice, at length, driven also by fear, lest he should keep the king waiting, he said: "I predicted that a contest of great, but not fruitless labour threatened; and it is not so much my art as

193

27 volentia tua¹ perturbat. Infirmitatem valitudinis
tuae video et quantum in uno te sit scio ; vereor, ne
28 praesenti fortunae tu sufficere non possis." Rex
iussit eum² confidere felicitati suae ; ut alias sibi ait³
29 gloriam concedere deos. Consultanti inde⁴ cum
eisdem quonam modo flumen transirent, supervenit
Aristander non alias laetiora exta vidisse se affirmans,
utique prioribus longe diversa ; tum sollicitudinis
causas apparuisse, nunc prorsus egregie litatum esse.
30 Ceterum, quae subinde nuntiata sunt regi, con-
tinuae felicitati rerum eius imposuerant labem.
31 Menedemum, ut supra dictum est, miserat ad ob-
sidendum Spitamenen, Bactrianae defectionis auctorem ; qui, comperto hostis adventu, ne muris urbis
includeretur, simul fretus excipi posse, qua eum⁵
32 venturum sciebat, consedit occultus. Silvestre iter
aptum insidiis tegendis erat ; ibi Dahas condidit.
Equi binos armatos vehunt, quorum invicem singuli
repente desiliunt et⁶ equestris pugnae ordinem tur-
33 bant. Equorum velocitati par est hominum pernicitas. Hos Spitamenes saltum circumire iussos pariter
et a lateribus et a fronte et a tergo hosti ostendit.
34 Menedemus undique inclusus, ne numero quidem
par, diu tamen resistit clamitans nihil aliud superesse

¹ tua *added by Hedicke.* ² iussit eum *Jeep;* iussum *A.*
³ ut alias sibi ait *Hedicke;* ad alia sibi ad *A.*
⁴ inde *Aldus;* mihi *A.* ⁵ qua eum *Stangl;* quem *A.*
⁶ et *added by Hedicke.*

a Arrian (iv. 4. 3) says that Aristander did not change his
predictions. *b* See vii. 6. 24.

27 affection for you that disturbs me. I see the weakness of your health, and I know how much depends on you alone. I fear that you cannot be equal to
28 the present fortune." The king bade him have confidence in his good fortune ; saying that, just as at
29 other times, the gods granted him glory. Then, as he was consulting with the same men as to what method they should use for crossing the river, Aristander appeared, declaring that at no other time had he seen more favourable entrails ; especially were they very different from the former ones ; that then causes for anxiety had appeared, but that now the sacrifice had turned out exceptionally favourable.[a]
30 But what was presently announced to the king had inflicted a stain on the continual good fortune of
31 his enterprises. He had sent Menedemus, as was said before,[b] to besiege Spitamenes, the author of the defection of the Bactriani ; Spitamenes, having learned of the coming of the enemy, in order not to be shut within the walls of the city, and at the same time trusting that Menedemus could be taken unawares, had secretly laid an ambuscade where he knew that
32 Menedemus would come. The road was covered with woods and adapted to conceal the ambush ; there he hid the Dahae. Each of their horses carries two riders, of whom in turn one suddenly dismounts
33 and confuses the order of a cavalry battle. The speed of the men is equal to the swiftness of their horses. These, which had been ordered to surround the woods, Spitamenes showed at the same time on the flanks,
34 in front, and in the rear of the enemy. Menedemus, hemmed in on all sides, although not even equal in numbers, yet resisted for a long time, crying that since they had been deceived by an ambuscade, no

locorum fraude deceptis quam honestae mortis
solacium ex hostium caede.

35 Ipsum praevalens equus vehebat, quo saepius in
cuneos barbarorum effusis habenis evectus, magna
36 strage eos fuderat. Sed cum unum omnes peterent,
multis vulneribus exsanguis Hypsiclem[1] quendam ex
amicis hortatus est ut in equum suum escenderet
et se fuga eriperet. Haec agentem anïma defecit,
37 corpusque ex equo defluxit in terram. Hypsicles
poterat quidem effugere, sed amisso amico mori
statuit. Una erat cura ne inultus occideret; itaque
subditis calcaribus equo in medios hostis se inmisit
38 et, memorabili edita pugna, obrutus telis est. Quod
ubi videre, qui caedi supererant, tumulum paulo
quam cetera editiorem capiunt ; quos Spitamenes
39 fame in deditionem subacturus obsedit. Cecidere
eo proelio peditum ii milia, ccc equites. Quam
cladem Alexander sollerti consilio texit, morte de-
nuntiata his qui ex proelio advenerant, si acta vul-
gassent.

VIII. Ceterum cum animo disparem vultum diutius
ferre non posset, in tabernaculum super ripam flu-
2 minis de industria locatum secessit. Ibi sine arbitris
singula animi consulta pensando noctem vigiliis
extraxit, saepe pellibus tabernaculi allevatis, ut
conspiceret hostium ignes, e quibus coniectare poterat
3 quanta hominum multitudo esset. Iamque lux appetebat, cum thoracem indutus, procedit ad milites,

---

[1] Hypsiclem *Eberhard;* suspiciens *A.*

---

a For *defluxit cf.* Livy ii. 20. 3.

solace was left for them except that of an honourable death, a solace arising from the slaughter of the enemy.

35 He himself rode a very powerful horse, by which often carried at full speed into solid blocks of barbarian
36 troops, he routed them with great carnage. But when they all attacked him alone, and he was drained of blood by many wounds, he urged Hypsicles, one of his friends, to mount his horse and save himself by flight. As he was saying this, life left him, and his body slipped down *a* from his horse to the ground.
37 Hypsicles could in fact have escaped, but after losing his friend he resolved to die. His only care was, not to fall unavenged ; therefore, spurring on his horse, he plunged into the midst of the enemy, and having fought a memorable fight, was overwhelmed by their
38 weapons. When those who had survived the carnage saw that, they took position on an eminence a little higher than the rest of the field ; there Spitamenes besieged them, hoping by starvation to drive
39 them to surrender. There fell in that battle 2000 foot and 300 horsemen. Alexander with crafty prudence concealed this disaster, threatening with death those who had returned from the battle, if they made public what had happened.

VIII. But when he could no longer bear an expression which belied his feelings, he withdrew to his tent, which he had purposely placed on the bank of the
2 river. There without witnesses, weighing his plans one by one, he spent the night sleepless, often raising the skins of the tent to look at the enemies' fires, from which he could calculate how great their number of
3 men was. And already daylight was at hand, when, putting on his cuirass, he went out to the soldiers,

4 tum primum post vulnus proxime acceptum. Tanta
erat apud eos veneratio regis, ut facile periculi, quod
horrebant, cogitationem praesentia eius excuteret.
5 Laeti ergo et manantibus gaudio lacrimis consalutant
eum et, quod ante recusaverant bellum feroces de-
6 poscunt. Ille se ratibus equitem phalangemque
transportaturum esse pronuntiat, super utres iubet
7 nare levius armatos. Plura nec dici res desideravit
nec rex dicere per valitudinem potuit. Ceterum
tanta alacritate militum rates iunctae sunt, ut intra[1]
triduum ad XII milia effecta sint.

8   Iamque ad transeundum omnia aptaverant, cum
legati Scytharum xx, more gentis per castra equis
vecti, nuntiare iubent regi, velle ipsos ad eum man-
9 data perferre. Admissi in tabernaculum iussique
considere, in vultu regis defixerant oculos ; credo,
quis magnitudine corporis animum aestimantibus
modicus habitus[2] haudquaquam famae par videbatur.
10 Scythis autem non, ut ceteris barbaris, rudis et in-
conditus sensus est ; quidam eorum sapientiam
quoque capere dicuntur, quantamcumque gens capit
11 semper armata. Sic, quae[3] locutos esse apud regem
memoriae proditum est abhorrent forsitan moribus
oratoribusque[4] nostris, et tempora et ingenia cultiora
sortitis. Sed, ut possit oratio eorum sperni, tamen

---

[1] intra *Hedicke;* in *A.*
[2] habitus *Acidalius;* animus *A.*
[3] Sic, quae *Halm;* sicque *C;* si qua *P.*
[4] oratoribus *added by Hedicke;* que *A.*

---

[a] But contrary to Roman custom.

for the first time since the recent wound which he
4 had suffered. So great was their veneration for the
king, that his presence readily dispelled all thought
5 of the danger which they dreaded. Happy therefore and shedding tears of joy, they saluted him, and
confidently demanded the battle which they had before
6 refused. He announced that he was going to transport the cavalry and the phalanx on rafts, and he
ordered the lighter-armed troops to swim, sup-
7 ported by inflated skins. The situation did not call
for more words, nor could the king say more because
of his illness. But the rafts were put together with
such enthusiasm on the part of the soldiers, that
within three days about 12,000 were finished.

8   And already they had prepared everything for
crossing, when twenty envoys of the Scythians, according to the custom of their race^a riding through
the camp on horseback, ordered announcement to be
made to the king that they desired to deliver a
9 message to him. Being admitted to the tent and
invited to be seated, they had fixed their eyes on
the king's face, because, I suppose, to those who
estimated spirit by bodily stature his moderate size
10 seemed by no means equal to his reputation. However, the comprehension of the Scythians is not so
rude and untrained as that of the rest of the barbarians ; in fact, some of them are even said to be
capable of philosophy, so far as a race that is always
11 in arms is capable of such knowledge. Hence what
they are reported to have said to the king is perhaps foreign to our customs and our orators, who
have been allotted more cultivated times and intel-
lects. But although their speech may be scorned,
yet our fidelity ought not to be ; and so we shall

fides nostra non debet ; quae, utcumque sunt tradita,
incorrupta proferemus.[1]

12 Igitur[2] unum ex his maximum natu locutum ac-
cepimus : " Si di habitum corporis tui aviditati animi
parem esse voluissent, orbis te non caperet ; altera
manu Orientem, altera Occidentem contingeres, et
hoc assecutus, scire velles ubi tanti numinis fulgor
13 conderetur. Sic quoque concupiscis quae non capis.
Ab Europa petis Asiam, ex Asia transis in Europam ;
deinde, si humanum genus omne superaveris, cum
silvis et nivibus et fluminibus ferisque bestiis gesturus
14 es bellum. Quid ? tu ignoras arbores magnas diu
crescere, una hora exstirpari ? Stultus est qui fructus earum spectat, altitudinem non metitur.[3] Vide,
ne, dum ad cacumen pervenire contendis, cum ipsis
15 ramis quos comprehenderis decidas. Leo quoque aliquando minimarum avium pabulum fuit, et ferrum
robigo consumit. Nihil tam firmum est, cui peri-
16 culum non sit etiam ab invalido. Quid nobis tecum
est ? Numquam terram tuam attigimus. Quis[4] sis,
unde venias, licetne ignorare in vastis silvis viventibus ? Nec servire ulli possumus nec imperare de-
17 sideramus. Dona nobis data sunt, ne Scytharum
gentem ignores iugum boum[5] et aratrum, sagitta,
hasta, patera. His utimur et cum amicis et adversus
18 inimicos. Fruges amicis damus boum labore quaesi-

---

[1] proferemus *Bentley;* perferemus *A.*
[2] igitur] *the Excerpta Rhenaugiensia (R) begin with this*
word.
[3] metitur *Lauer;* metit *A.*   [4] Quis *Kinch;* qui *A.*
[5] boum *Vindelinus;* bouem *PR;* boues *C.*

report their words without change, just as they have
been handed down to us.

12 Well then, we have learned that one of them, the
eldest, said : " If the gods had willed that your
bodily stature should be equal to your greed, the
world would not contain you ; with one hand you
would touch the rising, with the other the setting
sun, and having reached the latter, you would wish
to know where the brilliance of so great a god hides
13 itself. So also you desire what you cannot attain.
From Europe you pass to Asia, from Asia you cross
into Europe ; then, when you have subdued the
whole human race, you will wage war with the woods
14 and the snows, with rivers and wild beasts. Why,
do you not know that great trees are long in growing, but are uprooted in a single hour ? He is a fool
who looks at their fruits, but does not scan their
height. Beware lest, while you strive to reach the
top, you fall with the very branches which you have
15 grasped. Even the lion has sometimes been the
food of the smallest of birds, and rust consumes iron.
Nothing is so strong that it may not be in danger
16 even from the weak. What have we to do with
you ? We have never set foot in your lands. Are
not those who live in the solitary woods allowed to
be ignorant who you are, whence you come ? We
cannot obey any man, nor do we desire to rule any.
17 That you may know the Scythian nation, we have
received as gifts a yoke of oxen [a] and a plow, an
arrow, a spear, and a bowl. These we use both with
18 our friends and against our foes. We give grain to
our friends, acquired by the labour of our oxen,

* Cf. Hdt. iv. 5.

tas, patera cum eisdem[1] vinum dis libamus, inimicos
sagitta eminus, hasta comminus petimus.

"Sic Syriae[2] regem et postea Persarum Medorum-
que superavimus, patuitque nobis iter usque in
19 Aegyptum. At tu, qui te gloriaris ad latrones
persequendos venire, omnium gentium quas adisti
latro es. Lydiam cepisti, Syriam occupasti, Persidem
tenes, Bactrianos habes in potestate, Indos petisti ;
iam etiam ad pecora nostra avaras et insatiabiles[3]
20 manus porrigis. Quid tibi divitiis opus est, quae
esurire te cogunt ? Primus omnium satietate parasti
famem, ut, quo plura haberes, acrius quae non habes
21 cuperes. Non succurrit tibi, quam diu circum Bactra
haereas ? Dum illos subigis, Sogdiani bellare coeperunt. Bellum tibi ex victoria nascitur. Nam, ut
maior fortiorque sis quam quisquam, tamen alieni-
genam dominum pati nemo vult.

22 "Transi modo Tanain ; scies, quam late pateant,[4]
numquam tamen consequeris Scythas. Paupertas
nostra velocior erit quam exercitus tuus, qui praedam
tot nationum vehit. Rursus, cum procul abesse nos
credes, videbis in tuis castris. Eadem enim veloci-
23 tate et sequimur et fugimus. Scytharum solitudines
Graecis etiam proverbiis audio eludi ; at nos deserta

---

[1] isdem *PR;* hiis *B m. pr.;* iis *B corr. FL;* his *V.*
[2] Syriae *Modius;* scythiae *A* (scythae *B*, scythiae *F);*
greciae scithiae *R.*
[3] insatiabiles *Acidalius;* instabiles *AR.*
[4] pateant *Modius;* pateat *AR.*

---

[a] *i.e.* Assyria, as in v. 1. 35.
[b] *Cf.* the reply of the pirates to Alexander in Cic. *De Rep.*
iii. 14 ; Aug. *De Civ. Dei* iv. 4. 25.
[c] *Cf.* vii. 3. 19 ; Alexander had reached the Indian Caucasus (Parapanisus).

with them from the bowl we offer libation to the gods, we attack our foes from a distance with the arrow, with the spear hand to hand.

"It is thus that we have conquered the king of Syria [a] and later those of the Persians and the Medes, and that a way was opened for us even into Egypt.
19 But you, who boast that you are coming to attack robbers, are the robber [b] of all the nations to which you have come. You have taken Lydia, you have seized Syria, you hold Persia you have the Bactriani in your power, you have aimed at India [c]; already you are stretching your greedy and insatiable hands
20 for our flocks. What need have you for riches, which compel you to hunger for them? First of all men, you by a surfeit have produced a hunger wherein the more you have, the keener is your desire for
21 what you have not. Does it not occur to you how long you are delaying around Bactra? [d] While you are subduing the Bactriani the Sogdiani have begun to make war. For you victory is a source of war. For although you may be the greatest and bravest of all men, yet no one is willing to endure a foreign lord.
22 "Only cross the Tanais; you will learn how far the Scythians extend, yet you will never overtake them. Our poverty will be swifter than your army, which carries the pillage of so many nations. Again, when you believe us afar off, you will see us in your camp. For we both pursue and flee with the same
23 swiftness. I hear that the solitudes of the Scythians are made fun of even in Greek proverbs,[e] but we

[d] Curtius sometimes includes Sogdiana with Bactria south of the Oxus, but sometimes separates them; cf. vii. 4. 26.

[e] Σκυθῶν ἐρημία; see Aristoph. *Ach.* 704 and scholium.

et humano cultu vacua magis quam urbes et opulentos
24 agros sequimur. Proinde fortunam tuam pressis
manibus tene ; lubrica est nec invita teneri potest.
Salubre consilium sequens quam praesens tempus
ostendet melius. Impone felicitati tuae frenos ;
25 facilius illam reges. Nostri sine pedibus dicunt esse
Fortunam, quae manus et pinnas tantum habet ; cum
manus porrigit, pinnas quoque comprehende.[1]
26 " Denique, si deus es, tribuere mortalibus beneficia
debes, non sua eripere ; sin autem homo es, id quod
es semper esse te cogita. Stultum est eorum me-
27 minisse, propter quae tui obliviscaris. Quibus bellum non intuleris, bonis amicis poteris uti. Nam et
firmissima est inter pares amicitia, et videntur pares
28 qui non fecerunt inter se periculum virium. Quos
viceris amicos tibi esse, cave credas. Inter dominum
et servum nulla amicitia est ; etiam in pace belli
29 tamen iura servantur. Iurando gratiam Scythas
sancire ne credideris ; colendo fidem iurant. Graecorum ista cautio est, qui pacta[2] consignant et deos
invocant ; nos religionem in ipsa fide ponimus.[3] Qui
30 non reverentur homines, fallunt deos. Nec tibi
amico opus est de cuius benivolentia dubites. Ceterum nos et Asiae et Europae custodes habebis ;
Bactra, nisi dividat Tanais, contingimus, ultra Tanain
terras[4] usque ad Thraciam colimus, Thraciae Macedoniam coniunctam esse fama fert. Utrumne imperio

---

[1] comprehende *Jeep;* comprehendere *AR.*
[2] pacta *Bongars;* facta *AR.*
[3] ponimus *Foss;* nouimus *AR.*
[4] terras *Hedicke;* et *AR.*

---

[a] Cf. Sen. *Oedip.* 192 *amplexu presso.*
[b] Not the real Tanais (Don), but the Iaxartes.

seek after places that are desert and free from human cultivation rather than cities and rich fields.

24 Therefore hold your fortune with tight hands[a]; she is slippery and cannot be held against her will. Wholesome advice will be better shown by the future than by the present. Put curbs upon your good fortune;

25 you will manage it the more easily. Our people say that Fortune is without feet, she has only hands and wings; when she stretches out her hands, grasp her wings also.

26 "Finally, if you are a god, you ought to confer benefits on mankind, not strip them of those they have; but if you are a mortal man, always remember that you are what you are. It is folly to remember

27 those things which make you forget yourself. Those on whom you have not made war you will be able to use as friends. For friendship is strongest among equals, and those are regarded as equals who have

28 not made trial of one another's strength. Do not believe that those whom you have conquered are your friends. There is no friendship between master and slave; even in peace the laws of war are kept.

29 Believe not that the Scythians ratify a friendship by taking oath; they take oath by keeping faith. The oath is a caution of the Greeks, who jointly seal agreements and call upon the gods; our religion consists in good faith itself. Those who do not respect men

30 deceive the gods. And you have no need of a friend whose goodwill you may doubt. Moreover in us you will have guardians of both Asia and Europe; we touch upon Bactra, except that the river Tanais[b] is between us. Beyond the Tanais we inhabit lands extending to Thrace, and report says that the Macedonians border upon Thrace. Consider whether you

tuo finitimos hostes an amicos velis esse, considera."[1]
Haec barbarus.

IX. Contra rex fortuna sua et consiliis eorum se
usurum esse respondet ; nam et fortunam, cui con-
fidat, et consilium suadentium, ne quid temere et
2 audacter faciat, secuturum. Dimissisque legatis, in
praeparatas rates exercitum inposuit. In proris
clipeatos locaverat iussos in genua subsidere, quo
3 tutiores essent adversus ictus sagittarum. Post hos
qui tormenta intenderent stabant et ab utroque
latere et a fronte circumdati armatis. Reliqui, qui
post[2] tormenta constiterant, remigem lorica non tu-
4 tum[3] scutorum testudine armati protegebant. Idem
ordo in illis quoque ratibus quae equitem vehebant
servatus est. Maior pars a puppe nantes equos loris
trahebat. At illos quos utres stramento repleti
vehebant obiectae rates tuebantur.

5 Ipse rex cum delectis primus ratem solvit et in
ripam dirigi iussit. Cui Scythae admotos ordines
equitum in primo ripae margine opponunt, ut ne
6 applicari quidem terrae rates possent. Ceterum
praeter hanc speciem ripis praesidentis exercitus
ingens navigantes terror invaserat ; namque cursum
gubernatores, cum obliquo flumine impellerentur,
regere non poterant, vacillantesque milites et ne

---

[1] considera] *frag. R ends with this word.*
[2] qui post *J. Froben;* post qui *P;* post eos qui *C.*
[3] lorica non tutum *Hedicke;* loricam indutum *A.*

---

[a] See the description in Amm. xxiii. 4. 2 ff.
[b] That is by the force of the current.

wish enemies or friends to be neighbours to your
empire." So spoke the barbarian.

IX. In reply the king responded that he would
make use of his own fortune and of their advice ; for
he would follow his fortune, in which he had confidence, and the advice of those who persuaded him
2 not to do anything rash and reckless. Having dismissed the envoys, he embarked his army on the
rafts which he had prepared beforehand. On the
prows he had stationed those who carried bucklers,
with orders to sink upon their knees, in order that
they might be safer against the shots of arrows.
3 Behind these stood those who worked the hurling-
engines,[a] surrounded both on each side and in front
by armed men. The rest, who were placed behind
the artillery, armed with shields in testudo-forma-
tion, defended the rowers, who were not protected
4 by corselets. The same order was observed also on
those rafts which carried the cavalry. The greater
part of these let their horses swim astern, held by
the reins. But the men who were carried on skins
stuffed with straw were protected by the rafts that
came between them and the foe.

5 The king himself with a select band of troops was
the first to cast off a raft and to order it to be directed
against the opposite bank. To him the Scythians
opposed ranks of horsemen moved up to the very
margin of the bank, that the rafts might not be
6 able even to reach the land. Moreover, besides the
sight of the army guarding the banks, great terror
had seized those who were managing the rafts ; for
the steersmen could not direct their course, since
they were driven in a slanting direction,[b] and the
soldiers, who kept their feet with difficulty and were

excuterentur solliciti, nautarum ministeria turbave-
7 rant. Ne tela quidem conati nisu vibrare poterant,
cum prior standi sine periculo quam hostem incessendi cura esset. Tormenta saluti fuerunt, quibus in
confertos ac temere se offerentes haud frustra excussa
8 sunt tela. Barbari quoque ingentem vim sagittarum
infudere ratibus, vixque ullum fuit scutum quod non
9 pluribus simul spiculis perforaretur. Iamque terrae
rates applicabantur, cum acies clipeata consurgit et
hastas certo ictu, utpote libero nisu, mittit e ratibus.
Et ut territos recipientesque equos videre, alacres
mutua adhortatione in terram desilire et[1] turbatis
10 acriter pedem inferre coeperunt. Equitum deinde
turmae, quae frenatos habebant equos, perfregere
barbarorum aciem. Interim ceteri, agmine dimican-
11 tium tecti, aptavere se pugnae. Ipse rex quod
vigoris[2] aegro adhuc corpori deerat animi firmitate
supplebat. Vox adhortantis non poterat audiri,
nondum bene obducta cicatrice cervicis, sed dimican-
12 tem cuncti videbant. Itaque ipsi quidem[3] ducum
fungebantur officio, aliusque alium adhortati, in
hostem salutis immemores ruere coeperunt.
13   Tum vero non ora, non arma, non clamorem hostium barbari tolerare potuerunt omnesque effusis
habenis—namque equestris acies erat—capessunt

[1] desilire et *Hedicke;* desiliere *A.*
[2] vigoris *Lauer;* uigori *A.*
[3] quidem *Vindelinus;* quod *A.*

* *Cf.* iv. 3. 18.

worried by fear of being shaken overboard, threw
7 into confusion[a] the work of the boatmen. Although
making every effort the soldiers could not even hurl
their javelins, since they thought rather of keeping
their footing without danger than of attacking the
enemy. Their safety was the hurling-engines, from
which bolts were hurled with effect against the enemy,
who were crowded together and recklessly exposed
8 themselves. The barbarians also poured such a great
amount of arrows upon the rafts, that there was hardly
a single shield that was not pierced by many of their
9 points at the same time. And now the rafts were
being brought to land, when those who were armed
with bucklers rose in a body and with sure aim, since
they had firm footing, hurled their spears from the
rafts. And as soon as they saw that the horses were
terrified and drawing back, inspired by mutual
encouragement, they began to leap to land and
10 vigorously to charge the disordered barbarians. Then
the troops of horsemen, who had their horses bridled,
broke through the enemies' line. In the meantime
the rest, being covered by those who were fighting,
11 prepared themselves for battle. The king himself
by the vigour of his courage made up for what he still
lacked in bodily strength because of his illness. His
words of encouragement could not be heard, since the
old wound on his neck was not yet wholly healed, but
12 all saw him fighting. And so they themselves played
the part of leaders, and urging one another against
the enemy, they began to rush upon them, regardless
of their lives.
13 Then truly the barbarians could not endure the
faces, the arms, nor the shouts of the enemy, but all
with loose rein—for it was an army of cavalry—took

fugam. Quos rex, quamquam vexationem invalidi
corporis pati non poterat, per LXXX tamen stadia
14 insequi perseveravit. Iamque linquente animo suis
praecepit, ut, donec lucis aliquid superesset, fugientium tergis inhaererent ; ipse, exhaustis etiam animi
15 viribus, in castra se recepit ibique[1] substitit. Transierant iam Liberi Patris terminos, quorum monumenta
lapides erant crebris intervallis dispositi arboresque
16 procerae, quarum stipites hedera contexerat. Sed
Macedonas ira longius provexit ; quippe media fere
nocte in castra redierunt, multis interfectis, pluribus
captis, equosque M et DCCC abegere. Ceciderunt
autem Macedonum equites LX, pedites C fere, M saucii fuerunt.
17 Haec expeditio deficientem magna ex parte Asiam
fama tam opportunae victoriae domuit. Invictos
Scythas esse crediderant ; quibus fractis, nullam
gentem Macedonum armis parem fore confitebantur.
Itaque Sacae[2] misere legatos qui pollicerentur gen-
18 tem imperata facturam ; moverat eos regis non
virtus magis, quam clementia in devictos Scythas.
Quippe captivos omnes sine pretio remiserat, ut
fidem faceret sibi cum ferocissimis gentium de forti-
19 tudine, non de ira fuisse certamen. Benigne igitur
exceptis Sacarum legatis comitem Euxenippon[3] dedit,
adhuc admodum iuvenem, aetatis flore conciliatum

---

[1] ibique *Freinshem;* reliquum *A.*
[2] Sacae *J. Froben;* sagae *A.*
[3] Euxenippon *Hedicke;* excipinon *C;* escipinon *P.*

---

[a] The influence of the report of the victory is greatly
exaggerated ; *cf.* Arr. iv. 4. 8-9.
[b] This name is here applied to the Scythians east of the
Iaxartes. *Cf.* also viii. 4. 20, and note.

flight. The king, although he was unable to endure
the tossing of his ailing body, yet persisted in pur-
14 suing them for eighty stadia. And when finally his
strength gave out, he ordered his men, so long as any
light remained, to follow at the backs of the fugitives,
he himself, having exhausted even his strength of
mind, returned to the camp and remained there.
15 Already they had passed the bounds of Father
Bacchus, which were marked by stones set up at
frequent intervals and by tall trees whose trunks
16 were covered with ivy. But the wrath of the Macedonians carried them still farther; for it was nearly
midnight when they returned to camp, after having
slain many and taken still more prisoners, and they
drove off 1800 horses. But of the Macedonians there
fell sixty horsemen and about one hundred foot-
soldiers; 1000 were wounded.
17 This campaign by the fame of so opportune a
victory completely subdued Asia, which in great
part was revolting.[a] They had believed that the
Scythians were invincible; after their defeat they
confessed that no nation would be a match for the
Macedonians. Accordingly the Sacae [b] sent envoys
18 to promise that they would submit; the valour of
the king had not influenced them more than his
clemency towards the conquered Scythians. For he
had sent back all the prisoners without a ransom,
in order to make it appear that his rivalry with the
most warlike nations was in bravery and not in
19 blind rage. Therefore he received the envoys of the
Sacae courteously and gave them Euxenippus to
accompany them; he was still very young and a
favourite of the king because of his youthful beauty,
but although in handsome appearance he was equal

211

sibi, qui cum specie corporis aequaret Hephaestionem,
ei[1] lepore haud sane virili par non erat.

20   Ipse Cratero cum maiore parte exercitus modicis
itineribus sequi iusso, adiit[2] Maracanda urbem. Inde[3]
Spitamenes, comperto eius adventu, Bactra per-
21 fugerat. Itaque quadriduo rex longum itineris spatium emensus, pervenerat in eum locum, in quo
Menedemo duce duo milia peditum et ccc equites
amiserat. Horum ossa tumulo contegi iussit et
22 inferias more patrio dedit. Iam Craterus, cum
phalange subsequi iussus, ad regem pervenerat ;
itaque, ut omnes qui defecerant pariter belli clade
premerentur, copias dividit urique agros et interfici
puberes[4] iubet.

X. Sogdiana regio maiore ex parte deserta est ;
octingenta[5] fere stadia in latitudinem vastae soli-
2 tudines tenent. Ingens spatium rectae regionis est,
per quam amnis—Polytimetum vocant incolae—fertur. Torrentem eum ripae in tenuem alveum cogunt,
3 deinde caverna accipit et sub terram rapit. Cursus
absconditi indicium est aquae meantis sonus, cum
ipsum solum, sub quo tantus amnis fluit, ne modico
4 quidem resudet humore. Ex captivis Sogdianorum
ad regem xxx nobilissimi corporum robore eximio
perducti erant ; qui ubi[6] per interpretem cognove-

---

[1] ei *Heinse;* et *A.*   [2] adiit *Hedicke;* ad *A.*
[3] Inde *Hedicke;* inqua *A.*   [4] puberes *Lauer;* pubes *A.*
[5] octingenta *Glareanus;* lxxx *A.*
[6] ubi *added by Hedicke.*

---

[a] Samarcand.   According to Arrian (iv. 6. 3), this march
followed immediately after the disaster of vii. 7. 30.
[b] Apparently the city which Arr. (iv. 1. 5) calls Zariaspa :
whether that was another name for Bactra is uncertain.

212

to Hephaestion, he was not his match in a charm which was indeed not manly.

20 The king himself, having ordered Craterus with the greater part of the army to follow by moderate marches, went on to the city of Maracanda.[a] From there Spitamenes, on learning of his coming, had 21 fled to Bactra.[b] Accordingly the king, having in four days traversed a great extent of country, had reached the place where, under the lead of Menedemus, he had lost 2000 foot-soldiers and 300 cavalry. He ordered the bones of these to be covered with a mound and offered sacrifice to the spirits of the dead [c] 22 in the Macedonian fashion. Now Craterus, who had been ordered to follow with the phalanx, had rejoined the king; accordingly, in order that all who had revolted might alike be visited with the disasters of war, he divided his forces and gave orders that the fields should be set on fire and that all who were of military age should be killed.

X. The region of Sogdiana is for the greater part deserted; desert wastes occupy a width of 800 2 stadia. It extends straight on for a vast distance, through which flows a river which the natives call the Polytimetus.[d] This is at first a torrent, since its banks force it into a narrow channel, then a cavern 3 receives it, and hurries it off under the ground. Its hidden course is revealed only by the noise of the flowing waters, since the soil itself under which so great a river [e] flows does not exude even a slight 4 moisture. Of the prisoners of the Sogdiani thirty of the noblest born, men of extraordinary strength of body, had been brought in to the king; when these

---

[a] For *inferias dedit* cf. x. 1. 30.   [d] The modern Koi.
[e] On the size of the river see Arr. iv. 6. 7.

runt iussu regis ipsos ad supplicium trahi, carmen
laetantium modo canere tripudiisque et lasciviori
corporis motu gaudium quoddam animi ostentare
5 coeperunt. Admiratus rex tanta magnitudine animi
oppetere mortem, revocari eos iussit, causam tam
effusae laetitiae, cum supplicium ante oculos habe-
6 rent, requirens. Illi, si ab alio occiderentur, tristes
morituros fuisse respondent; nunc a tanto rege,
victore omnium gentium, maioribus suis redditos
honestam mortem, quam fortes viri voto quoque
expeterent, carminibus sui moris laetitiaque cele-
7 brare.[1]

Tantam[2] rex admiratus magnitudinem animi:
" Quaero," inquit,[3] " an vivere velitis non inimici
8 mihi, cuius beneficio victuri estis." Illi numquam
se inimicos ei, sed bello lacessitos se inimicos hosti
fuisse respondent; si quis ipsos beneficio quam iniuria
experiri maluisset, certaturos fuisse ne vincerentur
9 officio. Interrogantique quo pignore fidem obligaturi
essent, vitam quam acciperent pignori futuram esse
dixerunt; reddituros quandoque repetisset. Nec
promissum fefellerunt. Nam qui remissi domos
erant fide continuere populares; quattuor inter
custodes corporis retenti, nulli Macedonum in regem
caritate cesserunt.
10 In Sogdianis Peucolao cum III milibus peditum—
neque enim maiore praesidio indigebat—relicto,
Bactra pervenit. Inde Bessum Ecbatana duci iussit

---

[1] celebrare *Giunta;* celebrarent *A.*
[2] Tantam *Hedicke;* tum *A.*
[3] inquit *Grunauer;* itaque *A.*

---

[a] Diod. xvii. 22 originally related this; *cf.* Contents κβ:
οἱ πρωτεύοντες Σωγδιανῶν ἀπαγόμενοι πρὸς τὸν θάνατον παρα-
δόξως ἐσώθησαν.

learned through an interpreter that they were being
led to execution by order of the king, they began to
sing a song [a] as if rejoicing, and to show a kind of
pleasure by dances and by wanton movements of their
5 bodies. The king, surprised at their facing death
with such greatness of spirit, ordered them to be
recalled, and inquired the reason for such transports
of joy when they had execution before their eyes.
6 They replied that if they were to be killed by anyone
else they would have died sorrowful; as it was, being
restored to their ancestors by so great a king, conqueror of all nations, they were celebrating by their
usual songs and with rejoicing a glorious death,
which brave men might even pray for.
7   Admiring such great courage, Alexander said:
" I ask you whether you would wish to live on condition of not being unfriendly to me to whose favour
8 you will owe your lives." They replied that they had
never been unfriendly to him, but that when pro-
voked to war they were enemies of their foe. If
one had preferred to try them with kindness rather
than with injury, they would have striven not to be
9 outdone in courtesy. And when asked by what
pledge they would bind their loyalty, they said that
the life which was granted them would be their
pledge; that they would pay it when he demanded
it. And they kept their promise. For those who
were then sent to their homes have by their good
faith held their fellow-citizens together; four, who
were retained as a part of his body-guard, yielded to
none of the Macedonians in affection for the king.
10   Having left Peucolaüs among the Sogdiani with
3000 infantry—for he needed no larger force—Alexander came to Bactra. From there he ordered

11 interfecto Dareo poenas capite persoluturum. Eisdem fere diebus Ptolomaeus[1] et Melanidas[2] peditum
IIII milia et equites M adduxerunt, mercede milita-
12 turos. Asander[3] quoque ex Lycia cum pari numero
peditum et D equitibus venit. Totidem ex Syria
Asclepiodorum sequebantur. Antipater Graecorum
13 VIII milia, in quis DC equites erant, miserat. Itaque
exercitu aucto, ad ea quae defectione turbata erant
componenda processit, interfectisque consternationis
auctoribus, quarto die ad flumen Oxum perventum
est. Hic, quia limum vehit, turbidus semper, in-
14 salubris est potui. Itaque puteos miles coeperat
fodere, nec tamen, humo alte egesta, exsistebat
humor. Tandem[4] in ipso tabernaculo regis conspectus est fons ; quem quia tarde notaverant, subito
exstitisse finxerunt, rexque ipse credi voluit, deum[5]
15 donum id fuisse. Superatis deinde amnibus Ocho et
Oxo, ad urbem Margianam[6] pervenit. Circa eam VI
oppidis condendis electa sedes est, duo ad meridiem
versa, IIII spectantia orientem ; modicis inter se
spatiis[7] distabant, ne procul repetendum esset mu-
tuum auxilium. Haec omnia sita sunt in editis
16 collibus. Tunc[8] velut freni domitarum gentium, nunc
originis suae oblita, serviunt quibus imperaverunt.

XI. Et cetera quidem pacaverat rex. Una erat

[1] Ptolomaeus *Hedicke;* ptolomeus *C;* ptholomeus *P.*
[2] Melanidas *Hedicke;* maenidas *A.*
[3] Asander *Schmieder;* alexander *FLP;* aelexander *B m. pr. V.*
[4] Tandem *Kinch;* tamen *A.*   [5] deum *added in I.*
[6] Marginam *Ortel;* marganiam *A* (marginiam *B*).
[7] spatiis *J. Froben;* stadiis *A.*
[8] Tunc *Hedicke;* tum *A.*

[a] *Cf.* Arr. iv. 7. 3.
[b] *Cf.* Arr. iv. 7.   [c] See

Bessus to be taken to Ecbatana,[a] to expiate with
11 his life his murder of Darius. At about the same
time Ptolemy and Melanidas [b] brought the king
4000 infantry and 1000 horsemen, to serve as mer-
12 cenaries. Asander [c] also came from Lycia with an
equal number of foot-soldiers and 500 horsemen. The
same number followed Asclepiodorus from Syria.
Antipater had sent 8000 Greeks, among whom were
13 600 cavalry. With his army thus increased the king
marched forth to set in order the provinces which had
been disordered by the revolt ; and after putting to
death the ringleaders of the disturbance, he returned
on the fourth day to the river Oxus. This river,
because it carries silt, is always turbid and unwhole-
14 some to drink. Therefore the soldiers had begun to
dig wells; yet, although they excavated the soil to
a great depth, they found no water. At length a
spring was found right in the king's tent,[d] and because
they had been late in perceiving it, they spread
the report that it had suddenly appeared, and the
king himself wished it to be believed that it was a
15 gift of the gods. Then he crossed the rivers Ochus [e]
and Oxus and came to the city of Margiana. Round
about it six sites were chosen for founding towns,
two facing south and four east ; they were distant
from one another only a moderate space, so that they
might be able to aid one another without seeking
help from a distance. All these were situated on
16 high hills. At that time they served as curbs upon
the conquered nations; to-day, forgetful of their
origin, they serve those over whom they once ruled.
XI. And everything else the king had subdued.

---

[d] Arr. iv. 15. 7 says οὐ μακρὰν τῆς σκηνῆς, " not far from
the tent."   [e] See Strabo xi. 11. 5.

petra, quam Ariamazes[1] Sogdianus cum xxx milibus
armatorum obtinebat, alimentis ante congestis quae
tantae multitudini vel per biennium suppeterent.
2 Petra in altitudinem xxx eminet stadia, circuitu c
et L complectitur ; undique abscisa et abrupta semita
3 perangusta aditur.   In medio altitudinis spatio habet
specum, cuius os artum et obscurum est ; paulatim
deinde ulteriora panduntur, ultima etiam altos[2] recessus habent.   Fontes per totum fere specum
manant, e quibus collatae aquae per prona montis
4 flumen emittunt.   Rex loci difficultate spectata,
statuerat inde abire ; cupido deinde incessit animo
5 Naturam quoque fatigandi.   Prius tamen quam fortunam obsidionis experiretur, Cophen[3]—Artabazi hic
filius erat—misit ad barbaros qui suaderet ut dede-
rent rupem.   Ariamazes loco fretus, superbe[4] multa
respondit, ad ultimum, an Alexander etiam volare
posset interrogat.
6   Quae nuntiata regi sic accendere animum, ut,
adhibitis cum quibus consultare erat solitus, indicaret
insolentiam barbari eludentis ipsos, quia pinnas non
haberent ; se autem proxima nocte effecturum, ut
7 crederet Macedones etiam volare.   " ccc," inquit,
" pernicissimos iuvenes ex suis quisque copiis per-
ducite ad me, qui per calles et paene invias rupes
8 domi pecora agere consueverant."[5]   Illi praestantes
et levitate corporum et ardore animorum strenue
adducunt.   Quos intuens rex : " Vobiscum," inquit,

---

[1] Ariamazes *Hedicke;* arimazes *A.*
[2] altos *I;* altus *A.*   [3] Cophen *J. Froben;* cophan *A.*
[4] superbe *I;* superba *P;* superbiae *C.*
[5] consueverant *C;* consuerant *P.*

---

[a] *Cf.* Arr. iv. 18. 6.

There was one rock, which Ariamazes, a native of
Sogdiana, was holding with 30,000 armed men,
having previously stored there provisions sufficient
2 to support so great a force for fully two years. The
rock rises to a height of 30 stadia, and embraces
a circuit of 150 ; it is scarped on every side and
3 approached by a very steep and narrow path. In the
middle of its ascent it has a cavern, the entrance of
which is narrow and obscure ; then farther in it
gradually widens, and finally even contains deep
recesses. Springs flow almost everywhere in the
cavern, and the waters which gather in these send
forth a river down the steep sides of the mountain.
4 The king, having seen the difficulty of the place, had
decided to leave it ; then a desire entered his mind
5 to wear out even Nature's strength. Nevertheless,
before trying the fortune of a siege, he sent Cophes
—he was a son of Artabazus—to the barbarians, to
persuade them to surrender the rock. Ariamazes,
trusting to his position, made several arrogant replies,
and finally asked whether Alexander could even fly.[a]
6 When this was reported to the king, it so inflamed
his mind, that summoning those with whom he was
wont to consult, he told them of the insolence of
the barbarian, who mocked at them because they did
not have wings ; but that he on the following night
would make him believe that the Macedonians
7 could even fly. " Let each of you," said he, " bring
me 300 of the most active young men from your
forces, who at home were accustomed to drive their
flocks over mountain pastures and almost impass-
8 able rocks." They quickly brought that number,
who excelled in bodily agility and in ardour of courage. The king, looking them over, said : " It is with

" o iuvenes et mei aequales, urbium invictarum ante
me munimenta superavi, montium iuga perenni nive
obruta emensus sum, angustias Ciliciae intravi, Indiae
sine lassitudine vim frigoris sum perpessus. Et mei
9 documenta vobis dedi et vestra habeo. Petra quam
videtis unum aditum habet, quem barbari obsident,
cetera neglegunt ; nullae vigiliae sunt, nisi quae
10 castra nostra spectant. Invenietis viam, si sollerter
rimati fueritis aditus ferentis ad cacumen. Nihil tam
alte natura constituit quo virtus non possit eniti.
Experiendo quae ceteri desperaverunt,[1] Asiam habe-
11 mus in potestate. Evadite in cacumen ; quod cum
ceperitis, candidis velis signum mihi dabitis ; ego,
copiis admotis, hostem in nos a vobis convertam.
12 Praemium erit ei qui primus occupaverit verticem
talenta x, uno minus accipiet qui proximus ei venerit,
eademque ad decem homines servabitur portio.
Certum[2] autem habeo vos non tam liberalitatem
intueri meam quam voluntatem."
13   His animis regem audierunt, ut iam cepisse verticem viderentur ; dimissique ferreos cuneos, quos
inter saxa defigerent, validosque funes parabant.
14 Rex circumvectus petram, qua minime asper ac
praeruptus aditus videbatur, secunda vigilia, quod
bene verteret, ingredi iubet. Illi, alimentis in biduum sumptis, gladiis modo atque hastis armati,
15 subire coeperunt. Ac primo pedibus ingressi sunt ;

---

[1] desperaverunt *J. Froben;* desperauerint *A.*
[2] Certum *J. Froben;* ceterum *A.*

---

[a] See vii. 8. 19, note *c.*
[b] *Cf.* Arr. iv. 18. 7, who says twelve.
[c] Iron wedges to ram between the steeper rocks and thus
provide footholds. Arrian (iv. 19. 1) speaks of tent-pegs, to
be fixed in the snow, or in the ground where it was bare
of snow.

you, O youths, my comrades, that I have overcome
the fortifications of cities that before now were
unconquered, that I have traversed the heights of
mountains buried in perpetual snow, that I entered
the passes of Cilicia, and have endured the intense
cold of India [a] without fatigue.   I have given you
9 proofs of myself, and I have had proofs of you.   The
rock which you see has only one approach, which the
barbarians beset, they neglect the rest ; they have
no sentinels except those that are watching our
10 camp.   You will find a way, if you seek carefully for
paths leading to the top.   Nature has placed nothing
so high, that valour cannot overcome it.   It is by
trying what others have despaired of that we have
11 Asia in our power.   Go up to the summit ; when you
have attained it, you will give me a signal with white
cloths.   I will bring up forces and divert the enemy
12 from you to us.   The reward for him who first reaches
the top will be ten talents [b] ; he who comes next
will receive one less, and the same proportion will
be maintained up to the number of ten men.   But
I am sure that you will have an eye, not so much to
the reward, as to my desire."
13   They heard the king with such alacrity, that it
seemed that they had already attained the summit ;
and when dismissed they prepared iron wedges to
14 insert between the stones,[c] and strong ropes.   The
king rode around the rock, and where the approach
seemed least rough and steep he ordered them to
set out in the second watch, uttering a prayer to the
gods for success.[d]   They, taking food sufficient for
two days, and armed only with swords and lances,
15 began to climb up.   And at first they advanced on

[d] *Cf.* v. 4. 12, note.

deinde, ut in praerupta perventum est, alii manibus
eminentia saxa complexi levavere[1] semet, alii adiectis
funium laqueis evasere, quidam[2] cum cuneos inter
saxa defigerent, gradus subdidere[3] quis insisterent.

16 Diem inter metum laboremque consumpserunt. Per
aspera enisis[4] duriora restabant, et crescere altitudo
petrae videbatur. Illa vero miserabilis erat facies,
cum ii quos instabilis gradus fefellerat ex praecipiti
devolverentur ; mox eadem in se patienda alieni

17 casus ostendebat exemplum. Per has tamen difficultates enituntur in verticem montis, omnes fatigatione continuati laboris affecti, quidam mulcati parte
membrorum, pariterque eos et nox et somnus op-

18 pressit. Stratis passim corporibus in inviis et asperis
saxorum, periculi instantis obliti, in lucem quieve-
runt ; tandemque, velut ex alto sopore excitati, oc-
cultas subiectasque ipsis valles rimantes,[5] ignari, in
qua parte petrae tanta vis hostium condita esset,
fumum specu[6] infra se ipsos evolutum notaverunt.

19 Ex quo intellectum illam hostium latebram esse.
Itaque hastis imposuere quod convenerat signum ;
totoque e numero II et XXX in ascensu interisse
agnoscunt.

20 Rex non cupidine magis potiundi loci quam vice
eorum quos ad tam manifestum periculum miserat

---

[1] levavere *Wagener;* leuare *A.*
[2] quidam *Hedicke;* quibus *A.*
[3] subdidere *Foss;* subinde *A.*
[4] aspera enisis *Lauer;* asperenisi *P;* aspera nisi *BVF
m. pr.;* aspera nisu *F corr. L m. pr.*
[5] rimantes *Lauer;* rimantis *C;* rimantium *P.*
[6] specu *Mützell;* specui *P;* specus *C.*

---

[a] See p. 220 note *c.*   [b] *Cf.* viii. 14. 27 ; viii. 11. 12.
[c] *Cf.* Cic. *Verr.* ii. 4, 43. 94 : Amm. xxix. 1. 33.

foot; then, when they came to very steep places, some grasped projecting stones with their hands and pulled themselves up, others made their way by using nooses of rope, still others drove wedges between the stones and made steps [a] on which to stand.

16 They spent a day amid fear and toil. After having struggled over rough places, still harder ones awaited them, and the height of the rock seemed to grow. That indeed was a pitiful sight,[b] when those whom their unsteady step had betrayed were hurled down a sheer drop; and the example of others' disaster showed that they must soon suffer the same fate.

17 Nevertheless, through all these difficulties they mounted to the top of the mountain, all worn out by the fatigue of constant toil, some maimed [c] in a part of their limbs, and night and sleep came upon them

18 together. With their bodies stretched here and there on the pathless and rough rocks, they forgot their dangerous situation and slept until daybreak [d]; and when at last they awakened as from a deep slumber, examining the hidden valleys that lay below them, and not knowing in what part of the rock so great a force of the enemy was hidden, they saw smoke rolling out from a cavern below them.

19 From this they knew that it was the hiding place of the enemy. Therefore they raised on their spears the signal which had been agreed upon; and they found that out of their whole number thirty-two had perished during the ascent.

20 The king, harassed not more from desire of taking the place than for the possible fate of those whom he had sent into such evident danger, stood during the

[d] According to Arrian (iv. 19. 3), they made the ascent in one night; Curtius' account seems more probable.

sollicitus, toto die cacumina montis intuens restitit,
noctu demum, cum obscuritas conspectum oculorum
21 ademisset, ad curandum corpus recessit.   Postero die
nondum satis clara luce primus vela, signum capti
verticis, conspexit.   Sed, ne falleretur acies, dubitare
cogebat varietas caeli, nunc internitente lucis fulgore,
nunc condito.[1]   Verum ut liquidior lux apparuit
22 caelo, dubitatio exempta est ; vocatumque Cophen,
per quem barbarorum animos temptaverat, mittit ad
eos qui moneret nunc saltem salubrius consilium
inirent, sin autem fiducia loci perseverarent, ostendi *a*
23 tergo iussit qui ceperant verticem.   Cophes admissus suadere coepit Ariamazi petram tradere, gratiam
regis inituro, si tantas res molientem in unius rupis
obsidione haerere non coegisset.   Ille ferocius super-
biusque quam antea locutus, abire Cophen iubet ;
24 at is prensum manu barbarum rogat ut secum extra
specum prodeat.   Quo impetrato, iuvenes in cacu-
mine ostendit et[2] eius superbiae haud immerito
illudens, pinnas habere ait milites Alexandri.
25   Iamque e[3] Macedonum castris signorum concentus
et totius exercitus clamor audiebatur.   Ea res, sicut
pleraque belli, vana et inanis[4] barbaros ad deditionem
traxit ; quippe occupati metu, paucitatem eorum qui
26 a tergo erant aestimare non poterant.   Itaque Cophen

[1] nunc condito *Freinshem;* conditor *P;* conditi *C.*
[2] et *added by Vogel.*   [3] e *added in I.*
[4] inanis *Hedicke;* inania *C;* inaniania *P.*

a Cf. Arr. iv. 19. 3.
[1] *Cf.* viii. 4. 3.   *c Cf.* iv. 13. 5.

whole day, looking at the summit of the mountain;
not until night, when darkness prevented him from
21 seeing, did he withdraw for repose. On the following day,[a] before it was yet broad daylight, he was
the first to see the cloths that showed that the top was
taken. But the changing sky, where now a gleam
of light shown through, which again was hidden,[b]
compelled him to doubt whether his eyes did not
deceive him. But as a clearer light appeared in the
22 heavens, his doubt was dispelled; and having summoned Cophes, through whom he had tested the
feelings of the barbarians, he sent him to them, to
warn them now at least to adopt a better purpose;
but if they persisted through confidence in their
situation, he ordered that those who had taken possession of the summit should be pointed out to them.
23 Cophes, being admitted, began to urge Ariamazes to
surrender the rock, saying that he would gain the
king's favour if, while he was engaged in such great
enterprises, he should not delay him in the siege of
a single rock. He, speaking more proudly and arro-
24 gantly than before, ordered Cophes to depart; but
he took the barbarian by the hand and asked him to
go with him outside the cave. When he had com-
plied, Cophes showed him the young men on the
summit, and with good reason mocking his arrogance,
said that the soldiers of Alexander had wings.
25 And now from the camp of the Macedonians the
notes of the trumpets and the shouts of the whole
army were heard. This, like many other things in
war, although vain and empty,[c] moved the barbarians
to surrender; for seized with fear, they were unable
to estimate rightly the small number of those who were
26 in their rear. Therefore they quickly recalled Cophes,

—nam trepidantes reliquerat—strenue revocant et cum eo xxx principes mittunt, qui petram tradant

27 et ut incolumibus abire liceat paciscantur. Ille quamquam verebatur, ne conspecta iuvenum paucitate, deturbarent eos barbari, tamen et fortunae suae confisus et Ariamazi superbiae infensus,[1] nullam

28 se condicionem deditionis accipere respondit. Ariamazes, desperatis magis quam perditis rebus, cum propinquis nobilissimisque gentis suae descendit in castra; quos omnis verberibus affectos sub ipsis radi-

29 cibus petrae crucibus iussit affigi. Multitudo deditorum incolis novarum urbium cum pecunia capta dono data est, Artabazus in petrae regionisque quae apposita esset ei tutelam[2] relictus.

---

[1] infensus *added in I.*
[2] tutelam *Hedicke;* tutela *A.*

who had left them in their confusion, and sent with
him thirty of their leading men, to surrender the rock
and to stipulate that they should be allowed to retire
27 unharmed.   The king, although he feared that, seeing
the fewness of the young men,[a] the barbarians might
dislodge them, yet trusting to his fortune and incensed by the arrogance of Ariamazes, replied that
he would accept only an unconditional surrender.
28 Ariamazes, believing that his situation was desperate, whereas it was in fact not hopeless, came down
to the king's camp with his relatives and the principal
nobles of his race ; Alexander ordered all these to be
scourged and crucified at the very foot of the rock.
29 A multitude of those who had surrendered, together
with the booty in money, was given to the settlers in
the new cities.[b]   Artabazus was left to govern the
rock and the region adjacent to it.

[a] *i.e.* those who had reached the summit.
[b] The six that had been newly founded; see vii. 10. 15.

BOOK VIII

CONTENTS OF BOOK VIII

HISTORY OF ALEXANDER, VIII

Alexander marches into India. A description of the country : its rivers, climate, animals, and wealth ; the various classes of its people ; the luxury of the kings, the manner of life and the wisdom of the gymnosophists (ix).

Alexander receives the submission of some of the princes of India, and conquers various cities and regions which resist him. He is wounded in the siege of Magazae, and admits that he is mortal, though called the son of Jupiter (x).

After much toil he takes the city of Hora and the crag of Aornus, formerly vainly attempted by Hercules (xi).

He crosses the Indus and restores his rule to Omphis, who had surrendered himself and his kingdom. The kings exchange gifts (xii).

Alexander encamps at the river Hydaspes and makes war on Porus ; by a clever stratagem he divides Porus' forces and crosses the river and takes possession of the opposite bank (xiii).

The hard-fought battle of the Macedonians and the Indi ; Porus is defeated but shows a lofty spirit, which wins Alexander's clemency and friendship (xiv).

LIBER VIII

I. Alexander, maiore fama quam gloria in dicionem redacta petra, cum propter vagum hostem spargendae manus essent, in tres partes divisit exercitum. Hephaestionem uni, Coenon[1] alteri duces dederat, 2 ipse ceteris praeerat. Sed non eadem mens omnibus barbaris fuit; armis quidam subacti, plures ante certamen imperata fecerunt. Quibus eorum qui in defectione perseveraverant urbes agrosque iussit at- 3 tribui. At exsules Bactriani cum DCCC Massagetarum equitibus proximos vicos vastaverunt. Ad quos coercendos Attinas, regionis eius praefectus, CCC equites insidiarum quae parabantur ignarus,[2] 4 eduxit. Namque hostis in silvis—et erant forte campo[3] iunctae—armatum militem condidit, paucis propellentibus pecora, ut improvidum ad insidias 5 praeda perduceret. Itaque incomposito agmine solutisque ordinibus Attinas praedabundus sequebatur;

---

[1] Coenon *Aldus;* Cenon *A.*

[2] ignarus] *the frag. Herbipolitanum* (**H**) *begins with this word.*

[3] et erant forte campo *P;* quae erant forte campo *B F corr.* *L corr. V;* et quae erant forte campo *F m. pr.;* equae et erant forte campo *L m. pr.;* et forte campo erant *H.*

232

BOOK VIII

I. ALEXANDER, having brought the rock under his sway with more fame than glory,[a] divided the army into three parts, since the roving nature of the enemy made it necessary for him to spread his forces about.[b] He gave the lead of one part to Hephaestion, of a second to Coenus, and he himself commanded the 2 third. But the barbarians were not all of the same mind; some were subdued by his arms, still more submitted without a contest. To the latter he ordered to be assigned the cities and lands of those 3 who had persisted in rebellion. But the Bactriani who had been dispossessed devastated, in company with 900 horsemen of the Massagetae, the neighbouring villages. To check them, Attinas,[c] the governor of that region, led out 300 horsemen, being unaware of the ambuscade that was being laid. 4 For in the woods—and it chanced that they were close to a plain—the enemy hid an armed force, while a few drove flocks before them, in order that the hope of booty might lead Attinas unawares into the 5 snare. Accordingly he, marching in disorder and in loose formation, was following them, thinking only

---

[a] Cf. Cic. De Inv. ii. 55. 166 ; Pro Sest. lxvi. 139 ; also ix. 10. 24, and note.   [b] Cf. v. 13. 18 ; Arr. iv. 16. 3.
[c] Otherwise unknown. With the whole account cf. Arr. iv. 16. 4 ff.

quem praetergressum silvam qui in ea consederant ex improviso adorti, cum omnibus interemerunt.

6 Celeriter ad Craterum huius cladis fama perlata est, qui cum omni equitatu supervenit. Et Massagetae quidem iam refugerant, Dahae M oppressi sunt ; quorum clade totius regionis finita defectio est.

7 Alexander quoque, Sogdianis rursus subactis, Maracanda repetit. Ibi Derdas,[1] quem ad Scythas super Bosphorum colentes miserat, cum legatis gentis

8 occurrit. Phrataphernes quoque, qui Chorasmiis[2] praeerat, Massagetis et Dahis regionum confinio adiunctus, miserat qui facturum imperata pollicerentur.

9 Scythae petebant, ut regis sui filiam matrimonio sibi iungeret ; si dedignaretur adfinitatem, principes Macedonum cum primoribus suae gentis conubio coire pateretur ; ipsum quoque[3] regem

10 venturum ad eum pollicebantur. Utraque legatione benigne audita, Hephaestionem et Artabazum operiens stativa habuit ; quibus adiunctis, in regionem quae appellatur Bazaira pervenit.

11 Barbarae opulentiae in illis locis haud ulla sunt maiora indicia quam magnis nemoribus saltibusque

12 nobilium ferarum greges clusi. Spatiosas ad hoc eligunt silvas crebris perennium aquarum fontibus amoenas ; muris nemora cinguntur turresque habent

13 venantium receptacula. Quattuor continuis aetatibus intactum saltum fuisse constabat, cum[4] Alex-

---

[1] Derdas *Hedicke;* berdes *AH.*
[2] Chorasmiis *Rader;* Choras *A.*
[3] regum (*before* quoque) *deleted by Lauer.*
[4] cum *Hedicke;* quem *A.*

---

[a] *Cf.* Arr. iv. 17. 1.   [b] On *super* see vi. 2. 13, note.
[c] *Cf.* Arr. iv. 15. 4.   Perhaps the dwellers in Khiva.

of plunder ; but when he had passed by the woods,
those who had taken post there suddenly attacked
him and slew him with all his men.

6   The report of this disaster was quickly brought to
Craterus, who came to the spot [a] with all his cavalry.
The Massagetae, for their part, had already fled, but
1000 of the Dahae were slain, and by their slaughter
7 the rebellion of the whole region was ended.   Alexander also, having again subdued the Sogdiani,
returned to Maracanda.   There Derdas, whom he
had sent to the Scythians dwelling east of the
Bosphorus,[b] met him with envoys of that people.
8 Phrataphernes also, satrap of the Chorasmii,[c] a neighbour to the Massagetae and the Dahae, had sent
9 messengers to promise his obedience. The Scythians
asked that he should marry the daughter of their
king ; if he considered her unworthy of the alliance,
that he should suffer the leading men of the Macedonians to contract marriages with the great ladies
of his race [d] ; they promised that the king himself
10 also would come to him. Both deputations were
courteously heard and Alexander remained in camp
for a few days, waiting for Hephaestion and Artabazus ; when they joined him, he passed into the
district called Bazaira.[e]

11   There are no greater indications of the wealth of
the barbarians in those regions than their herds of
noble wild beasts, confined in great woods and parks.
12 For this purpose they choose extensive forests made
attractive by perennial springs ; they surround the
woods with walls and have towers as stands for
13 the hunters. The forest was known to have been
undisturbed for four successive generations, when

[d] *Cf.* Arr. iv. 15. 2-3.   [e] Near Samarcand ?

ander cum toto exercitu ingressus agitari undique
14 feras iussit. Inter quas cum leo magnitudinis rarae
ipsum regem invasurus incurreret, forte Lysimachus,
qui postea regnavit, proximus Alexandro venabulum
obicere ferae coeperat; quo rex repulso et abire
iusso, adiecit tam a semet uno quam a Lysimacho
15 leonem interfici posse. Lysimachus enim quondam,
cum venarentur in Syria, occiderat quidem eximiae
magnitudinis feram solus, sed laevo humero usque ad
16 ossa lacerato, ad ultimum periculi pervenerat. Id
ipsum exprobrans ei, rex fortius quam locutus est
fecit; nam feram non excepit modo, sed etiam uno
vulnere occidit.
17 Fabulam quae obiectum leoni a rege Lysimachum
temere vulgavit ab eo casu quem supra diximus
18 ortam esse crediderim. Ceterum Macedones, quamquam prospero eventu defunctus erat Alexander,
tamen scivere gentis suae more,[1] ne aut[2] pedes
venaretur aut[3] sine delectis[4] principum atque ami-
19 corum. Ille, IIII milibus ferarum deiectis, in eodem
saltu cum toto exercitu epulatus est.
Inde Maracanda reditum est; acceptaque aetatis
excusatione ab Artabazo, provinciam eius destinat
20 Clito. Hic erat qui apud Granicum amnem nudo

---

[1] more *Vindelinus;* morem *A.*
[2] ne aut *Mützell;* nam ut *A.*   [3] aut *Aldus;* haud *A.*
      [4] delectis *Vindelinus;* dilectis *A.*

---

[a] See x. 10. 4.
[b] It is accepted by Justin xv. 3; Pliny, *N.H.* viii. 16. 21;
Sen. *De ira* iii. 17. 2, *De clem.* i. 25.
[c] Bactriana.
[d] He commanded the ἴλη βασιλική of the Companion

Alexander, entering it with his whole army, ordered
14 an attack on the wild beasts from every side. Among
these when a lion of extraordinary size rushed to
attack the king himself, it happened that Lysimachus, who was afterwards a king,[a] being beside
Alexander, began to oppose his hunting-spear to the
animal ; but the king pushed him aside and ordered
him to retire, adding that a lion could be killed by
15 himself alone as well as by Lysimachus. And in
fact Lysimachus, once when they were hunting in
Syria, had indeed alone killed a lion of remarkable
size, but had had his left shoulder torn to the bone
16 and thus had come into great peril of his life. The
king, taunting him with this very experience, acted
more vigorously than he spoke ; for he not only met
the wild beast, but killed him with a single wound.
17 I am inclined to believe that the story which without evidence spread the report [b] that Lysimachus
was exposed by the king to the attack of a lion arose
from the incident which we have just mentioned.
18 But the Macedonians, although Alexander had been
successful in his attempt, nevertheless voted in the
manner of their nation that he should neither hunt
on foot nor without being accompanied by selected
19 officers or friends. He, after having laid low 4000
wild beasts, banqueted in that same park with his
entire army.

From there the king returned to Maracanda ;
and having accepted Artabazus' excuse of old age, he
20 made over his province [c] to Clitus. It was he, an old
soldier of Philip and distinguished by many exploits
in war,[d] who at the river Granicus [e] covered the

Cavalry, and later shared with Hephaestion the command of
the whole troop.   [e] See Arr. i. 15. 8.

capite regem dimicantem clipeo suo texit et Rhosacis manum capiti regis imminentem gladio amputavit, vetus Philippi miles multisque bellicis operibus clarus.

21 Hellanice,[1] quae Alexandrum educaverat, soror eius, haud secus quam mater a rege diligebatur. Ob has causas validissimam imperii partem fidei eius tutelae-

22 que commisit. Iamque iter parare in posterum iussus, sollemni et tempestivo adhibetur convivio. In quo rex cum multo incaluisset mero, immodicus aestimator sui, celebrare quae gesserat coepit, gravis etiam eorum auribus qui sentiebant vera memorari.

23 Silentium tamen habuere seniores, donec Philippi res orsus obterere, nobilem apud Chaeroneam victoriam sui operis fuisse iactavit ademptamque sibi malignitate et invidia patris tantae rei gloriam.

24 Illum quidem, seditione inter Macedones milites et Graecos mercenarios orta, debilitatum vulnere quod in ea consternatione acceperat iacuisse, non alia re[2] quam simulatione mortis tutiorem ; se corpus eius protexisse clipeo suo, ruentesque in illum sua manu

25 occisos. Quae patrem numquam aequo animo esse confessum, invitum filio debentem salutem suam. Atque[3] post expeditionem quam sine eo fecisset ipse in Illyrios victorem scripsisse se patri fusos fugatosque

26 hostes ; nec adfuisse usquam Philippum. Laude

---

[1] hellanice *A;* et Lanice *Hedicke.*
[2] alia re *Zumpt;* alias *A.*   [3] Atque *Hedicke;* itaque *A.*

---

[a] In Arrian (iv. 9. 3) Lanicê.
[b] See v. 10. 3.   [c] See vi. 2. 2, note.
[d] For *obterere* in this sense *cf.* Livy xxiii. 43. 10.
[e] 338 B.C. Plut. *Alex.* ix. 2 and Diod. xvi. 86. 3 say that Alexander was first to break the line of the Thebans and put them to flight.
[f] Nothing is said of this elsewhere.

king with his shield when he was fighting bareheaded,
and with his sword cut off the hand of Rhosaces, when
21 it threatened the king's life. And Hellanicê,[a] his
sister, who had reared Alexander, was loved by the
king as dearly as if she were his own mother. It was
for these reasons that he entrusted to Clitus' faith
and protection the strongest part of his empire.[b]
22 And now, after being bidden to prepare for a march
on the following day, Clitus was invited to one of the
king's usual prolonged banquets.[c] There, when
the king had been heated by an abundance of wine,
having an immoderate opinion of himself, he began to
boast of his exploits, to the displeasure even of the
ears of those who knew that what he said was true.
23   But the older men remained silent until he began
to belittle [d] the deeds of Philip and to boast that the
famous victory at Chaeronea [e] had been his work, but
that the glory of so great a battle had been taken from
him by the grudgingness and jealousy of his father.
24 That Philip, when a quarrel had arisen between the
Macedonian soldiers and the Greek mercenaries,
being disabled by a wound which he had suffered
during that disturbance, had fallen to the ground and
could find no other expedient to protect himself better
than feigning death; but that he had protected his
father's body with his shield, and with his own hand
25 had slain those who were rushing upon him. This
Philip could never bring himself to admit, being unwilling to be indebted for his life to his son. Also,
that after the campaign which he himself had made
without Philip against the Illyrians,[f] when victorious
he had written to his father that the enemy had
been routed and put to flight; and that Philip had
26 nowhere been present. He said that praise was due,

dignos esse, non qui Samothracum initia viserent
cum Asiam uri vastarique oporteret, sed eos qui
magnitudine rerum fidem antecessissent.

27 Haec et his similia laeti audiere iuvenes; ingrata
senioribus erant, maxime propter Philippum, sub quo
28 diutius vixerant, cum Clitus, ne ipse quidem satis
sobrius, ad eos qui infra ipsum cubabant conversus
Euripidis rettulit carmen, ita ut sonus magis quam
29 sermo exaudiri posset[1] a rege, quo significabatur male
instituisse Graecos, quod tropaeis regum dumtaxat
nomina inscriberent; alieno enim sanguine partam
gloriam intercipi. Itaque rex, cum suspicaretur
malignius habitum esse sermonem, percontari proxi-
30 mos coepit quid ex Clito audissent. Et illis ad
silendum obstinatis, Clitus paulatim maiore voce
Philippi acta bellaque in Graecia gesta commemorat,
31 omnia praesentibus praeferens. Hinc inter iuniores
senesque orta contentio est. Et rex, velut patienter
audiret quis Clitus obterebat laudes eius, ingentem
32 iram conceperat. Ceterum cum animo videretur imperaturus si finem procaciter orto sermoni Clitus
imponeret, nihil eo remittente[2] magis exasperabatur.
33 Iamque Clitus etiam Parmenionem defendere
audebat et Philippi de Atheniensibus victoriam
Thebarum praeferebat excidio, non vino modo, sed

---

[1] posset *Lauer;* possit *A.*
[2] eo remittente *Acidalius;* eorum omittente *A.*

---

[a] Its Mysteries ranked next to those of Eleusis; it was
at his initiation that Philip had met and married Olympias;
cf. Plut. *Alex.* ii.
[b] *Androm.* 684.   [c] See viii. 1. 23, note.

not to those who had witnessed the initiatory rites
of Samothrace *a* at a time when Asia should have
been laid waste by fire, but to those who by the
greatness of their deeds had surpassed belief.

27 These and similar things the young soldiers heard
with pleasure, but they were odious to the older
men, especially because of Philip, under whom they

28 had lived longer, when Clitus, who was himself by no
means wholly sober, turned to those who were reclining below him, and quoted a line of Euripides *b* in
such a tone that the sound could be heard by the king

29 rather than the words made out, to the effect that it
was a bad custom of the Greeks to inscribe on their
trophies only the names of kings; for the kings stole
the glory won by the blood of others. Therefore
Alexander, for he suspected that the words had been
somewhat malicious, began to ask those next to him

30 what they had heard Clitus say. And when they
maintained an obstinate silence, Clitus, gradually
raising his voice, spoke of the deeds of Philip and
the wars which he had waged in Greece, rating them

31 all higher than the present victories. From this
there arose a dispute between the younger and the
older soldiers. And the king, although he appeared
to hear with patience the words in which Clitus be-

32 littled his glory, had become exceedingly angry. But
when it seemed that he would control himself if Clitus
would put an end to the talk which he had wantonly
begun, as he did not in any way moderate it, the
king became more exasperated.

33 And now Clitus even ventured to defend Parmenion
and extolled the victory of Philip over the Athenians *c*
above the destruction of Thebes, being carried away,
not only by wine, but by a perverse spirit of conten-

241

34 etiam animi prava contentione provectus. Ad ultimum : " Si moriendum," inquit, " est pro te, Clitus
est primus ; at cum victoriae arbitrium agis,[1] praecipuum ferunt qui procacissime patris tui memoriae
35 illudunt. Sogdianam regionem mihi attribuis, totiens
rebellem et non modo indomitam, sed quae ne subigi
quidem possit. Mittor ad feras bestias, praecipitia
36 ingenia sortitas. Sed, quae ad me pertinent, transeo.
Philippi milites spernis oblitus, nisi hic Atarrhias
senex iuniores pugnam detrectantes[2] revocasset,
37 adhuc nos circa Halicarnasum haesuros fuisse. Quomodo igitur Asiam totam[3] cum istis iunioribus subegisti ?[4] Verum est, ut opinor, quod avunculum
tuum in Italia dixisse constat, ipsum in viros in-
cidisse, te in feminas."
38 Nihil ex omnibus inconsulte ac temere iactis regem
magis moverat quam Parmenionis cum honore mentio
illata. Dolorem tamen repressit,[5] contentus iussisse
39 ut convivio excederet. Nec quicquam aliud adiecit
quam forsitan eum, si diutius locutus foret, expro-
braturum sibi fuisse vitam a semetipso datam; hoc
40 enim superbe saepe iactasse. Atque illum cunctan-
tem adhuc surgere, qui proximi ei cubuerant, iniectis
manibus, iurgantes monentesque conabantur ab-
41 ducere. Clitus cum abstraheretur, ad pristinam

[1] agis *Acidalius;* magis *A.*
[2] detrectantes *Aldus;* detractantes *A.*
[3] totam *Bentley;* etiam *A.*
[4] subegisti *I;* subiecisti *A.*
[5] repressit *Acidalius;* rex pressit *A.*

---

[b] Bactriana, rather, first assigned to Artabazus, later to
Clitus ; *cf.* vii. 5. 1, viii. 1. 19, Arr. iv. 15. 5; also p. 203,
note *d.*   [b] See v. 2. 5.

34 tion. Finally he said: "If someone must die for you, Clitus is the first choice; but when you award the prizes of a victory, those bear off the palm who most wantonly mock the memory of your father.

35 You assign to me the province of Sogdiana,[a] so often rebellious, and not only untamed but not even capable of being subdued. I am sent to wild beasts, to which

36 Nature has given incorrigible recklessness. But of what concerns me I have nothing to say. You scorn the soldiers of Philip, forgetting that if old Atarrhias[b] here had not called back the younger men when they shrank from battle, we should still be lingering around

37 Halicarnassus. How then would you have subdued all Asia with those young men of yours? That is true, in my opinion, which your uncle[c] is known to have said in Italy, that he had encountered men, you women."[d]

38 Nothing among all the taunts which Clitus had ill advisedly and rashly uttered had more aroused the king than the honourable mention made of Parmenion.[e] Yet he restrained his resentment, content

39 with ordering Clitus to leave the banquet. And he added nothing else than that perhaps if Clitus had spoken at greater length, he would have taunted him with having saved his life; for of this he had often

40 arrogantly boasted. And when Clitus still delayed to rise, those who had reclined next to him laid hands upon him and with remonstrances and warning were

41 trying to lead him from the room. As he was being taken away, anger also was added to his former

[c] Alexander Molossus, ruler in Epirus, brother of Olympias, Alexander's mother.
[d] See Gell. 17. 21; Livy ix. 19. 10-11.
[e] Referring to § 33 *supra*.

vinolentiam[1] ira quoque adiecta, suo pectore tergum
illius esse defensum, nunc, postquam tanti meriti
praeterierit tempus, etiam memoriam invisam esse
42 proclamat. Attali quoque caedem obiciebat et ad
ultimum Iovis, quem patrem sibi Alexander assere-
ret, oraculum eludens, veriora se regi quam patrem
eius respondisse dicebat.

43 Iam tantum irae conceperat rex quantum vix
sobrius ferre potuisset. Enimvero, olim mero sensi-
44 bus victis, ex lecto repente prosiluit. Attoniti amici,
ne positis quidem, sed abiectis poculis, consurgunt
in eventum rei quam tanto impetu acturus esset
45 intenti. Alexander, rapta lancea ex manibus armigeri, Clitum adhuc eadem linguae intemperantia
furentem percutere conatus, a Ptolomaeo et Perdicca
46 inhibetur. Medium complexi et obluctari perseverantem morabantur, Lysimachus et Leonnatus etiam
47 lanceam abstulerant; ille militum fidem implorans
comprehendi se a proximis amicorum, quod Dareo
nuper accidisset, exclamat signumque tuba dari ut
ad regiam armati coirent iubet.

48 Tum vero Ptolomaeus et Perdiccas, genibus advo-
luti, orant, ne in tam praecipiti ira perseveret
spatiumque potius animo det; omnia postero die
49 iustius executurum. Sed clausae erant aures, obstrepente[2] ira; itaque impotens animi, procurrit in

---

[1] vinolentiam *J. Froben;* uiolentiam *A.*
[2] obstrepente *I;* obstrepentes *A.*

---

^a Cf. vi. 9. 18, note.   ^b Cf. Arr. iv. 8. 8.

drunkenness, and he shouted that the king's back
had been protected by his own breast, but that now,
after the time of so great a service had passed, even
42 the memory of it was odious. Then he also re-
proached the king with the murder of Attalus,[a] and
finally, mocking the oracle of Jupiter, whom Alexander claimed as his father, he said that he himself
had spoken to the king more truly than his " father "
had done.

43   By now Alexander was filled with such great wrath
as he could hardly have mastered when sober.   In
fact, his senses having long since been overcome by
44 wine, he suddenly leaped from his couch. His friends,
in a panic, having not even put down their cups but
thrown them aside, arose in a body, their thoughts
centred upon the result of the act which he was about
45 to commit with such impetuosity. Alexander, wrest-
ing a lance from the hands of one of his guards, and
attempting to kill Clitus, who was still raging with the
same unbridled language, was prevented by Ptolemy
46 and Perdiccas.   Throwing their arms about his waist,
they kept holding him back while he continued to
struggle ; Lysimachus and Leonnatus had even taken
47 away the lance ; the king, invoking the loyalty of his
soldiers, cried that he was being seized by his closest
friends, as had lately happened to Darius,[b] and ordered the signal to be given with the trumpet for the
soldiers to take arms and come to the royal quarters.
48   Then truly Ptolemy and Perdiccas threw themselves at his knees and besought him not to persist
in such unrestrained anger, but rather to take time
for reflection ; that to-morrow he would manage the
49 whole matter with more justice. But his ears were
closed, deafened by wrath ; and so, beside himself,

regiae vestibulum et, vigili excubanti hasta ablata,
constitit in aditu, quo necesse erat his qui simul
50 cenaverant egredi. Abierant ceteri, Clitus ultimus
sine lumine exibat, cum[1] rex quisnam esset interrogat. Eminebat etiam in voce sceleris quod parabat
51 atrocitas. Et ille iam non suae, sed regis irae memor,
52 Clitum esse et de convivio exire respondit. Haec
dicentis latus hasta transfixit morientisque sanguine
aspersus : " I nunc," inquit, " ad Philippum et
Parmenionem et Attalum."

II. Male humanis ingeniis Natura consuluit, quod
plerumque non futura, sed transacta perpendimus.
Quippe rex, postquam ira mente decesserat, etiam
ebrietate discussa, magnitudinem facinoris sera aesti-
2 matione perspexit. Videbat tunc immodice[2] libertate
abusum, sed alioqui egregium bello virum et, nisi
erubesceret fateri, servatorem sui, occisum. De-
testabile carnificis ministerium occupaverat rex, verborum licentiam, quae vino poterat imputari, nefanda
3 caede ultus. Manabat toto vestibulo cruor paulo
ante convivae ; vigiles attoniti et stupentibus similes
procul stabant, liberioremque paenitentiam solitudo
4 eliciebat.[3] Ergo hastam ex corpore iacentis evolsam
retorsit in semet. Iamque admoverat pectori, cum
advolant vigiles et repugnanti e manibus extorquent

---

[1] cum *Hedicke;* quam *B m. pr. FL m. pr. P m. pr.
V m. pr.*
[2] immodice *Hedicke;* immodica *A.*
[3] eliciebat *Hedicke;* excipiebat *A.*

---

[a] Curtius' account is less favourable to Alexander than
those of Arrian, Plutarch, and Justin, who represent him as
killing Clitus more in the heat of passion, at table or when
he first rushed back into the dining-room.
[b] For *discussa cf.* vi. 8. 22.

he rushed into the vestibule of the royal quarters, and
snatching a lance from the sentinel on guard, stood
at the entrance where those who had dined with
50 him must pass out. The rest had gone, and Clitus
was coming out last without a light, when the king
asked who it was. Even his voice clearly indicated
51 the ferocity of the crime which he meditated. And
Clitus, no longer mindful of his own anger, but remembering that of the king, replied that it was Clitus
52 and that he was leaving the banquet. As he was
saying this the king ran the lance into his side, and
bespattered with the blood of the dying man, cried :
" Go now [a] to Philip and Parmenion and Attalus ! "

II. Nature has dealt ill with men's minds, in that
we generally weigh acts, not beforehand, but after
they are done. For the king, after anger had left
his mind and even his intoxication had been dispelled,[b] clearly perceived, but too late, the enormity
2 of his crime. He saw then that he had killed a man
who had indeed immoderately abused freedom of
speech, but who in any case was eminent in warfare,
and if he was not ashamed to admit it, the saviour of
his life. A king had usurped the detestable function
of an executioner, and had punished licence in
language, which might have been imputed to wine,
3 by an abominable murder. The whole vestibule
swam with the blood of one who but now had been his
guest, the sentinels stood aloof from him, amazed and
as if stupefied, and solitude gave freer opportunity
4 for repentance. Therefore, tearing the lance from
the body of the prostrate man, he turned it upon
himself. And he had already brought it against his
breast, when the sentinels flew to him, and in spite of
his resistance wrested it from his hand, lifted him up,

247

QUINTUS CURTIUS

5 adlevatumque in tabernaculum deferunt. Ille humi
prostraverat corpus, gemitu eiulatuque[1] miserabili
tota personante[2] regia. Laniare deinde os unguibus
et circumstantes rogare ne se tanto dedecori super-
stitem esse paterentur.

6   Inter has preces tota nox extracta est. Scrutan-
temque num ira deorum ad tantum nefas actus esset,
subit anniversarium sacrificium Libero Patri non
esse redditum stato[3] tempore. Itaque inter vinum
et epulas caede commissa, iram dei fuisse mani-
7 festam. Ceterum magis eo movebatur, quod omnium
amicorum animos videbat attonitos ; neminem cum
ipso sociare[a] sermonem postea ausurum, vivendum
esse in solitudine velut ferae bestiae terrenti alias
8 timentique. Prima deinde luce tabernaculo corpus,
sicut adhuc cruentum erat, iussit inferri. Quo posito
ante ipsum, lacrimis obortis : " Hanc," inquit, " nutrici meae gratiam rettuli, cuius duo filii apud Miletum
pro mea gloria occubuere mortem, hic frater, unicum
orbitatis solacium, a me inter epulas occisus est.
9 Quo nunc se conferet misera ? Omnibus eius unus
supersum, quem solum aequis oculis videre non
poterit. Et ego, servatorum meorum latro, revertar
in patriam, ut ne dexteram quidem nutrici sine
10 memoria calamitatis eius offerre possim ! " Et cum
finis lacrimis querellisque non fieret, iussu amicorum
corpus ablatum est.

      [1] eiulatuque *Vindelinus;* heiulatuque *A.*
      [2] personante *Modius;* personans *A.*
      [3] stato *Modius;* statuto *A.*

---

   [a] *sociare sermonem* is poetic; see Val. Flacc. v. 281 and 516.
   [b] Hellanicê; see viii. 1. 21; Arr. iv. 9. 3. One son was
Proteas, Athen. iv. 129 a.

5 and carried him into his tent. He had thrown himself on the ground, while all the whole royal quarters rang with his groans and piteous wailing. Then he tore his face with his nails, begging those who stood around him not to suffer him to survive such a disgrace.

6 Amid prayers like these the whole night was spent. And while he was considering whether he had been driven to commit such a great crime by the anger of the gods, it occurred to him that he had not paid the annual sacrifice to Father Liber at the appointed time. Hence it was evident that the murder committed amid wine and feasting was a manifestation

7 of the anger of that god. But the king was still more disturbed because he saw that the minds of all his friends were terror-stricken, that no one would dare hereafter to converse *a* with him, but he must live in solitude like a savage beast which now inspires terror in other beasts and at other times is itself in fear

8 of them. Later, at dawn, he ordered the body to be taken into his tent, all bloody as it still was. When it was placed before him, he said with eyes filled with tears : " This is my requital to my nurse,*b* whose two sons met death at Miletus for my glory, this her brother, the sole comfort of her bereave-

9 ment, I have slain at a banquet. Where will the poor woman turn now ? Of all her kindred I alone am living, and I am the only one whom she will not be able to look upon with kindly eyes. And I, the assassin of my preservers, shall return to my native land without being able even to offer my hand to my nurse without reminding her of her bereavement ! "

10 And since he did not put an end to his tears and laments, by order of his friends the body was removed.

11 Rex triduum iacuit inclusus. Quem ut armigeri corporisque custodes ad moriendum obstinatum esse cognoverunt, universi in tabernaculum irrumpunt diuque precibus ipsorum reluctatum aegre vicerunt,
12 ut cibum caperet. Quoque minus caedis puderet, iure interfectum Clitum Macedones decernunt, sepultura quoque prohibituri, ni rex humari iussisset.
13 Igitur, x diebus maxime ad confirmandum pudorem apud Maracanda consumptis, cum parte exercitus Hephaestionem in regionem Bactrianam misit, com-
14 meatus in hiemem paraturum. Quam Clito ante[1] destinaverat provinciam, Amyntae dedit ; ipse Xenippa pervenit. Scythiae confinis est regio habitaturque pluribus ac frequentibus vicis, quia ubertas terrae non indigenas modo detinet, sed etiam advenas
15 invitat. Bactrianorum exsulum qui ab Alexandro defecerant receptaculum fuerat ; sed, postquam regem adventare compertum est, pulsi ab incolis,
16 ii milia fere et d congregantur. Omnes equites erant, etiam in pace latrociniis assueti ; tum ferocia ingenia non bellum modo, sed etiam veniae desperatio efferaverat. Itaque ex improviso adorti Amyntan, praetorem Alexandri, diu anceps proelium fecerant ;
17 ad ultimum dcc suorum amissis, quorum ccc hostis

ante *Eberhard;* autem *A.*

---

[a] *Cf.* Arr. iv. 9. 3.
[b] The decree is not mentioned elsewhere ; *cf.* Arr. iv. 9. 7.
[c] Of 328–327 b.c. Curtius adds in viii. 8. 21 that after the execution of the " conspirators " whom the Macedonians agreed to be guilty the king had the Olynthian philosopher Callisthenes tortured to death.
[d] The name and the location are uncertain. McCrindle, *Ancient India,* p. 43, places it " on the skirts of the Noura

250

11 The king lay in seclusion for three days.[a] When his attendants and body-guards knew that he was resolved upon dying, they all burst into the tent, and although for a long time he resisted their entreaties, they with difficulty prevailed upon him to take food.

12 And in order that he might feel less shame for the murder, the Macedonians decreed [b] that Clitus had been justly put to death, and that they would even have deprived him of funeral rites, if the king had not ordered that he be buried.

13 Then, after having spent ten days near Maracanda, chiefly that he might recover from his shame, he sent Hephaestion with a part of the army into the region

14 of Bactriana to prepare supplies for the winter.[c] The province which he previously had intended for Clitus he gave to Amyntas. He himself came to Xenippa [d]; this is a place bordering on Scythia, and it is occupied by many populous villages, since the fertility of the soil not only holds the natives but also attracts new-

15 comers. It had been the refuge of the Bactrian exiles who had revolted from Alexander; but after it was learned that the king was coming, these were driven out by the natives and were gathered together

16 to the number of about 2500. They were all horse-men, accustomed to brigandage even in time of peace; at that time too their proud natures had been made more reckless, not only by the war, but also by despair of pardon. Hence they made an unlooked-for attack upon Amyntas, a general of Alexander, and for a long time had held the contest in balance;

17 finally, after having lost 700 of their number, of whom the enemy took 300 prisoners, they turned

mountains, a range that runs from east to west about ten miles north of Bokhara."

cepit, dedere terga victoribus, haud sane inulti;
quippe LXXX Macedonum interfecerunt, praeterque
18 eos CCC et L saucii facti sunt. Veniam tamen etiam
post alteram defectionem impetraverunt.

19 His in fidem acceptis, in regionem, quam Nautaca[1]
appellant, rex cum toto exercitu venit. Satrapes erat
Sisimithres, duobus ex sua matre filiis genitis; quippe
apud eos parentibus stupro coire cum liberis fas est.
20 Is,[2] armatis popularibus, fauces regionis, qua in
artissimum cogitur, valido munimento saepserat.[3]
Praeterfluebat torrens amnis, terga[4] petra claudebat;
21 hanc manu perviam incolae fecerant, sed aditu specus
accipit lucem, interiora nisi illato lumine obscura
sunt.[5] Perpetuus cuniculus iter praebet in campos
22 ignotum[6] nisi indigenis. At Alexander, quamquam
angustias naturali situ munitas valida[7] manu barbari
tuebantur, tamen, arietibus admotis, munimenta,
quae manu adiuncta erant, concussit fundisque et
sagittis propugnantium plerosque deiecit.

Quos ubi dispersos fugavit, ruinas munimentorum
23 supergressus ad petram admovit exercitum. Ceterum interveniebat fluvius, coeuntibus aquis ex
superiore fastigio in vallem, magnique operis vide-
24 batur tam vastam voraginem explere; caedi tamen
arbores et saxa congeri iussit. Ingensque barbaros

---

[1] Nautaca *Glareanus;* nauta (amittam *F m. pr.*) *C.*
[2] Is *Modius;* ii *A.*   [3] saepserat *Modius;* sepserant *A.*
[4] terga *Acidalius;* tergo *A.*
[5] obscura sunt *Vindelinus;* obsunt *A.*
[6] campos ignotum *Lauer;* campo signorum *A.*
[7] valida *J. Froben;* ac ualidas *A.*

---

[a] On the first see vii. 6. 13, 7. 31, 10. 10.

their backs to the victors, but by no means unavenged : for they killed eighty of the Macedonians, and 350
18 besides those suffered wounds. Yet they received pardon even after a second revolt.[a]
19 After these had been received in surrender, the king with his whole army came into the region which they call Nautaca.[b] The satrap was Sisimithres, who had two sons born of his own mother ; for among those people it is lawful for parents to cohabit with
20 their children. He, having armed his subjects, had blocked the narrowest part of the entrance to the region with a strong fortification. Near by flowed a torrential river, which a crag in its rear protected ;
21 through this the natives had made artificially a road ; but whereas at either entrance a cave receives light, the inner parts are dark unless a light has been carried in. A continuous passage, known only
22 to the natives, gives access to the plains. Although the barbarians with a strong force were guarding the pass, which was protected by its natural situation, nevertheless Alexander, bringing up his battering-rams, shattered the fortifications which had been artificially added, and laid low many of the defenders with slings and arrows.

When he had scattered these and put them to flight, passing over the ruins of the fortifications, he
23 brought his army to the crag. But the river inter-vened, where the waters from the summit came together and flowed into the valley, and it seemed a
24 task of great labour to fill up so vast an abyss ; never-theless he ordered trees to be felled and rocks to be brought together. And great panic had struck the

[b] A place in the middle of Sogdiana ; Arr. iii. 28. 9 ; iv. 18. 2.

pavor, rudes ad talia opera, concusserat excitatam
25 molem subito cernentes. Itaque rex ad deditionem
metu posse compelli ratus, Oxarten misit nationis
eiusdem, sed dicionis suae, qui suaderet duci ut
26 traderet petram. Interim ad augendam formidinem
et turres admovebantur et excussa tormentis tela
micabant. Itaque verticem petrae, omni alio prae-
27 sidio damnato, petiverunt. At Oxartes trepidum
diffidentemque rebus suis Sisimithren coepit hortari
ut fidem quam vim Macedonum mallet experiri neu
moraretur festinationem victoris exercitus in Indiam
tendentis ; cui quisquis semet offerret, in suum caput
alienam cladem esse versurum.
28   Et ipse quidem Sisimithres deditionem non[1] abnuebat, ceterum mater eademque coniunx morituram se
ante denuntians quam in ullius veniret potestatem,
barbari animum ad honestiora quam tutiora converterat, pudebatque libertatis maius esse apud
29 feminas quam apud viros pretium. Itaque, dimisso
internuntio pacis, obsidionem ferre decreverat. Sed
cum hostis vires suasque pensaret, rursus muliebris
consilii, quod praeceps magis quam necessarium esse
30 credebat, paenitere eum coepit. Revocatoque
strenue Oxarte, futurum se in regis potestate respondit, unum id precatus,[2] ne voluntatem et consilium
matris suae proderet, quo facilius venia illi quoque
31 impetraretur.   Praemissum igitur Oxarten cum

---

[1] non abnuebat *Kinch;* abnuebat *P;* annuebat *C.*
[2] id precatus *Heinse;* inprecatus *A.*

---

[a] This seems doubtful ; Arr. iv. 21. 3 ff. tells of an attempt
on the rock of Chorienes, where similar difficulties made the
work very slow. It might have seemed quick to the barbarians.

barbarians, who were unfamiliar with such works,
25 when they saw a dam quickly^a raised. As a result
the king, thinking that they could be forced by fear
to surrender, sent Oxartes, of that same nation but
under his sway, to persuade their leader to deliver
26 over the crag. Meanwhile, to increase the dread,
at the same time towers were brought up and bolts
hurled from artillery leapt about. Accordingly, the
enemy made for the top of the crag, disapproving all
27 other defence. But Oxartes began to urge Sisimithres, who was fearful and distrustful of his affairs,
to try the faith rather than the strength of the Macedonians, and not to delay the haste of a victorious
army which was on its way to India ; for anyone who
opposed it would bring upon his own head the disaster
aimed at others.
28 And Sisimithres for his part was not disinclined to
surrender, but his mother, who was also his wife,
declaring that she would die rather than come into
the power of any other, turned the mind of the
barbarian to what was more honourable than
safe, and he felt ashamed that freedom was more
highly valued among the women than among the
29 men. Accordingly, dismissing the intermediary for
peace, he had decided to stand a siege. But when
he had repeatedly measured the strength of the
enemy against his own, he began to regret having
followed the advice of the woman, which seemed to
30 be rash rather than necessary, and quickly recalling
Oxartes, he replied that he would surrender to the
king, begging only this one thing, that he would not
betray the advice and wish of his mother, in order that
he might more easily obtain pardon for her also.
31 Therefore, sending Oxartes ahead, he followed with

matre liberisque et totius cognationis grege sequebatur, ne expectato quidem fidei pignore quod
32 Oxartes promiserat. Rex, equite praemisso, qui
reverti eos iuberet opperirique praesentiam ipsius,
supervenit et, victimis Minervae Victoriae[1] caesis,
imperium Sisimithri restituit, spe maioris etiam pro-
vinciae facta, si cum fide amicitiam ipsius coluisset.
33 Duos illi iuvenes, patre tradente, secum militaturos
sequi iussit.

Relicta deinde phalange ad subigendos qui defece-
34 rant, cum equite processit. Arduum et impeditum
saxis iter primo utcumque tolerabant, mox equorum
non ungulis modo attritis, sed corporibus etiam fatigatis, sequi plerique non poterant, et rarius subinde
agmen fiebat, pudorem, ut fere fit, immodico labore
35 vincente. Rex tamen, subinde equos mutans, sine
intermissione fugientes insequebatur. Nobiles iuvenes comitari eum soliti defecerant praeter Philippum ; Lysimachi erat frater tum primum adultus et,
36 quod facile appareret, indolis rarae. Is pedes, incredibile dictu, per D stadia vectum regem comitatus
est, saepe equum suum offerente Lysimacho, nec
tamen, ut digrederetur a rege, effici potuit, cum
lorica indutus arma gestaret.
37 Idem, cum perventum esset in saltum, in quo se
barbari abdiderant, nobilem edidit pugnam regemque
38 comminus cum hoste dimicantem protexit. Sed

[1] Minervae Victoriae *Stangl;* mineruae auictoriae P m.
pr.; mineruae ac uictoriae C.

---

[a] 'Aθήνη Nίκη; see iv. 13. 15, note.
[b] At Nautaca. [c] Cf. Pliny, N.H. xi. 37. 45.
[d] Cf. Cic. De Nat. Deorum i. 41. 114.
[e] See viii. 5. 1.

his mother and children and with a band of all his kindred, not even waiting for the pledge of parole which
32 Oxartes had promised. The king, after sending on a horseman to order them to return and await his presence, came up, and having sacrificed victims to Minerva Victoria,[a] restored his rule to Sisimithres, giving him hope of a still greater province if he culti-
33 vated his friendship with loyalty. He ordered Sisimithres' two sons, whom their father had delivered to him, to follow, in order to serve as soldiers with him.

Then, having left [b] the phalanx to subdue those
34 who had revolted, he went on with the cavalry. The road, which was steep and impeded by rocks, they endured at first as well as they could; presently, when not only were the hooves of the horses worn down,[c] but their bodies also were wearied, many were unable to follow and the line became thinner from time to time, the excessive toil overcoming
35 their shame, as usually happens. Yet the king, from time to time changing horses, pursued the fugitives without interruption.[d] The young nobles who were accustomed to attend him [e] had given out except Philippus; he was a brother of Lysimachus, and had just arrived at manhood, and, as was readily apparent,
36 a youth of a rare character. He, incredible to relate, on foot for 500 stadia accompanied the mounted king, and although Lysimachus often offered him his horse, yet he could not be induced to leave Alexander's side, although he wore a cuirass and was carrying his arms.
37 This same youth, when they had come to the wood in which the barbarians had hidden, made a splendid fight and protected the king as he fought hand to
38 hand with the enemy. But after the barbarians left

postquam barbari, in fugam effusi, deseruere silvas,
animus, qui in ardore pugnae corpus sustentaverat,
liquit, subitoque ex omnibus membris profuso sudore,
39 arboris proximae stipiti se applicuit. Deinde ne illo
quidem adminiculo sustinente, manibus regis excep-
40 tus est; inter quas collapsus exstinguitur. Maestum
regem alius haud levis dolor excepit. Erigyius inter
claros duces fuerat; quem exstinctum esse paulo
ante quam reverteretur in castra cognovit. Utriusque funus omni apparatu atque honore celebra-
tum est.

III. Dahas deinde statuerat petere; ibi namque
Spitamenen esse cognoverat. Sed hanc quoque
expeditionem, ut pleraque alia, fortuna, indulgendo
2 ei numquam fatigata, pro absente transegit. Spitamenes uxoris immodico amore flagrabat, quam aegre
fugam[1] et nova subinde exsilia tolerantem, in omne
discrimen comitem trahebat. Illa, malis fatigata,
identidem muliebres adhibere blanditias, ut tandem
fugam sisteret victorisque Alexandri clementiam
3 expertus placaret, quem effugere non posset. Tres
adulti erant liberi ex eo geniti; quos cum pectori
patris admovisset, ut saltem eorum misereri vellet
orabat: et, quo efficaciores essent preces, haud
4 procul erat Alexander. Ille se prodi, non moneri
ratus, et formae profecto fiducia cupere eam quam
primum dedi Alexandro, acinacem strinxit, per-

---

[1] aegre fugam *Giunta;* aegram fuga *A.*

the wood in scattered flight, the spirit which had
sustained the young man's body in the ardour of
battle left him, and suddenly a sweat broke out on
all his body and he leaned against the nearest tree-
39 trunk. Then, when he was not sustained even by that
support, he was taken in the king's arms, and there
40 swooned and died. In the midst of his sorrow another
severe grief came to the king. Erigyius had been
one of his illustrious generals[a] ; and he learned,
a little before his return to the camp, that he had
died. The funeral of each was performed with every
splendour and honour.

III. Next he had decided to attack the Dahae ;
for he had learned that Spitamenes was there. But
this affair, like many others, Fortune, never wearied
in indulging him, finished for him in his absence.
2 Spitamenes burned with immoderate love for his
wife, whom he dragged with him as his companion
into every danger, although she could hardly endure
the toil of flight and constant changes of exile. She,
worn out by hardships, from time to time made use
of a woman's blandishments to persuade her husband
at last to cease his flight, and having experienced
Alexander's clemency, to placate one whom he could
3 not escape. She had borne him three children, who
were now grown to manhood ; having put these in
their father's arms, she begged him to consent at
least to pity them : and it gave greater effect to her
4 prayers that Alexander was not far off. Spitamenes,
thinking that he was being betrayed, not advised,
and that undoubtedly through confidence in her
beauty his wife desired as soon as possible to be
surrendered to Alexander, drew his scimitar and

See especially vii. 4. 32 ff.

cussurus uxorem, nisi prohibitus esset fratrum eius occursu.

5   Ceterum abire e conspectu iubet, addito metu mortis si se oculis eius obtulisset, et ad desiderium
6 levandum noctes agere inter pelices coepit. Sed penitus haerens amor fastidio praesentium accensus est. Itaque rursus uni ei deditus, orare non destitit, ut tali consilio abstineret patereturque sortem, quamcumque eis Fortuna fecisset ; sibi mortem deditione
7 esse leviorem. At illa purgare se, quod quae utilia esse censebat muliebriter forsitan, sed fida tamen mente suasisset ; de cetero futuram in viri potestate.
8 Spitamenes, simulato captus obsequio, de die convivium apparari iubet vinoque et epulis gravis et semi-
9 somnus in cubiculum fertur. Quem ut alto et gravi somno sopitum esse sensit uxor, gladium, quem veste occultaverat, stringit caputque eius abscisum, cruore
10 respersa, servo suo conscio facinoris tradit. Eodem comitante, sicuti erat cruenta veste, in Macedonum castra pervenit nuntiarique Alexandro iubet, esse
11 quae ex ipsa deberet agnoscere. Ille protinus barbaram iussit admitti. Quam ut respersam cruore conspexit, ratus ad deplorandam contumeliam venisse,
12 dicere quae vellet iubet. At illa servum, quem in vestibulo stare iusserat, introduci desideravit.

---

would have slain her if he had not been prevented
by the hurried intervention of her brothers.

5 However he ordered her to quit his sight, adding
a threat of death if she should show herself before
his eyes, and to satisfy his longing he began to

6 pass his nights with concubines. But his deep-seated
love was inflamed through disgust with his present
associates. Therefore, again devoted to his wife alone,
he did not cease to beg her to refrain from giving such
advice, and to endure whatever lot Fortune should
offer them, saying that to him death was a lighter

7 thing than surrender. But she excused herself for
having advised what she thought expedient, perhaps
with feminine weakness, but yet in a loyal spirit,
saying that for the future she would submit to

8 her husband's authority. Spitamenes, won by this
feigned compliance, ordered a prolonged ^a banquet
to be prepared, from which he was carried to his

9 chamber heavy with wine and half-asleep. As soon
as his wife saw that he was sunk in a deep and heavy
slumber, she drew a sword which she had hidden
under her robe, cut off his head, and, bespattered
with blood, handed it to a slave who had been her

10 accomplice in the crime. Attended by the slave,
with her robe all blood-stained as it was, she came
into the camp of the Macedonians and ordered it to be
announced to Alexander that there was something

11 that he ought to hear from her own lips. He at once
ordered the barbarian woman to be admitted. When
he saw her bespattered with blood, thinking that she
had come to complain of some outrage, he bade her

12 tell him what she wished. But she desired that the
slave whom she had ordered to stand in the vestibule
should be brought in.

Qui, quia caput Spitamenis veste tectum habebat,
13 suspectus scrutantibus quid occuleret ostendit. Con-
fuderat oris exsanguis notas pallor, nec quis esset
nosci satis poterat; ergo rex certior factus, humanum
caput afferre eum, tabernaculo excessit percontatus-
14 que quid rei sit illo profitente cognoscit. Variae hinc
cogitationes invicem animum diversa agitantem com-
moverant. Meritum ingens in semet esse credebat,
quod transfuga et proditor, tantis rebus, si vixisset,
iniecturus[1] moram, interfectus esset ; contra facinus
ingens aversabatur, cum virum[2] optime meritum de
ipsa, communium parentem liberum per insidias
15 interemisset. Vicit tamen gratiam meriti sceleris
atrocitas, denuntiarique iussit ut excederet castris,
ne[3] licentiae barbarae exemplar in Graecorum mores
et mitia ingenia transferret.
16 Dahae, Spitamenis caede comperta, Dataphernen,
defectionis eius participem, vinctum Alexandro seque
dedunt. Ille, maxima praesentium curarum parte
liberatus, convertit animum ad vindicandas iniurias
eorum quibus a praetoribus suis avare ac superbe
17 imperabatur. Ergo Phratapherni Hyrcaniam et
Mardos[4] cum Tapuris[5] tradidit mandavitque, ut
Phradaten cui succedebat ad se in custodiam mitteret.
Arsami, Drangarum[6] praefecto, substitutus est
Stasanor,[7] Arsaces in Mediam missus ut Oxydates

[1] iniecturus *Giunta;* inuecturus *A.*
[2] virum *added by Hedicke.*   [3] ne *Hedicke;* neu *A.*
[4] et Mardos *Modius;* eardos *A.*
[5] Tapuris *Aldus;* taphiris *A.*
[6] Drangarum *Freinshem;* dramearum *A.*
[7] Stasanor *Aldus;* tamsanor *A* (tamsonor *B*).

[a] *Cf.* Arr. iv. 18. 2.

Because the slave had the head of Spitamenes hidden under his robe, he was suspected, and when some men searched him, he showed them what he was 13 hiding. A pallor had made the features of the blood-less face unrecognizable, and it could not be known who it was ; therefore the king, being informed that the slave was bringing a man's head, came out of his tent, and upon inquiring what had happened, learned 14 the truth from the slave's confession. Thereupon, as he considered the varied aspects of the case, his mind was moved by conflicting thoughts. He believed that it was a great service to him that a deserter and a traitor, who, if he had lived, would have caused delay to his important affairs, had been killed ; on the other hand, he was repelled by the great crime, in that the woman had treacherously killed a husband who deserved well of her, the father of their common 15 children. Yet the atrocity of the deed prevailed over gratitude for the service, and he ordered notice to be given her to leave the camp, lest by this example of barbarian lawlessness she might affect the character and mild dispositions of the Greeks.

16 The Dahae, learning of the murder of Spitamenes, bound Dataphernes, his partner in the revolt, and surrendered him and themselves to Alexander. He, thus freed from the greatest part of his present cares, turned his attention to avenging the wrongs of those who were being ruled greedily and tyrannically by his 17 governors. As a result, he made over to Phrata-phernes Hyrcania and the Mardi with the Tapuri, and commanded him to send him under a guard Phradates, whose successor he was.[a] For Arsames, governor of the Drangae, Stasanor was substituted, while Arsaces was sent to Media, in order that Oxy-

inde discederet. Babylonia, demortuo **Mazaeo**, Stameni[1] subiecta est.

IV. His compositis, tertio mense ex hibernis movit exercitum, regionem, quae Gazaca[2] appellatur, adi-
2 turus. Primus dies quietum iter praebuit, proximus ei nondum quidem procellosus et tristis, obscurior tamen pristino, non sine minis crescentis mali prae-
3 teriit, tertio ab omni parte caeli emicare fulgura et, nunc internitente luce, nunc condita, non oculos modo meantis exercitus, sed etiam animos terrere
4 coeperunt. Erat prope continuus caeli fragor, et passim cadentium fulminum species visebatur, attonitisque auribus, stupens agmen nec progredi nec
5 consistere[3] audebat ; cum[4] repente imber grandinem incutiens torrentis modo effunditur. Ac primo quidem armis suis tecti exceperant, sed iam nec retinere arma lubrica rigentes manus[5] poterant nec ipsi destinare in quam regionem obverterent corpora, cum undique tempestatis violentia maior quam vita-
6 batur occurreret. Ergo, ordinibus solutis, per totum saltum errabundum agmen ferebatur, multique, prius metu quam labore defetigati, prostraverant humi corpora, quamquam imbrem vis frigoris concreto gelu
7 astrinxerat. Alii se stipitibus arborum admoverant ; id plurimis et adminiculum et suffugium erat.
8 Nec fallebat ipsos morti locum eligere se,[b] cum

---

[1] Stameni *Zumpt;* ditameni *A.*
[2] Gazaca *Hedicke;* gazaba *A.*
[3] consistere *Acidalius;* considere *A.*
[4] cum *Hedicke;* tum *C; P omits.*
[5] arma lubrica rigentes manus *Modius;* arma lubricae et rigentes manus *A.*   [6] se *added by Hedicke.*

---

[a] At Nautaca, viii. 2. 19.
[b] *Cf.* Arr. iv. 17. 4.   [c] *Cf.* iv. 6. 25.

dates might be recalled from there. In place of Mazaeus, who had died, Stamenes was made governor of Babylonia.

IV. After these matters had been arranged, he withdrew the army from winter quarters [a] after two months' stay, intending to go to the region which is
2 called Gazaca.[b] The first day allowed a quiet march, the following day was, it is true, not yet stormy and gloomy, yet it was darker than the preceding one, and did not pass without threat of growing trouble,
3 on the third, lightning flickered from every quarter of the heavens, and the light which now shone through and now was hidden, began, not only to dazzle the eyes of the advancing army, but even to
4 terrify them. There were almost continual peals of thunder, and bolts of lightning striking everywhere were seen, so that the army, stunned and deafened,
5 dared neither to halt nor to advance ; then suddenly a rain-storm bombarding them with hail poured upon them like a torrent. At first indeed they had received the hail successfully on the cover afforded by their shields, but finally their stiffened hands could no longer hold their slippery weapons,[c] nor could they themselves determine in what direction to turn their bodies, since on every side greater violence of the storm met them than that which they were trying to
6 avoid. Hence, having broken ranks, the army went wandering all through the woods, and many, worn out by fear (not yet by toil), had thrown themselves upon the ground, although the extreme cold had
7 hardened the rain and hail into solid ice. Others had leaned against the trunks of trees ; this served as a
8 support and refuge for very many. But it did not escape them that they were choosing a place to die,

immobilis vitalis calor linqueret ; sed grata erat
pigritia corporum fatigatis, nec recusabant exstingui
quiescendo. Quippe non vehemens modo, sed etiam
pertinax vis mali insistebat, lucemque, naturale
solacium, praeter tempestatem haud disparem nocti,
silvarum quoque umbra suppresserat.

9 Rex unus tanti mali patiens circumire milites, con-
trahere dispersos, allevare prostratos, ostendere
procul evolutum ex tuguriis fumum, hortarique ut
10 proxima quaeque suffugia occuparent. Nec ulla res
magis saluti fuit, quam quod multiplicato labore
sufficientem malis quis[1] ipsi cesserant regem deserere
11 erubescebant. Ceterum, efficacior in adversis necessitas quam ratio, frigoris remedium invenit ; dolabris
enim silvas sternere aggressi passim acervos struesque
12 accenderunt. Continenti incendio ardere crederes
saltum et vix inter flammas agminibus relictum
locum. Hic calor stupentia membra commovit,
paulatimque spiritus quem continuerat rigor meare
13 libere coepit. Excepere alios tecta barbarorum,
quae in ultimo saltu abdita necessitas investigaverat,
alios castra, quae in humido quidem, sed iam caeli
mitescente saevitia locaverunt. Duo milia[2] militum
atque lixarum calonumque pestis illa consumpsit.
14 Memoriae proditum est quosdam applicatos arborum

---

since when they ceased to move, the vital heat left them; but inactivity of body was welcome to them in their weariness, nor did they shrink from dying as the price of resting. As a matter of fact, the force of the disastrous storm was not only violent but also persistent, and the light, that natural solace, in addition to the tempest, which was like night, was obscured also by the shade of the woods.

9 The king, who alone was able to endure such a disaster, went about among the soldiers, brought together those that were scattered, lifted up those who had fallen, and pointing out the distant smoke that rolled up from some huts, urged each man to resort to

10 the nearest places of refuge. And nothing contributed more to their safety than that they were ashamed to fail the king, who in spite of redoubled toil was able to endure the hardships to which they themselves

11 had succumbed. Moreover, necessity, which in adversity is more effective than reason, found a remedy for the cold ; for they began to cut down the woods everywhere with adzes and set fire to the heaps

12 and piles of wood. You would have thought that the forest was ablaze with a continuous conflagration and that amid the flames hardly room was left for the troops. This heat aroused their benumbed bodies, and gradually their breath, which the cold had

13 checked, began to pass freely. Some took refuge in the huts of the barbarians, which necessity had tracked out though they were hidden in the inmost part of the woods, others in the camp which they pitched on ground that was indeed wet, but already the severity of the weather was moderating. That plague destroyed 2000 soldiers, not counting sutlers

14 and batmen. It is reported that some were seen

truncis et non solum viventibus, sed etiam inter se
colloquentibus similis, esse conspectos, durante adhuc
habitu in quo mors quemque deprenderat.

15 Forte Macedo gregarius miles seque et arma male[1]
sustentans tamen in castra pervenerat ; quo viso rex,
quamquam ipse tum maxime admoto igne refovebat
artus, ex sella sua exsiluit torpentemque militem et
vix compotem mentis, demptis armis, in sua sede
16 iussit considere. Ille diu nec ubi requiesceret, nec
a quo esset exceptus agnovit. Tandem, recepto
calore vitali, ut regiam sedem regemque vidit, terri-
17 tus surgit. Quem intuens Alexander : " Ecquid
intellegis, miles," inquit, " quanto meliore sorte quam
Persae sub rege vivatis ? Illis enim in sella regis
consedisse capital foret, tibi saluti fuit."
18 Postero die, convocatis amicis copiarumque ducibus, pronuntiari iussit ipsum omnia quae amissa
essent redditurum. Et promisso fides exstitit.
19 Nam Sisimithres multa iumenta et camelorum ii milia
adduxit pecoraque et armenta ; quae distributa pari-
20 ter militem et damno et fame liberaverunt. Rex
gratiam sibi relatam a Sisimithre perlaetus,[2] sex
dierum cocta cibaria ferre milites iussit, Sacas petens.
Totam hanc regionem depopulatus, xxx milia pecorum ex praeda Sisimithri dono dat.
21 Inde pervenit in regionem, cui Oxyartes,[3] satrapes

[1] male added by Hedicke.
[2] perlaetus Hedicke; praefatus A.
[3] Oxyartes Aldus; cohortandus A.

[a] For the same story see Val. Max. v. 1, ext. 1 ; Front.
Strat. iv. 6. 3.
[b] iumenta (horses, asses, and mules) are here distinguished
from camels ; see Amer. Jour. of Phil. lvii. p. 138, note.
[c] Apparently dwelling in the eastern part of Hissar, or
east of Hissar.

stuck to the trunks of trees, looking as if they were not only alive but even talking together, still keeping the posture in which death had overtaken them.

15 It chanced that a Macedonian common soldier, hardly able to stand up and hold his weapons, had nevertheless reached the camp. On seeing him the king, although he himself was just then warming himself beside a fire, leaped up from his chair, and taking his armour from the exhausted and hardly

16 conscious soldier, bade him sit in his own seat. For a long time the man did not realize where he was resting nor by whom he had been rescued. At last, when he had recovered his vital heat and saw the

17 royal seat and the king, he arose in terror. Alexander, looking kindly at him, said : " Do you understand, soldier, how much better a life you all have under a king than the Persians have ? For with the Persians, to have sat in the king's seat would have been a capital crime, with you it has saved your life." [a]

18 On the next day, having called together his friends and the leaders of his forces, he ordered it to be proclaimed that he himself would make good all that

19 had been lost. And he kept his promise. For Sisimithres had brought in many pack-animals [b] and 2000 camels, besides flocks and herds ; these were distributed equally and saved the soldiers both from

20 loss and from hunger. The king, greatly pleased by the requital made him by Sisimithres, on his way to the Sacae [c] ordered the soldiers to carry with them cooked food enough for six days. Having devastated all that region, he gave Sisimithres a gift of 30,000 cattle from the booty.

21 From there he came into the province governed by

nobilis, praeerat, qui se regis potestati fideique permisit. Ille, imperio ei reddito, haud amplius quam
ut duo ex tribus filiis secum militarent exegit.
22 Satrapes etiam eo qui penes ipsum relinquebatur
tradito,[1] barbara opulentia convivium, quo regem
23 accipiebat, instruxerat; id cum multa comitate
celebraretur, introduci xxx nobiles virgines iussit.
Inter quas erat filia ipsius, Roxane nomine, eximia
corporis specie et decore habitus in barbaris raro.
24 Quae quamquam inter electas processerat, omnium
tamen oculos convertit in se, maxime regis, minus iam
cupiditatibus suis imperantis inter obsequia Fortunae,
25 contra quam non satis cauta mortalitas est. Itaque
ille, qui uxorem Darei, qui duas filias virgines, quibus
forma praeter Roxanen comparari nulla potuerat,
haud alio animo quam parentis aspexerat, tunc in
amorem virgunculae, si regiae stirpi compararetur
ignobilis, ita effusus est, ut diceret ad stabiliendum
regnum pertinere Persas et Macedones conubio
iungi; hoc uno modo et pudorem victis et superbiam
26 victoribus detrahi posse. Achillem quoque, a quo
genus ipse deduceret, cum captiva coisse; ne inferri
nefas arbitrentur victi,[2] matrimonii iure velle iungi.
27 Insperato gaudio elatus[3] pater sermonem eius
excipit, et rex in medio cupiditatis ardore iussit

---

[1] tradito *Modius;* tradit *C;* tradi *P.*
[2] victi *Hedicke;* ita *A.*   [3] elatus *Hedicke;* laetus *A*

---

[a] For the name *cf.* Arr. iv. 19. 5.
[b] For *in* and the accusative with *effusus cf.* v. 1. 37 ; Livy
xxix. 23. 4.   [c] Briseïs.

Oxyartes,[a] an illustrious satrap, who submitted himself to the power and good faith of the king. Alexander restored his dominion to him, and made no further requirement than that two of the satrap's
22 three sons should serve as his soldiers. Oxyartes delivered to him also the son who was left with him, and prepared a banquet of oriental magnificence, at
23 which he entertained Alexander; while this was being celebrated with great friendliness, the satrap ordered thirty high-born maidens to be brought in. Among these was his own daughter, Roxanê by name, a maiden of remarkable beauty of person, and of a dignity of bearing uncommon among barbarians.
24 She, although she had entered among an elite group, yet drew the eyes of all to her, especially of the king, who by now had less mastery over his passions amid the constant indulgence of Fortune, against whom
25 mortal man is not sufficiently on his guard. And so he, who had looked upon the wife of Darius and his two maiden daughters, to whom none save Roxanê could be compared in beauty, with no other feeling than that of a father, was then so transported [b] with love for this little maiden, of obscure birth in comparison with royal stock, that he said that it was important for establishing his empire that Persians and Macedonians be joined in wedlock; that only in that way could shame be taken from the conquered and
26 haughtiness from the victors. Achilles also, he said, from whom he traced his ancestry, had united with a captive maiden [c]; lest the vanquished should think that a wrong was being done to them, he wished to be joined with Roxanê in lawful wedlock.
27 The father was elated with unexpected joy on hearing the king's words and Alexander, in the full

afferri patrio more panem—hoc erat apud Macedonas
sanctissimum coeuntium pignus—quem divisum gla-
28 dio uterque libabat.   Credo eos qui gentis mores
condiderunt parco et parabili victu ostendere voluisse
iungentibus opes quantulo contenti esse deberent.
29 Hoc modo rex Asiae et Europae introductam inter
convivales ludos matrimonio sibi adiunxit, ex[1] captiva
30 geniturus qui victoribus imperaret.   Pudebat amicos
super vinum et epulas socerum ex deditis esse delec-
tum, sed post Cliti caedem libertate sublata, vultu,
qui maxime servit, assentiebantur.

   V. Ceterum Indiam et inde Oceanum petiturus, ne
quid a tergo quod destinata impedire posset, moveretur, ex omnibus provinciis xxx milia iuniorum legi
iussit et ad se armata perduci, obsides simul habiturus
2 et milites.   Craterum autem ad persequendos Hausta-
nen et Catanen qui ab ipso defecerant misit ; quorum Haustanes captus est, Catanes in proelio occisus.
Polypercon quoque regionem, quae Bubacene appel-
3 latur, in dicionem redegit.   Itaque, omnibus compositis, cogitationes in bellum Indicum vertit.   Dives
regio habebatur non auro modo, sed gemmis quoque
margaritisque, ad luxum magis quam ad magnificen-
4 tiam exculta.   Periti militum res[2] auro et ebore

---

[1] ex *Kinch;* et *P;* e *C.*
[2] militum res *Hedicke;* militares *A.*

---

[a] *Cf.* vi. 1. 17 ; vii. 8. 1.
[b] *Cf.* vii. 5. 21.
[c] According to Arr. iv. 22. 1, Polypercon was in command of a part of Craterus' division of the army.
[d] Mentioned only by Curtius.
[e] *Cf.* v. 1. 23.

tide of his ardent passion, ordered a loaf of bread to
be brought in according to his country's custom—this
among the Macedonians was the most sacred pledge
of those contracting marriage—which was cut in two
28 with a sword and tasted by each. I suppose that
those who established the customs of the race wished
by a frugal and common food to show to those who
were about to unite their resources with how little
29 they ought to be contented. In this way the king of
Asia and of Europe took to himself in wedlock a
woman who had been brought in among the entertainments of a banquet, intending to beget from a captive
30 a son who should rule over victors. His friends were
ashamed that a father-in-law had been chosen from
among the surrendered amid wine and feasting, but
since after the murder of Clitus freedom of speech had
been banned, they pretended assent by expression
of their faces,[a] which most readily play the slave.

V. But the king, intending to go on to India and
from there to the Ocean, lest there should be any
disturbance in his rear which could interfere with his
plans, ordered 30,000 of the younger men to be
selected from all the provinces and brought to him
under arms, intending to have them at once as host-
2 ages and as soldiers. Furthermore, he sent Craterus
in pursuit of Haustanes and Catanes,[b] who had revolted from him, of whom Haustanes was taken
prisoner, Catanes killed in battle. Polypercon[c] also
reduced to submission the region which is called
3 Bubacenê.[d] Accordingly, when everything was in
order, he turned his thoughts towards an Indian war.
That region was considered rich, not only in gold, but
also in gems and pearls, and was highly developed
4 rather for luxury than for magnificence.[e] Those who

273

fulgere dicebant ; itaque, necubi vinceretur, cum
ceteris praestaret, scutis argenteas laminas, equis
frenos aureos addidit, loricas quoque alias auro, alias
argento adornavit. cxx milia armatorum erant, quae
regem ad id bellum sequebantur.

5 Iamque omnibus praeparatis, ratus[1] quod olim
prava mente conceperat tunc esse maturum, quonam
modo caelestes honores usurparet coepit agitare.
Iovis filium non dici tantum se, sed etiam credi volebat, tamquam perinde animis imperare posset ac
6 linguis, iussitque[2] more Persarum Macedonas venerabundos ipsum salutare prosternentes humi corpora.
Non deerat talia concupiscenti perniciosa adulatio,
perpetuum malum regum, quorum opes saepius as-
7 sentatio quam hostis evertit. Nec Macedonum haec
erat culpa—nemo enim illorum quicquam ex patrio
more libare sustinuit—sed Graecorum, qui profes-
sionem honestarum artium malis corruperant mori-
8 bus, Agis[3] quidem Argivus, pessimorum[4] carminum
post Choerilum conditor, et ex Sicilia Cleo, hic quidem
non ingenii solum, sed etiam nationis vitio adulator,
et cetera urbium suarum purgamenta, quae propinquis etiam maximorumque exercituum ducibus a
rege inserebantur.[5] Hi tum caelum illi aperiebant,

---

[1] ratus *added by Freinshem.*
[2] iussitque *Jeep;* itaque *A.*   [3] Agis *Aldus;* hages *A.*
[4] pessimorum *Lauer;* piissimorum *A.*
[5] inserebantur *Hedicke;* ferebantur *A.*

---

[a] Alexander's army was so large at no other time. Plut.
Alex. lxvi. 2 gives the same figure.   [b] *Cf.* iv. 7. 30.
[c] Going a step farther than in iv. 7. 30.
[d] *Cf.* Cic. *De Orat.* iii. 32. 127 ; *De Off.* i. 42. 151.

knew said that the equipment of the soldiers gleamed
with gold and ivory ; consequently Alexander, not to
be outdone in anything, since he surpassed all other
men, added silver plates to the shields and put
golden bits on his horses, and adorned the cuirasses
also, some with gold, others with silver. There
were 120,000 armed men [a] who followed the king
to that war.

5 And now, when all was ready in advance, thinking
that the time was then ripe for what he had long
perversely planned,[b] he began to consider how he
might usurp divine honours. He wished, not only
to be called,[c] but to be believed to be the son of
Jupiter, as if he could rule men's minds as well as their
6 tongues, and he ordered the Macedonians to pay
their respects to him in the Persian fashion and to
salute him by prostrating themselves on the ground.
In his desire for such things he did not lack pernicious
adulation, the constant evil of kings, whose power is
more frequently overthrown by flattery than by foes.
7 And this was not the fault of the Macedonians—for
none of them could endure to impair any jot of his
native customs—but of the Greeks, who had debased
their profession of the liberal arts [d] by evil habits :—
8 Agis,[e] an Argive, the composer of the worst of poems
next after Choerilus,[f] and Cleo,[g] from Sicily, the
latter indeed a flatterer, from a defect not only in his
own nature, but also in his nation, and other sweep-
ings [h] of their own cities ; these were mingled by
the king even with his nearest friends and the leaders
of his greatest armies. These at that time were

* An epic poet ; *cf.* Arr. iv. 9. 9.
[f] Hor. *Epist.* ii. 1. 232 ff. ; *Ars Poet.* 357.
Not otherwise known.   [h] *Cf.* vi. 11. 2.

Herculemque et Patrem Liberum et cum Polluce
Castorem novo numini cessuros esse iactabant.

9 Igitur festo die omni opulentia convivium exornari
iubet, cui non Macedones modo et Graeci, principes
amicorum, sed etiam hostium[1] nobiles adhiberentur.
Cum quibus cum discubuisset rex, paulisper epulatus
10 convivio egreditur. Cleo, sicut praeparatum erat,
sermonem cum admiratione laudum eius instituit.
Merita deinde percensuit ; quibus uno modo referri
gratiam posse, si, quem intellegerent deum esse,
confiterentur, exigua turis impensa tanta beneficia
11 pensaturi. Persas quidem non pie solum, sed etiam
prudenter reges suos inter deos colere ; maiestatem
enim imperii salutis esse tutelam. Ne Herculem
quidem et Patrem Liberum prius dicatos deos, quam
vicissent secum viventium invidiam ; tantum de quoque posteros credere, quantum praesens aetas spo-
12 pondisset. Quodsi ceteri dubitent, semetipsum, cum
rex inisset convivium, prostraturum humi corpus.
Debere idem facere ceteros et in primis sapientia
praeditos ; ab illis enim cultus in regem exemplum
esse prodendum.
13 Haud perplexe in Callisthenen dirigebatur oratio.
Gravitas viri et prompta libertas invisa erat regi,
quasi solus Macedonas paratos ad tale obsequium
14 moraretur. Is tum, silentio facto, unum illum in-

---

[1] hostium *added by Hedicke.*

---

[a] *Cf.* Arr. iv. 10. 5-6, where on a similar occasion the
sophist Anaxarchus uses like language.
[b] *Cf.* Arr. iv. 8. 3.

opening Heaven to him, boasting that Hercules and
Father Liber and Castor with Pollux would give place
to the new deity.

9   Therefore on a festal day he ordered a banquet to
be prepared with all magnificence, to which not only
Macedonians and Greeks, the chief of his friends, but
also nobles of the enemy were invited. When the
king had taken his place at table with these, after
10 feasting for a little while he left the banquet. Cleo,
as had been prearranged,[a] began the conversation by
expressing admiration for the king's glorious deeds.
Then he enumerated their obligations to him ; these,
he said, could be requited in only one way, namely,
since they knew that he was a god, by admitting
it and paying for such great favours by the slight
11 expense of incense. The Persians indeed were not
only loyal but also wise in worshipping their kings
among the gods ; for the majesty of the empire was
the protector of its safety. Not even Hercules and
Father Liber had been acknowledged as gods until
they had overcome the jealousy [b] of those who lived
with them : future generations believed only so
much about each man as his own time had vouched
12 for. But if the rest of the company were in doubt,
he himself would prostrate himself on the ground
when the king entered the banquet. The rest
ought to do the same, and especially those endowed
with wisdom ; for it was by those that a precedent
in worshipping the king ought to be shown.
13   Quite clearly this speech was directed against
Callisthenes. The austerity of the man and his ready
freedom of speech were odious to the king, as if
he alone were delaying the Macedonians, who were
14 prepared for such obsequiousness. He then, when

277

tuentibus ceteris : " Si rex," inquit, " sermoni tuo
adfuisset, nullius profecto vox responsuri tibi deside-
raretur ; ipse enim peteret, ne in peregrinos ritus
externosque[1] degenerare se cogeres neu rebus felicis-
sime gestis invidiam tali adulatione contraheres.

15 Sed quoniam abest, ego tibi pro illo respondeo, nullum
esse eundem et diuturnum et praecoquem fructum,
caelestesque honores non dare te[2] regi, sed auferre.
Intervallo enim opus est, ut credatur deus, semperque

16 hanc gratiam magnis viris posteri reddunt. Ego
autem seram immortalitatem precor regi, ut et[3] vita
diuturna sit et aeterna maiestas. Hominem conse-
quitur aliquando, numquam comitatur divinitas.

17 " Herculem modo et Patrem Liberum consecrata
immortalitati exempla referebas. Credisne illos unius
convivii decreto deos factos ? Prius ab oculis mortalium amolita natura est, quam in caelum Fama

18 perveheret. Scilicet ego et tu, Cleo, deos facimus,
a nobis divinitatis suae auctoritatem accepturus est
rex. Potentiam tuam experiri libet ; fac aliquem
regem, si deum potes facere ! Facilius est caelum

19 dare quam imperium ? Di propitii sine invidia quae
Cleo dixit audierint eodemque cursu, quo fluxere
adhuc res, ire patiantur. Nostris moribus velint nos
esse contentos. Non pudet patriae, nec desidero ad
quem modum rex mihi colendus sit discere a victis.[4]

---

[1] ritus externosque *P;* externosque ritus *C* (*B omits* externosque).   [2] te *Lauer;* se *A.*
[3] ut et *Modius;* et ut *A.*   [4] a victis *added by Hedicke.*

silence ensued and the rest were looking at him alone, said : " If the king had been present at your talk, surely the words of no one would be needed to reply to you ; for he himself would beg that you should not force him to descend to foreign and alien rites, nor would you expose his highly successful exploits to
15 odium by such flattery. But since he is not present, I am replying to you in his behalf that no fruit is at the same time both durable and prematurely ripened,[a] and that you are not giving divine honours to your king, but taking them from him. For there is need of time for a man to be believed to be a god, and it is always thus that future generations requite great
16 men. But I pray for a late immortality for the king, in order that his life may be long and his majesty eternal. Divinity sometimes overtakes a man, it never accompanies him.
17 " You mentioned Hercules and Father Liber just now as examples of consecration to immortality. Do you believe that they were made gods by the decree of a single banquet ? Their mortal nature was removed from sight before Fame transported them
18 to Heaven. Forsooth you and I, Cleo, make gods, from us the king will receive endorsement of his divinity ! I should like to try your power ; make someone a king, if you can make a god. Is it easier
19 to bestow heaven than empire ? May the propitious gods have heard without offence what Cleo said, and suffer things to go on in the same course in which they have flowed up to now. May they allow us to be content with our habits. I am not ashamed of my fatherland, nor do I desire to learn from the vanquished how I ought to do honour to my king.

[a] Cf. iv. 15. 11.

Quos equidem victores esse confiteor, si ab illis lege
quis vivamus accipimus."

20   Aequis auribus Callisthenes veluti vindex publicae
libertatis audiebatur. Expresserat non assensionem
modo, sed etiam vocem, seniorum praecipue, quibus
21 gravis erat inveterati moris externa mutatio. Nec
quicquam eorum quae invicem iactata erant rex
ignorabat, cum post aulaea, quae lectis obduxerat,
staret. Igitur ad Agin et Cleonem misit, ut, sermone finito, barbaros tantum, cum intrasset, procumbere suo more paterentur, et paulo post, quasi potiora
22 quaedam egisset, convivium repetit. Quem vene-
rantibus Persis, Polypercon, qui cubabat super regem,
unum ex eis mento contingentem humum per ludibrium coepit hortari, ut vehementius id quateret ad
terram, elicuitque iram Alexandri quam olim animo
23 capere non poterat. Itaque rex : " Tu autem,"
inquit, " non veneraberis me ? An tibi uni digni
videmur esse ludibrio ? " Ille nec regem ludibrio
24 nec se contemptu dignum esse respondit. Tum
detractum eum lecto rex praecipitat in terram et,
cum is pronus corruisset : " Videsne," inquit, " idem
te fecisse, quod in alio paulo ante ridebas ? " Et
tradi eo in custodiam iusso convivium solvit.

VI. Polyperconti quidem postea custodito[1] diu
ignovit ; in Callisthenen olim contumacia suspectum

---

[1] custodito *Kinch;* castigato *A.*

---

[a] *Cf.*   6 .24.

For my part, I admit that they are the victors if we accept from them the laws under which we live."

20 Callisthenes was heard with favourable ears ^a as a defender of the public liberty. He had forced, not only assent, but also words, especially of the older men, to whom the change of their long-standing 21 customs to those of strangers was distasteful. And the king was not unaware of anything that was said on one side and the other, since he was standing behind the curtains which he had caused to be spread round the couches. Therefore he sent word to Agis and Cleo to put an end to the discussion and to allow only the barbarians, when he entered, to prostrate themselves after their custom, and a little later, as if he had transacted some unusually important business, 22 he returned to the banquet. When the Persians paid reverence to him, Polypercon, who was reclining above the king, in mockery began to urge one of them, who touched the ground with his chin, to strike it harder against the earth, and thus aroused the anger of Alexander, which he had already been 23 unable to contain. Accordingly he said : " You, then, will not adore me ? To you alone do we seem to be deserving of ridicule ? " Polypercon replied that the king did not seem to deserve ridicule, nor he 24 himself contempt. Then the king dragged him from his couch, hurled him to the ground, and when he had fallen on his face, said : " Do you not see that you have done the same thing which a little while before you ridiculed in another ? " And ordering that he should be put in prison, he broke up the banquet.

VI. Polypercon, indeed, he pardoned after he had been held in custody for a long time ; against Callisthenes, who had formerly been suspected because of

pervicacioris irae fuit. Cuius explendae matura
2 obvenit occasio. Mos erat, ut supra dictum est,
principibus Macedonum adultos liberos regibus
tradere ad munia haud multum servilibus ministeriis
3 abhorrentia. Excubabant, servatis noctium vicibus,
proximi foribus eius aedis, in qua rex acquiescebat.
Per hos pelices introducebantur alio aditu quam
4 quem armati obsidebant. Eidem acceptos ab aga-
sonibus equos, cum rex ascensurus esset, admovebant
comitabanturque et venantem et in proeliis, omnibus
5 artibus studiorum liberalium exculti. Praecipuus
honor habebatur, quod licebat sedentibus vesci cum
rege. Castigandi eos verberibus nulli potestas
6 praeter ipsum erat. Haec cohors velut seminarium
ducum praefectorumque apud Macedonas fuit ; hinc
habuere posteri reges, quorum stirpi post multas
aetates Romani opes ademerunt.
7　Igitur Hermolaus, puer nobilis ex regia cohorte,
cum aprum telo occupasset, quem rex ferire destinaverat, iussu eius verberibus affectus est. Quam
ignominiam aegre ferens deflere apud Sostratum
8 coepit. Ex eadem cohorte erat Sostratus, amore eius
ardens ; qui cum laceratum corpus, in quo deperibat,
intueretur, forsitan olim ob aliam quoque causam regi
infestus, iuvenem sua sponte iam motum, data fide
acceptaque, perpulit, ut occidendi regem consilium

---

^a See v. 1. 42 ; the custom was established by Philip
(Arr. iv. 13. 1) ; *cf.* Val. Max. iii. 3.

^b This is a contrast with *servilibus ministeriis* in section 2,
but corresponds with *seminarium ducum* in 6.

^c For a similar use of *seminarium cf.* Cic. *In Cat.* ii. 10. 23.

^d Arr. iv. 13. 2 gives a different version.

^e *deflere* is a strong expression, and seems to favour the
version of Arrian (see preceding note).

insubordination, his anger was more persistent. For
2 satisfying this an opportunity soon arose. It was the
custom, as was said before,[a] for the leading men of
the Macedonians to entrust their sons to the king on
their coming of age for duties not very different from
3 the services of slaves. They kept watch at night in
turn close to the doors of the room in which the king
slept. By these youths concubines were brought in
by a different entrance from that before which the
4 armed guards were posted. They also received the
horses from the grooms, brought them to the reign-
ing king when he was about to mount, and accompanied him in the chase and in battle, besides being
thoroughly trained in all the accomplishments of
5 liberal studies. The special honour was paid them
of being allowed to sit at table with the king.[b] No
one had the power of chastising them by flogging
6 except the king himself. This troupe among the
Macedonians was a kind of training-school[c] for
generals and governors of provinces; from these
also their posterity had the kings from whose stock
after many ages the Romans took away all power.
7   So then, Hermolaüs, a high-born boy belonging to
this royal band, because he had been first to attack
a wild boar[d] which the king had intended to strike,
by his order was punished by scourging. Being
indignant at this disgrace, he began to complain[e]
8 about it to Sostratus. Sostratus was a member of
the same troupe and an ardent lover of Hermolaüs;
when he saw the lacerated body of which he was
enamoured, perhaps being already angered with the
king for some other reason also, he induced Hermolaüs, who was already incensed on his own account,
to give and receive a pledge to join with him in form-

9 secum iniret.   Nec puerili impetu rem exsecuti sunt;
quippe sollerter legerunt, quos in societatem sceleris
adsciscerent.   Nicostratum, Antipatrum, Asclepio-
dorumque et Philotan placuit assumi ; per hos adiecti
10 sunt Anticles et Aphthonius[1] et Epimenes.   Ceterum
agendae rei haud sane facilis patebat via ; opus erat
eadem omnis coniuratos nocte excubare, ne ab ex-
pertibus consilii impedirentur, forte autem alius alia
11 nocte excubabat.   Itaque in permutandis stationum
vicibus ceteroque apparatu exsequendae rei, xxx et
duo dies absumpti sunt.
12   Aderat nox, qua coniurati excubare debebant,
mutua[2] fide laeti, cuius documentum tot dies fuerant.
Neminem metus spesve mutaverat ; tanta omnibus
13 vel in regem ira vel fides inter ipsos fuit.   Stabant
igitur ad fores aedis eius in qua rex vescebatur, ut
14 convivio egressum in cubiculum deducerent.   Sed
fortuna ipsius simulque epulantium comitas provexit
omnes ad largius vinum ; ludi etiam convivales ex-
traxere tempus, nunc laetantibus coniuratis, quod
sopitum aggressuri essent, nunc sollicitis, ne in lucem
15 convivium extraheret.   Quippe alios in stationem
oportebat prima luce succedere, ipsorum post septimum diem reditura vice, nec sperare poterant in
16 illud tempus omnibus duraturam fidem.   Ceterum

---

[1] et Aphthonius *Hedicke;* elaphthonius *P;* elaptonius *C.*
[2] mutua *Giunta;* multa *A.*

---

[a] Arr. iv. 13. 4 gives a somewhat different list of names.
[b] See Arr. iv. 13. 4.   The number of guards and their
duties are uncertain.

9 ing a plot to kill the king. And they did not execute the plan with youthful impetuosity; for they chose with care those whom they would admit as associates in the intended crime. They decided to include Nicostratus, Antipater, Asclepiodorus and Philotas [a]; through these there were added Anticles and Aphtho-

10 nius and Epimenes. But for carrying out the plan no easy road at all lay open; for it was necessary that all the conspirators should be on guard the same night, in order not to be interfered with by those who were not in the plot, but it happened that they

11 were on watch on different nights. Therefore in changing the order of guard-duty,[b] and in other preparations for carrying out their design, thirty-two days were spent.

12 The night had come on which the conspirators were due to be on guard, rejoicing in their common fidelity, of which the lapse of so many days had been a proof. Not one had hope or fear changed; so great among all was either their anger against the king or their

13 loyalty to one another. They were standing, then, at the door of the room in which the king was dining, in order to escort him to his bedchamber when he

14 had left the table. But his own good fortune, as well as the good company of the diners, led all to be lavish with their wine; games at the banquet also extended the time, while the conspirators now rejoiced because they would attack him when sleepy, and now were anxious lest he should prolong the feast

15 until daylight. For others were due to take their places as guards at dawn, and their turn would not come again until after seven days, and they could not hope that the fidelity of all would endure until

16 that time. But when daylight was already at hand,

cum iam lux appeteret, et convivium solvitur et
coniurati exceperunt regem laeti occasionem exse-
quendi sceleris admotam ; cum mulier attonitae, ut
creditum est, mentis, conversari in regia solita, quia
instinctu videbatur futura praedicere, non occurrit
modo abeunti, sed etiam semet obiecit vultuque et
oculis motum praeferens animi, ut rediret in con-
17 vivium, monuit.   Et ille per ludum, bene deos suadere respondit, revocatisque amicis, in horam diei
ferme secundam convivii tempus extraxit.

18   Iam alii ex cohorte in stationem successerant ante
cubiculi[1] fores excubituri, adhuc tamen coniurati
stabant vice officii sui expleta ; adeo pertinax spes
19 est, quam humanae mentes devoraverunt.   Rex
benignius quam alias allocutus, discedere eos ad
curanda corpora, quoniam tota nocte perstitissent,
iubet.   Data singulis L sestertia, collaudatique,[2]
quod, etiam aliis tradita vice, tamen excubare per-
20 severassent.   Illi tanta spe destituti, domos abeunt.
Et ceteri quidem expectabant stationis suae noctem ;
Epimenes sive comitate regis, qua ipsum inter coniuratos exceperat, repente mutatus, sive quia coeptis
deos obstare credebat, fratri suo Eurylocho, quem
antea expertem esse consilii voluerat, quid pararetur
21 aperit.   Omnibus Philotae supplicium in oculis erat ;
itaque protinus inicit fratri manum et in regiam

---

[1] cubiculi *I;* cubili *A.*
[2] conlaudatique *J. Froben;* conlaudatisque *A.*

---

[a] *Cf.* Arr. iv. 13. 5-6.
[b] Arr. iv. 13. 7 follows a different tradition.

the banquet came to an end and the conspirators received the king, rejoicing that the opportunity was offered for committing their crime, when a woman,[a] of unsound mind, as it was thought, who was accustomed to haunt the royal quarters because she seemed by inspiration to foretell the future, not only met the king as he came out, but put herself in his way, and showing disturbance of mind in her face and eyes, warned him to return to the banquet.

17 He jestingly replied that the gods gave good advice, and recalling his friends, extended the time of the entertainment until nearly the second hour of the day.

18 Now the others of the troupe had taken over their posts, to watch before the door of the king's bedchamber, yet the conspirators remained there, although their turn of duty was completed ; so persistent is a hope which human minds have eagerly

19 conceived. The king, addressing them more kindly than usual, bade them go and rest themselves, since they had stood watch all night. He gave each man fifty sestertia and praised them because even after their turn had passed to others they had continued

20 on guard. And they, deprived of their great hope, went to their homes. The others for their part waited for the night of their guard-duty; Epimenes, either because of the affability with which the king had received him along with the other conspirators, or because he believed that the gods opposed their design, had a sudden change of heart and disclosed the plan to his brother Eurylochus,[b] whom before

21 he had wished to have no part in the plot. All had the torture of Philotas before their eyes, and so Eurylochus at once took his brother by the hand and

287

pervenit, excitatisque custodibus corporis, ad salutem
22 regis pertinere quae afferret affirmat. Et tempus
quo venerant et vultus haud sane securi animi index
et maestitia e duobus alterius Ptolomaeum ac Leonnatum excubantes ad cubiculi limen excitaverunt.
Itaque, apertis foribus et lumine illato, sopitum mero
ac somno excitant regem. Ille paulatim mente
23 collecta, quid afferrent interrogat. Nec cunctatus
Eurylochus non ex toto domum suam aversari deos
dixit, quia frater ipsius, quamquam impium facinus
ausus foret, tamen et paenitentiam eius ageret et
per se potissimum profiteretur indicium ; in eam
ipsam noctem, quae decederet insidias comparatas
fuisse, auctores[1] scelesti consilii esse quos minime
24 crederet rex. Tum Epimenes cuncta ordine con-
sciorumque nomina exponit. Callisthenen non ut
participem facinoris nominatum esse constabat, sed
solitum puerorum sermonibus vituperantium crimi-
25 nantiumque regem faciles aures praebere. Quidam
adiciunt, cum Hermolaus apud eum quoque verbera-
tum se a rege quereretur, dixisse Callisthenen meminisse debere eos iam viros esse ; idque ad consolandam
patientiam verberum an ad incitandum iuvenum
dolorem dictum esset in ambiguo fuisse.
26   Rex animi corporisque sopore discusso, cum tanti
periculi quo evaserat[2] imago oculis oberraret, Eury-

---

[1] auctores *Lauer;* acturos *A.*
[2] evaserat *L m. sec.;* euaserit *A.*

---

[a] *Cf.* viii. 9. 30.   [b] For *ex toto cf.* Sen. *De Ira* ii. 6.
   [c] *p. e. ageret,* a rare form of expression.
       [d] *Cf.* Arr. iv. 14. 1.

came into the royal quarters, then having aroused
the body-guard, he declared that what he had to say
22 concerned the king's life. Both the time at which
he had come and the anxious expression of both
brothers, betraying surely a troubled mind, as well
as the sadness of one of them, alarmed Ptolemy and
Leonnatus, who were on watch at the door of the
king's bedchamber. Therefore opening the doors
and bringing in a light, they awoke the king whom
wine had buried*a* in deep sleep. He gradually col-
lected his thoughts and asked them what they had to
23 say. Without delay Eurylochus said that the gods
had not entirely *b* turned against their family, since his
brother, although he had dared an impious crime,
yet repented of it *c* and through himself rather than
anyone else would reveal it; that the conspiracy had
been planned for that very night which was passing,
the ringleaders of the abominable design were those
24 whom the king would least suspect. Then Epimenes explained everything in order and gave the
names of the participants. It is certain that Callisthenes was not named as taking part in the plot,*d* but
it was said that he was accustomed to lend ready ears
to the boys when they abused the king and criticized
25 his conduct. Some add that when Hermolaüs
complained to him also that he had been flogged,
Callisthenes had said that they ought to remember
that they were now men; but whether that was said
to console him for suffering lashes, or to excite the
resentment of the youths, was uncertain.
26 The king, awakened in mind and body, when he
pictured the great danger which he had escaped,*e* at

* For the ablative *cf.* Livy xxi. 33. 5. He also has the
accusative.

lochum L talentis et cuiusdam Tiridatis[1] opulentis
bonis protinus donat fratremque, antequam pro
27 salute eius precaretur, restituit, sceleris autem auctores interque eos Callisthenen vinctos asservari
iubet. Quibus in regiam adductis, toto die et nocte
28 proxima mero ac vigiliis gravis acquievit. Postero
autem frequens consilium adhibuit, cui patres pro-
pinquique eorum de quibus agebatur intererant, ne
de sua quidem salute securi ; quippe Macedonum
more perire debebant omnium devotis capitibus, qui
29 sanguine contigissent reos.[2] Rex introduci coniuratos praeter Callisthenen iussit ; atque quae agitave-
30 rant sine cunctatione confessi sunt. Increpantibus
deinde universis, eos ipse rex, quo suo merito tantum
in semet cogitassent facinus, interrogat.

VII. Stupentibus ceteris Hermolaus : " Nos vero,"
inquit, " quoniam, quasi nescias, quaeris, occidendi
te consilium iniimus,[3] quia non ut ingenuis imperare
2 coepisti, sed quasi in mancipia dominari."[4] Primus
ex omnibus pater ipsius Sopolis, parricidam etiam
parentis sui clamitans esse, consurgit, et ad os manu
obiecta, scelere et malis insanientem ultra negat
3 audiendum. Rex, inhibito patre, dicere Hermolaum
iubet, quae ex magistro didicisset Callisthene. Et
Hermolaus : " Utor,"[5] inquit, " beneficio tuo et dico
4 quae nostris malis didici. Quota pars Macedonum
saevitiae tuae superest ? quotus quidem non e[6]

---

[1] Tiridatis *Vogel;* tyridatis *A.*   [2] reos *Heinse;* eos *A.*
[3] iniimus *Kinch;* inimus *P;* inivimus *C.*
[4] dominari *Vogel;* dominaris *A.*
[5] utor] *the Excerpta Rhenaugiensia* (R) *begin with this
word.*   [6] e *I;* a *AR.*

---

[a] *Cf.* vi. 11. 20.
[b] *Cf.* x. 7. 2 ; Cic. *Pro Sest.* xvii. 39 ; Livy xl. 15. 10.
[c] A Sopolis is mentioned by Arr. iv. 18. 3.

once gave Eurylochus fifty talents and the rich estate
of a certain Tiridates and restored his brother to him
27 even before he begged for his life, but the authors of
the crime, and among them Callisthenes, he ordered
to be kept in fetters. When these had been brought
into the royal quarters, since he was wearied by wine
and loss of sleep he rested all day and the following
28 night. But on the next day he called a general
assembly, at which the fathers and relatives of those
concerned were present, who were not without
anxiety even for their own lives, for according to the
law of the Macedonians *a* they were doomed to die,
since the lives of all were forfeit who were related by
29 blood to the guilty parties. The king ordered the
conspirators except Callisthenes to be brought in,
and without hesitation they confessed what they had
30 planned. Then, when all cried out against them, the
king himself asked what he had done to deserve the
plotting *b* of such a crime against him.

VII. The rest were struck dumb, but Hermolaüs
said : " We verily, since you ask as if you did not
know, made a plot to kill you because you have begun,
not to rule us as free men, but to lord it over us as if
2 we were slaves." First of all his own father Sopolis,*c*
crying out that he was also the murderer of his parent,
arose and putting his hand over his son's mouth,
declared that one who was crazed by his crime and
his misfortunes ought not to have a further hearing.
3 But the king, silencing the father, ordered Hermolaüs
to tell what he had learned from his master Callisthenes, and Hermolaüs said : " I take advantage of
your favour and tell you what I have learned from
4 our own calamities. How small a part of the Macedonians survive your cruelty ; how few too of the

291

vilissimo sanguine ?   Attalus et Philotas et Parmenio
et Lyncestes Alexander et Clitus quantum ad hostes
pertinet vivunt, stant in acie et[1] clipeis suis te
protegunt et pro gloria tua, pro victoria vulnera
5 excipiunt.   Quibus tu egregiam gratiam rettulisti ;
alius mensam tuam sanguine suo aspersit, alius ne
simplici quidem morte defunctus est.   Duces exercituum tuorum in eculeum impositi Persis, quos vice-
rant, fuere spectaculo.   Parmenio indicta causa
6 trucidatus est, per quem Attalum occideras.   Invicem enim miserorum uteris manibus ad expetenda
supplicia et, quos paulo ante ministros caedis habuisti
subito ab aliis iubes trucidari.''
7   Obstrepunt subinde cuncti Hermolao, pater super
eum[2] strinxerat ferrum, percussurus haud dubie, ni
inhibitus esset a rege ; quippe Hermolaum dicere
iussit petiitque,[3] ut causas supplicii augentem patien-
8 ter audirent.   Aegre ergo coercitis,[4] rursus Hermolaus : `` Quam liberaliter, ' inquit, `` pueris rudibus
ad dicendum agere permittis ! at Callisthenis vox
9 carcere inclusa est, quia solus potest dicere.   Cur
enim non producitur, cum etiam confessi audiuntur ?
nempe quia liberam vocem innocentis audire metuis
10 ac ne vultum quidem pateris.   Atqui nihil eum fecisse
contendo.   Sunt hic qui mecum rem pulcherrimam
cogitaverunt ; nemo est qui conscium fuisse nobis
Callisthenen dicat, cum morti olim destinatus sit a

---

[1] et *Hedicke;* te *A.*
[2] super eum *Hedicke;* supremum *C;* suppremum *AR.*
[3] petiitque *J. Froben;* petitque *AR.*
[4] coercitis *Vindelinus;* coercitus *CR;* cohercitus *P.*

---

[a] This is not in harmony with iii. 12. 19 and with Curtius'
account of the slaying of Clitus ; but it may be a general
term.   [b] *Cf.* Tac. *Ann.* i. 8 ; Cic. *Ad Att.* xiv. 11.

noblest blood ?   Attalus and Philotas and Parmenion
and Lyncestes Alexander and Clitus, so far as our
enemies are concerned still live, they stand firm in
battle and protect you with their bucklers, and for
your glory, for your victory they suffer wounds.
5 These you have magnificently requited ; one stained
your table ^a with his blood, another died not even a
simple death.   The leaders of your armies, stretched
upon the rack, furnished entertainment to the Persians, whom they had conquered.   Parmenion was
butchered without a trial, the man through whom you
6 had slain Attalus.   For in turn you use the hands of
the wretched to inflict death, and those who shortly
before served as the tools of your murders you suddenly order to be butchered by others."
7   Thereupon all cried out at Hermolaüs, his father
had drawn his sword against him and beyond doubt
would have slain him if he had not been prevented by
the king ; for indeed he ordered Hermolaüs to continue, and asked that they should hear with patience
one who was adding to the reasons for his punishment.
8 Therefore, when they had been with difficulty restrained, Hermolaüs went on : " How generously,"
said he, " do you permit boys inexperienced in speaking to plead ! But the voice of Callisthenes is shut up
9 in a dungeon, because he alone is able to speak. For
why is not he brought before you, when even those
who have confessed are heard ? No doubt because
you fear to hear the free words of an innocent man,
10 and cannot even endure his look. And yet I insist that
he is guilty of nothing. They are here who with me
planned a glorious deed ^b ; there is none who says
that Callisthenes was implicated with us, although he
has been marked out for death by the most just

QUINTUS CURTIUS

11 iustissimo et patientissimo rege. Haec ergo sunt
Macedonum praemia, quorum ut supervacuo et sor-
dido abuteris sanguine ! At tibi xxx milia mulorum
captivum aurum vehunt, cum milites nihil domum
praeter gratuitas cicatrices relaturi sint.

12 " Quae tamen omnia tolerare potuimus, antequam
nos barbaris dederes et novo more victores sub iugum
mitteres. Persarum te vestis et disciplina delectant,
patrios mores exosus es. Persarum ergo, non Macedonum regem occidere voluimus et te transfugam

13 belli iure persequimur. Tu Macedonas voluisti
genua tibi ponere venerarique te ut deum, tu Philippum patrem aversaris et, si quis deorum ante Iovem

14 haberetur, fastidires etiam Iovem. Miraris, si liberi
homines superbiam tuam ferre non possumus ? Quid
speramus ex te, quibus aut insontibus moriendum
est aut, quod tristius morte est, in servitute viven-

15 dum ? Tu quidem, si emendari potes, multum mihi
debes. Ex me enim scire coepisti, quid ingenui
homines ferre non possint. De cetero propinquorum[1]
orbam senectutem suppliciis ne oneraveris ; nos iube
duci ut, quod ex tua morte petieramus, consequamur
ex nostra." Haec Hermolaus.

VIII. At rex : " Quam falsa sint,"[2] inquit, " quae
iste tradita a magistro suo dixit, patientia mea osten-
2 dit. Confessum enim ultimum facinus tamen non
solum ipse audivi, sed ut vos[3] audiretis expressi, non
imprudens,[4] cum permisissem latroni huic dicere,

[1] propinquorum *Kinch;* parce quorum *A.*
[2] sint *I;* sunt *AR.*
[3] audivi, sed ut vos *added by Mützell.*
[4] imprudens *Lauer;* impudens *AR.*

[a] *Cf.* iv. 6. 28.
[b] *duci* is used absolutely in judicial language.

11 and long-suffering of kings. These, then, are the rewards of the Macedonians, whose blood you use up as if it were superabundant and mean. But for you 30,000 mules carry captured gold, while your soldiers will bring home nothing save scars got without reward.

12 "Yet we could have endured all these things until you delivered us to the barbarians and by a novel fashion made the victors pass under the yoke. It is the Persians' garb and habits that delight you; you have come to loathe the customs of your native land. Therefore it was the king of the Persians, not of the Macedonians, that we wished to kill, and by the law

13 of war we justly pursue you as a deserter. You wished the Macedonians to bow the knee to you [a] and to venerate you as a god, you reject Philip as a father, and if any of the gods were regarded as greater

14 than Jupiter, you would disdain even Jupiter. Do you wonder if we, who are free men, cannot endure your haughtiness? What do we hope for from you, since we must either die when innocent, or, what is more

15 dismal than death, must live in slavery? You truly, if you can have a change of heart, owe much to me. For from me you have begun to know what honourable men cannot endure. For the rest, do not load with punishment the bereaved old age of our near of kin. Order us to be led to execution,[b] so that we may accomplish by our death what we had sought from yours." Thus spoke Hermolaüs.

VIII. But the king replied: "My patience shows how false is what that wretch has said, taught by his

2 master. For although he has pleaded guilty to the worst of crimes, I have not only heard him, but I have compelled you to hear him, knowing well that when I allowed this brigand to speak he would show the same

usurum eum rabie, qua compulsus est, ut me, quem
3 parentis loco colere deberet, vellet occidere. Nuper
cum procacius se in venatione gessisset, more patrio
et ab antiquissimis Macedoniae regum usurpato,
castigari eum iussi. Hoc et oportet[1] fieri et ferunt[2]
a tutoribus pupilli, a maritis uxores ; servis quoque
4 pueros huius aetatis verberare concedimus. Haec
est saevitia in ipsum mea, quam impia caede voluit
ulcisci. Nam in ceteros, qui mihi permittunt uti
ingenio meo, quam mitis sim non ignaris[3] commemo-
rare supervacuum est.

5 " Hermolao parricidarum supplicia non probari,
cum eadem ipse meruerit, minime, hercule, admiror.
Nam cum Parmenionem et Philotan laudat, suae
6 servit causae. Lyncestem vero Alexandrum, quamvis[4] insidiatum capiti meo a duobus indicibus litterisque[5] suis convictum, per triennium tamen distuli,
donec vos postularetis ut tandem debito supplicio
scelus lueret. Attalum, antequam rex essem, hostem meo capiti fuisse meministis. Clitus utinam non
coegisset me sibi irasci ! cuius temerariam linguam
probra dicentis mihi et vobis diutius tuli quam ille
8 eadem me dicentem tulisset. Regum ducumque
clementia non in ipsorum modo, sed etiam in illorum
qui parent ingeniis sita est. Obsequio mitigantur
imperia ; ubi vero reverentia excessit animis et

---

[1] oportet *J. Froben;* oportere *A;* oportere eum *R.*
[2] ferunt *Acidalius;* ut *A;* *R omits.*
[3] ignaris *Hedicke;* ignoratis *AR.*
[4] quamvis *Hedicke;* bis *AR.*
[5] litterisque suis *Hedicke;* liberavi rursus *AR.*

---

[a] See viii. 6. 7. [b] *Cf.* viii. 6. 2-6, and notes.
[c] When in charge of children.
[d] *Cf.* vii. 1. 5-6. [e] *Cf.* vi. 9. 18.

madness by which he was driven to wish to kill me,
3 whom he ought to have honoured as a father. Lately
when he conducted himself so insolently [a] in the
chase, I ordered him to be chastised according to the
custom of our country, one which was practised by
the most ancient of the kings of Macedonia.[b] This
both ought to be done, and pupils endure it from
their teachers, wives from their husbands ; we allow
4 even slaves [c] to flog boys of his age. This is my
cruelty towards him, for which he wished to avenge
himself by an impious murder. For towards the rest,
who permit me to follow my natural disposition,
how mild I am it is superfluous to say to those who
are not unaware of it.

5 "That Hermolaüs does not approve the punishments of traitors, since he himself has deserved the
same treatment, by Heaven ! I am not at all surprised. For when he praises Philotas and Parmenion,
6 he is helping his own cause. As for Lyncestes
Alexander,[d] although he was convicted by two witnesses and by his own letter of having plotted against
my life, I put off his punishment for three years, until
you demanded that at last he should atone for his
crime by the penalty which he had deserved.
7 Attalus,[e] before I became king you remember to have
been an enemy to my life. As for Clitus, would that
he had not forced me to be angry with him ! I
endured his rash tongue, as he abused you and me,
longer than he would have put up with me if I had
8 said the same things. The clemency of kings and
leaders depends not only upon their own dispositions,
but also upon those of their subjects. Commands are
made mild by obedience, but when men's minds have
lost reverence and no distinction is observed between

297

summa imis confunduntur,[1] vi opus est, ut vim repel-
9 lamus. Sed quid ego mirer istum crudelitatem mihi
obiecisse, qui avaritiam exprobrare ausus sit ? Nolo
singulos vestrum excitare, ne invisam mihi liberalitatem meam faciam, si pudori vestro gravem fecero.
Totum exercitum aspicite ; qui paulo ante nihil
praeter arma habebat, nunc argenteis cubat lectis,
mensas auro onerant, servorum greges ducunt, spolia
de hostibus sustinere non possunt.

10   " At enim Persae, quos vicimus, in magno honore
sunt apud me ! Mihi[2] quidem moderationis meae
certissimum indicium est, quod ne victis quidem
superbe impero.   Veni enim in Asiam, non ut fundi-
tus everterem gentes nec ut dimidiam partem terrarum solitudinem facerem, sed ut illos quos bello
11 subegissem victoriae meae non paeniteret.   Itaque
militant vobiscum, pro imperio vestro sanguinem
fundunt qui superbe habiti rebellassent.   Non est
diuturna possessio, in quam gladio inducimur ; bene-
12 ficiorum gratia sempiterna est.   Si habere Asiam,
non transire volumus, cum his communicanda est
nostra clementia ; horum fides stabile et aeternum
faciet imperium.   Et sane plus habemus, quam
capimus.[3]   Insatiabilis autem avaritiae est adhuc
13 implere velle quod iam circumfluit.   Morem[4] tamen

---

[1] confunduntur *Mützell;* confundimus *AR.*
[2] Mihi *added by Hedicke.*
[3] capimus *Acidalius;* cupimus *AR.*
[4] Morem *Hedicke;* uerum *AR.*

---

[a] An exaggeration, so far as the common soldiers are
concerned.
[b] *Inducimur* is judicial language, as in *inducimur in
possessionem.*

the highest and the lowest, force is needed to resist
9 force. But why should I wonder that that fellow has
charged me with cruelty when he has dared to re-
proach me with avarice? I am unwilling to call you
up one by one, for fear of making my generosity
odious to me, if I make it offensive to your modesty.
Just look at our whole army; those who before had
nothing except their arms now sleep on silver couches,
load their tables with gold, possess troupes of slaves,[a]
and cannot carry the weight of the spoils taken from
the enemy!

10 " But, he says, the Persians, whom we have conquered, are in high honour with me! In my opinion
at least, the surest indication of my moderation is
that I do not rule even the vanquished tyrannically.
For I came into Asia, not in order to overthrow
nations and make a desert of a half part of the world,
but in order that those whom I had subdued in war
11 might not regret my victory. Therefore those are
serving in the army with you and are shedding blood
in defence of your empire, who, if they had been
treated tyrannically would have rebelled. That
possession is not lasting of which we are made
owners [b] by the sword; the gratitude for acts of
12 kindness is everlasting. If we wish to hold Asia, not
merely to pass through it, our [c] clemency must be
shared with its people; their faith in us will make a
stable and lasting empire. And it is certainly true
that we have more than we can carry. But it is the
way of insatiable avarice to wish to fill still fuller a
13 vessel which is already overflowing. Yet I am accused
of transferring the customs of the vanquished to the

[c] *nostra* is plural of majesty, referring to Alexander,
although *volumus* refers to the Macedonians as a whole.

eorum in Macedonas transfundo !¹ In multis enim
gentibus esse video quae non erubescamus imitari ;
nec aliter tantum imperium apte regi potest, quam ut
quaedam et tradamus illis et ab eisdem discamus.

14 " Illud paene dignum risu fuit, quod Hermolaus
postulabat a me ut aversarer Iovem cuius oraculo
agnoscor.ᵃ An etiam, quid di respondeant in mea
15 potestate est ? Obtulit nomen filii mihi ; recipere
ipsis rebus quas agimus haud alienum fuit. Utinam
Indi quoque deum esse me credant ! Fama enim
bella constant, et saepe etiam, quod falso creditum
16 est veri vicem obtinuit. An me luxuriae indulgen-
tem putatis arma vestra auro argentoque adornasse ?
Assuetis nihil vilius hac videre materia volui ostendere, Macedonas invictos ceteris ne auro quidem
17 vinci. Oculos ergo primum eorum sordida omnia et
humilia despectantium² capiam, et docebo nos non
auri aut argenti cupidos, sed orbem terrarum sub-
acturos venire. Quam gloriam tu, parricida, inter-
cipere voluisti et Macedonas, rege adempto, devictis
gentibus dedere.

18 " At nunc mones me ut vestris parentibus parcam !
Non oportebat quidem vos scire quid de his statuis-
sem, quo tristiores periretis, si qua vobis parentum
memoria et cura est ; sed olim istum morem occidendi
cum scelestis insontes propinquos parentesque solvi,ᵇ

¹ transfundo *Giunta;* transeundo *AR.*
² despectantium *Bentley;* spectantium *AR.*

ᵃ This absolute use of *agnoscor* is rare.
ᵇ *Cf.* vi. 11. 20.

Macedonians! True, for I see in many nations things which we should not blush to imitate; and so great an empire cannot fitly be ruled without contributing some things to the vanquished and learning from them.

14 " That was almost enough to make one laugh, when Hermolaüs demanded of me that I should oppose Jupiter by whose oracle I am recognized as his son.[a] Have I control even of the responses of the

15 gods ? He offered me the title of son ; to accept it was not unfavourable to the very plans in which we are engaged. Would that the people of India may believe me to be a god. For wars depend upon reputation, and often even what has been falsely

16 believed has gained the place of truth. Do you think it was to gratify my luxury that I adorned your arms with gold and silver ? I wished to show to those who are accustomed to nothing cheaper than those metals that the Macedonians, who are invincible in other things, cannot be outdone even in gold.

17 Therefore I will first of all captivate the eyes of those who despise everything that is usual and humble and will show them that we are coming, not because we are desirous of gold and silver, but to subdue the whole world. It is this glory, parricide that you are, that you wished to interrupt and to deliver the Macedonians to the conquered nations by killing their king !

18 " But now you urge me to spare your relatives ! You all certainly ought not to have known what I had resolved to do about them, in order that you might die with greater grief, if you have any memory and regard for your near of kin ; but I long ago abandoned [b] that custom to which you refer, of killing the innocent kinsmen and relatives along with the

301

et profiteor in eodem honore futuros omnes eos in
19 quo fuerunt. Nam tuum[1] Callisthenen, cui uni vir
videris, quia latro es, scio cur produci velis ut coram
his probra, quae in me modo iecisti, modo audisti,
illius quoque ore referantur. Quem, si Macedo esset,
tecum introduxissem, dignissimum te discipulo
magistrum ; nunc Olynthio non idem iuris est."
20 Post haec consilium dimisit tradique damnatos
hominibus qui ex eadem cohorte erant iussit. Illi,
ut fidem suam saevitia regi approbarent, excruciatos
21 necaverunt. Callisthenes quoque tortus interiit, initi
consilii in caput regis innoxius, sed haudquaquam[2]
22 aulae et assentantium accommodatus ingenio. Itaque nullius caedes maiorem apud Graecos Alexandro
excitavit invidiam, quod praeditum optimis moribus
artibusque, a quo revocatus ad vitam erat cum interfecto Clito mori perseveraret, non tantum occiderit,
23 sed etiam torserit, indicta quidem causa. Quam
crudelitatem sera paenitentia consecuta est.

IX. Sed ne otium serendis rumoribus natum aleret,
in Indiam movit, semper bello quam post victoriam
2 clarior. India tota ferme spectat orientem, minus
3 in latitudinem quam recta regione spatiosa. Quae

---

[1] tuum *Vindelinus;* cum *PRV m. pr.;* tuum cum *BFLV*
corr.
[2] haudquaquam] utquaquam *PR;* haudquam *F.*

---

[a] That is, of being admitted to a council of Macedonians.
[b] Varying accounts of his death are given by Arr. iv. 14. 3
and others.

guilty parties, and I guarantee that they will all
19 hold the same rank that they had before. Now as
to your Callisthenes, to whom alone you seem to be
a man because you are an assassin, I know why you
wish him to be given audience; it is that in the
presence of this company those reproaches which
you have sometimes hurled at me and sometimes
heard may be repeated from his lips. If he were a
Macedonian, I should have presented him along with
you, a master most worthy of such a pupil; as it is,
being an Olynthian, he has not the same privilege." [a]

20 After these words he dismissed the assembly, and
ordered those who had been condemned to be handed
over to the men who belonged to the same cohort.
They put them to death with torments, in order by
21 cruelty to show their loyalty to the king. Callisthenes [b]
also expired in torture, although he was guiltless of
forming any design against the king's life; but he
was by no means suited to a court and to the character
22 of flatterers. Therefore there was no one whose
death roused greater hatred of the king among the
Greeks, because he had not only put to death a man
endowed with noble character and accomplishments,
one who had called him back to life when he had
resolved to die after the death of Clitus, but had
23 even tortured him, and that without a trial. This
act of cruelty, when it was too late, was followed by
repentance.

IX. But in order not to foster idleness, which
naturally sows gossip, he set out for India, being
always more illustrious in war than after a victory.
2 Almost all India looks towards the east, being less
3 extensive in width than in a straight line. [c] The

[c] Cf. recta plaga, vi. 2. 13.

austrum accipiunt in altius terrae fastigium exce-
dunt ; plana sunt cetera, multisque inclitis amnibus
Caucaso monte ortis, placidum per campos iter
4 praebent. Indus gelidior est quam ceteri ; aquas
vehit a colore maris haud multum abhorrentes.
5 Ganges, omnium ab Oriente fluvius maximus,[1] ad
meridianam regionem[2] decurrit et magnorum mon-
6 tium iuga recto alveo stringit ; inde[3] eum obiectae
rupes inclinant ad orientem. Uterque Rubro mari
accipitur. Indus[4] ripas multasque arbores cum
7 magna soli parte exsorbet, saxis quoque impeditus,
quis[5] crebro reverberatur; ubi mollius solum repperit,
stagnat insulasque molitur. Acesines eum[6] auget.
8 Ganges decursurum Iomanen[7] intercipit, magnoque
motu amnis uterque colliditur ; quippe Ganges
asperum os influenti obicit, nec repercussae aquae
9 cedunt. Diardines minus celeber auditu est, quia
per ultima Indiae currit ; ceterum non crocodillos
modo, uti Nilus, sed etiam delphinos ignotasque aliis
10 gentibus beluas alit. Ethymantus, crebris flexibus
subinde curvatus, ab accolis rigantibus campos[8] carpi-
tur ; ea causa est cur tenues reliquias iam sine nomine
11 in mare emittat. Multis praeter hos amnibus tota

[1] maximus *Modius;* eximiis *P;* exnmiis *R;* eximius *C.*
[2] ad meridianam regionem *Freinshem;* a meridiana regione *A;* a meridiana oregione *R.*
[3] inde *Freinshem;* in *AR.*
[4] Indus *Bentley;* findens *AR.*
[5] quis *Mützell;* quia *CP m. sec. R;* qua *P m. pr.*
[6] Acesines eum *Erasmus;* acesineum *AR.*

parts which receive the south wind rise to a higher
level of ground ; the rest of the country is flat and
allows a quiet course through plains to many famous
4 rivers rising in Mount Caucasus.[a] The Indus is
colder than the rest ; it carries waters which do not
5 differ much from the sea in colour. The Ganges,
greatest of all the rivers of the Orient, flows towards
the south and in a straight channel grazes the great
6 mountain ranges. Then rocks in its course deflect it
towards the east. Both rivers flow into the Red Sea.[b]
The Indus carries away its banks along with many
7 trees and a great part of the soil, and is also checked
by rocks, from which it often rebounds; where it
finds a softer soil it is quiet, and forms islands. The
8 Acesines [c] increases it. The Ganges intercepts the
Iomanes[d] in its downward course, and the two unite
with a great commotion of their waters ; for the
Ganges opposes a rough mouth to the inflowing river
and the waters which are hurled back do not yield.
9 The Diardines [e] is less frequently heard of, because it
runs through the remotest part of India, but it breeds
not only crocodiles, as does the Nile, but also dolphins
10 and sea beasts unknown to other nations. The
Ethymantus, curved from time to time into many
windings, is made use of by the neighbouring peoples
for irrigating their fields; that is why it sends out
scanty remains of its waters, now without a name,
11 into the sea. The whole region is cut up by many

[a] Here refers to all the range north of India, which had
several names.   [b] See iii. 2. 9, note.
     [c] The modern Chenab.   [d] The modern Jumnâ.
     [e] The Brahmaputra.

---

[7] Iomanen *Hedicke;* in mare *A.*
[8] campos *added by Hedicke.*

regio dividitur, sed ignobilibus, quia non adita[1]
interfluunt.

12 Ceterum quae propiora sunt mari aquilone maxime
deuruntur[2]; is[3] cohibitus iugis montium, ad interiora
13 non penetrat, ita alendis frugibus mitia.[4] Sed adeo
in illa plaga mundus statas temporum vices mutat,
ut, cum alia fervore solis exaestuant, Indiam nives
obruant, rursusque, ubi cetera rigent, illic intoleran-
dus aestus existat. Nec, cur verterit[5] se Natura,
14 causa. Mare certe quo[6] alluitur ne colore quidem
abhorret a ceteris. Ab Erythro rege inditum est
nomen ; propter quod ignari rubere aquas credunt.
15 Terra lini ferax ; inde plerisque sunt vestes. Libri
arborum teneri haud secus quam chartae litterarum
16 notas capiunt. Aves ad imitandum humanae vocis
sonum dociles sunt. Animalia invisitata ceteris
17 gentibus nisi invecta. Eadem terra rhinocerotas
aliis ignotos[7] generat. Elephantorum maior est vis
quam quos in Africa domitant, et viribus magni-
18 tudo respondet. Aurum flumina vehunt, quae leni
19 modicoque lapsu segnes aquas ducunt. Gemmas
margaritasque mare litoribus infundit ; neque alia
illis maior opulentiae causa est, utique postquam
vitiorum commercium vulgavere in exteras gentes.

[1] adita *Bentley;* adeo *AR.*
[2] aquilone maxime deuruntur *Foss;* aquiloni maxime
decurrunt *AR.*   [3] is *Zumpt;* his *AR.*
[4] mitia *Acidalius;* mitis *AR.*
[5] verterit *Novák;* ubi *C;* ibi *P;* ubri *R.*
[6] quo *Giunta;* quod *AR.*
[7] aliis ignotos *Hedicke;* alit non *AR.*

[a] Sixty, according to Seneca in Pliny, *N.H.* vi. 17. 21.
[b] Or Erythras; Strabo xvi. 3. 5; Pliny, *N.H.* vi. 13. 28;
Arr. *Indica* xxxvii. 3; Pliny, *N.H.* xix. 1. 2.
[c] Probably cotton is meant.

rivers [a] besides these, but they are unknown to fame, because they flow through regions unapproached as yet by us.

12 But the parts which are nearer the sea are greatly parched by the north wind ; this is checked by the mountain ranges and does not penetrate into the interior, which in consequence is mild for bearing

13 fruits. But in that quarter the earth so varies the established order of the seasons that when other places are burning with the heat of the sun, snows bury India, and on the other hand, when other places are stiff with frost, intolerable heat prevails there. Nor is there any reason why Nature should have changed her

14 course. Certainly the sea by which India is washed does not differ even in colour from other seas. Its name was given it from King Erythrus [b] ; for which reason the ignorant believe that its waters are red.

15 The land is rich in flax [c] ; most of the inhabitants have their garments made of it. The bark of the trees is tender and can receive writing just as papyrus

16 does. [d] There are birds which can be taught to imitate the sound of the human voice. [e] The animals are unknown to other nations, except such as are im-

17 ported from that country. The same land produces rhinoceroses, which are unknown to other peoples. The strength of its elephants is greater [f] than those which men tame in Africa, and their size corresponds

18 to their strength. The rivers which flow sluggishly

19 in a mild and moderate course carry gold. The sea casts upon its shores gems and pearls ; and they have no greater source of wealth, especially since they have made their vices common among foreign nations.

[d] The most ancient writing was on palm leaves.
Cf. Pliny, *N.H.* x. 42. 55.   [f] Strabo xv. 1. **44.**

Quippe aestimantur purgamenta exaestuantis freti pretio quod libido constituit.

20 Ingenia hominum, sicut ubique, apud illos locorum
21 quoque situs format. Corpora usque pedes carbaso velant, soleis pedes, capita linteis vinciunt, lapilli ex auribus pendent ; brachia quoque et lacertos auro colunt, quibus inter populares aut nobilitas aut opes
22 eminent. Capillum pectunt saepius quam tondent ; mentum semper intonsum est, reliquam oris cutem
23 ad speciem levitatis exaequant. Regum tamen luxuria, quam ipsi magnificentiam appellant, super omnium gentium vitia. Cum rex semet[1] in publico conspici patitur, turibula argentea ministri ferunt totumque iter per quod ferri destinavit odoribus com-
24 plent. Aurea lectica·margaritis circumpendentibus recubat ; distincta sunt auro et purpura carbasa quae indutus est ; lecticam sequuntur armati corporisque
25 custodes, inter quos ramis aves pendent, quas cantu
26 seriis rebus obstrepere docuerunt. Regia auratas columnas habet ; totas eas vitis auro caelata percurrit, aviumque, quarum visu maxime gaudent, argenteae effigies opera distinguunt.[2]
27 Regia adeuntibus patet, cum capillum pectit atque ornat ; tunc responsa legationibus, tunc iura popularibus reddit. Demptis soleis, odoribus illinuntur
28 pedes. Venatus maximus labor est inclusa vivario

---

[1] semet *Foss;* sene *PR;* sane *C.*
[2] distinguunt *I;* distingunt *AR.*

---

[a] Pliny, *N.H.* xxxvii. 6. 23 ; ix. 35. 60.
[b] See note *c* on p. 306.
[c] The connexion is not very clear, but *cf.* Strabo xv. 1. 69.

Indeed this refuse of the surging sea is valued at the price which desire sets upon it. [a]

20 There, as everywhere, so also with them, the situation of the country affects the character of the men.

21 They veil their bodies in linen robes as far as the feet, clothe their feet in sandals, bind their heads in linen, and precious stones hang from their ears ; those who are eminent among the people for high birth or wealth adorn their wrists also and arms with gold.

22 They comb their hair more frequently than they shear it ; the chin is always unshorn, the rest of the skin of the face they shave close, so that it appears 23 smooth. Nevertheless the luxury of their kings, which they themselves call magnificence, surpasses the vices of all other nations. When the king allows himself to be seen in public, his attendants carry before him silver pans of incense, and fill with perfumes the whole road over which he has decided to be 24 borne. He reclines in a golden litter adorned with pearls hanging on every side ; the linen [b] robe which he wears is embroidered with gold and purple ; his litter is followed by armed men and by his body-guard, 25 among whom [c] on branches of trees birds perch, which they have trained by song to divert him from 26 serious affairs. His palace has gilded columns ; over all of these runs a vine carved in gold, and silver figures of birds, in the sight of which they take the greatest pleasure, adorn the structure.

27 The palace is open to all comers, when the king is having his hair combed and adorned ; it is then that he gives replies to deputations, then that he administers justice to his countrymen. When his sandals are taken off, his feet are bathed in perfumes.

28 His favourite exercise is the chase, which consists in

animalia inter vota cantusque pelicum figere. Binum
cubitorum sagittae sunt, quas emittunt maiore nisu
quam effectu ; quippe telum, cuius in levitate vis
29 omnis est, inhabili pondere oneratur. Breviora
itinera equo conficit ; longior ubi expeditio est,
elephanti vehunt currum, et tantarum beluarum
corpora tota contegunt auro. Ac, ne quid perditis
moribus desit, lecticis aureis pelicum longus ordo
sequitur ; separatum a reginae ordine agmen est
30 aequatque luxuriam. Feminae epulas parant. Ab
eisdem vinum ministratur, cuius omnibus Indis
largus est usus. Regem mero somnoque sopitum, in
cubiculum pelices referunt, patrio carmine noctium
invocantes deos.

31   Quis credat inter haec vitia curam esse sapientiae ?
Unum agreste et horridum genus est, quod sapientes
32 vocant.   Apud hos occupare fati diem pulchrum, et
vivos se cremari iubent quibus aut segnis[1] aetas aut
incommoda valetudo est; exspectatam mortem pro
dedecore vitae habent, nec ullus corporibus, quae senectus solvit, honos redditur; inquinari putant ignem,
33 nisi qui spirantes[2] recipit.   Illi, qui in urbibus pub-
licis muneribus[3] degunt, siderum motus scite spectare dicuntur et futura praedicere.   Nec quemquam

---

[1] aut segnis *J. Froben;* autem segnis *AR* (autem segnes
P m. pr. V m. pr.).
[2] spirantes *R;* sperantes *A.*
[3] muneribus *Hedicke;* moribus *A.*

---

[a] *i.e.* for his success.   [b] *Cf.* viii. 14. 19.
[c] Curtius does not take account of the lighter material.
[d] Perhaps Indras is thought of, the god of the entire
heaven and the stars.

shooting with arrows animals shut up in a preserve amid the prayers [a] and songs of his concubines. The arrows are two cubits in length, and they discharge them with more effort than effect [b]; for a weapon whose whole power depends upon lightness is bur-

29 dened by its unsuitable weight.[c] Shorter journeys he makes on horseback; when he undertakes a longer expedition, he rides in a chariot drawn by elephants, and the entire bodies of such huge brutes are covered with gold. Also, that nothing may be lacking in his abandoned habits, a long line of con-cubines follows in golden litters; this train is separ-ated from that of the queen, but equals it in luxury.

30 Women prepare his food. They also serve his wine, the use of which is lavish with all the Indian peoples. When the king is overcome by wine and drowsiness, concubines take him to his chamber, invoking the gods of the night [d] in a song, after the custom of the country.

31 Who would believe that amid such vices there would be regard for philosophy? There is one rude

32 and hideous class which they call sages.[e] These consider it glorious to anticipate the day of fate,[f] and those whose life is feeble or whose health is impaired give orders to be burned alive; to wait for death they regard as a disgrace to life, and no honour is paid to the bodies of those who die of old age; they believe that the fire [g] is sullied unless it receives

33 them while still breathing. Those who pass their lives in public services in the city are said skilfully to study the courses of the stars and to predict future

[e] Probably the sect of gymnosophists, similar to the modern *yogi*.
[f] See Strabo xv. 1. 68. [g] Of the funeral pyre.

admovere leti diem credunt cui exspectare interrito
34 liceat. Deos putant quidquid colere coeperunt,
35 arbores maxime, quas violare capital est. Menses in
quinos denos discripserunt[1] dies, anni plena spatia
36 servantur. Lunae cursu notant tempora, non, ut
plerique, cum orbem sidus implevit, sed cum se cur-
vare coepit in cornua, et idcirco breviores habent
menses, quia[2] spatium eorum ad hunc lunae modum
37 dirigunt. Multa et alia traduntur, quibus morari
ordinem rerum haud sane operae[3] videbatur.

X. Igitur Alexandro finis Indiae ingresso, gentium
finitimarum[4] reguli occurrerunt, imperata facturi,
illum tertium Iove genitum ad ipsos pervenisse memorantes ; Patrem Liberum atque Herculem fama
2 cognitos esse, ipsum coram adesse cernice. Rex
benigne exceptos sequi iussit, eisdem itinerum ducibus usurus.[5] Ceterum cum amplius nemo occurreret,
Hephaestionem et Perdiccan cum copiarum parte
praemisit ad subigendos qui aversarentur imperium,
iussitque ad flumen Indum procedere et navigia
facere, quis in ulteriora transportari posset exercitus.

---

[1] discripserunt *Hedicke;* descripserunt *AR.*
[2] quia *Koehler;* qui *A.*
[3] sane operae *Giunta;* sine opere *AR.*
[4] finitimarum *Hedicke;* suarum *AR.*
[5] usurus] *frag. R ends with this word.*

---

[a] Thus differing from the *agreste genus* of section 31.
[b] Each month being divided into two halves; see Bohlen,
Indien ii. p. 287.
[c] A solar year, consisting of twelve months of 30, 31,
and 29 days ; in all, 365 days, 15 hours, 31 minutes, and
15 seconds; Bohlen, *l.c.* ii. pp. 284 f.
[d] We find *operae est* in the sense of *vacat* in Livy iv. 8. 3
and elsewhere ; but here the meaning is different.
[e] Curtius omits the account of the march from Bactra

events. And they believe that no one hastens the
34 day of death who can wait for it unterrified.[a] They
regard as gods whatever they have begun to care for,
especially trees, the violation of which is a capital
35 offence. They have divided the months into periods
of fifteen days,[b] but the full duration of the year is
36 observed.[c] They reckon time by the course of the
moon, not, as most do, when it has filled its orb, but
when it has begun to curve into horns, and therefore
they have shorter months, because they reckon their
37 duration according to that phase of the moon. Also
many other things are related, for which it did
not seem to be worth while [d] to delay the course of
our history.

X. So, then, when Alexander had entered the
bounds of India,[e] the petty kings of the neighbouring
races met him intending to submit to him, saying[f]
that he was the third son of Jupiter who had arrived
in their land ; that Father Liber and Hercules were
known to them only by repute, but that Alexander
2 was present among them and was seen. The king
received them courteously and bade them follow
him, intending to use them as guides for his routes.
But when no one else presented himself, he sent on
Hephaestion and Perdiccas [g] with a part of his forces
to subdue those who rejected his rule, and ordered
them to proceed to the Indus River and make boats
by which his army could be transported to places

through the Cabul valley (Arr. iv. 22. 3-4). *Fines Indiae*
shows that the writers whom Curtius followed count the
mountain range which separates Iran from India as a part
of India.

[f] Strabo xv. 1. 9 says that this came from his flatterers,
to whom many of his older historians belonged.

[g] *Cf.* Arr. iv. 22. 7.

3 Illi, quia plura flumina superanda erant, sic iunxere
naves ut solutae plaustris vehi possent rursusque
4 coniungi. Ipse,[1] Cratero cum phalange iusso sequi,
equitatum ac levem armaturam eduxit, eosque qui
occurrerunt levi proelio in urbem proximam compulit.
5 Iam supervenerat Craterus ; itaque, ut principio
terrorem incuteret genti nondum arma Macedonum
expertae, praecipit ne cui parceretur munimentis
6 urbis quam obsidebat incensis. Ceterum, dum
obequitat moenibus, sagitta ictus. Cepit tamen
oppidum, et, omnibus incolis eius trucidatis, etiam
in tecta saevitum est.
7   Inde, domita ignobili gente, ad Nysam urbem pervenit. Forte, castris ante ipsa moenia in silvestri
loco positis, nocturnum frigus vehementius quam
alias horrore corpora affecit, opportunumque re-
8 medium ignis oblatum est. Caesis quippe silvis,
flammam excitaverunt, quae lignis[2] alita oppidanorum sepulcra comprehendit. Vetusta cedro erant
facta conceptumque ignem late fudere, donec omnia
9 solo aequata sunt. Et ex urbe primum canum latra-
tus, deinde etiam hominum fremitus auditus est.
Tunc et oppidani hostem et Macedones ad urbem
10 ipsos venisse cognoscunt. Iamque rex eduxerat
copias et moenia obsidebat, cum hostium qui dis-

---

[1] Ipse *Stangl;* post se *A.*   [2] lignis *Faber;* igni *A.*

---

[a] More exactly Arr. iv. 23. 1.
[b] Arr. iv. 23. 3 puts the city east, Curtius west, of the Choaspes (the Attock).
[c] *Cf.* Livy xxx. 31. 10 *in delubra saevisse.*
[d] Because of the elevation, not the season.

3 farther on. Those men, because several other rivers had to be crossed, joined ships together, but in such a way that they could be taken apart and carried on
4 wagons and again joined together. He himself after having directed Craterus to follow with the phalanx led out the cavalry and the light-armed troops,[a] and in a slight battle drove those who
5 opposed him into the nearest city.[b] And now Craterus had arrived ; and so, in order in the beginning to strike with terror a nation which had not yet experienced the arms of the Macedonians, the king ordered him to spare no one, having set fire to the
6 fortifications of the city which he was besieging. But while Alexander was riding up to the walls he was struck by an arrow. Nevertheless he took the town, and having butchered all its inhabitants, even vented his anger on its buildings.[c]

7   Next, after subduing this unknown people, he came to the city of Nysa. It chanced that when he had pitched a camp before the very walls in a wooded place, a coldness severer than they had experienced at any other time[d] chilled their bodies, and fire offered
8 a convenient remedy. Therefore they cut down trees and raised a flame, which, fed by logs, caught the sepulchres of the inhabitants. These had been built of old cedar, and widely spread the fire which had been started, until all were levelled with the
9 ground. And from the city first the barking of dogs, then the noise of men was heard. Then the townspeople knew that the enemy had come, and the Macedonians themselves, that they had reached the
10 city. And already the king had led out his troops and was laying siege to the place, when those of the enemy who had attempted a sortie were over-

crimen temptaverant obruti telis sunt. Aliis ergo
deditionem, aliis pugnam experiri placebat.

Quorum dubitatione comperta, circumsederi tan-
11 tum eos et abstineri caedibus iussit; tandemque
obsidionis malis fatigati, dedidere[1] se. A Libero
Patre conditos se esse dicebant; et vera haec origo
12 erat. Sita est urbs[2] sub radicibus montis, quem
Meron incolae appellant; inde Graeci mentiendi
traxere licentiam, Iovis femine Liberum Patrem esse
13 celatum. Rex, situ montis cognito ex incolis, cum
toto exercitu, praemissis commeatibus, verticem eius
ascendit. Multa hedera vitisque toto gignitur
14 monte, multae perennes aquae manant. Pomorum
quoque varii salubresque suci sunt, sua sponte for-
tuitorum germinum[3] fruges humo nutriente. Lauri
buxique[4] et myrti[5] in illis rupibus agrestis est silva.
15 Credo equidem non divino instinctu, sed lascivia esse
provectos ut passim hederae ac vitium folia decer-
perent redimitique fronde toto nemore similes bac-
16 chantibus vagarentur. Vocibus ergo tot milium
praesidem nemoris eius deum adorantium iuga montis
vallesque[6] resonabant, cum orta licentia a paucis, ut
17 fere fit, in omnes se repente[7] vulgasset. Quippe
velut in media pace per herbas aggestamque frondem

---

[1] dedidere *B m. sec.;* dedere *A.*
[2] urbs *added by Eberhard.*
[3] germinum *Heinse;* segeminum *B m. pr. P;* seugemi-
num *V;* seugerminum *B m. sec. FL corr.*
[4] buxique *Hedicke;* baceque *P V;* bacaeque *BFL.*
[5] myrti *Hedicke;* multa *A.*
[6] vallesque *Hedicke;* collesque *A.*
[7] omnes se repente *Giunta;* homines serpente *A* (homines
serpentes *F*).

---

* Gk. μηρός, "thigh."

whelmed by weapons. In consequence some favoured surrender, others the trial of battle.

When their hesitation became known, Alexander directed that they should merely be beleaguered and 11 not killed, and at last, exhausted by the hardships of a siege, they gave themselves up. They said that they had been founded by Father Liber ; and this 12 was in fact their origin. The city is situated at the foot of a mountain which the natives call Meros *a*; from this the Greeks took the liberty of inventing the fable *b* that Father Liber had been hidden in the 13 thigh of Jupiter. Alexander, having learned from the natives the situation of the mountain, had supplies sent in advance, and ascended to its summit *c* with his whole army. Ivy and vines in abundance grow all over the height, and many perennial springs 14 gush forth. There are also fruits of a varied and wholesome flavour, since the earth without cultivation produces crops from the seeds that chance to fall there. Laurel, box, and myrtle form a natural grove 15 on those rocks. Carried away, as I for my part believe, not by divine inspiration but by a spirit of playfulness, they plucked the foliage of the ivy and the vines everywhere, and wreathed with garlands made from the leaves, wandered here and there through the whole grove like so many bacchantes. 16 Hence the mountain heights and valleys rang with the shouts of so many thousands, as they invoked the god who presided over that grove, since as soon as this wantonness was begun by a few, as commonly happens it quickly spread to the whole company. 17 In fact, as if they were in full enjoyment of peace, they threw themselves on the grass and the leaves

b See Pliny, *N.H.* vi. 21. 23.   *c* *Cf.* Arr. v. 2. 5.

QUINTUS CURTIUS

prostravere corpora. Et rex, fortuitam laetitiam non aversatus, large ad epulas omnibus praebitis, per x dies Libero Patri operatum habuit exercitum.

18 Quis neget eximiam quoque gloriam saepius fortunae quam virtutis esse beneficium ? Quippe ne epulantes quidem et sopitos mero aggredi ausus est hostis, haud secus bacchantium ululantiumque fremitu perterritus quam si proeliantium clamor esset auditus. Eadem felicitas ab Oceano revertentes temulentos comissantesque inter ora hostium texit.

19 Hinc ad regionem quae Daedala vocatur perventum est. Deseruerant incolae sedes et in avios silvestresque montes confugerant. Ergo Acadira transit aeque[1] vasta[2] et destituta incolentium fuga.

20 Itaque rationem belli necessitas mutavit. Divisis enim copiis, pluribus simul locis arma ostendit, oppressique ubi[3] non exspectaverant hostem omni clade

21 perdomiti sunt. Ptolomaeus plurimas urbes, Alexander maximas cepit ; rursusque quas distribuerat copias iunxit.

22 Superato deinde Choaspe amne Coenon in obsidione urbis opulentae—Beiram incolae vocant—reliquit, ipse ad Mazagas venit. Nuper Assacano, cuius regnum fuerat, demortuo, regioni urbique

---

[1] aeque *J. Froben;* atque *A.*
[2] vasta *Acidalius;* usta *A.*   [3] ubi *Bongars;* urbi *A.*

---

[a] *Cf.* Tibull. ii. 6. 95.
[b] *i.e.* from the Indus mouth through southern Iran; see ix. 10. 24 ff. ; for the language *cf.* ix. 10. 26 ; Livy ix. 17. 17.
[c] See *montes Daedalos*, Justin xii. 7 ; otherwise unknown.
[d] Otherwise unknown : *cf.* Arr. iv. 33. 5 Ἄνδακα.
[e] See Arr. iv. 24 ff., who apparently follows Ptolemy's own account.   [f] The modern Attock.
[g] See Arr. iv. 27. 5, who calls it Bazira. Its location is unknown.

that they had heaped together. And the king, not averse to this opportunity for revelry, furnished in abundance everything needed for feasting, and for ten days kept the army engaged in the service of

18 Bacchus.[a] Who would deny that distinguished glory also is more often the gift of Fortune than of merit? For the enemy did not venture to attack them even while they were feasting or in a drunken sleep, being as greatly terrified by the noise of their rioting and howling as if they had heard the shouts of men going to battle. The same good fortune on their return from the Ocean protected them in their drunken revelry before the faces of their enemies.[b]

19 From here they came to the region which is called Daedala.[c] The inhabitants had deserted their homes and had fled to the inaccessible and forest-covered mountains. Accordingly the king passed by Acadira,[d] which was equally abandoned and deserted by the

20 flight of its inhabitants. And so necessity changed his plan for war. For dividing his forces, he showed his arms in many places at the same time, and when the natives had been crushed where they had not looked for the enemy, they were thoroughly subdued

21 through general bloodshed. Ptolemy took the most cities,[e] Alexander the greatest; then the king united again the forces which he had distributed.

22 Next, having passed over the Choaspes[f] River, he left Coenus engaged in the siege of a rich city—the inhabitants call it Beira[g]—and he himself came to the country of the Mazagae.[h] Assacenus, whose realm it had been, had lately died, and his mother

---

[h] Arr. iv. 26. 1, who has (τὰ) Μάσσαγα. It was the largest city of the Assaceni, at the junction of the Cabul and the Indus.

23 praeerat mater eius Cleophis. xxxviii milia peditum
tuebantur urbem non situ solum, sed etiam opere
munitam. Nam qua spectat orientem, cingitur amne
torrenti, qui praeruptis utrimque ripis aditum ad
24 urbem impedit. Ad occidentem ac meridiem[1] veluti[2]
de industria rupes praealtas obmolita natura est,
infra quas cavernae et voragines longa vetustate in
altum cavatae iacent, quaque desinunt, fossa ingentis
25 operis obiecta est. xxxv stadium[3] murus urbem
complectitur, cuius ima[4] saxo, superiora crudo latere
sunt structa. Lateri vinculum lapides sunt, quos
interposuere ut duriori materiae fragilis incumberet,
26 simulque terra humore diluta. Ne tamen universa
consideret, impositae erant trabes validae, quibus
iniecta tabulata muros et tegebant et pervios fecerant.
27 Haec munimenta contemplantem Alexandrum
consiliique incertum, quia nec cavernas nisi aggere
poterat implere nec tormenta aliter muris admovere,
28 quidam e muro sagitta percussit ; et[5] forte in suram
incidit telum. Cuius spiculo evolso, admoveri equum
iussit, quo vectus, ne obligato quidem vulnere, haud
29 segnius destinata exsequebatur. Ceterum cum crus
saucium penderet, et cruore siccato frigescens vulnus
aggravaret dolorem, dixisse fertur se quidem Iovis

[1] ac meridiem *Kinch;* a meridie *P;* et a meridie *C.*
[2] veluti *Hedicke;* uelut in *P m. pr.;* uelut *C.*
[3] stadium *Zumpt;* stadia *A.*
[4] ima *Vogel;* iam *P;* inferiora *C.*
[5] et *Hedicke;* cum *P;* tum *C.*

[a] Arr. iv. 25. 5 says "over 30,000."
[b] *Cf.* Plut. *Alex.* xxviii.

23 Cleophis ruled the city and the region. The city was garrisoned by 38,000 infantry [a] and was fortified, not only by its situation, but also by art. For where it looks towards the east it is girt by a very rapid river, which, having precipitous banks on both sides, makes

24 approach to the city difficult. Towards the west and the south Nature, as if by design, has thrown up towering crags, below which lie caverns and abysses which have been deeply hollowed by long lapse of time, and where they come to an end ditches have been

25 interposed with enormous labour. The city is surrounded by a wall of thirty-five stadia, the lower part of which is constructed of stone, the upper part of sun-dried brick. The brick work is so bound together by stones which they have interposed and at the same time by earth soaked in water, that the weaker part

26 rests on a stronger material. Nevertheless, in order that the whole structure might not settle, strong beams were placed upon it, on which galleries were raised, which both protected the walls and at the same time afforded a passage through them.

27 As Alexander was reconnoitring these fortifications and was uncertain what to do, since he could not fill up the caverns except by a mound, nor move up his siege-engines to the walls in any other way, someone from the wall shot at him with an arrow, and, as it happened, the weapon struck him in the

28 calf of his leg. When the barb had been pulled out he ordered a horse to be brought and riding upon it, without even binding up the wound, he continued no less vigorously to carry on what he had undertaken.

29 But since the wounded leg hung down, and when the blood dried the stiffening of the wound aggravated the pain, he is reported to have said [b] that he was

30 filium dici, sed corporis aegri vitia sentire. Non
tamen ante se recepit in castra, quam cuncta perspexit et quae fieri vellet edixit. Ergo, sicut imperatum erat, alii extra urbem tecta demoliebantur[1]
ingentemque vim materiae faciendo aggeri detrahe-
bant, alii magnarum arborum stipites cum ramis[2] ac
31 moles saxorum in cavernas deiciebant. Iamque
agger aequaverat summae fastigium terrae ; itaque
turres erigebantur,[3] quae opera ingenti militum
ardore intra nonum diem absoluta sunt.

Ad ea visenda rex, nondum obducta vulneri cicatrice, processit, laudatisque militibus, admoveri
machinas iussit, e quibus ingens vis telorum in pro-
32 pugnatores effusa est. Praecipue rudes talium
operum terrebant mobiles turres, tantasque moles,
nulla ope quae cerneretur adiutas, deorum numine
agi credebant ; pila quoque muralia et excussas
tormentis praegraves hastas negabant convenire
33 mortalibus. Itaque, desperata urbis tutela, con-
cessere in arcem. Inde, quia nihil obsessis praeter
deditionem patebat,[4] legati ad regem descenderunt,
34 veniam petituri. Qua impetrata, regina venit cum
magno nobilium feminarum grege aureis pateris vina
35 libantium. Ipsa, genibus regis parvo filio admoto,
non veniam modo, sed etiam pristinae fortunae impetravit decus ; quippe appellata regina est. Et

---

[1] demoliebantur *Giunta;* em. *P;* am. *C.*
[2] cum ramis *Freinshem;* cumulis *A.*
[3] erigebantur *P;* erigebant *C.*
[4] patebat *Eberhard;* placebat *A.*

indeed called the son of Jupiter, but that he felt the
30 effects of an ailing body. Yet he did not return to
the camp until he had carefully examined everything
and had ordered what he wished to be done. Accordingly, just as had been commanded, some were de-
molishing the houses outside the city and were
bringing a great amount of timber for making the
mound ; others were throwing trunks of great trees,
with their branches, and masses of stone into the
31 caverns. And already the mound had risen to the
level of the surface of the ground ; therefore they
erected towers, and such was the ardour of the
soldiers that these tasks were finished within the
ninth day.

To inspect these works the king went out before a
scab had covered his wound, and after praising the
soldiers he ordered them to push forward the siege-
engines, from which a mighty mass of weapons was
32 poured upon the defenders. The movable towers
especially terrified men who were unacquainted with
such devices, and they believed that such massive
structures, aided by no visible power, were moved
by the will of the gods; the mural pikes also, and
the heavy spears hurled by the engines, they said
33 were not compatible with mortal power. Therefore,
despairing of defending the city, they withdrew to
the citadel. From there, because nothing but surrender was open to the besieged, envoys came down
34 to the king to ask for pardon. When this was
granted, the queen came with a great train of noble
ladies, making libations of wine from golden cups.
35 She herself, placing her little son at the king's knees,
obtained, not only pardon, but also the splendour of
her former fortune ; indeed, she was addressed as

credidere quidam plus formae quam miserationi
36 datum; puero quoque certe postea, ex ea utcumque
genito, Alexandro fuit nomen.

XI. Hinc Polypercon ad urbem Horam[1] cum exercitu missus, inconditos oppidanos proelio vicit intra
munimenta compulsos secutus, urbem in dicionem
2 redegit. Multa ignobilia oppida, deserta a suis,
venere in regis potestatem. Quorum incolae armati
petram, Aornum[2] nomine, occupaverunt. Hanc ab
Hercule frustra obsessam esse terraeque motu coac-
3 tum absistere, fama vulgaverat. Inopem consilii
Alexandrum, quia undique praeceps et abrupta rupes
erat, senior quidam peritus locorum cum duobus filiis
adiit, si pretium operae esset,[3] aditum se monstratu-
4 rum esse promittens. LXXX talenta constituit daturum
Alexander et, altero ex iuvenibus obside retento,
5 ipsum ad exsequenda quae obtulerat dimisit. Leviter armatis dux datus est Myllinas,[4] scriba regis.
Hos enim circuitu quo[5] fallerent hostem in summum
iugum placebat evadere.

6 Petra non, ut pleraeque, modicis ac mollibus clivis
in sublime fastigium crescit, sed in metae maxime
modum erecta est, cuius ima spatiosiora sunt, altiora
in artius coeunt, summa in acutum cacumen exsur-

[1] Horam *Hedicke;* nram *P m. pr.;* noram *CP m. sec.*
[2] Aornum *J. Froben;* aorni in *LPV;* aorini in *B;* aorni *F.*
[3] operae esset *Letellier;* obpesset *BFP;* obpreesset *LV;*
uel operis esset *C in marg.* (*in text F*).
[4] Myllinas *Hedicke;* mullinus *A.*
[5] quo *Freinshem;* qui *A.*

[a] Justin xii. 7 speaks more decidedly about this.
[b] Justin *l.c.* says : *postea regnum Indorum potitus est.*
[c] Ὦρα, Arr. iv. 27. 7-9, of a city in the same neighbourhood.
[d] So Diod. xvii. 85. 2   Arr. iv. 28. 1-4 expresses doubt
about the story.

queen. And some believed [a] that this was granted
rather to her beauty than because of compassion ;
36 also it is certain that a son who was born to her,
whoever his father was, was called Alexander.[b]

XI. Then Polypercon, who had been sent to the
city of Hora [c] with an army, defeated the townsmen
in a battle when they made a disorderly sortie ; having driven them within their fortifications, he followed
2 and reduced the city to subjection. Many obscure
towns, which had been deserted by their inhabitants,
came into the power of the king. The inhabitants
of these armed themselves and occupied a crag called
Aornus. That this had been beset by Hercules without success and that he had been compelled by an
earthquake to abandon the attempt was a widespread
3 report.[d] When Alexander was at a loss, because the
rock was steep and abrupt on all sides, an old man
who was acquainted with the neighbourhood came to
him with two sons, promising that if it were made
4 worth his while he would show him a way up. Alexander agreed that he would give him eighty talents
and having retained one of the young men as a host-
age, sent the father to carry out what he had offered
5 to do. Myllinas,[e] the king's secretary, was made
the leader of a light-armed troop. For Alexander
wished these to go to the summit by a circuitous
route, in order to escape the notice of the enemy.
6 The rock did not, like many others, rise by moderate and gentle slopes to a lofty summit, but elevated
itself very much in the manner of a turning-block, of
which the lower parts are wider, but become narrower
as they rise higher and force the highest parts into

[e] The name is doubtful ; according to Arr. iv. 29. 1,
Ptolemy led this division.

QUINTUS CURTIUS

7 gunt. Radices eius Indus amnis subit, praealtus,
utrimque asperis ripis ; ab altera parte voragines
eluviesque praeruptae sunt. Nec alia expugnandi
8 patebat via, quam ut replerentur. Ad manum silva
erat ; quam rex ita caedi iussit, ut nudi stipites
iacerentur ; quippe rami fronde vestiti impedissent
ferentes. Ipse primus truncam arborem iecit, cla-
morque exercitus,[1] index alacritatis, secutus est, nullo
9 detrectante munus quod rex occupavit. Sic[2] intra
septimum diem cavernas expleverant, cum rex sagittarios et Agrianos iubet per ardua niti. Iuvenesque
10 promptissimos ex sua cohorte xxx delegit; duces his
dati sunt Charus et Alexander, quem rex nominis,
quod sibi cum eo commune esset, admonuit. Ac
primo, quia tam[3] manifestum periculum erat, ipsum
11 regem discrimen subire non placuit, sed ut signum
tuba datum est, vir audaciae promptae conversus ad
corporis custodes, sequi se iubet primusque invadit in
rupem. Nec deinde quisquam Macedonum substitit,
relictisque stationibus, sua sponte regem sequebantur.
12 Multorum miserabilis fuit casus, quos ex praerupta
rupe lapsos amnis praeterfluens hausit, triste spectaculum etiam non periclitantibus ; cum vero alieno
exitio quid ipsis timendum foret admonerentur, in
metum misericordia versa, non exstinctos, sed semetipsos deflebant.

[1] se (*after* exercitus) *deleted by Giunta.*
[2] occupavit. Sic *Hedicke;* occupauisset *A.*
[3] tam *C;* iam *P.*

---

[a] Cut out by the water.
[b] The *regia cohors* ; *cf.* viii. 6. 7.

7 a sharp point. The Indus River comes close up to its base, and is very deep with steep banks on both sides ; on the other side there are deep abysses and chasms.[a] There was no other way open for storming the place 8 except by filling these. There was a forest at hand ; this the king ordered to be cut in such a way that the tree-trunks should be thrown in stripped bare ; for the branches covered with leaves would have hampered those who carried them. Alexander himself trimmed and threw in the first tree, and the army's shouting which followed was an indication of their eagerness, since no one shirked the task in which the 9 king had taken the lead. In this way before the seventh day they had wholly filled the caverns, when the king ordered the archers and the Agriani to try to mount the heights. Also he chose thirty of the 10 most active men of his own cohort.[b] As leaders he gave them Charus and Alexander, and the king exhorted the latter to remember the name which he had in common with himself. And at first, because the danger was so evident, the king himself decided 11 not to run the risk, but when the signal was given by the trumpet, that prince of ready daring, turning to his guards, ordered them to follow him, and was the first to climb upon the rock. Then not one of the Macedonians stayed behind, but leaving their posts 12 of their own accord, they followed the king. Many met a wretched death, for they slipped from the steep rock, and the river which flowed by swallowed them up, a sad sight even for those who were not at the moment in danger ; but when by the death of others they were reminded what they themselves had to fear, compassion changing to dread, they lamented, not the dead, but themselves.

13 Et iam eo perventum erat, unde sine pernicie nisi
victores redire non possent, ingentia saxa in sub-
euntes provolventibus barbaris, quis[1] perculsi instabili
14 et lubrico gradu praecipites recidebant. Evaserant
tamen Alexander et Charus, quos cum xxx delectis
praemiserat rex, et iam pugnare comminus coeperant ; sed cum superne tela barbari ingererent,
15 saepius ipsi feriebantur quam vulnerabant. Ergo
Alexander, et nominis sui et promissi memor, dum
acrius quam cautius dimicat, confossus undique
16 obruitur. Quem ut Charus iacentem conspexit, ruere
in hostem omnium praeter ultionem immemor coepit
multosque hasta, quosdam gladio interemit; sed cum
tot unum incesserent manus, super amici corpus
17 procubuit exanimis. Haud secus quam par erat,
promptissimorum iuvenum ceterorumque militum
18 interitu commotus, rex signum receptui dedit. Saluti
fuit quod sensim et intrepidi se receperunt, et barbari hostem depulisse contenti, non institere cedenti-
19 bus. Ceterum Alexander cum statuisset desistere
incepto—quippe nulla spes potiundae petrae offere-
batur—tamen speciem ostendit in obsidione[2] perseverantis. Nam et itinera obsideri iussit et turres
admoveri et fatigatis alios succedere.
20 Cuius pertinacia cognita, Indi per biduum quidem
ac duas noctes cum ostentatione non fiduciae modo,
sed etiam victoriae epulati sunt, tympana suo more

---

[1] quis *Freinshem;* qui *A.*
[2] obsidione *Lauer;* obsidionem *A.*

---

[a] See viii. 11. 10.
[b] So only Curtius ; Diodorus and Arrian differ.

13 And now they had gone so far that except as victors, they could not return without destruction, since the barbarians were rolling down huge stones upon them as they went up, and when struck by these while their footing was unsteady and slipping,
14 they fell back headlong. Nevertheless Alexander and Charus, whom the king had sent ahead with thirty selected men, had gained the height and were already fighting hand to hand ; but since the barbarians showered javelins upon them from above, they themselves were wounded more often than they
15 inflicted wounds. Therefore Alexander,[a] remembering his name and his promise, while fighting more fearlessly than cautiously, was struck from every side
16 and overwhelmed. When Charus saw him lying prostrate, unmindful of everything except revenge he began to rush upon the enemy and killed many with his lance, some with his sword ; but when so many assailed one man, he fell lifeless upon the body
17 of his friend. The king, troubled as was natural by the death of these most valiant young men and of the
18 rest of his soldiers, gave the signal for retreat. They saved themselves by withdrawing gradually and unterrified, and the barbarians, content with having dislodged the enemy, did not follow them up as they
19 gave ground. But although Alexander had decided to abandon the attempt [b]—for no hope was offered of getting possession of the rock—yet he made a show of persisting in the siege. For he ordered the roads to be beset, and the towers to be advanced, and others to take the place of the wearied.
20 When his persistence was known, the Indi feasted for two days and two nights with a display, not only of confidence, but even of victory, beating drums

21 pulsantes ; tertia vero nocte tympanorum quidem
strepitus desierat audiri, ceterum ex tota petra faces
refulgebant, quas accenderant barbari ut tutior esset
22 ipsis fuga obscura nocte per invia saxa cursuris. Rex,
Balacro qui specularetur praemisso, cognoscit petram
fuga Indorum esse desertam. Tum dato signo ut
universi conclamarent, incomposite fugientibus me-
23 tum incussit; multique, tamquam adesset hostis, per
lubrica saxa perque invias cotes praecipitati occi-
derunt, plures, aliqua membrorum parte mulcati, ab
24 integris deserti sunt. Rex, locorum magis quam
hostium victor, tamen magnae victoriae speciem[1]
sacrificiis et cultu deum fecit. Arae in petra locatae
25 sunt Minervae Victoriae.[2] Ducibus itineris quo[3]
subire iusserat leviter armatos, etsi promissis minora
praestiterant, pretium cum fide redditum est, petrae
regionisque ei adiunctae Sisocosto tutela permissa.

XII. Inde processit Ecbolima et, cum angustias
itineris obsideri xx milibus armatorum ab Erice
quodam comperisset, gravius agmen exercitus Coeno
2 ducendum modicis itineribus tradidit, ipse prae-
gressus per[4] funditores ac sagittarios, deturbatis qui
obsederant[5] saltum, sequentibus se copiis viam fecit.
3 Indi[6] sive odio ducis sive gratiam victoris inituri,
Ericen fugientem adorti interemerunt, caputque eius

---

[1] speciem *added by Mützell.*
[2] Victoriae *Stangl;* uictoriaeque *A.*
[3] quo *Zumpt;* quos *A.*   [4] per *added by Bentley.*
[5] obsederant *Giunta;* obsiderant *A.*
[6] Indi *J. Froben;* inde *A.*

---

[a] See Arr. iii. 12. 3 ; iii. 13. 5 ; iv. 4. 6. Which one of
three or more of this name is referred to is uncertain.
[b] *Cf.* Arr. iv. 30. 4, where Sisicottos.
[c] See Arr. iv. 28. 7, but the location is uncertain.
[d] The name is uncertain.

21 according to their custom; but on the third night the noise of the drums had ceased to be heard, but from the whole rock torches gleamed, which the barbarians had lighted in order that their flight might be safer, since they would have to run over pathless rocks

22 in the darkness of night. The king, having sent Balacrus [a] to reconnoitre, learned that the rock was deserted and the Indi in flight. Then, when the signal had been given for all to raise a shout, he struck

23 fear into them as they fled in disorder; and many, as if the enemy were at hand, were killed by throwing themselves over the slippery stones and pathless crags, still more, disabled in some part of their limbs,

24 were deserted by those who escaped injury. The king, although victor rather over the locality than over the enemy, yet made the show of a great triumph by sacrifices and worship of the gods. Altars to

25 Minerva Victoria were set up on the rock. To the guides of the road by which he had ordered the light-armed troops to go up, although they had accomplished less than they had promised, the reward was faithfully paid, and the government of the rock, and of the district adjoining it, was entrusted to Sisocostus.[b]

XII. From there the king went on to Ecbolima,[c] and when he had found that a narrow part of the road was blocked by a certain Erices [d] with 20,000 armed men, he turned over the heavier part of the army to

2 Coenus to be led at a moderate pace, and he himself, going ahead, dislodged by slingers and archers those who had beset the narrows, and make a way for the

3 forces which were following him. The Indi, either through hatred of their leader, or with the object of entering the good graces of the victor, attacked

atque arma ad Alexandrum detulerunt. Ille facto
impunitatem dedit, honorem denegavit exemplo.

4 Hinc ad flumen Indum sextisdecumis castris pervenit omniaque, ut praeceperat, ad traiciendum praeparata ab Hephaestione repperit. Regnabat in ea
regione Omphis, qui patri quoque fuerat auctor

5 dedendi regnum Alexandro et post mortem parentis
legatos miserat, qui consulerent eum regnare se
interim vellet an privatum opperiri eius adventum.

6 Permissoque,[1] ut regnaret, non tamen ius datum
usurpare sustinuit. Is benigne quidem exceperat
Hephaestionem gratuitum frumentum copiis eius
admensus, non tamen ei occurrerat, ne fidem ullius

7 nisi regis experiretur. Itaque venienti obviam cum
armato exercitu egressus est, elephanti quoque per
modica intervalla militum agmini immixti procul

8 castellorum fecerant speciem. Ac primo Alexander
non socium, sed hostem adventare credebat, iamque
et ipse arma milites capere et equites discedere[2] in
cornua iusserat, paratus ad pugnam.

At Indus, cognito Macedonum errore, iussis subsistere ceteris, ipse concitat equum quo vehebatur;
idem Alexander quoque fecit, sive hostis sive amicus

9 occurreret, vel sua virtute vel illius fide tutus. Coiere,[3]
quod ex utriusque vultu posset intellegi, amicis

---

[1] Permissoque *Modius;* praemissoque *P;* permissusque
BFL; permissique *V.*
[2] discedere *J. Froben;* descendere *A.*
[3] Coiere *Wagener;* coiret *A.*

---

[a] See viii. 10. 2.
[b] *Cf.* Diod. xvii. 86. 6; Arr. iv. 22. 6 says nothing of him.
He was son and successor of Taxiles.

Erices, who was in flight, killed him, and bore his head and armour to Alexander. He granted impunity to the deed, but refused any honour to the example.

4 From here he came on the sixteenth day to the river Indus, and found, as he had directed,ᵃ that everything had been prepared by Hephaestion for crossing it. In that region Omphis was king,ᵇ who had induced his father also to surrender his kingdom 5 to Alexander and after the death of his parent had sent envoys to ask Alexander whether he wished him to reign in the interim, or as a private citizen to await 6 his coming. But although he was allowed to be king, he nevertheless did not have the courage to use the privilege which was granted him. He indeed had received Hephaestion courteously, had measured out grain free of charge to his troops, yet had not met him, fearing to test the good faith of anyone except 7 the king. And so, when Alexander was coming near, he went out to meet him with his army equipped for action, in which he had also at moderate intervals between the companies of soldiers placed elephants, which at a distance gave the appearance of castles. 8 And Alexander at first thought that not an ally but an enemy was coming, and he also had already ordered his soldiers to take arms and the cavalry to withdraw to the wings, and was prepared for battle.

But the Indian, perceiving the mistake of the Macedonians, ordered the rest of his force to halt and himself put spurs to the horse which he was riding ; Alexander did the same, whether he came as an enemy or a friend feeling safe either through his own 9 valour or the prince's good faith. They met, as could be judged from the expression of each, in a

animis. Ceterum sine interprete non poterat conseri
sermo ; itaque, adhibito eo, barbarus occurrisse se
dixit cum exercitu, totas imperii vires protinus tradi-
turum nec exspectasse[1] dum per nuntios daretur fides.
10 Corpus suum et regnum permittere illi quem sciret
gloriae militantem nihil magis quam famam timere
perfidiae. Laetus simplicitate barbari, rex et dexteram, fidei suae pignus, dedit et regnum restituit.
11 lvi elephanti erant quos tradidit Alexandro, multaque pecora eximiae magnitudinis, tauros ad iii milia,
pretiosum in ea regione acceptumque animis regnan-
tium armentum.
12 Quaerenti Alexandro, plures agricultores haberet
an milites, cum duobus regibus bellanti sibi maiore
militum quam agrestium manu opus esse respondit.
13 Abisares et Porus erant, sed in Poro eminebat auctoritas. Uterque ultra Hydaspen amnem regnabat
et belli fortunam, quisquis arma inferret, experiri
14 decreverat. Omphis, permittente Alexandro, et
regium insigne sumpsit et more gentis suae nomen
quod patris fuerat ; Taxilen appellavere populares,
sequente nomine imperium in quemcumque transiret.
15 Igitur cum per triduum hospitaliter Alexandrum
accepisset, quarto die et quantum frumenti copiis
quas Hephaestion duxerat praebitum a se esset
ostendit, et aureas coronas ipsi amicisque omnibus,

---

[1] expectasse *Lauer;* spectasse *A.*

---

   a Sacred bulls are usual in India to-day.
   b His kingdom corresponded to modern Lahore.
   c The Jhelum.   *d* *Cf.* viii. 12. 6.
334

spirit of friendship. However, they could not talk together without an interpreter; accordingly, when one had been furnished, the barbarian said that he had met Alexander with his army, intending at once to deliver to him all the forces of his empire, and had not waited for a pledge of safety to be given through

10 messengers. He said that he entrusted his person and his realm to a prince whom he knew to be fighting for glory and to fear nothing more than a reputation for treachery. Pleased by the sincerity of the barbarian, the king gave him his hand as a pledge of

11 good faith, and restored his kingdom to him. There were fifty-six elephants, which he presented to Alexander, besides many head of sheep of extraordinary size and about 3000 bulls, a herd highly valued in that region [a] and pleasing to the minds of rulers.

12 When Alexander inquired whether he had more field-labourers or soldiers, Omphis replied that since he was at war with two kings, he needed a greater

13 force of soldiers than of farmers. These kings were Abisares and Porus,[b] but Porus was the more powerful. Both reigned beyond the river Hydaspes,[c] and they had decided to try the fortune of war against

14 anyone who attacked them. Omphis with the permission of Alexander assumed the royal diadem, and according to the usage of his race took the name which his father had had; the people called him Taxiles, a name which went with the sovereignty

15 of whoever succeeded to it. Having then entertained Alexander as his guest for three days, on the fourth day he both made known how much grain he had furnished to the forces which Hephaestion had brought,[d] and gave golden crowns to Alexander

praeter haec signati argenti LXXX talenta dono dedit.

16 Qua benignitate eius Alexander mire laetus, et quae is dederat remisit et M talenta ex praeda quam vehebat adiecit, multaque convivalia ex auro et argento vasa, plurimum Persicae vestis, XXX equos ex suis cum eisdem insignibus quis assueverant cum ipsum veherent.

17 Quae liberalitas, sicut barbarum obstrinxerat, ita amicos ipsius vehementer offendit. E quibus Meleager super cenam, largiore vino usus, gratulari se Alexandro dixit quod saltem in India repperisset

18 dignum talentis M. Rex haud oblitus quam aegre tulisset quod Clitum ob linguae temeritatem occidisset, iram quidem tenuit, sed dixit invidos nomines nihil aliud quam ipsorum esse tormenta.

XIII. Postero die legati Abisarae adiere regem ; omnia dicioni eius, ita ut mandatum erat, permittebant, firmataque invicem fide, remittuntur ad regem.

2 Porum quoque nominis sui fama ratus ad deditionem posse compelli, misit ad eum Cleocharen qui denuntiaret ei ut stipendium penderet et in primo suorum finium aditu occurreret regi. Porus alterum ex his facturum sese respondit, ut intranti regnum suum

3 praesto esset, sed armatus. Iam Hydaspen Alexander superare decreverat, cum Barzaentes,[1] defectionis Arachosiis auctor, vinctus trigintaque elephanti

---

[1] Barzaentes *Letellier;* barzaentis *F corr. LP;* barzentis *BV;* barzentis *F m. pr.*

---

[a] *Cf.* iii. 13. 16.   [b] *Cf.* Plut. *Alex.* lix. 3.
[c] Arr. v. 8. 3.   [d] See vi. 6. 36.

and to all his friends, and besides these eighty talents
16 of coined silver [a] as a gift. Alexander, wonderfully
pleased by his generosity, both returned what he had
given and added 1000 talents from the booty which
he was carrying, besides many gold and silver vessels
for use at table, a quantity of Persian robes, and
thirty of his own horses with the same trappings to
which they were accustomed when he himself rode
them.

17 This liberality, although it put the barbarian under
an obligation, yet seriously offended the king's
friends.[b] One of them, Meleager, having indulged
too freely in wine, said at table that he congratulated
Alexander that at least in India he had found a man
18 deserving of 1000 talents. The king, not forgetting
how deeply he had regretted having killed Clitus
because of his rash language, restrained his anger,
but said that jealous men were nothing less than
self-tormentors.

XIII. On the following day envoys [c] of Abisares
came to the king. They, according to their orders,
surrendered everything into his power; and having
given and received a pledge of good faith, they were
2 sent back to their king. Thinking that Porus also
could be forced to surrender by the fame of his name,
Alexander sent Cleochares to him to demand that he
should pay tribute and meet Alexander at the frontier
of his territories. Porus replied that he would com-
ply with the second of these demands, that he would
be on hand when Alexander entered his realm, but it
3 would be in arms. Alexander had already decided
to cross the Hydaspes River, when Barzaentes,[d] the
instigator of the revolt of the Arachosii, was brought
to him in fetters, as well as thirty elephants which

simul capti perducuntur, opportunum adversus Indos auxilium; quippe plus in beluis quam in exercitu
4 spei ac virium illis erat. Damaraxus quoque,[1] rex
exiguae partis Indorum, qui Barzaenti se coniunxerat,
5 vinctus adductus est. Igitur, transfuga et regulo in
custodiam, elephantis autem Taxili traditis, ad
amnem Hydaspen pervenit, in cuius ulteriore ripa
Porus consederat, transitu prohibiturus hostem.
6 LXXX et V elephantos obiecerat eximio corporum
robore ultraque eos currus CCC et peditum XXX fere
milia, in quis erant sagittarii, sicuti ante dictum est,
gravioribus telis, quam ut apte excuti possent.
7   Ipsum vehebat elephantus super ceteras beluas
eminens, armaque auro et argento distincta corpus
rarae magnitudinis honestabant. Par animus robori
corporis et, quanta inter rudes poterat esse, sapientia.
8 Macedonas non conspectus hostium solum, sed etiam
fluminis quod transeundum erat magnitudo terrebat. IIII in latitudinem stadia diffusus profundo
alveo et nusquam[2] vada aperiente speciem vasti
9 maris fecerat. Nec pro spatio aquarum late stagnan-
tium impetum coercebat, sed quasi in artum coeuntibus ripis, torrens et elisus ferebatur, occultaque saxa
inesse ostendebant pluribus locis undae repercussae.
10 Terribilior facies erat ripae, quam equi virique compleverant. Stabant ingentes vastorum corporum
moles et, de industria irritatae, horrendo stridore

---

[a] *Cf.* viii. 14. 13 ; Plut. *Alex.* lx. ; Arr. v. 19. 1.
[b] On the size of the rivers of India at the time of Alexander's march see Arr. v. 9. 4.
[c] That is, it was not less rapid for being wide.
[d] *i.e.* elephants.

had been captured at the same time with him, a timely aid against the Indi ; for they had more hope and strength in those beasts than in their army.

4 Damaraxus also, the king of a small district of India, who had allied himself with Barzaentes, was brought

5 to Alexander in fetters. Accordingly, when the deserter and the prince had been put under guard and the elephants given to Taxiles, Alexander came to the river Hydaspes, on whose farther bank Porus had taken position, intending to prevent the enemy

6 from crossing. Porus had put in front eighty-five elephants of extraordinary strength of body, and behind these 300 chariots and about 30,000 foot-soldiers, among whom were archers with heavier arrows, as was said before, than they could shoot to advantage.

7 Porus himself was mounted upon an elephant towering above the rest of the brutes, and armour decorated with gold and silver adorned a body of unusual stature.[a] His courage was equal to his strength of body, and his wisdom was as great as

8 could be found among uncultivated folk. Not merely the appearance of the enemy, but also the size [b] of the river that must be crossed terrified the Macedonians. Extending to a width of four stadia, with a deep channel which nowhere disclosed a ford, it gave

9 the impression of a vast sea. And it did not check its swift course in proportion to the extent of its widely spread waters,[c] but as if confined by its banks to a narrow channel, it rushed on in a foaming torrent, and rebounding billows revealed hidden

10 rocks in many places. Still more formidable was the appearance of the bank, which had been filled with horses and men. There stood huge masses of vast bodies,[d] and when they were purposely irritated they

11 aures fatigabant. Hinc amnis, hinc hostis, capacia
quidem bonae spei pectora et saepe sane[1] experta,
improviso tamen pavore percusserant. Quippe instabiles rates nec dirigi ad ripam nec tuto applicari
posse credebant.

12 Erant in medio amne insulae crebrae, in quas et
Indi et Macedones nantes, levatis super capita armis,
transibant. Ibi levia proelia conserebantur, et uterque rex parvae rei discrimine summae experiebatur

13 eventum. Ceterum in Macedonum exercitu temeritate atque audacia insignes fuere Hegesimachus et
Nicanor, nobiles iuvenes et perpetua partium felici-

14 tate ad spernendum omne periculum accensi ; quis
ducibus promptissimi iuvenum, lanceis modo armati,
transnavere in insulam quam frequens hostis tenebat, multosque Indorum, nulla re melius quam

15 audacia armati, interemerunt. Abire cum gloria
poterant, si umquam temeritas felix[2] inveniret
modum ; sed dum supervenientes contemptim et
superbe quoque exspectant, circumventi ab eis qui

16 occulti enaverant eminus obruti telis sunt. Qui
effugerant hostem aut impetu amnis ablati sunt
aut verticibus[3] impliciti. Eaque pugna multum Pori
fiduciam erexit cuncta cernentis e ripa.

17 Alexander inops consilii tandem ad fallendum
hostem talem dolum intendit. Erat insula in flumine

---

[1] sane *Hedicke;* se *A.*   [2] infelix *C.*
[3] verticibus *C;* uorticibus *A.*

---

[a] *Cf.* iv. 2. 9.   [b] *Cf.* iv. 16. 4.
[c] Arr. v. 11. ff. ; Plut. *Alex.* lx. 1 from Alexander's own
Memoirs ; see C. A. Robinson, *The Ephemerides of Alexander's Expedition,* Providence, Brown University, 1932, and
bibliography, p. 7.   [d] Arr. v. 11. 1.

11 wearied the ears with their hideous trumpeting. On
one hand the river, on the other the enemy had
nevertheless struck unlooked-for terror into breasts
which were indeed capable of good hope and had
surely often seen such hope realized. For they
thought that the unsteady [a] boats could not be
steered to the bank nor landed there in safety.

12   There were in midstream numerous islands, to
which both the Indi and the Macedonians crossed by
swimming, raising their weapons over their heads.
There light skirmishing took place, and both kings
by the decision of these small contests were testing

13 the outcome of the main struggle. Now there were
in the army of the Macedonians Hegesimachus and
Nicanor, high-born youths conspicuous for rashness
and daring, aroused by the constant good fortune of

14 their side [b] to despise all dangers ; under their lead
the most active of the young men, armed only with
lances, swam across to an island which a crowd of the
enemy held and, armed with nothing better than

15 daring, slew many of the Indi. They might have
come off with glory if successful rashness were ever
capable of moderation; but while they were awaiting
contemptuously and even haughtily those who were
coming against them, they were surrounded by those
who had secretly swum out and were overwhelmed

16 by weapons hurled at long range. Those who had
escaped the enemy were swept away by the force of
the river or swallowed up in the whirlpools. And
this battle greatly increased the confidence of Porus,
who saw the whole event from the bank.

17   Alexander, uncertain what to do, finally devised
the following stratagem [c] to deceive the enemy.
There was an island [d] in the river larger than the

amplior ceteris, silvestris eadem et tegendis insidiis
apta, fossa quoque praealta haud procul ripa quam
tenebat ipse non pedites modo sed etiam cum equis
18 viros poterat abscondere; igitur ut a custodia huius
opportunitatis oculos hostium averteret, Ptolemaeum
omnibus turmis obequitare iussit procul insula et
subinde Indos clamore terrere, quasi flumen transna-
19 turus foret. Per complures dies Ptolemaeus id fecit
eoque consilio Porum quoque agmen suum ei parti
quam se petere simulabat coegit advertere. Iam
20 extra conspectum hostis insula erat. Alexander in
diversa parte ripae statui suum tabernaculum iussit
assuetamque comitari ipsum cohortem ante id tabernaculum stare et omnem apparatum regiae magnifi-
21 centiae hostium oculis de industria ostendi. Attalum
etiam, aequalem sibi et haud disparem habitu oris
et corporis, utique cum procul viseretur, veste regia
exornat, praebiturum speciem ipsum regem illi ripae
praesidere nec cogitare[1] de transitu.
22   Huius consilii effectum primo morata tempestas
est, mox adiuvit, incommoda quoque ad bonos even-
23 tus vertente Fortuna. Traicere amnem cum ceteris
copiis in regionem insulae de qua ante dictum est
parabat, averso hoste in eos, qui cum Ptolemaeo
inferiorem obsederant ripam, cum procella imbrem
24 vix sub tectis tolerabilem effundit. Obrutique

[1] cogitare *Vogel;* agitare *A.*

---

[a] According to Arr. v. 13. 1, Ptolemy remained with the
king.   [b] Arrian says nothing of this.
[c] For details see Arr. v. 12. 2.

rest, wooded also and suitable for concealing an ambuscade, moreover in a very deep ditch not far from the bank which he himself held he could conceal not only foot-soldiers but even men and their horses;

18 therefore, in order to distract the enemy's attention from guarding against this advantageous place, he ordered Ptolemy [a] with all his cavalry to ride to a point far from that island, and from time to time to alarm the Indi by shouts, as if they were going to

19 swim across the river. For many days Ptolemy did this, and by this device compelled Porus also to turn his army to that part at which he pretended to be aiming. Already the island was out of the enemy's

20 sight. Alexander ordered his tent to be pitched on a different part of the bank, and the cohort which usually attended him to stand before that tent and all the equipment of royal magnificence to be purposely

21 displayed before the eyes of the foe. Attalus [b] also, of the same age as himself and not unlike him in face and figure, especially when he was seen from a distance, he adorned with the royal robe, in order to give the impression that the king himself was encamped on that part of the bank and was not thinking of crossing.

22 The carrying out of this plan was first delayed then furthered by a storm, since Fortune turned even

23 obstacles to good results. He was preparing to cross the river with the rest [c] of his forces to the shore near the island of which mention was made before, having diverted the attention of the enemy against those who, with Ptolemy, had occupied a part of the bank farther down the river, when a tempest poured out rain which was scarcely to be endured by people

24 under cover. And the soldiers, overwhelmed by the

milites nimbo in terram refugerunt, navigiis ratibus-
que desertis, sed tumultuantium fremitus, obstre-
pentibus ventis, ab hoste non poterat audiri. Deinde
momento temporis repressus est imber, ceterum adeo
spissae intendere se nubes, ut conderent lucem
vixque colloquentium inter ipsos facies noscitarentur.
25 Terruisset alium obducta nox caelo, cum ignoto amne
navigandum esset, forsitan hoste eam ipsam ripam
26 quam caeci atque improvidi petebant tenente. At[1]
rex, periculo gloriam accersens et[2] obscuritatem quae
ceteros terrebat suam occasionem ratus, dato signo
ut omnes silentio escenderent in rates,[3] eam qua
27 ipse vehebatur primam iussit expelli. Vacua erat
ab hostibus ripa quae petebatur ; quippe adhuc
Porus Ptolomaeum tantum intuebatur. Una ergo
navi, quam petrae fluctus illiserat, haerente ceterae
evadunt, armaque capere milites et ire in ordines[4]
iussit.

XIV. Iamque agmen in cornua divisum ipse ducebat, cum Poro nuntiatur armis virisque ripam ob-
tineri et rerum adesse discrimen. Ac primo humani
ingenii vitio spei suae indulgens, Abisaren belli
socium—et ita convenerat—adventare credebat.
2 Mox liquidiore luce aperiente aciem[5] hostium, c
quadrigas et IIII milia equitum venienti agmini

[1] petebant tenente. At rex *Jeep;* et ex *A.*
[2] accersens et *Jeep;* accerserant *A.*
[3] rates *J. Froben;* ratem *A.*
[4] ordines *Acidalius;* ordinem *A.*
[5] aciem *Bentley;* hostem *A.*

a Arr. v. 12. 3.
b According to Plut. *Alex.* lx. 2, the attempt was made
by night.
c See Arr. v. 13. 1.   d *Cf.* viii. 13. 1.

storm, fled back to the land, deserting the boats and the rafts, but the uproar made by the bustling men was drowned*a* by the noisy gusts of wind and could not be heard by the enemy. Then in a moment the rain ceased,*b* but such thick clouds overspread the sky that they hid the light, and men who were talking together 25 could scarcely recognize each other's faces. The night that darkened the sky would have terrified anyone else, since it was necessary to sail upon an unknown river, when perhaps the enemy were holding that very bank at which they were blindly and recklessly 26 aiming. But the king, inviting glory by courting danger, and thinking that the obscurity which terrified the rest was his opportunity, having given the signal for all silently to embark in the boats, ordered the one in which he himself was carried to be 27 pushed off first. The bank at which they aimed was deserted *c* by the enemy; for Porus was still watching Ptolemy only. Therefore only one boat, which a wave had dashed upon a rock, was stranded ; the rest reached their goal, and Alexander ordered his soldiers to arm themselves and take their places in the ranks.

XIV. And now the army had formed its wings and the king himself was leading it, when it was announced to Porus that the bank was held by armed men and that a dangerous moment was at hand. And at first, by that defect of the human mind which indulges wishful thinking, he believed that Abisares, his ally in the war, was coming,*d* for so it 2 had been agreed. But presently, as the light grew clearer and revealed the enemy's battle line, Porus sent 100 four-horse chariots and 4000 horsemen to oppose the advancing column. The leader of the

obiecit.   Dux erat copiarum quas praemisit Spitaces,[1]
3 frater ipsius, summa virium in curribus; senos viros
singuli vehebant, duos clipeatos, duos sagittarios ab
utroque latere dispositos, aurigae erant ceteri, haud
sane inermes ; quippe iacula complura, ubi comminus proeliandum erat, omissis habenis, in hostem
4 ingerebant.   Ceterum vix ullus usus huius auxilii
eo die fuit.   Namque, ut supra dictum est, imber
violentius quam alias fusus, campos lubricos et
inequitabiles fecerat, gravesque et propemodum
immobiles currus illuvie ac voraginibus haerebant.
5 Contra Alexander expedito ac levi agmine strenue
invectus est.   Scythae et Dahae primi omnium in-
vasere Indos ; Perdiccam deinde cum equitibus in
dextrum cornu hostium emisit.
6   Iam undique pugna se moverat, cum ei qui currus
agebant illud ultimum auxilium suorum rati, effusis
7 habenis in medium discrimen ruere coeperunt.   Anceps id malum utrisque erat.   Nam et Macedonum
pedites primo impetu obterebantur, et per lubrica
atque invia immissi currus excutiebant eos a quibus
8 regebantur.   Aliorum turbati equi non in voragines
modo lacunasque, sed etiam in amnem praecipitavere
9 curricula, pauci telis[2] hostium exacti, penetravere ad
Porum acerrime pugnam cientem.   Is, ut dissipatos
tota acie currus vagari sine rectoribus vidit, proximis
10 amicorum distribuit elephantos.   Post eos posuerat

---

[1] Spitaces *Anspach;* hages *A.*
[2] telis *Snakenburg;* tenus *C;* tamen *P m. pr. B m. sec.*

---

[a] Porus' son, according to Arr. v. 14. 3.
[b] Arr. v. 13. 1 ; v. 12. 2.
[c] *pugna se moverat* is a unique expression, but with some
analogies.

troops which he sent was Spitaces, his brother,[a] and the greater part of his strength was in his chariots ;

3 each of these carried six men, two with bucklers, two archers stationed on each side, the rest were the drivers, who were by no means unarmed ; for when it was necessary to fight hand to hand, they dropped the reins and poured a shower of javelins upon the enemy.

4 However, on that day this aid was of hardly any use ; for, as was said above, the rain which had fallen with greater violence than usual had made the plains slippery and unfit for riding, and the heavy and almost immovable chariots stuck fast in the muck and

5 mudholes. On the other hand, Alexander with his unencumbered and light-armed force charged them vigorously. The Scythians and the Dahae first of all attacked the Indi ; then Alexander sent Perdiccas [b] with the cavalry against the right wing of the enemy.

6 And already the battle had begun [c] everywhere, when those who drove the chariots, thinking it the last possible aid for their side, began to rush with loose

7 rein into the midst of the contest. This was a common evil for both sides. For the foot-soldiers of the Macedonians were trampled at the first attack, and the chariots sent over the slippery and impassable ground

8 shook off those who guided them. The frightened horses of others dragged the chariots not only into

9 the mudholes and pools, but even into the river, a few, driven by the enemy's weapons, made their way to Porus, who was vigorously urging on the fight. He, when he saw the chariots wandering all over the field without drivers, distributed [d] the elephants to

10 those of his friends who were nearest to him. Behind

---

[a] Arr. v. 14. 4 ff. gives a clear and full account of Porus' army.

peditem ac sagittarios et[1] tympana pulsare solitos;
id pro cantu tubarum Indis erat, nec strepitu eorum
movebantur, olim ad notum sonum auribus mitigatis.

11 Herculis simulacrum agmini peditum praeferebatur;
id maximum erat bellantibus incitamentum, et
deseruisse gestantis militare flagitium habebatur.

12 Capitis etiam sanxerant poenam eis[2] qui ex acie non
rettulissent, metu quem ex illo hoste quondam con-
ceperant etiam in religionem venerationemque
converso. Macedonas non beluarum modo, sed

13 etiam ipsius regis aspectus parumper inhibuit. Beluae
dispositae inter armatos speciem turrium procul
fecerant, ipse Porus humanae magnitudinis prope
modum excesserat; speciem[3] magnitudini Pori
adicere videbatur belua qua vehebatur tantum inter
ceteras eminens quanto aliis ipse praestabat.

14 Itaque Alexander contemplatus et regem et agmen Indorum : " Tandem," inquit, " par animo meo
periculum video cum bestiis simul et cum egregiis

15 viris res est." Intuensque Coenon : " Cum ego,"
inquit, " Ptolomaeo Perdiccaque et Hephaestione
comitatus in laevum hostium cornu impetum fecero,
viderisque me in medio ardore certaminis, ipse ad[4]
dextrum move et turbatis signa infer. Tu, Antigene,

---

[1] et *added in* I.   [2] iis *Vindelinus;* his *A.*
[3] speciem *Hedicke;* formam *A.*   [4] ad *added by Capps.*

---

[a] There seems to be no evidence for this ; probably the
Indian god Vishnu is meant.

[b] That is, behind them but fitting into the intervals (100
feet) between them (Arr. v. 15. 4 ff.).

[c] According to Arrian (v. 19. 1), it was " over five cubits "

these he had stationed the infantry and the archers, as well as those who were accustomed to beat the drums; this with the Indi took the place of the sound of trumpets, and the elephants were not terrified by the noise, since their ears had been long since trained
11 to the familiar sound. A statue of Hercules [a] was carried at the head of the infantry force ; this was a very great incentive to the combatants, and to have abandoned those who were carrying it was held
12 to be a military disgrace. They even decreed the penalty of death to those who should not bring it back from the field of battle, since the fear which they had once felt of that enemy had been changed even to adoration and veneration. The Macedonians were checked for a time, by the sight not only of the elephants but of the king himself.
13 The beasts, stationed [b] between lines of armed men, at a distance looked like towers, while Porus himself had almost exceeded the measure of human stature [c] ; the beast on which he rode seemed to add to his height, since it rose as much higher than the other elephants as he did above the rest of his men.
14 Accordingly Alexander, contemplating both the king and the army of the Indi, said : " At last I behold a danger worthy of my spirit ; I am dealing at the same time with beasts and with remarkable
15 men." Then, looking at Coenus, he said : " When I, attended by Ptolemy, Perdiccas, and Hephaestion, have made a charge against the left wing of the enemy and you see me in the thick of the brunt of battle, do you move to the right wing and attack the enemy while they are in disorder. You, Antigenes,

(7 feet, 6 inches) ; according to Plut. *Alex.* lx. 6, four cubits and a span (6 feet, 3 inches).

et tu, Leonnate, et Tauron, iam invehemini[1] in
16 mediam aciem et urgebitis frontem. Hastae nostrae
praelongae et validae non alias magis quam adversus beluas rectoresque earum usui esse poterunt;
deturbate eos qui vehuntur et ipsas confodite.
Anceps genus auxilii est et in suos acrius furit ; in
hostem enim imperio, in suos pavore agitur."
17 Haec elocutus concitat equum primus. Iamque,
ut destinatum erat, invaserat ordines hostium, cum
18 Coenus ingenti vi in laevum cornu invehitur. Phalanx
quoque mediam Indorum aciem uno impetu perrupit.
At Porus, qua equitem invehi senserat, beluas agi
iussit ; sed tardum et paene immobile animal equo-
19 rum velocitatem aequare non poterat. Ne sagittarum quidem ullus erat barbaris usus. Quippe
longas[2] et praegraves, nisi prius in terra statuerunt[3]
arcum, haud satis apte et commode imponunt, tum,
humo lubrica et ob id impediente conatum, molientes
20 ictus celeritate hostium occupantur. Ergo spreto
regis imperio—quod fere fit, ubi turbatis acrius
metus quam dux imperare coepit—totidem erant
21 imperatores quot agmina errabant ; alius iungere
aciem, alius dividere, stare quidam et nonnulli cir-
cumvehi terga hostium iubebant ; nihil in medium
22 consulebatur. Porus tamen cum paucis quibus metu

---

[1] iam invehemini *Hedicke;* non inuaehimini *P;* inuehi-
mini *C.*   [2] longas *J. Froben;* longae *A.*
[3] statuerunt *Kinch,* -erent *A.*

---

[a] With *ad dextrum move* in § 15 Curtius is intelligible and
consistent with Arrian v. 16. 3. Coenus had his own and
Demetrius' troops.
[b] *Cf.* viii. 9. 28, and note *c.*   [c] *Cf.* Diod. xvii. 88.

and you, Leonnatus, and Tauron, will at the same
time advance against the centre and attack their front.

16 Our spears, which are very long and strong, will never
serve us better than against these beasts and their
drivers; bring down those who are mounted on them
and stab the brutes. It is a doubtful kind of
strength, and rages more violently against its own
men; for it is driven against the enemy by command,
against its own men by fear."

17 Having said this, he was the first to put spurs to
his horse. And already, as had been planned, he had
plunged into the ranks of the enemy, when Coenus

18 with mighty force charged the left wing.[a] The
phalanx too at the first onset burst through the
middle of the line of the Indi. But Porus, where
he saw that the cavalry were charging, ordered the
elephants to be advanced, but that animal, being
slow and well-nigh immovable, could not equal the

19 speed of the horses. The barbarians too could make
no use of their arrows. For since these were long and
very heavy, they could not safely and conveniently
fit them to the bow[b] unless they first rested its end
upon the earth, and as the ground was slippery and
therefore interfered with attempting this, by the time
they were ready to take aim they were overtaken

20 by the speed of the enemy. Therefore, disregarding[c]
the king's order—which generally happens when it is
fear rather than a leader that begins to issue the
sharper commands to men who are in great confusion
—there were as many commanders as there were

21 scattered bands; one was giving orders to unite the
line of battle, another to divide it, some to stand fast,
and others to envelop the enemy from behind;

22 there was no general plan of action. Porus, how-

potior fuerat pudor colligere dispersos, obvius hosti
ire pergit elephantosque ante agmen suorum agi
23 iubet. Magnum beluae iniecere terrorem, insolitus-
que stridor non equos modo, tam pavidum ad omnia
animal, sed viros quoque ordinesque turbaverat.
24 Iam fugae circumspiciebant locum paulo ante
victores, cum Alexander Agrianos et Thracas leviter
armatos, meliorem[1] concursatione quam comminus
25 militem, emisit in beluas. Ingentem hi vim telorum
iniecere et elephantis et regentibus eos. Phalanx
26 quoque instare constanter territis coepit. Sed quidam avidius persecuti beluas in semet irritavere
vulneribus. Obtriti ergo pedibus earum ceteris ut
27 parcius instarent fuere documentum. Praecipue
terribilis illa facies erat, cum manu arma virosque
28 corriperent et super se regentibus traderent. Anceps
ergo pugna nunc sequentium, nunc fugientium
elephantos, in multum diei varium certamen extraxit,
donec securibus—id namque genus auxilii praepara-
29 tum erat—pedes amputare coeperunt. Copidas
vocabant gladios leviter curvatos, falcibus similes,
quis appetebant beluarum manus. Nec quicquam
inexpertum non mortis modo, sed etiam in ipsa morte
novi supplicii timor omittebat.
30 Ergo elephanti vulneribus tandem fatigati, suos
impetu sternunt, et qui rexerant eos praecipitati in

---

[1] meliorem *Lauer;* meliore *A.*

---

[a] Changing the position they held in viii. 14. 13.
[b] Diod. xvii. 88 gives a vivid description.
[c] For *obtriti pedibus cf.* vii. 11. 16.

352

ever, with a few over whom shame had more power
than fear, proceeded to collect his scattered forces
and to advance against the foe, giving orders that
the elephants be put in front of his line of troops.[a]

23 The brutes caused great terror, and their trumpeting
not only threw into confusion the horses, animals so
fearful of everything, but also the men and the ranks.

24 And already those who shortly before were victors
were looking about for an opportunity for flight,
when Alexander sent against the elephants the light-
armed Agriani and the other Thracians, troops

25 better in a rapid attack[b] than in close combat. These
cast a great shower of weapons both upon the elephants and upon those who were guiding them. The
phalanx also began steadily to attack the terrified

26 animals. But some, who pursued the elephants too
eagerly, so irritated them by wounds that they
turned upon them. Hence, being trampled under
foot,[c] they served to the rest as a lesson to attack

27 with greater caution. It was a particularly awful
spectacle when with their trunks they seized men and
their weapons and passed them over their heads to

28 the drivers. As a result, the shifting battle, as they
now pursued and now fled from the elephants, prolonged the undecided contest until late in the day,
when with axes—for that kind of help had been prepared beforehand—they began to cut off their feet.

29 With slightly curved swords, like sickles, which they
called *copides*, they attacked the brutes' trunks.
And their fear left nothing untried, not only in dealing death, but also in new ways of making death
itself painful.

30 Therefore the elephants, at last worn out by
wounds, rushed upon and overthrew their own men,

terram, ab ipsis obterebantur. Iamque[1] pecorum
modo magis pavidi quam infesti ultra aciem exige-
31 bantur, cum Porus, destitutus a pluribus, tela multa[2]
ante praeparata in circumfusos ex elephanto suo
coepit ingerere. Multisque eminus vulneratis, expo-
32 situs ipse ad ictus undique petebatur. Novem iam
vulnera hinc tergo, illinc pectore exceperat, multoque
sanguine profuso, languidis manibus magis elapsa
33 quam excussa tela mittebat. Nec segnius belua
instincta rabie, nondum saucia, invehebatur ordinibus, donec rector beluae regem conspexit, fluentibus
membris omissisque armis, vix compotem mentis.
34 Tum beluam in fugam concitat, sequente Alexandro ·
sed equus eius, multis vulneribus confossus defi-
ciensque, procubuit, posito magis rege quam effuso.
35 Itaque, dum equum mutat, tardius insecutus est.
Interim frater Taxilis, regis Indorum, praemissus
ab Alexandro, monere coepit Porum, ne ultima ex-
36 periri perseveraret dederetque se victori. At ille,
quamquam exhaustae erant vires deficiebatque sanguis, tamen ad notam vocem excitatus: " Agnosco,"
inquit, " Taxilis fratrem, imperii regnique sui pro-
ditoris," et telum, quod unum forte non effluxerat,
contorsit in eum ; quod per medium pectus pene·

---

[1] Iamque *Mützell;* itaque *A.*   [2] multa *Vogel;* multo *A.*

---

[a] Only when they believed that Porus was dead, Diod.
xvii. 88. 7.
[b] *fluentibus membris* ; *cf.* Livy xxxviii. 17. 7.

and those who had guided them were hurled to the
ground and trampled to death by them. And now
like cattle, more frightened than dangerous, they
31 were being driven off the field of battle, when Porus,
abandoned by very many of his followers,[a] began from
his own elephant to pour upon those who surrounded
him many javelins which had been made ready in
advance. And although he wounded many at long
range, he himself was exposed to shots from every
32 side. He had already suffered nine wounds, now in
his back, now in his breast, and had lost so much
blood that his arms were weak and the weapons
which he tried to throw rather fell from his hands
33 than were hurled with any force. His elephant too,
roused to madness and not yet wounded, charged
with no less vigour against the enemy's ranks, until
the driver of the beast saw that the king had
collapsed,[b] had dropped his weapons, and was hardly
34 conscious. Then he urged the monster to flight,
pursued by Alexander ; but the king's horse, which
had been pierced by many shafts and was giving out,
fell under him, rather dismounting him than throwing
him off. And so, while he was changing his horse he
35 pursued more slowly. Meanwhile the brother of
Taxiles, king of the Indi, being sent ahead by Alexander, began to advise Porus not to persist in resisting
to the bitter end, but to surrender himself to the
36 victor. But he, although his strength was exhausted
and he had lost much blood, nevertheless, aroused by
the familiar voice, said : " I recognize the brother of
Taxiles, the betrayer of his kingdom and his country,"
and hurled at him the only javelin which, as it
happened, had not fallen from his hands ; and it
passed through the middle of his breast and came

37 travit ad tergum. Hoc ultimo virtutis opere edito, fugere acrius coepit. Sed elephantus quoque, qui multa exceperat tela, deficiebat; itaque sistit fugam peditemque sequenti hosti obiecit.

38 Iam Alexander consecutus erat et, pertinacia Pori cognita, vetabat resistentibus parci. Ergo undique et in pedites et in ipsum Porum tela congesta sunt,

39 quis tandem[1] gravatus labi ex belua coepit. Indus qui elephantum regebat descendere eum ratus, more solito elephantum procumbere iussit in genua ; qui ut se submisit, ceteri quoque—ita enim instituti erant —demisere corpora in terram. Ea res et Porum et

40 ceteros victoribus tradidit. Rex spoliari corpus Pori, interemptum esse credens, iubet, et, qui detraherent loricam vestemque, concurrere, cum belua dominum tueri et spoliantes coepit appetere levatumque corpus eius rursus dorso suo imponere. Ergo telis undique obruitur, confossoque[2] eo, in vehiculum Porus imponitur.

41 Quem rex ut vidit allevantem oculos, non odio, sed miseratione commotus : " Quae, malum," inquit, " amentia te coegit, rerum mearum cognita fama, belli fortunam experiri, cum Taxilis esset in deditos clementiae meae tam propinquum tibi exemplum ? "

42 At ille : " Quoniam," inquit, " percontaris, respon-

---

[1] tandem *Giunta;* tantum A.
[2] confossoque *Aldus;* conpositoque *A.*

---

[a] Plut. *Alex.* lx. 7 follows a strange tradition.
[b] See Strabo xv. 1. 42.
[c] A somewhat strange expression under the circumstances, probably reproducing the Greek τί παθών, "what possessed you?" But see Cicero, *De Off.* ii. 15. 53.

37 out at his back. After performing this last feat of
valour Porus began to flee with greater speed. But
the elephant also, which had received many spear-
wounds, began to give out; hence Porus checked
his flight and opposed the infantry to the pursuing
enemy.

38   Already Alexander had come up with him and,
perceiving Porus' obstinacy, ordered that no quarter
be given to those who resisted. Therefore weapons
were hurled from every side both upon the foot-
soldiers and upon Porus himself, by which he was at
last overwhelmed and began to slide off his beast.

39 The Indian who was managing the animal,[a] thinking
that the king was dismounting in the usual manner,
ordered the elephant to kneel; when he did so, the
rest of the animals also—for so they had been trained
—let down their bodies to the ground. This action
delivered Porus and the rest of his company to the

40 victors. The king, believing that Porus had been
killed, ordered his body to be stripped of its armour,
and men were running up to take off his cuirass and
his robe, when the elephant began to protect [b] his
master, and to attack the spoilers, and lifting the
king's body, to place it upon his back. Therefore
the beast was overwhelmed with weapons from all
sides, and when he had been killed Porus was placed
in a chariot.

41   When the king saw him lifting his eyes, moved by
pity, not by hatred, he said: "What the mischief [c]
was the madness which forced you, knowing the fame
of my exploits, to try the fortune of war, when you had
Taxiles, so near a neighbour, as an example of my clem-

42 ency to those who submit?" But Porus answered:
"Since you ask me, I will reply with that frankness

857

debo ea libertate quam interrogando fecisti ; neminem me fortiorem esse censebam. Meas enim
noveram vires, nondum expertus tuas ; fortiorem
esse te belli docuit eventus. Sed ne sic quidem
43 parum felix sum, secundus tibi.'' Rursus inter-
rogatus quid ipse victorem statuere debere censeret:
" Quod hic," inquit, " dies tibi suadet, quo[1] expertus
44 es quam caduca felicitas esset." Plus monendo
profecit quam si precatus esset ; quippe magnitudinem animi eius interritam ac ne fortuna[2] quidem
infractam non misericordia modo, sed etiam honore
45 excipere dignatus est. Aegrum curavit haud secus
quam si pro ipso pugnasset ; confirmatum contra
spem omnium, in amicorum numerum recepit, mox
46 donavit ampliore regno quam tenuit. Nec sane
quicquam ingenium eius solidius aut constantius
habuit quam admirationem verae laudis et gloriae ;
simplicius tamen famam aestimabat in hoste quam
in cive. Quippe a suis credebat magnitudinem suam
destrui posse, eandem clariorem fore, quo maiores
fuissent quos ipse vicisset.

[1] quo *Lauer;* quod *A.*
[2] fortuna *Giunta;* fortunam *A.*

which you have granted me in asking your question.
I thought that no one was stronger than I. For I
knew my strength, but had not yet tried yours. The
outcome of war has shown that you are the stronger.
But not even so am I unhappy in being second to
43 you." Being further asked how he thought the
victor ought to treat him, he replied: "As this
day advises you, on which you have learned how
44 perishable good fortune is."[a] Porus effected more
by his admonition than if he had resorted to prayers;
for the greatness of his spirit, unterrified and un-
broken even by misfortune, Alexander saw fit to
treat, not merely with compassion, but even with
45 honour. He had the wounded man attended to as
if he had fought for him. When, contrary to the
expectation of all, he recovered, Alexander received
him into the number of his friends, and presently
gave him a kingdom greater than he had held before.[b]
46 And truly there was no stronger and more consistent
characteristic of his nature than admiration for true
merit and glory; yet he estimated fame more frankly
in an enemy than in a fellow citizen. For he believed
that by his own countrymen his greatness could be
impaired, but that it would be the more illustrious
the greater those had been whom he had conquered.

[a] Cf. Arr. v. 19. 2, who says "treat me as a king"
(βασιλικῶς μοι χρῆσαι).
[b] Cf. Arr. v. 19. 3; Plut. Alex. lx. 8.

BOOK IX

CONTENTS OF BOOK IX

Alexander advances to the Hypasis River; he subdues many nations and cities, whose manners and customs are described (i).

When he prepares to cross the Hypasis and attack two powerful nations, his soldiers show signs of weariness and reluctance to go farther. The king appeals to their devotion in an eloquent speech (ii).

Coenus replies to the king in the name of the soldiers. Alexander finally turns back after setting up twelve altars as a memorial of his expedition, and founding Nicaea and Bucephala. He prepares a fleet and sails down the Hypasis. Coenus falls ill and dies (iii).

Alexander subdues the Sibi. He suffers great peril at the confluence of the Hydaspes and the Acesines, but reaches the land of the Malli. The soldiers show renewed signs of disaffection, but a speech of the king rouses their enthusiasm. He defeats the barbarians, and in spite of the warning of a seer attacks their city (iv).

He leaps from the wall of the citadel into the midst of the enemy and, after fighting against great odds, is severely wounded but is rescued by members of his body-guard (v).

Before his wound is healed the king appears in public. His friends urge him to have more consideration for his own and the public safety. He expresses gratitude, but persists in his determination to conquer the whole world (vi).

Disturbances among the Greeks in Bactriana. Envoys from the Malli and the Sudracae offer submission. Alexander gives them a banquet, at which Dioxippus, an Athenian and Corratas, a Macedonian, fight a duel. The Greek is victor, but kills himself because of the calumnies of his enemies (vii).

Alexander sails down the Indus to Patala and subdues the neighbouring tribes. Ptolemy is wounded by a poisoned arrow, and is miraculously cured (viii).

Alexander at last satisfies his longing to reach the Ocean, not without danger from the tides and the inexperience of his sailors (ix).

Leaving Nearchus to explore the Ocean with the fleet and come back by sea, Alexander returns through the great deserts of Cedrosia, where the army suffers greatly from hunger and disease. At length they reach Carmania and pass through it in a bacchanalian procession (x).

LIBER IX

I. Alexander tam memorabili victoria laetus, qua sibi Orientis finis apertos esse censebat, Soli victimis caesis, milites quoque, quo promptioribus animis reliqua belli obirent, pro contione laudatos, docuit quidquid Indis virium fuisset, illa dimicatione prostra-
2 tum ; cetera opimam praedam fore celebratasque[1] opes in ea regione eminere quam peterent. Proinde iam vilia et obsoleta esse spolia de Persis ; gemmis margaritisque et auro atque ebore Macedoniam Graeciamque, non suas tantum domos repleturos.[2]
3 Avidi milites et pecuniae et gloriae, simul quia numquam eos affirmatio eius fefellerat, pollicentur operam ; dimissisque cum bona spe navigia exaedificari iubet, ut, cum totam Asiam percucurrisset,[3]
4 finem terrarum, mare, inviseret. Multa materia navalis in proximis montibus erat ; quam caedere aggressi magnitudinis invisitatae repperere serpentes.

---

[1] celebratasque *Lauer;* celebratesque *A.*
[2] repleturos *I;* repleturum *A.*
[3] percucurrisset *C;* percurrisset *P.*

---

[a] Diodorussays (xvii. 89. 3) that it was because that god had given him victory over the Orient. Arrian (v. 20 . merely says " to the gods."

BOOK IX

I. ALEXANDER, rejoicing in so memorable a victory, by which he believed that the bounds of the Orient were opened to him, sacrificed victims to the Sun[a]; then, in order that his soldiers also might meet the rest of the war with readier minds, he called an assembly, and after praising them informed them that whatever strength the Indi had possessed had 2 been overthrown in the recent battle; that hereafter there would be nothing but rich booty, and that world-renowned riches were conspicuous in that region to which they were on their way. Furthermore, he said that the spoils taken from [b] the Persians were now cheap and shabby, that his hearers would fill, not only their homes, but all Macedonia and Greece with gems and pearls and gold and ivory.
3 The soldiers, being eager both for wealth and for glory, and at the same time because no assertion of his had ever disappointed them, engaged their service; and when they had been dismissed full of good hope, he ordered ships to be built, in order that, when they had overrun all Asia, they might visit the 4 world's end, the sea. There was an abundance of timber[c] for ships in the neighbouring mountains, and when they began to attack it they found snakes

[b] *Cf. spolia de hostibus*, viii. 8. 9; ix. 10. 12.
[c] Especially cedar, Diod. xvii. 89. 4; Strabo xv. 1. 29.

5 Rhinocerotes quoque, rarum alibi animal, in eisdem
montibus erant. Ceterum hoc nomen beluis inditum
a Graecis; sermonis eius ignari Indi[1] aliud lingua
sua usurpant.

6 Rex, duabus urbibus conditis in utraque fluminis
quod superaverat ripa, copiarum duces coronis et
M aureis singulos donat; ceteris quoque pro portione
aut gradus[2] quem in amicitia obtinebant, aut navatae
7 operae, honos habitus est. Abisares, qui, priusquam
cum Poro dimicaretur, legatos ad Alexandrum miserat, rursus alios misit pollicentes omnia facturum
quae imperasset, modo ne cogeretur corpus suum
dedere; neque enim aut sine regio imperio victurum
8 aut regnaturum esse captivum. Cui Alexander
nuntiari iussit, si gravaretur ad se venire, ipsum ad
eum esse venturum.

Hinc, praerapido[3] amne superato, ad interiora
9 Indiae processit. Silvae erant prope in immensum
spatium diffusae procerisque et in eximiam altitu-
10 dinem editis arboribus umbrosae. Plerique rami
instar ingentium stipitum flexi in humum, rursus qua
se curvaverant erigebantur, adeo ut species esset non
rami resurgentis, sed arboris ex sua radice generatae.
11 Caeli temperies salubris; quippe et vim solis umbrae

---

[1] Indi *added by Hedicke.*   [2] gradus *Acidalius;* gradu *A.*
[3] praerapido *Hedicke;* poro *A.*

---

[a] Diod. xvii. 90. 1 says sixteen cubits in length; they were
pythons.
[b] *Cf.* viii. 9. 17, but the truth of the statement is doubtful.
[c] Nicaea and Bucephala, named in ix. 3. 23.
[d] A somewhat rare expression; *cf.* Livy vii. 1. 8; xxxiv.
50. 7. So also *pro rata portione,* Pliny, *N.H.* xi. 15 (40).

5 of unheard-of size.[a] There were in those mountains rhinoceros also, an animal rare elsewhere.[b] This, however, was the name given to the beasts by the Greeks ; the Indi, being unacquainted with that tongue, use another word in their own language.

6 The king, having founded two cities,[c] one on each bank of the river which he had crossed, presented each of the leaders of his forces with a crown of gold and a thousand gold-pieces ; and to the rest also, in proportion [d] to the rank which they held in his friendship or to their services, honour was

7 paid. Abisares, who had sent envoys to Alexander before he fought with Porus, again sent others, promising that he would do everything that the king should order, provided only that he might not be compelled to surrender his person; for he would not live without royal power, nor reign as a captive.

8 To him Alexander ordered it to be announced that if Abisares was reluctant to come to him, he himself would come to Abisares.

Then, after crossing a very rapid river, he advanced

9 into the interior of India. There were forests [e] extending over an almost immeasurable space and given shade by trees towering to an enormous height.

10 Most of their branches, which were as huge as great trunks, being bent down to the earth, rose again from where they had curved, so that the appearance was, not of a branch rising again, but of a tree sprung

11 from its own roots.[f] The temperature of the air is wholesome ; for the shade tempers the force of the sun, and there is an abundant flow of water from

---

[e] This shows that his march was at first towards the north.

[f] Cf. Strabo xv. 1. 21. The description fits the banyan (*Ficus Indica*); see also Arr. *Indica* 11. 7.

12 levant et aquae large manant e fontibus. Ceterum
hic quoque serpentium magna vis erat, squamis ful-
gorem auri reddentibus. Virus haud ullum magis
noxium est ; quippe morsum praesens mors seque-
13 batur donec ab incolis remedium oblatum est. Hinc
per deserta ventum est ad flumen Hyraotim.[1] Iunc-
tum erat flumini nemus, opacum arboribus alibi
invisitatis agrestiumque pavonum multitudine fre-
14 quens. Castris inde motis, oppidum haud procul
positum corona capit, obsidibusque acceptis, stipendium imponit.

Ad magnam deinde, ut in ea regione, urbem pervenit, non muro solum, sed etiam palude munitam.
15 Ceterum barbari, vehiculis inter se iunctis, dimicaturi
occurrerunt ; tela aliis hastae, aliis secures erant,
transiliebantque in vehicula strenuo saltu, cum suc-
16 currere laborantibus suis vellent. Ac primo insolitum
genus pugnae Macedonas terruit, cum eminus vul-
nerarentur ; deinde spreto tam incondito auxilio, ab
utroque latere vehiculis circumfusi, repugnantes
17 fodere coeperunt. Et vincula quis conserta erant
iussit incidi, quo facilius singula circumvenirentur.
Itaque, VIII milibus suorum amissis, in oppidum re-
18 fugerunt. Postero die, scalis undique admotis, muri
occupantur. Paucis pernicitas saluti fuit ; qui ubi,[2]
cognito urbis excidio, paludem transnavere, in vicina

---

[1] Hyraotim *Hedicke;* hiarotim *A.*
[2] ubi *added by Hedicke.*

---

[a] *Cf.* Diod. xvii. 90. 5.
[b] His march had turned southward, see note *e* on p. 367.
368

12 springs. But here also there was a great quantity
of serpents,[a] whose scales shone with the brilliance
of gold. No poison is more dangerous; for instant
death followed their bite unless an antidote was
13 furnished by the natives. From there over deserts [b]
they came to the river Hyraotis.[c] Close to the river
was a shady grove, abounding in trees not seen else-
14 where and in a quantity of wild peafowl. Having
moved his camp from there, Alexander took a near-
by town by encirclement, and after receiving hostages
imposed tribute upon it.

Next he came to a great city, for that region,
protected not only by a wall but also by a marsh.[d]
15 But the barbarians sallied forth to battle with chariots
joined together; some were armed with lances,
others with axes, and they leaped rapidly from chariot
to chariot, when they wished to aid their men who
16 were under difficulties. And at first the unusual
kind of battle terrified the Macedonians, when they
were wounded from a distance; then, scorning such
a disorderly device, they surrounded the chariots on
17 both sides and began to kill those who resisted. And
Alexander gave orders that the bonds by which the
chariots were held together should be cut, in order
that one by one they might be more easily surrounded. And so the enemy, after losing 8000 of
18 their number, fled back to the town. On the following day ladders were planted on all sides and the
walls were carried by assault. A few were saved by
their swiftness, and when these, knowing of the
destruction of the city, swam across the marsh, they

[c] Hydraotis, Arr. v. 4. 2; the modern Ravi.
[d] This indicates that the city was probably in the vicinity
of modern Lahore.

oppida ingentem intulere terrorem invictum exercitum et deorum profecto advenisse memorantes.

19 Alexander, ad vastandam eam regionem Perdicca cum expedita manu misso, partem copiarum Eumeni tradidit, ut is quoque barbaros ad deditionem compelleret; ipse ceteros ad urbem validam, in quam
20 aliarum quoque confugerant incolae, duxit. Oppidani, missis qui regem deprecarentur, nihilo minus bellum parabant. Quippe orta seditio in diversa consilia diduxerat[1] vulgum; alii omnia deditione potiora, quidam nullam opem in ipsis esse ducebant.
21 Sed dum nihil in commune consulitur, qui deditioni
22 imminebant apertis portis hostem recipiunt. Alexander, quamquam belli auctoribus iure poterat irasci, tamen omnibus venia data et obsidibus acceptis, ad
23 proximam deinde urbem castra movit. Obsides ducebantur ante agmen; quos cum ex muris agnovissent, utpote gentis eiusdem, in colloquium incolae vocaverunt.[2] Illi clementiam regis simulque vim commemorando ad deditionem eos compulere; ceterasque urbes simili modo domitas in fidem accepit.
24 Hinc in regnum Sopithis[3] perventum est. Gens, ut barbari credunt, sapientia excellet bonisque moribus
25 regitur. Genitos liberos non parentum arbitrio tollunt aluntque, sed eorum quibus spectandi infantum

---

[1] diduxerat *J. Froben;* deduxerat *A.*
[2] incolae vocaverunt *Damsté;* collocauerunt *P;* conuo-cauerunt *C.*   [3] Sopithis *Mützell;* sophites *A.*

---

[a] *Cf.* Arr. v. 24. 6.   [b] *Cf.* Arr. vi. 2. 2.
[c] Comeliness and vigour the criteria; *cf.* Diod. xvii. 91. 5.

struck great terror into the neighbouring towns by
declaring that an invincible army, surely made up
of gods, had come.

19 Alexander sent Perdiccas with a light-armed band,
to devastate that region, and delivered a part of the
forces to Eumenes,[a] in order that he also might force
the barbarians to surrender ; Alexander himself led
the rest to a strong city, in which the natives also of
20 other cities had taken refuge. The besieged sent
envoys to beg the king for mercy, but nevertheless
prepared for war. For a disagreement had arisen,
which had divided the common people into divers
opinions ; some thought anything preferable to surrender, others that they had no power in themselves.
21 But while they could not come to an agreement, those
who were eager for surrender opened the gates and
22 let in the enemy. Alexander, although he might
justly have been angry with those who advocated
war, having nevertheless pardoned them all and
received hostages, moved his camp from there to the
23 next city. The hostages were led at the head of the
army ; when the inhabitants recognized them from
the walls, since they were of the same nation they
summoned them to a conference. The hostages by
telling them of the king's clemency and at the same
time of his power drove them to surrender ; and he
subdued the rest of the cities in a similar manner
and received them under his protection.

24 From there he came into the realm of Sopithes.[b]
That nation, as the barbarians believe, excels in
wisdom and is governed in accordance with good
25 customs. The children that are born [c] they acknowledge and rear, not according to the discretion of
their parents, but of those to whom the charge of

habitum cura mandata est. Si quos vitiis[1] insignes
aut aliqua parte membrorum inutiles notaverunt,
26 necari iubent. Nuptiis coeunt non genere ac nobilitate coniunctis, sed electa corporum specie, quia
27 eadem aestimatur in liberis. Huius gentis oppidum,
cui Alexander admoverat copias, ab ipso Sopithe
obtinebatur. Clausae erant portae, sed nulli in
muris turribusque se armati ostendebant, dubita-
bantque Macedones deseruissent urbem incolae an
28 fraude se occulerent; cum subito, patefacta porta,
rex Indus cum duobus adultis filiis occurrit, multum
29 inter omnes barbaros eminens corporis specie. Vestis
erat auro purpuraque distincta, quae etiam crura
velabat, aureis soleis inseruerat gemmas, lacerti quo-
30 que et brachia margaritis ornata erant, pendebant
ex auribus insignes candore ac magnitudine lapilli,
baculum aureum berylli distinguebant. Quo tradito,
precatus ut sospes acciperet, se liberosque et gentem
suam dedidit.

31 Nobiles ad venandum canes in ea regione sunt;
latratu abstinere dicuntur, cum viderunt feram,
32 leonibus maxime infesti. Horum vim ut ostenderet
Alexandro, in consaeptum[2] leonem eximiae magnitudinis iussit emitti et quattuor omnino admoveri
canes. Qui celeriter feram occupaverunt; tum ex eis[3]

---

[1] vitiis *added by Hedicke.*
[2] consaeptum *Mützell;* conseptu *A* (conspectu *B m. pr.*).
[3] iis *I;* his *A.*

---

[a] *Cf.* Diod. xvii. 91. 7 ; Strabo xv. 1. 30.
[b] See Pliny, *N.H.* ix. 56 (113).

the physical examination of children has been committed. If these have noted any who are conspicuous for defects or are crippled in some part of their limbs, they give orders to put them to death. 26 They marry, not because of consideration of family or rank, but of exceptional personal beauty, because 27 that is what is valued in the children. A town of this nation, against which Alexander had moved his forces, was held by Sopithes himself. The gates were shut, but no armed men showed themselves on the walls and in the towers, and the Macedonians were in doubt whether the inhabitants had deserted the city or had hidden themselves treacherously; 28 when suddenly a gate was opened and the Indian king with two grown-up sons presented himself, a man far surpassing all other barbarians in physical 29 attractiveness.[a] His robe, which covered his legs as well as the rest of his body, was embroidered with gold and purple, he wore golden sandals studded with gems, his shoulders and arms were adorned 30 with pearls and from his ears hung pearls conspicuous for whiteness [b] and size, his golden sceptre was ornamented with beryl. This he handed to Alexander with a prayer that he might receive it with good fortune and surrendered himself and his children along with his nation.

31   There are in that region dogs famous for hunting; they are said to abstain from barking when they have seen a wild beast, and they are especially enemies to 32 lions. In order to display their strength to Alexander, Sopithes ordered a lion of extraordinary size to be let into an enclosed space and only four dogs to be brought in. They quickly attacked the wild beast; then one of those who were accustomed to such ser-

qui assueverant talibus ministeriis unus[1] canis leoni
cum aliis inhaerentis crus avellere et, quia non seque-
33 batur, ferro amputare coepit. Ne sic quidem pertinacia victa, rursus aliam partem secare institit et
inde non segnius inhaerentem ferro subinde caedere;
at[2] ille in vulnere ferae dentes moribundus quoque
infixerat. Tantam in illis animalibus ad venandum
cupiditatem ingenerasse naturam memoriae proditum
34 est. Equidem plura transcribo quam credo; nam
nec affirmare sustineo de quibus dubito, nec sub-
35 ducere quae accepi. Relicto igitur Sopithe in suo
regno, ad fluvium Hypasin processit, Hephaestione
36 qui diversam regionem subegerat coniuncto. Phegeus[3] erat gentis proximae rex; qui popularibus
suis colere agros, ut assueverant, iussis, Alexandro
cum donis occurrit, nihil quod imperaret detrectans.
II. Biduum apud eum substitit rex. Tertio die
amnem superare decreverat, transitu difficilem non
spatio solum aquarum, sed etiam saxis impeditum;
2 percontatus[4] igitur Phegea quae noscenda erant, xii[5]
dierum ultra flumen per vastas solitudines iter esse
cognoscit, excipere deinde Gangen, maximum totius
3 Indiae fluminum, ulteriorem ripam colere gentes
Gangaridas et Prasios[6] eorumque regem esse Ag-
grammen, xx milibus equitum ducentisque peditum

[1] unus *Giunta;* unius *A.*
[2] caedere; at *Hedicke;* caedebat *A.*
[3] Phegeus *I;* phegelis *A.*
[4] percontatus *J. Froben;* percunctatus *A.*
[5] xii *Vogel;* xi *A.*
[6] Prasios *Salmasius;* pharrasios *C;* pharassios *P.*

---

[a] This spelling has better authority than *Hyphasis.* The
river is the Beas, before it joins the Sutlej.
[b] *Cf.* Diod. xvii. 93. 1.

vices began to pull away the leg of a dog that with
the others was clinging to the lion, and then, because
the animal did not let go, to cut the leg off with a
33 knife. When even then the dog's persistency was
not overcome, he began to cut another part, and
when the dog held fast with equal strength, to make
cuts at the dog's body as well; but the dog even
in dying kept his teeth fixed in the lion's wound.
Such is the eagerness for the chase which Nature is
34 reported to have implanted in those animals. As
for myself, I report more things than I believe; for
I cannot bring myself to vouch for that about which
I am in doubt, nor to suppress what I have heard.
35 Alexander then, leaving Sopithes in his kingdom,
advanced to the river Hypasis,[a] joined by Hephaes-
36 tion, who had subdued a different region. Phegeus[b]
was king of the next nation; he gave orders to his
subjects to work in the fields as they had been accustomed and went on to meet Alexander, refusing
nothing which he should order.

II. The king remained with Phegeus for two days.
On the third day he had decided to pass over the river,
which was difficult to pass, not only because of the
extent of its waters, but also because it was encum-
2 bered with rocks. Accordingly, having inquired of
Phegeus what he needed to know, he learned that
beyond the river there was a journey of twelve days
through desert wastes and that then they came to
3 the Ganges, the greatest river of all India, and that
on its farther bank dwelt the races called Gangaridae
and Prasii; that their king was Aggrammes[c] and
that he was blocking the roads with 20,000 cavalry

[c] The name (='Aγγράμμηs=Angrammes) is doubtful; Diod.
xvii. 93. 2 has *Sandrames*.

4 obsidentem vias. Ad hoc quadrigarum II milia
trahere et, praecipuum terrorem, elephantos, quos
III milium numerum explere dicebat.

5   Incredibilia regi omnia videbantur ; igitur Porum
—nam cum eo erat—percontatur an vera essent quae
6 dicerentur. Ille vires quidem gentis et regni haud
falso iactari affirmat, ceterum, qui regnaret, non
modo ignobilem esse, sed etiam ultimae sortis ; quippe
patrem eius, tonsorem vix diurno quaestu propulsan-
tem famem, propter habitum haud indecorum cordi
7 fuisse reginae. Ab ea in propiorem eius qui tum
regnasset amicitiae locum admotum, interfecto eo
per insidias, sub specie tutelae liberum eius invasisse
regnum, necatisque pueris hunc qui nunc regnat
generasse, invisum vilemque popularibus, magis
8 paternae fortunae quam suae memorem. Affirmatio
Pori multiplicem animo regis iniecerat curam. Hostem beluasque spernebat, situm locorum et vim
9 fluminum extimescebat ; relegatos in ultimum paene
rerum humanarum persequi terminum et eruere
arduum videbatur, rursus avaritia gloriae et insatiabilis cupido famae nihil invium, nihil remotum videri
10 sinebat. Et interdum dubitabat an Macedones tot
emensi spatia terrarum, in acie et in castris senes
facti, per obiecta flumina, per tot naturae obstantes
difficultates secuturi essent ; abundantes onustosque
praeda magis parta frui velle quam acquirenda[1]

    [1] adquirenda *J. Froben;* adquerenda *A.*

---

        [a] For *eruere* cf. ix. 3. 8.
  [b] A poetic expression ; cf. Hor. *Ars Poet.* 323 ff.
   [c] This did not apply to the whole army.

4 and 200,000 infantry. Besides this, he was leading 2000 chariots, and, a special cause of terror, elephants, of which Phegeus said that he had as many as 3000.

5 All this seemed incredible to Alexander; therefore he asked Porus—for he was with him—whether

6 what was said was true. Porus assured him that the strength of the nation and of the kingdom was not exaggerated, but that the ruler was not only of humble, but of the lowest condition; in fact, his father, a barber whose daily profit barely kept him from starving, because he was not bad looking had

7 been beloved by the queen. By her he had been advanced to intimate friendship with the king who then reigned, and having treacherously killed him, had usurped the throne under the pretext of guardianship of the king's children; then, having murdered the children, he had begotten the present king, who was hated and despised by his subjects and mindful

8 of his father's fortune than of his own. Porus' declaration had filled the king's mind with varied anxiety. He scorned the enemy and his beasts, but dreaded the nature of the terrain and the violence of

9 the rivers; it seemed a hard task to follow up and dislodge ^{a} those who had been relegated almost to the utmost limit of the human race, on the other hand, his eager thirst ^{b} for glory and his insatiable longing for renown allowed nothing to seem inacces-

10 sible, nothing remote. Also he doubted sometimes whether the Macedonians, after having traversed such an extent of country and grown old ^{c} in battle and in camp, would follow him over opposing rivers and through so many difficulties put in their way by nature; he feared that sated and laden with booty they would prefer to enjoy what they had obtained

377

11 fatigari. Non idem sibi et militibus animi ; sese[1]
totius orbis imperium mente complexum adhuc in
operum suorum primordio stare, militem labore
defetigatum proximum quemque fructum, finito
tandem periculo, expetere.

12 Vicit ergo cupido rationem, et ad contionem vocatis
militibus, ad hunc maxime modum disseruit : " Non
ignoro, milites, multa quae terrere vos possent ab
incolis Indiae per hos dies de industria esse iactata ;

13 sed non est improvisa vobis mentientium vanitas.
Sic Ciliciae fauces, sic Mesopotamiae campos, Tigrim
et Euphraten, quorum alterum vado transiimus,

14 alterum ponte, terribiles[2] fecerant Persae. Numquam[3] ad liquidum Fama perducitur ; omnia illa
tradente maiora sunt vero. Nostra quoque gloria,
cum sit ex solido, plus tamen habet nominis quam

15 operis. Modo quis beluas offerentes moenium
speciem, quis Hydaspem amnem, quis cetera auditu
maiora quam veriora[4] sustineri[5] posse credebat ?
Olim, hercules, fugissemus ex Asia si nos fabulae
debellare potuissent.

16 " Creditisne elephantorum greges maiores esse
quam usquam armentorum sunt, cum et rarum sit
animal nec facile capiatur multoque difficilius miti-

---

[1] sese *Hedicke;* esse *A.*
[2] terribiles *Bentley;* terribilem *A.*
[3] numquam *A (Post defends);* nil umquam *Damsté.*
[4] veriora *Hedicke, ed. min.;* uero *A.*
[5] sustineri *Bentley;* sustinere *A.*

---

[a] *Cf.* ix. 3. 9.
[b] For *ad liquidum cf.* Livy xxxv. 8. 7 ; Quint. v. 14. 28.

rather than wear themselves out by acquiring more.
11 He realized that his mind and that of his soldiers was not the same ; he embraced in his thoughts the rule of the whole world and still stood at the beginning [a] of his task, but the soldiers, exhausted by toil, now that the danger was finally at an end sought the fruit of their labour which was nearest at hand.
12 Therefore ambition prevailed over reason, and having called the soldiers together, he addressed them in about these terms : " I know well, soldiers, that many things which may well alarm you have been spread abroad with that intent by the peoples
13 of India during recent days ; but such artifices of falsifiers are not unknown to you. It is thus that the Persians described as terrible the passes of Cilicia, the plains of Mesopotamia, the Tigris and Euphrates, one of which we crossed by a ford, the
14 other by a bridge. Repute is never transmitted with certainty [b] ; all things that she reports are exaggerated. Even our glory, although it rests on a solid
15 foundation,[c] is greater in name than in fact. But now, who could believe that beasts looking like walls,[d] that the river Hydaspes, that other obstacles greater to hear of than in reality, could be surmounted ? Long ago, by Heaven ! we should have fled from Asia if mere tales could have vanquished us.
16 " Do you believe that there are greater herds of elephants in India than of cattle anywhere else, although the elephant is a rare beast, is not easy to capture, and is tamed with still greater difficulty ? [e]

    [c] Cf. Cic. De Fin. i. 18. 61 solido nomine.
    [d] Cf. Amm. xxiv. 6. 8.
    [e] This is denied by Strabo xv. 1. 42, and Pliny, N.H. viii. 7. 7 (23).

17 getur? Atqui eadem vanitas copias peditum equitum-
hoc numeravit. Nam flumen, quo latius fusum est,
hoc placidius stagnat; quippe angustis ripis coercita
et in angustiorem alveum elisa torrentes aquas inve-
18 hunt, contra spatio[1] alvei segnior cursus est. Praeterea in ripa omne periculum est, ubi applicantes
navigia hostis exspectat. Ita, quantumcumque flumen intervenit, idem futurum discrimen est evaden-
19 tium in terram. Sed omnia ista vera esse fingamus;
utrumne nos[2] magnitudo beluarum an multitudo
hostium terret? Quod pertinet ad elephantos,
praesens habemus exemplum; in suos vehementius
quam in nos incucurrerunt; tam vasta corpora securi-
20 bus falcibusque mutilata sunt. Quid autem interest,
totidem sint quot[3] Porus habuit, an III milia cum,
uno aut altero vulnerato, videritis[4] ceteros in fugam
21 declinari? Dein paucos aegre[5] et incommode
regunt; congregata vero tot milia ipsa se elidunt,
ubi nec stare nec fugere potuerint inhabiles vastorum
corporum moles. Equidem sic animalia ista con-
tempsi, ut, cum haberem ipse, non opposuerim, satis
gnarus plus suis quam hostibus periculi inferre.
22   "At enim equitum peditumque multitudo vos
commovet! Cum paucis enim pugnare soliti estis et

---

[1] spatio *Francine;* statio *B VL;* stacio *FP.*
[2] nos *P;* vos *C.*   [3] quot *Lauer;* quod *A.*
[4] vulnerato, videritis *Hedicke;* uulneratis *A.*
[5] aegre *Bentley;* quoque *A.*

---

^a After the battle of Arbela (Gaugamela) and in India.

17 And yet it is with the same untruthfulness that they
have numbered their forces of infantry and cavalry.
Indeed, the wider the extent of a river, the more
quietly it flows ; for when restrained by banks that
are close together, and hence dashed into a narrower
channel, they carry torrential waters, and on the
contrary their course is more sluggish in a spacious
18 channel. Besides this, all the danger is at the bank,
where the enemy awaits us as we are landing our
boats. Hence, however great the river that inter-
venes, the danger will be the same when we dis-
19 embark on the land. But let us imagine that all
those things are true ; does the great size of the beasts
or the multitude of the enemy terrify us ? So far as
the elephants are concerned, we have a recent experience before our eyes ; they rushed with greater
fury against their own men than against us ; their
bodies, great as they are, were mutilated by axes and
20 sickles. But what difference does it make whether
they are as many as Porus had, or that there are
3000, when you have seen that after one or two are
21 wounded the rest are turned to flight ? Furthermore,
they manage even a few elephants with difficulty
and inconvenience ; but, when so many thousands are
gathered together, they trample one another—where
such huge and unwieldy masses of bodies have been
able neither to stand nor to flee. For my part, I so
despised those animals that after I had them,[a] I did
not make use of them against the enemy, knowing
well enough that they inflicted more damage on their
own side than on the enemy.
22   " But, one may say, it is the multitude of infantry
and cavalry which appals you ! For you have been
accustomed to fight against small forces and now

23 nunc primum inconditam sustinebitis turbam. Testis
adversus multitudinem invicti Macedonum roboris
Granicus amnis et Cilicia inundata cruore[1] Persarum
et Arbela, cuius campi devictorum a nobis ossibus
24 strati sunt. Sero hostium legiones numerare coepistis,
postquam solitudinem in Asia vincendo fecistis. Cum
per Hellespontum navigaremus de paucitate nostra
cogitandum fuit ; nunc nos Scythae sequuntur, Bactriana auxilia praesto sunt, Dahae Sogdianique inter
25 nos militant. Nec tamen illi turbae confido ; vestras
manus intueor, vestram virtutem rerum quas gesturus
sum vadem praedemque habeo. Quamdiu vobiscum
in acie stabo nec mei nec hostium exercitus numero ;
vos modo animos mihi plenos alacritatis ac fiduciae
26 adhibete. Non in limine operum laborumque nos-
trorum, sed in exitu stamus ; pervenimus ad solis
ortum et Oceanum. Nisi obstat ignavia, inde victores,
perdomito fine terrarum, revertemur in patriam.

" Nolite, quod pigri agricolae faciunt, maturos
27 fructus per inertiam amittere e manibus. Maiora
sunt periculis praemia ; dives eadem et imbellis est
regio. Itaque non tam ad gloriam vos duco quam
ad praedam. Digni estis qui opes quas illud mare
litoribus invehit referatis in patriam, digni qui nihil
28 inexpertum, nihil metu omissum relinquatis. Per
vos gloriamque vestram, qua humanum fastigium
exceditis, perque et mea in vos et in me vestra merita,

---

[1] cruore *Lauer;* feruore *A.*

---

[a] *Cf.* Aristoph. *Eq.* 570 οὐ γὰρ οὐδεὶς πώποτ' αὐτῶν τοὺς
ἐναντίους ἰδὼν ἠρίθμησεν.

[b] *Cf.* ix. 4. 18 *trahi extra sidera et solem.*

[c] This does not agree with ix. 2. 3-4, nor with Arr. v.
25. 24.

[d] The pearls ; see Amm. xxiii. 6. 85.

for the first time will have to withstand a disorderly
23 throng! Testimony to the invincible strength of the
Macedonians against a superior number is given
by the river Granicus, by the flooding of Cilicia
with the blood of the Persians, and by Arbela, whose
plains are strewn with the bones of those whom we
24 decisively defeated. You are late in having begun to count[a] the enemy's legions, after you have
made a desert in Asia by your victories. When we
were sailing through the Hellespont was the time to
think of our small numbers; now the Scythians follow
us, we have Bactrian auxiliaries at hand, the Dahae
25 and the Sogdiani are fighting in our ranks. Yet it is
not in that mob that I trust. To your hands I look,
your valour I have as a bail and a surety for what I
am about to accomplish. So long as I shall stand in
battle with you I do not number my army nor that
of the enemy; do you only furnish me with hearts full
26 of enthusiasm and confidence. We stand, not on the
threshold of our labours and toils, but at the end; we
have come to the rising sun[b] and the Ocean. If
cowardice does not stand in our way we shall return
from there in triumph to our native land after subduing the whole world.

" Do not, as lazy husbandmen do, through negli-
27 gence let the ripe crop escape your grasp. The
prizes are greater than the dangers; that region is
both rich and unwarlike.[c] Therefore I am leading
you not so much to glory as to booty. You deserve to bear back to your native land the wealth
which that sea casts upon its shores,[d] you deserve
to leave nothing untried, nothing neglected through
28 fear. By yourselves and your glory, in which you
rise above human heights, and by your services

quibus invicem[1] contendimus, oro quaesoque ne
humanarum rerum terminos adeuntem alumnum
commilitonemque vestrum, ne dicam regem, desera-
29 tis. Cetera vobis imperavi ; hoc unum debiturus
sum. Et is vos rogo qui nihil umquam vobis praecepi
quin[2] primus me periculis obtulerim,[3] qui saepe aciem
clipeo meo texi. Ne infregeritis in manibus meis
palmam, qua Herculem Liberumque Patrem, si
30 invidia afuerit, aequabo. Date hoc precibus meis et
tandem obstinatum silentium rumpite. Ubi est ille
clamor, alacritatis vestrae index ? ubi ille meorum
Macedonum vultus ? Non agnosco vos, milites, nec
agnosci videor a vobis. Surdas iam dudum aures
pulso, aversos animos et infractos excitare conor."
31 Cumque illi, in terram demissis capitibus, tacere
perseverarent : " Nescio quid," inquit, " in vos imprudens deliqui, quod me ne intueri quidem vultis.
In solitudine mihi videor esse. Nemo respondet,
32 nemo saltem negat. Quos alloquor ? quid autem
postulo ? Vestram gloriam et magnitudinem vindicamus.[4] Ubi sunt illi quorum certamen paulo ante
vidi contendentium qui potissimum vulnerati regis
corpus exciperent ? Desertus, destitutus sum, hos-
33 tibus deditus. Sed solus quoque ire perseverabo.
Obicite me fluminibus et beluis et illis gentibus

---

[1] invicem *Bentley;* inuicti *A.*   [2] quin *Giunta;* qui *A.*
       [3] obtulerim *Giunta;* obtuli *A.*
    [4] vindicamus *J. Froben;* indicamus *A.*

---

[a] Cf. iii. 5. 8 *eundem regem et commilitonem.*
[b] Cf. Sen. *Phoeniss.* 638 *frangenda palma est.*
[c] *vindicamus* is a plural of majesty, *vestram* is an ordinary
plural.
384

to me and mine to you, in which we rival each other,
I beg and implore you not to desert your foster-child
and fellow soldier, not to say your king,[a] as he is
29 approaching the ends of the universe. All the rest
I have ordered you to do ; this one thing I shall
owe you. And I who ask this of you am one who
has never ordered you to do anything without first
exposing himself to its dangers, one who has often
covered the army with his shield. Do not break the
palm [b] that is in my hands, with which I shall equal
Hercules and Father Liber, if Nemesis withhold her
30 hands. Grant this to my prayers, and at last break
your persistent silence. Where are those shouts, the
sign of your eagerness ? Where is that look on the
faces of my Macedonians ? I do not recognize you,
my soldiers, nor do I seem to be recognized by you.
For a long time I have been knocking at deaf ears, I
have been trying to arouse estranged and broken
spirits."
31   And when, with faces lowered towards the earth,
they persisted in keeping silence, he continued : " I
have unintentionally failed you, in some way or other,
that you do not wish even to look upon me. I seem
to myself to be in a desert. No one replies, no one
32 at least refuses. To whom am I speaking ? And
what am I asking ? It is your own glory and greatness that we [c] are upholding. Where are those whom
but now I saw vying with one another as to who
should have the honour of carrying the body of their
wounded king ? I am deserted, abandoned, given
33 up to the enemy. But even alone I shall persist in
going on.[d] Expose me to the rivers, the beasts, and

[d] He speaks more bitterly in Arr. v. 28. 2, cf. Curt. x.
2. 25-29.

quarum nomina horretis ; inveniam qui desertum a
vobis sequantur. Scythae Bactrianique erunt me-
34 cum, hostes paulo ante, nunc milites nostri. Mori
praestat quam precario imperatorem esse. Ite
reduces domos ! ite deserto rege ovantes ! Ego hic
aut[1] vobis desperatae victoriae aut honestae morti
locum inveniam."

III. Ne sic quidem ulli militum vox exprimi potuit.
Exspectabant ut duces principesque ad regem per-
ferrent, vulneribus et continuo labore militiae fati-
gatos, non detrectare munia, sed sustinere non posse.
2 Ceterum illi, metu attoniti, in terram ora defixerant.
Igitur primo fremitus sua sponte, deinde gemitus
quoque oritur, paulatimque liberius dolor egeri[2]
coepit, manantibus lacrimis, adeo ut rex ira in misericordiam versa ne ipse quidem, quamquam cupiebat,[3]
3 temperare oculis potuerit. Tandem, universa contione effusius flente, Coenus[4] ausus est, cunctantibus
ceteris, propius tribunal accedere, significans se loqui
4 velle. Quem ut videre milites detrahentem galeam
capiti—ita enim regem alloqui mos est—hortari
5 coeperunt ut causam exercitus ageret. Tum Coenus:
" Dii prohibeant," inquit, " a nobis impias mentes !
Et profecto prohibent ; idem animus est tuis, qui
fuit semper, ire quo iusseris, pugnare, periclitari,

---

[1] aut *Bentley;* a *A.*   [2] egeri *Gebhard;* erigi *A.*
[3] cupiebat *Kinch;* cupierat *P;* cuperat *C.*
[4] Coenos *Aldus;* poenus *A* (*so below*).

---

[a] For *precario cf.* iv. 7. 1.

those nations whose mere names you dread. I shall
find men to follow me, deserted though I am by you.
With me will be the Scythians and the Bactriani, a
34 while ago our enemies, now our soldiers. It is better
to die than to command on sufferance.[a] Go then
back to your homes. Go in triumph after having
abandoned your king. Here I shall find either the
victory of which you despair or opportunity for an
honourable death."

III. Not even thus could a word be forced from any
of the soldiers. They were waiting for their generals
and chief officers to bear the news to the king that,
worn out by wounds and the unremitting toil of
military service, they did not refuse their duties, but
2 were no longer able to endure them. But the
generals, overwhelmed with fear, kept their eyes
riveted on the ground.

Then first an involuntary murmur, then also groans
were heard, and little by little sadness began to be
shown more freely by such floods of tears that the
king's anger was turned to compassion, and he himself, though he strove to do so, could not control his
3 eyes. At length, when the whole assembly was
dissolved in tears, Coenus, while the rest hesitated,
ventured to approach nearer to the tribunal, indi-
4 cating that he desired to speak. When the soldiers saw him removing his helmet from his head—
for so it is customary to address the king—they
began to urge him to plead the cause of the army.
5 Then Coenus said : " The gods forbid that we should
have impious thoughts. And surely they do forbid it ;
the feelings of your soldiers are the same that they
always have been, namely, to go wherever you order,
to fight, to incur danger, at the price of our blood to

387

sanguine nostro commendare posteritati tuum nomen.
Proinde, si perseveras, inermes quoque et nudi et
exsangues, utcumque tibi cordi est sequimur vel
antecedimus.

6 " Sed si audire vis non fictas tuorum militum voces,
verum necessitate ultima expressas, praebe, quaeso,
propitias aures imperium atque auspicium tuum con-
stantissime secutis et quocumque pergis secuturis.

7 Vicisti, rex, magnitudine rerum non hostes modo, sed
etiam milites. Quidquid mortalitas capere poterat,
implevimus. Emensis maria terrasque, melius nobis
quam incolis omnia nota sunt. Paene in ultimo

8 mundi fine consistimus. In alium orbem paras ire
et Indiam quaeris Indis quoque ignotam. Inter
feras serpentesque degentes eruere ex latebris et
cubilibus suis expetis, ut plura quam sol videt vic-

9 toria lustres. Digna prorsus cogitatio animo tuo, sed
altior nostro. Virtus enim tua semper in[1] incremento

10 erit, nostra vis iam in fine est. Intuere corpora
exsanguia, tot perfossa vulneribus, tot cicatricibus
putria. Iam tela hebetia sunt, iam arma deficiunt.

" Vestem Persicam induti,[2] quia domestica subvehi
non potest, in externum degeneravimus cultum.

11 Quoto cuique lorica est ? quis equum habet ? Iube
quaeri quam multos servi ipsorum persecuti sint,[3]
quid[4] cuique supersit ex praeda. Omnium victores

---

[1] in *added in I.*
[2] induti *Kinch;* induit *P;* indui *C (adding in marg.* mus
or ∗Λ∗ induimus).
[3] sint *Zumpt;* sunt *A.*   [4] quid *J. Froben;* quod *A.*

---

[a] Not wholly exaggeration, because of the deep and dark
valleys in the mountains.
[b] *Cf. exsanguis senectus,* Lucan i. 343.

hand your name down to future generations. Therefore, if you persist, we, even unarmed, naked, and
worn out, follow wherever you desire, or lead the way.
6 "But if you are willing to hear from your soldiers
words that are not false, but are wrung from them by
dire necessity, lend, I beg you, propitious ears to
those who have most faithfully followed your command and your auspices and will follow them whither-
7 soever you go. You have conquered, my king, by
the greatness of your exploits, not the enemy alone,
but also your own soldiers. Whatever mortals were
able to endure we have fulfilled. We have traversed
seas and lands, and everything there is better known
to us than to the natives. We stand almost at the
8 very end of the world. You are preparing to go into
another world, and to seek an India unknown even to
the Indi. You seek to bring out of their lurking-
places and lairs those who dwell among wild beasts
and serpents, in order that you may survey in vic-
9 tory more places than the sun looks upon.[a] The
thought is most worthy of your spirit, but too lofty
for ours. For your valour will ever be on the increase,
10 our strength is already at an end. Look upon these
bodies drained of blood,[b] pierced by so many wounds,
rotted by so many scars. Already our weapons are
dull, already our armour is giving out.[c]

"Clad in Persian dress, because that of our own
country cannot be brought to us, we have degener-
11 ated into foreign ways. How many of us have a
cuirass? Who has a horse? Bid it be asked how
many are attended by their own slaves, what each
man has left from his booty. Victors over all, we

[c] Some armour was so old that it had to be burned:
ix. 3. 22.

omnium inopes sumus. Nec luxuria laboramus, sed
12 bello instrumenta belli consumpsimus. Hunc tu
pulcherrimum exercitum nudum obicies beluis ?
Quarum ut multitudinem augeant de industria barbari, magnum tamen esse numerum etiam ex men-
13 dacio intellego. Quodsi adhuc penetrare in Indiam
certum est, regio a meridie minus vasta est ; qua
subacta, licebit decurrere in illud mare, quod rebus
14 humanis terminum voluit esse natura. Cur circuitu
petis gloriam quae ad manum posita est ? Hic quoque occurrit Oceanus. Nisi mavis errare, pervenimus
15 quo tua fortuna ducit. Haec tecum quam sine te
cum his loqui malui, non uti inirem circumstantis
exercitus gratiam, sed ut vocem loquentium potius
quam gemitum murmurantium audires."
16 Ut finem orationi Coenus imposuit, clamor undique
cum ploratu oritur, regem, patrem, dominum con-
17 fusis appellantium vocibus. Iamque et alii duces
praecipueque seniores, quis ob aetatem et excusatio
honestior erat et auctoritas maior, eadem precaban-
18 tur. Ille nec castigare obstinatos nec mitigari[1]
poterat iratus ; itaque inops consilii desiluit ex[2]
tribunali claudique regiam iussit, omnibus praeter

---

[1] mitigari *Kinch;* mitigare *C;* mig*are *P.*
[2] ex *Hedicke;* et *P;* e *C.*

---

[a] The distance is greatly minimized ; it took Alexander
almost a year to cover it ; *cf.* Strabo xv. 1. 17.

lack everything. And we are not suffering because of luxury, but it is in war that we have used up the
12 equipment for war. Will you expose this most noble army naked to wild beasts? Of these, although the barbarians purposely exaggerate the multitude, yet even from their false report I know that the number
13 is great. But if you are still determined to penetrate farther into India, the southern part of that region is less immense; when that has been subdued, you may run down to that sea which Nature has decreed
14 should be be the boundary of human affairs. Why do you seek glory by a long circuit when it lies at your hand? [a] Here too the Ocean meets you. Unless you prefer to wander about, we have reached
15 the place to which your fortune is leading you. I have preferred to say these things in your presence rather than to discuss them with the men in your absence, not with a view to gaining favour with the army here assembled, but that you might hear from my lips the voice of those who speak out rather than the groans of those who grumble."
16 When Coenus had ended his address, shouts arose from every side mingled with lamentations, as in a medley of voices they called out "king," "father"
17 and "lord." And now also the other generals, and especially the older ones, for whom because of their age it was both more honourable to ask for an excuse and whose authority was greater, gave
18 utterance to the same entreaties. Alexander found himself unable either to rebuke them for their obstinacy or to be appeased in his anger; therefore, being at a loss what to do, he leaped down from the tribunal, ordered the royal quarters to be closed, and all to be refused admission except his regular

391

19 assuetos adire prohibitis. Biduum irae datum est ;
tertio die processit erigique[1] duodecim aras ex quadrato saxo, monumentum[2] expeditionis suae, munimenta quoque castrorum iussit extendi cubiliaque
amplioris formae quam pro corporum habitu relinqui,
ut speciem omnium augeret, posteritati fallax miraculum praeparans.

20 Hinc repetens quae emensus erat, ad flumen
Acesinen[3] locat castra. Ibi forte Coenus morbo
exstinctus est ; cuius morte ingemuit quidem rex,
adiecit tamen propter paucos dies longam orationem
eum exorsum, tamquam solus Macedoniam visurus

21 esset. Iam in aqua classis quam aedificari iusserat
stabat. Inter haec[4] Memno ex Thracia in supplementum equitum v milia, praeter eos ab Harpalo
peditum vii milia adduxerat armaque xxv milibus

22 auro et argento caelata pertulerat. Quis distributis,
vetera cremari iussit. Mille navigiis aditurus Oceanum, discordesque et vetera odia retractantes Porum

---

[1] erigique *J. Froben;* e regia qui *A.*
[2] monumentum *J. Froben;* munimentum *A.*
[3] Acesinen *Hedicke;* acaestimen *P;* acasatimem *BF;*
acestimem *LV.*   [4] Inter haec *Giunta;* in hac *A.*

---

[a] Also in hope that the soldiers would change their minds.
Diod. xvii. 94. 3-4 says that he offered the soldiers an opportunity to plunder the rich country on the river, and made
presents to their wives and children.
[b] Diodorus, Plutarch, and Justin agree with this. Arrian
(v. 29. 1) says nothing of it, but speaks of the altars as of
great size.
[c] The Chenab. But in fact Alexander, having turned back
at the Hypasis, marched as far as the Hydaspes ; see p. 394,
note *a*, Strabo xv. 1. 32, and Aristobulus in Strabo xv. 1.
17. Curtius' error is shared by Diodorus and Justin, who in

19 attendants. Two days were spent in anger[a]; on the third day he came out and ordered twelve altars of squared stone to be erected as a memorial of his expedition. He also gave directions that the fortifications of the camp be extended, and couches of a larger size than were used by men of ordinary stature be left there, in order that by exaggerating the proportion of everything he might prepare a deceptive wonder for posterity.[b]

20 From here he retraced the ground which he had covered and encamped near the river Acesines.[c] There, as it chanced, Coenus was taken ill and died.[d] The king was in fact grieved by his death, but could not forbear to remark that Coenus for the sake of a few days[e] had begun a long harangue, as if he alone

21 were destined to see Macedonia again. Already the fleet which he had ordered to be built was afloat in the river.[f] Meanwhile Memnon had brought from Thrace a reinforcement of 5000 horsemen, and besides these 7000 foot-soldiers from Harpalus, for 25,000 men

22 sets of armour inlaid with gold and silver. These Alexander distributed and ordered the old ones to be burned. Intending to make for the Ocean with a thousand ships,[g] he left Porus and Taxiles, the Indian

general follow the same sources as he. The Hypasis (Beas) and the Hydaspes (Sutlej) become one river in due course.

[d] According to Arrian vi. 2. 1, Coenus died when Alexander had reached the Hydaspes and prepared his fleet.

[e] Curtius is more rhetorical than exact; the time was considerably more than " a few days."

[f] The Hydaspes, not the Acesines. See Arr. vi. 1. 1, and for what Alexander did at the Acesines v. 29. 3.

[g] According to Arrian vi. 2. 4, the number of ships and boats was nearly 2000, of which 80 had thirty oars each ; so also Diod. xvii. 95. 5, who agrees with Curtius as to the whole number.

et Taxilen, Indiae reges, firmatae per affinitatem gratiae reliquit in suis regnis, summo in aedificanda
23 classe amborum studio usus. Oppida quoque duo condidit; quorum alterum Nicaeam appellavit, alterum Bucephala,[1] equi quem amiserat memoriae ac
24 nomini dedicans urbem. Elephantis deinde et impedimentis terra sequi iussis, secundo amne defluxit quadraginta ferme stadia singulis diebus procedens, ut opportunis locis exponi subinde copiae possent.

IV. Perventum erat in regionem in qua Hydaspes
2 amnis Acesini[2] committitur; hinc decurrit in fines Siborum.[3] Hi de exercitu Herculis maiores suos esse memorant; aegros relictos[4] cepisse sedem quam ipsi
3 obtinebant. Pelles ferarum pro veste, clavae tela erant, multaque etiam, cum Graeci mores exolevis-
4 sent, stirpis ostendebant vestigia. Hinc escensione facta, cc et l stadia excessit depopulatusque regionem,
5 oppidum, caput eius, corona cepit. xl milia peditum alia gens in ripa fluminum opposuerat; quae, amne superato, in fugam compulit inclusosque moenibus expugnat. Puberes interfecti sunt, ceteri venierunt.
6 Alteram deinde urbem expugnare adortus, magnaque

---

[1] Bucephala *Hedicke;* bucephalum *A* (bucefalum *V*).
[2] Acesini *Modius;* acessino *A*.
[3] Siborum *Zumpt;* soborum *A*.
[4] relictos *Acidalius;* relictos esse *C;* relictos se *P*.

---

[a] These are the ones named in ix. 1. 6, see note. In the source followed by Curtius and Diodorus, either the Acesines was confused with the Hydaspes, or the account of the march from the Acesines to the Hydaspes was omitted.

[b] Inaccurate; *cf.* Diod. xvii. 96. 1; Arr. vi. 2. 2.

[c] *Sibae*, Arr. and Strabo xv. 1. 8 and 1. 33, but the Sanscrit is *Sivi*, showing the v-sound of β at this time.

[d] *Cf.* viii. 14. 11, note.

kings, who had been at odds and reviving old feuds,
in friendly relations strengthened by an alliance by
marriage, and established each in his own sovereignty
because he had received the greatest service from
23 them in building his fleet. He also founded ^a two
towns, of which he called one Nicaea and the other
Bucephala, dedicating the latter to the name and
24 memory of the horse which he had lost. Then, having
given orders that the elephants and the baggage
should follow by land,^b he sailed down the river,
advancing about forty stadia each day, to allow the
troops to be landed from time to time where there
were convenient places.

IV. They had come into the country where the
2 Hydaspes unites with the Acesines. From there the
river flows into the country of the Sibi.^c These
people allege that their forefathers belonged to the
army of Hercules^d; that being left behind on account
of sickness, they had gained possession of the abode
3 in which their posterity were living. They dressed
in the skins of wild beasts, their weapons were clubs,
and they also showed many traces of their origin,
although Greek customs had become obsolete.
4 Having made a landing there, he went on for a
distance of two hundred and fifty stadia, and after
devastating the region, by an assault on all sides took
5 the town which was its capital. Another nation had
opposed 40,000 foot-soldiers on the bank of the
rivers^e; Alexander crossed the Acesines, drove them
within their walls, and took their town by assault.
Those of military age were put to death, the rest
6 were sold. Then, having attempted to storm a

^e The united Acesines and Hydaspes; *amne* refers prob-
ably to the former.

vi defendentium pulsus, multos Macedonum amisit.
Sed cum in obsidione perseverasset, oppidani, desperata salute, ignem subiecere[1] tectis seque[2] ac
7 liberos coniugesque incendio cremant. Quod cum
ipsi augerent, hostes exstinguerent, nova forma
pugnae erat; delebant incolae urbem, hostes defendebant.[3] Adeo etiam naturae iura bellum in
contrarium mutat.[4]
8 Arx erat oppidi intacta, in qua praesidio invalidos
reliquit. Ipse est[5] navigiis circumvectus arcem.
Quippe III flumina tota India praeter Gangen maxima
munimento arcis applicant undas ; a septentrione
Indus alluit, a meridie Acesines Hydaspi confunditur.
9 Ceterum amnium coetus maritimis similes fluctus
movet, multoque ac turbido limo, quod aquarum
concursu subinde turbatur, iter qua meatur[6] navigiis
10 in tenuem alveum cogitur. Itaque cum crebri fluctus
se inveherent et navium hinc proras, hinc latera
pulsarent, subducere nautae vela coeperunt. Sed
ministeria eorum hinc aestu,[7] hinc praerapida celeri-
11 tate fluminum occupantur. In oculis omnium duo
maiora[8] navigia submersa sunt ; leviora, cum et ipsa
nequirent regi, in ripam tamen innoxia expulsa sunt.
Ipse rex in rapidissimos vertices incidit, quibus
intorta navis obliqua et gubernaculi impatiens age-
12 batur. Iam vestem detraxerat corpori, proiecturus

---

[1] subiecere *I;* subicere *A.* [2] seque *Hedicke;* se quoque *A.*
[3] defendebant *J. Froben;* extinguebant *A.*
[4] mutat *Lauer;* mutant *A.* [5] est *added by Hedicke.*
[6] meatur *Heinse;* meat *A.* [7] aestu *Jeep;* cetu *A.*
[8] omnium duo maiora *Acidalius;* duo maiora omnium *C;*
duo maiora *P.*

---

[a] Diod. xvii. 96. 4 f. gives a different account.
[b] *i.e.* to brail up ; see *Class. Jour.* vi. 75-77.

second city, but being repulsed by the great strength
of its defenders, he lost many of the Macedonians.
But when he had persisted in besieging it, the inhabitants, despairing of safety, set fire to their houses and
burned to death in the flames themselves and their

7 wives and their children.[a] Since they themselves
were spreading the fire, while the enemy were trying
to put it out, a novel kind of battle took place ; the
inhabitants were trying to destroy their city, the
enemy were defending it. So completely does war
invert even the laws of Nature.

8 The citadel of the town was unharmed, and in it
Alexander left his sick as a garrison. He himself
sailed around the fortress in his ships. For the three
greatest rivers of all India except the Ganges protect
its fortifications with their waters ; on the north the
Indus washes them, on the south the Acesines unites

9 with the Hydaspes. Moreover, the union of the
rivers raises billows like those of the sea, and the
abundance of turbid silt, which is constantly shifted
by the confluent waters, compresses the way where it

10 is navigable by boats into a narrow channel. Therefore, since wave after wave met them, and struck
now the prows and now the sides of the ships, the
sailors began to furl[b] the sails. But their efforts
were thwarted, partly by the surging waves, partly

11 by the very rapid flow of the rivers. In the sight of
all two of the greater ships were sunk ; the lighter
ones, although they also could not be managed,
were nevertheless driven on the bank uninjured.
The king himself met with the swiftest of the eddies,
by which his ship was turned sidewise and driven

12 on without obeying its helm. Already he had
taken off his clothing, intending to plunge into

397

semet in flumen, amicique, ut exciperent **eum,** haud
procul nabant, apparebatque anceps periculum tam
13 naturi quam navigare perseverantis ; ergo ingenti
certamine concitant remos, quantaque vis humana
esse poterat admota est, ut fluctus, qui se invehebant,
14 everberarentur. Findi crederes undas et retro gur-
gites cedere. Quibus tandem navis erepta, non
tamen ripae applicatur, sed in proximum vadum
illiditur. Cum amne bellum fuisse crederes. Ergo
aris pro numero fluminum positis sacrificioque **facto,**
xxx stadia processit.

15 Inde ventum est in regionem Sudracarum Mallo-
rumque, quos alias bellare inter se solitos, tunc
periculi societas iunxerat. Nonaginta milia iuniorum
peditum in armis erant, praeter hos equitum x milia
16 nongentaeque quadrigae. At Macedones, qui omni
discrimine iam defunctos se esse crediderant, postquam integrum bellum cum ferocissimis Indiae gentibus superesse cognoverunt, improviso metu territi,
rursus seditiosis vocibus regem increpare coeperunt :
17 Gangen amnem et quae ultra essent coactos trans-
mittere non tamen finisse, sed mutasse bellum.
Indomitis gentibus se obiectos, ut sanguine suo
18 aperirent ei Oceanum. Trahi extra sidera et solem
cogique adire quae mortalium oculis Natura subduxerit.[1] Novis identidem armis novos hostes exsis-

---

[1] subduxerit *Acidalius;* subduxerat *A.*

---

[a] The number is uncertain ; Diod. xvii. 98. 1 makes it more
than 80,000.
[b] *Cf.* ix. 4. 24 ; Arr. vi. 4. 3 ; Plut. *Alex.* lxiii. 1.
[c] *Cf.* iv. 8. 3. [d] *Cf.* Sen. *Suas.* i. 4.

the river, and his friends were swimming near by
ready to pick him up, and it appeared equally
dangerous either to take to swimming or to persist
13 in sailing on ; therefore they plied the oars with
mighty rivalry, and did all that human power could
do to break through the waves which dashed upon
14 them. You might have thought that the billows
were cloven and that the surges were forced to
retreat. When at last the ship was saved from
these, it nevertheless could not be brought to the
bank, but was dashed upon the nearest shoal. You
would have thought that a war had been waged
with the river. Accordingly, Alexander set up as
many altars as there were streams, and having offered
sacrifice, went on for thirty stadia.

15 From there he came into the land of the Sudracae
and the Malli, who at other times were usually at war
with each other, but then had united in the face of
the common danger. They had 90,000 younger
foot-soldiers,[a] and besides these 10,000 horsemen
16 and 900 chariots. But when the Macedonians, who
believed that they had already encountered every
danger, knew that a fresh war with the most warlike nations of India [b] still remained, they were
struck with sudden fear, and began again to upbraid
17 the king with mutinous language : that after being
compelled to cross the Ganges and the regions beyond
it, they had nevertheless not ended, but only shifted,
the war. They were exposed to unconquered nations
in order that at the cost of their blood they might
18 open a way for him to the Ocean. They were being
dragged beyond the constellations and the sun [c] and
forced to approach places which Nature had withdrawn from the sight of mortals.[d] For their new arms

tere. Quos ut omnes fundant fugentque, quod
praemium ipsos manere ? caliginem ac tenebras et
perpetuam noctem profundo incubantem mari, repletum immanium beluarum gregibus fretum, immobiles
undas, in quibus emoriens natura defecerit.

19 Rex non sua, sed militum sollicitudine anxius,
contione advocata, docet imbelles esse, quos metuant.
Nihil deinde praeter has gentes obstare quominus
terrarum spatia emensi, ad finem simul mundi labo-
20 rumque[1] perveniant. Concessisse[2] illis metuentibus
Gangen et multitudinem nationum quae ultra amnem
essent ; declinasse iter eo ubi par gloria minus
21 periculum esset. Iam prospicere se Oceanum, iam
perflare ad ipsos auram maris ; ne inviderent sibi
laudem quam peteret. Herculis et Liberi Patris
terminos transituros illos, regi suo parvo impendio
immortalitatem famae daturos. Paterentur se ex
India redire, non fugere.

22 Omnis multitudo et maxime militaris mobilis[3]
impetu effertur[4] ; ita seditionis non remedia quam
23 principia maiora sunt. Non alias tam alacer clamor
ab exercitu est redditus ; iubent eum ducere[5] dis
secundis, aequareque[6] gloria quos aemularetur.
Laetus his acclamationibus, ad hostes protinus castra
24 movit. Validissimae Indorum gentes erant et bellum
impigre parabant ducemque ex natione Sudracarum

---

[1] laborumque *I;* laboremque *A.*
[2] Concessisse *Hedicke;* cessisse *A.*
[3] mobilis *Hedicke;* mobili *A.*
[4] effertur *Vindelinus;* adfertur *A.*
[5] iubent eum ducere *Hedicke;* iubentium duceret *A.*
[6] aequareque *Hedicke;* aequaretque *A.*

---

[a] A rhetorical exaggeration ; see ix. 9. 3.
[b] *i.e.* Hercules and Father Liber ; see ix. 4. 21, above.

new enemies constantly appeared. Granted that
they routed and put to flight all these, what reward
awaited them ? Gloom and darkness, and perpetual
night brooding over an unplumbed sea, a deep teem-
ing with schools of savage sea-monsters, stagnant
waters in which expiring Nature had met her end.

19 The king, disturbed by anxiety, not for himself but
for his soldiers, having called an assembly, told them
that those whom they feared were unwarlike ; that
after these no other nations stood in their way of
traversing all the wide spaces which remained and
coming to the end of the world and at the same time to
20 the end of their labours. The Ganges and the multitude of nations which were beyond that river he had
sacrificed to their fears ; he had diverted his arms to
a quarter where there was equal glory but less danger.
21 Already they were in sight of the Ocean,ª already the
breezes of the sea were wafted to them ; let them not
begrudge him the renown which he sought. They
would pass the bournes of Hercules and Father Liber,
and thus give their king immortal fame at little cost
to themselves. Let them allow him to return from
India, not to leave it in flight.
22 Every assemblage, especially one of soldiers, is
fickle and carried away by impulse; thus is sedition
23 no harder to quell than to arouse. Never before
were such cries of joy sent forth by the army ; they
bid him lead on with the favour of the gods, and to
equal in glory those whom he is emulating.ᵇ Alexander, elated by these acclamations, at once broke
24 camp and moved against the enemy. These were
the strongest nations of the Indi ; they were making
vigorous preparations for war and had chosen as
their leader one of the nation of the Sudracae, a

spectatae virtutis elegerant ; qui sub radicibus
montis castra posuit lateque ignes, ut speciem multitudinis augeret, ostendit, clamore quoque ac sui
moris ululatu identidem acquiescentes Macedonas
25 frustra terrere conatus. Iam lux appetebat, cum
rex fiduciae ac spei plenus alacres milites arma capere
et exire in aciem iubet. Sed—haud[1] traditur metune
an oborta seditione inter ipsos—subito profugerunt
barbari certe et[2] avios montes et impeditos occupaverunt. Quorum agmen rex frustra persecutus,
impedimenta cepit.

26   Perventum deinde est ad oppidum Sudracarum, in
quod plerique confugerant, haud maiore fiducia
27 moenium quam armorum. Iam admovebat rex,
cum vates monere eum coepit, ne committeret aut
certe differret obsidionem ; vitae eius periculum
28 ostendi. Rex Demophontem—is namque vates erat
—intuens : " Si quis," inquit, " te arti tuae intentum
et exta spectantem sic interpellet, non dubitem quin
29 incommodus ac molestus videri tibi possit." Et cum
ille ita prorsus futurum respondisset : " Censesne,"
inquit, " tantas res, non pecudum fibras ante oculos
habenti ullum esse maius impedimentum quam
30 vatem superstitione captum ? " Nec diutius quam
respondit moratus, admoveri iubet scalas, cunctanti-
busque ceteris, evadit in murum. Angusta muri

---

[1] haud *Acidalius;* ut *A.*   et *added by Hedicke.*

---

[a] Really, of the Malli ; Arr. vi. 11. **3.**

man of tried valour; he had encamped at the foot
of a mountain and showed fires far and wide in order
to increase the impression of his numbers, also vainly
trying after the fashion of his nation from time to
time by shouts and yells to terrify the unperturbed
25 Macedonians. And daylight was already approaching, when the king, now confident and full of hope,
ordered his eager soldiers to arm themselves and go
forth to battle. But the barbarians—it is not known
whether through fear or because a disagreement
had arisen among them—at any rate suddenly took
to flight and gained the mountains, which were remote and full of obstacles. The king vainly pursued
their army, but took their baggage.

26 Next they arrived at a town of the Sudracae [a] in
which many of the enemy had taken refuge, although
they had no greater confidence in their walls than
27 in their arms. The king was already approaching
them, when a soothsayer began to warn him not to
enter on a siege, or at any rate to postpone it; that
28 danger to his life was indicated. The king, fixing
his gaze upon Demophon—for that was the soothsayer's name—said: " If anyone should thus interrupt you when you were intent upon your art and
were inspecting the entrails, I doubt not that he
29 would impress you as tactless and annoying." And
when Demophon replied that it would most certainly
be so, Alexander rejoined: " Do you think that to me,
having before my eyes such important affairs, and not
the entrails of animals, anything could be a greater
hindrance than a seer enslaved by superstition ? "
30 And with no longer delay than making this answer
required, he ordered the scaling ladders to be applied,
and while the rest hesitated, himself mounted the

corona erat; non pinnae sicut alibi fastigium eius
distinxerant, sed perpetua lorica obducta transitum
31 saepserat. Itaque rex haerebat magis quam stabat
in margine, clipeo undique incidentia tela propulsans;
32 nam ipse[1] eminus ex turribus petebatur, nec subire
milites poterant, quia superne vi telorum obrueban-
tur. Tandem magnitudinem[2] periculi pudor vicit;
quippe cernebant cunctatione sua dedi hostibus
33 regem. Sed festinando morabantur auxilia. Nam
dum pro se quisque certat evadere, oneravere scalas;
quis non sufficientibus, devoluti unicam spem regis
fefellerunt. Stabat enim in conspectu tanti exercitus velut in solitudine destitutus.

V. Iamque laevam, qua clipeum ad ictus circum-
ferebat, lassaverat, clamantibus amicis ut ad ipsos
desiliret, stabantque excepturi; cum ille rem ausus
est incredibilem atque inauditam multoque magis ad
2 famam temeritatis quam gloriae insignem. Namque
in urbem hostium plenam praecipiti saltu semet ipse
immisit, cum vix sperare posset dimicantem certe et
non inultum esse moriturum; quippe, antequam
3 assurgeret, opprimi poterat et capi vivus. Sed forte
ita libraverat corpus ut se pedibus exciperet; itaque
stans init pugnam. Et ne circumiri posset[3] fortuna

---

[1] ipse *Hedicke;* ubique *C;* ubi *P.*
[2] telorum (*after* magnitudinem) *deleted by J. Froben.*
[3] posset *Lauer;* possit *C.*

---

[a] See Arr. vi. 9. 2-3, who says that he entered the city
through a gate, and then mounted on a ladder to the citadel.
[b] That is, the towers of the citadel.
[c] According to Arrian (vi. 9. 3-4), Peucestes and Leonnatus came up the same ladder as the king, and Abreas by
another ladder.
[d] See Arr. vi. 9. 5 and Diod. xvii. 99. 1, who give the king's
motive more clearly.

wall.[a] The crown of the wall was narrow and its summit was not marked by battlements, as is usually the case, but a parapet was built all along it and pre-
31 vented assailants from crossing it. Hence the king was rather clinging to this parapet than standing on its edge, defending himself with his buckler from the
32 spears that fell upon him from every side; for he was being attacked at long range from the towers [b] and his soldiers could not come up [c] because they were overwhelmed by a storm of weapons from above. But at last shame overcame the greatness of their peril; for they saw that by their delay the king was
33 being abandoned to the enemy. But their help was delayed by their hurry; for while each man strove to be the first to reach the top of the wall they overloaded the ladders; and when these could not hold the burden put upon them, they fell and thus deprived the king of his sole hope. For in the sight of so great an army he stood alone, as if left utterly deserted.

V. By this time he had tired his left hand, by which he was shifting his shield about to parry the shots, and his friends were shouting to him to leap down to them, and were standing ready to catch him; when he dared an incredible and unheard-of deed, one which added much more to his reputation for rashness
2 than to his glory. For with a headlong leap he threw himself into the city filled with enemies, although he could hardly hope [d] that he would at least die fighting and not unavenged; for before he could rise to his feet, he was likely to be overpowered and taken
3 prisoner. But by good luck he had balanced his body so well that he alighted on his feet; hence he was standing erect when he began to fight. Fortune

405

4 providerat. Vetusta arbor haud procul muro ramos
multa fronde vestitos, velut de industria regem protegentes, obiecerat ; huius spatioso stipiti corpus, ne
circumiri posset, applicuit, clipeo tela quae ex adverso
5 ingerebantur excipiens. Nam cum[1] summa vi unum
procul tot manus peterent, nemo tamen auderet[2]
propius accedere missilia ramis plura quam clipeo
incidebant.

6   Pugnabat pro rege primum celebrati nominis fama,
deinde desperatio, magnum ad honeste moriendum in-
7 citamentum. Sed cum subinde hostis afflueret, iam
ingentem vim telorum exceperat clipeo, iam galeam
saxa perfregerant, iam continuo labore gravata genua
8 succiderant. Itaque contemptim et incaute, qui
proximi steterant incurrerunt; e quibus duos gladio
ita excepit, ut ante ipsum exanimes procumberent.
Nec cuiquam deinde propius incessendi eum animus
9 fuit ; procul iacula sagittasque mittebant. Ille ad
omnes ictus expositus, non aegre tamen[3] exceptum
poplitibus corpus tuebatur, donec Indus duorum
cubitorum sagittam—namque Indis, ut antea diximus, huius magnitudinis sagittae erant—ita excussit,
ut per thoracem paulum super latus dextrum in-
10 figeret. Quo vulnere afflictus, magna vi sanguinis
emicante, remisit arma moribundo similis adeoque
resolutus ut ne ad vellendum quidem telum sufficeret
dextra. Itaque ad spoliandum corpus qui vulnera-

---

[1] comminus (*after* cum) *deleted by Aldus.*
[2] auderet *Bentley;* audebat *A.*   [3] tamen *Jeep;* iam *A.*

---

[a] So Diodorus and Justin; Arrian does not mention the
tree.   [b] viii. 9. 28.

had also provided that he could not be surrounded ;
4 for an aged tree,ᵃ standing close to the wall, had
thrown out its branches, thickly clothed with leaves,
as if for the very purpose of protecting the king ;
against the huge trunk of this he took his place, in
such a way as not to be surrounded, receiving on his
buckler all the weapons that were hurled at him in
5 front. For although he was single-handed and so
many men were attacking him with extreme violence
from a distance, yet none dared to come nearer, and
more missiles fell in the branches than on his shield.
6 The king was protected in the first place by the
widespread fame of his name, and secondly by
7 desperation, a great incentive to die gloriously. But
as constantly new enemies came pouring on, by this
time he had caught a vast number of weapons on his
shield, his helmet was shattered by stones, and already
his knees, wearied by protracted toil, had sunk under
8 him. On seeing this, those who stood nearest rushed
upon him incautiously and in contempt of the danger ;
two of these he ran through with his sword and laid
them dead at his feet. After that no one had the
courage to go nearer him, but they assailed him with
9 javelins and arrows from afar. But although a mark
for every shot, yet on his knees he had no difficulty
in defending himself, until an Indian discharged an
arrow two cubits long—for, as I have said,ᵇ the Indi
had arrows of that length—with so good an aim that
it passed through his cuirass and was fixed in his body
10 a little above his right side. On suffering this wound,
from which a great jet of blood gushed forth, he let
his armour drop as if dying, not even having the
strength to draw out the weapon with his right hand.
On seeing this, the man who had wounded him ran

11 verat alacer gaudio accurrit. Quem ut inicere corpori suo manus sensit, credo, ultimi dedecoris
indignitate commotus, linquentem revocavit animum
et nudum hostis latus subrecto[1] mucrone hausit.

12 Iacebant circa regem tria corpora, procul stupentibus ceteris. Ille ut, antequam ultimus spiritus
deficeret, dimicans tamen[2] exstingueretur, clipeo se

13 allevare conatus est et, postquam ad conitendum
nihil supererat virium, dextera impendentes ramos
complexus temptabat assurgere. Sed ne sic quidem
potens corporis, rursus in genua procumbit, manu

14 provocans hostes, si quis congredi auderet. Tandem
Peucestes, per aliam oppidi partem deturbatis pro-
pugnatoribus muri, vestigia persequens regis super-

15 venit. Quo conspecto, Alexander iam non vitae
spem,[3] sed mortis solacium supervenisse ratus, clipeo
fatigatum corpus excepit. Subinde[4] Timaeus et
paulo post Leonnatus, huic Aristonus supervenit.

16 Indi quoque, cum intra moenia regem esse com-
perissent, omissis ceteris, illuc concurrerunt urge-
bantque protegentes eum. E quibus[5] Timaeus,
multis adverso corpore vulneribus acceptis, egregia-

17 que edita pugna cecidit ; Peucestes quoque, tribus
iaculis confossus, non se tamen scuto sed regem

---

[1] subrecto *Acidalius;* subiecto *A.*
[2] tamen *Vogel;* iam *A.*   [3] spem *Bentley;* suae *A.*
[4] subinde *P;* subit inde *C.*
[5] E quibus *Kinch;* cum quibus *P;* ex quibus *C.*

---

[a] According to Arrian, Peucestes was with him from the
first ; see ix. 4. 32, note.
[b] *vestigia* is used generally not literally ; Peucestes
followed along the wall until he came to him ; Heinse read
muri vestigia. But see note *a.*
[c] *Cf.* Arr. vi. 28. 4. Abreas, whom Arrian (vi. 9. 3)
names among those who came to the king's help, is not else-

11 forward with eager joy to strip his body. No sooner
did the king feel him lay hand on his person, than
aroused, I suppose, by the disgrace of this supreme
indignity, he recalled his failing spirits, and plunged
his sword upward into his enemy's naked side.

12 Three bodies lay dead around the king, while the
rest of his assailants stood in stupefaction afar off.
He tried to lift himself with his shield, that he might
at any rate die fighting before his last breath failed

13 him, but finding that not enough strength remained
for that effort, he laid hold of the overhanging
branches with his right hand and tried to rise. But
not even then being able to control his body, he again
fell upon his knees, waving his hand as a challenge
to the enemy to meet him in single combat, if any-

14 one dared. At last Peucestes, having dislodged
the defenders of the wall in another part of the
town, followed [a] in the king's footsteps [b] and came

15 to him. Alexander, on seeing him, thinking that
not hope of life but consolation in death had
arrived, allowed his wearied body to fall on his
shield. Then Timaeus appeared, and a little later

16 Leonnatus, and after him Aristonus.[c] The Indi
also, having learned that Alexander was within
the walls, left the others, ran to the spot, and assailed
those who were protecting him. Of these Timaeus,[d]
after receiving many wounds in front and fighting a

17 glorious battle, fell. Peucestes also, though pierced
by three javelins, nevertheless with his shield was

where mentioned. Arrian (vi. 11. 7) says that there was
difference of opinion about Leonnatus and Abreas ; so also
in the details of the king's battle with his foes.

[d] Apparently identical with Limnaeus, Plut. *Alex.* lxiii.
4, note.

tuebatur ; Leonnatus, dum avide ruentes barbaros
submovet, cervice graviter icta, semianimis procubuit
18 ante regis pedes. Iam et Peucestes vulneribus fatigatus submiserat clipeum ; in Aristono spes ultima
haerebat. Hic quoque graviter saucius tantam vim
hostium ultra sustinere non poterat.

19 Inter haec ad Macedonas regem cecidisse fama
perlata est. Terruisset alios quod illos incitavit.
Namque periculi omnis[1] immemores dolabris perfregere murum et qua moliti erant aditum irrupere
in urbem Indosque plures fugientes quam congredi
20 ausos ceciderunt. Non senibus, non feminis, non
infantibus parcitur ; quisquis occurrerat, ab illo
vulneratum regem esse credebant. Tandemque
internecione hostium iustae irae parentatum est.
21 Ptolomaeum, qui postea regnavit, huic pugnae adfuisse auctor est Clitarchus et Timagenes, sed ipse,
scilicet gloriae suae non refragatus, afuisse se, missum in expeditionem, memoriae tradidit. Tanta
componentium vetusta[2] rerum monimenta vel securi-
tas vel, par huic vitium, credulitas fuit.

22 Rege in tabernaculum relato, medici lignum sagittae corpori infixae,[3] ita ne spiculum moveretur,
23 abscidunt. Corpore deinde nudato, animadvertunt
hamos inesse telo nec aliter id sine pernicie corporis
extrahi posse quam ut secando[4] vulnus augerent.

---

[1] omnis *Modius;* omnes *A.*
[2] vetusta *Giunta;* uetustate *A.*
[3] infixae *Vogel;* infixum *A.*
[4] secando *J. Froben;* secundo *A.*

---

[a] He was not killed ; see ix. 10. 6.
[b] On *parentatum est* see v. 6. 1.
[c] *i.e.* of Egypt ; see x. 10. 1.
[d] In his *Memoirs*; see L.C.L. *Arrian,* Prefatory Note, p. xi.

protecting not himself but the king; Leonnatus, while
he was vigorously repulsing the eagerly charging barbarians, was severely wounded in the neck and fell
18 half-dead *a* at the king's feet. Now Peucestes also,
exhausted by his wounds, had lowered his shield ;
the last hope remained in Aristonus. He too was
badly wounded and could no longer hold out against
so great a number of foemen.

19 Meanwhile news was brought to the Macedonians
that the king had been killed. What would have
terrified other men animated them. For regardless
of all danger, they broke through the wall with
mattocks, and when they had made a breach, rushed
into the city and cut down the Indi, more of whom fled
20 than dared to engage them. They spared neither
old men, women, nor children ; whoever met them
they believed to be the person by whom the king
had been wounded. And at length by the slaughter
of the enemy they appeased *b* their just anger.

21 Clitarchus and Timagenes are our authorities for the
statement that Ptolemy, who was later king,*c* was
present at this battle, but he himself, who certainly
was not inclined to depreciate his own glory, has
written *d* that he was not there, since he had been sent
on an expedition. Such was the carelessness of those
who composed the old records, or their credulity,*e*
which is an equally great fault.

22 Alexander was carried to his tent and the physicians cut off the shaft of the arrow, which was firmly
fixed in his body, taking care not to stir the point.
23 Then, when his clothing had been removed, they perceived that the arrow was barbed, and that it could
not be extracted without injury unless the wound

See ix. 1. 34.

24 Ceterum, ne secantes profluvium sanguinis occuparet verebantur; quippe ingens telum adactum erat et
25 penetrasse in viscera videbatur. Critobulus, inter medicos artis eximiae, sed in tanto periculo territus, manus[1] admovere metuebat, ne in ipsius caput parum
26 prosperae curationis recideret[2] eventus. Lacrimantem eum ac metu[3] et sollicitudine propemodum exsanguem rex conspexerat: "Quid," inquit, "quodve tempus exspectas et non quam primum hoc dolore me saltem moriturum liberas? An times ne
27 reus sis, cum insanabile vulnus acceperim?" At Critobulus, tandem vel finito vel dissimulato metu, hortari eum coepit ut se continendum praeberet, dum spiculum evelleret; etiam levem corporis motum
28 noxium fore. Rex cum affirmasset nihil opus esse eis qui semet continerent, sicut praeceptum erat, sine motu praebuit corpus.

Igitur, patefacto latius vulnere, et spiculo evolso, ingens vis sanguinis manare coepit linquique animo rex et, caligine oculis offusa, velut moribundus ex-
29 tendi. Cumque profluvium medicamentis frustra inhiberent, clamor simul atque ploratus amicorum oritur regem exspirasse credentium. Tandem constitit sanguis, paulatimque animum recepit et circum-
30 stantes coepit agnoscere. Toto eo die ac nocte quae secuta est armatus exercitus regiam obsedit, confessus

---

[1] manus *added by J. Froben.*
[2] recideret *I;* reccident *A.*
[3] metu *Bentley;* metuentem *A.*

---

a See Pliny, *N.H.* vii. 37. 37 (124), but Arrian (vi. 11. 1) gives the same as Critodemus.

b *linqui* may not be dependent on *coepit,* as *manare*

24 was enlarged by the knife. But they feared that the
flow of blood could not be staunched by those who
performed the operation; for the arrow was very
long and seemed to have penetrated the vital parts.
25 Critobulus,[a] who was a physician of distinguished
skill, but was terrified in the face of such great risk,
dreaded to put his hand to the work, lest the result
of the treatment, if unsuccessful, might recoil upon
26 his own head. The king observed that he was weeping
and near to fainting from fear and anxiety and said :
" For what event or moment are you waiting, and why
do you not free me as soon as possible from this pain
and let me at least die ? Do you perhaps fear that
you may be blamed because I have received an incur-
27 able wound ? " But Critobulus, having at last ended
his fear, or concealed it, began to urge that he let
himself be held while he was withdrawing the point ;
that even a slight movement of his body would be
28 dangerous. When the king had assured him that
there was no need of any to hold him, he kept his
body motionless, as had been ordered.

So when the wound had been laid open and the
barb extracted, a copious amount of blood proceeded
to flow, the king to swoon,[b] darkness veiled his eyes,
29 and he lay stretched out as if he were dead. And
while they were vainly trying to staunch the flow of
blood by applications, his friends began to cry out and
to weep, believing that he had breathed his last. At
last the blood ceased to flow, and the king gradually
recovered his senses and began to recognize those
30 who stood around him. All that day and the following night the army stood under arms before the royal

is, but may be the infinitive of vivid narration, the so-called
" historical infinitive."

omnes unius spiritu vivere. Nec prius recesserunt,
quam compertum est somno paulisper acquiescere.
Hinc certiorem spem salutis eius in castra rettulerunt.

VI. Rex, vii diebus curato vulnere, necdum obducta cicatrice, cum audisset convaluisse apud barbaros famam mortis suae, duobus navigiis iunctis,
statui in medium undique conspicuum tabernaculum
iussit, ex quo se ostenderet perisse credentibus,
conspectusque ab incolis spem hostium falso nuntio
2 conceptam inhibuit. Secundo deinde amne defluxit
aliquantum intervalli a cetera classe praecipiens,
ne quies perinvalido adhuc necessaria pulsu remorum
impediretur.

3   Quarto postquam navigare coeperat die pervenit
in regionem desertam quidem ab incolis, sed frumento et pecoribus abundantem. Placuit is locus et
4 ad suam et ad militum requiem. Mos erat principibus amicorum et custodibus corporis excubare ante
praetorium quotiens adversa regi valetudo incidisset;
hoc tum quoque more servato, universi cubiculum
5 eius intrant. Ille sollicitus ne quid novi afferrent,
quia simul venerant, percontatur num hostium recens
6 nuntiaretur adventus. At Craterus, cui mandatum
erat ut amicorum preces perferret ad eum : " Cre-

---

pavilion, confessing that they all lived by his breath alone,[a] and they did not leave until they learned that he was quietly sleeping for a time. Then they returned to the camp with more assured hope of his recovery.

VI. The king, after his wound had been treated for seven days but had not yet cicatrized, hearing that the report of his death had gained strength among the barbarians, ordered two ships to be lashed together, and his tent to be set up in the centre, where it would be conspicuous to everyone, in order that from it he might show himself to those who believed that he was dead, and, being seen by the inhabitants, he put an end to the enemies hope which they had conceived from the false report.

2 Then he went on down the river,[b] keeping some distance ahead of the rest of the fleet, in order that the quiet which he still needed in his very weak condition might not be interfered with by the beat of the oars.

3 On the fourth day after he had begun his voyage he came into a region which was indeed deserted by all its inhabitants, but abounded in grain and cattle. The place suited him for resting both himself and his 4 soldiers. It was the custom for the principal men among the king's friends and for his body-guard to keep watch before his tent whenever he had fallen ill ; since this custom was being observed at that time 5 as usual, they all entered his chamber. Alexander, anxious lest they brought some serious news, because they had all come at once, asked whether an immediate approach of the enemy was being reported. 6 But Craterus, who had been intrusted to convey to him the prayers of his friends, replied : " Do you

415

disne," inquit, " adventu magis hostium, ut iam in
vallo consisterent, sollicitos esse quam cura salutis
7 tuae, ut nunc est, tibi vilis ? Quantalibet vis omnium gentium conspiret in nos, impleat armis virisque
totum orbem, classibus maria consternat, invisitatas
8 beluas inducat, tu nos praestabis invictos. Sed quis
deorum hoc Macedoniae columen ac sidus diuturnum
fore polliceri potest, cum tam avide manifestis periculis offeras corpus, oblitus tot civium animas trahere
9 te in casum ? Quis enim tibi superstes aut optat
esse aut potest ? Eo pervenimus auspicium atque
imperium secuti tuum, unde nisi te reduce nulli ad
penates suos iter est.
10 " Quodsi adhuc de Persidis regno cum Dareo dimi-
cares, etsi nemo vellet, tamen ne admirari quidem
posset tam promptae esse te ad omne discrimen
audaciae ; nam ubi paria sunt periculum ac praemium, et secundis rebus amplior fructus est et ad-
11 versis solacium maius. Tuo vero capite ignobilem
vicum emi quis ferat, non tuorum modo militum, sed
ullius gentis barbarae civis qui tuam magnitudinem
12 novit ? Horret animus cogitationem rei, quam paulo
ante vidimus. Eloqui timeo invicti corporis spolia
inertissimas manus fuisse infecturas,[1] nisi te interceptum misericors in nos Fortuna servasset.
" Totidem proditores, totidem desertores sumus,
13 quot te non potuimus persequi. Universos licet

---

[1] infecturas *Zumpt;* iniecturas *A.*

---

[a] *Cf.* Hor. *Odes* ii. 17. 4 ; i. 12. 46 f.
[b] Minimized for rhetorical effect. It was not the capital
of the Malli, but was far from being *ignobilis vicus.*

imagine that we are more disturbed by the coming
of the enemy, although they even now stood on
our rampart, than through care for your safety, on
7 which you seem to set little store? However great
a force of all nations should unite against us, should
fill the whole world with arms and men, should cover
the sea with their fleets, should bring against us
beasts never seen before, it is you that will make us
8 invincible. But who among the gods can promise
that this prop and star *a* of Macedonia will be lasting,
when you so eagerly expose your person to evident
dangers, forgetting that you draw into disaster the
9 lives of so many citizens? For who desires to be, or
can be, your survivor? Following your auspices and
command, we have come to a place from which none
of us can find a way to his hearth and home except
under your lead.

10 "But if you were still contending with Darius for the
dominion of Persia, although no one could wish it, yet
one could not even wonder that you are of such ready
daring in the face of every danger; for when the peril
and its reward are equal, the gain is not only more
ample in case of success, but the solace is greater in
11 case of defeat. But that an obscure village *b* should
be bought at the price of your life who could endure,
not to mention your own soldiers, but even the citizen
of any barbarous nation who knows your greatness?
12 My soul shudders at the thought of the scene which
we witnessed a short time ago. I fear to mention
that the most worthless of hands would have polluted
the spoils stripped from your invincible body, had not
Fortune been compassionate and saved you for us.

"We are so many traitors, so many deserters, all of
13 us who were not able to keep up with you. Although

milites ignominia notes, nemo recusabit luere id quod
14 ne admitteret praestare non potuit. Patere nos,
quaeso, alio modo esse viles tibi. Quocumque iusseris, ibimus. Obscura pericula et ignobiles pugnas
nobis deposcimus ; temet ipsum ad ea serva, quae
magnitudinem tuam capiunt. Cito gloria obsolescit
in sordidis hostibus, nec quicquam indignius est quam
15 consumi eam ubi non possit ostendi." Eadem fere
Ptolomaeus et similia his ceteri. Iamque confusis
vocibus flentes eum orabant ut tandem ex satietate[1]
laudi modum faceret ac saluti suae, id est publicae,
parceret.

16 Grata erat regi pietas amicorum ; itaque singulos
familiarius amplexus, considere iubet, altiusque ser-
17 mone repetito : " Vobis quidem," inquit, " o fidis-
simi piissimique civium atque amicorum, grates ago
habeoque, non solum eo[2] nomine quod hodie salutem
meam vestrae praeponitis, sed quod a primordiis belli
nullum erga me benivolentiae pignus atque indicium
omisistis, adeo ut confitendum sit numquam mihi
vitam meam fuisse tam caram, quam esse coepit, ut
18 vobis diu frui possim. Ceterum non eadem est
cogitatio eorum qui pro me mori optant, et mea, qui
pridem[3] hanc benivolentiam vestram virtute meruisse
me iudico. Vos enim diuturnum fructum ex me,

---

[1] ex satietate *Bentley;* exacietate *F;* exsatiatae *BVL;*
exsaciatae *P.*   [2] eo *Francine;* meo *A.*
[3] et mea, qui pridem *Hedicke;* meam et quidem *C;* et
quidem meam *P.*

---

[a] *praestare* is frequent in juristic Latin, in the sense of
" guarantee."   [b] *Cf.* Sen. *Suas.* i. 3.
[c] Antony's use of *piissimus* is criticized as un-Latin by
Cicero, *Philipp.* xiii. 19. 43, but occurs frequently in later
Latin.

you should brand your soldiers with ignominy, no
one will refuse to pay that penalty for the guilt which
14 he could not avoid [a] incurring. I pray you, allow us
to be worthless in your sight in a different way.
Whithersoever you bid us we will go. We demand for
ourselves the obscure dangers and inglorious battles;
save yourself for those which are worthy of your
greatness. Glory gained over mean enemies quickly
fades, and nothing is more unworthy than for it to
15 be wasted when it cannot be displayed." Ptolemy
spoke too about the same purport, and the rest
used similar language. And now with mingled
tears and cries all besought him that at last from
satiety he should set a limit [b] to the pursuit of
glory and have regard for his safety, that is, the
safety of the state.

16 The affection of his friends was gratifying to the
king; accordingly, having embraced them one after
the other with unusual tenderness, he bade them
be seated and, seeking words of deeper feeling,
17 said : " To you indeed, most faithful and most
loyal [c] of my fellow citizens and friends, I feel and
express gratitude, not only for the reason that to-
day you value my safety more than your own, but
also because from the outset of this war there is
no pledge and proof of your affection for me which
you have omitted, so much so that I must confess
that my life has never been so dear to me as it
has begun to be now that I can enjoy your com-
18 panionship for a long time. But the thought of
those who wish to die for me is not the same as my
own, since I think that I have long since won this
goodwill of yours through deeds of valour. For you
would wish to enjoy me for a long time, and perhaps

forsitan etiam perpetuum percipere cupiatis ; ego
19 me metior non aetatis spatio, sed gloriae. Licuit
paternis opibus contento, intra Macedoniae terminos
per otium corporis exspectare obscuram et ignobilem
senectutem. Quamquam ne pigri quidem sibi fata
disponunt, sed unicum bonum diuturnam vitam
existimantes saepe acerba mors occupat. Verum
ego, qui non annos meos, sed victorias numero, si
munera Fortunae bene computo, diu vixi.
20   " Orsus a Macedonia imperium Graeciae teneo,
Thraciam et Illyrios subegi, Triballis Maedisque
imperito, Asiam, qua Hellesponto, qua Rubro mari
subluitur, possideo. Iamque haud procul absum fine
mundi, quem egressus aliam Naturam, alium orbem
21 aperire mihi statui. Ex Asia in Europae terminos
momento unius horae transivi. Victor utriusque
regionis post nonum regni mei, post vicesimum atque
octavum annum vitae,[1] videorne vobis in excolenda
gloria, cui me uni devovi, posse cessare ? Ego vero
non deero et, ubicumque pugnabo, in theatro ter-
22 rarum orbis esse me credam. Dabo nobilitatem
ignobilibus locis, aperiam cunctis gentibus terras,
quas Natura longe submoverat.
   " In his operibus exstingui mihi, si fors ita feret,
pulchrum est ; ea stirpe sum genitus, ut multam[2]
23 prius quam longam vitam debeam optare. Obsecro
vos, cogitate nos pervenisse in terras quibus feminae
ob virtutem celeberrimum nomen est. Quas urbes

---

[1] vitae *added by Jeep.*   [2] multam *J. Froben;* multa *A.*

---

[a] *Cf.* Livy v. 7. 3.
[b] It was really the tenth year of his reign and the thirtieth
of his age.

forever, whereas I measure myself by the extent of
19 my glory rather than that of my life. I might, content with the kingdom of my sire, within the limits
of Macedonia amid idleness have awaited an obscure
and inglorious old age. And yet even the indolent
cannot control their destiny, but a premature death
often surprises those who consider length of days the
only blessing. But I, who count not my years but
my victories, if I keep a correct account of Fortune's
favours, have already had a long life.

20 "Beginning my reign in Macedonia, I hold dominion
over Greece, I have subdued Thrace and the Illyrians,
I rule the Triballi and the Maedi, I possess Asia from
where it is washed by the Hellespont to the shores of
the Red Sea. And now I am not far from the end
of the world, and passing beyond this, I have resolved
to open to myself a new realm of Nature, a new
21 world. From Asia I crossed into the bounds of
Europe in a single hour.[a] Having conquered both
continents in the ninth year of my reign and the
twenty-eighth of my life,[b] does it seem to you that
I can pause in the task of completing my glory, to
which alone I have devoted myself? I at least shall
not be found wanting, and wherever I shall fight, I
shall believe that I am in the theatre of the whole
22 world. I will give fame to unknown places. I will
open to all nations lands which Nature had moved
to a distance.

"To end my life amid these enterprises, if chance
shall so will it, is in my opinion glorious; I am born
from such stock that I am bound to desire an
23 abundant life rather than a long one. I pray you,
think that you have come to lands in which the name
of a woman is renowned because of her valour. What

Samiramis condidit ! quas gentis redegit in potestatem ! quanta opera molita est ! Nondum feminam aequavimus gloria, et iam nos laudis satietas cepit ?
24 Di faveant, maiora adhuc restant. Sed ita nostra erunt quae nondum adiimus,[1] si nihil parvum duxerimus in quo magnae gloriae locus est. Vos modo me ab intestina fraude et domesticorum insidiis praestate securum ; belli Martisque discrimen impavidus subibo.
25 " Philippus in acie tutior quam in theatro fuit ; hostium manus saepe evitavit,[2] suorum effugere non valuit. Aliorum quoque regum exitus si reputaveritis, plures a suis quam ab hoste interemptos
26 numerabitis. Ceterum, quoniam olim rei agitatae in animo meo nunc promendae occasio oblata est, mihi maximus laborum atque operum meorum erit fructus, si Olympias mater immortalitati consecretur quan-
27 doque excesserit vita. Hoc, si licuerit, ipse praestabo ; hoc, si me praeceperit fatum, vos mandasse me[3] mementote." Ac tum quidem amicos dimisit. Ceterum per complures dies ibi stativa habuit.

VII. Haec dum in India geruntur, Graeci milites nuper in colonias a rege deducti circa Bactra, orta inter ipsos seditione, defecerant non tam Alexandro
2 infensi quam metu supplicii. Quippe, occisis quibusdam popularium, qui validiores erant arma spectare

---

[1] adiimus *P;* attigimus *and* atigimus *C.*
[2] evitavit *Hedicke;* uitauit *A.*   [3] me *added by Eussner.*

---

[a] The exploits of Samiramis are given in Diod. ii. 4 ff., especially ii. 16 ff.
[b] Where he was assassinated by Pausanias ; see Diod. xvi. 94. 1-3.

cities did Samiramis build ! What nations did she reduce to submission ! What great works did she accomplish ! [a] We have not yet equalled a woman in glory, and has a satiety of renown already seized us ? Let the gods favour us, and still greater things
24 await us. But those which we have not yet undertaken will be ours only if we consider nothing small in which there is room for great glory. Do you only keep me safe from intestine treachery and domestic plots ; I will meet unterrified the hazard of war and of Mars.

25 " Philip was safer on the field of battle than in the theatre.[b] He often evaded the hands of the enemy, but he could not escape those of his own countrymen. If you think also of the deaths of other kings, you will count more that were slain by their own
26 people than by the foe. But since an opportunity has now been offered of setting forth a matter which I have long agitated in my thoughts, let me say that I shall receive the greatest reward for my labours and my toils if my mother Olympias shall be consecrated to immortality when she departs from life.
27 This, if it shall be allowed me, I myself will effect ; if Fate shall anticipate me, remember that I have entrusted this duty to you." And then indeed he dismissed his friends. But for many days he remained there in the same camp.

VII. While this was going on in India, the Greek soldiers who had lately been established by the king in colonies round about Bactra, since disagreement had arisen among them, had revolted, not so much through hostility to Alexander, as from fear of punish-
2 ment. For the stronger faction, having killed some of their countrymen, began to think of armed action,

coeperunt et Bactriana arce, quae quasi tuta[1] negle-
gentius asservata erat, occupata, barbaros quoque
3 in societatem defectionis impulerant. Athenodorus
erat princeps eorum, qui regis quoque nomen assumpserat, non tam imperii cupidine quam in patriam
revertendi cum eis,[2] qui auctoritatem ipsius seque-
4 bantur. Huic Biton[3] quidam nationis eiusdem, sed
ob aemulationem infestus, comparavit insidias in-
vitatumque ad epulas per Boxum quendam Bactria-
5 num[4] in convivio occidit. Postero die contione
advocata, Biton ultro insidiatum sibi Athenodorum
plerisque persuaserat ; sed aliis suspecta erat fraus
Bitonis, et paulatim in plures coepit manare suspicio.
6 Itaque Graeci milites arma capiunt, occisuri Bitonem
si daretur occasio ; ceterum[5] principes eorum iram
multitudinis mitigaverunt.
7 Praeter spem suam Biton, praesenti periculo ereptus, paulo post est insidiatus auctoribus salutis suae.
Cuius dolo cognito, et ipsum comprehenderunt et
8 Boxum. Ceterum Boxum protinus placuit interfici,
Bitonem etiam per cruciatum necari. Iamque corpori
tormenta admovebantur, cum Graeci—incertum, ob
quam causam—lymphatis similes ad arma discurrunt.
9 Quorum fremitu exaudito, qui torquere Bitonem
iussi erant omisere, veriti ne id facere tumultuantium
10 vociferatione prohiberentur. Ille, sicut nudatus erat,[a]
pervenit ad Graecos, et miserabilis facies supplicio
destinati in diversum animos repente mutavit, dimit-

---

[1] tuta *added by Hedicke.*   [2] cum iis *Aldus;* cunctis *A.*
[3] Biton *Hedicke;* bicon *A (similarly below).*
[4] Bactrianum *Bentley;* macerianum *A.*
[5] ceterum *Acidalius;* ceteri *A.*

---

[a] *sicut nudatus:* cf. iv. 14. 9 ; viii. 3. 10.

and after having seized the citadel of Bactra, which through belief in its safety had been carelessly guarded, they had forced the barbarians also to join
3 in their revolt. Their chief was Athenodorus, who had even assumed the title of king, not so much from a desire for power, as for returning to his fatherland along with those who acknowledged his authority.
4 Against him a certain Biton of the same nation, but hostile to Athenodorus because of rivalry, laid a plot, and having invited him to a banquet, had him assassinated at table by a Bactrian called Boxus.
5 On the following day Biton called an assembly and convinced the majority that Athenodorus without provocation had plotted to take his life ; but others suspected imposture on the part of Biton and the
6 suspicion gradually began to spread to more. Accordingly, the Greek soldiers armed themselves, intending to kill Biton if an opportunity offered ; but their leading men appeased the wrath of the multitude.
7 Biton, rescued from imminent danger contrary to his expectation, a little later plotted against those who had saved him. But when his treachery became
8 known, they seized both him and Boxus. The latter they ordered to be put to death at once and Biton also, but after suffering torture. And they were already applying the instruments of torture to his body, when the Greeks—for what reason is uncertain
9 —as if crazed, rushed to arms. When their tumult was heard, those who had been ordered to torture Biton, left him, for fear that they would be prevented from carrying out their orders by the cries of the
10 rioting soldiers. He, stripped naked as he was,[a] came to the Greeks, and the pitiable aspect of the man who had been condemned to death suddenly changed their

11 tique eum iusserunt. Hoc modo poena bis liberatus,
cum ceteris qui colonias a rege attributas reliquerunt
revertit in patriam. Haec circa Bactra et Scytharum
terminos gesta.

12 Interim regem duarum gentium de quibus ante
dictum est c legati adeunt. Omnes curru vehebantur
eximia magnitudine corporum, decoro habitu ; lineae

13 vestes intexto auro purpuraque distinctae. Ei se
dedere ipsos, urbes agrosque referebant, per tot
aetates inviolatam libertatem illius primum fidei
dicionique permissuros ; deos sibi deditionis auctores,
non metum ; quippe intactis viribus iugum excipere.

14 Rex, consilio habito, deditos in fidem accepit stipen-
dio, quod Arachosiis utraque natio pensitabat,
imposito ; praeterea II milia et D equites imperat.

15 Et omnia oboedienter a barbaris facta. Invitatis
deinde ad epulas legatis gentium regulisque, exornari
convivium iussit. c aurei lecti modicis intervallis
positi erant, lectis circumdederat aulaea purpura
auroque fulgentia, quidquid aut apud Persas vetere
luxu aut apud Macedonas nova inmutatione corrup-
tum erat, confusis utriusque gentis vitiis, in illo
convivio ostendens.

6 Intererat epulis Dioxippus Atheniensis, pugil no-

---

^a This shows some uncertainty on Curtius' part of the
geography of Bactra.

^b Malli and Sudracae ; see Arr. vi. 14. 1.

^c Really, cotton.   ^d Arr. vi. 14. 2.

^e This is not consistent with *inviolatam libertatem*, above.

feelings to pity, and they gave orders to let him go.
11 Twice freed from punishment in this way, he returned to his native land with the rest who had left the colonies established by Alexander. This is what happened in the region of Bactra and the frontiers of Scythia.[a]

12 In the meantime a hundred envoys came to the king from the two nations of which mention has been made.[b] All rode in chariots and were men of uncommon stature and dignified bearing ; their robes were of linen,[c] embroidered with inwrought gold and
13 purple. They said that they surrendered to him themselves, their cities, and their lands, and would entrust[d] for the first time the liberty which they had preserved inviolate for so many ages to his protection and authority ; that it was the gods that advised their submission to him, not fear, since they assumed the yoke while their strength was unim-
14 paired. The king, after holding a council, admitted the surrendered peoples into his protection, imposing upon them the tribute which both nations were paying to the Arachosii[e] ; besides, he ordered them to furnish 2500 horsemen. All these commands
15 were faithfully carried out by the barbarians. Then he invited the envoys and the petty kings of the nations to a banquet, and ordered a magnificent feast to be prepared. A hundred golden couches had been placed at a small distance from each other ; the couches he had hung about with purple tapestries gleaming with gold, displaying in that banquet all that was corrupt in the ancient luxury of the Persians or in the new fashions adopted by the Macedonians, thus intermingling the vices of both nations.
16 There was present at the feast Dioxippus, an

bilis et ob eximiam virtutem virium iam et regi[1]
pernotus et gratus. Invidi malignique increpabant
per seria et ludum saginati corporis sequi inutilem
beluam ; cum ipsi proelium inirent, oleo madentem
17 praeparare ventrem epulis. Eadem igitur in convivio Corratas[2] Macedo iam temulentus exprobrare
ei coepit et postulare, ut, si vir esset, postero die
secum ferro decerneret ; regem tandem vel de sua
18 temeritate vel de illius ignavia iudicaturum. Et a
Dioxippo contemptim militarem eludente[3] ferociam,
accepta condicio est. Ac postero die rex, cum etiam
acrius certamen exposcerent, quia deterrere non
19 poterat, destinata exsequi passus est. Ingens vis[4]
militum, inter quos erant Graeci, Dioxippo studebant.
Macedo iusta arma sumpserat, aereum clipeum hastamque[5]—sarisam vocant—laeva tenens, dextera
lanceam gladioque cinctus, velut cum pluribus simul
20 dimicaturus ; Dioxippus oleo nitens et coronatus,
laeva puniceum amiculum, dextra validum nodosum-
que stipitem praeferebat. Ea ipsa res omnium
animos expectatione suspenderat ; quippe armato
congredi nudum dementia, non temeritas videbatur.
21 Igitur Macedo, haud dubius eminus interfici posse,
lanceam emisit. Quam Dioxippus cum exigua cor-

---

[1] et regi *Stangl;* a rege *A.*
[2] Corratas *Hedicke;* horrotas *A.*
[3] eludente *Aldus;* eludentem *A.*   [4] vis *Jeep;* hic *A.*
[5] hastamque *Gertz;* hastam quam *A.*

---

[a] *virtutem virium* is an uncommon expression, but is
justified by the etymological meaning of *virtus,* and makes
an effective alliteration.
[b] *Cf.* iii. 1. 17 ; vii. 4. 14.

Athenian, a celebrated boxer, and because of the extraordinary greatness [a] of his strength already both well known to the king and a favourite of his. Some through jealousy and malice carped at him with mingled seriousness and jest, saying that they had as a companion a useless brute with an over-fed body ; that while they entered battle, he, dripping

17 with oil, was preparing his belly for feasts. Thus it was that at the banquet Corratas, a Macedonian, already overcome by wine, began to upbraid Dioxippus, and to demand that, if he were a man, he should fight with him on the following day with swords ; that the king at last would have an opportunity to judge of Corratas' rashness or the other's

18 cowardice. And the challenge was accepted by Dioxippus, who contemptuously made sport of the soldier's bravado. And on the next day the king, since they even more earnestly demanded the contest, and he was unable to dissuade them, allowed

19 what they desired to be carried out. A great number of soldiers, including the Greeks, favoured Dioxippus. The Macedonian had assumed his usual arms, holding in his left hand a bronze shield and a spear—they call it *sarisa*—in his right a lance, and girt with a sword, as if he were going to fight with

20 several men at once ; Dioxippus, gleaming with oil and wearing a garland, displayed a purple cloth in his left hand, and in his right a stout knotted club. This very thing had filled the minds of all with eager anticipation [b] ; since for a naked man to fight with one in full armour seemed not only rashness, but madness.

21 Then the Macedonian, not doubting that his foe could be killed at long range, hurled his lance. Diox-

poris declinatione vitasset, antequam ille hastam
transferret in dextram, assiluit et stipite mediam
22 eam fregit. Amisso utroque telo, Macedo gladium
coeperat stringere, cum[1] occupatum, complexu pedibus repente subductis, Dioxippus arietavit in terram,
ereptoque gladio, pedem super cervicem iacenti
imposuit stipitem intentans elisurusque eo victum,
ni prohibitus esset a rege.

23 Tristis spectaculi eventus non Macedonibus modo,
sed etiam Alexandro fuit, maxime quia barbari
adfuerant ; quippe celebratam Macedonum fortitu-
24 dinem ad ludibrium recidisse querebatur.[2] Hinc ad
criminationem invidorum adapertae sunt regis aures.
Et post paucos dies inter epulas aureum poculum ex
composito subducitur, ministrique, quasi amisissent
25 quod amoverant, regem adeunt. Saepe minus est
constantiae in rubore, quam in culpa ; coniectum
oculorum, quibus ut fur destinabatur, Dioxippus ferre
non potuit et, cum excessisset convivio, litteris con-
scriptis, quae regi redderentur, ferro se interemit.
26 Graviter mortem eius tulit rex, existimans indigna-
tionis esse, non paenitentiae testem, utique postquam
falso insimulatum eum nimium invidorum gaudium
ostendit.

VIII. Indorum legati dimissi domos paucis post
diebus cum donis revertuntur. ccc erant equites,

---

[1] cum *Bentley;* quam *A.*
[2] querebatur *Meiser;* uerebatur *A.*

---

[a] Diod. xvii. 101. 3 attributes this to friends of the king.

ippus avoided it by a slight movement of his body, and before the other could transfer his spear to his right hand, leaped upon him and broke the spear in
22 two with his club. Having lost both his missiles, the Macedonian had begun to draw his sword, when Dioxippus seized him in his arms, suddenly knocked his feet from under him, and butted him to the ground ; then snatching his sword from him, he set his foot upon the Macedonian's neck as he lay prostrate, and poising his club to strike him, would have crushed his defeated adversary with it, had he not been prevented by the king.
23 The result of this spectacle was displeasing, not only to the Macedonians, but to the king, especially because the barbarians had witnessed it ; for he regretted that the famous valour of the Macedonians was
24 exposed to ridicule. For this reason the ears of the king were opened to the calumnies of jealous rivals. And a few days later at a feast a golden cup was purposely abstracted,[a] and the attendants went to the king, pretending to have lost what they had
25 actually hidden. Often there is less firmness in innocent embarrassment than in genuine guilt. Dioxippus could not endure the gaze of all eyes by which he was marked as a thief, and leaving the banquet, he wrote a letter to be delivered to the king, and
26 killed himself with his sword. The king was greatly grieved by his death, believing it to be a sign of indignation rather than of repentance, especially after the excessive joy of his rivals showed that he had been falsely accused.

VIII. After the envoys of the Indians had been sent home, they returned a few days later with gifts. These consisted of 300 horsemen, 1030 chariots, each

MXXX currus, quos quadriiugi equi ducebant, lineae
vestis aliquantum, mille scuta Indica et ferri candidi
talenta c leonesque rarae magnitudinis et tigres,
2 utrumque animal ad mansuetudinem domitum,
lacertarum quoque ingentium pelles et dorsa testudi-
3 num. Cratero deinde imperat rex haud procul amne
per quem erat ipse navigaturus, copias duceret; eos
autem, qui comitari eum solebant, imponit in naves
et in fines Mallorum¹ secundo amne devehitur.

4 Inde Sambagras² adiit, validam Indiae gentem,
quae populi, non regum imperio regebatur. LX milia³
peditum habebant, equitum VI milia⁴; has copias
currus D sequebantur. III duces spectatos virtute
5 bellica elegerant. At qui in agris erant proximis⁵
flumini—frequentes autem vicos maxime in ripa
habebant—ut videre totum amnem qua prospici
poterat navigiis constratum et tot militum arma
fulgentia, territi nova facie deorum exercitum et
alium Liberum Patrem, celebre in illis gentibus
6 nomen, adventare credebant. Hinc militum clamor,
hinc remorum pulsus variaeque nautarum voces
7 hortantium pavidas aures impleverant. Ergo universi ad eos qui in armis erant currunt, furere clami
tantes et cum dis proelium inituros; navigia non

¹ Mallorum *Lauer;* malliorum *A.*
² Sambagras *Hedicke;* sebarcas *A.*
³ LX milia *Freinshem;* VI milia *A.*   ⁴ VI milia] VI *C.*
⁵ proximis *Quicherat;* proximi *A.*

ᵃ *i.e.* cotton.
ᵇ The exact meaning of *ferrum candidum* is not clear;

drawn by four horses abreast, a quantity of linen [a] cloth, 1000 Indic shields, 100 talents of white iron, [b]

2 lions and tigers of unusual size (both species of animals being broken in and tamed), also some skins

3 of huge lizards, and shells of tortoises. Then the king ordered Craterus to lead on his forces at no great distance from the river down which he was going to sail, but those who were accustomed to attend him he embarked upon ships and sailed downstream to the lands of the Malli. [c]

4 From there he went on to the Sambagrae, [d] a strong race of India, which was governed by the will of the people, not the power of kings. They had 60,000 infantry and 6000 cavalry; these forces were followed by 500 chariots. They had chosen three leaders

5 distinguished for valour in war. But the people in the fields adjoining the river—and they had many villages, especially on its bank—when they saw the whole stream as far as they could see covered [e] with ships, and shining arms of so many soldiers, stunned by the novel sight, believed an army of gods was coming and another Father Liber, a name celebrated

6 among those nations. Hence the shouting of the soldiers, hence the beat of the oars and the confused cries of the rowers, as they encouraged one another,

7 had filled their ears [f] with terror. Therefore they all ran to those who were under arms, crying that they were mad and were about to do battle with gods; that

like *plumbum candidum* and *aes candidum*, it denotes the presence of an alloy, but whether for increasing the beauty or the strength of the iron is uncertain.

[c] Probably modern Multan.

[d] The name is variously given by Arrian and Diodorus.

[e] For *constratum cf.* ix. 6. 7.

[f] *impleverat aures*, an unusual locution; *cf.* iv. 12. 20, note.

posse numerari quae invictos viros veherent. Tan-
tumque in exercitum suorum intulere terroris, ut
legatos mitterent gentem redituros.

8 His in fidem acceptis, ad alias deinde gentes quarto
die pervenit. Nihilo plus animi his fuit quam ceteris
fuerat. Itaque oppido ibi condito, quod Alexandream
appellari iusserat, fines eorum qui Musicani appellan-
9 tur intravit. Hic de Teriolte satrape, quem Parapanisadis[1] praefecerat, eisdem arguentibus cognovit
multaque avare ac superbe fecisse convictum interfici
10 iussit. Oxyartes,[2] praetor Bactrianorum, non absolutus modo, sed etiam iure amoris, amplioris imperii
donatus est finibus. Musicanis deinde in dicionem
redactis urbi eorum praesidium imposuit.

11 Inde per silvas ad asperam[3] Indiae gentem perventum est. Porticanus rex erat, qui se munitae urbi
cum magna manu popularium incluserat. Hanc
Alexander tertio die quam coeperat obsidere, expug-
12 navit. Et Porticanus, cum in arcem confugisset,
legatos de condicione deditionis misit ad regem. Sed
antequam adirent eum, duae turres cum ingenti
fragore prociderant ; per quarum ruinas Macedones
evasere in arcem. Qua capta, Porticanus cum paucis
repugnans occiditur.

13 Diruta igitur arce, et omnibus captivis venundatis,

[1] Parapanisadis *Hedicke;* caracamisadis *A.*
[2] Oxyartes *Aldus;* oxartes *A.*
[3] per silvas ad asperam *Hedicke;* praestos et ipsam *A.*

---

[a] So called from the name of their king Musicanus (Arr.
vi. 15. 5 ; Diod. xvii. 102. 5) ; *cf.* viii. 10. 22.
[b] The name is corrupted and uncertain ; *cf.* Arr. vi. 15. 3.

the ships were innumerable and carried invincible heroes. And they struck such terror into the army of their countrymen that they sent envoys to surrender the nation.

8 When these had been received in submission, Alexander came next on the fourth day to another nation. These had no more courage than the others had had. Accordingly, after founding a town there, which he ordered to be called Alexandria, he entered the territories of those who are called the

9 Musicani.[a] Here, because of charges made by the Parapanisadae, he tried the satrap Terioltes,[b] whom he had made their governor, and since he was convicted of many acts of greed and arrogance, ordered

10 him to be put to death. Oxyartes,[c] ruler of the Bactriani, was not only acquitted, but because of his tie of affection with the king was given the territories of a more extensive rule. Then, having reduced the Musicani to submission, Alexander put a garrison in charge of their capital.

11 From there he came through forests to a rude race of India. Its king was Porticanus, who with a great force of his subjects had shut himself up in a fortified city. This Alexander took by assault on the third

12 day after he had begun to besiege it. And Porticanus, having taken refuge in the citadel, sent envoys to the king to discuss conditions of surrender. But before they reached Alexander two towers had fallen with a mighty crash, and through their ruins the Macedonians burst into the citadel. After this had been taken, Porticanus, who was resisting with a few of his men, was slain.

13 Having therefore razed the citadel, and sold all the

[c] The name appears in varied forms ; cf. viii. 4. 21.

Sambi regis fines ingressus est, multisque oppidis in
fidem acceptis, validissimam gentis urbem cuniculo
14 cepit. Barbaris simile monstri visum est, rudibus
militarium operum; quippe in media ferme urbe
armati terra exsistebant, nullo suffossi specus ante
15 vestigio facto. LXXX milia[1] Indorum in ea regione
caesa Clitarchus est auctor multosque captivos sub
16 corona venisse. Rursus Musicani defecerunt; ad
quos opprimendos missus est Pithon,[2] qui captum
principem gentis, eundemque defectionis auctorem,
adduxit ad regem. Quo Alexander in crucem sublato, rursus amnem, in quo classem exspectare se
iusserat, repetit.
17 Quarto deinde die secundo amne pervenit ad
oppidum quod in regno imo[3] erat Sambi. Nuper se
ille dediderat, sed oppidani detrectabant imperium
18 et clauserant portas. Quorum paucitate contempta,
rex D Agrianos moenia subire iussit et sensim
recedentes elicere extra muros hostem, secuturum
19 profecto, si fugere eos crederet. Agriani, sicut imperatum erat, lacessito hoste, subito terga verterunt;
quos barbari effuse sequentes, in alios, inter quos
ipse rex erat, incidunt. Renovato ergo proelio, ex
III milibus barbarorum DC caesi sunt, M capti, ceteri
20 moenibus urbis inclusi. Sed non ut prima specie
laeta victoria, ita eventu quoque fuit; quippe bar-

[1] LXXX milia *Rader;* D̄C̄C̄C̄ *P;* DCCC *C.*
[2] Pithon *J. Froben;* phyton *A.*
[3] regno imo *Jeep;* regnum *A.*

[a] See Arr. vi. 16. 3.   [b] Sindimana; Arr. vi. 16. **4.**
[c] For this sense of *specus* see iv. 6. 8.
[d] See Arr. vi. 15. 4; vi. 17. 1-2.

prisoners, Alexander entered the domain of King
Sambus,[a] and after receiving many towns in surrender
took the strongest city [b] of the nation by a subter-
14 ranean passage. To the barbarians, who were inexperienced in military operations, this seemed like
a prodigy ; for armed men came up out of the earth
almost in the middle of the city, no indication having
been given beforehand of the digging of the passage-
15 way.[c] Clitarchus states that 80,000 Indi were killed
in that region, and many captives sold at auction.
16 Again the Musicani revolted ; Pithon [d] was sent to
subdue them, captured the principal man of the
race, who was also the instigator of the rebellion and
brought him to Alexander. The king had him crucified, and returned again to the river, on which he
had ordered the fleet to wait for him.
17 Then, three days later, he sailed down the river to
a town at the extremity of the realm of Sambus.
That king had lately given himself up, but the people
of the city rejected his authority and had closed the
18 gates of the town. The king, despising the small-
ness of their number, ordered 500 of the Agriani to
advance to the wall, and by slowly retiring to lure
the enemy outside of the town ; for they would be
sure to follow, if they believed that the Agriani were
19 in flight. The Agriani, as had been ordered, after
attacking the enemy, suddenly turned their backs ;
the barbarians, hotly pursuing them, fell in with
other troops, among whom was King Alexander himself. Hence the battle was renewed, and of 3000
barbarians 600 were killed, 1000 captured, and the
20 rest shut within the walls of the city. But the victory
was not so happy in its outcome as it appeared to be
at first sight ; for the barbarians had poisoned their

bari veneno tinxerant gladios. Itaque saucii[1]
subinde expirabant, nec causa tam strenuae mortis
excogitari poterat a medicis, cum etiam leves plagae
insanabiles essent.

21   Barbari autem speraverant incautum et temerarium regem excipi posse. Sed[2] forte inter promp-
22 tissimos dimicans intactus evaserat. Praecipue
Ptolomaeus, laevo humero leviter quidem saucius,
sed maiore periculo quam vulnere affectus, regis sollicitudinem in se converterat. Sanguine coniunctus
erat, et quidam Philippo genitum esse credebant;
23 certe pelice eius ortum constabat. Idem corporis
custos promptissimusque bellator et pacis artibus
quam militiae maior et clarior; modico civilique cultu,
liberalis imprimis adituque facili, nihil ex fastu regiae
24 assumpserat. Ob haec regi an popularibus carior
esset, dubitari poterat; tum certe primum expertus
suorum animos, adeo ut fortunam in quam postea
ascendit in illo periculo Macedones ominati esse
videantur.

25   Quippe non levior illis Ptolomaei fuit cura quam
regi.[3] Qui et proelio et sollicitudine fatigatus, cum
Ptolomaeo assideret, lectum in quo ipse acquiesceret
26 iussit inferri. In quem ut se recepit, protinus altior
insecutus est somnus. Ex quo excitatus, per quietem

---

[1] saucii *I;* socii *A.*   [2] Sed *Kinch;* et *A.*
        [3] regi *Freinshem;* regis *A.*

---

[a] For *strenuus* in about this sense see iii. 6. 2.
[b] See Pausanias i. 6. 2.
[c] One of the seven officers of the body-guard; see Arr. vi.
28. 4.
[d] He became king of Egypt; see x. 10. 1 and 20.

438

swords. In consequence the wounded died one
after the other, and no cause for so speedy [a] a death
could be imagined by the physicians, since even
slight wounds were incurable.

21 Now the barbarians had hoped that the incautious
and rash king might be one of the victims. But
although he fought among the foremost, he was
22 fortunate enough to escape untouched. Ptolemy,
who was wounded in the left shoulder, slightly it is
true but with greater danger than that caused by
the wound, had caused the king special anxiety.
He was a blood-relation, and some believed him to be
a son of Philip [b]; at any rate it was known for certain
that he was the offspring of one of that king's con-
23 cubines. He was also a member of Alexander's
body-guard [c] and a most valiant warrior, and even
greater and more distinguished in the arts of peace
than in those of war ; modest and affable in his
manner of life, particularly generous and easy of
access, he had assumed none of the haughtiness of
24 royal origin. Because of these qualities it could be
doubted whether he was dearer to the king or to the
people ; at all events, it was at that time that he first
realized the affection of his countrymen ; which was
so great that in that time of his peril the Macedonians
seemed to have presaged the rank to which he afterwards rose.[d]

25 Indeed their solicitude for Ptolemy was no
weaker than that of the king. For when Alexander,
wearied by fighting and by anxiety, had taken his
place beside Ptolemy, he ordered a bed for himself
26 to sleep on to be brought in. As soon as he lay
down upon it, he immediately fell into a profound
sleep. When he awoke, he said that in a dream a

vidisse se exponit speciem draconis oblatam herbam
ferentis ore, quam veneni remedium esse monstrasset;
27 colorem quoque herbae referebat agniturum, si quis
repperisset, affirmans. Inventam deinde—quippe a
multis simul erat requisita—vulneri imposuit, pro-
tinusque dolore finito, intra breve spatium cicatrix
28 quoque obducta est. Barbaros ut prima spes fefellerat, se ipsos urbemque dediderunt.

Hinc in proximam gentem Patalium[1] perventum
est. Rex erat Soeris,[2] qui, urbe deserta, in montes
29 profugerat; itaque Alexander oppido potitur agrosque populatur. Magnae inde praedae actae sunt
pecorum armentorumque, magna vis reperta fru-
30 menti. Ducibus deinde sumptis amnis peritis,
defluxit ad insulam medio ferme alveo enatam.

IX. Ibi diutius subsistere coactus, quia duces
socordius asservati profugerant, misit qui conquire-
rent alios. Nec repertis, pervicit[3] cupido visendi
Oceanum adeundique terminos mundi sine regionis
peritis flumini ignoto caput suum totque fortissi-
2 morum virorum salutem permittere; navigabant
ergo omnium per quae ferebantur ignari. Quantum
inde abesset mare, quae gentes colerent, quam placi-

---

[1] Patalium *Hedicke;* pataliam *A.*
[2] Soeris *Lassen;* moeris *A* (meris *V*).
[3] pervicit *Bentley;* peruicax *A.*

---

[a] Diod. xvii. 103. 7 says that the snake told the king where
the herb was to be found.

[b] In the delta of the Indus; Strabo xv. 1. 33; Pliny,
N.H. vi. 23 (71); ii. 73. 75 (184). Perhaps the modern
Tatta, but the changes in the low and alluvial country make
identifications difficult.

[c] Arrian (vi. 17. 2) says that the king, whom he does not
name, came earlier and offered to submit to Alexander;
later he fled (vi. 17. 5).

serpent had appeared to him, carrying an herb in its
mouth, which it had indicated to be a cure for the
27 poison; and the king declared too that he would recognize the colour of the herb if anyone could find it.
Then, when it was found—for it was sought by many
at the same time [a]—he placed it upon the wound;
and immediately the pain ceased and within a short
28 time the wound was scabbed over. The barbarians,
since their first hope had proved vain, surrendered
themselves and the city.

From there they came to the next nation, that of
the Patalii.[b] Their king was Soeris,[c] who had abandoned his city, and taken refuge in the mountains.
29 Alexander took the town and pillaged the fields.
From there great booty was driven off, in the form of
flocks and herds, and a great store of grain was found.
30 Then, taking guides acquainted with the river, he
sailed down to an island which arose in about the
middle of the channel.[d]

IX. Being compelled to stay there for a longer
time, because the guides, who had been carelessly
guarded, had made their escape, he sent men to look
for others. When none were found, the desire of
visiting the Ocean and going to the ends of the world
prevailed upon him, without guides who knew the
region, to entrust his own life and the safety of so
2 many valiant men [e] to an unknown river; and so
they sailed on, knowing nothing of the country
through which they were being carried. How far
off from there the sea was, what nations dwelt there,

[d] The great number of islands makes it impossible to
identify this one.
[e] He was attended only by a small part of the army; see
Arr. vi. 18. 3.

dum amnis os, quam patiens longarum navium esset,
anceps et caeca aestimatio augurabatur ; unum erat
temeritatis solacium perpetua felicitas.

3 Iam cccc stadia processerant, cum gubernatores
agnoscere ipsos auram maris et haud procul videri
4 sibi Oceanum abesse indicant regi.   Laetus ille hortari nauticos coepit : incumberent remis ;   adesse
finem laboris omnibus votis expetitum ;   iam nihil
gloriae deesse, nihil obstare virtuti, sine ullo Martis
discrimine, sine sanguine oram[1] terrae ab illis capi ;
ne Naturam quidem longius posse procedere ; brevi
5 incognita nisi immortalibus esse visuros.   Paucos
tamen navigio emisit in ripam, qui agrestes vagos
exciperent, e quibus certiora nosci posse sperabat.
Illi, scrutati[2] omnia tuguria, tandem latentes rep-
6 perere.   Qui interrogati quam procul abessent mari,
responderunt nullum ipsos mare ne fama quidem
accepisse ;   ceterum tertio die perveniri posse ad
aquam amaram, quae corrumperet dulcem.

Intellectum est mare destinari ab ignaris naturae
7 eius.   Itaque ingenti alacritate nautici remigant, et
proximo quoque die quo propius spes admovebatur,
crescebat ardor animorum.   Tertio iam die mixtum
flumini subibat mare, leni adhuc aestu confundente
8 dispares undas.   Tum aliam insulam medio amni
sitam evecti paulo lentius,[3] quia cursus aestu reverberabatur,[4] applicant classem et ad commeatus

---

[1] oram *Eberhard;* orbem *A.*
[2] scrutati *Vindelinus;* scrutata *A.*
[3] lentius *Acidalius;* lenius *A.*
[4] reverberabatur *B m. sec.;* reuererbrabatur *P m. pr.;*
reuerabatur *C* (reuerebatur *B m. pr.*).

how quiet the mouth of the river was, whether it was
navigable by ships of war, was divined by uncertain
and blind conjecture ; the sole consolation for the
rash enterprise was the king's perpetual good fortune.
3 Already they had gone on for 400 stadia, when the
pilots made known to the king that they felt sea air
4 and that the Ocean was not far distant. He, filled
with joy, began to urge the sailors to bend to the
oars, saying that the end of their labours, so ardently
desired, was at hand ; now nothing was wanting to
complete their glory, nothing left to oppose their
valour, without any decision of Mars, without bloodshed, they were taking the very edge of the world ; not
even Nature could go farther; soon they would see what
5 was unknown except to the immortals. Nevertheless he sent a few men ashore in a boat, to take some
of the peasants who were roving about, from whom
he hoped to get more accurate information. They,
after searching all the huts, at last found some hidden
6 in them. These, when asked how far away the sea
was, answered that they had never even heard of
any sea ; but that on the third day they could reach
bitter water, which spoiled the fresh water.

It was clear that this was a description of the sea
by those who were not acquainted with its nature ;
7 and so the boatmen rowed on with great eagerness,
and each succeeding day, as the fulfilment of their
hopes drew nearer, their ardour increased. By the
third day sea water mixed with the river met them, as
the tide, which was still gentle, mingled the different
8 waters. Then carried to another island, situated in
the middle of the river, somewhat more slowly
because their speed being retarded by the tide, they
brought their fleet to the shore and ran about to

petendos discurrunt, securi casus eius, qui supervenit
9 ignaris. Tertia ferme hora erat, cum stata vice
Oceanus exaestuans invehi coepit et retro flumen
urgere. Quod primo coercitum, deinde vehementius
pulsum, maiore impetu adversum agebatur quam
10 torrentia praecipiti alveo incurrunt. Ignota vulgo
freti natura erat, monstraque et irae deum indicia
cernere videbantur, identidem intumescens mare et
in campos paulo ante siccos descendere superfusum.
11 Iamque levatis navigiis, et tota classe dispersa, qui
expositi erant, undique ad naves trepidi et improviso
12 malo attoniti recurrunt. Sed in tumultu festinatio
quoque tarda est. Hi[1] contis navigia pellebant, hi,
13 dum remos aptari prohibebant, consederant, quidam
enavigare properantes, sed non exspectatis qui simul
esse debebant, clauda et inhabilia navigia languide
moliebantur, aliae navium inconsulte ruentes omnes
receperant[2]; pariterque et multitudo et paucitas
14 festinantes morabatur. Clamor hinc exspectare,
hinc ire iubentium dissonaeque voces numquam idem
atque unum tendentium non oculorum modo usum,
15 sed etiam aurium abstulerant. Ne in gubernatoribus
quidem quicquam opis erat, quorum nec exaudiri vox
a tumultuantibus poterat nec imperium a territis
incompositisque servari.
16 Ergo collidi inter se naves abstergerique invicem

[1] Hi *Lauer;* II *A.*
[2] non (*before* receperant) *deleted by Hedicke.*

---

[a] *Cf.* v. 1. 22.
[b] The phenomenon known as a " bore," such as that in
the river Severn,or that in th e Bay of Fundi.
[c] There is very little rise and fall of tide in the Mediterranean, but the nature of the tides was known to the highly
educated.
[d] " Haste makes waste "; " more haste, less speed."

look for supplies, with no thought of the accident
9 which befell them in their ignorance. It was nearly
the third hour, when the Ocean, in its regular change,[a]
began to be carried on a flood-tide into the river,
and pushed it back. The stream, at first checked and
then pushed more violently, was driven upstream with
greater speed than that of torrents [b] running in a
10 precipitous channel. The nature of the sea was
unknown to the common soldiers,[c] who thought that
they were witnessing portents and signs of the anger
of the gods when the sea continually swelled and
overflowed to flood fields that shortly before were dry.
11 Now the ships were lifted and the whole fleet was
scattered, and those who had gone on shore, alarmed
and amazed by the unexpected calamity, ran from
12 every side back to the ships. But in times of confusion even haste is slow.[d] Some were pushing at the
ships with poles, others had taken their seats while
13 they prevented the oars from being put in place, some
in their haste to sail, without waiting for those
who ought to have been with them, were weakly struggling with crippled and unmanageable ships,[e] other
ships had taken all those who rushed inconsiderately
into them; and equally too great and too small num-
14 bers delayed their haste. Here some were shouting
to wait, there others, to go on, and the contradictory
cries of those who never demanded one and the same
action had prevented the use, not only of the eyes,
15 but also of the ears. And there was no help even in
the pilots, for their voice could not be heard in the
tumult, nor could their orders be carried out by the
frightened and disordered sailors.
16 Hence the ships began to be dashed together, and

* From want of sufficient oarsmen.

remi et alii aliorum navigia urgere coeperunt. Crederes non unius exercitus classem vehi, sed duorum
17 navale inisse certamen. Incutiebantur puppibus
prorae, premebantur a sequentibus qui antecedentes
turbaverant; iurgantium ira perveniebat etiam ad
manus.

18 Iamque aestus totos circa flumen campos inun-
daverat, tumulis dumtaxat eminentibus velut insulis
parvis, in quos plerique trepidi, omissis navigiis,
19 enare properant. Dispersa classis partim in praealta
aqua stabat qua subsederant valles, partim in vado
haerebat, utcumque inaequale terrae fastigium
occupaverant undae, cum subito novus et pristino
20 maior terror incutitur. Reciprocari coepit mare
magno tractu,ᵃ aquis in suum fretum recurrentibus,
reddebatque terras paulo ante profundo salo mersas.
Igitur destituta navigia alia praecipitantur in proras,
alia in latera procumbunt. Strati erant campi sarcinis, armis, avulsarum tabularum remorumque frag-
21 mentis. Miles nec egredi in terram nec in nave[1]
subsistere audebat identidem praesentibus graviora
quae sequerentur exspectans. Vix quae perpetie-
bantur videre ipsos credebant, in sicco naufragia, in
amni mare.

22 Nec finis[2] malorum; quippe aestum paulo post
mare relaturum quo navigia allevarentur, ignari
famem et ultima sibimet ominabantur. Beluae

[1] nave *Scheffer;* naves *A.* [2] finis *Lauer;* fines *A.*

ᵃ For *magno tractu* cf. *leni tractu,* ix. 9. 25.

the oars to be shorn off in turn, and the crews to
foul one another's ships. You would have supposed,
not that it was the fleet of one army, but that the
fleets of two armies were engaged in a sea-fight.
17 Prows were dashed against sterns, those ships that
damaged ships in front of them were in turn injured
by ships behind them; from angry words they even
came to blows.

18 And now the tide had flooded all the plains about
the river except for mounds projecting like small
islands, to which many in their trepidation hastened
19 to swim, deserting the ships. The scattered fleet
stood, a part in very deep water, where valleys had
made low ground, a part were stranded on shoals,
wherever the waters had covered land of uneven
but rising level; when on a sudden a new cause
of terror, greater than the former one, surprised
20 them. The sea began to flow back with great
pull,[a] as the waters ran back to their own channel
and restored the lands which a little before had
been submerged in deep surge. Hence some of
the ships, being thus stranded, were thrown upon
their prows, others fell upon their sides. The fields
were strewn with baggage, arms, and fragments of
21 broken planks and oars. The soldiers dared neither
to land nor to stay aboard, since they were awaiting
more serious calamities than the present that might
follow at any time. They could hardly believe that
they actually beheld what they were experiencing,
shipwreck on dry land, the sea in the river.

22 And there was no end to their troubles; for since
they did not know that the sea would a little later
bring back the tide by which their ships would be
floated, they foresaw famine and the utmost extremi-

quoque fluctibus destitutae terribiles vagabantur
23 Iamque nox appetebat, et regem quoque desperatio
salutis aegritudine affecerat. Non tamen invictum
animum curae obruunt quin tota nocte persederet in
speculis equitesque praemitteret ad os amnis, ut,
cum mare rursus exaestuare sensissent, praecederent.
24 Navigia quoque et lacerata refici et eversa fluctibus
erigi iubet, paratosque esse et intentos, cum rursus
25 mare terras inundasset. Tota ea nocte inter vigilias
adhortationesque consumpta, celeriter et equites
ingenti cursu refugere et secutus est aestus. Qui
primo, aquis leni tractu subeuntibus, coepit levare
navigia, mox, totis campis inundatis, etiam impulit
classem.
26   Plaususque militum nauticorumque[1] insperatam
salutem immodico celebrantium gaudio, litoribus
ripisque resonabat. Unde tantum redisset subito
mare, quo pridie refugisset, quaenam esset eiusdem
elementi[2] natura, modo discors, modo imperio tem-
27 porum obnoxia, mirabundi requirebant. Rex cum
ex eo quod acciderat coniectaret post solis ortum
statum tempus esse, media[3] nocte, ut aestum occuparet, cum paucis navigiis secundo amne defluxit
evectusque os eius, cccc stadia processit in mare,

---

[1] que *added by Giunta.*
[2] elementi *B m. sec.;* mentis *A.*
[3] esse, media *J. Froben;* esset media *P;* esse et media *C.*

---

[a] *Cf.* Arr. vi. 19. 5, Plut. *Alex.* lxvi. 1.

ties. Horrible sea-beasts too, left by the tide, were
23 roaming about. And already night was drawing
near, and despair of safety had disturbed even the
king himself. However his cares did not so master
his indomitable spirit as to keep him from spending
the whole night on the watch and sending horsemen
ahead to the mouth of the river, in order that when
they saw that the tide was rising again, they might
24 outstrip it. He also gave orders that the ships which
were damaged should be repaired, that those which
had been overturned by the waves should be raised,
and that everyone should be prepared and alert
25 when the sea had again flooded the lands. When
all that night had been spent in watching and in
encouraging the army, at the same time the horsemen came fleeing for safety at top speed, and the
tide followed. This at first, as the waters came
under them with gentle flow, began to lift the ships,
and then, when all the fields were flooded, even set
the fleet in motion.
26 Then the hand-claps and cheers of the soldiers and
boatmen, hailing with unrestrained joy the unexpected safety, made the shores and banks resound.
In wonder they asked one another whence so great a
sea had suddenly returned, whither it had fled the
day before, what was the nature of this same element
which was at one moment at variance with the strict
laws of time, and at another so subject to them.
27 The king, since from what had happened he con-
jectured that the regular time was after sunrise, in
the middle of the night, in order to anticipate the
tide, with a few ships went down the river and,
carried [a] out to its mouth, proceeded 400 stadia
into the sea, at last accomplishing the object of his

tandem voti sui compos. Praesidibusque et maris et
locorum dis sacrificio facto, ad classem rediit.

X. Hinc adversum flumen subit classis et altero die
appulsa est haud procul lacu salso, cuius incognita
natura plerosque decepit temere ingressos aquam.
Quippe scabies corpora invasit, et contagium morbi
2 etiam in alios vulgatum est. Oleum remedio fuit.
Leonnato deinde praemisso, ut puteos foderet qua
terrestri itinere ducturus exercitum videbatur—
quippe sicca erat regio—, ipse cum copiis subsistit
3 vernum tempus exspectans. Interim et urbes plerasque condidit, et[1] Nearcho atque Onesicrito, nauticae
rei peritis, imperavit ut validissimas navium deducerent in Oceanum, progressique quoad tuto possent,
naturam maris noscerent; vel eodem amne vel
Euphrate subire eos posse, cum reverti ad se vellent.
4 Iamque mitigata hieme, et navibus quae inutiles
5 videbantur crematis, terra ducebat exercitum. Nonis
castris in regionem Arabiton,[2] inde totidem diebus
in Cedrosiorum perventum est. Liber hic populus
concilio habito dedidit se, nec quicquam deditis
6 praeter commeatus imperatum est. Quinto hinc die
venit ad flumen; Arabum[3] incolae appellant. Regio

---

[1] et *added by Kinch.*   [2] Arabiton *Bentley;* aboriton *A.*
[3] Arabum *Aldus;* barbarum *A.*

---

[a] Arrian does not mention this; it may be identical with
the λίμνη μεγάλη mentioned by Arrian on the left branch of
the Indus (vi. 20. 3). There is evidently a gap in the narrative of Curtius.

[b] According to Aristobulus, in Strabo xv. 1. 17 (see also
xv. 2. 3), and Arr. vi. 21. 1-2, it was already towards the end
of July.

[c] Nearchus was the commander, Onesicritus the pilot, or
steersman. On the former see, *e.g.,* Arr. iii. 6. 5 and 6.

prayers. Then, after sacrificing to the gods presiding over the sea and the region, he returned to the fleet.

X. Next the fleet went up the river, and on the second day was moored near a salt lake,[a] the unknown nature of which deceived those who rashly entered its waters. For a scabby itch attacked their bodies and the contagion of the ailment was com-
2 municated also to others. A remedy was oil. Then Leonnatus was sent ahead, to dig wells along the route by which he seemed likely to lead the army in a march by land—for the region was dry—while Alexander himself with his troops remained where he was,
3 waiting for the springtime.[b] Meanwhile he both founded several cities and ordered Nearchus and Onesicritus, who were skilled in navigation,[c] to sail the strongest ships down to the Ocean, and having gone as far as they safely could, to make themselves acquainted with the nature of the sea, saying that when they wished to return to him, they could come up either by that same river or by the Euphrates.
4 And when the winter was nearly over, he burned the ships which seemed useless, and led the army
5 by land.[d] On the ninth day he came into the region of the Arabitae, and from there in the same number of days into that of the Cedrosii. This free people, after having held a council, surrendered themselves, and nothing was demanded of the surrendered
6 except supplies. Next, on the fifth day, he came to a river which the natives call the Arabus.[e] A region

[a] This account is unclear and inexact, but the same faults are found in Diodorus (xvii. 104); cf. Arr. vi. 17. 3; 27. 3; 21. 3, etc.
[e] The form of the name is variously given; it has been identified by many with the Purali.

451

deserta et aquarum inops excipit; quam emensus in
Horitas[1] transit. Ibi maiorem exercitus partem
Hephaestioni tradidit, levem armaturam cum Ptolo-
7 maeo Leonnatoque partitus est. Tria simul agmina
populabantur Indos, magnaeque praedae actae sunt;
maritimos Ptolomaeus, ceteros ipse rex et ab alia
parte Leonnatus, urebant. In hac quoque regione
urbem condidit, deductique sunt in eam[2] Arachosii.
8 Hinc pervenit ad maritimos Indos. Desertam
vastamque regionem late tenent ac ne cum finitimis
9 quidem ullo commercii iure miscentur. Ipsa solitudo
natura quoque immitia efferavit ingenia; prominent
ungues numquam recisi, comae hirsutae et intonsae
10 sunt. Tuguria conchis et ceteris purgamentis maris
instruunt. Ferarum pellibus tecti, piscibus sole
duratis et maiorum quoque beluarum, quas fluctus
11 eiecit, carne vescuntur. Consumptis igitur alimentis
Macedones primo inopiam, deinde ad ultimum famem
sentire coeperunt, radices palmarum—namque sola
12 ea arbor gignitur—ubique rimantes. Et[3] cum haec
quoque alimenta defecerant iumenta caedere aggressi ne equis quidem abstinebant. Et cum dees-
sent quae sarcinas veherent, spolia de hostibus
propter quae ultima Orientis peragraverant, crema-
bant incendio.

---

[1] Horitas *J. Froben;* noritas *A.*
[2] in eam *J. Froben;* inam *A.*   [3] Et *Hedicke;* sed *A*

---

[a] So Diod. xvii. 104. 5 ; *cf.* Arr. vi. 21. 3.
[b] The former Rambacia, Arr. vi. 21. 5.
• The Ichthyophagi.   [d] *Cf.* Diod. xvii. 105. 4.

barren and poor in water met him ; having passed
through this, he crossed into the land of the Horitae.
There he handed over the greater part of the army
to Hephaestion and shared the light-armed troops
7 with Ptolemy [a] and Leonnatus.   Three armies at the
same time were pillaging the Indi, and a great
amount of booty was driven off ; Ptolemy was burning the maritime regions, the king himself and in
another direction Leonnatus, the rest of the country.
In this region also he founded a city,[b] and colonized
it with Arachosii.
8   From there he came to the Indi who dwell along
the sea-coast.[c] They occupy a great extent of country
which is barren and desolate, and mingle in no kind of
9 intercourse even with their neighbours.   Their very
solitude has made quite wild their dispositions, which
are savage even by nature ; their nails grow long, never
having been cut, their hair is shaggy and unshorn.
10 They adorn their huts with shells [d] and other things
thrown up by the sea.   Clad in the skins of wild
beasts, they feed upon fish cured in the sun, and
also on the flesh of larger animals cast up by the sea.
11 Therefore, since their supplies were used up,[e] the
Macedonians began to suffer at first scarcity, and
finally starvation, grubbing everywhere for the roots
of palms—for that is the only kind of tree that grows
12 there.   And when even this nourishment had failed
them, they began to kill their draught animals, not
even abstaining from the horses.   And when they
had nothing to carry their packs, they burned the
spoils taken from the enemy, for the sake of which
they had traversed the remotest parts of the Orient.

[e] On the march through Cedrosia along the coast of Persia
toward the entrance to the Persian Gulf; cf. Arr. vi. 24. 4 ff.

QUINTUS CURTIUS

13 Famem deinde pestilentia secuta est. Quippe insalubrium ciborum noxii[1] suci, ad hoc itineris labor et aegritudo animi vulgaverant morbos, et nec manere sine clade nec progredi poterant ; manentes fames,
14 progressos acrior pestilentia urguebat. Ergo strati erant campi paene pluribus semivivis quam cadaveribus. Ac ne levius quidem aegri sequi poterant ; quippe agmen raptim agebatur, tantum singulis ad spem salutis ipsos proficere credentibus, quantum
15 itineris festinando praeciperent. Igitur qui defecerant notos ignotosque ut allevarentur orabant ; sed nec iumenta erant quibus excipi possent, et miles vix arma portabat, imminentisque et ipsis[2] facies mali ante oculos erat. Ergo saepius revocati, ne respicere quidem suos sustinebant, misericordia in formidinem
16 versa. Illi relicti deos testes et sacra communia regisque implorabant opem, cumque frustra surdas aures fatigarent, in rabiem desperatione versi, parem suo exitum similesque ipsis amicos et contubernales precabantur.
17 Rex dolore simul ac pudore anxius, quia causa tantae cladis ipse esset, ad Phrataphernen,[3] Parthyaeorum satrapen, misit, qui iuberet camelis cocta cibaria afferri, aliosque finitimarum regionum prae-
18 fectos certiores necessitatis suae fecit. Nec cessatum

---

[1] noxii *Cornelissen;* noui *A.*
[2] ipsis *J. Froben;* ipsius *A.*
[3] ad Phrataphernen] affrapernen *A.*

---

[a] Alexander is accused by Strabo xv. 2. 5 of an unworthy ambition to outdo Samiramis and Cyrus; so also Arr. vi. 24. 2-3 ; *cf.* Curtius ix. 6. 23.

13　Then pestilence followed hunger.　For the harmful juices of the unwholesome viands, added to the labour of marching and anxiety of mind, had spread diseases, and they could neither remain where they were nor advance without danger of death ; if they remained, famine, if they went on, a deadlier enemy, pesti-
14 lence, assailed them.　Hence the plains were strewn with almost more bodies of the dying than of the dead.　And not even those who were slightly ill were able to follow ; for the army was led on rapidly, since each man believed that the army was making the more progress towards the hope of safety, the more
15 they cut short their journey by hurrying.　Therefore those who had given out besought those whom they knew, and strangers as well, to succour them ; but there were no animals by which they could be taken on, and the soldiers could barely carry their arms and the sight of the evil which threatened themselves was before their eyes.　Therefore, though often called back, they could not endure even to look upon their comrades, but pity was overcome by fear.
16 Those others, being left behind, called upon the gods as witnesses, on their common sacred rites, and on the aid of the king, and when they found that they were wearying deaf ears to no purpose, despair turned to madness and they prayed that those to whom they appealed might have a fate like their own and friends and comrades as cruel as themselves.
17　The king, oppressed by grief, and at the same time by shame,[a] because he himself was the cause of such a great disaster, sent messengers to Phrataphernes, satrap of the Parthyaei, to order cooked food to be brought on camels, and informed other governors of
18 neighbouring regions of his necessities.　And they

est ab his. Itaque fame dumtaxat vindicatus, exercitus tandem in Cedrosiae fines perducitur. Omnium rerum solo fertili[1] regio est ; in qua stativa habuit,
19 ut vexatos milites quiete firmaret. Hic Leonnati litteras accepit, conflixisse ipsum cum VIII milibus peditum et CCCC equitibus Horitarum prospero eventu. A Cratero quoque nuntius venit Ozinen et Zariaspen, nobilis Persas, defectionem molientes, oppressos a
20 se in vinculis esse. Praeposito igitur regioni Sibyrtio[2] —namque Menon, praefectus eius, nuper interierat
21 morbo—in Carmaniam ipse processit. Astaspes[3] erat satrapes gentis, suspectus res novare voluisse, dum in India rex est ; quem occurrentem, dissimulata ira, comiter allocutus, dum exploraret quae delata erant, in eodem honore habuit.
22 Cum inde praefecti, sicut imperatum erat, equorum iumentorumque[4] iugalium vim ingentem ex omni quae sub imperio erat regione misissent, quibus deerant
23 impedimenta restituit. Arma quoque ad pristinum refecta sunt cultum quippe haud procul a Perside aberant, non pacata modo, sed etiam opulenta.
24 Igitur, ut supra dictum est, aemulatus Patris Liberi

---

[1] solo fertili *Acidalius;* sola fertilis *A.*
[2] regioni Sibyrtio *Freinshem;* regionis iburtio *A* (regionis iburcio *V*).
[3] Astaspes *Fuhr;* aspastis *A.*
[4] que *added by Lauer.*

---

[a] According to the usual, well-supported, account, the sufferings of the army were undergone in Cedrosia, and ended on their arrival in its capital—Pura, modern Punpoor (?).
[b] *Cf.* Arr. vii. 5. 5.
[c] Diod. xvii. 105. 8 disagrees, but *cf.* Arr. *l.c.*

did not delay. And so the army, saved at least from starvation, was at last led into the country of Cedrosia.[a] That is a land with a soil productive of all fruits ; there he encamped for some time, in order
19 to recuperate the suffering soldiers with rest. Here he received a letter from Leonnatus,[b] saying that he had fought with 8000 infantry and 400 cavalry of the Horitae with successful result.[c] From Craterus also came the news that he had defeated Ozines and Zariaspes, Persian nobles who were attempting
20 a revolt, and that they were in fetters. Therefore, having made Sibyrtius [d] governor of that region—for Menon, its prefect, had lately fallen ill and died—
21 he himself advanced into Carmania. The satrap of that nation was Astaspes,[e] who was suspected of having wished to revolt while the king was in India. When Astaspes came to meet him, Alexander dissembled his anger, and, addressing him graciously, kept him in his same rank until he could inquire into what had been reported.
22 Then, when the governors, as had been ordered, had sent a great supply of horses and yoked draughtcattle from all the region which was under their rule, the king restored their equipment [f] to those who
23 lacked it. Their arms also were replaced with equally handsome ones ; for they were not far from Persia,
24 which was not only subdued, but also rich. Therefore, as was said before, rivalling not only the glory of

[d] So also Arr. vi. 27. 1.

[e] Otherwise unknown ; he is not mentioned by Arrian in vi. 27. 1.

[f] *impedimenta* here means *iumenta*; *cf.* Arr. vi. 27. 6. That meaning is not rare in military language ; see *e.g.* Livy xxxviii. 41. 3 *in eo proelio cum et impedimentorum pars . . . cecidissent.*

non gloriam solum, quam ex illis gentibus deporta-
verat, sed etiam pompam,[1] sive illud triumphus fuit
ab eo primum institutus sive bacchantium lusus,
statuit imitari animo super humanum fastigium elato.

25 Vicos per quos iter erat floribus coronisque sterni
iubet, liminibus aedium creterras vino repletas et alia
eximiae magnitudinis vasa disponi, vehicula deinde
constrata, ut plures capere milites possent, in taberna-
culorum modum ornari, alia candidis velis, alia veste
pretiosa.

26 Primi ibant amici et cohors regia, variis redi-
mita floribus coronisque ; alibi tibicinum[2] cantus,
alibi lyrae sonus audiebatur ; item vehiculis pro
copia cuiusque adornatis, comissabundus exercitus,
armis quae maxime decora erant circumpendentibus. Ipsum convivasque currus vehebat creterris
aureis eiusdemque materiae ingentibus poculis prae-

27 gravis. Hoc modo per dies vii bacchabundum agmen
incessit, parata[3] praeda, si quid victis saltem adversus
comissantes animi fuisset ; mille, hercule, viri modo et
sobrii vii dierum crapula graves in suo triumpho

28 capere potuerunt. Sed Fortuna, quae rebus famam
pretiumque constituit, hoc quoque militiae probrum
vertit in gloriam. Et praesens aetas et posteritas
deinde mirata est per gentes nondum satis domitas

[1] pompam *Meiser;* famam *A.*
[2] tibicinum *Freinshem;* tubicinum *A.*
[3] parata *J. M. Palmer;* parta *A.*

---

[a] Reading Meiser's *pompam* for *famam*; for *fama* and
gloria see viii. 1. 1, note *a.*
[b] Here *amici* refers to the most intimate of his body-guard
(see note on ix. 8. 23) ; *regia cohors,* to the rest of the body-

Father Liber which he had carried off from those nations, but also his procession,[a] whether that was a triumph first invented by that god or the sport of drunken revellers, he decided to imitate it, in a spirit 25 raised above the level of human greatness. To this end, he ordered the villages through which his route lay to be strewn with flowers and garlands, mixing-bowls filled with wine, and other vessels of unusual size to be placed everywhere on the thresholds of the houses, then carriages to be spread, so that each might hold many soldiers, and to be equipped like tents, some with white curtains, and others with costly tapestries.

26 At the head marched the king's friends and the royal troop,[b] wreathed with chaplets made of a variety of flowers ; on one side was heard the music of flute-players, on another the notes of the lyre ; the army also joined the revels in vehicles adorned according to the means of each man and hung around with their most beautiful arms. The king and his companions rode in a chariot loaded down with golden 27 bowls and huge beakers of the same material. In this way the army for seven days marched in a riotous procession, an easy prey if the conquered had had any courage even against revellers ; a single thousand, by Heaven !, provided they were real men and sober, could have captured in the midst of their triumph those who for seven days had been heavy with 28 drunkenness. But Fortune, who assigns renown and value to actions, turned to glory even this disgrace to an army. Both the age of that time, and afterwards posterity, regarded it as wonderful that they marched

guard, probably including the young men referred to in viii. 6. 2 ff.

incessisse temulentos, barbaris quod temeritas erat
29 fiduciam esse credentibus. Hunc apparatum carnifex
sequebatur : quippe satrapes Astaspes, de quo ante
30 dictum est, interfici iussus est ; adeo nec luxuriae
quicquam crudelitas nec crudelitati luxuria obstat.

---

[a] See ix. 10. 21.

drunken through nations not wholly subdued, and
that the barbarians took this rash conduct for con-
29 fidence. This splendid exhibition was followed by
the executioner ; for it was ordered that the satrap
Astaspes, of whom mention was made before,[a] should
30 be put to death ; so true is it that cruelty is no
obstacle whatever to luxury, nor luxury to cruelty.

BOOK X

CONTENTS OF BOOK X

464

to a banquet. Then all the weaker soldiers are mustered out with pay for past services and a talent each for travelling expenses. He gives orders that all sons begotten from Asiatic wives be left with him. More than 10,000 veterans, led by Craterus, are discharged and sent to Greece. Antipater is directed to give them special honours and privileges. Craterus is made governor of Macedonia, and Antipater is ordered to come to Alexander with reinforcements. Because of discord between Antipater and Olympias the king is suspicious of Antipater as being too important for a prefect. After making changes in the army, Alexander comes to Celonae, a town occupied by the descendants of Boeotians driven from their homes by Xerxes. A quarrel arises between Eumenes and Hephaestion. Alexander comes to Media, celebrated for its fine horses. At Ecbatana he offers sacrifices and celebrates games, and relaxes his mind with banquets. Hephaestion is taken ill and dies. His body is taken to Babylon and given a magnificent funeral. Alexander orders mourning for Hephaestion throughout the empire, and his friends vie with him in honouring Hephaestion ; he is persuaded that Hephaestion is a god and Agathocles, a Samian, falls into great danger by weeping for him as if he were dead. Alexander marches against the Cossaei, a rude and warlike nation ; he subdues them within 40 days. He founds cities and marches to Babylon. Nearchus warns him not to enter the city, but he scorns the prediction of the Chaldeans. He sails on the river Pallacopas to the land of the Arabians. He founds a city, in which he settled the aged and infirm Greeks and others who wished to remain there. In spite of many unfavourable omens, he enters Babylon. He is entertained by Nearchus at a banquet, and when he was about to retire was persuaded by Medius to attend a drinking-bout. After spending the night in drinking he is taken ill and within six days his strength is exhausted. The troops insist on being admitted to see him.

On his death-bed Alexander remained in the same posture until he had saluted every man in the army. He gives his ring to Perdiccas, and directs that his body be taken to Ammon. He dies, saying that he left his kingdom " to the best man." A summary of his good qualities and his defects. His invariable good fortune (v).

Consultation as to his successor, and the various opinions of the Macedonians (vi).

Meleager favours Alexander's brother Arrhidaeus. Pithon names Perdiccas and Leonnatus as regents for an expected son of Roxanê. Arrhidaeus with a guard of footsoldiers breaks into the king's quarters. Perdiccas and Leonnatus with their cavalry decide to leave the city (vii).

Meleager urges Arrhidaeus to kill Perdiccas. Perdiccas takes a position in the plains and afflicts Babylon with hunger. Arrhidaeus, desirous of peace, tries to quiet the disturbance (viii).

Perdiccas, while he is making a lustration of the army in the Macedonian manner, by a stratagem kills Meleager and about 30 other fomenters of discord (ix).

Perdiccas partitions Alexander's empire, giving the main part to Arrhidaeus and himself, the remainder to the leaders of the Macedonian forces. Rumour that Alexander was poisoned. The king's body is embalmed in the manner of the Egyptians and Chaldeans and taken by Ptolemy to Memphis and later to Alexandria (x).

LIBER X

I. Eisdem fere diebus Cleander et Sitalces et cum
Agathone Heracon superveniunt, qui Parmenionem
iussu regis occiderant. v milia peditum cum equitibus
2 M, sed et[1] accusatores eos e provincia cui praefuerant
sequebantur.   Nec tot facinora quot admiserant
compensare poterat caedis perquam gratae regi mini-
3 sterium.   Quippe cum omnia profana spoliassent, ne
sacris quidem abstinuerant, virginesque et principes
feminarum, stupra perpessae, corporum ludibria
4 deflebant.   Invisum Macedonum nomen avaritia
5 eorum ac libido barbaris fecerat.   Inter omnes tamen
eminebat Cleandri furor, qui nobilem virginem con-
stupratam servo suo pelicem dederat.
6   Plerique amicorum Alexandri non tam criminum
quae palam obiciebantur atrocitatem, quam memoriam occisi per illos Parmenionis, quod tacitum
prodesse reis apud regem poterat, intuebantur, laeti
reccidisse iram in irae ministros nec ullam potentiam

---

[1] sed et *C;* sed *P.*

---

    [a] Arr. vi. 27. 3 puts this event immediately after the
entrance of Alexander into Carmania (see ix. 10. 20) ; *eisdem
diebus* suggests that Curtius took the account of the seven
days' procession through Carmania from another source.
    [b] See Arr. iii. 26. 3 and on Agathon, iii. 12. 4.   Heracon
is mentioned nowhere else.

BOOK X

I. At about that same time [a] Cleander and Sitalces,[b] and Heracon with Agathon arrived, who at the king's
2 order had killed Parmenion. 5000 infantry with 1000 horsemen followed them, but also accusers from the provinces of which they had been governors. And the service rendered by the assassination, although very pleasing to the king, could not make amends for the many crimes which they had committed. For not only had they pillaged everything secular, but they had not even withheld their hands from sacred objects, and maidens and women of high station who had suffered violation were weeping for
4 the insult to their persons. Their greed and lust had made the name of the Macedonians hateful to the
5 barbarians. Among them all, however, the mad passion [c] of Cleander was preëminent, who after having assaulted a maiden of high birth had given her to one of his slaves as a concubine.
6 Very many of Alexander's friends had an eye, not so much to the atrocity of the crimes that were openly laid to the charge of these men, as to the memory that they had killed Parmenion, which might secretly help the accused with the king ; and they rejoiced that his anger had recoiled upon the tools of his anger, and that no power gained through crime was lasting

Cf. Sen. *Hippol.* 178 ; Val. Flacc. v. 427 *amore furens.*

7 scelere quaesitam cuiquam esse diuturnam. Rex,
cognita causa, pronuntiavit ab accusatoribus unum
et id maximum crimen esse praeteritum, desperationem salutis suae ; numquam enim talia ausuros
qui ipsum ex India sospitem aut optassent reverti
8 aut credidissent reversurum. Igitur hos quidem
vinxit, DC autem militum, qui saevitiae eorum ministri
9 fuerant, interfici iussit. Eodem die sumptum est
supplicium de eis quoque, quos auctores defectionis
Persarum Craterus adduxerat.
10   Haud multo post Nearchus et Onesicritus, quos
longius in Oceanum procedere iusserat, superveniunt.
11 Nuntiabant autem quaedam auditu, alia aditu[1] comperta ; insulam ostio amnis obiectam[2] auro abundare,
inopem equorum esse—singulos eos compererant ab
eis, qui ex continenti traicere auderent, singulis
12 talentis emi—plenum esse beluarum mare ; aestu secundo eas ferri magnarum navium corpora aequantes,
tubae[3] cantu deterritas sequi classem, cum magno
aequoris strepitu velut demersa navigia subisse aquas.
13   Cetera incolis crediderant, inter quae : Rubrum
mare non a colore undarum, ut plerique crederent,
14 sed ab Erythro rege appellari ; esse haud procul a
continenti insulam palmetis[4] frequentibus consitam
et in medio fere nemore columnam eminere, Erythri

---

[1] aditu *added by Hedicke, ed. min.*
[2] amnis obiectam *Scheffer;* amni subiectam *A.*
[3] tubae *Sebisius;* truci *A.*
[4] palmetis *Modius;* palmitis *P;* palmis *C.*

---

[a] Arrian says nothing of this ; *cf.* Pliny, *N.H.* vi. 23. 80.
[b] Arr. viii. 30 ; Strabo xv. 2. 12. Pliny, *N.H.* vi. 26. 99
speaks of *hydri marini* twenty cubits in length.
[c] See viii. 9. 14, and note.

7 for anyone. The king, having examined the case, declared that the accusers had passed over one crime, and that the greatest of all, namely, despair of his safety ; for they never would have ventured on such conduct, if they had either wished him to return safely from India or had believed that he would 8 return. Therefore he bound these men in fetters, but ordered the 600 soldiers who had been the instru-9 ments of their cruelty to be put to death. On the same day punishment was inflicted upon those also whom Craterus had brought in, who were responsible for the revolt of the Persians.

10 Not long afterwards Nearchus and Onesicritus arrived, whom he had ordered to advance some dis-11 tance into the Ocean. They reported some things from hearsay, others which they had learned from observation : that there was an island opposite the mouth of the river, which abounded in gold, but lacked horses *a*—these, they had learned, were bought at a talent apiece from those who ventured to bring them from the mainland—that the sea was full of 12 whales *b* ; that these, huge as great ships, floated with the course of the tide, and when frightened off by the blast of the trumpet, from following the ships, plunged under the water with a great roaring of the sea, like so many sunken vessels.

13 As to other matters they had taken the word of the natives ; that the Red Sea was so called, not from the colour of its waters, as most people believed, but 14 from a King Erythrus *c*; that there was, not far from the mainland, an island thickly planted with palm-groves, and that in about the middle of the wood a lofty column arose, marking the grave of King Erythrus and inscribed in the characters of that

471

15 regis monumentum, litteris gentis eius scriptam. Adiciebant navigia, quae lixas mercatoresque vexissent, famam auri secutis gubernatoribus, in insulam esse
16 transmissa[1] nec deinde ab eis postea visa. Rex, cognoscendi plura cupidine accensus, rursus eos terram legere iubet, donec ad Euphratis os[2] appellerent classem ; inde adverso amne Babylona subituros.
17 Ipse, animo infinita complexus, statuerat, omni ad orientem[a] maritima regione perdomita, ex Syria petere Africam, Carthagini infensus, inde, Numidiae solitudinibus peragratis, cursum Gadis dirigere—ibi namque
18 columnas Herculis esse fama vulgaverat—Hispanias deinde, quas Hiberiam Graeci a flumine Hibero vocabant, adire et praetervehi Alpes Italiaeque oram,
19 unde in Epirum brevis cursus est. Igitur Mesopotamiae praetoribus imperavit[3] materia in Libano monte caesa devectaque ad urbem Syriae Thapsacum, septingentarum[4] carinas navium ponere ; septemremis[5] omnes esse deducique Babylona. Cypriorum regibus imperatum ut aes stuppamque et vela praeberent.
20 Haec agenti Pori et Taxilis regum litterae traduntur, Abisaren morbo, Philippum, praefectum ipsius, ex vulnere interisse, oppressosque qui vulnerassent
21 eum. Igitur Philippo substituit Eudaemonem—

---

[1] transmissa *Lauer;* transmissam *A.*
[2] os *added by Acidalius.*
[3] ut (*after* imperavit) *deleted by J. Froben.*
[4] Thapsacum, septingentarum *Zumpt;* thapsagas et ingentarumque *A.*
[5] septemremis *Hedicke;* vii remis *A.*

---

[a] For *ad orientem cf.* Pliny, *Epist.* ix. 12. 11.
[b] Because of its connexion with Tyre and its encouragement of the Tyrians in the war with Alexander.

15 nation. They added that ships carrying sutlers and merchants, whose pilots had followed the report of gold, had crossed to the island, but after that had
16 never been seen by them again. The king, fired with eagerness to know more, bade them go back and coast along the shore until they brought the fleet to the mouth of the Euphrates ; from there they would go up the river to Babylon.

17 Alexander himself, having embraced infinite plans in his mind, had determined, after thoroughly subduing the entire seacoast of the Orient,[a] to cross from Syria to Africa, being incensed against the Carthaginians,[b] then passing through the deserts of Numidia, to direct his course to Gades—for the report had spread abroad that the pillars of Hercules were there
18 —then to visit Spain, which the Greeks called Hiberia from the river Hiberus, to approach and skirt the Alps and the seacoast of Italy, from which it is
19 only a short voyage to Epirus. With this in view he ordered the governors of Mesopotamia to cut timber on Mt. Libanus, transport it to Thapsacus, a city of Syria, and lay the keels of 700 ships ; all were to be septiremes, and to be taken to Babylon. The kings of the Cypriotes [c] were ordered to furnish copper, hemp and sails.

20 While he was thus engaged, letters of Kings Porus and Taxiles were delivered to him, reporting that Abisares [d] had died a natural death, and Philippus, his satrap, as the result of a wound, and that those who had wounded the latter had been punished.
21 Accordingly, he appointed, in place of Philippus

[c] On Cyprus as a source of naval supplies see Amm. xiv. 8. 14.
[d] See ix. 1. 7.

dux erat Thracum—Abisaris regnum filio eius attribuit.

22 Ventum est deinde Parsagada[1]; Persica est gens, cuius satrapes Orsines erat, nobilitate ac divitiis inter
23 omnes barbaros eminens. Genus ducebat a Cyro, quondam rege Persarum ; opes et a maioribus traditas habebat et ipse longa imperii possessione cumu-
24 laverat. Is regi cum omnis generis donis, non ipsi modo ea, sed etiam amicis eius daturus, occurrit. Equorum domiti greges sequebantur currusque argento et auro adornati, pretiosa supellex et nobiles gemmae, aurea magni ponderis vasa vestesque pur-
25 pureae, et signati argenti talentum III milia. Ceterum tanta benignitas barbaro causa mortis fuit. Nam cum omnes amicos regis donis super ipsorum vota coluisset, Bagoae spadoni, qui Alexandro obsequio corporis
26 devinxerat sibi, nullum honorem habuit, admonitusque a quibusdam Bagoam[2] Alexandro cordi esse, respondit amicos regis, non scorta se colere, nec moris esse Persis mares ducere qui stupro effeminarentur.
27 His auditis, spado potentiam flagitio et dedecore quaesitam in caput nobilissimi et insontis exercuit. Namque gentis eiusdem levissimos falsis criminibus clam struxit,[3] monitos tum demum ea deferre, cum
28 ipse iussisset. Interim, quotiens sine arbitris erat, credulas regis aures implebat, dissimulans causam

---

[1] Parsagada *Vogel;* persagara *A.*
[2] Bagoam *Jeep;* equam *C;* equa *P.*
[3] clam struxit *Hedicke;* adstruxit *A.*

---

[a] Arr. vi. 27. 2 has Εὔδημος ; Diod. xix. 14. 1 Εὔδαμος. After Alexander's death he slew Porus and usurped his kingdom ; Diod. *l.c.* 8.
[b] See vi. 5. 23.

Eudaemon *a*—he was a general of the Thracians—and
gave the kingdom of Abisares to that king's son.

22 From there they came to Parsagada ; that is a
Persian race, whose satrap was Orsines, prominent
among all the barbarians for high birth and wealth.

23 He traced his descent from Cyrus, formerly king of
the Persians ; he had wealth, both what he had
inherited from his forefathers and what he himself
had amassed during long possession of sovereignty.

24 He met the king with gifts of every kind, intending
to give presents not only to Alexander but to his
friends as well. Troops of tamed horses followed
him and chariots adorned with silver and gold, costly
furniture and splendid gems, golden vases of great
weight, purple vestments, and 3000 talents of coined

25 silver. But this great generosity of the barbarian was
the cause of his death. For when he had honoured
all the friends of the king with gifts beyond their
highest hopes, to Bagoas,*b* a eunuch who had won
the regard of Alexander through prostitution, he

26 paid no honour, and on being admonished by some
that Bagoas was dear to Alexander, replied that he
was honouring the friends of the king, not his harlots,
and that it was not the custom of the Persians to
mate with males who made females of themselves
by prostitution.

27 On hearing this, the eunuch exercised the power
which he had gained by shame and disgrace against
the life of an eminent and guiltless man. For he
secretly supplied the most worthless fellows of that
same nation with false accusations, warning them not
to make them public until he himself should have

28 given the word. Meanwhile, whenever no witnesses
were present, he filled the credulous ears of the king

29 irae, quo gravior criminantis auctoritas esset. Nondum suspectus erat Orsines, iam tamen vilior ; reus
enim in secreto agebatur latentis periculi ignarus.
Et importunissimum scortum ne in stupro quidem
et dedecoris patientia fraudis oblitum, quotiens
amorem regis in se accenderat, Orsinen modo avaritiae, interdum etiam defectionis arguebat.

30 Iam matura erant in perniciem innocentis mendacia,
et Fatum, cuius inevitabilis sors est, appetebat. Forte
enim sepulchrum Cyri Alexander iussit aperiri, in quo
erat conditum eius corpus, cui dare volebat inferias.

31 Auro argentoque conditorium[1] repletum esse cre-
diderat—quippe ita fama Persae vulgaverant—, sed
praeter clipeum eius putrem et arcus duos Scythicos

32 et acinacem nihil repperit. Ceterum, corona aurea
imposita, amiculo cui assuerat ipse solium in quo
corpus iacebat velavit, miratus tanti nominis regem
tantis praeditum opibus haud pretiosius sepultum

33 esse, quam si fuisset e plebe. Proximus erat lateri
spado, qui regem intuens : " Quid mirum," inquit,
" est inania sepulchra esse regum, cum satraparum
domus aurum inde egestum capere non possint ?

34 Quod ad me attinet, ipse hoc bustum antea non
videram, sed ex Dareo ita accepi, III milia talentum

35 condita esse cum Cyro. Hinc illa benignitas in te, ut

---

[1] conditorium *Heinse;* conditum *A.*

ª For *in secreto cf.* vii. 1. 13.
ᵇ See Strabo xv. 3. 7 ; Arr. vi. 29. 4-11 ; also Ker Porter
Travels, quoted by Mützell.
476

with lies, concealing the reason for his anger, in order to add greater weight to his accusations.

29 Orsines as yet was not suspected, but nevertheless was already less esteemed; for he was secretly [a] being incriminated without being aware of the hidden danger. And that most shameless harlot, not forgetting his deception even amid debauchery and the endurance of shame, whenever he had aroused the king's passion for himself, charged Orsines now with avarice, sometimes even with treason.

30   And now the calumnies were ripe for the ruin of a blameless man, and Fate was on hand, whose will is inescapable. For it chanced that Alexander ordered the tomb of Cyrus [b] to be opened, in which his body had been laid at rest, and to which Alexander wished

31 to pay funereal honours. He had believed it to be a storehouse filled with gold and silver—for that was common rumour among the Persians—, but except the king's mouldering shield, two Scythian bows,[c]

32 and a scimitar he found nothing. However, having placed a crown of gold upon the coffin in which the body lay, he covered it over with the robe which he himself was accustomed to wear, expressing surprise that a king of such renown and endowed with such power had been buried no more sumptuously than

33 if he had been one of the common folk. The eunuch was at Alexander's side; looking significantly at him, he said : " What wonder if the tombs of kings are empty, when the houses of their satraps cannot contain the gold that they have amassed from them ?

34 For my part, I had never seen the tomb before, but I learned from Darius that 3000 talents of gold were

35 buried with Cyrus. Hence that generosity to you,

[c] See Amm. xxii. 8. 10, note.

quod impune habere non poterat Orsines, donando
etiam gratiam iniret."

36 Concitaverat iam animum in iram, cum ei[1] quibus
negotium idem dederat superveniunt. Hinc Bagoas,
hinc ab eo subornati, falsis criminibus occupant aures.

37 Antequam accusari se suspicaretur Orsines, in vincula
est traditus. Non contentus supplicio insontis, spado
ipse morituro manum iniecit. Quem Orsines intuens :
" Audieram," inquit, " in Asia olim regnasse feminas ;

38 hoc vero novum est, regnare castratum ! " Hic fuit
exitus nobilissimi Persarum nec insontis modo, sed

39 eximiae quoque benignitatis in regem. Eodem tempore Phradates, regnum affectasse suspectus, occiditur. Coeperat esse praeceps ad repraesentanda

40 supplicia, item ad deteriora credenda ; scilicet res
secundae valent commutare naturam, et raro quisquam erga bona sua satis cautus est. Idem enim
paulo ante Lyncestem Alexandrum, delatum a duo-

41 bus indicibus, damnare non sustinuerat, humiliores
quoque reos contra suam voluntatem quia ceteris
videbantur insontes, passus absolvi, hostibus victis

42 regna reddiderat[2] ; ad ultimum vitae tantum[3] ab
semetipso degeneravit, ut invicti[4] quondam adversus
libidinem animi, arbitrio scorti aliis regna daret, aliis
adimeret vitam.

43 Eisdem fere diebus litteras a Coeno accipit de rebus

---

[1] ii *Vindelinus;* hii *A* (hi *F*).
[2] regna reddiderat *Freinshem;* regnare duxerat *A.*
[3] vitae tantum *Heraeus;* traiectum *A.*
[4] invicti *Hedicke;* in *A.*

---

[a] See Arr. vi. 30. 1, who does not tell this story, but charges
Orsines (Orxines) with many crimes.
[b] See vi. 5. 21 : viii. 3. 17.
[c] For *erga cf.* Tac. *Ann.* iv. 74. [d] See vii. 1. 5-9.

in order that what Orsines could not keep with safety, he might even curry favour by giving away."

36 He had already aroused the king's mind to anger, when those to whom he had entrusted the same business arrived. On one side Bagoas, on the other those whom he had suborned, filled the king's ears

37 with false charges. Before Orsines suspected that he was being accused he was delivered into bondage. Not content with the punishment of an innocent man,[a] the eunuch laid his hand upon him as he was about to be executed. Orsines with a glance at him said : " I had heard that women once reigned in Asia; this however is something new, for a eunuch to

38 reign ! " Such was the end of one of the noblest of the Persians, who was not only blameless but of remark-

39 able kindness towards the king. At the same time Phradates,[b] suspected of aspiring to royal power, was put to death. Alexander had begun to be too hasty in inflicting prompt punishment, and also in

40 believing calumnies ; so true is it that success is able to change one's nature, and that rarely is any-one cautious enough towards his own good fortune.[c] For this same man shortly before had not been able to bring himself to punish Lyncestes Alexander [d]

41 though he had been charged by two witnesses, had even suffered humbler criminals to be acquitted against his desire because the rest believed them innocent, and had restored their thrones to van-

42 quished enemies ; but towards the end of his life he had so degenerated from his true self, that though formerly of a mind proof against lust, at the caprice of a catamite he gave kingdoms to some and took life from others.

43 At about that same time Alexander received a

in Europa et Asia gestis, dum ipse Indiam subigit.
44 Zopyrio, Thraciae praepositus, cum expeditionem in
Getas[1] faceret, tempestatibus procellisque subito co-
45 ortis, cum toto exercitu oppressus erat. Qua cognita
clade, Seuthes Odrysas, populares suos, ad defectionem compulerat. Amissa propemodum Thracia, ne
Graecia quidem[2] *tumultibus inconcussa mansit. Nam
Alexander, punita insolentia satraparum quorundum, qui
dum in extremo orbe Indorum armis retinetur, summa
scelera atque flagitia in provinciales exercuerant, ceteris
metum iniecerat. Hi in paribus delictis eandem facino-
rum poenam veriti, ad mercennariorum militum fidem
confugerunt, illorum manibus, si ad supplicium posceren-
tur, se tutaturi, aut pecunia quanta poterat coacta, fuga
salutem petiverunt. Qua re cognita, litterae ad omnes
Asiae praetores missae sunt, quibus inspectis, e vestigio
omnes peregrinos milites, qui stipendia sub ipsis facerent,
dimittere iubebantur.*

*Erat inter eos Harpalus, quem Alexander, quod propter
ipsius amicitiam olim a Philippo eiectus solum verterat,
inter fidissimos habebat, et post Mazaei mortem satrapeam
Babyloniae attribuerat thesaurorumque custodiae praefecerat. Is igitur cum fiduciam, quam in singulari regis
gratia habere poterat, magnitudine flagitiorum consump-*

---

[1] Getas *Vindelinus;* gestas *A.*
[2] quidem] *the words which follow are added by Freinshem.
In A the next words are* igitur ***, x. 2. 1. C adds in margin*
hic desunt II lineae.

---

[a] Curtius forgets that Coenus had died in India; see ix.
3. 20. Or more probably, as Warmington suggests, the
Greek originally had ἀπὸ τοῦ κοινοῦ (=ab commune or ab
commune), meaning from the Macedonian commune (=
government). See also Mützell ad loc.
[b] According to Justin, they were destroyed by the Getae,
not by the storms. Cf. Justin xii. 1. 4.

letter from Coenus [a] about what had happened in Europe and Asia while the king subdued India. 44 Zopyrion, governor of Thrace, while making an expedition against the Getae, had been overwhelmed with his whole army by tempests and gales which 45 suddenly arose.[b] On learning of this disaster Seuthes had forced his subjects the Odrysae to revolt. While Thrace was almost lost, Greece also [c] *did not remain unshaken by disturbances. For Alexander, by punishing the insolence of certain satraps who, while he was detained at the end of the world by war with the Indi, had practised the greatest and most disgraceful crimes against the provincials, had inspired fear in the rest. These, being guilty of like offences and fearing the same punishment for their crimes, took refuge in the protection of the mercenary soldiers, expecting by such troops as these to defend themselves if they should be demanded for punishment, or after exacting as much money as they could, sought safety in flight. After this was known, letters were sent to all the governors of Asia, and when these were read, they found that they were ordered to disband on the spot all the foreign soldiers who were serving under them.*

Among these was Harpalus. Alexander, because years before Philip, just on account of the friendship between Harpalus and his son, had driven him out and Harpalus had fled the country, regarded him as one of his most faithful friends. And after the death of Mazaeus he had made him satrap [d] of Babylon and had appointed him custodian of the royal treasures.[e] Harpalus, then, having by his flagrant offences lost the confidence which he could have felt in the remarkable favour of the king, abstracted 5000 talents [f]

[c] See crit. note 2.
[a] See Plut. *Alex.* xxv. [b] See Arr. iii. 19. 7.
[f] Diod. xvii. 108. 6.

*sisset, quinque milia talentorum ex gaza regia abstulit,
conductaque sex milium mercennariorum manu, in Europam evasit. Iampridem enim luxu et libidinibus in
praeceps tractus, desperataque regis venia, adversus iram
eius alienum subsidium circumspexerat et Athenienses,
quorum cum potentiam et auctoritatem apud ceteros
Graecos, tum occultum in Macedonas odium norat, sedulo
coluerat. Itaque spem suis ostendit Athenienses, adventu
suo cognito, copiisque et pecuniis quas adduceret coram
inspectis, protinus arma consiliaque esse sociaturos. Nam
a populo imperito et mobili per homines improbos et venales
omnia se muneribus consecuturum existimabat.*

II. Igitur xxx navibus Sunium transmittunt—promuntorium est Atticae terrae—unde portum urbis
2 petere decreverant. His cognitis, rex Harpalo
Atheniensibusque iuxta infestus, classem parari iubet,
3 Athenas protinus petiturus. Quod consilium clam
agitanti litterae redduntur, Harpalum intrasse quidem Athenas, pecunia conciliasse sibi principum animos; mox, concilio plebis habito iussum urbe excedere
ad Graecos milites pervenisse, navibus inde Cretam
transvectum, amico quodam[1] auctore interemptum
4 per insidias. His laetus, in Europam traiciendi consilium omisit, sed exsules praeter eos, qui civili
sanguine aspersi erant, recipi ab omnibus Graecorum
5 civitatibus quis pulsi erant iussit. Et Graeci, haud

---

[1] navibus ... quodam *Hedicke;* quibus interceptum trucidatum a quodam *A.*

---

[a] The Piraeus.
[b] Especially the orators ; see Plut. *Demos.* xxv.
[c] See Plut. *l.c.*
[d] See Diod. xvii. 108. 8 ; his name was Thibron.
[e] More than 20,000 ; Diod. xviii. 8. 5.

from the royal treasure, hired a band of 6000 mercenaries, and escaped to Europe. For long since, driven headlong by extravagance and his passions, and despairing of pardon from the king, he had looked about for help from others against Alexander's anger, and had sedulously courted the Athenians, whose power and influence with the rest of the Greeks he knew, as well as their secret hatred of the Macedonians. Therefore he pointed out to his followers that the Athenians, knowing of his arrival and seeing before their eyes the forces and the money which he was bringing, would join forces and plans with them at once. For he thought that from an inexperienced and fickle people by making use of unprincipled and venal persons he could gain everything by bribes.

II. Therefore with thirty ships they cross to Sunium—it is a promontory of the land of Attica—from which they had decided to go to the port [a] of 2 the city. Alexander, having learned this, and being equally incensed at Harpalus and the Athenians, ordered a fleet to be made ready, intending to go 3 at once to Athens. As he was secretly considering this plan, a letter was delivered to him, saying that Harpalus had in fact entered Athens, and by his money had won the support of the leading men [b] but that presently, after an assembly of the people had been held, he was ordered to leave the city [c] and had taken refuge with his Greek soldiers; then he had crossed to Crete in his ships and at the instigation of a friend [d] had been treacherously slain. 4 Alexander, rejoicing at this, gave up his design of crossing into Europe, and issued orders that the exiles,[e] except such as were stained by the blood of citizens, should be received by all the Greek cities 5 from which they had been banished. **And the**

ausi imperium aspernari, quamquam solvendarum
legum id principium esse censebant, bona quoque,
6 quae exstarent, restituere damnatis. Soli Athenienses, non sui[1] modo, sed etiam Graeciae[2] vindices,
colluvionem ordinum[3] hominumque[4] aegre ferebant,
non regio imperio, sed legibus moribusque patriis regi
7 assueti ; prohibuere igitur exsules finibus, omnia
potius toleraturi quam purgamenta quondam urbis
suae, tunc etiam exsilii admitterent.

8   Alexander, senioribus militum in patriam remissis,
xiii milia peditum et ii milia equitum quae in Asia
retineret eligi iussit, existimans modico exercitu continere posse Asiam, quia pluribus locis praesidia dis-
posuisset, nuperque conditas urbes colonis replesset
9 res retinere[5] cupientibus. Ceterum priusquam excer-
neret quos erat retenturus, edixit, ut omnes milites
aes alienum profiterentur. Grave plerisque esse compererat et, quamquam ipsorum luxu contractum erat,
10 dissolvere tamen ipse decreverat. Illi temptari ipsos
rati, quo facilius ab integris sumptuosos discerneret,
prolatando aliquantum extraxerant temporis. Et rex
satis gnarus, professioni aeris pudorem, non contumaciam obstare, mensas totis castris[6] poni iussit et x
11 milia talentum proferri. Tum demum cum[7] fide facta

---

[1] sui *Jeep;* suo *A.*   [2] Graeciae *Hedicke;* publice *A.*
[3] ordinum *Zumpt;* ordinem *A.*
[4] hominumque *Jeep;* hominum quia *A* (hominem quia *F*).
[5] retinere *Hedicke;* renouare *A.*
[6] *P omits at the end of a folio the words which follow, as far
as x. 5. 8* nec se ipsos, *two folios apparently being lost.*
[7] cum *added by Jeep.*

---

[a] Rather a favourite word with Curtius ; *cf.* vi. 11. 2;
viii. 5. 8.
[b] 10,000 in number ; Diod. xvii. 109. 1.

Greeks, not daring to disregard his order, although they thought that it marked the beginning of the breakdown of their laws, even restored to those who had been condemned such of their property as was
6 left. The Athenians alone, defenders not only of themselves but also of Greece, could not tolerate such a cesspool of classes and men, being accustomed to be governed, not by the command of a king, but
7 by the laws and ancestral customs; therefore they shut out the exiles from their territories, preferring to endure anything rather than admit what was once the off-scourings [a] of their city, and then even of their places of exile.

8   Alexander, having sent the older of his soldiers [b] to their native land, ordered 13,000 infantry and 2000 horsemen to be selected for him to retain in Asia, thinking that Asia could be held by an army of moderate size, because he had distributed garrisons in many places and had filled the newly founded cities with colonists desirous of maintaining
9 the *status quo*. But before selecting those whom he intended to retain, he ordered all the soldiers to make a declaration of their debts. He had learned that many had heavy indebtedness, and although it had been contracted by their own extravagance, he had nevertheless decided to liquidate it himself.
10 The soldiers, thinking that they were being tested, in order that he might more easily separate the wastrels from the frugal, had delayed for some time in making their reports. And the king, knowing well that it was shame and not stubbornness which kept them from confessing their indebtedness, ordered tables to be set up throughout the whole
11 camp, and 10,000 talents to be brought out. Then

professio est.   Nec amplius ex tanta pecunia quam c
et xxx talenta superfuere.   Adeo ille exercitus, tot
divitissimarum gentium victor, plus tamen victoriae
quam praedae deportavit ex Asia.

12   Ceterum ut cognitum est alios remitti domos, alios
retineri, perpetuam eum regni sedem in Asia habiturum rati, vaecordes et disciplinae militaris immemores, seditiosis vocibus castra complent regemque
ferocius quam alias adorti, omnes simul missionem
postulare coeperunt, deformia ora cicatricibus cani-

13 tiemque capitum ostentantes.   Nec aut praefectorum[1]
castigatione aut verecundia regis deterriti,[2] tumultuoso clamore et militari violentia volentem loqui
inhibebant, palam professi nusquam inde nisi in

14 patriam vestigium esse moturos.   Tandem silentio
facto, magis quia motum esse credebant quam quia
ipsi moveri poterant, quidnam acturus esset, exspectabant, cum[3] ille :

15   " Quid haec," inquit, " repens consternatio et tam
procax atque effusa licentia denuntiat ?   Eloqui
metuo, palam certe ; rupistis imperium, et precario
rex sum, cui non alloquendi, non noscendi monendi-

16 que aut intuendi vos ius reliquistis.   Equidem cum
alios dimittere in patriam, alios mecum paulo post
deportare statuerim,[4] tam illos acclamantes video qui
abituri sunt, quam hos cum quibus praemissos sub-

17 sequi statui.   Quid hoc est rei ? dispari in causa

---

[1] praefectorum *I;* profectorum *A.*
[2] deterriti *Lauer;* deterritum *A.*
[3] cum *added by Hedicke.*
[4] statuerim *J. Froben;* statuerem *A.*

at last, when they were satisfied that he was in earnest, they declared their debts. And out of so great a sum of money not more than 130 talents remained. To such an extent had that army, though victor over so many of the richest nations, yet carried off from Asia more victory than booty.

12 But when it was known that some were being sent home and others retained, the soldiers, thinking that he would establish the permanent seat of his kingdom in Asia, frenzied and forgetful of military discipline, filled the camp with mutinous talk, and assailing the king more boldly than ever before, began all together to demand their discharge, displaying their faces dis-
13 figured with scars and their hoary heads. Prevented by neither the rebukes of their officers nor by respect for the king, with rebellious shouts and military violence they interrupted Alexander when he wished to speak, and openly declared that they would move a step from there in no direction except towards
14 their native land. At last, when silence had been made rather because they thought that he had been influenced than because they could be, they were waiting to see what he would do, when he said :

15 "What does this sudden disturbance and such insolent and furious lawlessness threaten ? I fear to speak, at least plainly ; you have broken my author-ity and I am king on sufferance, to whom you have not left the privilege of addressing you, of knowing and advising you, or even of looking you in the face.
16 In fact, when I have decided to send some to their native land and a little later to take others with me, I witness the same uproar from those who are to go as from those with whom I decided to follow those
17 who had been sent in advance. What does this

idem omnium clamor est! Pervelim scire utrum qui discedunt,[1] an qui retinentur, de me querantur."

18 Crederes uno ore omnes sustulisse clamorem ; ita pariter ex tota contione responsum est omnes queri.

19 Tum ille : " Non, hercule," inquit, " potest fieri ut adducar querendi simul omnibus hanc causam esse quam ostenditis, in qua maior pars exercitus non est, utpote cum plures dimiserim quam retenturus sum.

20 Subest nimirum altius malum quod omnes avertit a me. Quando enim regem universus deseruit exercitus ? Ne servi quidem uno grege profugiunt dominos, sed est quidam[2] in illis pudor a ceteris

21 destitutos relinquendi. Verum ego tam furiosae consternationis oblitus, remedia insanabilibus conor adhibere. Omnem, hercule, spem quam ex vobis conceperam, damno nec ut cum militibus meis—iam enim esse desistis—, sed ut cum ingratissimis operis[3]

22 agere decrevi. Secundis rebus, quae circumfluunt vos, insanire coepistis obliti status eius, quem beneficio exuistis meo, digni, hercule, qui in eodem consenescatis, quoniam facilius est vobis adversam quam secundam regere fortunam.

23 " En insolentiam ![4] Illyriorum paulo ante et Persarum tributariis Asia et tot gentium spolia fastidio sunt ! modo sub Philippo seminudis amicula ex purpura sordent ! aurum et argentum oculi ferre non

---

[1] discedunt *Lauer;* descendunt *A.*
[2] sed est quidam *J. Froben;* sedem quidem *A.*
[3] operis *Ruben;* oportet *A.*
[4] insolentiam *Hedicke;* tandem *A.*

---

[a] Diod. xvi. 2. 2.   [b] Justin vii. 3. 1.
              [c] Arr. vii. 9. 2.

mean ? The shouting of all is the same for different reasons ! I should very much like to know whether it is those who are to go, or those who are to be retained who complain of me."

18 You would have believed that all with one voice raised a shout; so unanimously came the reply from
19 the whole assembly that they all complained. Then the king continued : " By Heaven ! it is impossible for me to be led to believe that you all have the reason for complaint which you allege, in which the greater part of the army does not join, inasmuch as I dismissed more than I am intending to retain.
20 Undoubtedly there is some deeper evil which turns you all from me. For when has a whole army abandoned its king ? Not even slaves run away from their masters in a single body, but even they feel some shame in leaving those who have been
21 deserted by the rest. But I, forgetting such mad mutiny, am trying to apply remedies to those that are incurable. By Heaven ! I reject all the hope which I had conceived from you, and I have decided to treat with you, not as with my soldiers—for that you have already ceased to be—but as the most ungrate-
22 ful of hired hands. You have begun to be crazed by the prosperity which surrounds you, forgetting the condition from which you were saved by my kindness, in which, by Heaven ! you deserve to grow old, since it is easier for you to master bad fortune than good.
23 " There's insolence ! You, who a short time ago were paying tribute to the Illyrians *a* and the Persians,*b* are disdainful of Asia and the spoils of so many nations. Those who but now were half-naked *c* under Philip find purple robes mean ! Their

489

possunt! Lignea enim vasa desiderant et ex cratibus
24 scuta robiginemque[1] gladiorum. Hoc cultu nitentes
vos accepi et D talenta aeris alieni, cum omnis regia
supellex esset[2] haud amplius quam LX talenta,[3] meorum mox operum fundamenta. Quibus tamen—
absit invidia—imperium maximae terrarum parti
25 imposui. Asiaene pertaesum est quae vos gloria
rerum gestarum dis pares fecit? In Europam ire
properatis rege deserto, cum pluribus vestrum de-
futurum viaticum fuerit, ni aes alienum luissem,
26 nempe in Asiatica praeda. Nec pudet profundo
ventre devictarum gentium spolia circumferentes
reverti velle ad liberos coniugesque, quibus pauci
praemia victoriae potestis ostendere; nam cetero-
rum, dum etiam spei vestrae obviam istis, arma
quoque pignori sunt.

27 "Bonis vero militibus cariturus sum, pelicum
suarum concubinis, quibus hoc solum ex tantis opibus
superest, in quod impenditur! Proinde fugientibus
me pateant limites! facessite hinc ocius! ego cum
Persis abeuntium terga tutabor. Neminem teneo;
28 liberate oculos meos, ingratissimi cives! Laeti vos
excipient parentes liberique sine vestro rege re-
deuntes! obviam ibunt desertoribus transfugisque!
29 Triumphabo, mehercule, de fuga vestra et, ubicumque
ero, expetam poenas hos cum quibus me relinquitis

---

[1] robiginemque *Hedicke;* rubiginemque *A.*
[2] esset *added by Hedicke.*
[3] talenta, meorum mox *Hedicke;* talentorum mox *A.*

---

[a] Arr. vii. 9. 6; Plut. *Alex.* xv. 1 says seventy.
[b] That is, of returning home.
[c] *quod, i.e. pelices.*   [d] *i.e.* from the sight of you.

eyes cannot endure gold and silver! For they desire wooden bowls, wicker shields, and rusty swords!

24 Such was the splendid equipment in which I received you, besides a debt of 500 talents, when the whole royal equipment was not more than 60 talents,[a] the foundation of the deeds which I afterwards accomplished. With which nevertheless—may envy withhold her hand!—I imposed my rule upon the

25 greatest part of the earth. Are you wearied of Asia, which by the glory of your deeds has made you equal to the gods? You are in a hurry to desert your king and go into Europe, when to very many of you your travelling expenses would have been lacking if I had not liquidated your debts, and that too in booty from

26 Asia. And you are not ashamed, carrying about in your bottomless bellies the spoils of conquered nations, to wish to return to your wives and children, to whom few of you can show the fruits of victory; for of the rest your very arms have been pawned, even while you are on the way to the realization of your hopes.[b]

27 " Fine soldiers truly I am going to lose, bed-mates of mistresses; men to whom this alone remains out of such great riches, and on this, wealth is being spent.[c] Therefore let the ways be opened for those who desert me! Get out from here! And quickly too! I with the Persians will protect your backs as you flee. I detain no one; free my eyes,[d] most

28 ungrateful of citizens! Joyfully will your parents and children receive you, returning without your king! They will come out to meet deserters and

29 runaways! I shall triumph, by Heaven! in your flight, and wherever I shall be, I shall punish you by honouring and preferring to you those with

491

colendo praeferendoque vobis. Iam autem scietis, et
quantum sine rege valeat exercitus, et quid opis in
30 me uno sit." Desiluit deinde frendens de tribunali
et in medium armatorum agmen se immisit, notatos
quoque qui ferocissime oblocuti erant, singulos manu
corripuit[1] nec ausos repugnare xiii asservandos custodibus corporis tradidit.

III. Quis crederet saevam paulo ante contionem
2 obtorpuisse subito metu, etiam cum[2] ad supplicium videret trahi nihilo[3] ausos graviora quam ceteros ?[4] . . .
3 Sive nominis, quod gentes quae sub regibus vivunt
reges[5] inter deos colunt, sive propria ipsius veneratio
sive fiducia tanta vi exercentis imperium conterruit
4 eos ; singulare certe ediderunt patientiae exemplum
adeoque non sunt accensi supplicio commilitonum,
cum sub noctem interfectos esse cognossent, ut nihil
omiserint quod singuli magis oboedienter et pie
5 facerent. Nam cum postero die prohibiti aditu fuissent,[6] Asiaticis modo militibus admissis, lugubrem
totis castris edidere clamorem, denuntiantes protinus
6 sese[7] morituros, si rex perseveraret irasci. At ille
pervicacis ad omnia quae agitasset animi, peregri-

---

[1] corripuit *Lauer;* corripit *A.*
[2] etiam cum *Bentley;* et cum *A.*
[3] nihilo *Acidalius;* nihil *A.*
[4] ceteros] *a lacuna after this word was assumed by*
Freinshem.
[5] vivunt reges *added by Stangl.*
[6] fuissent *Bentley;* uenissent *A.*
[7] sese *Hedicke;* esse *A.*

whom you leave me. Moreover, you will soon know
how much an army is worth without a head, and
30 what help there is in my single person." Then in
a rage he leaped down from the tribunal and plunged
into the midst of the array of armed soldiers, and
having noted those who had spoken most mutin-
ously, he seized them [a] one by one, none daring to
resist, and handed over thirteen of them to his body-
guard to be kept in custody.

III. Who would have believed that an assemblage
2 recently so savage was paralysed by sudden fear, even
when they saw those who had dared nothing more
serious than the rest dragged off to punishment? . . .
3 Whether veneration for the mere name, since nations
which live under kings honour their kings among the
gods, or a particular veneration for Alexander himself, or the confidence with which he exercised his
authority with such force, struck them all with
4 terror; at any rate, they showed a remarkable
instance of patience, and were so far from being
exasperated by the execution of their fellow-soldiers
when towards nightfall they learned that they had
been put to death, that there was nothing that they
left undone to make each man act with more obedi-
5 ence and loyalty. For on the following day, when
they had been refused access to the king,[b] and only
Asiatic soldiers were admitted, they uttered mourn-
ful cries throughout the whole camp, declaring that
they wished to die forthwith if the king persisted
6 in being angry. But he, determined to carry out
everything upon which he had resolved, ordered an

[a] According to Arr. vii. 8. 3, this happened before his
speech.
[b] See Arr. vii. 11. 1.

norum militum contionem advocari iubet, Macedonibus intra castra cohibitis, et, cum frequentes
coissent, adhibito interprete, talem orationem habuit:

7 "Cum ex Europa traicerem in Asiam, multas
nobiles gentes, magnam vim hominum imperio meo
me additurum esse sperabam. Nec deceptus sum quod
8 de his credidi famae. Sed ad illa hoc quoque accessit,
quod video fortes viros erga reges suos pietatis in-
9 victae. Luxu omni[1] fluere credideram et nimia
felicitate mergi in voluptates; at, hercules, munia
militiae hoc animorum corporumque robore[2] aeque
impigre toleratis et, cum fortes viri sitis, non forti-
10 tudinem magis quam fidem colitis. Hoc ego vero[3]
nunc primum profiteor, sed olim scio. Itaque et
dilectum e vobis iuniorum habui et vos meorum
militum corpori immiscui. Idem habitus, eadem
arma sunt vobis; obsequium vero et patientia imperii
longe praestantior est quam ceteris.

11 "Ergo ipse Oxyartis Persae filiam mecum matrimonio[4] iunxi, non dedignatus ex captiva liberos
12 tollere. Mox deinde cum stirpem generis mei latius
propagare cuperem, uxorem Darei filiam duxi, proxi-
misque amicorum auctor fui ex captivis generandi
liberos, ut hoc sacro foedere omne discrimen victi et
13 victoris excluderem. Proinde genitos esse vos mihi,

---

[1] omni *Hedicke;* omnia *A.*
[2] robore *Francine;* robor *A.*   [3] vero *Hedicke;* non *A.*
[4] in (*before* matrimonio) *deleted by Hedicke.*

---

[a] That is, Persians in the wide sense of the word; *cf.* Arr.
vii. 11. 1 ff.
[b] Rather, Bactrian; Arr. vii. 4. 4.
[c] Barsinê, Arr. vii. 4. 6; Statira, Diod. xvii. 105. 6.
[d] Arr. vii. 4. 5-6 mentions seven by name, and refers to
80 besides.

assembly of the foreign [a] troops to be called, while the Macedonians were kept within their camp, and when the foreign troops had come together in great numbers, he summoned an interpreter and addressed them as follows :

7 " When I was crossing from Europe into Asia, I hoped that I should add many famous nations and a great force of men to my kingdom. And I was not deceived in believing what was reported about them.

8 But to that report this also is added, that I behold brave men of invincible loyalty towards their kings.

9 I had supposed that luxury prevailed everywhere, and that by excess of good fortune you were plunged into pleasures ; but, by Heaven ! you endure with equal indefatigability, such is that strength of yours of both mind and body, the duties of military service, and while you are brave men, you cultivate loyalty

10 no less than courage. This, it is true, I now declare for the first time, but have long known it. Therefore I have both made a selection from the men of military age among you, and have incorporated them with my soldiers. You have the same equipment, the same arms ; but in obedience and submission to discipline you are far superior to the rest.

11 " It is for this reason that I myself united in marriage with me Roxanê, daughter of the Persian [b] Oxyartes, not disdaining to rear children from a

12 captive. Then later, when I desired to propagate the stock of my race more extensively, I took to wife a daughter [c] of Darius and set the example to my nearest friends [d] of begetting children from captives, in order that by this sacred alliance I might abolish all distinction between vanquished and victor.

13 Therefore believe that in my eyes you are soldiers

non ascitos milites credite ! Asiae et Europae unum
atque idem regnum est ; Macedonum vobis arma do,
inveteravi peregrinam novitatem ; et cives mei estis
14 et milites. Omnia eundem ducunt colorem ; nec
Persis Macedonum morem[1] adumbrare nec Macedonibus Persas imitari indecorum. Eiusdem iuris
esse debent, qui sub eodem rege victuri sunt."[2] *Hac
oratione habita, Persis corporis sui custodiam credidit,
Persas satellites, Persas apparitores fecit. Per quos cum
Macedones, qui huius seditionis principes erant, vincti,
ad supplicia traherentur, unum ex eis, auctoritate et aetate
gravem, ad regem ita locutum ferunt :*

IV. " Quousque," inquit, " animo tuo etiam per
supplicia et quidem externi moris obsequeris ?[3]
Milites tui, cives tui, incognita causa, et[4] captivis
suis ducentibus, trahuntur ad poenam. Si mortem
meruisse iudicas, saltem ministros supplicii muta."
2 Amico animo, si veri patiens fuisset, admonebatur,
sed in rabiem ira pervenerat. Itaque rursus—nam
parumper, quibus imperatum erat, dubitaverant—
3 mergi in amnem, sicut vincti erant, iussit. Ne[5] hoc
quidem supplicium seditionem militum movit. Namque copiarum duces atque amicos eius manipuli
adeunt petentes, ut, si quos adhuc pristina noxa iudi-

---

[1] morem *Vindelinus;* more *A.*
[2] victuri sunt] *the words which follow, as far as the
beginning of ch. 4, were added by J. Froben. In A a considerable space is left vacant, and in BL a corrector has
written* hic deest.
[3] obsequeris *Giunta;* exsequeris *A.*
[4] et *Stangl;* a *A.*   [5] Ne *Zumpt;* nec *A.*

---

[a] See crit. note 2.

of our blood, not brought in from outside. Asia
and Europe now belong to one and the same kingdom ; I give you the arms of the Macedonians, I
have made you old soldiers instead of new and
foreign ones ; you are both my citizens and my
14 soldiers. All things take on the same colour ; it is
neither unbecoming for the Persians to simulate the
manners of the Macedonians, nor for the Macedonians to copy those of the Persians. Those ought
to have the same rights who are to live under the
same sovereign." *After* [a] *having made this address,
Alexander entrusted to Persians the guardianship of his
person, made his attendants Persians, his servants Persians. When the Macedonians who were leaders in this
mutiny were being led by these in bonds to execution,
they say that one of them, a man of weight in authority
and in years, spoke as follows to the king :*

IV. "How long will you gratify your mind even
with punishments, and those too of a foreign kind ?
Your soldiers, your citizens, without a trial and led
by their captives, are dragged off to death. If it is
your judgement that we deserve death, at least
2 change those who inflict the penalty." The king was
admonished in a friendly spirit, if he had been willing
to listen to the truth, but his wrath had changed to
madness. Therefore he ordered again—for those to
whom the order had been given had hesitated—that
the mutineers be drowned in the river, bound as
3 they were.[b] Not even such a punishment as this
roused mutiny among the soldiers. On the contrary,
the companies went to the leaders of the forces and
to the king's friends, asking that if he judged that

[b] According to Arr. vii. 8, this took place at Opis on the
Tigris.

caret esse contactos, iuberet interfici. Offerre se corpora irae ; trucidaret.[1] *Tandem prae dolore vix mentis
compotes, universi concurrunt ad regiam, armisque ante
fores proiectis, tunicati astantes, ut nuda et obnoxia poenis
corpora admitterentur, flentes orabant. Non se deprecari,
quin suppliciis sontium expiarentur quae per contumaciam
deliquissent. Regis iracundiam sibi morte tristiorem esse.*

   *Cumque dies noctesque ante regiam persistentes miserabili
clamore habituque paenitentiam suam approbarent, biduum
tamen adversus humillimas suorum preces iracundia regis
duravit. Tertio die victus constantia supplicum, processit,
incusataque leniter exercitus immodestia, non sine multis
utrimque lacrimis in gratiam se cum ipsis redire professus
est. Digna tamen res visa est quae maioribus hostiis
expiaretur. Itaque sacrificio magnifice perpetrato, Macedonum simul Persarumque primores invitavit ad epulas.
Novem milia eo convivio excepisse proditum est memoriae,
eosque omnes, invitante rege, ex eadem creterra libavisse,
Graecis barbarisque vatibus cum alia fausta vota prae-
euntibus, tum imprimis, ut utriusque imperii societas in
idem corpus coalita perpetua esset. Maturata deinde est
missio, et infirmissimus quisque exauctorati. Amicorum
quoque seniorum quibusdam commeatum dedit. Ex quibus Clitus cognomine Albus Gorgiasque et Polydamas et
Antigenes fuere. Abeuntibus non modo praeteriti tem*

---

[1] irae; trucidaret *Modius;* ira retrucidaret *A. The words
which follow, as far as the beginning of ch. 5, were added by
Freinshem. In A no part of the page is left vacant, but
either in the line itself (FL m. pr. V) or in the margin
(BL corr.) a corrector added* hinc deest.

---

there were any besides who were stained with the same guilt, he should order them to be put to death ; that they offered their bodies to his anger ; let him slaughter them. *At last,[a] almost beside themselves with grief, they ran to the royal quarters in a body, and throwing down their arms before the doors and standing in their tunics, begged with tears that their bodies, unarmed and submissive to punishment, might be admitted. That they did not refuse by the punishment of the guilty to expiate the faults that they had committed through insubordination. That the anger of the king was to them more terrible than death.*

But although, continuing to stand day and night before the royal quarters, they manifested their repentance by pitiful outcries and attire, yet the king's wrath held out for two days against his men's most abject prayers. On the third day, overcome by their constant entreaties, he came out, and after mildly censuring the lack of discipline of the army, declared, not without the shedding of many tears by both sides, that he was reconciled with them. Nevertheless the event seemed to call for expiation by greater victims. Accordingly, after offering a splendid sacrifice, he invited the chief men of the Macedonians and at the same time those of the Persians to a feast. It is reported that he entertained 9000 men at that banquet, and that they all, at the king's invitation, made libation from the same bowl, while the priests of the Greeks and of the barbarians dictated not only other propitious prayers, but especially that a union of the two kingdoms should be consolidated for all time in the same body. Then the discharge was hastened, and all the weakest soldiers were mustered out. He also granted a furlough to some of his friends of greater age.[b] Among these were Clitus, surnamed Albus, Gorgias, Polydamas, and Antigenes. To those who left

*poris stipendia cum fide persolvit, verum etiam talentum
adiecit in singulos milites viatici nomine.*

*Filios ex Asiaticis uxoribus susceptos—ad decem milia
fuisse traduntur—apud se relinqui iussit, ne in Macedoniam cum parentibus transgressi et coniugibus liberisque
prioribus permixti, familias contentionibus et discordiis
implerent ; sibi curae fore pollicitus, ut patrio more instituti militiae artes edocerentur. Ita plus decem milia
veteranorum dimissa sunt, additusque est qui eos deduceret
Craterus, ex praecipuis regis amicis. Cui si quid humani
accidisset, Polyperconti parere iussi sunt. Litteris etiam
ad Antipatrum scriptis, honorem emeritis haberi iussit, ut
quotiens ludi atque certamina ederentur, in primis ordinibus coronati spectarent, utque fato functorum liberi im-
puberes in paterna stipendia succederent. Craterum
Macedoniae finitimisque regionibus cum imperio praeesse
placuit, Antipatrum autem cum supplemento iuniorum
Macedonum ad regem venire. Verebatur enim ne per
discordiam praefecti cum Olympiade gravis aliqua clades
acciperetur. Nam multas ad Alexandrum epistulas mater,
multas Antipater miserat, vicissimque alter alterum arro-
ganter et acerbe pleraque facere criminabantur, quae ad
dedecus aut detrimentum regiae maiestatis pertinerent.
Postquam enim rumor occisi regis, temere vulgatus, in
Macedonian manavit, mater eius sororque Cleopatra*

---

    a See Arr. vii. 12. 1.   *b* Justin xii. 12. 8.
        c Cf. Arr. vii. 12. 3 f.
    d Cf. Arr. vii. 13. 4 : Justin xii. 12. 4.

he not only faithfully gave pay for their past services, but also added a talent to each soldier for travelling expenses.[a]

He gave orders that the sons whom they had begotten from Asiatic wives—they are said to have numbered about 10,000—should be left with him, for fear that if they returned to Macedonia with their fathers and mingled with the former wives and children of these, they might fill the families with strife and discord; he promised that he would take care that the children should be trained in the customs of their country and taught the principles of military service. So, more than 10,000 veterans were discharged, and Craterus,[b] one of the king's special friends, was appointed to lead them. If anything to which humanity is liable should befall him, they were ordered to obey Polypercon. A letter was also written to Antipater with orders that honour should be paid to the discharged veterans, so that whenever games and athletic contests were celebrated, they should witness them from the first rows of seats and with garlands on their heads, and that the ungrown children of those who should have died should inherit their fathers' pay. He appointed Craterus governor of Macedonia and the adjacent districts,[c] but gave orders that Antipater [d] should come to the king with a reinforcement of younger Macedonians. For he feared that through the discord between the governor and Olympias some grave calamity might be suffered. For his mother had sent many letters to Alexander, and Antipater many, in which they charged each other with numerous arrogant and hostile acts which tended to the disgrace or the impairment of the royal majesty. For after the rumour of the king's death, which had been falsely spread abroad, had seeped into Macedonia, his mother and his sister Cleopatra [e] had set on foot a revolu-

• Plut. *Alex.* lxviii. 3.

501

*tumultum moverant, et haec quidem paternum regnum,
Olympias Epirum occupaverat.*

*Forte, dum eiusmodi litterae redduntur, Hephaestion,
qui omnium arcanorum particeps haberetur, resignatas ab
Alexandro simul inspiciebat. Neque retinuit eum rex, sed
detractum digito anulum ori legentis admovit, nihil eorum
quae perscripta essent in alios efferendum significans.
Incusasse autem ambos fertur et matris insolentia per-
motus exclamasse, eam pro habitatione decem mensium,
quam in utero sibi praebuisset, gravem mercedem exigere,
Antipatrum vero suspectum habuisse, parta ex Spartanis
victoria, tollere animos et imperio tot iam annos prorogato
supra praefecti modum esse elatum. Itaque cum eius
gravitas atque integritas a quibusdam praedicaretur, respondit exterius quidem album videri, sed si penitus
introspiceretur, totum esse purpureum. Pressit tamen
suspicionem suam neque ullum manifestius abalienati
animi indicium protulit. Credidere tamen plerique Antipatrum, arcessi se supplicii causa ratum, impiis insidiis
mortis regis, quae paulo post secuta est, auctorem exstitisse.*

*Interea rex, ut imminuti exercitus detrimenta sarciret,
optimum quemque Persarum in Macedonicos ordines al-
legit ; mille etiam praestantissimos segregavit ad corporis
custodiam ; aliam hastatorum manum, haud pauciores
decem milibus, ad regium tabernaculum excubias agere
iussit. Haec agenti Peucestes supervenit cum viginti mili-*

ᵃ Macedonia, see note ᵉ on p. 501.
ᵇ Plut. *Apophtheg.* 39 ; Arr. vii. 12. **6.**
ᶜ *Cf.* Diod. xvii. 101. 3.

tion, and his sister had taken possession of her **father's** kingdom,[a] and Olympias, of Epirus.

It happened that while letters of that kind were being delivered, Hephaestion, who was wont to be regarded as the confidant of all the king's secrets, was at the same time looking over the letters that had been opened by Alexander. And the king did not prevent him, but taking off his ring from his finger, he laid it upon the reader's lips, signifying that nothing of what had been written should be communicated to others. But he is said to have railed at them both, and, angered by the insolence of his mother, to have said that she for a lodging of ten months which she had furnished him in her womb was exacting a heavy price,[b] but that he had held Antipater in suspicion, on the ground that having gained a victory over the Spartans he was growing arrogant, and because of power already prolonged over so many years had risen above the conduct becoming a prefect. Accordingly, when Antipater's dignity and uprightness were praised by certain men, Alexander replied that he seemed white on the outside, but if he was looked into deeply, he was all purple. Nevertheless he concealed his suspicion and showed no clearer indication of an alienated feeling. Yet very many believed that Antipater, thinking that he was summoned for punishment, was responsible by disloyal plots for the death of the king, which followed shortly afterward.

Meanwhile the king, in order to patch up the losses in his diminished army, mustered all the best of the Persians into the ranks of the Macedonians [c]; he also set aside a thousand of the most distinguished for a body-guard; another troop of spearmen, not fewer than 10,000, he ordered to keep watch by night at the royal quarters. As he was doing this, Peucestes appeared with 20,000 archers

bus sagittariorum funditorumque, quos ex sua provincia coegerat. His per exercitum distributis, profectus est Susis et, Pasitigri amne traiecto, apud Caras castra metatus est. Inde, quadriduo per Sittacenen ductis copiis, Sambana processit ibique per septem dies substitit. Tridui deinde itinere emenso, Celonas perventum est. Oppidum hoc tenent Boeotia profecti, quos Xerxes ex sedibus suis excitos in Orientem transtulit ; servabantque argumentum originis peculiarem sermonem ex Graecis plerumque vocibus constantem, ceterum propter commercii necessitatem finitimorum barbarorum lingua utebantur. Inde in Bagistanen ingressus est, regionem opulentam et abundantem arborum amoeno et fecundo fetu ceterisque ad vitae non usum modo, verum etiam delectationem pertinentibus.

Gravis inter haec Eumeni cum Hephaestione simultas inciderat. Nam servos Eumenis e deversorio quod pro domino suo occupaverant, Hephaestio proturbavit, ut Euius tibicen eo reciperetur. Neque multo post, cum iam sopita odia viderentur, nova orta contentione, adeo recruduerunt, ut etiam in atrox iurgium et acerba utrimque convicia prorumperent. Sed Alexandri intercessione imperioque inimicitiae saltem in speciem abolitae sunt, cum ille Hephaestioni etiam minatus esset, qui in summa regis gratia Eumenem quamvis cupidum reconciliationis pertinacius aversabatur.

Perventum deinde est in Mediae campos, ubi maximi equorum greges alebantur; Nisaeos appellant, magnitudine et specie insignes. Plus quinquaginta milia ibi reperta

---

[a] Egypt ; see iv. 8. 4.
[b] Really the Eulaeus ; *cf.* v. 3. 1.
[c] See Amm. xxiii. 6. 30, note.

504

and slingers which he had mustered from his own province.[a] *When these had been distributed through the army, the king set out from Susa, and, having crossed the Pasitigris*[b] *River, measured off a camp at Carae. Then, having led his forces for four days through Sittacenê, he advanced to Sambana, and remained there for seven days. Then, after making a march of three days, he arrived at Celonae. This town is occupied by people from Boeotia, whom Xerxes drove from their homes and transferred to the Orient ; and they retained as a proof of their origin a language of their own, consisting for the most part of Greek words, but because of the necessity of commerce they used the speech of the neighbouring barbarians. Then he entered Bagistanê, a rich region, abounding in a handsome and prolific growth of trees, and in other things which contribute not only to the necessities, but also to the enjoyment of life.*

Meanwhile a serious quarrel had arisen between Eumenes and Hephaestion. For Hephaestion had evicted Eumenes' slaves from the lodging of which they had taken possession for their master, in order that Evius, a flute-player, might be put up in it. And not long afterwards, when their hatred seemed to be already put to sleep, through a new cause of strife that arose it revived to such an extent that they even broke out into a dreadful wrangle and bitter abuse of each other. But by the intervention of Alexander and at his command their enmity was ended, at least in appearance, after he had even threatened Hephaestion, who, since he enjoyed the king's greatest favour, persistently repulsed Eumenes, although the latter was desirous of a reconciliation.

Then they came to the plains of Media, where very great herds of horses were bred ; they call them Nisaean and they are conspicuous for their size and beauty.[c] *More*

*esse, cum Alexander eo transiret, a comitibus eius anno-
tatum est ; olim triplicem numerum fuisse, sed inter
bellorum turbas maximam eorum partem praedones ab-
egisse. Ad triginta dies ibi substitit rex. Eo Atropates,
Mediae satrapes, centum barbaras mulieres adduxit equi-
tandi peritas peltisque et securibus armatas ; unde quidam
crediderunt Amazonum ex gente reliquias fuisse. Septimis
deinde castris Ecbatana, Mediae caput, pervenit. Ibi
sollemnia dis sacrificia fecit ludosque edidit et conviviis
festisque diebus laxavit animum, ut ad nova opera validior
esset.*

*Sed ista volventem, velut iniecta manu, Fatum alio traxit
vitamque carissimo amicorum eius neque multo post ipsi
quoque regi eripuit. Pueros in stadio certantes spectabat,
cum nuntiatum est deficere Hephaestionem, qui ex crapula
septimum iam diem aeger cubabat. Exterritus amici periculo statim surrexit et ad hospitium eius celeriter se contulit. Neque tamen prius eo pervenit, quam illum mors
occupavit. Id regi omnium quae in vita pertulerat adver-
sorum luctuosissimum accidisse certum habetur, eumque
magnitudine doloris in lacrimas et lamenta victum, multa
animi de gradu deiecti argumenta edidisse. Sed ea quidem
varie traduntur; illud inter omnes constat, Alexandrum, ut
quam decentissimas exsequias ei duceret, noluisse Ecbatanis
eum sepeliri, sed Babylonem quo ipse profecturus esset a*

ᵃ Diod. xvii. 110. 6 ; Arr. vii. 13. 1.
ᵇ Arr. vii. 14. 1.   ᶜ Arr. *l.c.*
ᵈ *Cf.* Arr. vii. 14. 1-3.
ᵉ Plut. *Alex.* lxxii. 2 ; Arr. vii. 14 ; Diod. xvii. 110. 8.

*than 50,000 were found there when Alexander crossed
into that country, as was noted by his companions ; that
formerly there had been three times that number, but amid
the confusion of the wars brigands had driven off the
greatest part of them.   There the king halted for about
thirty days.[a]   Thither Atropates, satrap of Media,
brought a hundred barbarian women [b] skilled in horse-
manship and armed with round shields and axes ; this
equipment led some to believe that they were survivors of
the race of the Amazons.   Then in seven days he came
to Ecbatana, the capital of Media.   There he offered
solemn sacrifices to the gods,[c] exhibited games, and
relaxed his mind with banquets and festal days, in order
to be stronger for new tasks.*

*But as he was meditating on these tasks, Fate, as if
laying her hand upon him, drew him elsewhere and snatched
away the life of the dearest of his friends, and not long
afterwards of the king himself.   He was viewing the
boys contesting in the stadium [d] when it was announced
that Hephaestion was failing ; he had already been sick
abed for seven days from over-indulgence in wine.
Alarmed by the danger of his friend, the king at once
rose from his seat and quickly went to Hephaestion's
lodging.   Yet he did not reach there before death had
anticipated him.   This is certainly regarded as the most
grievous of all the losses which Alexander had suffered
in his whole lifetime,[e] and that he was so overcome by
the greatness of his sorrow as to burst into tears and
lamentations gave strong proof of a loss of his usual
spirit.   But there are various reports of his conduct ; this
much is agreed by all, that Alexander, in order to give
his friend the most splendid obsequies, did not wish him
to be buried at Ecbatana, but to be taken by Perdiccas to
Babylon, to which place he himself was on the point of*

*Perdicca deferri ; ibique funus inaudito exemplo duo-
decim milibus talentum locavisse. Per universum certe
imperium lugeri eum iussit et, ne memoria eius in exercitu
exolesceret, equitibus quibus praefuerat nullum praefecit
ducem, sed Hephaestionis alam appellari voluit et quae ille
signa instituisset, ea non immutari. Funebria certamina ludosque, quales numquam editi fuissent, meditatus,
tria milia artificum coegit ; qui non multo post in ipsius
exequiis certasse traduntur.*

*Nec amici tam effuso affectu ad conciliandam eius
gratiam segniter usi, certatim repperere per quae memoria
defuncti clarior honoratiorque fieret. Eumenes igitur cum
se ob simultatem cum Hephaestione in regis indignationem
incurrisse sensisset, multis auctor fuit seque et arma sua
Hephaestioni consecrandi pecuniasque ad cohonestandum
funus large contulit. Hoc exemplum imitati sunt ceteri ;
eoque processit assentantium impudentia, ut regi maerore
et desiderio defuncti insanienti persuasum tandem sit,
deum esse Hephaestionem.*

*Quo quidem tempore ex copiarum ducibus Agathocles
Samius in extremum periculum venit, quod eius tumulum praeteriens illacrimasse visus est. Ac nisi Perdiccas
venanti sibi Hephaestionem apparuisse ementitus per deos
omnes ipsumque Hephaestionem deierasset ex ipso se cog-
novisse, Agathoclem non ut mortuum et vanae divinitatis
titulis frustra ornatum flevisse, verum propter memoriam*

---

^a He was general of the Companion cavalry, Arr. vii.
14. 10.
^b Arr. vii. 14. 10 says that an image modelled on Hephaes-
tion was carried before it.

going ; and that there he had arranged for a funeral of unheard-of splendour at a cost of 12,000 talents. Certain it is that he gave orders for Hephaestion to be mourned throughout the whole empire, and in order that his memory might not be lost in the army, Alexander appointed no leader of the cavalry which he had commanded,[a] but wished it to be called the troop of Hephaestion, and that the standards that he had established there should not be changed.[b] The king planned funereal contests and games such as had never been given before, and brought together 3000 artists; and these not long after are said to have competed at Alexander's own funeral.

The king's friends also, not lacking in zeal to win his favour by such lavish demonstrations of sympathy, vied with one another in devising means of making the memory of the deceased more glorious and more honoured. Accordingly Eumenes, since he felt that he had incurred the king's indignation because of his quarrel with Hephaestion, induced many men to consecrate themselves and their arms to Hephaestion and he himself contributed generously to join in honouring his funeral. The rest followed this example, and their shameless flattery went so far that the king, insane with grief and longing for his dead friend, was at last persuaded that Hephaestion was a god.

At that time, indeed, among the leaders of the forces Agathocles the Samian fell into extreme danger because when passing the tomb of Hephaestion he was seen to have wept over him. And had not Perdiccas falsely said that while he was hunting Hephaestion had appeared to him, and had he not sworn by all the gods and by Hephaestion himself that he had learned from him that Agathocles had not wept as over a dead mortal who had vainly been honoured with the title of divinity, but that it was because

509

*pristinae sodalitatis lacrimas non tenuisse, vir fortis et
de rege bene meritus pietatis in amicum graves poenas
innoxius pependisset.*

*Ceterum ut paulisper a luctu avocaret animum, in
Cossaeorum terram expeditionem suscepit. Iuga Mediae
vicina Cossaei tenent, aspera et bellicosa et rapto vivere
assueta gens. Ab his Persarum reges annuo tributo pacem
redimere solebant, ne in subiectam terram decurrentes
latrociniis regionem facerent infestam. Nam vim tem-
ptantes Persas facile reppulerant asperitate locorum de-
fensi, in quae se recipiebant, quotiens armis superati erant.
Eidem muneribus quotannis placabantur, ut regi Ecbatanis, ubi aestiva solebat agere, Babylonem remigranti
tutus per ea loca transitus esset. Hos igitur Alexander,
bipartito agmine, aggressus intra quadraginta dies per-
domuit. Nam ab ipso rege et Ptolomaeo, qui partem
exercitus ducebat, saepe victi, ut captivos suos reciperent
permisere se victori.*

*Ille validas urbes opportunis locis condi iussit, ne abducto
exercitu fera gens iugum exueret. Motis inde castris, ut
militem expeditione recenti fessum reficeret, lento agmine
Babylonem processit. Iamque vix triginta ab urbe stadia
aberat, cum Nearchus occurrit, quem per Oceanum et
Euphratis ostia Babylonem praemiserat, oravitque ne fata-*

ª Diod. xvii. 111. 5 ; Arr. vii. 15. 1-2.

of the memory of their former comradeship that he had been unable to restrain his tears, a brave man, who had deserved well of the king, although blameless, would have suffered severe punishment because of his affection for his friend.

But in order for a time to call away his mind from grief, the king undertook an expedition into the land of the Cossaei.[a] They dwell in the mountains near Media, a rude and warlike race, accustomed to live by plunder. From that people the kings of the Persians were wont to purchase peace by an annual tribute, to prevent them from running down into the land below them and infesting it with brigandage. For when the Persians resorted to force they had easily defeated them, defended as they were by the ruggedness of the places in which they took refuge whenever they were overcome by arms. They were also placated by annual gifts, in order that the king on his return to Babylon from Ecbatana, where he regularly spent the summer, might have a safe passage through those lands. These people, then, Alexander attacked with his force in two divisions, and completely subdued them within forty days. For after being often defeated by the king himself and by Ptolemy, who was leading one part of the army, they surrendered to the victor, in order to recover their men who had been made prisoner.

Alexander gave orders that strong cities be founded in strategic places, for fear that when the army was withdrawn the savage race might throw off the yoke. Then he moved his camp, and in a leisurely march, in order to give rest to the soldiers, who were wearied by the recent campaign, he went on to Babylon. And already he was only thirty stadia distant from the city, when Nearchus, whom he had sent ahead to Babylon by way of the Ocean and the mouths of the Euphrates, met him, and entreated

511

lem sibi urbem vellet ingredi. Compertum id sibi ex
Chaldaeis, qui multarum iam praedictionum eventu artis
suae fidem abunde probavissent. Rex fama eorum hominum constantique asseveratione motus, dimissis in urbem
amicorum plerisque, alia via praeter Babylonem ducit ac
ducenta inde stadia stativa collocat. Sed ab Anaxarcho
philosopho edoctus, contemptis Chaldaeorum monitis, quorum disciplinam inanem aut supervacuam arbitrabatur,
urbem intrat. Legationes eo ex universo ferme orbe con-
fluxerant. Quibus per complures dies studiose auditis,
deinceps ad Hephaestionis exsequias animum advertit.
Quae summo omnium studio ita celebratae sunt ut nullius
ad id tempus regis feralia magnitudine sumptuum appa-
ratusque celebritate non vicerint.

Post haec cupido incessit regi, per Pallacopam amnem
ad Arabum confinia navigandi ; quo delatus, urbi condendae commoda sede reperta, Graecorum aetate aut
vulneribus invalidos et, si qui sua sponte remanserant, ibi
collocat. Quibus ex sententia perfectis, iam futuri securus,
Chaldaeos irridebat, quod Babylonem non ingressus tantum esset incolumis, verum etiam excessisset. Verum
enimvero revertenti per paludes, quas Euphrates in Pallacopam effusus efficit, foedum omen oblatum est. Quippe
rami desuper impendentes detractum capiti regis diadema
proiecerunt in fluctus. Cum deinde alia atque alia prodigia

---

[a] So also Diod. xvii. 112. 4 ; Arr. vii. 16. 5 says that the
warning came directly from the Chaldeans.

[b] Cf. Arr. vii. 15. 4 : Diod. xvii. 113. 1 ff., who give fuller
details.　　　　　　　　　　　　　[c] Cf. Arr. vii. 22. 1.

[d] Cf. Arr. vii. 21. 1-7, who tells us that it was a canal from
the Euphrates and not a river.

*him not to think of entering the city, which was destined
to be fatal to him. He said that he had learned this from
the Chaldeans, who had already abundantly proved the
credibility of their art by the result of many predictions.[a]
The king, influenced by the reputation of the Chaldeans
and by their persistent assertion, having sent many of his
friends to the city, led the army by another road past
Babylon and pitched a permanent camp 200 stadia from
the city. But, advised by the philosopher Anaxarchus,
he scorned the warnings of the Chaldeans, whose teach-
ings he thought false or superfluous, and entered the city.
Thither deputations from almost the whole world [b] had
flocked together. After giving attentive audience to these
for several days, he then turned his thoughts to the
obsequies of Hephaestion. These were celebrated with
such great and general devotion that there was no king
up to that time whose funeral rites they did not surpass
in the greatness of their cost and the magnificence of their
equipment.*

*After this a longing seized the king to sail over the river
Pallacopas to the lands of the Arabians ; having arrived
there and having discovered a suitable site for founding
a city, he settled in it those of the Greeks who were disabled by age or by wounds, as well as any who had
remained behind of their own volition. When these things
had been finished to his satisfaction, now at ease about
the future, he laughed at the Chaldeans because he had
not only entered Babylon but also had left it unharmed.[c]
But in fact, as he was returning through the marshes
which the Euphrates makes by pouring into the Pallacopas,[d]
a direful omen was offered. For some overhanging
branches dragged the diadem from the king's head and
cast it into the river. When after this prodigies were
announced one after the other, continual sacrifices were*

*nuntiarentur, procurandis eis Graeco simul barbaroque ritu
continua sacra facta sunt.*

*Neque tamen expiari nisi morte regis potuere. Qui cum
Nearchum excepisset convivio iamque cubitum iturus esset,
Medii Larisaei obnixis precibus dedit, ut ad eum comissa-
tum veniret. Ubi postquam tota nocte perpotavit, male
habere coepit. Ingravescens deinde morbus adeo omnes
vires intra sextum diem exhausit, ut ne vocis quidem
potestas esset. Interea milites sollicitudine desiderioque
eius anxii, quamvis admonentibus ducibus ne valetudinem
regis onerarent, expresserunt ut in conspectum eius admitterentur.*

V. Intuentibus lacrimae obortae praebuere speciem
iam non regem, sed funus eius visentis exercitus ;
2 maeror tamen circumstantium lectum eminebat.
Quos ut rex aspexit[1] : " Invenietis," inquit, " cum
3 excessero, dignum talibus viris regem ? " Incredibile
dictu audituque, in eodem habitu corporis in quem
se composuerat cum admissurus milites esset, du-
rasse, donec a toto exercitu illud ultimum persalutatus
est.   Dimissoque vulgo, velut omni vitae debito
4 liberatus, fatigata membra reiecit, propiusque as-
sidere[2] iussis amicis—nam et vox deficere iam coeperat—detractum anulum digito Perdiccae tradidit,
adiectis mandatis ut corpus suum ad Hammonem ferri
iuberent.
5   Quaerentibusque his cui relinqueret regnum, respondit,[3] ei qui esset optimus ; ceterum providere[4]

[1] rex aspexit] respexit *A*.   [2] adsidere *Hedicke;* adire *A*.
[3] respondit *Lauer;* respondet *A*.
[4] providere *Modius;* prouide *A*.

---

[a] *Cf.* Arr. vii. 24. 4 ; 25. 1 ff.
[b] *Cf.* Justin xii. 15 ; Diod. xvii. 117. 3.
[c] Arr. vii. 26. 3 and Diod. xvii. 117. 4 have τῷ κρατίστῳ.

offered to avert them, at the same time by Greek and by barbarian rites.

Nevertheless they could not be expiated except by the king's death. And when he had entertained Nearchus with a banquet and he was already about to go to bed, he yielded to the urgent entreaties of Medius of Larissa [a] *that he would come to him for a drinking-bout. After he had drunk deeply there all night, he began to feel ill. Then his illness grew so much worse that within six days it had so exhausted all his strength that he could not even speak. Meanwhile the troops, overcome by anxiety and longing to see him, although their leaders warned them not to burden the king in his illness, extorted permission to be admitted to his presence.*

V. As they gazed at him, their rising tears gave the impression no longer of an army looking upon its
2 king, but of one attending his funeral; yet the grief of those who stood about his couch was still greater. When the king saw them he said : " After I am gone
3 will you find a king worthy of such men ? " Incredible to tell and to hear of, he continued to hold his body in the same attitude in which he had composed himself when he was about to admit the soldiers, until he had been saluted by the whole army for that last time. And having dismissed the common throng, as if he had discharged every debt to life, he threw
4 back his exhausted frame, and after bidding his friends to seat themselves—for his voice too had already begun to give out—he drew his ring from his finger [b] and handed it to Perdiccas, adding instructions that they should order his body to be taken to Ammon.
5 When they asked to whom he left his kingdom, he replied, to him who was the best man, [c] but that he

iam se, ob id certamen magnos funebres ludos parari
6 sibi.   Rursus Perdicca interrogante quando caelestes
honores haberi sibi vellet, dixit tum velle cum ipsi
felices essent.   Suprema haec vox fuit regis, et paulo
post exstinguitur.

7   Ac primo, ploratu lamentisque et planctibus tota
regia personabat; mox, velut in vasta solitudine
omnia tristi silentio muta torpebant, ad cogitationes
8 quid deinde futurum esset dolore converso.   Nobiles
pueri custodiae corporis eius assueti nec doloris magnitudinem capere nec se[1] ipsos intra vestibulum regiae
tenere potuerunt.   Vagique et furentibus similes
tantam urbem luctu ac maerore compleverant, nullis
questibus omissis, quos in tali casu dolor suggerit
9 ergo, qui extra regiam astiterant, Macedones pariter;
barbarique, concurrunt.   Nec poterant victi a victoribus in communi dolore discerni ; Persae iustissimum
ac mitissimum dominum, Macedones optimum ac
fortissimum regem invocantes, certamen quoddam
maeroris edebant.

10   Nec maestorum solum, sed etiam indignantium
voces exaudiebantur, tam viridem et in flore aetatis
fortunaeque invidia deum ereptum esse rebus humanis.   Vigor eius et vultus educentis in proelium
milites, obsidentis urbes, evadentis in muros, fortes
11 viros pro contione donantis occurrebant oculis.   Tum
Macedones divinos honores negasse ei paenitebat,

---

[1] capere nec se *Freinshem;* canecse *B m. pr., corr. in
marg.* carere; canecse *L m. pr., corr. in marg.* canere;
carere nece *F m. pr.;* carere nesce *F corr.;* carere *V.*

---

[a] May 22 or 24, 323.

[b] *Cf.* viii. 2. 5.   [c] See v. 1. 42.

already foresaw that because of that contest great
6 funeral games were in preparation for him. Again,
when Perdiccas asked when he wished divine honours
to be paid to him, he said that he wished it at
the time when they themselves were happy. These
were the king's last words, and shortly afterwards
he died.[a]

7 And at first the whole royal quarters rang[b] with
wailing, lamentation, and beating of breasts; presently, as if in a desert waste, everything was mute
and torpid, since grief was changed to thoughts of
8 what would happen next. The high-born boys who
were his regular body-guard[c] could neither contain
the greatness of their grief nor keep themselves
within the vestibule of the royal quarters. Wandering about and as if crazed, they had filled that city,
great as it was, with grief and sorrow, omitting
no plaints which sorrow suggests in such a disaster;
9 therefore those who had stood without the royal
quarters, Macedonians and foreigners alike, rushed
together. And in their common sorrow the vanquished could not be distinguished from the victors;
the Persians, calling upon a most just and mild lord,
the Macedonians upon the best and bravest of kings,
exhibited, as it were, a contest in mourning.

10 And not only words of sorrow were heard, but also
of indignation, that through the envy of the gods a
man so vigorous and in the flower of his youth and
his fortune had been torn from mankind. His vigour
and his aspect as he led his soldiers to battle, besieged
cities, scaled walls, and rewarded brave men before
the assembled army, were before their minds' eye.

11 Then the Macedonians repented of having denied him
divine honours, and they confessed that they had been

517

impiosque et ingratos fuisse se confitebantur, quod
aures eius debita appellatione fraudassent. Et cum
diu nunc in veneratione, nunc in desiderio regis hae-
12 sissent, in ipsos versa miseratio est. Macedonia profecti ultra Euphraten in[1] mediis hostibus novum
imperium aspernantibus destitutos se esse cernebant ;
sine certo regis herede, sine herede regni publicas
vires ad se quemque tracturum.
13 Bella deinde civilia quae secuta sunt mentibus
augurabantur ; iterum non de regno Asiae, sed de
rege ipsorum[2] ipsis sanguinem esse fundendum, novis
14 vulneribus veteres rumpendas cicatrices ; senes, de-
biles, modo petita missione a iusto[3] rege, nunc
morituros pro potentia forsitan satellitis alicuius
15 ignobilis. Has cogitationes volventibus nox supervenit terroremque auxit. Milites in armis vigilabant,
Babylonii, alius e muris, alius culmine sui quisque
16 tecti prospectabant, quasi certiora visuri. Nec quisquam lumina audebat accendere et, quia oculorum
cessabat usus, fremitus vocesque auribus captabant
ac plerumque vano metu territi per obscuras semitas,
aliis alii occursantes, invicem suspecti ac solliciti
ferebantur.
17 Persae, comis suo[4] more detonsis, in lugubri veste
cum coniugibus ac liberis, non ut victorem et modo
hostem,[5] sed ut gentis suae iustissimum regem vero

[1] in *added by Zumpt.*
[2] ipsorum *added by Warmington.*
[3] a iusto *B m. sec.;* iusto *A.*
[4] comis suo *J. M. Palmer;* commisso *A.*
[5] ut (*before* hostem) *deleted by Vindelinus.*

[a] *Cf.* viii. 12. 9. [b] *Cf.* vi. 8. 19.
[c] *i.e.* in time of mourning.

impious and ungrateful in having cheated his ears
of the title due him. And after they had continued
for a long time, now in veneration, now in longing
for the king, their pity was diverted to themselves.

12 Having left Macedonia, they saw themselves abandoned beyond the Euphrates and in the midst of foes
dissatisfied with the new rule ; without a sure heir
to their king, without an heir to the throne, each
man would be trying to draw the public forces [a] into
his own power.

13 Then they foresaw the civil wars that followed.
Again they would have to pour out their blood, old
scars must be broken by new wounds ; not to gain
the rule of Asia, but to appoint a king to reign

14 over themselves. Aged and infirm, they who had
recently asked their discharge from a legitimate king
would now die perhaps in defence of the power of

15 some obscure subordinate.[b] As they were turning
over such thoughts in their minds, night came on
and increased their alarm. The soldiers kept vigil
under arms, the Babylonians, some from the walls,
others from the roof of their own houses, were each
looking out as if to get more certain information.

16 And none dared to light their lamps, but because they
could not use their eyes, they caught with their ears
the noise and outcries, and often terrified by unfounded fear, they ran through the dark streets, and
as they met one another were in turn suspected
and apprehensive.

17 The Persians, having shaved their hair according
to custom,[c] in mourning garb with their wives and
children grieved for the king, not as their conqueror
and recently their enemy, but with genuine longing
as their own nation's most just ruler, and used as

519

QUINTUS CURTIUS

desiderio lugebant, ac sueti sub rege vivere, non alium
qui imperaret ipsis digniorem fuisse confitebantur.

18 Nec muris urbis luctus continebatur, sed proximam regionem ab ea, deinde magnam partem Asiae
19 cis Euphraten tanti mali fama pervaserat. Ad Darei
quoque matrem celeriter perlata est ; abscissa ergo
veste quam induta erat lugubrem sumpsit, laceratis-
20 que crinibus, humi corpus abiecit. Assidebat ei
altera ex neptibus[1] nuper amissum Hephaestionem,
cui nupserat, lugens, propriasque causas doloris in
21 communi maestitia retractabat.[2] Sed omnium suorum mala Sisigambis una capiebat ; illa suam, illa
neptium vicem flebat. Recens dolor etiam praeterita
revocaverat. Crederes modo amissum Dareum et
pariter miserae duorum filiorum exequias esse du-
22 cendas. Flebat simul mortuos vivosque. Quem
enim puellarum acturum esse curam ? quem alium
futurum Alexandrum ? iterum esse se captas, iterum
excidisse regnum.[3] Qui mortuo Dareo ipsas tueretur
repperisse, qui post Alexandrum respiceret utique
non reperturas.

23 Subibat inter haec animum LXXX fratres suos eodem
die ab Ocho, saevissimo regum, trucidatos adiectum-
que stragi tot filiorum patrem, e septem liberis quos
genuisset ipsa unum superesse, ipsum Dareum flo-
24 ruisse paulisper, ut crudelius posset exstingui. Ad

[1] neptibus *Lauer;* nepotibus *A.*
[2] retractabat *Freinshem;* retractabant *A.*
[3] regnum *P m. pr.;* regno *CP m. sec.*

[a] For *proximam ab* (next, reckoning from) *cf.* vi. 11. 28 :
Suet. *Aug.* 31. 5 ; etc. [b] *Cf.* Justin xiii. 1.
[c] Arr. vii. 4. 4 and Diod. xvii. 107. 6 give her name as
Drypetis.
[d] See Justin x. 3. 1 ; Val. Max. ix. 2, ext. 7.
[e] See iii. 11. 8.

they were to live under a king, they confessed that
none other had been more worthy to rule them.

18   And their grief was not confined within the walls
of the city, but the report of so great a disaster had
spread through the region nearest to *a* Babylon and
then through a great part of Asia on the hither side
19 of the Euphrates. The news was quickly brought
also to the mother of Darius ; she, rending the
garments which she wore, put on mourning garb
and, tearing her hair, threw herself on the ground.*b*
20 Beside her sat one of her granddaughters, mourning
for the recent loss of Hephaestion, whom she had
married,*c* and in the general sorrow was renewing her
21 own reasons for grief. But Sisigambis alone felt the
misfortune that had befallen all her family ; she
wept for her own loss and for that of her granddaughters. This recent grief too had revived the
sorrows of the past. You might think that she had
just lost Darius, and that the unhappy woman had
to perform the funeral rites of two sons ; she wept at
22 once for the dead and for the living. For who would
have a care for her girls ? Who would be a second
Alexander ? Again they were taken prisoner, again
they had lost royal rank. After the death of Darius they had found someone to protect them, but
after Alexander they assuredly would find none to
do so.*d*
23   Amid these thoughts it entered her mind that her
eighty brothers had been killed on one and the same
day by Ochus,*d* most savage of kings, and that their
father had been added to the slaughter of so many
sons, and that of the seven children that she herself
had borne only one *e* was left. Even Darius had
flourished for a time, only that he might meet a more

ultimum dolori succubuit, obvolutoque capite, acci-
dentis genibus suis neptem nepotemque aversata,
cibo pariter abstinuit et luce.   Quinto postquam mori
25 statuerat die exstincta est.   Magnum profecto Alexandri indulgentiae in eam, iustitiaeque in omnes
captivos, documentum est mors huius ; quae cum
sustinuisset post Dareum vivere, Alexandro esse
superstes erubuit.

26   Et, hercule, iuste aestimantibus regem, liquet bona
27 naturae eius fuisse, vitia vel fortunae vel aetatis.   Vis
incredibilis animi, laboris patientia propemodum
nimia, fortitudo non inter reges modo excellens, sed
28 inter illos quoque quorum haec sola virtus fuit, liberalitas saepe maiora tribuens[1] quam a dis petuntur,
clementia in devictos, tot regna aut reddita quibus
29 ademerat[2] bello aut dono data, mortis cuius metus
ceteros exanimat perpetua contemptio, gloriae laudis-
que ut iusto maior cupido, ita in iuvene[3] et in tantis
30 neglegenda[4] rebus, iam pietas erga parentes, quorum Olympiada immortalitati consecrare decreverat,
31 Philippum ultus erat, iam in omnes fere amicos
benignitas, erga milites benevolentia, consilium par
magnitudini animi et, quantam vix poterat aetas eius
32 capere, sollertia, modus[5] inmodicarum cupiditatum,
veneris intra naturale desiderium usus, nec ulla

[1] tribuens *Bentley;* tribuentis *A.*
[2] ademerat *Bentley;* eadem erat *P;* eademserat *C.*
[3] in iuvene *Jeep;* ut iuueni *A.*
[4] neglegenda *Hedicke;* nec amittenda *A.*
[5] modus *Lauer;* modum *A.*

---

[a] For a general characterization of Alexander see Arr.
xvii. 28-30.

24 cruel death. At last she gave way to grief and
veiling her head and turning away from her granddaughter and her grandson, who fell at her knees,
she at the same time abstained from food and
shunned the light of day. The fifth day after she
25 had resolved to die, she passed away. Surely her
death is a strong testimony to Alexander's indulgence
towards her and to his just treatment of all the
captives ; for she who had had the fortitude to live
after Darius was ashamed to survive Alexander.

26   And, by Heaven! to those who judge the king [a]
fairly it is clear that his good qualities were natural,
27 his faults due to his fortune or to his youth. He
possessed incredible strength of mind, an endurance
of toil which was almost excessive, a courage excelling
not only among kings but among those whose sole
28 merit it is, a generosity that often bestowed greater
gifts than are asked of gods in prayer, clemency
towards the vanquished, shown either by returning
so many kingdoms to those from whom he had taken
29 them in war or by giving them as gifts, a constant
contempt of death, the fear of which appals the rest
of mankind, a desire for glory and renown which,
although it was greater than was proper, yet was to
be overlooked in a young man who had done such
30 glorious deeds ; also his devotion to his parents, of
whom he had decided to consecrate Olympias among
31 the immortals and had avenged Philip, his kindness
to almost all his friends, his goodwill to his soldiers,
32 his wisdom equal to the greatness of his spirit, and
a keenness of judgement of which one of his years
could hardly have been capable, a restraint of immoderate desires, the indulgence of passion only
within natural requirements, and to have enjoyed

nisi ex permisso voluptas, ingenii[1] profecto dotes
erant.

33   Illa fortunae : dis aequare se et caelestes honores
accersere et talia suadentibus oraculis credere et
dedignantibus venerari ipsum vehementius, quam par
esset, irasci, in externum habitum mutare corporis
cultum, imitari devictarum gentium mores, quos[2] ante
34 victoriam spreverat. Nam iracundiam et cupidinem
vini sicuti iuventa irritaverat, ita senectus mitigare
35 potuisset. Fatendum est tamen, cum plurimum
virtuti debuerit, plus debuisse Fortunae, quam solus
omnium mortalium in potestate habuit. Quotiens
illum a morte revocavit ! quotiens temere in pericula
36 vectum perpetua felicitate protexit ! Vitae quoque
finem eundem illi quem gloriae statuit ; exspectavere
eum Fata, dum, Oriente perdomito aditoque Oceano,
quidquid mortalitas capiebat impleret.

37   Huic regi ducique successor quaerebatur, sed maior
moles erat quam ut unus subire eam posset ; itaque
nomen quoque eius et fama rerum in totum propemodum orbem reges ac regna diffudit ; clarissimique sunt
habiti qui etiam minimae parti tantae fortunae ad-
haeserunt.

VI. Ceterum Babylone—inde enim devertit oratio
—corporis eius custodes in regiam principes amicorum
ducesque copiarum advocavere. Secuta est militum
turba cupientium scire in quem Alexandri fortuna

---

[1] ingenii *Acidalius;* ingentes A.   [2] quos *I;* quas *A.*

---

        a *Cf.* iii. 6. 20 ; Pliny, *Epist.* iii. 3. 4.
            b *Cf.* Livy ix. 18. 4 ; Justin ix. 8.
     c In a different sense of Cato Uticensis in Vell. ii. 35. 2.
                    d At x. 5. 18.

no pleasures except such as were lawful, were certainly gifts of his own nature.[a]

33 The following qualities were attributable to his fortune : to equal himself with the gods and to aspire to divine honours, to trust to oracles which advised such conduct, and to be more angry than was fitting with those who refused to venerate him, to change his attire to that of foreign nations, to imitate those customs of the conquered [b] races which he had scorned 34 before his victory. As for his hot temper and his love of wine, just as these were intensified by youth, 35 greater age might have moderated them. Yet it must be confessed that although he owed much to his own merit, yet he owed still more to Fortune, over whom he alone of all mortals had control.[c] How often did she save him from death ! How often, when rashness brought him into danger, did she protect 36 him by perpetual good luck ! She likewise fixed the same end for his life and for his glory ; the Fates waited for him until, having thoroughly subdued the Orient, and having reached the Ocean, he fulfilled every task of which mortality was capable.

37 This was the king and leader for whom a successor was sought, but the burden was too great for the shoulders of one man ; hence even his name and the fame of his exploits spread kings and kingdoms throughout almost the whole world, and those were considered most glorious who had retained even the least part of so great a fortune.

VI. But in Babylon—for it was from there that I made a digression [d]—his body-guards called to the royal quarters the chief of the king's friends and the leaders of his forces. A throng of soldiers followed, eager to know to whom the fortune of Alexander

2 esset transitura. Multi duces, frequentia militum exclusi, regiam intrare non poterant, cum praeco exceptis qui nominatim citarentur adire prohiberet.
3 Sed precarium spernebatur imperium. Ac[1] primum eiulatus ingens ploratusque renovatus est, deinde futuri exspectatio, inhibitis lacrimis, silentium fecit.
4 Tunc Perdicca, regia sella in conspectum volgi data, in qua diadema vestisque Alexandri cum armis erant, anulum sibi pridie traditum a rege in eadem sede posuit.

Quorum aspectu rursus obortae omnibus lacrimae
5 integravere luctum, et Perdicca : " Ego quidem," inquit, " anulum quo ille regni atque imperii res[2] obsignare erat solitus, traditum ab ipso mihi, reddo
6 vobis. Ceterum quamquam nulla clades huic qua affecti sumus par ab iratis dis excogitari potest, tamen magnitudinem rerum quas egit intuentibus credere licet, tantum virum deos accommodasse rebus humanis, quarum sorte completa, cito repeterent eum
7 suae stirpi. Proinde quoniam nihil aliud ex eo superest quam quod semper ab immortalitate seducitur, corpori utique[3] quam primum iusta solvamus, haud obliti in qua urbe, inter quos simus, quali praeside ac rege
8 spoliati. Tractandum est, commilitones, cogitandumque,[4] ut victoriam partam inter hos de quibus

---

[1] Ac *Lauer;* ad *A.*
[2] res *Scheffer;* uires *A (cf. x. 5. 12).*
[3] utique *Hedicke;* nominique *A.*
[4] cogitandumque *Vindelinus;* cogitantumque *A* (cogitatumque *V*).

---

^a *Cf.* iii. 8. 2 ; viii. 12. 9.   ^b *i.e.* the physical body.

2 would pass. Many generals, shut out by the great
number of soldiers, had been unable to enter the royal
quarters, since a herald forbade access except to those
who had been summoned by name. But this order,
3 being of uncertain origin, was disregarded. And first
of all the great wailing and lamentation was renewed,
then expectation of what was coming checked their
4 tears and caused silence. Then Perdiccas, having
put in view of the public the royal throne, on which
were the diadem and the robe of Alexander together
with his arms, placed on the same throne the ring
which had been handed to him the day before by
the king.

At the sight of these the whole assembly again
burst into tears and renewed the mourning, and Per-
5 diccas said : " For my part, I return to you the ring
handed to me by the late king himself, with which he
was wont to seal the documents pertaining to his
6 kingdom and his power.[a] Furthermore, although no
calamity equal to this which has befallen us can be
devised by the angry gods, yet those who consider the
greatness of what he accomplished may well believe
that so great a man was merely loaned to mankind
by the gods, in order that, when his allotted service
to humanity was completed, they might quickly take
7 him back into their own family. Therefore, since
nothing else is left of him except what is always
separated from immortality,[b] let us pay as soon as
possible the rites due to his body at least, not forgetting in what city and among whom we are, and
of what a chief and what a king we have been
8 despoiled. We must therefore, fellow-soldiers, give
attention and consider how we may secure the victory
which he has won among those from whom it was

parta est obtinere possimus. Capite opus est ; hoc
nominare[1] in vestra potestate est. Illud scire debetis,
militarem sine duce turbam corpus esse sine spiritu.

9 Sextus mensis est ex quo Roxane praegnans est ;
optamus, ut marem enitatur, cuius regnum dis approbantibus sit[2] futurum, quandoque adoleverit.
Interim a quibus regi velitis destinate." Haec Perdicca.

10 Tum Nearchus Alexandri modo sanguinem ac stirpem regiae maiestati convenire, neminem ait posse

11 infitiari,[3] ceterum exspectari nondum ortum regem,
et qui iam sit praeteriri, nec animis Macedonum
convenire nec tempori eorum.[4] Esse e Barsine[5] filium

12 regis ; huic diadema dandum. Nulli placebat oratio ;
itaque suo more hastis scuta quatientes obstrepere
perseverabant. Iamque prope ad seditionem per-
venerant, Nearcho pervicacius tuente sententiam,

13 cum[6] Ptolomaeus : " Digna prorsus est suboles,"
inquit, " quae Macedonum imperet genti Roxanes
vel Barsines filius, cuius nomen quoque Europam

14 discere[7] pigebit maiore ex parte captivi ! Est cur
Persas vicerimus, ut stirpi eorum serviamus, quod
iusti illi reges, Dareus et Xerxes, tot milium agmini-

15 bus tantisque classibus nequiquam petiverunt ? Mea
sententia haec est, ut sede Alexandri in regia posita,
qui consiliis eius adhibebantur, coeant quotiens in
commune consulto opus fuerit, eoque quod maior pars

---

[1] hoc nominare *Bentley;* hocine uno an *A.*
[2] sit *added by Hedicke.*   [3] infitiari *Bentley;* mirari *A.*
[4] eorum *Hedicke;* rerum *A.*
[5] e Barsine *J. Froben;* abarsine *A.*
[6] cum *Hedicke;* tum *A.*   [7] discere *Heinse;* dicere *A.*

---

[a] See Justin xiii. 2. Referring to the daughter of Artabazus, and not to the elder daughter of Darius, whose name
was really Statira ; see Arr. vii. 4. 6.

528

won. We have need of a head ; to name one is in your power. One thing you must know, that a throng of soldiers without a leader is a body without

9 a soul. It is five months from the time when Roxanê became with child ; we pray that she may bear a son, who shall rule over us with the gods' approval, when he comes of age. Determine by what men you wish to be ruled in the meantime." Thus spoke Perdiccas.

10 Then Nearchus said that no one could deny that only the blood and stock of Alexander was suited to

11 royal majesty, but that to wait for a king who was not yet born, and to pass over one who was already living, suited neither the desires of the Macedonians nor their exigencies ; that the king had a son by Barsinê [a] ; he ought to be presented with the crown.

12 His speech was approved by no one ; and so, clashing their shields with their spears after their custom, they persisted in uproar. And already, as Nearchus maintained his opinion too persistently, they had almost reached the point of mutiny, when Ptolemy

13 said : " Truly a most worthy stock to rule the race of the Macedonians is the son of Roxanê or Barsinê, whose very name Europe will be ashamed to hear, since it is that of one who is in greater part a captive.

14 Is that why we have conquered the Persians, that we may serve their stock, a thing which those legitimate kings, Darius and Xerxes, sought in vain with armies of so many thousands and such great fleets ?

15 My advice is this, that the throne of Alexander be set up in the royal quarters, and that those who were summoned to his counsels should come together whenever there shall be need of general consultation, and that what the majority of them shall decide shall

529

QUINTUS CURTIUS

eorum decreverit stetur, duces praefectique copiarum
his pareant."

16 Ptolomaeo quidam, pauciores Perdiccae assentiebantur. Tum Aristonus orsus est dicere, Alexandrum
consultum cui relinqueret regnum, voluisse optimum
deligi ; iudicatum autem ab ipso optimum Perdiccam
17 cui anulum tradidisset. Neque enim unum eum as-
sedisse morienti, sed circumferentem[1] oculos ex
turba amicorum delegisse cui traderet. Placere igi-
18 tur, summam imperii ad Perdiccam deferri. Nec
dubitare quin vera censeret. Itaque universi procedere in medium Perdiccam et regis anulum tollere
iubebant. Haerebat inter cupiditatem pudoremque
et, quo modestius quod spectabat[2] appeteret, per-
19 vicacius oblaturos esse credebat; itaque cunctatus
diuque quid ageret incertus ad ultimum tamen recessit et post eos qui sedi erant[3] proximi constitit.
20 At Meleager, unus e ducibus, confirmato animo,
quem Perdiccae cunctatio erexerat : " Nec di sierint,"
inquit, " ut Alexandri fortuna tantique regni fastigium in istos humeros ruat; homines certe non ferent.
Nihil dico de nobilioribus, quam hic est, sed de viris
21 tantum, quibus invitis, nihil perpeti necesse est. Nec
vero interest, Roxanes filium, quandoque genitus erit,
an Perdiccan regem habeatis, cum iste sub tutelae
specie regnum occupaturus sit. Itaque nemo ei rex

[1] circumferentem *Giunta;* circumferenti *A.*
[2] spectabat *Hedicke;* expectabat *A.*
[3] sedi erant *Kinch;* sederant *A.*

---

[a] See Livy vii. 35. 2 ; xxvii. 6. 9.   [b] See ix. 5. 15.
[c] But *cf.* x. 7. 8, of Perdiccas and Leonnatus.

530

stand approved,[a] and that the generals and commanders of troops shall obey those men."

16 Some agreed with Ptolemy, fewer with Perdiccas. Then Aristonus [b] began to speak, saying that Alexander, when he was asked to whom he left his kingdom, wished the best man to be chosen ; moreover, he had himself judged that Perdiccas, to whom he

17 had handed his ring, was the best man. For he was not the only one who sat by Alexander when he was dying, but, the king, looking about, had chosen him from his throng of friends to give it to. Therefore it was Alexander's wish that the supreme power

18 should be bestowed upon Perdiccas. And there was no doubt that Aristonus' opinion was the truth. Therefore all bade Perdiccas to come forward and take up the king's ring. He wavered between inclination and shame, and believed that the more modestly he sought what he coveted the more persistently they

19 would press it upon him. So, after delaying and being for a long time uncertain what to do, he finally retired to the back part of the assembly, and stood behind those who were nearest to the throne.

20 But Meleager, one of the generals, taking the courage which the hesitation of Perdiccas had aroused, said : " May the gods themselves not permit that the fortune of Alexander and the burden of so great a kingdom should fall upon such shoulders ; certainly men will not allow it. I say nothing of those of nobler birth [c] than this fellow, but only of brave men, who need to endure nothing against their

21 will. And truly it makes no difference whether you have for king the son of Roxanê, whenever he shall be born, or Perdiccas, since that fellow will usurp the royal power under the guise of regency.

placet, nisi qui nondum natus est, et in tanta omnium
festinatione non iusta modo, sed etiam necessaria,
exactos menses solus exspectat et iam divinat marem
esse conceptum. Quem vos dubitetis paratum esse
22 vel subdere ? Si, me dius fidius, Alexander hunc
nobis regem pro se reliquisset, id solum ex eis[1] quae
23 imperasset non faciendum esse censerem. Quin
igitur ad diripiendos thesauros discurritis ? harum
enim opum regiarum utique populus est heres."
24 Haec elocutus, per medios armatos erupit, et qui
abeunti viam dederant, ipsum ad pronuntiatam[2] praedam sequebantur.

VII. Iamque armatorum circa Meleagrum frequens
globus erat, in seditionem ac discordiam versa contione,[3] cum quidam plerisque Macedonum ignotus ex
infima plebe : " Quid opus est," inquit, " armis
civilique bello habentibus regem quem quaeritis ?[a]
2 Arrhidaeus, Philippo genitus, Alexandri paulo ante
regis frater, sacrorum caerimoniarumque consors
modo, nunc solus heres, praeteritur a vobis. Quo suo
merito ? quidve fecit, cur etiam gentium communi
iure fraudetur ? Si Alexandro similem quaeritis, num-
3 quam reperietis ; si proximum, hic solus est." His
auditis, contio primo silentium velut iussa habuit,
conclamant deinde pariter Arrhidaeum vocandum[4]

---

[1] iis *Vindelinus;* his *A.*
[2] pronuntiatam *Freinshem;* praenuntiantem *A.*
[3] contione *Vindelinus;* contio *A.*
[4] vocandum *Aldus;* uocatum *A.*

---

[a] *i.e.* to choose a king.
[b] Thirty, according to x. 9. 18.
[c] See Plut. *Alex.* lxxvii. 5.
[d] That is, of the royal family, rather than the people in
general.

That is why no king pleases him except one who is not yet born, and amid the great haste [a] of all, which is not only reasonable but even necessary, he alone waits for the completion of months, and already divines that a male child has been conceived. And could you doubt that he is even ready to suborn one ?
22 If, by the God of Faith ! Alexander had left this man to be king in his place, that would be the only one of his commands that I should think ought not
23 to be obeyed. Why then do you not run to plunder the treasures ? for surely the people alone are the
24 heirs to these riches of the king." Having said this, he burst through the midst of the armed men, and those who had made way for him when he left followed him to the booty which had been proclaimed.

VII. And already there was a large body of armed men [b] around Meleager, and the assembly was on its way to sedition and discord, when a man unknown to most of the Macedonians, one of the lowest of the common people, said : " What need is there of arms and civil war, when you have the king whom you
2 seek ? Arrhidaeus, [c] son of Philip, brother of Alexander, who was shortly before king, recently his associate in sacrifices and ceremonies, [d] and now his sole heir, is passed over by you. Why has he deserved this ? Or what has he done to be cheated even of the common law of nations ? [e] If you seek a king like Alexander, you will never find one ; if one next in blood, Arrhidaeus is the only choice."
3 After hearing these words the assembly at first kept silence, as if ordered to do so, then they shouted with one voice that Arrhidaeus ought to be summoned,

[e] This was not valid against the children of Roxanê and Statira.

esse mortemque meritos qui contionem sine eo
habuissent.

4 Tum Pithon, plenus lacrimarum, orditur dicere,
nunc vel maxime miserabilem esse Alexandrum, qui
tam bonorum civium militumque fructu et praesentia
fraudatus esset. Nomen enim memoriamque regis
5 sui tantum intuentes, ad cetera caligare eos. Haud
ambigue tum in eum[1] cui regnum destinabatur, ingessit probra ; at[2] quae obiecerat magis ipsi odium
quam Arrhidaeo contemptum attulerunt. Quippe
6 dum miserentur, etiam favere coeperunt. Igitur non
alium regem se quam eum, qui ad hanc spem genitus esset, passuros, pertinaci acclamatione declarant
7 vocarique Arrhidaeum iubent. Quem Meleager,
infestus invisusque Perdiccae, strenue perducit in
regiam : et milites Philippum consalutatum regem
appellant.

8 Ceterum haec vulgi erat vox, principum alia sententia. E quibus Pithon consilium Perdiccae exsequi
coepit tutoresque destinat filio ex Roxane futuro
9 Perdiccam et Leonnatum, stirpe regia genitos. Adiecit, ut in Europa Craterus et Antipater res ad-
ministrarent. Tum iusiurandum a singulis exactum,
10 futuros in potestate regis geniti Alexandro. Meleager
—haud iniuria metu supplicii territus, cum suis[3] se-
cesserat — rursus Philippum trahens secum irrupit
regiam, clamitans suffragari spei[4] de novo rege paulo

---

[1] tum in eum *Hedicke;* iuuenem *A.*
[2] ingessit probra ; at *Hedicke;* impensa probra *A.*
[3] suis *Giunta;* his *A.*   [4] spei *Hedicke;* rei publicae *A.*

and that those who had held an assembly without
him deserved death.

4 Then Pithon,[a] bathed in tears, began to say that now
Alexander was more than ever to be pitied, since he
had been defrauded of the use and company of such
good citizens and soldiers. For having an eye only
to the name and the memory of their king, they were
5 blind to all else. Then in plain language he heaped
abuse upon the one to whom the throne was being
awarded, but his insulting words brought more hatred
upon himself than contempt upon Arrhidaeus. For
in pitying him the assembly began to favour him.
6 Therefore with persistent acclamation they declared
that they would tolerate no other king than one
who had been born to such a hope, and they ordered
7 Arrhidaeus to be called. Him Meleager, being
hostile to Perdiccas, whom he hated, promptly
brought into the royal quarters, and the soldiers
hailed him as king under the name of Philippus.
8 But this was the voice of the common people, the
opinion of the chief men was different. Of these
Pithon began to follow the plan of Perdiccas, and
named Perdiccas and Leonnatus, both born of royal
stock, as guardians of the son to be born of Roxanê.
9 He added that Craterus and Antipater should have
direction of affairs in Europe. Then an oath was
exacted of each man that they would submit to a
10 king begotten of Alexander. Meleager—naturally
terrified for fear of punishment, he had withdrawn
with his partisans—again burst into the royal
quarters dragging Philippus with him and crying
that his vigorous youth favoured the hope which

[a] One of the seven officers of the body-guard, later increased to eight ; *cf.* Arr. vi. 28. 4.

ante conceptae robur aetatis ; experirentur modo
stirpem Philippi, filium[1] ac fratrem regum duorum ;
sibimet ipsis potissimum crederent.

11 Nullum profundum mare, nullum vastum fretum
et procellosum tantos ciet fluctus, quantos multitudo
motus habet, utique si[2] nova et brevi duratura liber-

12 tate luxuriat.[3] Pauci Perdiccae modo electo, plures
Philippo quem spreverant[4] imperium dabant. Nec
velle nec nolle quicquam diu poterant, paenitebatque
modo consilii, modo paenitentiae ipsius. Ad ultimum

13 tamen in stirpem regiam inclinavere studiis. Cesserat ex contione Arrhidaeus, principum auctoritate
conterritus, et abeunte illo conticuerat magis quam
elanguerat militaris favor ; itaque revocatus, vestem
fratris, eam ipsam quae in sella posita fuerat induitur.

14 Et Meleager, thorace sumpto, capit arma, novi regis
satelles. Sequitur phalanx hastis clipeos quatiens,
expletura se sanguine illorum qui affectaverant nihil

15 ad ipsos pertinens regnum. In eadem domo familia-
que imperii vires remansuras esse gaudebant ; hereditarium imperium stirpem regiam vindicaturam ;
assuetos esse nomen ipsum colere venerarique, nec
quemquam id capere nisi genitum ut regnaret.

16 Igitur Perdicca territus, conclave in quo Alexandri
corpus iacebat, obserari[5] iubet ; DC cum ipso erant

---

[1] et (*before* filium) *deleted by Hedicke.*
[2] si *Giunta;* etsi *C;* ipsi *P.*
[3] luxuriat *Lauer;* luxuria *A.*
[4] quem spreverant *Acidalius;* quam sperauerant *A.*
[5] obserari *J. M. Palmer;* obseruari *A.*

---

[a] *Cf.* x. 6. 5.

they had just conceived for the new king ; let them only try the offspring of Philip, son and brother to two kings; let them trust their own judgement rather than that of others.

11 No deep sea, no vast and storm-swept ocean rouses such great billows as the emotions of a multitude, especially if it is exulting in a liberty which is new 12 and destined to be short-lived. A few were for giving the power to Perdiccas, who had recently been chosen, more to Philippus, whom they had scorned. But they could not favour nor oppose anything for long, and now repented of their resolution, and now of the very fact of having repented. At last, however, their 13 favour inclined to the royal stock. Arrhidaeus had left the assembly greatly alarmed by the authority of the leading men, and as he went out the favour of the soldiers was rather silenced than diminished ; hence, on being recalled he put on the robe of his brother, the very one which had been placed upon 14 the throne. And Meleager, having put on his cuirass, armed himself as an attendant upon the new king. The phalanx followed his example, clashing their spears against their shields as a sign that they would sate themselves with the blood of those who 15 aspired to a rule to which they had no claim. They rejoiced that the strength of the empire *a* would remain in the same house and family ; that the inheritance of empire would defend the royal stock ; they were accustomed to honour and venerate the name itself, and no one assumed it unless born to rule.

16 Therefore Perdiccas in terror ordered the room in which the body of Alexander was lying to be bolted ; he had with him 600 men of tried valour, Ptolemy

spectatae virtutis, Ptolomaeus quoque se adiunxerat
17 ei, puerorumque regia cohors. Ceterum haud difficulter a tot milibus armatorum claustra perfracta sunt.
Et rex quoque irruperat, stipatus satellitum turba,
quorum princeps Meleager ibat ; itaque[1] Perdicca hos
18 qui Alexandri corpus tueri vellent sevocat. Sed qui[2]
irruperant eminus tela in ipsum iaciebant. Multisque
vulneratis, tandem seniores, demptis galeis, quo facilius nosci possent, precari eos, qui cum Perdicca
erant coepere, ut absisterent bello regique et pluribus
19 cederent. Primus Perdicca arma deposuit, ceterique
idem fecere. Meleagro deinde suadente ne a corpore
Alexandri discederent, insidiis locum quaeri rati,
diversa regiae parte ad Euphraten fugam intendunt.
20 Equitatus qui ex nobilissimis iuvenum constabat
Perdiccam et Leonnatum frequens sequebatur, place-
21 batque excedere urbe et tendere in campis. Sed
Perdicca ne pedites quidem secuturos ipsum despera-
bat ; itaque, ne abducendo equites abrupisse a cetero
exercitu videretur, in urbe subsistit.

VIII. At Meleager regem monere non destitit, ius
imperii Perdiccae morte sanciendum esse ; ni[3] occu-
petur impotens animus, res novaturum. Meminisse
eum quid de rege meruisset, neminem autem ei satis
2 fidum esse, quem metuat. Rex patiebatur magis
quam assentiebatur ; itaque Meleager silentium pro

---

[1] ibat ; itaque *Hedicke;* iratusque *A.*
[2] Sed qui *I;* sequi *C;* sequi qui *P.*
[3] ni *Modius;* ne *A.*

---

a That is, Arrhidaeus, the newly chosen king.

17 also had joined him and the royal band of pages. But
the barriers were easily broken through by so many
thousands of soldiers. And the king^a also had rushed
in, surrounded by a throng of attendants, of whom
18 Meleager took the lead ; accordingly, Perdiccas called
aside those who wished to protect the body of Alexander. But those who had broken in were throwing
javelins at him at long range. And after many had
been wounded, at last the older men, taking off their
helmets in order to be more easily recognized, began
to entreat those who favoured Perdiccas to cease
from war and yield to the king and to superior
19 numbers. Perdiccas was the first to lay down his
arms, and the rest followed his example. Then, when
Meleager tried to persuade them not to leave the
body of Alexander, they, thinking that he was looking
for an opportunity for treachery, through another
door of the palace took flight in the direction of the
20 Euphrates. The cavalry, which was composed of
the noblest of the youth, in great numbers followed
Perdiccas and Leonnatus, and advised leaving the
21 city and encamping in the plains. But Perdiccas did
not give up hope that even the infantry would follow
him ; and therefore, for fear that by leading away
the horsemen he might seem to have separated from
the rest of the army, he remained in the city.

VIII. But Meleager did not cease to warn the
king that his right to rule ought to be confirmed by
the death of Perdiccas ; that if his ambitious spirit
were not checked, he would start a revolution. That
he remembered what he had deserved of the king,
and besides no one was wholly loyal to one whom he
2 feared. The king rather listened to than accepted
this advice ; accordingly Meleager took his silence

imperio habuit misitque[1] regis nomine qui **Perdiccam**
accerserent. Eisdem mandatum ut occiderent, si
3 venire dubitaret. Perdicca, nuntiato satellitum adventu, sedecim omnino pueris regiae cohortis comitatus, in limine domus suae constitit, castigatosque et
Meleagri mancipia identidem appellans, sic animi
vultusque constantia terruit, ut vix mentis compotes
4 fugerint. Perdicca pueros[2] equos iussit conscendere
et cum paucis amicorum ad Leonnatum pervenit, iam
firmiore praesidio vim propulsaturus, si quis inferret.
5 Postera die indigna res Macedonibus videbatur
Perdiccam ad mortis periculum adductum, et Meleagri temeritatem armis ultum ire decreverant.[3]
6 Atque ille, seditione provisa, cum regem adisset,
interrogare eum coepit, an Perdiccam comprehendi
ipse iussisset. Ille Meleagri instinctu se iussisse
respondit; ceterum non debere tumultuari eos;
7 Perdiccam enim vivere. Igitur, contione dimissa,
Meleager equitum maxime defectione perterritus
inopsque consilii—quippe in ipsum periculum rec-
ciderat, quod inimico paulo ante intenderat—tri-
8 duum fere consumpsit incerta consilia volvendo. Et
pristina quidem regiae species manebat; nam et
legati gentium regem adibant, et copiarum duces
aderant, et vestibulum satellites armatique com-
9 pleverant. Sed ingens sua sponte maestitia ultimae

[1] misitque *P;* misit *C.*
[2] pueros *Lauer;* pueris *A.*
[3] decreverant] *Hedicke suspected a lacuna after this word.*
540

as a command and sent men in the name of the king to summon Perdiccas. They were directed to kill

3 him if he hesitated to come. Perdiccas, when the arrival of the messengers was known, attended only by sixteen youths of the royal cohort, took his place on the threshold of his house, and after upbraiding the messengers and repeatedly calling them slaves of Meleager, he so terrified them by the firmness of his courage and his expression, that they fled almost

4 beside themselves. Perdiccas ordered the youths to mount their horses and came with a few of his friends to Leonnatus, intending now to ward off violence with a stronger force, if anyone should offer it.

5 On the following day it seemed to the Macedonians shameful that Perdiccas had been exposed to danger of death, and they decided to go and punish by arms

6 the rash act of Meleager. But he, having foreseen a revolt, when he had come to the king began to ask him whether he himself had ordered Perdiccas to be seized. The king replied that he had ordered it at the instigation of Meleager, but that they ought not to make a disturbance ; for Perdiccas was alive.

7 Therefore when the assembly had been dismissed, Meleager, terrified especially by the desertion of the cavalry and not knowing what to do—for he had fallen into the very danger which he had shortly before devised for his enemy—spent nearly three

8 days in considering uncertain plans. And in fact the former appearance of the royal quarters continued ; for envoys of the nations came to the king, and the leaders of the forces were present with him, and armed men and attendants had filled the vestibule.

9 But the great seriousness which involuntarily showed

541

desperationis index erat, suspectique invicem non
adire propius, non colloqui audebant, secretas cogitationes[1] intra se quoque volvente, et ex comparatione
regis novi desiderium excitabatur amissi.

10 Ubi ille esset cuius imperium, cuius auspicium
secuti erant, requirebant ; destitutos se inter infestas
indomitasque gentes, expetituras tot suarum cladium

11 poenas, quandoque oblata esset occasio. His cogita-
tionibus animos exedebant, cum annuntiatur equites
qui sub Perdicca essent, occupatis circa Babylona
campis, frumentum quod in urbem vehebatur reti-

12 nuisse. Itaque inopia primum, deinde fames esse
coepit, et qui in urbe erant aut reconciliandam cum
Perdicca gratiam aut armis certandum esse censebant.

13 Forte ita acciderat, ut qui in agris erant populationem
villarum vicorumque veriti, confugerent in urbem,
oppidani cum ipsos alimenta deficerent, urbe excederent,[2] utrique generi tutior aliena sedes quam sua

14 videretur. Quorum consternationem Macedones veriti, in regiam coeunt, quaeque ipsorum sententia
esset exponunt. Placebat autem legatos ad equites[3]

15 mitti de finienda discordia armisque ponendis[4] ; igitur
a rege legatur Pasias[5] Thessalus et Damyllus[6] Me-
galopolitanus et Perilaus. Qui cum mandata regis
edidissent, non aliter posituros arma equites quam

---

[1] secretas cogitationes *Giunta;* secretae cogitationis *A.*
[2] excederent *Hedicke;* et *A.*
[3] ad equites *Lauer;* et equites *A;* et, *before* mitti, *deleted
by Vindelinus.*
[4] ponendis] *codex P ends with this word, at the end of a folio.*
[5] Pasias *Hedicke;* Pasas *A.*
[6] Damyllus *Hedicke;* amissus *A.*

itself was a sign of extreme desperation, and suspecting one another, they did not dare to approach nor to talk with anyone, but turned over secret thoughts each in their own minds, and from comparison with the new king longing was aroused for the one whom they had lost.

10 They inquired where he was whose rule and auspices they had followed; they had been deserted amid hostile and unsubdued nations, who would seek to inflict punishment for their many disasters, when-

11 ever an opportunity was offered. They were eating their hearts out by such thoughts as these, when it was announced that the cavalry who were under Perdiccas, having taken possession of the plains around Babylon, had held back the grain which was

12 being transported into the city. In consequence, there began to be at first scarcity and then famine, and those who were within the city maintained that they ought to come to terms with Perdiccas or fight

13 with him. By chance it had so happened that those who had been in the fields, fearing a devastation of the farmhouses and villages, were fleeing to the city, and that the townspeople, as provisions were failing them, were going out of the city, since to both classes the abode of the others seemed safer than their own.

14 The Macedonians, fearing some disturbance from these, went in a body to the royal quarters and expressed their opinions. But it seemed best for envoys to be sent to the cavalry to discuss ending

15 the discord and laying down arms. Therefore the king sent Pasias the Thessalian and Damyllus of Megalopolis and Perilaüs. When these had delivered the king's message, they received the reply that the horsemen would not lay down their arms unless

si rex discordiae auctores dedidisset, tulere responsum.

16　His[1] renuntiatis, sua sponte arma milites capiunt.
Quorum tumultu e regia Philippus excitus : " Nihil,"
inquit, " seditione est opus ; nam inter se certantium
17 praemia, qui quieverint occupabunt.　Simul mementote rem esse cum civibus ; quibus spem gratiae cito
18 abrumpere ad bellum civile properantium est.　Altera
legatione an mitigari possint experiamur.　Et credo,
nondum regis corpore sepulto, ad praestanda ei iusta
19 omnis esse coituros.　Quod ad me attinet, reddere
hoc imperium malo quam exercere civium sanguine ;
et si nulla alia concordiae spes est, oro quaesoque,
eligite potiorem."

20　Obortis deinde lacrimis, diadema detrahit capiti
dexteram qua id tenebat protendens, ut, si quis se
21 digniorem profiteretur, acciperet.　Ingentem spem
indolis, ante eum diem fratris claritate suppressae,
tam moderata[2] excitavit oratio.　Itaque cuncti instare
22 coeperunt, ut quae agitasset exsequi vellet.　Eosdem
rursus legat petituros[3] ut Meleagrum tertium ducem
acciperent.　Haud aegre id impetratum[4] est ; nam
et abducere Meleagrum Perdicca a rege cupiebat et
23 unum duobus imparem futurum esse censebat.　Igitur
Meleagro cum phalange obviam egresso, Perdicca

---

[1] His *Lauer;* iis *BF;* is *L V.*
[2] suppressae, tam moderata *Hedicke;* suppressae et amo-
derata *A.*
[3] petituros *Lauer;* petiturus *A.*
[4] id impetratum] *frag. S (schedae Vindobonenses) begins
with this word, and continues to the end of the book.*

the king should surrender the ringleaders of the discord.

16 When this reply was announced, the soldiers of their own accord armed themselves. Philip, called from the royal quarters by their tumult, said : " There is no necessity for an outbreak ; for those who rest quiet will seize the prizes of those who engage in

17 mutual strife. At the same time remember that you are dealing with citizens, and that hastily to snatch from them the hope of grace is the part of

18 those eager for civil war. Let us try by a second deputation whether they can be reconciled. And I believe that, since the body of Alexander is not yet buried, all will unite to pay this pious duty which

19 we owe him. So far as I am concerned, I prefer to return this authority of mine rather than to exercise it at the expense of the blood of fellow-citizens ; and if there is no other hope of harmony, I beg and entreat you, choose a better man."

20 Then with tears in his eyes he took the diadem from his head, and extended his right hand, in which he was holding it, so that if anyone claimed to be

21 more worthy he might take it. This very moderate speech aroused great hope of his character, which before that day had been obscured by his brother's fame. Accordingly, all began to urge him to consent

22 to carry out what he had planned. Again he sent the same envoys, to ask that they should receive Meleager as a third leader. This was granted without difficulty ; for Perdiccas wished to separate Meleager from the king, and thought that alone he

23 would be no match for the other two. Therefore when Meleager came out to meet him with the phalanx, Perdiccas received him at the head of

equitum turmas antecedens occurrit. Utrumque
agmen, mutua salutatione facta, coit in perpetuum,
ut arbitrabantur, concordia et pace firmata.

IX. Sed iam Fatis admovebantur Macedonum
genti bella civilia ; nam et insociabile est regnum et
2 a pluribus expetebatur. Primum ergo collisere vires,
deinde disperserunt ; et cum pluribus corpus quam
capiebat onerassent, cetera membra deficere coeperunt, quodque imperium sub uno stare potuisset,
3 dum a pluribus sustinetur, ruit. Proinde iure meri-
toque populus Romanus salutem se principi suo debere
profitetur, qui noctis quam paene supremam habu-
4 imus novum sidus illuxit. Huius, hercule, non solis,
ortus lucem caliganti reddidit mundo, cum sine suo
5 capite discordia membra trepidarent. Quot ille tum
exstinxit faces ! quot condidit gladios ! quantam
tempestatem subita serenitate discussit ! Non ergo
6 revirescit solum, sed etiam floret imperium. Absit
modo invidia, excipiet huius saeculi tempora eiusdem
domus utinam perpetua, certe diuturna posteritas.
7 Ceterum, ut ad ordinem a quo me contemplatio
publicae felicitatis averterat redeam, Perdicca unicam
spem salutis suae in Meleagri morte reponebat[1] ; vanum eundem et infidum celeriterque res novaturum
8 et sibi maxime infestum occupandum esse. Sed
alta[2] dissimulatione consilium premebat, ut opprimeret

---

[1] reponebat *Heinse;* deponebat *A.*
[2] alta *Giunta;* alia *A.*

---

[a] For *insociabile regnum cf.* Tac. *Ann.* xiii. 17.
[b] For this use of *cetera* (and *alius*) see *Trans. Amer. Phil.
Assoc.* lx. p. 349.
[c] On the identity of this prince and its importance for the
date of Curtius see Introd., vol. i. p. xx.
[d] On the metaphor in *sidus cf.* Sen. *Consol. ad Polyb.* 32 ;
Livy vi. 17. 4 ; Tac. *Hist.* i. 11.

the squadrons of cavalry. Both armies exchanged salutations and united for ever, as they thought, in firm concord and peace.

IX. But already by the Fates civil wars were being forced upon the Macedonian nation ; for royal power desires no associate [a] and was being sought by many.
2 First therefore they brought their forces into collision, then separated them ; and when they had weighted the body with more than it could carry, the limbs [b] also began to give out, and an empire that might have endured under one man fell in ruins while it was
3 being upheld by many. Therefore the Roman people rightly and deservedly asserts that it owes its safety to its prince,[c] who in the night which was almost our
4 last shone forth like a new star.[d] The rising of this star, by Heaven! rather than that of the sun, restored light to the world in darkness, since lacking their head the limbs were thrown into disorder.
5 How many firebrands did it extinguish ! How many swords did it sheath ! How great a tempest did it dispel with sudden prosperity ! Therefore our empire
6 not only lives afresh but even flourishes. Provided only that the divine jealousy be absent, the posterity of that same house will continue the good times of this our age, it is to be hoped forever, at any rate for very many years.
7 But to return to the series of events from which the contemplation of the public happiness had diverted me, Perdiccas rested the sole hope of his safety on the death of Meleager ; he thought that a man who was vain, faithless and quick to revolt, and his own bitterest enemy, must be attacked first.
8 But he hid his design with deep dissimulation, in order to crush him when he was off his guard.

547

incautum. Ergo clam quosdam ex copiis quibus praeerat subornavit, ut, quasi ignoraret ipse, conquererentur palam Meleagrum aequatum esse Perdiccae. 9 Quorum sermone Meleager ad se relato furens ira Perdiccae, quae comperisset, exponit. Ille, velut nova re exterritus, admirari, queri,[1] dolentisque speciem ostentare ei coepit ; ad ultimum convenit, ut comprehenderentur tam seditiosae vocis auctores. 10 Agit Meleager gratias, amplexusque Perdiccam, 11 fidem eius in se ac benevolentiam collaudat. Tum communi consilio rationem opprimendi noxios ineunt.

Placet[2] exercitum patrio more lustrari ; et proba-12 bilis causa videbatur praeterita discordia. Macedonum reges ita lustrare soliti erant milites, ut discissae canis viscera ultimo in campo in quem deduceretur exercitus ab utraque abicerent parte, intra id spatium armati omnes starent, hinc equites, illinc phalanx. 13 Itaque eo die quem huic sacro destinaverant, rex cum equitibus elephantisque constiterat[3] contra pedites 14 quis Meleager praeerat. Iam equestre agmen movebatur, et pedites subita formidine ob recentem discordiam haud sane pacati, quicquam exspectantes, parumper addubitavere an in urbem subducerent 15 copias—quippe pro equitibus planities erat—ceterum

---

[1] queri] que se *S.*   [2] placet] placeat *S.*
[3] constiterat] constiterant *S m. pr.*

---

* See Livy xl. 6. 1-3, 5.

Therefore he secretly suborned certain men from the troops which he commanded, who were to make open complaint, as if he himself knew nothing of it, that Meleager had been placed on an equality with
9 Perdiccas. When their talk was reported to Meleager, furious with anger at Perdiccas, he told him what he had learned. He, as if terrified by something of which he knew nothing, began to give utterance to surprise and complaint, and to show a pretence of displeasure; finally, he agreed that the authors of such seditious
10 talk ought to be arrested. Meleager embraced and thanked Perdiccas, and strongly commended his
11 loyalty and goodwill towards him. Then after consulting together they formed a plan for chastising the guilty parties.

It was decided to purify the army after the native fashion, and the past discord seemed to furnish a
12 reasonable cause for this. The kings of the Macedonians had been accustomed to purify the soldiers in the following manner [a]; having disembowelled as dog in the farthest part of the plain into which they were going to lead the army, they throw the flesh on both sides; within that space all the soldiers stand under arms, on one side the cavalry, on the other
13 the phalanx. Accordingly on that day which they had appointed for this sacred ceremony the king with the horsemen and the elephants stood facing the
14 infantry which Meleager commanded. Already the cavalry force was advancing, and the infantry, not wholly recovered from the sudden fear caused by the recent discord and expecting something, hesitated for a time whether to withdraw their forces into the city—for the plain was advantageous for the horse-
15 men—; but fearing to condemn the good faith of

549

veriti ne temere commilitonum fidem damnarent,
substitere, praeparatis ad dimicandum animis, si quis
vim inferret.

Iam agmina coibant, parvumque intervallum erat
16 quod aciem utramque divideret ; itaque rex cum una
ala obequitare peditibus coepit, discordiae auctores,
quos tueri ipse debebat, instinctu Perdiccae ad supplicia deposcens, minabaturque omnes turmas cum
17 elephantis inducturum se in recusantes.[1] Stupebant
improviso malo pedites, nec plus in ipso Meleagro
erat aut consilii aut animi. Tutissimum ex praesentibus videbatur exspectare potius quam movere
18 fortunam. Tum Perdicca, ut torpentes et obnoxios
vidit, xxx[2] fere, qui Meleagrum erumpentem ex
contione quae prima habita est post mortem Alexandri secuti erant, a ceteris discretos elephantis in
conspectu totius exercitus obicit. Omnesque beluarum pedibus obtriti sunt, nec prohibente Philippo
19 nec auctore ; apparebatque id modo pro suo vin-
dicaturum, quod approbasset eventus.

Hoc bellorum civilium Macedonibus et omen et
20 principium fuit. Meleager, sero intellecta fraude
Perdiccae, tum quidem, quia ipsius corpori vis non
afferebatur, in agmine quietus stetit, sed[3] mox
21 damnata spe salutis, cum eius nomine quem ipse
fecerat regem in perniciem suam abutentis videret

---

[1] se in recusantes *B corr.;* sin recusantes *S;* sine recutes
V; se in recuntes *B m. pr.;* se in recutes *FL.*
[2] xxx *Bentley;* ccc *A.*   [3] sed *Hedicke;* et *A.*

their fellow-soldiers without sufficient reason, they
halted, their minds prepared for fighting if anyone
should offer violence.

Already the forces were coming together, and there
was only a short space which divided the two lines.
16 Then the king with one wing of the cavalry [a] began
to ride up to the infantry, demanding for punishment,
at the instigation of Perdiccas, the authors of the
discord, whom he himself was bound to protect, and
threatened to lead all his squadrons against them,
17 as well as the elephants, if they refused. The infantry were dumbfounded by the unexpected danger,
and not even Meleager himself had longer either
judgement or courage. It seemed safest in the
circumstances rather to await their fate than to
18 hasten it. Then Perdiccas, seeing them paralysed
and in his power, separated from the rest about thirty
who had followed Meleager when he rushed forth
from the first assembly which was held after the
death of Alexander, and in the sight of the whole
army cast them before the elephants. All were
trampled to death by the feet of the beasts, while
19 Philip neither prevented nor authorized it ; and it
was plain that he would not admit anything as his
own act except what the result should justify.

This was an omen and a beginning of civil wars
20 among the Macedonians. Meleager, learning too
late the treachery of Perdiccas, for the moment
calmly kept his place in the formation, since no
violence was offered to his own person, but pres-
21 ently, abandoning hope of safety, since he saw
that his enemies were usurping to effect his ruin
the name of the man whom he himself had made

[a] Apparently the *agema* ; see iv. 13. 26, note.

inimicos, confugit in templum, ac ne loci quidem
religione defensus, occiditur.

X. Perdicca, perducto in urbem exercitu, consilium
principum virorum habuit, in quo imperium ita dividi
placuit, ut rex quidem summam eius obtineret, satrapeam Ptolomaeus Aegypti et Africae gentium quae
2 in dicione erant ; Leomedonti Syria cum Phoenice
data est, Philotae Cilicia destinata, Lyciam cum
Pamphylia et Maiore Phrygia obtinere iussus Antigonus, in Cariam Cassander, Menander in Lydiam
missi ; Phrygiam Minorem Hellesponto adiunctam
3 Leonnati provinciam esse iusserunt. Cappadocia
Eumeni cum Paphlagonia cessit ; praeceptum est,
ut regionem eam usque ad Trapezunta[1] defenderet,
bellum cum Ariarathe[2] gereret : solus hic detrectabat
4 imperium. Pithon Mediam, Lysimachus Thraciam
appositasque Thraciae Ponticas gentes obtinere iussi.
Qui Indiae quique Bactris et Sogdianis ceterisque aut
Oceani aut Rubri maris accolis praeerant, quibus
quisque finibus habuisset, imperium obtinerent, de-
cretum est ; Perdicca ut cum rege esset copiisque
praeesset quae regem sequebantur.
5 Credidere quidam testamento Alexandri distribu-
tas esse provincias, sed famam eius rei, quamquam
ab auctoribus tradita est, vanam fuisse comperimus.

[1] Trapezunta *Aldus;* trapeiunta *A* (trapeiuncta *VB m.
sec.*).
[2] Ariarathe *Zumpt;* arbate *B;* harbate *FLV;* araba
tegeret *S.*

---

[a] Arrhidaeus.   [b] *Cf.* Justin xiii. 4.
[c] Diod. xviii. 3. 1.   [d] Philotas Augaeus, see v. 2. 5.
[e] The " Ocean " here meant is the Northern Ocean
supposed to lie not far north of the Himalayas and Iran ;
the " Red Sea " included the Persian Gulf, Arabian Sea, and
Indian Ocean.

king, he took refuge in a temple and there was killed, not being protected even by the sanctity of the place.

X. Perdiccas, having led the army into the city, held a council of the leading men, in which it was decided that the rule should be so shared that the king [a] should in fact hold the chief authority, that Ptolemy should be satrap of Egypt [b] and the African races which were under the jurisdiction of the
2 Macedonians ; to Leomedon [c] was given Syria with Phoenicia, to Philotas [d] Cilicia was assigned, Antigonus was ordered to hold Lycia with Pamphylia and Greater Phrygia, Cassander was sent to Caria, Menander to Lydia ; they ordered that Lesser Phrygia that borders upon the Hellespont should
3 be the province of Leonnatus. Cappadocia fell to Eumenes with Paphlagonia ; he was ordered to defend that region as far as Trapezus and to wage war with Ariarathes ; he alone declined his assign-
4 ment. Pithon was ordered to hold Media, Lysimachus Thrace and the Pontic nations adjoining Thrace. It was decided that those who were in charge of India, and those in charge of Bactra, the Sogdiani, and the others who dwell near either the Ocean or the Red Sea [e] should retain command and hold rule over the territories of which each had charge ; that Perdiccas should remain [f] with the king and command the forces which followed the king.
5 Some have believed that the provinces were distributed by Alexander in his will, but we have learned that the report of such action was false, although handed
6 down by some authorities. Furthermore, when the

[f] See Diod. xviii. 2. 4.

6 Et quidem suas quisque opes, divisis imperii partibus,
tuebantur ut ipsi[1] fundaverant, si umquam adversus
7 immodicas cupiditates terminus staret. Quippe paulo
ante regis ministri specie imperii alieni procurandi
singuli ingentia invaserant regna, sublatis certami-
num causis, cum et omnes eiusdem gentis essent et
8 a ceteris sui quisque imperii regione discreti. Sed
difficile erat eo contentos esse quod obtulerat occasio;
quippe sordent prima quaeque, cum maiora sperantur.
Itaque omnibus expeditius videbatur augere regna
quam fuisset accipere.
9 Septimus dies erat, ex quo corpus regis iacebat in
solio, curis omnium ad formandum publicum statum
10 a tam sollemni munere aversis. Et non alius quam
Mesopotamiae regionis fervidior aestas[2] exsistit, adeo
ut pleraque animalia quae in nudo solo deprehendit
extinguat; tantus est vapor solis et caeli, quo cuncta
11 velut igne torrentur. Fontes aquarum et rari sunt
et incolentium fraude celantur; ipsis usus patet,
ignotus est advenis. Traditum magis quam creditum
12 refero[3]; ut tandem curare corpus exanimum amicis
vacavit, nulla tabe, ne minimo quidem livore corrup-
tum videre qui intraverant. Vigor quoque qui constat
13 ex spiritu nondum destituerat vultum. Itaque Aegyptii
Chaldaeique, iussi corpus suo more curare, primo non

---

[1] tuebantur ipsi *A* (ut *inserted by Post*); ut videbantur
sibi *Hedicke.*

[2] alius quam Mesopotamiae regionis fervidior aestas
Jeep; aliis quam mesopotamiae regione feruidior aestus *C;*
alias quam mesopotamiae regione feruidior aestus *S.*

[3] refero *Vogel;* refert *A.*

---

[a] *Cf.* Cic. *Balb.* xiii. 31; *Rab. Post.* i. 1; *Paradoxa* i. 10.

parts of the empire were distributed, they each continued to protect their own holdings as they themselves had fixed[a] them, except that no landmark could ever remain fixed in the face of unlimited
7 ambition. To be sure they had not long since as servants of the king, under pretext of exercising a delegated authority, individually usurped huge kingdoms, occasions for controversy having disappeared, since they were all of the same race and each one was separated from the rest by the situation
8 of his province. But it was difficult to be content with what occasion had granted them; for all first possessions seem mean when greater ones are hoped for. Hence it appeared to them all more convenient to increase their realms than it would have been to accept them as they were.
9 It was the seventh day since the king's body had been lying in its coffin, for the attention of all was diverted from so solemn a duty to the establishment
10 of public order. And no more burning heat exists than that of the region of Mesopotamia, so great that it destroys many animals which it overtakes on the bare ground; such is the heat of sun and sky,
11 by which everything is burned as by fire. Springs of water are rare and are hidden by the deceit of the natives; their use is available to them, but is unknown to strangers. I report what is recorded
12 rather than believed: when at last his friends had leisure to care for Alexander's lifeless body, those who had entered the room saw it corrupted by no decay, nor even by the slightest discoloration. The vigour too which comes from the breath of life had
13 not yet left his face. And so the Egyptians and Chaldeans who were ordered to care for the body

sunt ausi admovere velut spiranti manus ; deinde
precati, ut ius fasque esset mortalibus attrectare
deum,[1] purgavere corpus, repletumque est odoribus
aureum solium et capiti adiecta fortunae eius insignia.

14   Veneno necatum esse credidere plerique ; filium
Antipatri inter ministros, Iollam nomine, patris iussu
dedisse. Saepe certe audita erat vox Alexandri,
Antipatrum regium affectare fastigium maioremque
esse praefecti opibus ac titulo Spartanae victoriae
15 inflatum omnia a se data asserentem sibi. Credebant
etiam Craterum cum veterum militum manu ad inter-
16 ficiendum eum missum. Vim autem veneni, quod in
Macedonia gignitur, talem esse constat,[2] ut ferrum
quoque exurat, ungulam iumenti dumtaxat patien-
17 tem esse suci ; Stygem appellant fontem, ex quo
pestiferum virus emanat. Hoc per Cassandrum al-
latum traditumque fratri Iollae et ab eo supremae
regis potioni inditum.

18   Haec, utcumque sunt credita, eorum quos rumor
asperserat mox potentia exstinxit ; regnum enim
Macedoniae Antipater et Graeciam quoque invasit,
19 suboles deinde excepit, interfectis omnibus quicum-

---

[1] deum *Rader;* eum *A* (*V ends with this word at the end of
a folio*).
[2] constat *deleted by Acidalius.*

---

[a] See Justin xii. 13. 4 ; Plut. *Alex.* lxxvii. 1 ; Arr. vii.
27. 1-2.
[b] For *titulo* in this sense see vi. 6. 33.

after their manner, at first, as if he were still breathing, did not dare to lay their hands upon him ; then after praying that it might be right and lawful for mortals to handle a god, they emptied the body of entrails, the golden coffin was filled with perfumes, and the emblem of his rank was placed upon the king's head.

14 Many believed that he had been slain by poison [a] ; that a son of Antipater among his attendants, Iollas by name, had administered it by his father's command.   Certain it is that Alexander was often heard to say that Antipater took upon himself the state of a king, that he was more powerful than a prefect ought to be, and that he was puffed up by the rich spoil and fame [b] of his Spartan victory while he claimed 15 as his own all that the king had given him.   They also believed that Craterus had been sent to kill 16 Alexander with a troop of the old soldiers.   Now it is a fact that the power of the poison which is produced in Macedonia is such that it even melts iron and that only the hoof of a draught-animal can 17 withstand the liquid [c] ; they call the fount from which the destructive poison flows the Styx.[d]   This was brought by Cassander and delivered to his brother Iollas, and by him was put in the last draught given to the king.

18 These tales, however much they were given credence, the power of those whom rumour had 19 aspersed presently suppressed ; for Antipater seized the rule of Macedonia [e] and of Greece as well, then his son succeeded him, after all who were related

[c] Plut. *Alex.* lxxvii. 2 ; Paus. *Arcadia* xviii. 4.
[d] See Pliny, *N.H.* xxx. 16. 53.
[e] See Diod. xvii. 118. 2.

que Alexandrum etiam longinqua cognatione con-
20 tigerant.   Ceterum corpus eius a Ptolomaeo cui
Aegyptus cesserat, Memphim et inde paucis post
annis Alexandream translatum est, omnisque memoriae ac nomini honos habetur.

to Alexander, even by a distant connexion, had been
20 killed. But Ptolemy, under whose control Egypt
had come, transported the king's body to Memphis,
and from there a few years later to Alexandria [a]
where every honour was paid to his memory and his
name.

* *Cf.* Diod. xviii. 28. 3 f.

GENERAL INDEX

Prepared by Dr. John Rowe Workman

The references are to the Volumes (I, II), *pages and sections of the Loeb edition.*

561

GENERAL INDEX

GENERAL INDEX

of); 123, 19; 293, 4;
297, 6; 479, 40
Alexander Molossus, brother
of Olympias, king of Epi-
rus—I, 22; II, 243, n. c
Alexander, general of Alex.
III, otherwise unidentified
—II, 327, 10 (leader of
party scaling Aornus);
329, 14 f. (overwhelmed)
Alexander, son of Cleophis—
II, 325, 36 (named for
Alex. III)
Alexandreis, a thirteenth-
century epic by Philip
Walter on material drawn
from Curtius about Alex.
—I, xiv
Alexandretta, modern Alex-
andria in Cilicia—I, 117,
n. d
Alexandria in Egypt—I, 237,
1 ff. (founding of); 239,
5 f. (populated); II, 559,
20 (final resting place of
Alex.)
Alexandria on the Iaxartes—
II, 185, 25 ff. (founding
of)
Alexandria (*ad Caucasum*)—
I, xxvi; 392, n. a; II,
151, 23 (founding of)
Alexandria, at Issus—I, 117,
n. d
Alexandria, in India—II,
435, 8
Alexandropolis, a city of the
Medari in Thrace, re-
populated by Alex.—I, 12
Alps, the—II, 473, 18 (Alex.
plans to skirt)
altars—I, 21 (erected by

Alex. after defeat of Ge-
tae); 38 (erected by Alex.
in Europe and Asia Minor
at place of crossing Hellespont); 81, 9 (of silver,
carrying sacred fire, in
Persian processional); 145,
27 (consecrated by Alex.
on bank of Pinarus);
II, 331, 24 (erected to
Minerva Victoria on Aor-
nus); 393, 19 (Alex.
orders 12 of squared stone
erected as memorial to his
expedition); 399, 14 (many
erected in country of Sibi
after ship of Alex. escapes
whirlpool)
Amanican Gates, entrance
to Cilicia from Syria, situated north of the Pinarus
River—I, 113, 13 (reached
by Darius and his army
before Issus)
Amardi, variant for Mardi
(*q.v.*), a rude people dwelling near Hyrcania—II, 42,
n. a
Amazons, female warriors
living on the Pontus and
on the Caspian (see n. c on
II, 36)—II, 37, 17 (on the
Caspian); 47, 24, 27
(dwelling in plains of
Themiscyra, description
of); 507 (female warriors
under Atropates believed
survivors of race of A.).
See also Thalestris
Ambraciots, inhabitants of
Ambracia, a town in
southern Epirus—I, 20

GENERAL INDEX

571

GENERAL INDEX

GENERAL INDEX

Bagophanes, Babylonian in charge of the citadel at Babylon, guardian of the royal funds—I, 333, 20 ; 343, 44

Balacrus, Macedonian general—I, 211, 13 ; 287, 28 ; II, 331, 22

Balkh, mod. name of Bactra —I, 391, n. *c* ; II, 159, n. *d*

Balkhab River = Bactrus— II, 159, n. *e*

Baluchistan—II, 145, n. *e*

banquets—I, xxx (of Alex. with Medius) ; 34 (at Dium) ; 137, 2 (after Issus) ; II, 17, 2 ff. ; 75, 16 (to which Philotas was invited : also II, 85, 26 and 91, 11) ; 151, 1 ff. (held by Bessus) ; 239, 22 ff. ; 243, 38 (Clitus ordered to leave) ; 261, 8 (ordered by Spitamenes) ; 271, 22 (ordered by Oxyartes) ; 273, 29 ; 277, 9 ; 279, 17 ; 281, 21, 24 ; 287, 16 ; 425, 4 ; 427, 15 (given by Alex. to envoys of the Sudracae and the Malli) ; 429, 17 ; 431, 25 ; 499 ; 507 (at Ecbatana) ; 515

banyan tree—II, 367, n. *f*

Barcani, an Asiatic people dwelling in Hyrcania—I, 73, 5

barley, used by Alex. to mark the boundaries of Alexandria in Egypt—I, 239, 6

Barsinê, daughter of Darius,

wife of Memnon, later of Alex.—II, 494, n. *c*

Barsinê, wife of Pharnabazus, captured at Issus— I, 151, 14 ; II, 529, 11, 13

Barzaentes, satrap of the Drangae and Arachosii— I, 402, n. *a* ; II, 59, 36 ; 337, 3 ; 339, 4

batmen—I, 87, 25 ; II, 77, 23 ; 267, 13

battering rams—II, 253, 22

Bay of Issus—I, 68, n. *a*

Bazaira, region of Bactriana —II, 235, 10

Bazira—II, 318, n. *g*

Beas River = Hypasis — II, 374, n. *a* ; 393, n. *c*

Beira, siege and description of—II, 319, 22 ff.

Belitae, an unknown Asiatic people in Darius' army—I, 273, 10

Belus, ancestral god of Darius—I, 85, 16 ; 335, 24 (founder of Babylon)

Bermion, Mount—I, xxiii

Bernouilli, J. J.—I, xxxiv

beryl, ornamenting the sceptre of Sopithes—II, 373, 30

Bessus, satrap of the Bactrians—I, xxvi ; 215, 2 ff. ; 271, 6 ; 301, 2 ; 391, 4 ; 397, 2 (his conspiracy with Nabarzanes) ; 399, 8, 10 ; 401, 11 (slips away from Darius with Nabarzanes) ; 401, 16 ; 402, n. *a* ; 403, 1 ff. (resolves to carry out conspiracy) ; 405, 12 f. ; 407, 2 ; 409, 7, 8 ; 411, 1,

GENERAL INDEX

GENERAL INDEX

nian envoy to Darius—I, 151, 15

Callisthenes of Olynthus, philosopher and historian in Alex.'s retinue—I, xv; xvi; 3; 10; 142, n. *b*; II, 250, n. *c*; 277, 13, 14 ff. (speech of); 281, 20; 281, 1 (Alex. angered at); 289, 24, 25; 291, 27, 29; 291, 3; 293, 8, 10 (freed of charge by Hermolaüs); 303, 19, 21 (expires in torture)

caltrops, booby-trap device, used at Arbela—I, 289, 36

Cambyses, immediate predecessor of Darius I, last of family of Cyrus the Great to rule Persia—I, 29

camels—I, 87, 24 (in Darius' procession); 381, 9 (at Persepolis); II, 137, 18 (used by Polydamas); 269, 19; 455, 17 (bear food to army of Alex.)

Camp of Alexander—I, 227, 2 (a halting-place of Alex. in Egypt, otherwise unidentified)

Camp of Cyrus, a halting-place of Cyrus the Great in Cilicia on his march to Lydia against Croesus—I, 89, 1

Cappadocia, country of Asia between Pontus and Cilicia —I, 44; 73, 24 (Alex. moves to); 89, 1 (Sabistamenes appointed governor); 98, n. *c*; II, 25, 3;

149, 20; 553, 3 (Eumenes receives)

Cappadocians—I, 173, 34 (in Darius' army); 275, 12 (at Arbela)

captives, Greek, taken and persecuted by the Persians return to Alex. at Persepolis—I, 371, 5 ff. See also Greeks, the

Carae, site of camp established by Alex., after crossing the Eulaeus—II, 505

Caranus, alleged founder of the Argive dynasty in Macedonia—I, xxiii; xxiv

Caranus, general of Alex.— II, 145, 2; 161, 32

Carduchean mountains—I, 254, n. *d*

Caria, lies between Lydia and Lycia—I, 52; 53; 54; II, 25, 3; 553, 2; Carians—I, 66, n. *a*

Carmania, lies east of Persia on the Persian Gulf—II, 457, 20; 468, n. *a*

carriages, decorated for procession—II, 459, 25

cart of Darius, a wagon in which Darius was borne secretly from the advancing Macedonians—I, 415, 16; 417, 20; 421, 15; 422, n. *a*; 423, 20; 425, 23

Carthage—I, 179, 10 f. (relation to Tyre); 192, n. *c*; 193, 20; 195, 20 (Tyrian wives and children removed to); 195, 22; 205,

GENERAL INDEX

GENERAL INDEX

Cybelê or Great Mother—I,
30

Cydnus, river of Cilicia—I,
91, 8 f.; 93, 1

Cymê, city off coast of Asia
near Lesbos—I, 373, 9

Cyprus—I, 171, 27; 189,
11; 190, n. a; II, 473,
n. c; Cypriotes—I, 191,
11; 241, 14; II, 473, 19;
Cyprian ships—II, 9

Cyrenê—I, 212, n. c; 229, 9

Cyropolis, city of Sogdiana
—II, 183, 16, 19

Cyrus the Great—I, 28; 29;
34; 89, 1; 273, 8; 297,
n. c; 299, 24; 383, 10;
427; II, 29, 12; 143, 1;
145, 3; 179, 11; 183, 20;
454, n. a; 475, 23; 477,
30, 34

Cyrus, Camp of—I, 89, 1

Cyzicus—I, 30; Cyziceni—I,
30; 31

Dactyli, the Idaean—I, 30

Daedala, a region of India—
II, 319, 19

Dahae, Scythian people
dwelling beyond the Cas-
pian Sea—I, 271, 6; II,
27, 9; 153, 6; 195, 32;
235, 6, 8; 259, 1; 263, 16
(surrender to Alex.); 347,
5; 383, 24

Damaraxus, king of an
Indian district—II, 339, 4

Damascus, city in Syria—I,
113, 12; 145, 27; 147, 2,
4, 6; 151, n. d; 153, n. a;
161, 4; 267, 11

Damyllus, native of Megalo-

polis in Arcadia—II, 543,
15

Danube River—I, 21; 267,
13; II, 187, 4

Darius I, son of Hystaspes—
I, 29; 39; 125, 8; 163,
10; 379, 1; II, 106, n. a
(contemporary of Alex-
ander Philhellen); 529, 14

Darius II, son of Artaxerxes
I (Macrochir)—I, 29

Darius III, son of Arsames—
I, xxvi; xxix; 8; 19; 27;
28 (ascends the throne);
32; 36; 40 (reaction to
Alex.'s invasion); 67, 8,
10; 71, 19; 73, 1 (as-
sumes command of the
Persians in line of battle);
73, 2 ff.; 75, 9; 77, 17 (disposition of); 79, 1, 2 ff.
(dream of); 81, 5, 6, 7;
83, 15 f.; 85, 17 ff. (attire
of); 87, 28; 95, 6; 97,
10, 12, 16; 99, 4; 105, 1
(crosses the Euphrates);
106, n. a; 109, 12; 109,
1; 111, 4 ff.; 113, 13 (arrives at Amanican Gates);
113, 15; 115, 16 (crosses
the Pinarus); 115, 17; 117,
23, 24; 119, 27; 119, 1, 4;
121, 10; 127, 1; 129, 7 ff.
(at Issus); 131, 11 (flees
chariot at Issus); 133, 18,
19; 135, 23, 24 (mother
and wife of); 137, 26;
137, 1, 4 (believed dead);
137, 5; 139, 6 (bewailed by
Alex.); 139, 11; 141, 12,
13; 143, 22; 145, 24, 26;
145, 1; 147, 3; 149, 10 ff.

590

GENERAL INDEX

Dascyleum, town in Phrygia —I, 48

Datapheres, partner of Spitamenes in his revolt —II, 169, 21 ff. ; 263, 16

debauchery—I, 339, 37 ff. (in Babylon) ; II, 477, 29 (of Bagoas)

debts, declaration of by Alex.'s soldiers—II, 485, 9 ; 487, 11

Dehâs River = Bactrus—II, 159, n.

deification of Alex., the—I, 235, 30 f.

Deli Chai= Pinarus River— I, 118, n. a

Delius, Ephesian who pleaded for the freedom of Greeks in Asia Minor—I, 33

Delphi—I, 20

Demades, Athenian orator and statesman—I, 27

Demaratus of Corinth, through whose efforts Alex. returned to Macedonia from Illyria after a reconciliation with Philip II—I, 17

Demetrius, member of Alex.'s body-guard, implicated in the plot of Dymnus—II, 63, 15 ; 79, 5 ; 109, 35 f. ; 111, 37

Democrates, Athenian among the Greek mercenaries in the Persian army—II, 41, 9

Demophon, soothsayer—II, 403, 28 f.

Demosthenes, orator and

statesman—I, 12 ; 14 ; 23 ; 27 ; 49

Derbices, a people dwelling between the Caspian Sea and the Oxus River—I, 75, 7

Derdas, friend of Alex. sent by him to the Scythians— II, 181, 12 ; 235, 7

deserters—I, 417, 2 (from Darius' army) ; 419, 7, 10 ; 421, 11, 12 ; II, 417, 12

de Vogelas—I, xxxiii

diadem—II, 51, 4 (purple, worn by Alex.) ; 335, 14 (of Omphis) ; Alex.'s— II, 513 (dragged from his head) ; 527, 4 ; 545, 20

Diana, her temple at Ephesus—I, 4

Diardines River—II, 305, 9 (bred dolphins)

Didymeon, temple called— II, 173, 28

dimachae—I, 419, 8

Dinochares or Dinocrates, reputed architect of Alexandria in Egypt—I, 236, n. c

Dinon, father o Clitarchus —I, xviii

Diodorus Siculus—I, ix ; xv ; 3

Diodotus of Erythrae, writer of *Ephemerides*, a contemporary of Alex.—I, xv

Diogenes of Sinopê—I, 20 (reported conversation with Alex.)

Diogenes, tyrant of Mitylenê —I, 59

592

GENERAL INDEX

Dionysus, see Bacchus: Liber

Dioxippus, celebrated Athenian boxer—II, 427, 16 ff. (falsely accused of stealing)

Dium, city in Macedonia—I, 34; 46

divine honours—I, 235, 28 (ordered by Ammonian priest for Alex.); II, 275, 5 (Alex. desired); 279, 15 (Callisthenes speaks of); 517, 6 (requested by Alex. after his death); 517, 11 (Macedonians repent of denying to Alex.); 525, 33 (Alex.'s aspiration for)

Dnieper River = Borysthenes—II, 21, n. g

Don River = Tanais—I, 207, n. f; II, 21, n. h; 152, n. b; 180, n. a; 204, n. b

Dorians—I, xxiii

Doriscus, Thracian town west of the Hebrus—I, 73, n. b

Drangae, warlike people of Asia—II, 59, 36; 143, 1; 263, 17

Drangiana—I, 402, n. a

Dropides, Athenian in Persian army—I, 151, 15

Dropides, father of Hellanicê nurse of Alex.—I, 5

Drypetis, daughter of Darius, wife of Hephaestion—II, 520, n. a

Dübner, Fr.—I, xv

Dymnus, participant in a conspiracy against Alex.—II, 61, 2 ff. (forms conspiracy with Nicomachus); 63, 12 ff. (threatens Nicomachus' life); 65, 24 (arrested by attendants of Alex.); 67, 29 f. (wounds himself and dies); 69, 34; 77, 26 (corpse of, displayed at trial); 79, 5, 8; 81, 16; 89, 6; 91, 9; 93, 19, 20, 21; 107, 30

Ecbatana, capital of Media—I, 8; 209, 8; 391, 1 (Darius reaches); 392, n. a; 417, 1; II, 217, 10; 507 (Alex. arrives at); 511

Ecbolima, city of India—II, 331, 1

eclipse—of the sun (September, 20/21, 331 B.C.)—I, 253, 2 ff. (effect upon Alex.'s troops at Arbela); of the moon near Arbela—I, 253, 22 ff.

Edessa, ancient capital of Macedonia—I, xxiii

Egypt—I, 107, 11; 171, 27 ff. (reached by Amyntas); 197, 1; 219, 13; 225, 30 (Alex. hastens to); 227, 2 ff.; 237, 3 ff.; 243, 1; 291, 1: II, 203, 18; 438, n. d; 504, n. a; 553, 1; 559, 20; Egyptians, the—I, 171, 28, 30 (fickleness of); 225, 1 ff. (reaction to Alex.'s arrival); 227, 3 (revolution of); 233, n. f; 253, 4 ff.; II, 555, 13 (entrusted with Alex.'s body)

Elaeus, on the Hellespont, site of tomb of Protesilaüs—I, 37

GENERAL INDEX

(Greek increased by booty at Chios); 389, 8 (Persian of 1000 ships in the fifth century); 395, 16; II, 393, 21 (ordered to be constructed on the Hydaspes); 395, 22; 415, 2; 437, 16; 443, 8; 445, 11 (scattered by rising tide on the Indus); 447, 19; 449, 25; 451, 27; 451, 1 (Alex.'s proceeds up the Indus from the sea); 473, 16 (ordered back to the sea by Alex.); 483, 2; 529, 14 (allusion to the great fleets of Darius I and Xerxes)

flute, music of—I, 27; flute-players—II, 459, 26 (in procession); 505 (Evius)

Fortune, used by Curtius in a sense closely approximating that of Destiny to indicate both good-fortune and ill-fortune, frequently personified (see n. *b* on I, 78)—I, xviii (in Clitarchus' history of Alex.); 23; 29; 31; 77, 17; 79, 18; 97, 11; 109, 2; 115, 20; 119, 29; 135, 23; 143, 20; 151, 12: 171, 29; 175, 40; 207, 2; 211, 12; 235, 29; 297, 19; 299, 21; 305, 11; 315, 10; 327, 3; 347, 10; 385, 19; 393, 6; 395, 15, 17; 397, 4; 411, 11; 417, 20; 423, 22; 429; II, 9; 13, 9; 97, 33; 205, 25; 259, 1; 261, 6; 271, 24; 319, 18   343, 22; 405, 3;

417, 12; 421, 19; **459,** 28; 525, 25

Freinshem, J.—I, ix; xiv; xxxii

Furies, the—II, 91, 14

Gades, early colony of Tyre in Spain at the Pillars of Hercules—I, 205, 19; II, 473, 17

games, public—I, 105, 3 ff. (in honour of Alex.'s recovery); II, 507 (at Ecbatana); 509 (for Hephaestion); 517, 5

Gangaridae, an Indian people dwelling beside the Ganges River—II, 375, 3

Ganges River—II, 305, 5, 8; 375, 2; 397, 8; 399, 17; 401, 20

" Gates, The," the natives' term for a pass in Cilicia, opening into the Camp of Cyrus—I, 89, 2; 91, 11 (Alex. enters)

Gaugamela, site of the Battle of Arbela—I, xxvi; xxviii; xxix; 245. n. *d*; II, 380, n. *a*

Gaza, city of Palestine—I, 58; 209, 10; 217, 7 (besieged by Alex.); 219, 14 (battle begins at); 223, 23; 225, 30 (losses at); 227, 2

gaza,Persian word for "king's money"—I, 147, 5

Gazaca, region of Sogdiana —II, 265, 1

Gedrosia, Gedrosii, see Cedrosia, Cedrosii

GENERAL INDEX

597

GENERAL INDEX

Gordyaei, people of Armenia
—I, 331, 14

Gorgias, Macedonian soldier
—II, 129, 38 ; 499

Gorgidas, Macedonian sol-
dier—II, 129, 38

Gortuae, the, a race from
Euboea transferred to
Susiana by the Persians—
I, 273, 11

Granicus River, in Asia,
famous for Alex.'s battle
there—I, 39 ; 42 ; 43 ff.
(battle of); 67, 9 ; 74, n. b;
125, 7 ; 251, 22 ; 291, 1 ;
295, 10 ; II, 237, 20 ;
383, 23

Grynion, town of Aeolis—I,
31

Gualterus, Philippus—I, 14

gymnosophists—II, 311, n. e

habits, foreign—II, 17, 2 ff.
(affect the Macedonian
troops); 49, 1 ff. (also
Alex.); 51, 10 (veterans
bewail)

Haemus, Mount—I, 20 ; 120,
n. b

Halicarnassus—I, 52 ; 53 ;
54 ; 58 ; 105, 4 (Persian
defeat at); 345, 5 (siege
of); II, 243, 36

Halys River—I, 207, 1 ; 265,
5

Hammon = Ammon—II, 97,
28 ; 101, 5

harlots—I, 387, 2 ff. (in
Alex.'s company); II, 17,
2 ; 475, 26

harpagones—I, 179, 12 ; 196,
n. b

Harpalus, prefect of Alex.
entrusted with money to
gain the support of the
Athenians—II, 393, 21 ;
481 ; 483, 2, 3

Haustanes, associate of Catanes—II, 273, 2

Hebrews, their sacred books
—I, 57

Hebrus River—I, 37 ; 73, n. b

Hecataeus, Macedonian soldier—I, 18 ; II, 129, 38

Hecatompylos, city of Parthienê—II, 21, 15

Hector, son of Parmenion—
I, 239, 7 ff. ; II, 85, 27

Hector, son of Priam—I,
39

Hedicke, Edmund—I, v ; vi ;
x ; xii ; xiii ; xviii

Hegelochus, general of Alex.
—I, 42 ; 71, 19 ; 211,
14 ff.; 213, 21. The same
man, apparently, was a
friend of Parmenion—II,
105, 22 ff. ; 107, 27, 28

Hegesimachus, a daring,
noble youth in Alex.'s
army—II, 341, 13 ff.

Hegesistratus, commander of
Milesian garrison—I, 51

Hellanicê, daughter of Dropides and sister of Clitus,
and nurse of Alex.—I, 5 ;
II, 239, 21 ; 248, n. b

Hellanicus, competitor in the
contests at Sittacenê—I,
345, 5

Hellespont—I, 37 (Alex.
crosses); 38 ; 43 ; 71, 19
(Alex.'s fleet at); 71, 20 ;
95, 7 ; 143, 18 ; 163, 10 ;

GENERAL INDEX

GENERAL INDEX

611

GENERAL INDEX

GENERAL INDEX

GENERAL INDEX

GENERAL INDEX

Samos—I, 51

Samothrace, an island off the coast of Thrace—II, 240, n. *a* (its Mysteries); 241, 26

Sangala, a town in India—I, xvii

Sangarius River—I, 69, 12

Sardis, capital of Lydia—I, 48; 49; 54; 139, 6; 343, 44

sarisa—II, 429, 19 (Macedonian lance); *sarisophori* —I, 305, 13

Sarmatians, people dwelling along the Tanais River— II, 187, 3

satellites—II, 74, n. *a*

Satibarzanes, satrap of the Arii—II, 53, 13; 55, 20, 21, 22; 57, 25; 59, 34; 143, 2; 161, 33; 163, 37

Satropates, general of Darius' cavalry—I, 245, 7; 251, 25

Saturn—I, 195, 23

scalae= κλῖμαξ—I, 361, n. *c*

scaling ladders—I, 179, 9 (at Tyre)

scenic plays—1, 34

Schmidt, E. F.—I, xxxiv

Schmieder, F.—I, xxxii

Scythia—II, 149, 19; 273, 11; 251, 14; Scythians— I, 271, n. *d* (the Dahae); II, 187, 3; 201, 17; Scythians in Europe—II, 187, 2; in general—I, 40; 215, 3; 243, 2; 279, 5; 291, 3; 305, 12 f.; 307, 18; 398, n. *b*; II, 21, 13 f.; 53, 13; 153, 6;

161, 32: 179, 11; 181, 12; 187, 1, 2; 187, n. *d*; 189, 6, 11; 191, 12, 15, 16; 199, 8, 10; 203, 22, 23; 207, 5; 210, n. *b*; 211, 17, 18; 235, 7, 9; 347, 5; 383, 24; 387, 33

sea= Indian Ocean—II, 365, 3; 391, 13; 443, 6; 447, 20; 449, 26, 27

sea beasts—II, 449, 22 (in the Indus at low tide); sea monster at Tyre—I, 199, 3 ff.

Seistan, city in India—I, xxvi; xxvii; xxviii

Seleucus, general of Alex., later a king and founder of the Syrian dynasty of Seleucids—I, xxxi

Semiramis, an early queen, founder of Babylon—I, 335, 24; II, 183, 20; 423, 23; 454, n. *a*

Seneca—I, xviii

Septimius Severus, the emperor—I, xix; xx

Serapis, temple of—I, xxxi

serpents—I, 4; 230, n. *a* (two at Ammon); II, 369, 12 (in India); 389, 8; 441, 26 (in Alex.'s dream)

sesame, juice from—II, 157, 23

Sestus, town on the Hellespont—I, 37

Seuthes, king of the Odrysae —II, 481, 45

Shahrud, Persian city (Darius died near)—I, xxvi; xxix

Shar range—I, xxiii

622

GENERAL INDEX

GENERAL INDEX

Darius—I, 86, n. *b*; 134, n. *b*

Stesilaüs, tyrant of Methymnê—I, 241, 11

Stiboetes River—II, 33, 4 ff.

stoning, an ancient custom of the Macedonians—II, 101, 10; 105, 20; 111, 38; 131, 1

Strabo—I, xxviii; xxix

Straton, king of Aradus—I, 161, 6

Straton, king of Sidon—I, 165, 16; 169, 26

Strattis of Olynthus—I, xvii; xviii

Strymon River (mod. Struma) —I, xxiv; 37

Styx, a spring in Macedonia —II, 557, 17

Sudracae—II, 399, 15; 401, 24; 403, 26; 426, n. *b*

Suetonius—I, xxi

suicide—I, 414, n. *a* (Roman view of) on I, 415 (Darius' disdain of)

Suidas—I, xvii

sulphur, smeared on objects to make them inflammable —I, 185, 2; 219, 11

Sun, the—I, 81, 8 (image of); 83, 11 (steed of); 194, n. *a* (god); 233, 22 (water of); 281, 12 (invoked before Arbela); II, 307, 13 (heat of in India); 365, 1 (Alex. sacrifices to); 383, 26

Sunium, promontory of Attica—II, 483, 1

superstition—I, 42; 195, 23; 255, 7 (sways the ommon herd); 359, 1;

II, 189, 8; 193, 21, 23; 403, 29

suppliant—I, 221, 15 (Arab); 333, 17 (Mazaeus); 355, 14 (Medates); II, 59, 34 (Artacanians); 173, 33 (Branchidae)

Susa, capital of Susiana—I, 8; 329, 7; 347, 8, 11; 349, 16; 351, 3; 381, 9; 392, n. *a*; II, 505

Susiana, the region—I, 273, n. *f*; 350, n. *c*; the Susiani —I, 271, 6; 351, 3; 357, 16

Susidan Gates—I, 357, 17

Sutlej River—II, 374, n. *a*; 393, n. *c*

Sykes, Percy—I, xxxiii

Syracuse, in Sicily—I, 195, 22; Syracusans, the—I, 192, n. *c*; 193, 20

Syr Darya = Iaxartes River = Tanais River—I, 207, n. *f*; II, 152, n. *b*; 174, n. *b*; 180, n. *a*

Syria—I, 113, 12, 13; 145, 27; 161, 4; 175, 1 f.; 177, 6; 209, 9; 218, n. *c*; 239, 9; 291, 1; 295, 10; 339, 35; 421, 11; II, 25, 3; 203, 18, 19; 217, 12; 237, 15; 473, 17, 19; 553, 2; the Syrians—I, 161, 5; 275, 12

Syrmus, king of the Triballi —I, 21; 22

Syrtes, dwellers near the Syrtes in northern Africa —I, 231, 19

Tabae, town of Paraetacenê —I, 417, 2

GENERAL INDEX

GENERAL INDEX

GENERAL INDEX

Printed by CLARK CONSTABLE, *Edinburgh, London, Melbourne*

THE LOEB CLASSICAL LIBRARY

VOLUMES ALREADY PUBLISHED

1

THE LOEB CLASSICAL LIBRARY

CICERO: IN CATILINAM, PRO MURENA, PRO SULLA, PRO
    FLACCO. New version by C. Macdonald.
CICERO: LETTERS TO ATTICUS. E. O. Winstedt. 3 Vols.
CICERO: LETTERS TO HIS FRIENDS. W. Glynn Williams,
    M. Cary, M. Henderson. 4 Vols.
CICERO: PHILIPPICS. W. C. A. Ker.
CICERO: PRO ARCHIA, POST REDITUM, DE DOMO, DE
    HARUSPICUM RESPONSIS, PRO PLANCIO. N. H. Watts.
CICERO: PRO CAECINA, PRO LEGE MANILIA, PRO CLUENTIO,
    PRO RABIRIO. H. Grose Hodge.
CICERO: PRO CAELIO, DE PROVINCIIS CONSULARIBUS, PRO
    BALBO. R. Gardner.
CICERO: PRO MILONE, IN PISONEM, PRO SCAURO, PRO
    FONTEIO, PRO RABIRIO POSTUMO, PRO MARCELLO, PRO
    LIGARIO, PRO REGE DEIOTARO. N. H. Watts.
CICERO: PRO QUINCTIO, PRO ROSCIO AMERINO, PRO ROSCIO
    COMOEDO, CONTRA RULLUM. J. H. Freese.
CICERO: PRO SESTIO, IN VATINIUM. R. Gardner.
[CICERO]: RHETORICA AD HERENNIUM. H. Caplan.
CICERO: TUSCULAN DISPUTATIONS. J. E. King.
CICERO: VERRINE ORATIONS. L. H. G. Greenwood. 2 Vols.
CLAUDIAN. M. Platnauer. 2 Vols.
COLUMELLA: DE RE RUSTICA, DE ARBORIBUS. H. B. Ash,
    E. S. Forster, E. Heffner. 3 Vols.
CURTIUS, Q.: HISTORY OF ALEXANDER. J. C. Rolfe. 2 Vols.
FLORUS. E. S. Forster.
FRONTINUS: STRATAGEMS AND AQUEDUCTS. C. E. Bennett
    and M. B. McElwain.
FRONTO: CORRESPONDENCE. C. R. Haines. 2 Vols.
GELLIUS. J. C. Rolfe. 3 Vols.
HORACE: ODES AND EPODES. C. E. Bennett.
HORACE: SATIRES, EPISTLES, ARS POETICA. H. R. Fairclough.
JEROME: SELECT LETTERS. F. A. Wright.
JUVENAL AND PERSIUS. G. G. Ramsay.
LIVY. B. O. Foster, F. G. Moore, Evan T. Sage, A. C.
    Schlesinger and R. M. Geer (General Index). 14 Vols.
LUCAN. J. D. Duff.
LUCRETIUS. W. H. D. Rouse. Revised by M. F. Smith.
MANILIUS. G. P. Goold.
MARTIAL. W. C. A. Ker. 2 Vols. Revised by E. H.
    Warmington.
MINOR LATIN POETS: from PUBLILIUS SYRUS to RUTILIUS
    NAMATIANUS, including GRATTIUS, CALPURNIUS, SICULUS
    NEMESIANUS, AVIANUS, with "Aetna," "Phoenix" and
    other poems. J. Wight Duff and Arnold M. Duff. 2 Vols.

THE LOEB CLASSICAL LIBRARY

THE LOEB CLASSICAL LIBRARY

VALERIUS FLACCUS. J. H. Mozley.
VARRO: DE LINGUA LATINA. R. G. Kent. 2 Vols.
VELLEIUS PATERCULUS AND RES GESTAE DIVI AUGUSTI. F. W. Shipley.
VIRGIL. H. R. Fairclough. 2 Vols.
VITRUVIUS: DE ARCHITECTURA. F. Granger. 2 Vols.

GREEK AUTHORS

ACHILLES TATIUS. S. Gaselee.
AELIAN: ON THE NATURE OF ANIMALS. A. F. Scholfield. 3 Vols.
AENEAS TACTICUS, ASCLEPIODOTUS AND ONASANDER. The Illinois Greek Club.
AESCHINES. C. D. Adams.
AESCHYLUS. H. Weir Smyth. 2 Vols.
ALICIPHRON, AELIAN AND PHILOSTRATUS: LETTERS. A. R. Benner and F. H. Fobes.
APOLLODORUS. Sir James G. Frazer. 2 Vols.
APOLLONIUS RHODIUS. R. C. Seaton.
THE APOSTOLIC FATHERS. Kirsopp Lake. 2 Vols.
APPIAN'S ROMAN HISTORY. Horace White. 4 Vols.
ARATUS. Cf. CALLIMACHUS: HYMNS AND EPIGRAMS.
ARISTIDES. C. A. Behr. 4 Vols. Vol. I.
ARISTOPHANES. Benjamin Bickley Rogers. 3 Vols. Verse trans.
ARISTOTLE: ART OF RHETORIC. J. H. Freese.
ARISTOTLE: ATHENIAN CONSTITUTION, EUDEMIAN ETHICS, VIRTUES AND VICES. H. Rackham.
ARISTOTLE: THE CATEGORIES. ON INTERPRETATION. H. P. Cooke; PRIOR ANALYTICS. H. Tredennick.
ARISTOTLE: GENERATION OF ANIMALS. A. L. Peck.
ARISTOTLE: HISTORIA ANIMALIUM. A. L. Peck. 3 Vols. Vols. I and II.
ARISTOTLE: METAPHYSICS. H. Tredennick. 2 Vols.
ARISTOTLE: METEOROLOGICA. H. D. P. Lee.
ARISTOTLE: MINOR WORKS. W. S. Hett. "On Colours," "On Things Heard," "Physiognomics," "On Plants," "On Marvellous Things Heard," "Mechanical Problems," "On Invisible Lines," "Situations and Names of Winds," "On Melissus, Xenophanes, and Gorgias."
ARISTOTLE: NICOMACHEAN ETHICS. H. Rackham.
ARISTOTLE: OECONOMICA AND MAGNA MORALIA. G. C. Armstrong. (With METAPHYSICS, Vol. II.)

4

THE LOEB CLASSICAL LIBRARY

ARISTOTLE: ON THE HEAVENS. W. K. C. Guthrie.

ARISTOTLE: ON THE SOUL, PARVA NATURALIA, ON BREATH. W. S. Hett.

ARISTOTLE: PARTS OF ANIMALS. A. L. Peck; MOVEMENT AND PROGRESSION OF ANIMALS. E. S. Forster.

ARISTOTLE: PHYSICS. Rev. P. Wicksteed and F. M. Cornford. 2 Vols.

ARISTOTLE: POETICS; LONGINUS ON THE SUBLIME. W. Hamilton Fyfe; DEMETRIUS ON STYLE. W. Rhys Roberts.

ARISTOTLE: POLITICS. H. Rackham.

ARISTOTLE: POSTERIOR ANALYTICS. H. Tredennick; TOPICS. E. S. Forster.

ARISTOTLE: PROBLEMS. W. S. Hett. 2 Vols.

ARISTOTLE: RHETORICA AD ALEXANDRUM. H. Rackham. (With PROBLEMS, Vol. II.)

ARISTOTLE: SOPHISTICAL REFUTATIONS. COMING-TO-BE AND PASSING-AWAY. E. S. Forster; ON THE COSMOS. D. J. Furley.

ARRIAN: HISTORY OF ALEXANDER AND INDICA. 2 Vols. New version. P. Brunt.

ATHENAEUS: DEIPNOSOPHISTAE. C. B. Gulick. 7 Vols.

BABRIUS AND PHAEDRUS (Latin). B. E. Perry.

ST. BASIL: LETTERS. R. J. Deferrari. 4 Vols.

CALLIMACHUS: FRAGMENTS. C. A. Trypanis; MUSAEUS: HERO AND LEANDER. T. Gelzer and C. Whitman.

CALLIMACHUS: HYMNS AND EPIGRAMS, AND LYCOPHRON. A. W. Mair; ARATUS. G. R. Mair.

CLEMENT OF ALEXANDRIA. Rev. G. W. Butterworth.

COLLUTHUS. *Cf.* OPPIAN.

DAPHNIS AND CHLOE. *Cf.* LONGUS.

DEMOSTHENES I: OLYNTHIACS, PHILIPPICS AND MINOR ORATIONS: I-XVII AND XX. J. H. Vince.

DEMOSTHENES II: DE CORONA AND DE FALSA LEGATIONE. C. A. Vince and J. H. Vince.

DEMOSTHENES III: MEIDIAS, ANDROTION, ARISTOCRATES, TIMOCRATES, ARISTOGEITON. J. H. Vince.

DEMOSTHENES IV-VI: PRIVATE ORATIONS AND IN NEAERAM. A. T. Murray.

DEMOSTHENES VII: FUNERAL SPEECH, EROTIC ESSAY, EXORDIA AND LETTERS. N. W. and N. J. DeWitt.

DIO CASSIUS: ROMAN HISTORY. E. Cary. 9 Vols.

DIO CHRYSOSTOM. 5 Vols. Vols. I and II. J. W. Cohoon. Vol. III. J. W. Cohoon and H. Lamar Crosby. Vols. IV and V. H. Lamar Crosby.

THE LOEB CLASSICAL LIBRARY

DIODORUS SICULUS. 12 Vols. Vols. I-VI. C. H. Oldfather.
Vol. VII. C. L. Sherman. Vol. VIII. C. B. Welles. Vols.
IX and X. Russel M. Geer. Vols XI and XII. F. R.
Walton. General Index. Russel M. Geer.

DIOGENES LAERTIUS. R. D. Hicks. 2 Vols. New Intro-
duction by H. S. Long.

DIONYSIUS OF HALICARNASSUS: CRITICAL ESSAYS. S. Usher.
2 Vols.

DIONYSIUS OF HALICARNASSUS: ROMAN ANTIQUITIES. Spel-
man's translation revised by E. Cary. 7 Vols.

EPICTETUS. W. A. Oldfather. 2 Vols.

EURIPIDES. A. S. Way. 4 Vols. Verse trans.

EUSEBIUS: ECCLESIASTICAL HISTORY. Kirsopp Lake and
J. E. L. Oulton. 2 Vols.

GALEN: ON THE NATURAL FACULTIES. A. J. Brock.

THE GREEK ANTHOLOGY. W. R. Paton. 5 Vols.

THE GREEK BUCOLIC POETS (THEOCRITUS, BION, MOSCHUS).
J. M. Edmonds.

GREEK ELEGY AND IAMBUS WITH THE ANACREONTEA. J. M.
Edmonds. 2 Vols.

GREEK LYRIC. D. A. Campbell. 4 Vols. Vol. I.

GREEK MATHEMATICAL WORKS. Ivor Thomas. 2 Vols.

HERODES. Cf. THEOPHRASTUS: CHARACTERS.

HERODIAN. C. R. Whittaker. 2 Vols.

HERODOTUS. A. D. Godley. 4 Vols.

HESIOD AND THE HOMERIC HYMNS. H. G. Evelyn White.

HIPPOCRATES AND THE FRAGMENTS OF HERACLEITUS. W. H. S.
Jones and E. T. Withington. 4 Vols.

HOMER: ILIAD. A. T. Murray. 2 Vols.

HOMER: ODYSSEY. A. T. Murray. 2 Vols.

ISAEUS. E. S. Forster.

ISOCRATES. George Norlin and LaRue Van Hook. 3 Vols.

[ST. JOHN DAMASCENE]: BARLAAM AND IOASAPH. Rev. G. R.
Woodward, Harold Mattingly and D. M. Lang.

JOSEPHUS. 10 Vols. Vols. I-IV. H. St. J. Thackeray. Vol.
V. H. St. J. Thackeray and Ralph Marcus. Vols. VI
and VII. Ralph Marcus. Vol. VIII. Ralph Marcus and
Allen Wikgren. Vols. IX-X. L. H. Feldman.

JULIAN. Wilmer Cave Wright. 3 Vols.

LIBANIUS: SELECTED WORKS. A. F. Norman. 3 Vols. Vols.
I and II.

LONGUS: DAPHNIS AND CHLOE. Thornley's translation revised by J. M. Edmonds; and PARTHENIUS. S. Gaselee.

LUCIAN. 8 Vols. Vols. I-V. A. M. Harmon. Vol. VI. K.
Kilburn. Vols. VII and VIII. M. D. Macleod.

THE LOEB CLASSICAL LIBRARY

Lycophron. *Cf.* Callimachus: Hymns and Epigrams.

Lyra Graeca. J. M. Edmonds. 2 Vols.

Lysias. W. R. M. Lamb.

Manetho. W. G. Waddell.

Marcus Aurelius. C. R. Haines.

Menander. New edition by W. G. Arnott.

Minor Attic Orators. 2 Vols. K. J. Maidment and J. O. Burtt.

Musaeus: Hero and Leander. *Cf.* Callimachus: Fragments.

Nonnos: Dionysiaca. W. H. D. Rouse. 3 Vols.

Oppian, Colluthus, Tryphiodorus. A. W. Mair.

Papyri. Non-Literary Selections. A. S. Hunt and C. C. Edgar. 2 Vols. Literary Selections (Poetry). D. L. Page.

Parthenius. *Cf.* Longus.

Pausanias: Description of Greece. W. H. S. Jones. 4 Vols. and Companion Vol. arranged by R. E. Wycherley.

Philo. 10 Vols. Vols. I-V. F. H. Colson and Rev. G. H. Whitaker. Vols. VI-X. F. H. Colson. General Index. Rev. J. W. Earp.

Two Supplementary Vols. Translation only from an Armenian Text. Ralph Marcus.

Philostratus: The Life of Apollonius of Tyana. F. C. Conybeare. 2 Vols.

Philostratus: Imagines; Callistratus: Descriptions. A. Fairbanks.

Philostratus and Eunapius: Lives of the Sophists. Wilmer Cave Wright.

Pindar: Sir J. E. Sandys.

Plato: Charmides, Alcibiades, Hipparchus, The Lovers, Theages, Minos and Epinomis. W. R. M. Lamb.

Plato: Cratylus, Parmenides, Greater Hippias, Lesser Hippias. H. N. Fowler.

Plato: Euthyphro, Apology, Crito, Phaedo, Phaedrus. H. N. Fowler.

Plato: Laches, Protagoras, Meno, Euthydemus. W. R. M. Lamb.

Plato: Laws. Rev. R. G. Bury. 2 Vols.

Plato: Lysis, Symposium, Gorgias. W. R. M. Lamb.

Plato: Republic. Paul Shorey. 2 Vols.

Plato: Statesman, Philebus. H. N. Fowler; Ion. W. R. M. Lamb.

Plato: Theaetetus and Sophist. H. N. Fowler.

Plato: Timaeus, Critias, Clitopho, Menexenus, Epistulae. Rev. R. G. Bury.

THE LOEB CLASSICAL LIBRARY

PLOTINUS. A. H. Armstrong. 7 Vols. Vols. I-V.
PLUTARCH: MORALIA. 16 Vols. Vols. I-V. F. C. Babbitt.
Vol. VI. W. C. Helmbold. Vol. VII. P. H. De Lacy and
B. Einarson. Vol. VIII. P. A. Clement, H. B. Hoffleit.
Vol. IX. E. L. Minar, Jr., F. H. Sandbach, W. C.
Helmbold. Vol. X. H. N. Fowler. Vol. XI. L. Pearson,
F. H. Sandbach. Vol. XII. H. Cherniss, W. C. Helmbold.
Vol. XIII, Parts 1 and 2. H. Cherniss. Vol. XIV. P. H.
De Lacy and B. Einarson. Vol. XV. F. H. Sandbach.
PLUTARCH: THE PARALLEL LIVES. B. Perrin. 11 Vols.
POLYBIUS. W. R. Paton. 6 Vols.
PROCOPIUS: HISTORY OF THE WARS. H. B. Dewing. 7 Vols.
PTOLEMY: TETRABIBLOS. F. E. Robbins.
QUINTUS SMYRNAEUS. A. S. Way. Verse trans.
SEXTUS EMPIRICUS. Rev. R. G. Bury. 4 Vols.
SOPHOCLES. F. Storr. 2 Vols. Verse trans.
STRABO: GEOGRAPHY. Horace L. Jones. 8 Vols.
THEOPHRASTUS: CHARACTERS. J. M. Edmonds; HERODES,
etc. A. D. Knox.
THEOPHRASTUS: DE CAUSIS PLANTARUM. G. K. K. Link and
B. Einarson. 3 Vols. Vol. I.
THEOPHRASTUS: ENQUIRY INTO PLANTS. Sir Arthur Hort.
2 Vols.
THUCYDIDES. C. F. Smith. 4 Vols.
TRYPHIODORUS. Cf. OPPIAN.
XENOPHON: ANABASIS. C. L. Brownson.
XENOPHON: CYROPAEDIA. Walter Miller. 2 Vols.
XENOPHON: HELLENICA. C. L. Brownson.
XENOPHON: MEMORABILIA AND OECONOMICUS. E. C. Mar-
chant; SYMPOSIUM AND APOLOGY. O. J. Todd.
XENOPHON: SCRIPTA MINORA. E. C. Marchant and G. W.
Bowersock.

DESCRIPTIVE PROSPECTUS ON APPLICATION

CAMBRIDGE, MASS.   LONDON
HARVARD UNIV. PRESS   WILLIAM HEINEMANN LTD.

DATE DUE

	261-2500		Printed in USA

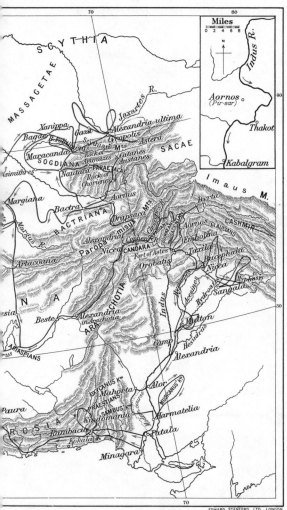

MASSAGETAE

SCYTHIA

Jaxartes R.

Miles
0 2 4 6 8

Aornos
(Pir-sar)

Indus R.

Thakot

40

Kabalgram

Xanippa
Bagae Fort Gazes
Maracanda Cyropolis
Alexandria ultima
Rock of Nautaca Ariamazes
SOGDIANA Astens
Petra PARAETACAE Catanes
Rock of Sisimithres Oxus
Chorienes

SACAE

Imaus M.

Margiana

Bactra

BACTRIANA
Margus
Aornus
Drapsaca

Artacoana

Alexandria
Paropamisus Mts.

Nicea CANDARA
Cophen R.
Fort of Astes

Orobatis

Aornos
Embolima
Taxila
Bucephala
Nicea

GLAUCANS
CASHMIR

Hyphasis
Sangala

N   A

Beste

Alexandria
in Arachotia
ARACHOTIA

Indus

Multan

Hesidrus

Camp
Alexandria

30

Paura

Mahorta OXICANUS Kd.
PRAESTIANS
SAMBUS Kd.
Sindomana MUSICANUS Kd.

ROSIA

Rambacia

Kokala

Alor

Harmatelia

Patala

Minagara

70

80

70

EDWARD STANFORD, LTD., LONDON